Lecture Notes in Computer Science 9459

Commenced Publication in 1973
Founding and Former Series Editors:
Gerhard Goos, Juris Hartmanis, and Jan van Leeuwen

More information about this series at http://www.springer.com/series/7408

Pekka Abrahamsson · Luis Corral
Markku Oivo · Barbara Russo (Eds.)

Product-Focused Software Process Improvement

16th International Conference, PROFES 2015
Bolzano, Italy, December 2–4, 2015
Proceedings

 Springer

Editors
Pekka Abrahamsson
Norwegian University of Science
    and Technology
Trondheim
Norway

Luis Corral
Free University of Bolzano
Bolzano
Italy

Markku Oivo
University of Oulu
Oulu
Finland

Barbara Russo
Free University of Bolzano
Bozen
Italy

ISSN 0302-9743   ISSN 1611-3349   (electronic)
Lecture Notes in Computer Science
ISBN 978-3-319-26843-9   ISBN 978-3-319-26844-6   (eBook)
DOI 10.1007/978-3-319-26844-6

Library of Congress Control Number: 2015955379

LNCS Sublibrary: SL2 – Programming and Software Engineering

Springer Cham Heidelberg New York Dordrecht London
© Springer International Publishing Switzerland 2015

Printed on acid-free paper

Springer International Publishing AG Switzerland is part of Springer Science+Business Media
(www.springer.com)

Preface

Welcome to the proceedings of the 16th International Conference on Product-Focused Software Process Improvement (PROFES 2015). The conference was held during December 2–4, 2015, and for the first time in Bolzano/Bozen, a charming town in South Tyrol, Italy.

PROFES 2015 provided an enthusiastic environment for practitioners, researchers, and educators to present and discuss experiences, ideas, innovations, as well as concerns related to professional software process improvement motivated by product and service quality needs. In a beautiful alpine winter atmosphere, PROFES encouraged the exchange of ideas to explore, understand, and model phenomena in software engineering in terms of process–product relationships. In these proceedings you will find the latest contributions to research and practice on the major topics of the conference including research contributions, research preview papers, and workshop papers.

To ensure that PROFES retains its high standards and keeps focusing on the most relevant research issues, the Program Committee applied a rigorous selection process, in which each submission received at least three peer reviews. Every paper that received only one or two positive reviews underwent further review in the form of discussion among the reviewers. The review process (and specially the discussion afterward) was very intensive; reviewers were very passionate and committed to ensuring the quality of the conference program. Finally, complete consensus was reached for all the papers submitted to the conference.

The Program Committee selected original research on current trends in software engineering addressing products and services, as well as studies reporting on the application of methods or technologies in real settings, replication studies, and systematic reviews. Overall, we received 50 submissions, 18 of which were selected as full papers. Ten more contributions were selected as research preview papers.

This volume presents the 28 peer-reviewed contributions of the main program of PROFES 2015. We organized the contents of the book in eight chapters, each one covering a relevant aspect of product-focused software process improvement: lessons learned from industry-research collaborations; instruments to improve the software development process; requirements, features, and release management; practices of modern development processes; human factors in modern software development; effort and size estimation validated by professionals; empirical generalization; and software reliability and testing in industry.

PROFES 2015 also had three co-located workshops that enriched and complemented the main track of the conference. We included in this volume three additional chapters including the papers presented at each workshop. The workshop main topics concerned: processes, methods, and tools for engineering embedded systems; human factors in software development processes; and software startups: state of the art and state of the practice.

We believe that the quality and relevance of the contributions included in this proceedings volume make it a valuable resource for all practitioners and researchers interested in a more in-depth understanding of the state of the art, the practice, and the future of product-focused software process improvement. We hope the reader finds it useful and insightful.

On behalf of the PROFES 2015 Organizing and Program Committees, we would like to thank the enthusiastic participation of our authors and the diligent effort of our reviewers, the generous contribution of our sponsors, and the dedication of the chairs. Finally, we would like to gratefully acknowledge the untiring support of the local organizers, publicity chairs, and all the members of the Organizing Committee who made the conference a success. A special thanks to the student volunteers, the Press and Event Management Office, and the Faculty of Computer Science of the Free University of Bozen/Bolzano, who kindly hosted the conference and provide all the facilities for its realization.

December 2015

Pekka Abrahamsson
Luis Corral
Markku Oivo
Barbara Russo

Organization

Organizing Committee

General Chair

Pekka Abrahamsson   Norwegian University of Science and Technology,
                                   Trondheim, Norway

Program Committee Co-chairs

Barbara Russo   Free University of Bozen-Bolzano, Italy
Markku Oivo   University of Oulu, Finland

Organizing Chairs

Gabriele Bavota   Free University of Bozen-Bolzano, Italy
Daniel Graziotin   Free University of Bozen-Bolzano, Italy

Research Preview Papers Chair

Martin Höst   Lund University, Sweden

Proceedings Chair

Luis Corral   Free University of Bozen-Bolzano, Italy

Workshops and Tutorials Chair

Paris Avgeriou   University of Groningen, Netherlands

Social Media Chair

Daniel Méndez Fernández   Technische Universität München, Germany
Davide Fucci   University of Oulu, Finland

Web Chairs

Carmine Giardino   Free University of Bozen-Bolzano, Italy
Emanuel Neumann   Free University of Bozen-Bolzano, Italy

Program Committee

Silvia Abrahão	Universidad Politecnica de Valencia (UPV), Spain
Sousuke Amasaki	Okayama Prefectural University, Japan
Maria Teresa Baldassarre	Università degli Studi di Bari A. Moro, Italy
Stefan Biffl	Technische Universität Wien, Austria
Andreas Birk	Software.Process.Management, Germany
Sjaak Brinkkemper	Universiteit Utrecht, The Netherlands
Luigi Buglione	Université du Québec, Canada
Gerardo Canfora	University of Sannio, Italy
Marcus Ciolkowski	Kaiserslautern University of Technology, Germany
Maya Daneva	University of Twente, The Netherlands
Oscar Dieste	Universidad Politécnica de Madrid, Spain
Tore Dybå	University of Oslo, Finland
Christof Ebert	University of Stuttgart, Germany
Davide Falessi	Cal Poly, USA
Daniel Graziotin	Free University of Bozen-Bolzano, Italy
Noriko Hanakawa	Hannan University, Japan
Jens Heidrich	Fraunhofer Institute, Germany
Yoshiki Higo	Osaka University, Japan
Frank Houdek	Ulm University, Germany
Hajimu Iida	Nara Institute of Science and Technology, Japan
Letizia Jaccheri	Politecnico di Torino, Italy
Andreas Jedlitschka	Fraunhofer Institute, Germany
Marco Kuhrmann	University of Southern Denmark, Denmark
Constanza Lampasona	Fraunhofer Institute, Germany
Casper Lassenius	Aalto University, Finland
Ricardo Jorge Machado	University of Minho, Portugal
Lech Madeyski	Wroclaw University of Technology, Poland
Tomi Mannisto	University of Helsinki, Finland
Jouni Markkula	University of Jyväskylä, Finland
Kenichi Matsumoto	Reitaku University, Japan
Emilia Mendes	Blekinge Institute of Technology, Sweden
Daniel Méndez Fernández	Technische Universität München, Germany
Jürgen Münch	University of Helsinki, Finland
Risto Nevalainen	Finland
Paolo Panaroni	INTECS, Rome, Italy
Oscar Pastor	Universidad Politécnica de Valencia, Spain
Dietmar Pfahl	University of Tartu, Estonia
Reinhold Plösch	Johannes Kepler Universität Linz, Austria
Bruno Rossi	Masaryk University, Brno, Czech Republic
Michael Stupperich	Daimler AG, Stuttgart
Marco Torchiano	Politecnico di Torino, Italy
Guilherme Travassos	University of Maryland, USA
Adam Trendowicz	Fraunhofer Institute, Germany

Burak Turhan   University of Oulu, Finland
Rini van Solingen   Delft University of Technology, The Netherlands
Sira Vegas   Technical University Madrid, Spain
Mathias Vierimaa   Finland
Stefan Wagner   University of Stuttgart, Germany
Dietmar Winkler   Vienna University of Technology, Austria
Xiaofeng Wang   Free University of Bozen-Bolzano, Italy
Jennifer Ferreira   Brunel University London, UK

Processes, Methods and Tools for Engineering Embedded Systems

Apostolos Ampatzoglou[1], Jukka Hemilä[2]

[1] Department of Comptuer Science and Mathematics, University of Groningen,
The Netherlands
[2] VTT Technical Research Centre, Finland
a.ampatzoglou@rug.nl, jukka.hemila@vtt.fi

Abstract. The processes, methods, and tools for engineering embedded systems (PROMOTE) workshop focuses on research topics on the intersection of software engineering and embedded systems. Nowadays embedded software plays an increasingly important role in embedded systems development, and urges for intense maintenance activities. Therefore, the embedded systems community is expected to benefit from sharing knowledge with the software engineering community, in the sense of applying accumulated experience in handling maintenance effort. However, successful software engineering processes, methods or tools are not usually found in the ES industry, whereas, others might not be even directly applicable, and require tailoring. PROMOTE attempts to bring together practitioners and researchers from both communities, to discuss progress on embedded software processes, methods and tools; to gather empirical evidence on their use; and to identify priorities for a research agenda.

1 Theme

Embedded software (ES), as a type of software targeting devices that are not typically thought of as computers, is usually specialized for one particular hardware (the one that it runs on) and therefore has hardware-specific run-time constraints (e.g., memory usage, processing power, etc.) [1]. The last decades, ES play an increasingly important role in the development process of embedded products: as suggested by Rauscher and Smith some embedded companies have increased the percentage of staff devoted to developing software in the organization—as much as 80 % in some software-intensive companies [2]. A possible explanation for that is software's negligible replication cost and its greater flexibility compared to hardware, which makes it easier to change. Thus, product development managers often allow for some software additions or changes late in the product development cycle to correct hardware problems or to add new functionality [2], urging for intense maintenance activities.

An additional challenge in embedded systems is a long lifetime expectancy, which is normally beyond one decade requiring the management of old systems in parallel to the design and implementation of new systems. State-of-the-art in electronics is advancing rapidly while old systems need to be maintained. Any decision to take advantage of novel hardware and software platforms means that companies need to manage many different configurations. This leads to issues of retaining skills and knowledge crossing decades hindering the work of current staff and rendering maintenance for ES extremely challenging. However, maintenance is one of the most effort consuming activities in the soft-ware lifecycle, since it consumes 50 – 75 % of the total time / effort budget of a typical software project [3]. In order for such maintenance activities to be efficient, the development of ES is expected to adopt software engineering processes, to apply software engineering methods and take advantage of sophisticated software engineering tools.

2   Goals

In this context, the topic of software engineering for Embedded Systems needs to receive more attention and research effort, considering that the software part of Embedded Systems is becoming increasingly larger and complex. However, there is a lack of forums that discuss the particularities of Embedded Software Engineering. To this end, the PROMOTE workshop aims to bring together researchers and practitioners from the software engineering and the embedded systems communities, so as to discuss the progress on embedded software-specific processes, methods and tools; gather empirical evidence on their use; and identify priorities for a research agenda. The main topics of interest include, but are not limited to:

- Process frameworks for embedded systems
- Processes for embedded systems development
- Software development for embedded systems
- Methods that are applied in ES architecture, design, and engineering
- Quality models for embedded systems
- Embedded software product quality improvement
- Business model innovations in embedded systems development
- Empirical studies (surveys, case studies, controlled experiments)

3   Accepted Papers

The workshop will include four accepted papers: (a) *Performance Engineering for Industrial Embedded Data-Processing Systems*, in which the authors present a model-based approach for performance engineering that has been applied in a printing industrial setting, (b) *Fault-prone Byte-code Detection Using Text Classifier*, in which the authors present a method for identifying fault-prone classes from java bytecode, (c) *Variability management strategies to support efficient delivery and maintenance of embedded systems*, in which the authors present a strategy for managing variability in communication industry, and (d) *Using Cross-Dependencies during Configuration of System Families*, in which the authors present a process for product configuration in the automotive industry.

Acknowledgement. This research has been partially funded by the ITEA2 project 11013 PROMES.

References

1. Stroustrup, B.: Abstraction and the C++ Machine Model. In: Wu, Z., Chen, C., Guo, M., Bu, J. (eds.) ICESS 2004. LNCS, vol. 3605, pp. 1–13. Springer, Heidelberg (2005)
2. Rauscher, T G., Smith, P.G.: From experience time-driven development of software in manufactured goods. J. Prod. Innov. Manag. **12**(3), 186–199 (1995)
3. van Vliet, H.: Software Engineering: Principles and Practice, 3 edn. Wiley, Chichester (2008)

Human Factors in Software Development Processes

Silvia Abrahao[1], Maria Teresa Baldassarre[2], Danilo Caivano[2],
Yvonne Dittrich[3], Rosa Lanzilotti[2], Antonio Piccinno[2]

[1] Universidad Politecnica de Valencia (UPV), Spain
[2] Università degli Studi di Bari, Italy
[3] IT University of Copenhagen, Denmark
sabrahao@dsic.upv.es, {mariateresa.baldassarre,
danilo.caivano,antonio.piccinno,rosa.lanzilotti}
@uniba.it, ydi@itu.dk

Abstract. Recent efforts have contributed to reduce the gap between Software Engineering and HCI for what concerns usability, however, this has not led to expected results and impacts in terms of the software development process where the debate is still open. The overall goal of this workshop has been to raise the level of engagement and discussion about human factors in software engineering and software development processes in order to identify opportunities to improve the quality of scientific results and improvements on human aspects of software development.

Keywords: Human computer interaction · Software engineering · Human factors · Development process

1 Introduction

Software development is a human intensive activity whatever the underlying production process it is based on. Though both software engineering (SE) and human-computer interaction (HCI) communities aim towards creating better software products, the two communities are still far from being synergic while they could both gain from a better integration. Recent efforts have contributed to increase the synergy between SE and HCI. Nevertheless, this has not led to expected results and impacts with respect to the software development process. Software product industry emphasizes the importance of contact with users and customers in order to understand requirements both regarding the functionality and the usability of software products. At the same time, multi layered software architectures are pursued in order to have robust and evolvable software products, according to the customers' needs, even if they were not properly taken into account at the beginning of the development process.

One might expect that such issues would lead to emphasize the core importance of human factors in software development. Unfortunately this has not been the case.

The overall goal of this interdisciplinary workshop has been to raise the level of engagement and discussion about human factors in software product engineering and development processes in order to identify opportunities to improve the quality of scientific results and improvements on human aspects of software product development. A further goal of the workshop has been to identify opportunities to improve the quality of scientific discourse and progress on human aspects of software development, as well as to identify opportunities able to educate researchers about how to conduct sound human-centered evaluations in the context of software engineering.

To achieve these goals, researchers and practitioners who face the problem of integrating human factors in software development processes and have tried effective methods to resolve it should be offered a place to discuss their experiences, lessons learned and future intentions. As so, this workshop has provided a forum to discuss the following research questions:

- What are the key methods that allow the integration of human factors in software development processes?
- What methods do current software development teams use to engage users in development processes?
- How can the level of human factor involvement be objectively verified during and after software development?
- How to educate researchers on performing human-centered evaluations in the software engineering processes?

2 Organization and Program Committee

The workshop has received a positive response from both HCI and SE communities and several interesting contributions have been submitted. Overall we have included 8 papers. The topics are likely to be of interest to several researches and studies in human-computer interaction and software engineering. The purpose of this interdisciplinary workshop was to bring together researchers and practitioners. The submissions were peer-reviewed by international committee members for their quality, topic relevance, innovation, and potentials to foster discussion.

- Silvia Acuña, Universidad Autónoma de Madrid, Spain
- Paolo Bottoni, Sapienza University of Rome, Italy
- Michel Chaudron, Chalmers & Gothenborg University, Sweden
- Daniela Fogli, University of Brescia, Italy
- Igor Garnik, Gdańsk University of Technology, Poland
- Marcela Genero, University of Castilla-La Mancha, Spain
- Ebba Hvannberg, University of Iceland, Iceland
- Emilia Mendes, Blekinge Institute of Technology, Sweden
- Marianna Obrist, University of Sussex
- Giuseppe Scanniello, Università della Basilicata, Italy
- Aaron Visaggio, University of Sannio, Italy
- Marco Winckler, University Paul Sabatier, France

Acknowledgment. We would like to thank the organizers of PROFES 2015 for giving us the opportunity to organize this workshop. We are also grateful to our international program committee of experts in the field for their reviews and collaboration.

Software Startups: State of the Art and State of the Practice (SSU2015)

Anh Nguyen-Duc[1], Syed Muhammad Ali Shah[2],
and Xiaofeng Wang[3]

[1] Norwegian University of Science and Technology, Norway
[2] SICS Swedish ICT AB, Sweden
[3] Free University of Bozen-Bolzano, Italy

The world has been witnessing the rapid spread of tech-entrepreneurship. Software startups are in the forefront of this big wave. A combination of infrastructure development, such as cloud computing, mobile software development, and easy-to-use tools have significantly accelerated the rise of software startups by reducing the cost of doing it. Besides, an increasing amount of accelerators, incubators and advisors provide the know-how, contributing to a growing number of software startups. Moreover, new ways of starting up software business are emerging, such as fund crowdsourcing, global startups, etc..

However, the landscape of software startups is extremely dynamic, unpredictable and even chaotic. Failure rate is very high. Many high-tech startups are still experiencing problems of lacking systematic methodologies on business, product, team and market development. To drive business through such a chaotic environment, software entrepreneurs need to improve the speed of their action, learning from failure in an economic way.

Software startups make a fascinating arena for both researchers and practitioners alike. The SSU2015 workshop is the very first workshop dedicated to software startup research and practice. The aim of the workshop is to gather industrial and academic minds together to explore the potentials and synergies from technical, methodological and operational perspectives. As a result of the workshop, we should have a clearer understanding on how they shape the future of software startups. The workshop has been strongly supported by the emerging Software Startup Research Network (www. softwarestarups.org).

Six papers addressing different aspects of software startups are presented at the SSU2015 workshop. They focus on different levels of investigation. Three paper investigate issues and challenges encountered by individual startups, such as pivoting, competence needs by entrepreneurial teams, and provision of software tools to support startup processes. The other three papers, instead, investigate startup phenomenon from the perspectives of community, large companies and ecosystems. The papers' research approach widely range from primary empirical studies, conceptual framework, industrial experience and previsions of future trends.

The workshop sessions are designed to be interactive, encouraging the participants to engage and contribute actively to the discussions of the presented papers. In addition to the paper presentations, the participants are also invited to collaboratively build a road map for future software startup research.

Contents

Empirical Generalization

Software Reliability and Testing in Industry

Workshop on Software Startups: State of the Art and State of the Practice

Lessons Learned from
Industry-Research Collaborations

Strategic Ecosystem Management:
A Multi-case Study in the B2B Domain

Helena Holmström Olsson[1](✉) and Jan Bosch[2]

[1] Department of Computer Science, Malmö University, Malmö, Sweden
helena.holmstrom.olsson@mah.se
[2] Department of Computer Science and Engineering, Chalmers University
of Technology, Gothenburg, Sweden
jan.bosch@chalmers.se

Abstract. In today's business environment, value creation is a collaborative effort in which companies depend on a number of external stakeholders. This implies a shift towards inter-organizational relationships and dependencies between companies. In this shift, companies seek strategies for how to effectively coordinate standardization efforts, share maintenance costs, and engage in open innovation initiatives, while at the same time increase control and accelerate development of differentiating functionality. On the basis of a multi-case study in six B2B software development companies, this paper explores the challenges involved in managing different ecosystem types. Based on the 'Three Layer Product Model' [1], we distinguish between innovation ecosystems, differentiating ecosystems and commoditizing ecosystems. We outline the challenges the companies experience in managing these, and we develop a model in which we identify the characteristics of each ecosystem type. Our model helps companies manage the different ecosystems they operate in. Finally, we present a framework in which we categorize the strategies employed by the case companies depending on the competitiveness of a specific product or product category.

Keywords: Business ecosystems · Ecosystem strategies · Challenges · Innovation ecosystem · Differentiating ecosystem · Commoditizing ecosystem

1 Introduction

Recently, business ecosystems have gained significant attention in the software engineering research community. Denoting the transition from the internals of an organization towards its external environment, it involves technical complexities as well as managerial challenges [2–4]. To be successful in this transition, companies need to shift focus from internal process efficiency towards strategic alignment of internal and external interests [5]. Also, companies need to better distinguish between the multiple ecosystems in which they operate, in order to select and combine the most competitive strategies for managing each of these. However, for most companies the selection of strategies is a challenging task due to the inherent differences in the ecosystems in which they operate. Typically, strategies that address challenges in relation to product

P. Abrahamsson et al. (Eds.): PROFES 2015, LNCS 9459, pp. 3–15, 2015.
DOI: 10.1007/978-3-319-26844-6_1

innovation do not apply for dealing with commoditized product functionality. Similarly, strategies that address challenges in relation to product differentiation do not help in maintaining commoditized products. Typically, there is insufficient guidance to support companies in deciding what strategies to use for maximizing the benefits of the ecosystems they operate in.

In this paper, and based on the 'Three Layer Product Model' [1], we distinguish between three types of ecosystems, i.e. the innovation ecosystem, the differentiating ecosystem and the commoditizing ecosystem. Based on a multi-case study at six B2B software development companies, we identify the challenges that these companies experience in relation to management of each of these ecosystems. Based on our empirical findings, we develop a model in which we identify the drivers of each ecosystem type, the purpose and stakeholders of each ecosystem type and the characteristics of each ecosystem type. In doing this, our model helps companies manage the activities associated with each ecosystem type, i.e. development of new functionality, optimization and extension of differentiating functionality, and reducing efforts related to commoditized functionality. Finally, and as a generalization of the approaches taken in the case companies, we present a framework in which we categorize the strategies employed by the companies depending on the competitiveness of a specific product or product category. The contribution of the paper is threefold. First, we identify the specific challenges related to innovation, differentiating and commoditizing ecosystems. Second, we develop a model that identifies the characteristics of each ecosystem type and helps companies select appropriate strategies for managing these. Third, we present a framework in which we categorize the strategies employed by the case companies depending on the competitiveness of a specific product or product category.

2 Background

2.1 Business Ecosystems

As recognized in previous research [4, 6–8], there are a number of reasons why companies increasingly operate in networks of stakeholders where joint interests drive product development and innovation. Typically, the opportunities to increase value and attractiveness to existing customers, at the same time as decreasing costs by sharing maintenance, are highlighted as the main advantages with a business ecosystem. In addition, and increasingly important, is the opportunity to accelerate innovation and to share costs of innovation with other actors in the ecosystem. Obviously, and as recognized in previous studies [2, 8], the benefits depend on what type of ecosystem you operate in and what type of relationship you have to other stakeholders. What is especially interesting in a commercial business ecosystem is the fact that two actors in the ecosystem might have mutual benefits, be in direct competition, be unaffected, or one being unaffected while the other is benefiting or harmed by the relationship. This situation makes business ecosystems complex in nature and therefore, an interesting phenomenon to study. In our study, we focus on the challenges involved when operating in a business ecosystem.

2.2 The 'Three Layer Product Model'

The 'Three Layer Product Model' (Table 1) was developed to better understand the complexity of system dimensions and interfaces that most companies experience. The model helps companies distinguish between distinct layers of system functionality in order to reduce architectural complexity [1]. The model distinguishes between the following functionality layers:

Table 1. Functionality layers as outlined in the Three Layer Product Model [1].

Functionality layer:	Description:
Innovative functionality layer	The focus of this layer is to develop functionality that has the potential to become value adding in the future. Functionality in this layer is under various stages of development, either in collaboration with external actors or by internally driven innovation initiatives
Differentiating functionality layer	This layer comprises functionality that differentiates the product from its competitors and offers newer, more specialized advantages with customer value. A product's market success or failure results from the functionality in this layer
Commoditized functionality layer	This layer comprises functionality necessary for system operation but that over time has become so integral to a system it no longer adds real customer value. It often combines internally built proprietary software with commercial and open source software solutions

In particular, the model recognizes a fundamental problem in that companies tend to treat these three layers of functionality as if they are equal and hence, ignore the fact that each layer has its specific characteristics. As a result of this, a number of problems occur, e.g. proprietary solutions are not replaced, commoditized functionality receive more resources than it warrants, the percentage of investments in differentiating functionality shrinks, and fewer development resources are devoted to enhancing system competitiveness etc. While this model was originally developed to help companies reduce architectural complexity, it recognizes the importance of distinguishing between different functionality layers. In our view, this distinction is equally important in order to understand the different ecosystems that companies operate in. Therefore, we use the 'Three Layer Product Model' as the theoretical foundation for our research. In our research, we distinguish between the innovation ecosystem, the differentiating ecosystem, and the commoditizing ecosystem, and based on a multi-case study research we explore challenges and characteristics of these.

3 Case Study Design

The research reported in this paper builds on a 14 months (January 2014 – February 2015) case study conducted in six software-intensive companies in the B2B domain. As a research method, case study research is used to contribute to our knowledge of individual, group, organizational and social phenomena, and is typically used to explain 'how' and 'why' and questions that require an extensive and in-depth understanding of the phenomenon [9]. As the objective of our study, we focused on the challenges the case companies experience when managing the different ecosystems, the strategies they apply and the way in which these strategies depend on product competitiveness. In our study, we conducted two rounds of group interviews, one round in April – May 2014 and the second round in October – November 2014. All interviews were two-hour sessions in which both authors were present. We shared the responsibility of taking notes so that we could merge and further discuss our findings after each interview. During analysis, the interviews notes were carefully read with the intention to identify recurring elements and concepts [10]. In the first round of interviews, we focused on the three ecosystem types and the ways-of-working that the companies employ in each of these. The main objective was to get an accurate understanding for the different stakeholders, the relationships between these and the ways in which each company viewed themselves within each ecosystem in terms of position, control and power. In the second round of interviews, we focused on the challenges involved when managing the different ecosystems. The main objective was to identify the specific challenges within each ecosystem, and to understand what strategies the companies deploy to manage these. In addition to the group interviews in each of the six case companies, we arranged four joint workshops to which all companies were invited. At these workshops, we planned our research activities, we presented preliminary results and we discussed our empirical findings. Also, two validation workshops were conducted at which all company representatives met to further discuss and validate the empirical findings. As this is on-going research, we have several research activities planned, and the focus for the spring (2015) is to explore further the many strategies that the companies deploy, how they select among these, and how different strategies can be efficiently combined to maximize the potential within each ecosystem layer.

3.1 Case Companies

Company A is a software company specializing in navigational information, operations management and optimization solutions. The company operates in a business domain where competition is fierce and where only a very limited number of actors provide the majority of customers with the solutions they need. For the purpose of this study, we met with a total of six people in the two rounds of interviews. The interviewees combined expertise in cloud services, SOA, and 'Devops', with significant experience of large-scale software development, agile software development and product lines.

Company B is a pump manufacturer producing pumps for heating and air conditioning, as well as pumps for e.g. water supply. The company is in a situation similar to many other embedded system companies, i.e. software is in the transition from being a supporting function to becoming the central differentiating technology of their products. For the purpose of this study, we met with a total of twelve people in the two rounds of interviews. The interviewees combined expertise in agile development, system architecture, project management, solutions and services development, marketing and sales and emerging technologies and connectivity.

Company C is world leading in network video and offers products such as network cameras, video encoders, video management software and camera applications. The company is regarded the keystone player in the domain. For the purpose of this study, we met with a total of fourteen people in the two rounds of interviews. The interviewees combined expertise in global sales, project management, product management, methods and tools, and system architecture.

Company D is a manufacturer and supplier of transport solutions for commercial use. The company operates in an ecosystem characterized by long-term relationships to a large number of suppliers, and where suppliers often are larger than the company itself and have a very strong position. For the purpose of this study, we met with a total of nine people in the two rounds of interviews. The interviewees had roles and expertise within the areas of user experience, concept and strategy, infotainment technology, interaction, and as technical lead within software engineering and management.

Company E is an automotive telematics service provider providing manufacturers of cars and commercial vehicles with complete telematics services to end-customers. For the purpose of this study, we met with a total of ten people in the two rounds of interviews. The interviewees had roles and expertise as domain owners, product owners, Scrum owners, technical management, platform delivery management and connectivity management.

Company F is a world-leading provider of telecommunication systems and equipment for mobile and fixed network operators. The company operates in a competitive ecosystem in which a number of new competitors have emerged during the recent years. Company F joined the study in November 2014 and consequently, we only met with this company in the second round of interviews. For the purpose of this study, we met with a total of eight people with roles such as line managers, strategy and portfolio managers, system architects and product managers.

3.2   Data Collection and Validity of Results

The research reported in this paper builds on group interviews in the six case companies, four joint workshop sessions and two joint validation sessions. In terms of data analysis, an interpretive approach was adopted [11]. While this approach has similarities with the qualitative grounded theory approach [10], it is not as strict in its coding process. Rather, the researcher documents his or her impressions during the research and when having an organized set of themes, the researcher carefully reflects on what implications can be drawn from the field data [11]. During our analysis we had close contact with each company to to avoid any misunderstandings of the empirical material. Also, the results were presented at validation sessions to which all company representatives were invited to discuss and validate the empirical findings.

Qualitative research rarely has the benefit of previously planned comparisons, sampling strategies, or statistical manipulations that control for possible threats [12].

Instead, researchers must try to rule out validity threats after the research has begun. To strengthen the validity of empirical research, triangulation is an important concept [13]. For the purpose of this study, we used data triangulation, i.e. more than one data source, and observer triangulation, i.e. more than one observer in the study. In addition, methodological triangulation was applied in that we used a combination of data collection methods e.g. interviews, workshops and validation sessions in order to avoid having one data source influence us to heavily.

4 Findings

In this section, we present the case study findings. We categorize our findings according to (1) innovation ecosystems, (2) differentiating ecosystems, and (3) commoditizing ecosystems. For each ecosystem type, we describe the current ways-of-working within each company, as described by the interviewees in the group interviews. We conclude the section by summarizing the challenges.

4.1 The Innovation Ecosystem

The innovation ecosystem is about hypothesizing about future differentiating functionality through customer interaction and analysis of competing products, as well as about brainstorming and other idea creation initiatives. In company A, each product line continuously proposes innovation initiatives as part of their strategy. Typically, innovations grow organically, but there are also examples of larger investments and more radical innovation initiatives where the company creates strategic partnerships with suppliers. This is noted by one of the product managers in the interview: *"When looking at large investments you typically want to share risks, so a "big jump" requires strategic partnerships"*. While the organic growth strategy is the most common, it is considered an inefficient way to grow. What is needed, and what is defined as critical by the interviewees, is a healthy balance between internal and external innovation. Due to its strong position in the business ecosystem, the company orchestrates other ecosystem players, and enjoys the opportunity of bringing externally developed functionality into its own product offering.

Company B has strong capabilities for internal and technology-driven innovation, and its strong market position is a result of rapid introduction of new technology. Typically, the engineers identify new high-end technologies and include them as part of the products. When included in the products, these new technologies allow for improved product characteristics that differentiate the company among its competitors. However, the company is experiencing a situation in which its traditional business of designing, building and manufacturing products is commoditizing. To respond to this, and to accelerate innovation, the company has defined a strategic business plan where the company aims to grow new businesses. To realize this plan, the company is moving more and more into collaborative forms of innovation, a transition that is recognized by one of the product managers: *"Our innovations are always started internally, i.e. only based on ideas from the company. We try to become more collaborative since we would benefit from more input."*

In company C, innovation is conducted in collaboration with partners. The company has a globally spanning partnership program in which they engage with external actors to drive innovation initiatives. Rather than focusing on generic feature sets for generic products, they focus on identifying specific customer needs in those niche markets. Similar to our other case study companies, the company has started to provide services and solutions surrounding their products. In doing this, they have to sustain a careful balance to maintain a good relationship with its current partners: *"We have to be careful and initially provide only basic solutions and services in our current partners' space, and only slowly improving these".*

Company D is experiencing challenging shift in that the product is becoming more and more software-intensive, and that new services that are introduced requires fundamentally new business models. As a result, company D is experiencing a number of new challenges as recognized in a quote from the group interview: *"When having innovations in terms of new services you run into interesting issues of responsibility... who is to blame when Spotify doesn't work in my car...?".* Recently, the company has started to involve in collaborations with stakeholders from very different domains, but that has the potential to have an impact on the future use of the product.

Company E acts as a supplier of telematics solutions to other key stakeholders. There is no direct connection to the consumers of their products and innovation is driven by internal initiatives. This makes innovation an expensive task, and so far, the company has been perceived as slow when it comes to innovation. This is mentioned by one of the interviewees when saying: *"We need to be better in picking up on others' ideas...to become quicker".*

Company F uses different ways-of-working depending on what type of products they target. For existing products to which they would like to add new functionality, the common approach is to focus on internal innovation in which ideas in the product backlog are developed and tested in-house. However, and as noted by one of the interviewees, the company is increasingly moving towards more collaborative innovation: *"We use the open source community as part of our innovation initiatives. We try things out there, or we build on top of what is there".* In this way, the company uses already existing infrastructures for their innovation initiatives. Typically, the more collaborative innovation approaches are used for new areas and new product development.

4.2   The Differentiating Ecosystem

The differentiating ecosystem is about identifying and incorporating new functionality into the core product offering. Company A operates using a business model that allows customers to modify and customize functionality to suit their specific business needs. As soon as modifications and customizations are done, they are pulled in as part of the core product offering in order to increase company control, and at the same time reduce complexity for customers. Typically, changes and improvements are made incrementally.

In company B, differentiation is achieved by the high quality of the products they deliver. However, and as emphasized during the interviews, their competitors are catching up in terms of quality: *"We are forced to increasingly seek differentiating advantages in our offering of systems, solutions and services. This, however, requires a radical change in our ways-of-working and company culture, and is an on-going transition that has only recently begun."* As this transition means forward integration in the value chain, it happens that the company runs into competitive challenges with stakeholders that used to be pure customers.

The main characteristic of company C's differentiating ecosystem is that it follows Moore's law, i.e. the amount of storage, the capacity of their products is constantly increasing. This allows for constant and rapid evolution of differentiating functionality in the products. To manage this, the company works closely with hardware suppliers, something that is recognized as critical: *"We work in very close collaboration with our hardware suppliers in order to make sure that they can stay competitive due to early access to new generation technology, and at price points that maintain the cost effectiveness to their solutions."*

Company D adopts an approach where functionality from the innovation layer is transferred to the differentiating layer as soon as it has proven valuable in internal prototyping and in prototyping with customers. Typically, the company works in an incremental fashion with the main intention to give functionality the typical "look and feel" of the brand, as described by one of the interviewees: *"Differentiation is usually standard solutions that we put a certain 'look and feel' to...95 % is standard solution and 5 % is our twist...".*

Company E puts the majority of its efforts on incremental improvements of internally developed functionality, and very little efforts on more radical improvements, as commented by one of the line managers: *"We do incremental improvements all the time, but we are very careful in doing more radical change".* This approach is seen as a result of the position the company has as a supplier within the ecosystem, and the interviewees describe a situation in which they are limited in what they can do.

Company F is very strong within its domain. Today, a large part of the revenue comes from applications, from support and from integration of services. To increase control by transferring innovations to the differentiating ecosystem is a prioritized activity: *"We push functionality to the differentiating layer when it is technically mature and when we have customers ask for it".* According to the interviewees, radical change of functionality is uncommon and new products typically build on existing ones.

4.3 The Commoditizing Ecosystem

The commoditized ecosystem is about incorporating functionality from the differentiating layer into the commoditized layer when it is no longer adding value to customers. Company A uses commercial-off-the-shelf solutions, as well as open source software to reduce the amount of investments spent on commoditized functionality. When it comes to letting go of functionality, i.e. 'push-out', the company rarely does so, but it happens in major system version upgrades and in new product development. Historically, company B has invested most of its development efforts in the commoditizing ecosystem. However, the company has started to look into replacing commodity functionality with commercial-off-the-shelf software and open source solutions. As this requires a change in culture, the company foresees a period in which a lot of attention will be put on internal change management.

Company C uses the Linux operating system as the basis for its products. As soon as differentiating functionality starts to commoditize, the company actively seeks to get this integrated into the main Linux stack. In this way, the company can efficiently reduce development and maintenance costs and focus their efforts on differentiating functionality. For the most software-intensive parts of the product, company D uses standard solutions that are slightly modified. The company engages in the development of open source software with the main intention to share development and maintenance costs with a broader community. Most common, however, is to share code and components between partners. Most of the resources within company E are allocated to development and maintenance of commoditized functionality. The company has a number of commercial off-the-shelf solutions in order to reduce their own development costs. Moreover, they are actively looking for incorporating their functionality in existing open source stacks.

A large part of the resources within company F are allocated to development and maintenance of commoditized functionality. However, the company is proactive in finding ways to share these costs. Both commercial-off-the-shelf and open source solutions are used to help replace components that are internally developed. In addition, company F outsources development to internal as well as external parties.

4.4   Summary of Ecosystem Challenges

Based on our empirical findings, we identified a number of challenges related to each ecosystem type. In Table 2, we summarize the most common challenges in relation to the different ecosystem types.

Table 2. Summary of the challenges the case companies experience in relation to the multiple ecosystems they operate in.

Ecosystem type:	Challenges:
Innovation ecosystem	• Efficient evaluation of innovation propositions and partners • Lack of metrics that facilitate innovation selection and prioritization • Managing limitations set by customer and technology maturity • High costs due to technology-driven innovation culture • Lack of continuous validation with customers • Adapting to new business models that transform the perception of the product
Differentiating ecosystem	• Timing the introduction of new technology to customers • Deciding when new technology is sufficiently mature to be introduced into new products

(Continued)

Table 2. (*Continued*)

Ecosystem type:	Challenges:
	• Transitioning of new technology into core offerings
	• Prediction of when to deploy certain functionality in certain markets
	• Keeping the products sufficiently differentiating, while at the same time not infringing too aggressively on current partners
	• Defining metrics to avoid investing in functionality that customers do not value as differentiating
Commoditizing ecosystem	• Establishing a culture where resources are allocated to differentiating functionality, rather than to development and maintenance of commoditized functionality
	• Deciding when to stop supporting functionality
	• Collection of product data that reveal product usage

5 Discussion

5.1 Ecosystem Characteristics: Case Study Findings

Internal and Incremental Innovation: Our interview findings reveal that all case companies find innovation a costly and time-consuming task. This is due to internal and technology-driven innovation where most of the ideas are generated and validated in-house. Although all companies engage in innovation initiatives with external partners such as suppliers and peers, they find it difficult to efficiently involve customers since customer- and technology maturity set limitations on innovation. Also, the companies lack mechanisms for continuous validation with customers and we see that incremental innovation is the common approach while disruptive innovation is scarce. Based on our findings, and the general approach taken at the case companies, we conclude that none of the companies are as effective in sharing the risks and costs of innovation with other stakeholders as they could be.

Safe and Careful Differentiation: Similar to their innovation approaches, all case companies do incremental improvements of their differentiating functionality rather than radical changes. They report on a situation in which they are very careful with introducing major changes to their products, and that they rather play safe than risk to upset existing customers. Challenges arise when deciding when to transfer innovations to the differentiation ecosystem, and when to further transfer functionality to the commoditizing ecosystem. Due to lack of metrics and governance for when this should be done, the companies spend too much time on developing functionality they think is important but that have stopped adding value to customers. Based on our findings, and the general approach taken at the case companies, we conclude that all companies struggle with defining metrics to avoid investing in functionality that customers do not value as differentiating. Also, timing the introduction of new technology to customers is a major challenge.

Don't – Let – Go" Commoditization: Most case companies report on internal and technology-driven company cultures. While commercial off-the-shelf solutions and open source software is available, most companies still struggle with efficiently utilizing these. Typically, the companies regard something as commodity when it stops generating money and when customers stop asking for it. However, the general feeling is that the majority of resources are allocated to functionality that could be considered commodity e.g. platform development. Also, and due to lack of metrics revealing feature usage, push-out of functionality is scarce. Based on our findings, and the general approach taken at the case companies, we conclude that none of the companies are as effective in establishing a culture where resources are allocated to differentiating functionality, rather than to commoditized functionality, as they could be.

5.2 Ecosystem Management

Based on our empirical findings, we develop a model in which we outline the defining characteristics of each ecosystem type (Fig. 1). In the model, we identify the drivers of each ecosystem type, the purpose and stakeholders of each ecosystem type and the characteristics of each ecosystem type. In outlining these different aspects of the ecosystem types, our model helps companies manage the activities associated with the different ecosystems they operate in.

During the interviews, it became evident that companies select different strategies and put different focus on the innovation, differentiation and commoditization aspects depending on where the product or product category finds itself from a competitive

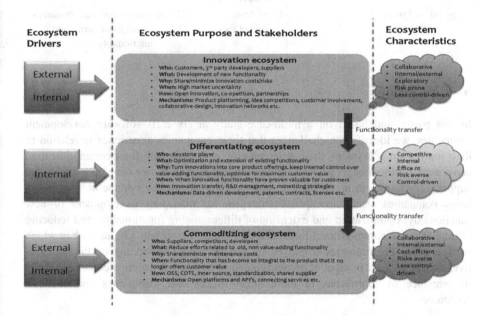

Fig. 1. The drivers, the purpose and stakeholders and the characteristics of the different ecosystem types.

perspective. In Table 3, and as a generalization of the approaches taken in the case companies, we present a framework in which we categorize the strategies employed by the companies depending on the competitiveness of a specific product or product category. As can be seen in this framework, companies deploy internally driven innovation and differentiating strategies for products and product categories that are considered market leading. Typically, selected suppliers are involved to validate innovative functionality and product differentiation is driven out of these initiatives. The more a product is 'on-par' with competition, i.e. equally good, the more collaborative companies get. Finally, for products and/or product categories that are considered 'laggards', the companies deploy a variety of strategies focusing on minimizing costs and resources, and in which copying from competitors is the way to drive potential differentiation.

Table 3. The different strategies deployed by the case companies in relation to the competitiveness of a product or product category.

	Innovation	Differentiation	Commoditization
Leader	Internal innovation and close collaboration with selected suppliers	Drive differentiation out of internal innovation initiatives	Aggressive commoditization to "kill off" potential differentiation by competitors
On-par	Collaborate with customers and ecosystem peers	Balance between innovation and copying from competitors	Commoditize to free up resources, but monetize as long as possible
Laggard	Ignore	Copy from competitors	Minimize cost and resources for acquiring commodity functionality

6 Conclusions

In this paper, and based on a multi-case study at six B2B software development companies, we identify the challenges that these companies experience in relation to their innovation ecosystem, their differentiation ecosystem and their commoditization ecosystem. Furthermore, and based on our empirical findings, we develop a model that supports companies in managing the different ecosystems they operate in. Our model helps companies select appropriate strategies for managing development of new functionality, optimization and extension of differentiating functionality, and reducing efforts related to commoditized functionality. Finally, we present a framework in which we categorize the strategies employed by the companies depending on the competitiveness of a specific product or product category. In future research, we intend to study the variance in approaches in more detail in the case companies and in other companies.

References

1. Bosch, J.: Achieving simplicity with the three-layer product model. IEEE Comput. **46**(11), 34–39 (2013)
2. Hanssen, G.K.: A longitudinal case study of an emerging software ecosystem: implications for practice and theory. J. Syst. Softw. **85**(7), 1455–1466 (2012)
3. Ritala, P., Agouridas, V., Assimakopoulos, D., Gies, O.: Value cration and capture mechanisms in innovation ecosystems: a comparative study. Int. J. Technol. Manage. **63** (3/4), 244–267 (2013)
4. Iansiti, M., Levien, R.: The Keystone Advantage: What the New Dynamics of Business Ecosystems Mean for Strategy, Innovation And Sustainability, p. 225. Harvard Business School Press (2004)
5. Olsson Holmström, H., Bosch, J.: Ecosystem-driven software development: a case study on the emerging challenges in inter-organisational R&D. In: Proceedings of the 5th International Conference on Software Business, pp. 16–18. Paphos, Cyprus, June 2014
6. Van den Berk, I., Jansen, S., Luinenburg, L.: Software ecosystems: a software ecosystem strategy assessment model. In: Proceedings of the 4th European Conference on Software Architecture: Companion Volume, pp. 127–134. ACM, New York, NY, USA (2010)
7. Bosch, J.: From software product lines to software ecosystems. In: Proceedings of the 13th International Software Product Line Conference (SPLC). San Francisco, CA, USA, 24–28 August 2009
8. Manikas, K., Hansen, K.M.: Software ecosystems: a systematic literature review. J. Syst. Softw. **86**, 1294–1306 (2013)
9. Yin, R.K.: Case Study Research. Design and Methods, 3rd edn. Sage, London (2003)
10. Corbin, J., Strauss, A.: Basics of Qualitative Research: Grounded Theory Procedures and Techniques. Sage, California (1990)
11. Walsham, G.: Doing Interpretive Reseach. Eur. J. Inf. Syst. **15**, 320–330 (2006)
12. Maxwell, J.A.: Qualitative Research Design: an Interactive Approach, 2nd edn. SAGE Publications, Thousands Oaks, CA (2005)
13. Stake, R.E.: The Art of Case Study Research. SAGE Publications, Thousands Oaks, CA (1995)

Early Value Argumentation and Prediction: An Iterative Approach to Quantifying Feature Value

Aleksander Fabijan[1(✉)], Helena Holmström Olsson[1], and Jan Bosch[2]

[1] Faculty of Technology and Society,
Malmö University, Östra Varvsgatan 11, 205 06 Malmö, Sweden
{Aleksander.Fabijan,Helena.Holmstrom.Olsson}@mah.se
[2] Department of Computer Science and Engineering,
Chalmers University of Technology,
Hörselgången 11, 412 96 Göteborg, Sweden
Jan.Bosch@chalmers.se

Abstract. Companies are continuously improving their practices and ways of working in order to fulfill always-changing market requirements. As an example of building a better understanding of their customers, organizations are collecting user feedback and trying to direct their R&D efforts by e.g. continuing to develop features that deliver value to the customer. We (1) develop an actionable technique that practitioners in organizations can use to validate feature value early in the development cycle, (2) validate if and when the expected value reflects on the customers, (3) know when to stop developing it, and (4) identity unexpected business value early during development and redirect R&D effort to capture this value. The technique has been validated in three experiments in two cases companies. Our findings show that predicting value for features under development helps product management in large organizations to correctly re-prioritize R&D investments.

Keywords: Continuous experimentation · EVAP · QCD · Data-driven development · Customer-driven development

1 Introduction

By introducing agile development practices [1], companies have taken the first step in being able to better cope with continuously changing market requirements [2, 3]. At the same time, organizations are striving to find systematic instructions that would guide them in re-prioritizing feature developments and assuring them to stop developing features when they don't deliver new value. Instead, what they wish for is a way to determine and validate feature value before it is fully developed in order to discover where to invest R&D efforts, or when to stop developing it [3, 17].

Known as customer experimentation, this is a common practice in the Business-to-Consumer (B2C) domain, while it is still to gain momentum in the Business-to-Business (B2B) domain. Data collection techniques in the B2B domain are typically designed for operational purposes and do not explicitly reveal the necessary

© Springer International Publishing Switzerland 2015
P. Abrahamsson et al. (Eds.): PROFES 2015, LNCS 9459, pp. 16–23, 2015.
DOI: 10.1007/978-3-319-26844-6_2

information for feature experimentation such as feature usage, role of the user etc. Today, and due to the fact that products are increasingly becoming connected, customer experimentation is gaining momentum also in B2B organizations [3, 11].

In this paper, and based on case study research in two B2B software-intensive companies, we investigate how feature value prediction and validation can be performed in a continuous experimentation setting in order to prevent companies from developing features that do not deliver value. We use as a foundation the QCD model [4] of customer-driven development and look into one aspect of it, e.g. how to validate hypotheses about feature value using customer data.

The contribution of this paper is the development and validation of the EVAP technique. With this technique we provide organizations with: (1) an actionable implementation of one of the aspects of the QCD model that practitioners can use to dynamically develop valuable product functionality, (2) a technique that helps teams develop just enough of a feature and stop when too little value is being created, (3) support to stop development of a when expected value is not realized, and (4) help to identify unexpected business value early during development and redirect R&D effort to capture this value.

2 Background

Von Hippel [5], coined the term 'Lead Users' in order to show that customers with strong needs often appear to be ahead of the market and that companies should involve them in order to validate concepts or emerge with new ideas. Learning and validating with users of the products is becoming increasingly important and organizations need to adapt their processes in order to take this source of feature validation into account [7, 8]. First seen in the B2C domain and recently also in B2B domain [6], products are becoming connected and by having data collection techniques in place, numerous new options are available to use this information.

2.1 The QCD Model: Qualitative and Quantitative Customer Validation

Recently, and as a model to help companies move away from early specification of requirements and towards continuous validation of hypotheses, the QCD model was introduced [4]. The model identifies a number of customer feedback techniques (CFT's) that can be used to validate feature value with customers. As seen in the model (Fig. 1), hypotheses are derived from business strategies, innovation initiatives, qualitative and quantitative customer feedback and results from on-going customer validation cycles.

The novel development approach as pictured in the QCD model captures, and expand further, on ideas that have been previously published [3, 12, 13]. In the QCD model quantitative, as well as qualitative feedback techniques are recognized.

Typically, and to initiate and experiment, a hypothesis is selected and validated on a set of customers. To support this process, numerous customer feedback collection techniques have been identified in the literature [9, 10]. In addition to the validation and

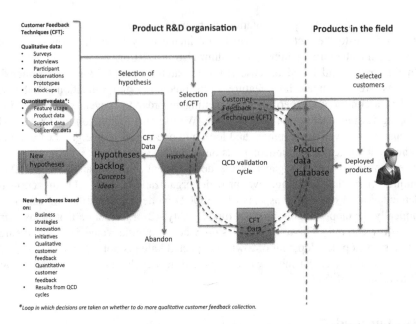

Fig. 1. The Qualitative/Quantitative Customer-driven Development (QCD) model [4].

confirmation of existing hypotheses, the data collected allows new hypothesis to be formed, making the QCD model an instrument for innovation of new features, for value discovery and for prediction of feature value.

Below, and in order to further illustrate the use of the QCD model, we specify one of its techniques, i.e. the 'Early Value Argumentation and Prediction' (EVAP).

3   Early Value Argumentation and Prediction Technique

Typically, and as recognized in previous research [17], product management (PdM) has to wait until the feature is fully developed in order to validate its expected value. To overcome this problem, and to be able to predict the value of a feature, we coin the term 'Early Value Argumentation and Prediction' (EVAP), to annotate a technique that practitioners can use in order to estimate what impact a feature will have when fully developed. We define value argumentation to be the ability to explicitly specify what the value of the feature will be when fully developed. And EVAP technique in particular works as a support for helping companies move away from early specification of requirements and towards dynamic feature prioritization (Fig. 2).

As a result of using the technique, companies can predict the value of a feature being developed, and decisions on whether to continue development or not can be taken based on real-time customer data. We illustrate this in Fig. 3, where we show the typical process of feature value validation and prediction.

In a continuous experimentation setting, a feature is first selected and its expected value is defined as a hypothesis. The product functionality is then iteratively developed

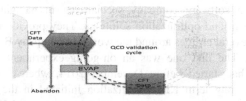

Fig. 2. 'EVAP' technique in the QCD model.

and validated on the customers. It may take several iterations of developing a minimal viable feature (MVF), referred to i*t(im) on Fig. 3, where 'i' denotes the number of iterations, before the expected value is confirmed. We annotate the time between identification of a feature expected value t(ex) and until its confirmation t(va), to be the 'value gap time' t(gap). This is the period where companies decide, using the customer data collected, whether to continue developing the functionality or stop and redirect R&D efforts.

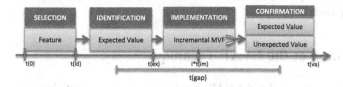

Fig. 3. 'Early Value Argumentation and Prediction' (EVAP) technique.

4 Research Method

We validated our model on a multiple-case study [14] that took place between December 2014 and June 2015. It builds on an ongoing work with two companies involved in large-scale development of software products. Case study methodology is an empirical method aimed at investigating contemporary phenomena in their context, and it is well suited for this kind of software engineering research [15]. Based on experience from previous projects on how to advance beyond agile practices [3, 9], we held two joint workshops with the companies involved in this research, and two individual workshops in-between. Since both participating companies collect quantitative as well as qualitative data, QCD model was the appropriate instrument. What companies struggled with, is an actionable implementation of one the aspects of the QCD model. We therefore completed the workshops with a concept that is now known as the EVAP technique.

4.1 Case Companies

Company A is a provider of telecommunication systems for mobile and fixed network operators. Together with company A, we performed one feature experiment focusing on a feature that reestablishes connections. Among the representatives we met were a product owner, a line and system manager and a developer.

Company B is a software company specializing in navigational information, operations management and optimization solutions. They provide nautical charts and airline avionics for several airlines around the world. In company B, we performed two feature experiments. The first one was an on-going experiment with a feature for adjusting schedule that started before December 2014, whereas the second feature experiment with the long term KPI visualization initiated in the beginning of this research. We met with a system architect, portfolio manager and UX Designer.

4.2   Data Collection and Analysis

The main data collection method in both of the joint workshops was semi-structured group interviews with open-ended questions [2]. Additionally, to the workshops, we had a number of Skype meetings, individual company visits and communicated via e-mail or Lync. In total, we met twice on joint workshops, twice at each of the companies individually, and communicated via emails at least once per month. The notes and workshop meeting minutes were analyzed following the qualitative content analysis approach [16].

5   Validation of the EVAP Technique

In company A, we validated EVAP in one feature experiment. Iteratively, and following EVAP technique, they tried different setting of the feature under development, until a significant difference in the measured counter (the number of detach requests on link failure) was visible. After the count of detaches stabilized, they were confident that the expected value of the feature is confirmed. Moreover, while validating feature value, company A monitored how the CPU load changes in time. Interestingly, they discovered that when this feature is active, the CPU load decreases.

In company B, we validated EVAP in two experiments. First, company B observed the customers using their scheduling feature. Company B wished that operators of the product use this functionality in order to improve the scenario proposed to better aid crew planner in doing the right tradeoffs between KPIs, and to compare different solutions. They discovered that the use of the feature in the first iteration was low, so they came-up with adjustments that they deployed in the next iteration. After another observation of the data collected, combined with the roles of users using this feature, they had enough evidence to argument that this feature delivers the hypothesized value. That is, the individual KPI improvements when manually adjusting a schedule.

In the third experiment, company B decided to validate if by visualizing performance indicators they could learn more about the customers and motivate them to take the improvements. Also, they did not know how well their product versions perform in reaching customers' KPIs. To overcome this, company B started to develop this functionality and show KPI trending prototypes and concepts to a test customer. First, company B visualized KPIs that they considered important. After analyzing the data, they did not see any significant difference in behavior of the customer. In the next iteration, Company B improved the feature by closely cooperating with the test

Table 1. Summary of the experiments.

	Company/Experiment	CFT and collected data	Expected and validated value	Predicted value
A	Network feature	Product logs that contain number of detaches, active users and sys. load	Reduced the number of detach requests	Reduces CPU load during a network hiccup
B	Scheduling feature	Service center logs with counts of feature usage and optimizations starts	Improving an individual KPI	Product-learning and improvements
B	Long term KPI visualization	Service center logs with counts of dashboard openings/interviews	/	Better alignment of the customers KPIs

customer and changed the visualizations so they reflect what companies consider as an important KPI. Now, customers are more interested in adopting this functionality and cooperating with Company B (Table 1).

6 Discussion and Conclusion

Organizations are struggling to know if and how much of the feature that they are developing, will actually deliver value to their customers. To overcome this problem, and to be able to predict and validate feature value, companies have to continuously be able to collect customer feedback and learn from the users [6, 10]. The QCD model, due to its nature of being very dynamic when forming hypotheses and able to handle both quantitative as well as qualitative data [4], is the current 'state of the art' instrument for continuous experimentation.

In this paper, we present EVAP technique as an actionable implementation of one aspects of the QCD model. Companies can use this technique in order to:

(1) *Dynamically develop valuable product functionality*

We illustrate this in the three feature experiments with the two case companies, showing how they both developed valuable functionalities. For example, company A successfully developed the network feature by proving that the number of detach requests iteratively reduced by validation on a test system. Similarly, company B developed the scheduling feature, by iteratively running feature experiments with their customers and validating the value. At the same time, company B started to develop the KPI visualization feature, which is showing positive validation results, giving company B a reason to continue developing this functionality.

(2) *Develop just enough of a feature and stop when too little value is being created*
    While iterating with the network feature, company A validated the functionality
    on the test system that mimics real-life environment and found out that by
    comparing the results of two consecutive iterations, the number of detach requests
    converged and developing further would not bring more value to the product.
    They stopped developing the parts of the feature that would further reduce detach
    requests.

(3) *Stop development of a feature and remove it from the system when expected value
    is not realized*
    Although this has not been the case during this research, companies could stop
    developing a feature and remove the already implemented parts from the system,
    if they had identified that measurable value of the feature is lower as expected.

(4) *Identify unexpected business value early during development and redirect R&D
    effort immediately to capture this value.*
    We can see from the experiments that both companies predicted the value of the
    feature even before they fully developed it. In Company A, they correctly pre-
    dicted the CPU load decrease and increasingly invested in further developing this
    functionality in order to capture this value. Similarly, company B predicted the
    value of their second experiment to be positive. They are increasing their efforts
    and further developing the functionality.

To conclude, we have demonstrated how continuous feature experimentation can
be conducted in two large B2B companies, in order to use the benefits of being
customer-driven to validate and predict feature value. We do this by exploring the QCD
validation cycle and developing an iterative technique that practitioners in organizations can use to dynamically develop valuable product functionality.

In future research we plan to further detail the different techniques that are used as
part of the QCD model, and we intend to validate these in our case companies.

References

1. Cockburn, A., Williams, L.: Agile software development: it's about feedback and change.
   Computer **36**, 0039–43 (2003)
2. Dzamashvili Fogelström, N., Gorschek, T., Svahnberg, M., et al.: The impact of agile
   principles on market-driven software product development. J. Softw. Maint. Evol. Res.
   Pract. **22**, 53–80 (2010)
3. Olsson, H.H., Bosch, J.: From opinions to data-driven software R&D: a multi-case study on
   how to close the 'open loop' problem. In: 2014 40th EUROMICRO Conference on Software
   Engineering and Advanced Applications (SEAA), pp. 9–16 (2014)
4. Olsson, H.H., Bosch, J.: Towards continuous customer validation: a conceptual model for
   combining qualitative customer feedback with quantitative customer observation. In:
   Fernandes, J.M., Machado, R.J., Wnuk, K. (eds.) ICSOB 2015. LNBIP, vol. 210, pp. 154–
   166. Springer, Heidelberg (2015)
5. Von Hippel, E.: Lead users: a source of novel product concepts. Manage. Sci. **32**, 791–805
   (1986)

6. Bosch, J., Eklund, U.: Eternal embedded software: towards innovation experiment systems. In: Margaria, T., Steffen, B. (eds.) ISoLA 2012, Part I. LNCS, vol. 7609, pp. 19–31. Springer, Heidelberg (2012)
7. McKinley, D.: (2012). http://mcfunley.com/design-for-Continuous-Experimentation
8. Davenport, T. H.: How to design smart business experiments. In: Strategic Direction, Emerald Group Publishing Limited, Bradford (2009)
9. Fabijan, A., Olsson, H., Bosch, J.: Customer feedback and data collection techniques in software R&D: a literature review. In: Fernandes, J.M., Machado, R.J., Wnuk, K. (eds.) ICSOB 2015. LNBIP, vol. 210, pp. 139–153. Springer, Heidelberg (2015)
10. Bosch, J.: Building products as innovations experiment systems. In: Proceedings of 3rd International Conference on Software Business, Cambridge, 18–20 June 2012
11. Lindgren, E., Münch, J.: Software development as an experiment system: a qualitative survey on the state of the practice. In: Lassenius, C., Dingsøyr, T., Paasivaara, M. (eds.) XP 2015. LNBIP, vol. 212, pp. 117–128. Springer, Heidelberg (2015)
12. Fagerholm, F., Guinea, A.S., Mäenpää, H., et al.: Building blocks for continuous experimentation, pp. 26–35 (2014)
13. Ries, E.: The Lean Startup: How Today's Entrepreneurs Use Continuous Innovation to Create Radically Successful Businesses. Random House LLC, New York (2011)
14. Walsham, G.: Interpretive case studies in IS research: nature and method. Eur. J. Inf. syst. **4**, 74–81 (1995)
15. Runeson, P., Höst, M.: Guidelines for conducting and reporting case study research in software engineering. Empirical Softw. Eng. **14**, 131–164 (2009)
16. Mayring, P.: Qualitative content analysis–research instrument or mode of interpretation. Role Researcher Qual. Psychol. **2**, 139–148 (2002)
17. Johansson, E., Bergdahl, D., Bosch, J., Olsson, H.H.: Quantitative requirements prioritization from a pre-development perspective. In: Rout, T., O'Connor, R.V., Dorling, A. (eds.) SPICE 2015. CCIS, vol. 526, pp. 58–71. Springer, Heidelberg (2015)

Challenges of Structured Reuse Adoption — Lessons Learned

Veronika Bauer[✉]

Technische Universität München, Munich, Germany
bauerv@in.tum.de

Abstract. Adoption of structured reuse approaches in practice often poses multiple challenges. Research-industry collaborations are considered as suitable vehicle to mitigate adoption difficulties as well as to validate the applicability of scientific results. However, research co-operations with industry do not always live up to the expectations of either of the partners. Unfortunately for researchers and practitioners alike, insights behind the scenes of failed adoption and cooperation are often difficult to obtain. This hinders discussions on lessons learned by organizations during the adoption process and delays improvements.

This paper aims to mitigate this issue by presenting lessons learned from interviews we conducted with practitioners in the context of a study on software reuse in industry. The study covered a wide range of aspects, including the process of reuse adoption. One of the participating companies had undertaken two attempts to adopt a form of structured reuse. However, both attempts did not succeed as expected. In our study, we identified tacit assumptions that were related to the encountered difficulties and present the lessons learned from the adoption approach. Furthermore, we report strategies that helped us to overcome the scepticism caused by a previous unsuccessful guided collaboration.

1 Introduction

Understanding and improving the adoption of research results in practice is an ongoing concern in the software engineering community [10]. To this end, one key challenge needs to be overcome: research does not operate under the same operational constraints as industry. As a result, it is usually difficult for researchers to "eat their own dog-food" and test their approaches under realistic circumstances. Furthermore, assumptions on significant context factors that need to be present for a successful adoption of the proposed approaches might remain implicit, with potential detrimental effects to adoption efforts. This is especially critical when proposing measures requiring significant and long-term changes in industry, such as large organizational restructuring [2]. Adoption of a structured reuse approach is a prime example for this case: approaches usually require substantial changes on the technical as well as the organizational level. These deep changes are very difficult to achieve [5]. Whilst abstracting a problem from its context is a necessity of scientific thought [6], as researchers we run the risk

© Springer International Publishing Switzerland 2015
P. Abrahamsson et al. (Eds.): PROFES 2015, LNCS 9459, pp. 24–39, 2015.
DOI: 10.1007/978-3-319-26844-6_3

of overestimating the applicability and the potential benefits of our results if we fail to explicate a clear relation to the assumed and envisioned application context.

Providing approaches that are applicable in practice is a challenge for researchers; successfully adopting these approaches might be even harder from an industrial perspective. Research-industry collaborations seem a suitable and popular vehicle to address and mitigate these challenges for both sides [1,5,21,25]. However, they are not free from challenges: one of the most obvious differences between academia and industry becomes apparent in the goals they typically bring to a collaboration: researchers wish for high quality data to validate their approaches, practitioners wish for a suitable, affordable, and fast solution for a specific issue [20,25]. Consequently, also successful technology adoption might have a different meaning for each party [3].

Structured reuse, by means of reusable components [15], Software Product Lines (SPL) [18], or the more pragmatic Inner Source [23] philosophy, have a long history of being considered a "silver bullet" [19] in research and practice alike. Virtually every paper on software reuse starts with a mantra-like declaration of abstract benefits (improved quality, decreased cost, decreased time to market) [11,13,14] and proceeds by adding several new aspects on how to achieve them. Often, the feasibility is demonstrated by the application of the approach in a small number of case studies. Whilst, from a researcher's perspective, this is a reasonable practice, it poses several problems for industry adoption: For instance, often-times the exact conditions under which the proposed solution is supposed to work are not mentioned in detail. Neither does the reader learn about all the preconditions and assumptions that make a solution applicable in the first place. Lastly, there is a tendency to advocate structured approaches as superior independently of a company's strategic context, business goals, or domain.

Several works have reported on adoption attempts of structured reuse in practice and proposed respective success and failure factors: Joos [12] reports on the experience of introducing a systematic reuse process at Motorola in the 1990s that succeeded due to management support, education of engineers, suitable incentives, tool support). Frakes and Fox [9] present a reuse failure mode model, derived from a questionnaire on (code) reuse answered by 113 people from 29 organizations. The authors mention four dimensions (managerial, economic, legal, technical) that need to be addressed when implementing systematic reuse. Lynex and Layzell [14] assess the management and organizational issues raised by the introduction of reuse programs in industry. They collect inhibitors to adoption gained from experiences from reuse projects reported in the literature, provide reasoning for causes and present possible solutions. Fichman and Kemerer [8] examine the extent to which the introduction of a formal and systematic reuse program was advanced in one large organization. They found that reuse was prevalent on an informal, local, scope but neglected on an inter-project, systematic, level due to an incentive conflict with respect to team priorities such as completing a project on time and on budget. Sherif and Vinze [22] report on barriers to reuse adoption, concluding that individual declination towards reuse was caused mainly by the organizational stance on reuse adoption. Morisio et al. [16] report on success factors for adopting or running company-wide reuse programs, collecting evidence from 24 reuse projects in European companies varying in size, business domain and culture. The authors identify underestimation of the required effort as main driver for failure and conclude that success of reuse projects depend on management commitment, awareness of human factors and modification of non-reuse processes according to the specific context of the company. Dubinsky et al. [7] investigate the reasons that cause companies to reluctantly move away from ad-hoc reuse in the form of code cloning to structured product line approaches. They identify efficiency, low overhead, short-term thinking, and lack of governance as main drivers.

Challenges that can occur when attempting to adopt structured reuse became apparent to us during a study on reuse in practice. To establish how reuse is currently effected in practice, we started a number of research-industry studies, of which 2 are currently completed. In their context, we so far interviewed approximately 30 practitioners from well established software companies (head count ≥ 5000, more than a decade of experience in the market). Especially in one company, issues during the adoption of research approaches were a consistent theme across departments and hierarchy. We therefore decided it worthwhile to extract and report lessons learned.

Goal and Contribution: Our goal is to create awareness of challenges of adopting structured reuse in practice. In this paper, we report practitioner accounts on several stages of a reuse adoption attempt, collect harmful patterns in the form of tacit and implicit assumptions and interpret them to identify lessons learned. Practitioners and researchers thus can consider this information and use it to counteract some of the challenges when driving a similar adoption attempt.

Outline: Section 2 introduces the context of the adoption situation of the given company. Section 3 details on the two previous adoption attempts. The findings are interpreted in Sect. 4. Section 5 reflects on the options of researchers and practitioners to improve collaboration in the context of research adoption. Section 6 concludes the paper.

2   Study Design

In the context of evaluating the state of the practice of reuse in industry, we so far completed two exploratory studies with two companies. At the current state of our research, we conducted 35 h of interviews and collected 138 questionnaire responses. This paper collects impressions from one specific company at which we conducted around 20 one-hour interviews and obtained 69 questionnaire responses. We report the impressions of our interview participants on the adoption of a structured reuse approach to their development practice.

In the following, we detail on the company context, summarized in Table 1[1], and line out the case study design and the main results. In addition, we provide pointers to supplementary material.

Company Characteristics: We can not disclose the names of the company and the involved partners in the previous research collaboration. However, we line out the characteristics of the company in order to give the reader an understanding of the circumstances: U is a national software house providing technical information services and business information products to their clients. The company was founded in the 1960s, emerged as a service provider and gradually moved to providing stand-alone software products and support services. Currently, U counts around 6000 employees.

Table 1. Company characteristics.

Characteristics	U
Established	1960s
Headcount	6000
Business model	Product
Field	business information systems
Organizational form	line
Scope	national
Distributed	locally
External requirements for release cycles	yes
Development context	
Development style	heterogeneous
Global requirements engineering	limited - none
Code ownership	exclusive
Code reviews	rarely
Testing	compulsory at product integration, else at developers' discretion
Infrastructure	local
Repositories	several local ones
Developer profiles	specialists
Work focus	single projects
Reuse characteristics	
Reuse strategy	ad-hoc in transition to structured
Current reuse scope	within division
Global incentives for reuse	no
Co-ordination of reuse	unofficial, within division
Co-ordination overhead for reuse	significant across divisions
Reuse consumer	within division
Reuse producer	within division
Pool of available artefacts for reuse	limited
Dedicated personnel for reuse	yes for basic product independent functionality
Reuse tool support	low
Accessibility of reusable artefacts	limited by organizational structure
Formal reuse assessment	no
Motivation for reuse	high
Satisfaction with current reuse benefits	limited
Study data	
Total number participants	~90
Participant average time in company	11-20 years

The company structure is hierarchical, structured along market segments within one specialized domain. The products have historically grown indepen-

---

[1] Please note that factors in the categories *development context* and *reuse characteristics* reflect tendencies and the state of the companies at the moment of the studies. Since the company aims to continuously improve their craft, this table does not necessarily reflect the situation at the time of reading.

dently over decades and contain a broad mix of technologies and various conventions in terms of architectural styles. In addition, many product varieties have been created to address niche markets, resulting in several hundred different products. This heterogeneity, furthermore, leads to a range of different required release dates.

Software development and maintenance is very heterogeneous across departments and teams, ranging from waterfall processes to tailored Scrum approaches. Also the level of development tool support, testing practices, and code ownership is highly diverse. As a result, product parts are integrated in a "big bang" style to prepare the respective releases. Developers usually work on specialized topics of a single product and tend to be responsible for the respective subsystems (Subsystem code ownership, see [17]).

Participants: We study the current practice of reuse at U by means of an exploratory study consisting of an interview phase with 20 participants, followed by questionnaire phase with 69 respondents.

To gain insight into contextual and strategic factors of reuse adoption, we drew interview participants from each of Us product and support development departments and all levels of the hierarchy between senior developers (including architects and user experience designers), higher, and top management (including the CTO and board members of the development department). The participants worked at U between 15 and more than 30 years. By means of qualitative data analysis, we extracted the context of reuse, involving roles, responsibilities, and reuse practices, i.e. reused artefacts and reuse realizations. We collected current issues, success factors, and ideas for improvement.

Questionnaire participants were invited by a newsletter and a post on a company news portal. Respondents came from 10 of the 13 departments. 44 % worked at U for at most 10 years, 20 % for 11–20 years, and 36 % for more than 20 years. 15 % reported their role as manager. The respondents job focus was mainly on development (78 %), and architecture (13 %). Respondents at U usually work within one product area and are organised in product departments over several hierarchical units. They are developing software most frequently in C# and SQL. In addition, they use Java and C++. The participants are software development professionals and managers with an experience ranging from 5 to 30 years. We selected them from a range of positions, hierarchy levels, and departments. Their participation was optional.

Methodology: As means of data collection, we used semi-structured interviews and online questionnaires.

The study contained semi-structured 1–2 h interviews always conducted by two researchers and an extensive online questionnaire containing mainly closed-questions. We analyzed the interviews by means of inductive content analysis. To extract relevant concepts, we coded the transcripts [4] and triaged the emerging concepts for relevance w.r.t. reuse. We conducted the study during 3 months in the time frame from September 2012 to February 2015.

Supplementary material shows the topics and sample questions of interviews and questionnaire[2]. For this paper, we focus on the interviews as the theme of technology adoption and a failed research collaboration mostly emerged during these sessions. We, therefore, extracted the related statements from the transcripts and present them in the following.

Goal of Our Collaboration: From the academic perspective, the goal for our research collaboration was to assess the state of reuse in practice. From the industrial perspective, the goal was to collect a neutral and honest account on the current perception of the reuse strategy, including improvement points.

3   Adoption of a Strategic Reuse Program

At the beginning of our study, we found the following situation with respect to reuse adoption: several years ago, management had decided to move from a range of independent products in the same or similar market segments to a more integrated version. This was a business decision based on feedback from clients and market requirements. In the process of pursuing this goal, a need for unification between products became apparent. To address this, the need for a structured reuse approach came into focus with the goal to improve software production, reducing errors, and providing customers and users with a homogeneous product. Two adoption attempts had taken place: one without guidance by researchers and one in collaboration with academia.

Reuse Goals and Targeted Approach: The company's reuse goals are: consistent extension of the .NET framework used by their products, consistent integration of existing products, lower maintenance costs. These goals should be reached by a structured company-wide reuse approach based on a shared platform, providing building blocks for products. The target vision of the reuse approach contained elements of SPL engineering and characteristics of Inner Source development.

Current State of Reuse: At the point of writing, reuse is mandated for an internal utility platform providing domain-independent functionality to products. In U, code is reused in a very heterogeneous way and mostly retrieved from colleagues on the basis of personal contact or, occasionally, by searching the web. In addition to code, style guides are reused.

Tacit Assumptions and Their Consequences on Adoption. At the company, many of the success factors mentioned in the literature for a transition to more strategic reuse were present: there was top management commitment, reuse was institutionalized by means of a visible workforce unit, the reason for reuse was founded on business needs, reuse was established as an explicit goal for developers, and a reuse champion was appointed [16]. However, in practice, we identified a number of assumptions tacitly held by key stakeholders of the

---

[2] Available at http://goo.gl/k9TWKE. Due to confidentiality of the data, we are unable to share the questionnaire raw response data.

adoption process which, from the beginning, significantly decreased the chances of a successful outcome.

In the following sections, we report the assumptions and their effects. We denote the roles which held the assumption in the following way: *HM* for *higher management*, *TM* for *top management*, *SD* for *senior developers*, followed by the number of the assumption.

In boxes, we contrast the respective assumptions with the participants' retrospective comments on their effect[3]. We denote the roles which provided the statements in the following way: *HM* for *higher management*, *TM* for *top management*, *SD* for *senior developers*, followed by the number of the statement. Furthermore, we distinguish between *product (P)* and *base platform (B)* participants.

3.1   Unguided Adoption Attempt — Company-Internal

Several measures were taken with the goal to establish a structured internal reuse approach: on the one hand, top management decided to build a generic base platform for all products the company was currently producing. For this task, a new department was founded and the use of that platform was mandated for all products. Furthermore, reuse became part of the developer goals with the intent of creating a reuse culture. Lastly, a designated reuse manager was appointed with the goal to identify potentially reusable entities and to build up a network of contributors.

Assumption 1, HM *"Successful transition to the new approach will not require deep organizational change."*

Based on this assumption, the department for base development was treated like any other product department. It was provided with a small to medium volume of resources (the weight between product development and base development is roughly 10:1) and assigned with a consulting status. Consequentially, recommendations for strategies or change, e.g. with respect to product architecture, were not binding for the products. As a consequence, significant energies were lost in the attempt to convince products to actively participate in the change. One senior developer summarized this by

SD1-B: "We have a rather political company culture, involving a lot of lobbying."

Furthermore, the company's heterogeneous development culture was not considered in terms of its impact on the reuse strategy. This meant that a platform approach should be adopted despite lacking central access points for source code and binding governance rules. Furthermore the infrastructure for code repositories, building, and testing was different in every department. Coordination was furthermore complicated by differing release time requirements of products.

---

[3] The quotes were translated into English. They are no longer verbatim, however we attempted to stay as closely as possible to the original meaning.

Lastly, the company relied on hierarchical communication paths and hindered exchange across the departments. Mending this was considered a key requirement for improvement by participants of product and base departments:

SD2-BP: "Increasing networking between the departments is a necessity."

Assumption 2, TM/SD *"Products will see the benefit of the platform and, therefore, will contribute."*

From the beginning, top-management was relying on active participation from products to contribute to the platform. This should, on the one hand, ensure the usefulness of the platform content, and on the other hand, educate every product department in the use of the platform. The contributing product developers, therefore, should serve as multiplicators. One of the tacit assumptions, however, was that middle management would provide resources when planning their efforts without further incentive. Senior product developers summarized the situation as follows:

SD3-P: "Top-management had a rather abstract interest in reuse. Middle management rather saw the cost than the potential. Workforce had varied views. We enjoyed [building for reuse] and could refer to the management goals. However, the architects were not enabled to create new structures."

The obvious discrepancies reportedly discouraged other developers from participating in the reuse initiative:

SD4-B: "Middle management occasionally even went out to punish developers that invested time in reuse contributions. [...] This quickly made many others loose interest [to participate]."

Assumption 3, TM/HM *"It is apparent to everyone how to do reuse."*

Reuse was never precisely defined, despite the platform use being mandated and despite reuse being explicated as a developer goal. The vagueness of the reuse initiative even lead to negative effects:

SD5-P: "During that time there was a massive focus on code reuse (also in the sense of copy and paste). Frequently, this lead to inadequate solutions for a given problem."

Consequentially, neither the scope of the platform and its intended use, nor the mechanisms for reuse on an individual level were explicitly discussed. Instead, product needs and product commonalities were assumed to be understood. This lead to a skewed implementation of the basis platform,

SD6-P: "Bigger departments and early collaborators dictated and shaped the platform to their needs."

as well as to a insufficiently focussed functionality.

SD7-P: "The basis unit is trying to do too much."

As a consequence, products reported a significant overhead in their deliverables, loss in performance of the product, and issues with dependencies.

SD8-B: "Products sit on a large bunch of code they don't really need."

Relying on the multiplicator model, the base development department assumed that extensive training in platform use was not necessary and that providing assistance, whenever asked for it, would be sufficient.

Assumption 4, HM *"One reuse manager can fully organize and coordinate reuse."*

The purpose of the reuse manager was to collect candidates for reusable entities from all development departments. In addition, they served as contact for anyone with inquiries or willingness to contribute to reuse. However, coordination was only intended as a part-time activity.

SD9-B: "Reuse coordination was always difficult. It stopped completely after I moved to a new role."

In the absence of a centralized code infrastructure, this identification and extraction of candidate reuse entities was a largely manual and infeasible process. The heterogeneity of the infrastructure as well as closed code repositories made the task more difficult.

SD10-P: "Source code analyses won't work here."

As a workaround, the reuse manager set up a wiki structure where reusable components could be registered with a description and a contributor contact. However, contributions remained scarce.

Effects of Unguided Adoption Attempt. After bringing the reuse initiative under way, top-management returned to everyday business. Since reuse was institutionalized to some extent, the platform was built and introduced. However, acceptance varied greatly among the products.

HM1-B: "If users don't like a platform, they will evade it and build their own things next to it. [...] This becomes apparent when changes in the platform have no effect in some of the products."

Furthermore, the voluntary co-operation between departments did not work as expected.

SD11-P: "Middle management enforced decisions that directly opposed the strategy of top management."

Summing up, the expectations towards the reuse efforts were only partially met.

3.2   Guided Adoption Attempt — Research Collaboration

To mend the weaknesses of the previous reuse adoption attempt, management initiated a research collaboration on the topic.

With interviews within the development organization, the researchers assessed the state of the current situation and proposed a new approach, based on principles of Open Source practices.

Assumption 5, HM *"A research collaboration will provide us with a tailored solution."*

As improvement, they proposed a model for reuse that required a significant restructuring of the entire organization. This idea was encountered with skepticism across all organizational ranks.

> TM1-BP: "The project and the idea were good in theory. However, [the researchers] did not take into account the company culture. [...] We were unable to adopt these ideas and maybe we were scared by the required effort and organizational risk. [...] They did not consider how to connect research to the company needs."

Assumption 6, HM/SD *"Collaborating researchers will align their goals with the organization."*

Furthermore, the attitude of the researchers caused significant irritation. Practitioners perceived them as disinterested towards the organizational risk as well as the long term applicability of the proposed approach.

> SD12-P: "The solution they proposed simply was unadoptable for us at that point in time: too risky, too expensive, unclear how we should even get there!"

This eroded trust and goodwill on the company side:

> SD13-P: "[The researchers] were pushing their approach, no matter if it was suitable for us or not. They went around the house interviewing people, but nothing really came from that."

> SD14-B: "They cared for their results and not so much for our needs."

Consequently, the case confirmed the assumption in practitioners that research results were no match for them. As a result, the collaboration was not continued.

> SD15-B: "We expected more from this collaboration."

Effects of Guided Adoption Attempt. Years later, the memory of this experience is still lingering in parts of the organization, resulting into tangible skepticism towards research(ers). On the one hand, this resulted in warnings from our industry contacts, such as:

> SD16-B: "Someone has done research on this context before, there is burned soil."

On the other hand, skepticism was outspoken:

> SD17-P: "Don't give us yet another tool."

> SD18-P: "Maybe this worked for someone else, but it won't work for us."

4   Lessons Learned — Adoption Attempts

In this section, we first sum up the core points of the encountered difficulties during research adoption. Then, we propose our lessons learned on how to avoid/mitigate these.

4.1 Company-Internal Adoption Difficulties

In the first reuse adoption attempt, several points caused the initiative to miss its goals: the understanding of the organizational, conceptual, and technical preconditions and requirements of the chosen approach was not deep enough. In this case, this lead to an underestimation of the necessary change, as well as to overly optimistic expectations regarding the benefits of the enterprise. In the end, the heterogeneity of the organizational context with respect to infrastructure, development processes, applicable mechanisms, communication culture, release dates etc. significantly reduced the benefits obtained from the platform approach.

Assumption 1 reveals that the company management fell for a well-known reuse myth: "reuse is for free" [24]. This misunderstanding highlights a typical danger of research adoption, as research papers as well as industry targeted publications oftentimes focus on the assumed benefits and general applicability of the approaches they propose. In this way, risks and necessary preconditions might be overlooked in the plan for adoption. In addition, the assumption expresses the desire to obtain a quick solution without investing significant resources. This desire partially prevented a thorough study of the organizational impact that a consistent application of the adoption was bound to have if it was meant to be successful. This aspect highlights the difficulty of motivating investments in research adoptions whose benefit can not be easily quantified.

Lesson 1. *A detailed assessment of the organizational factors is crucial to make a realistic estimate in terms of effort required to adopt a structured reuse approach.*

Assumption 2 shows that top management did not recognize the incompatibility of the current company and development structure and the planned adoption approach, which lead to an overly optimistic assessment on the effort required for a successful outcome. As a consequence, the adoption process stagnated when the company returned to everyday business. This highlights the need for top management to actively monitor the change process and compensate for the frictions induced by the change until the goal is reached.

Lesson 2. *Management commitment needs to exceed the initiation phase of a structural reuse adoption and provide long term support to reach the expected benefits.*

Assumption 3 highlights that the concrete implications of the approach were not understood in detail. One possible reason is that the concept to be adopted, strategical reuse, seemed so intuitive on an abstract level that the lack of methodology prescription on how to effect the adoption did not become apparent until it was too late. This highlights the need for a concrete adoption plan, including a selection of desired methods.

Assumption 4 provides a further example of how an abstract intuition for research adoption forms a mismatch with the details of a business environment. As a result, management did not assess the feasibility and practicality of the measure.

Lesson 3. *A rough and intuitive plan is not sufficient for structured reuse adoption. Instead the aimed for approach needs to be understood in detail to plan a successful adoption.*

4.2   Research-Industry Adoption Difficulties

Assumption 5 highlights the (mis)understanding of a research collaboration as a consultancy service. Whilst research collaborations *can* take that form, this oftentimes does not match the goals of the participating researchers, who (as in the present case) might look for feedback on or validation of a new approach. As a result, the approaches proposed by researchers might not always be the best match for the current situation of the industrial partner. Furthermore, the assumption shows the expectation that research approaches fit to a company without adjustment to the specific situation. Since research strives for general applicability, these two aspects are bound to collide if no explicit measures are taken. In this case, a part of the previous collaboration could, e.g., have consisted in a joint tailoring effort with industry delivering their concrete context and researchers providing support for an adoption strategy. Lastly, the assumption suggests that the goal for the cooperation might have been too ambitious in terms of scope.

Lesson 4. *It is important that researchers and practitioners alike be clear about their agendas, openly discussing goals and restrictions of their share of the adoption project to detect incompatibilities early on.*

Assumption 6 points to an expectation that is valid to a certain degree: if a collaboration is to be mutually beneficial, both parties might need to be flexible in terms of their goals. However, from the practitioners' perspective, their research partners did not show that kind of courtesy. The lack of interest in preconditions and context required for the adoption of the proposed approach caused frustration, since the suggested benefits seemed out of reach to practitioners. The attempt of pushing an approach onto a company for which it was not beneficial caused a lot of damage for the given and also future research-industry collaborations. It confirmed to several involved individuals the view of academia as theory-obsessed and practically irrelevant, a factor that increased skepticism towards software engineering research in general.

Lesson 5. *Sensitivity to the operational circumstances and restrictions of practitioners' work context is relevant to establish a trustful and beneficial relationship that is required to reach the collaboration goals.*

4.3   Threats to Validity

Reuse adoption was one of several aspects of our study. A dedicated study would have likely produced a more detailed picture. Nevertheless, the theme re-occurred reliably throughout the interviews so we consider the aspects as a useful starting point for further investigations.

This paper reports impressions from a single case study in a single company. Therefore, the results can not be considered general. However, several aspects coincide with experiences from other industry projects.

The participants were selected by a company insider. We invited to participate in the study by giving several talks within the company. This introduces a self-selection bias, which we tried to mitigate by selecting the volunteers according to their department and their position to obtain a varied picture.

The section on guided adoption is limited to the practitioners' perspective. Our scope was to highlight the difficulties encountered from their perspective and we did not want to adopt the position of an arbiter. Therefore, we did not contact the researchers of the previous collaboration.

5   Current Research Collaboration

Since the research adoption is still an active topic, the company agreed to participate in our study. The motivation on their part was to reflect on the adoption attempts of their reuse strategy, to evaluate the current state of how reuse is conducted across the different departments, and to use this information as the basis for improvement strategies. Our goals were data collection for a broader view on software reuse in current practice. In this case, the goals of industry and research aligned rather well and the scope of the collaboration was clear and of little risk. Being aware of the past research collaboration experience of this company, we invested strongly into communication, transparency, and expectation management. We could establish a close link between the company and research contacts, which keeps alive the cooperation and supports a regular exchange of findings.

5.1   Research Perspective

Establishing a trustful collaboration after a bad research adoption experience can be challenging. The following points helped us to overcome most of the encountered obstacles:

Transparency of Goals and Scope: From a research perspective, we were transparent about our goals and requirements with respect to results, publishing, and our position towards the company. We clearly communicated our minimum deliverables for success. At the same time, we carefully sourced the interests and agenda of the company stakeholders and clarified the expected deliverables as well as the legal restrictions on our research. Together with company contacts, we discussed the realizability of these goals and clarified potential legislative, moral, or scientific objections.

Knowledge About the Previous Failure: In the context of initiating the collaboration, we investigated the history of previous research adoptions and research-industry collaborations to find out when they took place, who was involved, which goals and results were achieved and which issues were encountered. This prepared us for potential apprehensions and helped us to address them whenever they surfaced.

Critical Distance to Research Approaches: Lastly, we could gain trust by displaying a flexible stance on our own research approaches. We reflected on the (implicit) preconditions that our solutions presupposed e.g. on the tool level, infrastructure, culture, goals and mapped this to the context of the specific company. In this way, we could reach a common understanding of potential next steps for the collaboration.

5.2 Industry Perspective

After two adoption attempts without satisfactory outcome, the company reflected thoroughly on the weaknesses of their previous strategies. In the current adoption attempt, the company has taken several measures to improve the process. The following aspects helped them to proceed:

Create Organizational Prerequisites: During reflection it became clear that the company did not yet fulfill several of the prerequisites that were necessary for a successful research adoption. For instance, the hierarchical communication structure was found to impair adoption: first, it caused a local prioritization of efforts, which counter-acted the strategy. Second, the lack of exchange between departments prevented the necessary distribution of knowledge and the homogenization of processes. To mitigate these issues, the company instantiated cross-department exchange forums for their technical experts. Via these forums, the company is guided through the changes needed to prepare a successful adoption. Management also realized that the adoption process needed a champion with decision power if the adoption process should be kept alive along every-day business. As a consequence, it provided the platform department with decision rights to push measures necessary for adoption.

Building and Instantiating a Long Term Adoption Strategy: To ensure a more successful adoption, the company hired an expert that had significant experience in leading similar adoption processes in larger software companies. The expert is now building up a concrete long term strategy to ensure beneficial adoption. At the same time, the company entered another research collaboration with the goal to obtain a complimentary and neutral viewpoint on the current situation of the adoption process.

6 Conclusion and Future Work

In the paper, we report the experience of a company attempting to adopt a structured reuse approach. We identify six assumptions that negatively impacted the adoption process and discuss their implications. We interpret the findings and derive lessons learned. In particular, we found that selecting a suitable approach for the current context and given goals is difficult since many factors need to be accounted for. In addition, the preconditions for research approaches often remain unclear. Furthermore, to execute a successful adoption, companies need support on how to guide change to experience benefits in the long run.

Research collaborations can potentially help with the adoption process. However, in our study we found that conflicts in short and long term goals as well as missing transparency of expectations erode the trust needed for a successful collaboration.

Lastly, we detail on aspects that helped our current research-industry cooperation to overcome some of the challenges from researcher and practitioner perspective.

Acknowledgements. Thanks go to the participants of our study for their time, frankness, and trust, to Annabelle Klarl and Daniel Mendez-Fernandez for helpful comments on previous versions of this work, and to Maximilian Junker for support with data collection. Parts of this work were funded by the Federal Ministry of Education and Research, Germany (BMBF).

References

1. Baldassarre, M.T., Caivano, D., Visaggio, G.: Empirical studies for innovation dissemination: ten years of experience. In: Proceedings of the 17th International Conference on Evaluation and Assessment in Software Engineering, EASE 2013, pp. 144–152. ACM, New York (2013)
2. Basili, V.R., Caldiera, G., Rombach, H.D.: The experience factory. In: Encyclopedia of Software Engineering (1994)
3. Bauer, V., Eckhardt, J., Hauptmann, B., Klimek, M.: An exploratory study on reuse at google. In: SER&IP's (2014)
4. Charmaz, K.: Constructing Grounded Theory: A Practical Guide Through Qualitative Analysis. Pine Forge Press, Newbury Park (2006)
5. Diebold, P., Vetrò, A.: Bridging the gap: SE technology transfer into practice: study design and preliminary results. In: Proceedings of the 8th ACM/IEEE International Symposium on Empirical Software Engineering and Measurement, ESEM 2014, pp. 52:1–52:4. ACM, New York (2014)
6. Dijkstra, E.W.: On the role of scientific thought. A personal Perspective, Texts and Monographs in Computer Science, In Selected Writings on Computing (1982)
7. Dubinsky, Y., Rubin, J., Berger, T., Duszynski, S., Becker, M., Czarnecki, K.: An exploratory study of cloning in industrial software product lines. In: CSMR 2013 (2013)
8. Fichman, R.G., Kemerer, C.F.: Incentive compatibility and systematic software reuse. J. Syst. Softw. **57**, 45–60 (2001)
9. Frakes, W.B., Fox, C.J.: Quality improvement using a software reuse failure modes model. IEEE Trans. Software Eng. **22**(4), 274–279 (1996)
10. Gorschek, T., Wohlin, C., Carre, P., Larsson, S.: A model for technology transfer in practice. IEEE Softw. **23**(6), 88–95 (2006)
11. Hislop, G.W.: Analyzing exsiting software for software reuse. J. Syst. Softw. **41**(1), 33–40 (1997)
12. Joos, R.: Software reuse at motorola. IEEE Softw. **11**(5), 42–47 (1994)
13. Lim, W.C.: Effects of reuse on quality, productivity, and economics. IEEE Softw. **11**(5), 23–30 (2002)

14. Lynex, A., Layzell, P.J.: Organisational considerations for software reuse. Ann. Softw. Eng. **5**, 105–124 (1998)
15. McILROY. M.D.: Mass produced soptware components. In: NATO Software Engineering Conference Report (1968)
16. Morisio, M., Ezran, M., Tully, C.: Success and failure factors in software reuse. IEEE Trans. Softw. Eng. **28**(4), 340–357 (2002)
17. Nordberg III, M.E.: Managing code ownership. IEEE Softw. **20**(2), 26–33 (2003)
18. Pohl, K., Böckle, G., van der Linden, F.J.: Software Product Line Engineering: Foundations, Principles and Techniques. Springer, Heidelberg (2005)
19. Ravichandran, T., Marcus, A.: Software reuse strategies and component markets. Commun. ACM **46**(8), 109–114 (2003)
20. Rodríguez, P., Kuvaja, P., Oivo, M.: Lessons learned on applying design science for bridging the collaboration gap between industry and academia in empirical software engineering. In: Proceedings of the 2nd International Workshop on Conducting Empirical Studies in Industry, CESI 2014, pp. 9–14. ACM, New York (2014)
21. Sandberg, A., Pareto, L., Arts, T.: Agile collaborative research: action principles for industry-academia collaboration. IEEE Softw. **28**(4), 74–83 (2011)
22. Sherif, K., Vinze, A.: Barriers to adoption of software reuse. a qualitative study. Inf. Manag. **41**, 159–175 (2003)
23. Stol, K.-J., Fitzgerald, B.: Inner source - adopting open source development practices in organizations: a tutorial. IEEE Softw. (2015)
24. Wasmund, M.: Reuse facts and myths. In: Proceedings of the 16th International Conference on Software Engineering, ICSE 1994, Los Alamitos, CA, USA, pp. 273–287. IEEE Computer Society Press (1994)
25. Wohlin, C., Aurum, A., Angelis, L., Phillips, L., Dittrich, Y., Gorschek, T., Grahn, H., Henningsson, K., Kagstrom, S., Low, G., Rovegard, P., Tomaszewski, P., van Toorn, C., Winter, J.: The success factors powering industry-academia collaboration. IEEE Softw. **29**(2), 67–73 (2012)

Instruments to Improve the Software Development Process

Software Process Improvement Implementation Risks: A Qualitative Study Based on Software Development Maturity Models Implementations in Brazil

Eliezer Dutra[1,2(✉)] and Gleison Santos[1]

[1] PPGI/UNIRIO, Universidade Federal do Estado do Rio de Janeiro,
Rio de Janeiro, Brazil
gleison.santos@uniriotec.br
[2] Centro Federal de Educação Tecnológica Celso Suckow da Fonseca,
Rio de Janeiro, Brazil
eliezer.goncalves@cefet-rj.br

Abstract. *Background:* Several problems affect software process improvement (SPI) initiatives planning and institutionalization. Past SPI initiatives provide valuable knowledge that can be used to identify risks that might affect new ones. *Aims:* In this article we aimed to identify risks that might affect SPI initiatives involving the adoption of software development maturity models such as CMMI-DEV and MR-MPS-SW. *Method:* We (i) conducted a systematic mapping study to identify potential risks sources in Brazilian SPI-related literature and (ii) performed a qualitative analysis of selected articles using coding procedures and thematic analysis. *Results:* From 86 articles discussing SPI-related problems we were able to identify 17 risk categories, or top-level risks, that might affect software development maturity models deployment. These 17 risk categories are decomposed on 135 first level risks. Each risk is associated to possible causes, consequences and events. Among the most critical risk categories identified are: inadequate process definition, lack of support or commitment, lack of human resources, resistance to SPI initiative and lack of knowledge.

Keywords: Software process improvement · Risk management · Qualitative analysis

1 Introduction

Software development organizations need to deliver products faster, cheaper, and with higher quality [1]. Therefore, they need to efficiently manage their software development processes and to continuously support their improvement. Software process improvement (SPI) has been a long-standing approach promoted by software engineering researchers, intended to help organizations develop higher-quality software more efficiently [4]. However, SPI initiatives are faced with risks that may prevent their goals from being fully accomplished. Many times such risks affect organizations'

© Springer International Publishing Switzerland 2015
P. Abrahamsson et al. (Eds.): PROFES 2015, LNCS 9459, pp. 43–60, 2015.
DOI: 10.1007/978-3-319-26844-6_4

ability to develop and deliver software with good quality [4], especially micro, small and medium-sized enterprises (mSME) due to natural constraints on this scenario.

Solving problems after they happen can be disruptive and expensive [1]. The failure to treat SPI programs as real projects prevent them benefit from known project management methods and techniques [3]. Therefore, good understanding of risks is vital to SPI initiatives success [4, 5]. Although most organizations nowadays plan and control SPI initiatives using project management best practices (including risk management practices and processes, in order to foster their success rate) reports about SPI initiatives low acceptance and limited success are not uncommon [4, 7, 14, 16].

In this paper we present a qualitative study aiming to identify risks that might affect SPI initiatives based on deployment of software development maturity models such as CMMI-DEV [1] and MR-MPS-SW [2]. We conducted a systematic mapping study to identify past SPI initiatives experience reports that could provide knowledge to the identification of SPI-related risks. Then, we used coding procedures [10] and thematic analysis [14] to identify risks that might affect SPI initiatives. We were able to identify 17 risk categories, or top-level risks, which expand to 135 first level risks. Each risk is associated to possible causes, consequences and events. Among the most critical risk categories identified are: inadequate process definition, lack of support or commitment, lack of human resources, resistance to SPI initiative and lack of knowledge. Although we used Brazilian conferences as source, we argue the results are applicable in other contexts, as problems associated with SPI initiatives implementations are common to other contexts.

This article is structured as follows: Sect. 2 presents theoretical background, Sect. 3 describes research methodology, Sect. 4 describes accomplished results, Sect. 5 presents limitations and threats to validity, Sect. 6 discusses related studies, and Sect. 7 presents our final considerations.

2 Theoretical Background

Maturity models, such as CMMI-DEV [1] and MR-MPS-SW [2], and international standards, such as ISO/IEC 15504 and ISO/IEC 12207, are used as guides to software process improvements (SPI) implementations. In Brazil, since 2005, more then 650 MR-MPS-SW appraisals have been conducted, most of them in micro, small and medium-sized enterprises (mSME) [8]. MR-MPS-SW, the Brazilian Reference Model for Software Process Improvement, is part of the Brazilian Software Process Improvement Program (MPS.BR Program), coordinated by Softex (Association for Promoting the Brazilian Software Excellence) [2]. MPS.BR aims at both, establishing reference models and disseminating them in the marketplace. MR-MPS-SW is: (i) in compliance with international standards ISO/IEC 12207 and ISO/IEC 15504; (ii) fully compatible with the CMMI-DEV; (iii) based on software engineering best practices; and (iv) focused primarily on mSME. Moreover, since 2007, 242 companies have been assessed in CMMI-DEV in Brazil [17].

Table 1 shows processes that comprise the MR-MPS-SW maturity levels (ML), which are defined in two dimensions (based on the requirements of ISO/IEC 15504) [8]: process dimension and process capability dimension (process attributes). The initial

MR-MPS maturity level is the level G constituted of the two most critical software processes to SMEs: Requirements Management and Project Management. Levels A and B are the highest MR-MPS-SW maturity levels focusing on continuous process improvement. All processes were defined based on their ISO/IEC 12207 counterpart and were supplemented by additions from CMMI-DEV as needed [8]. Processes in italic have no counterpart in CMMI-DEV. In addition, Table 1 shows CMMI maturity levels (CMMI ML) equivalence to MR-MPS-SW maturity levels. As MR-MPS-SW and CMMI-DEV have similar (but not equal) structures, processes and outcomes [8] we believe SPI initiatives based on those models face similar problems and concerns.

Table 1. MR-MPS-SW maturity levels (ML) structure (adapted from [8]).

ML	Processes	Process attributes	CMMI ML
A	(*no new processes are added*)	1.1, 2.1, 2.2, 3.1, 3.2, 4.1*, 4.2*, 5.1*, 5.2*	5
B	Project management (*new outcomes*)	1.1, 2.1, 2.2, 3.1, 3.2, 4.1*, 4.2*	4
C	Decision management, risk management, and *development for reuse*	1.1, 2.1, 2.2, 3.1, 3.2	3
D	Requirements development, product design and construction, product integration, verification, and validation	1.1, 2.1, 2.2, 3.1, 3.2	-
E	*Human resources management*, process establishment, process assessment and improvement, project management (*new outcomes*), and *reuse management*	1.1, 2.1, 2.2, 3.1, 3.2	-
F	Measurement, configuration management, acquisition, quality assurance, and *project portfolio management*	1.1, 2.1, 2.2	2
G	Requirements management and project management	1.1, 2.1	-

*These Process Attributes (PAs) are applicable only on selected processes. The others PAs must be applied on all processes

SPI-related literature provides several sources of critical factors of success or failure, difficulties, lessons learned or barriers, for instance, [6, 7, 14, 16], but few sources present SPI-related risks or propose risk-controlling measures in the context of SPI initiatives reported in literature [4, 5]. Iversen et al. [4] present an approach to understanding and managing risks in SPI teams comprising a framework to understand and choose different risk management approaches for specific contexts. Niazi [5] performed an exploratory study in literature to identify risks in SPI initiatives along with a survey with Australian professionals. Among the SPI risks identified, and generally considered critical by Australian practitioners, are: organizational politics, lack of support, lack of defined SPI implementation methodology, lack of awareness and lack of resources.

Some authors had identified SPI-related problems and difficulties based on surveys and interviews. As pointed out by Niazi [5], a disadvantage of the questionnaire survey method is that respondents are provided with a set list of possible issues, which limit those reported as respondents only focus on the factors provided in the list. An alternative is the use of practitioners' experiences and perceptions to be explored independently and without any suggestion from the researcher in interviews [5]. We have adopted other approach: we conducted a systematic mapping study [13] to find relevant source and the use of coding procedures and thematic analysis [10, 14] to identify relevant SPI-related risks.

3 Research Methodology

3.1 Systematic Mapping Study

A systematic mapping study aims to investigate, evaluate and interpret relevant papers for a specific research question or topic of interest [13]. We have defined a systematic mapping study protocol, following the guidelines presented in [13], and performed data analysis using coding procedures [10, 14] in order to identify possible risks in source material. Our main research question is: "What risks affect negatively SPI Brazilian initiatives based on MR-MPS-SW and CMMI-DEV models?" In order to answer the research question and aiming to identify the risks in a more detailed way, we defined two secondary questions: "What caused the risk?" and "Which were the perceived consequences?"

We extracted risks from software process improvements papers published in Brazilian major venues about this matter: SBQS (Brazilian Symposium on Software Quality), and WAMPS (MPS.BR Annual Workshop). Those are the two main forums in Brazil that link industry and academy to discuss problems and solutions about Software Quality. Traditionally, both events publish original technical research papers about software quality and software process improvement and also have industrial tracks were experience reports and case studies regarding SPI initiatives results are discussed. It is not uncommon that a research paper also present feedback gathered in industrial settings. All research papers are peer reviewed by at least three software engineering researchers, some of them also experienced on SPI consultancy and appraisals based on CMMI-DEV and MR-MPS-SW. Reviewers from industrial tracks also include experienced SPI practitioners (many of them also member of MPS.BR Program Technical Team [8]). Most experience reports involve authors from both academy and industry.

That way, we believe that our approach is an alternative to the use of surveys or interviews. The selected articles tend to present discussions from the point of view of academic researchers and industrial practitioners regarding actions taken and problems faced during the SPI initiatives depicted. Moreover, we were able to identify risks based on problems that happened during SPI initiatives based on a maturity model deployment. Also we were able to identify problems reported by several organizations, of different types and sizes, along the years.

In order to conduct the systematic mapping study we have defined the following scope criteria: (i) WAMPS and SBQS conference papers; (ii) papers published between 2004 and 2014 for SBQS and between 2005 and 2014 for WAMPS. Those periods are justified by the fact that the MR-MPS-SW business model was created in 2004, and that the first MR-MPS-SW consultants meeting, the event that originated WAMPS as it is named today, was held in 2005.

It is worth notice that we have chosen not to use a fixed search string, unlike usual systematic mapping [13]. In spite of our efforts, we were not able to define a search string capable of returning all relevant articles only by searching in titles and abstracts. Relevant publications would be missed even searching for very generic terms like "software process improvement" in papers' titles and abstracts. Moreover, a full text search was considered unproductive as it led to lots of false positives. Therefore, we decided to read and evaluate all published articles besides using inclusion and exclusion criteria to justify their selection or not.

We defined the following inclusion criteria: (i) only experience reports and technical papers related to SPI initiatives based on MR-MPS-SW or CMMI-DEV maturity models are to be considered; and (ii) only publications describing risks, difficulties, problems, barriers, lessons learned or negative actions that had influenced the design and/or implementation of a SPI initiative are to be considered. We defined two exclusion criteria: (i) publications in which no proposition present difficulties, problems, barriers or negative actions are not to be considered; and (ii) publications in which all prepositions are writing using subjective language that might hinder their interpretation are not to be considered.

All articles in the scope were read so the researcher was able to interpret whether they reported circumstances that had negatively influenced a SPI initiative based on MR-MPS-SW or CMMI-DEV. As our aim is to identify risks that might affect negatively a SPI initiative we did not codified events that led to positive effects. Therefore, despite a risk might be viewed as positive or negative, in this article "risk" and "negative risk" are used as synonyms. In case of doubt applying inclusion and exclusion criteria, another researcher was consulted in order to reach a consensus. After articles selection, we applied coding procedures [10] and thematic analysis steps [14] in order to identify and categorize the risks based on the elements in the proposed conceptual model (see Sect. 3.2 and Fig. 1).

Strauss and Corbin [10] state that coding is the analytical process by which data are divided, conceptualized and integrated to build a theory. Although the authors' objective is to describe how to build a theory, they argue that not all research projects aim that [10]. We have only used constant comparison to perform the coding [10]. That way, an incident (herein, mentioned as first level code) is compared to another incident in order to identify similarities and differences and also to group/associate an incident to a category. Constant comparison is not limited to comparing incident to incident though. Comparison is also related to theoretical comparison whose goal is to stimulate researcher's reasoning about the properties and dimensions specific to the incident category/theme [10].

Papers on scope were published during a 10 years interval. Thus some problems reported in early years of MR-MPS-SW and CMMI-DEV adoption in Brazil are not likely to appear in more recent years, such as problems caused by not conducting the SPI initiative as a real project. Nevertheless, we codified reported problems by the authors and did not judge their novelty or uniqueness. Moreover, use did not judge whether the codified risks are more likely to be present in implementations conducted by experienced or novice consultants or practitioners.

3.2 Risk Identification Structure

There is no consensus on the content and structure of a risk identification process. We used PMBOK [11], MR-MPS-SW [2], CMMI-DEV [1], and ISO 31000 [12] as basis for gathering essential requirements for the risk identification process. Both CMMI-DEV and MR-MPS-SW suggest that risk descriptions should include context, conditions, consequences, sources and categories. PMBOK proposes a framework for risks description using the following assumptions: an event can occur and cause an impact; or if there is a cause, an event can occur leading to an effect. Accordingly to ISO 31000 [12], an event represents an occurrence or a change in a specific set of circumstances, and a consequence represents the result of an event that affects objectives. ISO 31000's also states that the risk identification process promotes search, identification and description of risks aiming to generate a comprehensive list of risks based on events. Thus, it involves the identification of risk's sources, events, causes and potential consequences. ISO 31000 also states that a risk may have one or more events. PMBOK also defines that risk sources or project areas can be used to categorize risks.

In this sense, we can notice that PMBOK and ISO 31000 present an event-based risk description. Thus, Fig. 1 depicts the essential elements proposed by CMMI-DEV, MR-MPS-SW, PMBOK and ISO 31000 to guide the risk identification process. We used this structure to thoroughly and in a nutshell identify risks. Thus, a risk description is detailed by grouping events, causes and consequences. Categories are used to group risks with similar meaning. That way, a category may also represent a more generic description of a risk.

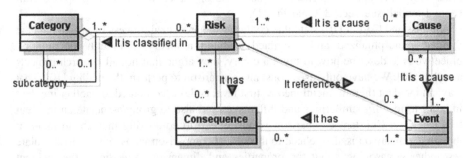

Fig. 1. Conceptual model.

The proposed structure does not intend to represent all involved concepts in the risk identification process. However, the use of a conceptual model allowed the extraction of essential elements and related concepts during risk identification process execution. For example, risks' source might be suggested by associated causes or events.

3.3 Data Collecting Using Coding Procedures and Thematic Analysis

During coding first phase, we only marked first level codes, i.e. those directly associated to text propositions, by identifying events, causes, and consequences (see Fig. 1). In this study, these elements represents themes [14] that are looked for in mapping study's selected articles' full text. During the coding phase the researcher do not infer the relationship between these concepts. The link must be established by the publication's prepositions.

During coding second phase, all articles were read again. Adjusts were made in first level code descriptions as needed. Also categories (i.e., more abstract codes) were grouped: events were grouped into risks; risks were grouped into risk categories; causes and consequences were grouped into more abstract codes of same names.

During coding, the procedures depicted in the systematic mapping study protocol were executed. One researcher read title and abstract of every article in scope to identify its type (i.e., experience report or technical research) and to assess whether it was related to at least one SPI initiative based on CMMI-DEV or MR-MPS-SW. If so, the article was completely and carefully read, line-by-line. Once the researcher had identified any proposition representing possible risks, difficulties, problems or barriers, he analyzed the reasoning depicted in the text in order to codify an event representing the main risk, difficulty, problem or barrier.

By using coding procedures, we were able to identify several events, causes and consequences, and to establish possible relationships between them. When possible we created codes using the exact same text depicted in the articles. However, sometimes we had to generalize the assumptions depicted. Moreover, as many papers described past events, sometimes text were adjusted to indicate future occurrence.

Figure 2 shows an experience report [15] excerpt translated from Portuguese, as an example. Text in bold indicates marks done by the researcher based on adopted coding procedures. The underlined expressions originated the following first level codes: "[EV114] Lack of communication between project leader and process owners", "[CA101] Project leader does not communicate software development project replanning to the team" and "[CO072] Organizational schedule regarding process deployment activities will be out of date or inconsistent". After analyzing the reasoning depicted in

---

During the configuration management process deployment we identified lack of communication between the project leader and the process owner [EV114], mainly after project replanning [CA101], because the organizational schedule regarding processes institutionalization activities was constantly out of date and, therefore, inconsistent [CO072].

Fig. 2. Text excerpt and coding example.

text we were able to establish a possible relationship between cause [CA101], event [EV114], and consequence [CO072].

Two researchers participated in the study for approximately one year. One of then was responsible to execute the systematic mapping study protocol and also to apply the coding procedures. Periodic meetings were carried out in order to analyze the quality of the coding process. Besides discussion about how to interpret articles' text, coding graphs (see Fig. 3) were analyzed to verify all marks and relationships between the codes. If the researchers interpreted differently the text, one of then had the article reanalyzed and notes were written to justify the consensual interpretation.

After all first level codes (events, causes, and consequences) were identified, the second coding phase began: codes were grouped into more generic ones (second level coding). Second level codes provide a more generic description to a first level code and also connect different first level codes identified in different articles excerpts. Figure 3 illustrates the codes identified in the excerpt presented in Fig. 2.

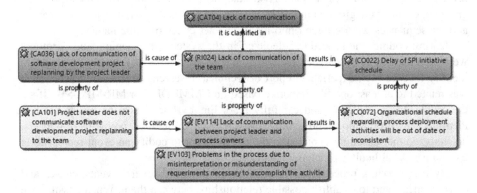

Fig. 3. Coding example showing risk category and associated first level risk.

Codes were grouped based on the structure depicted in Fig. 1: (i) first level risks are summarized in risk categories; (ii) first level risks are associated to possible causes, consequence and events. First level codes and second level codes are identified by square brackets and curly braces, respectively.

3.4   Auditing

In order to guarantee the overall quality of the coding process and the correct use of the coding procedures we have conducted two audits. Also codes were checked to verify whether events codified were really related to risks that might affect SPI initiatives based on maturity models such as MR-MPS-SW and CMMI-DEV.

During the first audit, three independent auditors verified if: (i) first level codes (for instance, cause, event or consequence) were grounded in propositions presented on articles, (ii) first level codes represented possible issues for SPI initiatives, and (iii) the researcher had associated cause, event and consequence accordingly. We made available to the auditors the digital file from the case tool used to perform the coding (Atlas.ti). We also made available two reports containing: (i) list of all markers (i.e., papers' original citations) along with all associated codes, and (ii) list of all events and their associated causes and consequences. This audit was performed by three researchers who (i) have knowledge about how to apply coding procedures [10], (ii) had previously published papers using Grounded Theory procedures as part of research method, and (iii) have knowledge about papers in search scope and software process improvement as well.

In the second audit, reports listing risks and associated events (as well as risk categories and their associated risks) were made available to the auditor. The auditor verified the coherence of (i) grouping events into first level risks, and (ii) categorizing first risks into second level risks (or risks categories). He also verified if identified risks, events, causes, and consequences were meaningful to SPI initiatives. The auditor is an experienced SPI consultant being responsible to conducting and managing SPI implementations based on CMMI-DEV and MR-MPS-SW in Brazil since 2003. He is also an official MR-MPS-SW competent assessor authorized to conducts assessment of any level, including the higher maturity ones (i.e., MR-MPS-SW levels B and A, equivalent to CMMI-DEV levels 4 and 5, respectively).

All remarks were checked and all required adjustments were made.

4   Results

We analyzed 527 technical research papers and experience reports from all SBQS and WAMPS proceedings. From those, 86 papers were included in the systematic mapping study scope comprising 56 papers from WAMPS and 30 papers from SBQS.

During the first level coding phase, we were able to identify 738 unique codes: 405 events, 156 causes and 177 consequences. Following the structure proposed in Fig. 1, first level codes (i.e., all risks, causes, events and consequences) were grouped accordingly to their characteristics into second level codes. The 156 first level causes were grouped into 85 second level causes. The 177 first level consequences were grouped into 87 second level consequences. The 405 events were grouped into 135 risks. Risks were classified and grouped into 17 risks categories. From those, 16 categories represent risks related to SPI initiative planning and execution and 1 of them ({CAT16}) represents risks associated to inadequate definition of processes. Category {CAT16} also comprises 15 subcategories associated to specific CMMI-DEV process areas or MR-MPS-SW processes (for instance, Requirements Management, Measurement etc.). We used subcategories (as depicted in the conceptual model in Sect. 3.3) to allow an intermediate abstraction dimension to represent the identified risks. In total, 1077 codes were identified; this large number prevents us from publishing all data due to lack of space. Table 2 shows the identified risk categories and quantity of risks and events associated. Table 2 also shows papers citations frequency count and percentage.

Five out of 17 categories comprise 64.7 % of citations: "{CAT16} Inadequate process definition (29,9 %)", "{CAT06} Lack of support or commitment (10,6 %)", "{CAT07} Lack of human resources (8,7 %)", "{CAT09} Resistance to SPI initiative (7,9 %)" e "{CAT02} Lack of knowledge (7,7 %)". It is worth notice that percentages

Table 2. Identified risk categories.

ID	Risk category	Risks	Events	Frequency	Frequency (%)
CAT01	Lack of tools	7	21	30	6.2
CAT02	Lack of knowledge	9	32	37	7.7
CAT03	Lack of training	2	5	6	1.2
CAT04	Lack of communication	3	10	10	2.1
CAT05	Lack of financial resources	2	10	13	2.7
CAT06	Lack of support or commitment	7	38	51	10.6
CAT07	Lack of human resources	3	24	42	8.7
CAT08	Turnover of employees	2	7	12	2.5
CAT09	Resistance to SPI initiative	5	26	38	7.9
CAT10	SPI initiative cancelation	1	2	2	0.4
CAT11	Organizational structure	5	15	17	3.5
CAT12	SPI initiative inadequate planning	7	21	23	4.8
CAT13	Inadequate planning of human resources	5	11	15	3.1
CAT14	Inadequate definition of training program	1	2	2	0.41
CAT15	Difficulties in SPI deployment in cooperative groups of organizations	4	11	13	2.7
CAT16	Inadequate process definition	59	139	144	29.9
CAT17	Difficulties in performing an official appraisal	13	27	27	5.6

indicated in this article do not represent judgment of value or expected impact to SPI initiatives.

Table 3 presents the first level risks associated to those 17 risks, showing the number of citations and citations percentage in parenthesis. Due to space limitations we are not able to present 55 risks associated to "{CAT16}" subcategories.

Category "{CAT16} Inadequate process definition" represent 29.9 % of total citation frequency, which evidence the need of defining software processes easy to understand (see for example "{RI038} Defined process is bureaucratic and difficult to understand" and "{RI111} Lack of adequate graphical view of activities and processes") and aligned to the organizational objectives (see for example "{RI053} Lack of alignment between organization goals and defined processes" and "{RI078} Lack of software development process tailored to specific situations"). Moreover, evidence defining and deploying several processes at once might hinder the SPI initiative (see for example "{RI059} Defining and deploying several software processes simultaneously").

Category "{CAT06} Lack of support or commitment" represents 10.6 % of total citation frequency. It indicates the importance of awareness of all involved stake-holders. Senior management support is one of the most important critical factors to SPI initiatives success. Nevertheless, we found that some initiatives were often obstructed

Table 3. Identified SPI-related risks.

Category	Risk
{CAT01}	{RI001} Lack of tools to support processes execution (11; 2.2 %)
{CAT01}	{RI002} Adoption of inadequate or discontinued tool to support processes execution (3; 0.6 %)
{CAT01}	{RI003} Lack of adequate tool to support SPI deployment based on agile methodologies (2; 0.4 %)
{CAT01}	{RI005} Lack of tools to support reuse management process (2; 0.4 %)
{CAT01}	{RI036} Lack of infrastructure or methodology to support diffusion of organizational memory (3; 0.6 %)
{CAT01}	{RI068} Lack of tools to support measurement process in high maturity (2; 0.4 %)
{CAT01}	{RI092} Inadequate analyzes of tools to support the software processes (7; 1.4 %)
{CAT02}	{RI006} Lack of knowledge on Software Engineering (9; 1.8 %)
{CAT02}	{RI007} Lack of knowledge on the adopted maturity model (10; 2 %)
{CAT02}	{RI008} Lack of knowledge on the SPI initiative (2; 0.4 %)
{CAT02}	{RI009} Lack of knowledge on the tools in use (1; 0.2 %)
{CAT02}	{RI010} Lack of knowledge on using measurement tools in high maturity organizations (2; 0.4 %)
{CAT02}	{RI011} Lack of knowledge on the deployed processes (8; 1.6 %)
{CAT02}	{RI012} Lack of understanding of reuse management process benefits (2; 0.4 %)
{CAT02}	{RI014} Lack of knowledge on requirements management (1; 0.2 %)
{CAT02}	{RI015} Lack of knowledge on project management (2; 0.4 %)
{CAT03}	{RI016} Lack of training (4; 0.8 %)
{CAT03}	{RI017} Inadequate or informal training (2; 0.4 %)
{CAT04}	{RI023} Lack of infrastructure to support communication (3; 0.6 %)
{CAT04}	{RI024} Lack of communication of the team (3; 0.6 %)
{CAT04}	{RI085} Lack of adequate involvement between senior management or organization's team and consultancy team (4; 0.8 %)
{CAT05}	{RI025} Lack of financial resources to execute the SPI initiative (8; 1.6 %)
{CAT05}	{RI026} SPI initiative inadequate scope (5; 1 %)
{CAT06}	{RI019} Lack of senior management support (8; 1.6 %)
{CAT06}	{RI020} Lack of support of middle-level management (4; 0.8 %)
{CAT06}	{RI022} Lack of support of clients (3; 0.6 %)
{CAT06}	{RI027} Lack of priority to SPI initiative activities (5; 1 %)
{CAT06}	{RI028} Lack of commitment (13; 2.6 %)
{CAT06}	{RI029} Lack of involvement on the SPI initiative (11; 2.2 %)
{CAT06}	{RI046} Demotivated organization team (7; 1.4 %)
{CAT07}	{RI031} Lack of human resources to execute the SPI initiative (25; 5.1 %)
{CAT07}	{RI032} Partially allocated human resources to the SPI initiative (14; 2.9 %)
{CAT07}	{RI107} Lack of consultants available to support the SPI initiative (3; 0.6 %)
{CAT08}	{RI033} Stakeholders turnover (8; 1.6 %)

(Continued)

Table 3. (*Continued*)

Category	Risk
{CAT08}	{RI034} Changes in sponsorship or senior management (4; 0.8 %)
{CAT09}	{RI037} Cultural resistance to software process adoption (17; 3.5 %)
{CAT09}	{RI039} Resistance to software process adoption (8; 1.6 %)
{CAT09}	{RI040} Rejection to the SPI initiative (2; 0.4 %)
{CAT09}	{RI041} Development team resistance to use the defined process (7; 1.4 %)
{CAT09}	{RI060} Team members think the defined process is an obstacle to execute their jobs (4; 0.8 %)
{CAT10}	{RI045} SPI initiative cancelation or suspension (2; 0.4 %)
{CAT11}	{RI035} Changes in organizational structure (2; 0.4 %)
{CAT11}	{RI055} Organization using a defined software development process for the first time (5; 1 %)
{CAT11}	{RI056} Inadequate organizational structure (5; 1 %)
{CAT11}	{RI074} Difficulties during contract formalization between consultancy firm and public organizations (2; 0.4 %)
{CAT11}	{RI075} Organization do not projectize maintenance operations (3; 0.6 %)
{CAT12}	{RI042} Pressure to perform official appraisals (3; 0.6 %)
{CAT12}	{RI044} Conflict of interest among organization's members (10; 2 %)
{CAT12}	{RI050} Adoption of new case tools (1; 0.2 %)
{CAT12}	{RI061} Consultancy firm deal with low experienced groups of organizations (1; 0.2 %)
{CAT12}	{RI088} Lack of prediction of pilot projects begin and end dates (1; 0.2 %)
{CAT12}	{RI100} Consultancy firm site distant from organization site (1; 0.2 %)
{CAT12}	{RI103} Difficulties to define, execute and understand the SPI initiative plans (6; 1.2 %)
{CAT13}	{RI076} Lack of availability of the team (1; 0.2 %)
{CAT13}	{RI079} Inadequate human resources allocation (1; 0.2 %)
{CAT13}	{RI087} Difficulties to allocate or keep an ideal composition of the software process expert group (7; 1.4 %)
{CAT13}	{RI089} Difficulties in planning the SPI initiative effort (1; 0.2 %)
{CAT13}	{RI133} Lack of a software process expert group member dedicated exclusively to the SPI initiative (5; 1 %)
{CAT14}	{RI109} Difficulties in defining or managing training programs (2; 0.4 %)
{CAT15}	{RI101} Lack of SPI activities coordination in the organization (1; 0.2 %)
{CAT15}	{RI102} Insufficient consultancy hours (1; 0.2 %)
{CAT15}	{RI105} Difficulties in planning the SPI initiative due to divergent interests and timing of organizations in a group (7; 1.4 %)
{CAT15}	{RI106} Difficulties in conciliating differences of the organizations in a group (4; 0.8 %)
{CAT16}	{RI018} Non-alignment between processes and organizational culture (4; 0.8 %)
{CAT16}	{RI038} Defined processes bureaucratic and difficult to understand (8; 1.6 %)
{CAT16}	{RI048} Processes defined without support of consultants (1; 0.2 %)

(*Continued*)

Table 3. (*Continued*)

Category	Risk
{CAT16}	{RI049} Organization might not be able to deploy the new processes in pilot projects (3; 0.6 %)
{CAT16}	{RI052} Defined process may change frequently (8; 1.6 %)
{CAT16}	{RI053} Lack of alignment between organization needs and defined processes (4; 0.8 %)
{CAT16}	{RI054} Lack of important activities in processes (1; 0.2 %)
{CAT16}	{RI057} Difficulties to execute organizational process quality evaluations (1; 0.2 %)
{CAT16}	{RI059} Defining and deploying several software processes simultaneously (2; 0.4 %)
{CAT16}	{RI078} Lack of software development process tailored to specific situations (2; 0.4 %)
{CAT16}	{RI080} Delay of processes definition (1; 0.2 %)
{CAT16}	{RI086} Defined process may reduce team productivity (2; 0.4 %)
{CAT16}	{RI099} Lack of objectivity during definition of software processes (3; 0.6 %)
{CAT16}	{RI108} Difficulties to define the best process architecture and the most adequate level of details (1; 0.2 %)
{CAT16}	{RI111} Lack of adequate graphical view of activities and processes (3; 0.6 %)
{CAT16}	{RI113} Software processes with lots of artifacts (1; 0.2 %)
{CAT16}	{RI124} Consultancy firm executes activities under the responsibility of the organization executing the SPI initiative (1; 0.2 %)
{CAT17}	{RI077} Lack of software development projects to execute an official appraisal (4; 0,8 %)
{CAT17}	{RI093} Structural difficulties in the SPI implementation (3; 0.6 %)
{CAT17}	{RI094} Lead appraiser might be late to the appraisal meeting (1; 0.2 %)
{CAT17}	{RI095} Organizational communication issues lead to interview schedule delays (1; 0.2 %)
{CAT17}	{RI096} Lack of information on how to get to appraisal site (1; 0.2 %)
{CAT17}	{RI097} Lack of time to execute the appraisal (1; 0.2 %)
{CAT17}	{RI098} SPI consultant, that also is an accredited appraiser, might act like an appraiser during the appraisal (1; 0.2 %)
{CAT17}	{RI110} Organization is not able to identify the adequate artifacts to evidence the maturity model outcomes (6; 1.2 %)
{CAT17}	{RI112} Organization may not understand important concepts involved in the appraisal (4; 0.8 %)
{CAT17}	{RI115} Organization is insecure on being appraised (1; 0.2 %)
{CAT17}	{RI116} Organization does not provide adequate infrastructure to the appraisal team (2; 0.4 %)
{CAT17}	{RI117} Pre-appraisal assessments may identify many weaknesses and improvement opportunities (1; 0.2 %)
{CAT17}	{RI118} Lack of personal on the organization to compose the appraisal team (1; 0.2 %)

by occurrence of risk "{RI019} Lack of senior management support". In many situations evidence shows that senior managers officially states support to the SPI initiative, but during deployment might reallocate the SPI team to software projects in order to deal with emergencies or unexpected issues. This is reality of some Brazilian micro and small organizations, in which "{CAT05} Lack of financial resources" and "{CAT07} Lack of human resources" also happen.

Category "{CAT07} Lack of human resources" represents 8.7 % of total citation frequency. Risk "{RI031} Lack of human resources to execute the SPI initiative" is the most cited (5.19 %) in this study. Risk "{RI031}" is caused by restrictions common to micro and small organizations. More than 70 % of the Brazilian organizations assessed in the MR-MPS-SW model are micro and small ones [8], therefore this risk should be taken in consideration during SPI initiative planning in such organizations. Other possible associated cause is not presenting to senior managers neither (i) resources needed to execute the SPI initiative, nor (ii) expected benefits of a successful SPI initiative.

Category "{CAT09} Resistance to SPI initiative" represents 7.9 % of total citation frequency, which evidences the need for awareness of all involved stakeholders. Intensive mentoring or workshop-like events for dissemination of the SPI initiative expected benefits are among the suggested examples of articles in scope. Involving stakeholders in decisions regarding the SPI initiative are likely to decrease the incidence of this risk.

Category "{CAT02} Lack of knowledge" represents 7.7 % of total citation frequency, which evidences the necessity of more effective and adequate training of project team in order to provide knowledge about organizational processes, software engineering and maturity models essential concepts. These trainings also are necessary to increase the necessary skills and abilities to perform SPI activities. Rocha et al. [9] also highlight low software engineering training level in universities and the presence of some undergraduate participants as possible causes for this risk.

We have created a sheet to each identified risk consolidating all information extracted from the publications on mapping study scope. An organization may use the risk sheets during the SPI initiative planning phase. The risk sheet presents risk's name, category, causes, and consequences. It also presents all identified events that originated the risk. Events may not have associated causes or consequences when they are not reported in the articles. It is worth notice that the associated events allow a broader understanding of the risk. Table 4 presents an example regarding risk "{RI024} Lack of communication of the team".

It is important to notice that each SPI initiative has different constraints, thus the lists provided in this paper must be carefully analyzed and used in each unique SPI context. The identified risks and risks categories can be used as input to SPI initiative planning activities. Moreover, prioritization on selected risks must be performed after qualitative and quantitative analyses. Finally, contingency and mitigation actions should be established to the most critical risks to both organization's and SPI initiative's goals.

Table 4. Risk sheet example.

Risk	{RI024} Lack of communication of the team	Category	{CAT04} Lack of communication
Cause	{CA036} Lack of communication of software development project replanning by the project leader {CA085} Lack of policy to execute activities	Consequence	{CO022} Delay of SPI initiative schedule {CO011} Productivity reduction
Events	[EV103] Problems in the process due to misinterpretation or misunderstanding of requirements necessary to accomplish the activities		
	[EV114] Lack of communication between project leader and process owners		
	[EV431] Miscommunication of activities planning to project team members		

5 Limitations and Threats to Validity

The exclusive use of technical papers and experience reports of the most important venues that discuss Software Quality and Software Process Improvement in Brazil to identify SPI-related risks may be interpreted as a validity threat to this study. But this strategy is grounded in CMMI-DEV [1], PMBOK [11] and Strauss and Corbin [10]. Both CMMI-DEV [1] and PMBOK [11] recommend the analysis of lessons learned documents during risk identification processes. Strauss and Corbin [10] argue that qualitative studies may be based on only one source, besides that the authors suggest that specialized literature might be considered.

Qualitative studies allow different interpretations from researchers [18]. Therefore, we have followed specific procedures to treat the limitations of our results [18]: dependability, confirmability, credibility (internal validity) and transferability (external validity). To treat dependability and confirmability we had two audits conducted by experienced researchers and by a SPI practitioner also an experienced researcher. We have addressed all identified problems. The triangularization of our results to risks presented literature [5] deal with credibility. We also presented details of the study planning, execution and data analysis. The coding performed throughout a detailed risk description treats transferability allowing the results to be analyzed and used in different contexts.

6 Related Works

Many articles present barriers or difficulties that may disturb SPI implementation initiatives [6, 7, 16], but few authors have described risks that affect SPI initiatives. Niazi [5] presented an exploratory study to identify risks in SPI initiatives. Five SPI risks were identified from the interview data that are generally considered critical by Australian practitioners: organizational politics, lack of support, lack of defined SPI implementation methodology, lack of awareness and lack of resources.

We were able to identify the top five critical risks presented in [5], but with different descriptions because of different methodologies to gather and analyze data and because of different methods to count citations frequency. For example, categories "{CAT05} Lack of financial resources" and "{CAT07} Lack of human resources" are described in [5] as "Lack of resources".

Niazi [5] conducted 34 interviews with Australian practitioners who were asked to provide a list of risks that can potentially undermine SPI implementation processes and in their opinion how these risks can be counteracted. We executed a systematic mapping study [13] to find relevant source information on articles that contains reports about SPI initiatives based on maturity models deployment, such as CMMI-DEV and MR-MPS-SW. In Niazi's study [5], more than 50 % of the interviewed practitioner's companies have been involved in SPI initiatives of any type over the last 5 years. Moreover interviewees were asked to say their opinion on which are critical risks for the implementation of SPI initiatives. We have collected all risks based on 86 articles that report facts about SPI initiatives conducted in Brazilian organizations.

Table 5 shows a comparison of the identified risks in both studies.

Table 5. Comparison to the top five critical risks identified by Niazi [5].

Niazi's rank	Niazi's risks	Our rank	Similar risks categories
1	Lack of support	2	{CAT06} Lack of support or commitment
2	Organizational politics	9	{CAT11} Organizational structure
3	Lack of awareness	2	{CAT06} Lack of support or commitment
4	Lack of defined SPI implementation methodology	10	{CAT13} Inadequate planning of human resources
		17	{CAT14} Inadequate definition of training program
		12	{CAT15} Deploying SPI on groups of organizations
		1	{CAT16} Inadequate process definition
5	Lack of resources	11	{CAT05} Lack of financial resources
		3	{CAT07} Lack of human resources

Risk category "{CAT06} Lack of support or commitment" represents the risks "Lack of support" and "Lack of awareness" identified by Niazi [5]. Risk "Lack of defined SPI implementation methodology" is represented by risk categories "{CAT13} Inadequate planning of human resources", "{CAT14} Inadequate definition of training program", "{CAT15} Deploying SPI on groups of organizations", "{CAT16} Inadequate process definition". These categories represent lack or inadequate definition of a methodology to conduct SPI initiatives. Risk category "{CAT15} Deploying SPI on groups of organizations" represents risks associated to a specific MPS.BR Business Model [2, 8] feature: part of resources is funded by public organizations to support SPI implementation in small groups of mSME across the country.

Other categories we have found, such as "{CAT10} SPI Initiative cancellation" (see Table 2), are not present in [5]. It represents events associated to loss of financial support, inappropriate relationship between top management and consulting, and project cancellation or interruption. Likewise we were not able to identify risks about "Negative/bad experience", and "SPI gets in the way of real work" presented in [5].

7 Conclusions and Future Work

We presented the results of a qualitative study aiming to identify risks that affect software process improvement (SPI) initiatives through Brazilian scientific software quality literature. After executing a systematic mapping study we applied coding procedures [10] and thematic analysis [14] on selected articles text to identify risks essential elements (event, cause and consequence) and later group them into risks and risk categories. Therefore, we were able to identify relevant SPI-related risks that might affect SPI initiatives based on a maturity model deployment. We expect organizations to use these risks as an input during the risk identification phase of a risk management process in order to increase the possibility of achieving SPI initiative success.

Among the most cited risk categories identified are: inadequate process definition, lack of support or commitment, lack of human resources, resistance to SPI initiative and lack of knowledge. The elements used to derive the risks were reported by several organizations, of different types and sizes along 11 years. Moreover, we argue that the identified risks can be used in different contexts and in other countries than Brazil.

As future work we will carry out further investigations to identify more SPI-related risks and to identify proper contingency and mitigation actions to them. Also we will expand the systematic mapping study scope to include articles published in different venues. Moreover we will evaluate and use our findings in an ongoing SPI initiative.

Acknowledgment. We would like to thank CAPES and FAPERJ (project E-26/110.438/2014) for the financial support to this research. We also thank Bianca Trinkenreich, Diego Cruz, Raphael Khoury, Patricia Lima and Tayana Conte for their valuable contributions.

References

1. CMMI Product Team: CMMI® for Development (CMMI-DEV), V1.3, Software Engineering Institute (2010). http://www.sei.cmu.edu/
2. SOFTEX: Brazilian Software Excellence Promotion Association, MR-MPS-SW – General Guide (2013). http://www.softex.br/mpsbr
3. Birk, D., Pfahl, D.: A systems perspective on software process improvement. In: International Conference on Product Focused Software Process Improvement, vol. 2559, pp. 4–18 (December 2002)

4. Iversen, J., Mathiassen, L., Axel, N.: Managing risk in SPI: an action research approach. MIS Q. Manag. Inform. Syst. **28**(3), 395–434 (2004)
5. Niazi, M.: An exploratory study of software process improvement implementation risks. J. Softw. Maint. Evol.: Res. Pract. **24**, 877–894 (2012)
6. Dyba, T.: Enabling software process improvement: an investigation of the importance of organizational issues. Empirical Softw. Eng. **7**(4), 387–390 (2002)
7. Rainer, A., Hall, T.: A quantitative and qualitative analysis of factors affecting software processes. J. Syst. Softw. **66**(1), 7–21 (2003)
8. Kalinowski, M., Weber K., Santos, G., et al.: Results of 10 years of software process improvement in Brazil based on the MPS-SW Model. In: 9th International Conference on the Quality of Information and Communications Technology (QUATIC), Guimarães, Portugal (2014)
9. Rocha, A.R., Montoni, M., Santos, G. et al.: Dificuldades e Fatores de Sucesso na Implementação de Processos de Software Utilizando o MR-MPS e o CMMI. (in portuguese) 2005. I Encontro de Implementadores MPS.BR, Brasília (2005)
10. Corbin, J., Strauss, A.: Basics of Qualitative Research: Techniques and Procedures for Developing Grounded Theory, 3rd edn. SAGE Publications, London (2008)
11. PMI: A Guide to the Project Management Body of Knowledge (PMBOK guide) (5th edn.), Project Management Institute, Inc (2013)
12. ISO 31000:2009: Risk Management—Principles and Guidelines. Geneva: International Standards Organisation (2009)
13. Kitchenham, B., Charters, S.: Guidelines for performing systematic literature reviews in software engineering. Technical Report EBSE 2007–001, Keele University and Durham University Joint Report (2007)
14. Baddoo, N.: Motivators and de-motivators in software process improvement: an emprical study. Ph.D. thesis, University of Hertfordshire, Hertfordshire, United Kingdom (2001)
15. Monteiro, R.W., Cabral, R., Alho, F., et al.: O Esforço Requerido para Institucionalização de Processos de Software na Prodepa. (in portuguese). In: ProQualiti – Qualidade na Produção de Software, vol. 4, no. 2, pp. 65–72 (2008)
16. O'Connor, R., Coleman, G.: An investigation of barriers to the adoption of software process best practice models. In: 18th Australasian Conference on Information Systems, pp. 780–789 (2007)
17. CMMI Institute: Maturity profile report: January 1, 2007–December 31, 2014. http://partners.clearmodel.com/cmmi-appraisals/process-maturity-profiles/
18. Recker, J.: Scientific Research in Information Systems: A Beginner's Guide. Springer, Berlin (2012)

Model-Driven Development for Multi-platform Mobile Applications

Rita Francese[1], Michele Risi[1]([✉]), Giuseppe Scanniello[2], and Genoveffa Tortora[1]

[1] Dipartimento di Informatica, Universitá di Salerno, Fisciano, Italy
{francese,mrisi,tortora}@unisa.it
[2] Dipartimento di Matematica, Informatica ed Economia,
Universitá della Basilicata, Potenza, Italy
giuseppe.scanniello@unibas.it

Abstract. In this paper, we propose an approach for the model-driven development of portable applications that use native device features. A model is based on a finite-state machine which specifies GUIs, transitions and data-flow among application screens. The source code is generated starting from that model. The state application logic is described by JavaScript. The approach has been developed within an integrated development environment.

Keywords: Multi-platform development · Mobile devices · Model-driven development · Visual development environment

1 Introduction

The market of mobile platforms is fragmented and it is rapidly changing [1]. These platforms are different from one another. As a consequence, to reach a wide audience of users there is the need of developing mobile applications (simply apps, from here on) for each platform and manually checking that the functionality is preserved across each of these platforms [2]. To do that, developers must have specific software skills and technology knowledge. A solution can be to develop an app as a Web application, obtaining the portability advantage peculiar of the Web, so that it will run on any device that has a Web browser. This approach reduces the development costs. However, this development strategy has the disadvantage that developed applications will not able to access to hardware features of mobile devices, such as camera, GPS, accelerometer and sensors [3]. The adoption of a multi-platform framework, such as PhoneGap[1] and Titanium,[2] partially solves this problem. These frameworks build hybrid applications for mobile devices using JavaScript, HTML5, and CSS3. These frameworks then compile the application exploiting native libraries for a specific platform and then generate an application for each target platform. However, developers are still in charge of designing and implementing data-flow, control flow,

---

[1] http://phonegap.com.
[2] http://www.appcelerator.com/titanium.

© Springer International Publishing Switzerland 2015
P. Abrahamsson et al. (Eds.): PROFES 2015, LNCS 9459, pp. 61–67, 2015.
DOI: 10.1007/978-3-319-26844-6_5

and interactions between user and app. To deal with these issues model-driven development (MDD) can be adopted to allow the developers to focus only on the problem and how to solve them, instead of focusing on technology details.

In this paper, we present an MDD approach and a supporting environment for the development of multi-platform mobile apps based on finite-state machine. In particular, the environment provides a finite-state machine editor and a generator, which produces source code starting from the model of the mobile app. The editor has been developed as an Eclipse plug-in, while the finite-state machine is implemented in JavaScript by using jQuery and jQueryMobile. The editor also exploits the PhoneGap functionalities to access the device native features and manages the app activities and the transitions between app screens. The dataflow and the control-flow of the application are automatically handled as well as the user's interaction. The state application logic is written in JavaScript. In this way, the developer only needs Web development skills to use our development environment. This reduces costs and risks for multi-platform development.

2 Background and Motivations

The limited resources of mobile devices represent critical aspects of mobile development (e.g., [4]). We recognize and summarize the following factors as critical aspects for mobile development:

Time-to market. It is often a disadvantage of mobile app development because it requires long time for the use of native platform development tools and for the porting to different platforms. There is the need of rapid development tools and capability for cross-platform mobile development.

Cost. Specific and advanced software skills are needed. Developers have to redesign and re-implement most of the applications. Low software reuse increases costs. Also several software configurations have to be maintained.

Quality. According to the results of the survey by Joorabchi *et al.* [2], it is challenging to port functionality across platforms and, when code is reused in another platform, the quality of the results is not satisfactory. Also documentation is not up-to-date due to the need of respecting strict deadlines.

Behavioral Consistency. A given mobile application should provide the same behavior independently from the operating system. To this aim, a generic design methodology for all the platforms should be provided.

To deal with the points mentioned before, MDD approaches could be successfully applied. For example, the problem of developing mobile applications with the same behavior on different platforms can be easily addressed by using MDD approaches [5]. A model is automatically transformed into the target application, without requiring the development of different software variants. MDD also offers a higher abstraction level than traditional programming languages. Under these conditions, MDD might be considered fast and cost effective. Indeed, it is faster (shorter time-to-market) because it should address the problem of redundancy of tasks. Cost reduction is also due to less people required, with less specialization. It is also easier to comprehend the application from its models and change it using these models with respect to modify the source code. This might reduce the cost related to maintenance operations. In addition, the documentation is always up-to date. The models are readable for domain experts and developers. The running application is generated starting from a high-level model; the application code quality can increase if the generator produces high quality code, that is if it has been developed by people with high programming experience/knowledge. MDD naturally provides *Behavioral Consistency* because models are independent from the platform. Only the back-end generation phase is platform-dependent.

3   Developing Multi-platform Mobile Applications

3.1   Finite-State Machine Diagram

Many definitions of state transition diagram (STD) exist in the literature. We based our proposal on the UML State Machine Diagrams [6]. An STD allows a developer to design the dynamic behavior of an application. In particular, it describes all the reachable states that implement the application and the events affecting each state. An STD is instantiated by a finite-state machine that executes the states and the state transitions. A state is executing when the State Machine waits until an event occurs for that state. In particular, an event occurs in case a specific trigger condition is satisfied or when the user interacts with the application. An event is a relation that links a source with a target state. These states are not necessarily distinct. If more than one event occurs at the same time, they are serialized using a priority scheme to execute one event at time. State Machine supports actions that depend on both the executing state and the triggering event. The development of an app also needs the definition of its GUI, which is generated starting from the definition of a state. We detail the elements of an STD and how they are mapped onto app elements.

- *State.* A state represents a screen of the app, i.e., what the user sees on the screen of his device. Each state has a type, i.e., *start, end, compute* and *intermediate*. It is depicted by a rounded rectangle and contains two attributes: name and stereotype. The latter is useful to specify the state type. A compute state has no GUIs and does not require interaction with it. It is in charge of performing an elaboration on data collected by the other states. The stereotype is absent for the intermediate states. Since the state represents a screen of the app, the description of its GUI has to be specified in terms of its widgets, such as buttons and edit texts. A state can use global variables to pass/acquire values to/from other states. Also device native functionalities can be associated to a state, such as *camera* to take a picture and *geolocation* to detect the GPS position of the mobile device.

    Users navigate through app screens and the STD moves in the corresponding states. Each state of the STD follows the life-cycle diagram shown in Fig. 1. In particular, a state S of the STD is initialized by *Create*, where *doDefineView*

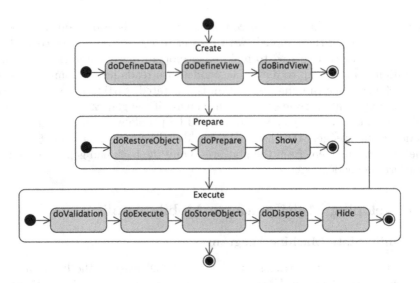

Fig. 1. The life-cycle of a state.

specifies the widgets to show in the GUI associated to S, *doDefineData* allows defining and initializing the variables of S, *doBindView* binds the events to the defined widgets to propagate fired events. Once S is created, the *Prepare* phase is executed. In particular, *doRestoreObjects* restores all the values of the variables of S. Successively, *doPrepare* initializes the widgets with the variable values and retrieves the needed information from database. Then, the GUI of S is shown and the user interacts with it (see *Execute*). *doValidation* validates the user's interaction (i.e., the input type correctness) and *doExecute* runs the business logic of S. *doStoreObjects* saves the attribute values in the device storage to let them available for the other states or when S is executed again. Finally, *doDispose* releases the allocated resources and the GUI of S is hidden.

– *Transition.* A transition is a directed relationship between a source state and a target state. Each transition has a label, specifying the event that induces state transition. A transition represents the passing from a screen to another. Thus, a transition occurs in correspondence of a user-generated event, such as the pressing of a GUI button. A transition can also occur automatically when a time-out is defined. In this case it is labeled by a number (i.e., the time). Between two states there could be more than one transition.

3.2   A Running Example

To better explain our proposal, we show how it supports the developer in the development of the *PictureEffect* app. This app accesses to the device camera, lets the user take a picture, and makes the picture preview by applying a graphical effect. The *PictureEffect* app has to be composed of the following three screens:

- *Home* contains two buttons: *Options*, to select the display options, and *Take Picture* to run the device camera;
- *Options* contains four input fields to set the roundness of the four corners of the image. The values associated to a perfect square are set as default values. Two buttons can be pressed: *Take Picture* to activate the device camera and *Back* to go backward to the previously shown screen.
- *TakePicture* allows taking a picture using device camera. The picture is then visualized with a graphical effect, by modifying the image shape considering the parameters set in the *Options* screen. Two buttons are available: *Take picture* and *Back*.

Each screen presents two buttons: *Home* and *Exit*. The former button lets a user go to the initial screen of the app, while the latter button allows to exit from the app. This example requires the use of a native functionality (camera) of the device and the specification of the application logic (the effect on the image). *PictureEffect* represents the experimental object used in our empirical study.

3.3   The Environment

Our development environment has been implemented as an Eclipse plug-in. It includes the STD Editor, which has been developed by using features offered by the Graphical Editing Framework[3] (GEF), a powerful tools for creating visual editors. The STD Editor is used to graphically specify finite-state machines. It manipulates one type of object, the state. It is possible to connect two states with one or more connections, the transitions.

The STD in Fig. 2 shows the finite-state machine associated to the *Picture-Effect* app. It is composed of four states: one for each screen specified before, with the addition of an ending state. On the top left side of Fig. 2, it is shown the development process menu. It is composed of four buttons:

- *Info*. It allows specifying general information on the app, such as name, author, and release data;
- *Generate*. It is responsible for the source code generation, of its syntactic and semantic checks;
- *Edit*. It allows modifying source code. In this case, HTML, JavaScript, CSS (Cascading Style Sheets), and jQueryMobile knowledge is needed.
- *Build*. It produces a project executable in the operating system of the app.

The editor allows the developer to specify additional properties for states and transitions, (i.e., GUI elements and variables), by adopting a form-based GUI. For example, a developer can define the GUI of a state by setting its widgets, as depicted in Fig. 3, where on the top left-hand side the buttons of the *Options* state are defined. Each button has an *id*, a *label*, and an associated *transition*. On the top right-hand side of Fig. 3 the editor generates transitions related to GUI events (pressing one of the two buttons). Also four input variables are defined,

---

[3] https://eclipse.org/gef/.

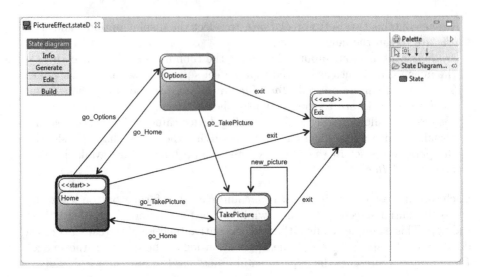

Fig. 2. An example of STD drawn with the generation environment.

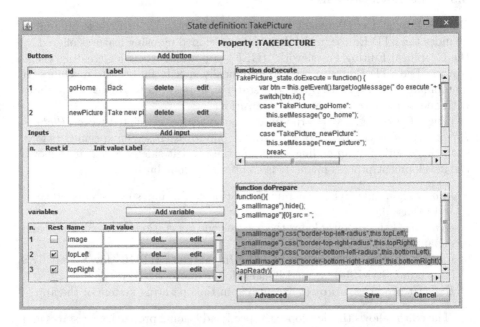

Fig. 3. The code manually added to the *doPrepare* method.

corresponding to the values to be used in the execution of the graphical effect on the taken image. The default value is 0 and indicates that the size of image is squared.

The editor allows the developer to exploit the native functionalities of a mobile device. To this end, it is possible to access a menu listing available functionalities, including camera, accelerometer, geolocation, network, and sensors. As an example, when *camera* is selected the logic for handle it is automatically generated. The editor GUI requires developer to specify variable names (e.g., *image* in Fig. 3). Developer can also provide a second not mandatory variable identifying the GUI widget where the picture is displayed.

The application logic (JavaScript code) is written in the *doPrepare* method. To complete the PictureEffect app, after having set all the variables, the developer edits *doPrepare* in the text area. The native camera functionality is provided by default, but to obtain the graphical effect on the picture there is the need of modifying the CSS of the image by inserting the code shown on the bottom right side of Fig. 3.

4   Conclusion

In this paper, we presented an approach and a development environment based on the design of a finite-state machine for supporting the generation of portable mobile apps. The definition of the data-flow and control-flow is managed by this environment. Web development skills are required to specifying application logic.

Future work will be also devoted to deeply assess the advantage offered by our approach by testing the generated apps on different devices. Also other types of widgets should be supported. To better support app development, also syntactic and semantic checks on the variable definitions and on their use will be took into considerations in the future versions of our environment.

References

1. Heitkötter, H., Hanschke, S., Majchrzak, T.A.: Evaluating cross-platform development approaches for mobile applications. In: Cordeiro, J., Krempels, K.-H. (eds.) WEBIST 2012. LNBIP, vol. 140, pp. 120–138. Springer, Heidelberg (2013)
2. Joorabchi, M., Mesbah, A., Kruchten, P.: Real challenges in mobile app development. In: ACM/IEEE International Symposium on Empirical Software Engineering and Measurement, pp. 15–24 (2013)
3. Heitkötter, H., Hanschke, S., Majchrzak, T.A.: Comparing cross-platform development approaches for mobile applications. In: Web Information Systems ans Technologies (WEBIST), pp. 299–311. SciTePress (2012)
4. Corral, L., Georgiev, A.B., Sillitti, A., Succi, G.: Can execution time describe accurately the energy consumption of mobile apps? an experiment in android. In: 3rd International Workshop on Green and Sustainable Software (GREENS), pp. 31–37 (2014)
5. Balagtas-Fernandez, F.T., Hussmann, H.: Model-driven development of mobile applications. In: 23rd IEEE/ACM International Conference on Automated Software Engineering (ASE), pp. 509–512. IEEE Computer Society (2008)
6. Group, O.M.G.: UML Specification, Version 2.0 (2005)

SINIS: A Method to Select Indicators for IT Services

Bianca Trinkenreich[1]([⊠]), Gleison Santos[1],
and Monalessa Perini Barcellos[2]

[1] Department of Computing, Federal University of the State of Rio de Janeiro
(UNIRIO), Rio de Janeiro, Brazil
{bianca.trinkenreich,gleison.santos}@uniriotec.br
[2] Ontology and Conceptual Modeling Research Group (NEMO),
Computer Science Department, Federal University of Espírito Santo (UFES),
Vitoria, Brazil
monalessa@inf.ufes.br

Abstract. Measurement initiatives support organizations in the control, management and improvement of their processes, products and services. IT services literature suggests proper identification of critical business processes and definition of relevant indicators to support decision-making. However, there is no clear direction about what should be the critical business processes and indicators. Moreover, most organizations consider indicators selection a difficult task. In this paper, we present SINIS, a method that supports the selection of indicators for IT services measurement. The research question that guided this work is: "How to support selection of IT services indicators at different levels and aligned with organizational goals?" We have conducted a case study in industry and the results showed that SINIS can be used to support IT service measurement. However, evidence suggests that it is still hard for organizations to define strategies and indicators to monitor and improve critical processes.

Keywords: Measurement · IT services · Indicators · GQM + Strategies · COBIT

1 Introduction

IT service management is a set of specialized organizational capabilities for providing value to customers through services. This practice is increasingly growing by adopting an IT management service-oriented approach to support applications, infrastructure and processes [4].

Guidance on how to develop and improve IT service maturity practices is a key factor to improve service performance and customer satisfaction [3]. Models such as CMMI-SVC [3] and MR-MPS-SV [9] have this purpose. They require appropriate measures to be identified in order to monitor processes executed for delivering service to customers. Thus, selection of processes to be measured must be aligned with organizational goals so that measurement results can provide relevant information for proper decision-making. However, there is no clear direction or strict suggestion about which critical processes and measures should be considered.

© Springer International Publishing Switzerland 2015
P. Abrahamsson et al. (Eds.): PROFES 2015, LNCS 9459, pp. 68–86, 2015.
DOI: 10.1007/978-3-319-26844-6_6

Aiming to identify measures that could be used to assess IT service quality, we carried out a systematic mapping study in which a set of measures was obtained [11]. Although the investigated papers suggested some measures applicable to IT services, there are no details about how these measures had been selected. After the study, we performed a case study in industry [12] to evaluate the applicability of the identified measures in a real context. The company where the case study was performed had corroborated that the selection of IT services measures is not an easy task.

The existence of a set of measures from which is possible to choose the ones useful to an organization can reduce effort and speedup selection [5, 18, 19]. However, it is not enough. It is necessary to define which ones will play the role of indicators, i.e., measures that help monitor a goal achievement [13]. Thus, it is necessary to align measures and goals and define indicators for IT services [20]. Alignment demands understanding stakeholders' information needs and the way IT services processes were designed and are executed in the organization, detecting IT services critical processes and choosing strategies that should be followed in order to achieve established goals. Considering that, we developed SINIS (Select Indicators for IT Services), a method to support selection of indicators for IT services aligned with organizational goals. SINIS is based on GQM + Strategies [1], COBIT [4], the set of measures for IT services defined in [11] and the Reference Software Measurement Ontology [13].

This paper presents SINIS and a case study at the Infrastructure Department of a global company. Section 2 provides presents the theoretical background, Sect. 3 presents SINIS, Sect. 4 describes the case study and its results, Sect. 5 discusses related works, and Sect. 6 presents our final considerations.

2 Background

In general, definitions of service reflect, at a certain level, the point of view of the academic disciplines and/or of the economic sectors wherein it was defined. Service is "a logical representation of a repeatable activity that has a specified outcome. It is self-contained and is a 'black box' to its consumers" [4, 15]. IT services are defined to support business realization [15] and are important means towards establishing Business-IT alignment [16]. There are several approaches devoted to IT services, such as COBIT [4], CMMI-SVC [3], MR-MPS-SV [9] and ITIL [21], which address processes related to IT services (e.g., Incident Management, Change Management, Problem Management, etc.) and provide guidelines to their implementation.

In order to assess and improve services quality, quality of processes performed to deliver services needs to be evaluated [3]. Measurement plays a key role in process quality improvement initiatives. In general, effective service measurements are planned based on few vital and meaningful indicators (i.e., measures used to quantitatively verify goals achievement [14]) that are quantitative, economical and adequate to support the desired results. Thus, it is important to define what indicators are suitable to support services quality monitoring and customer satisfaction goals [4]. Moreover, it is necessary to focus on indicators related to critical processes and aligned to organizational goals, but this is not an easy task.

There are some proposals that deal with this issue. COBIT Goals Cascade [4] provides a catalog with 17 enterprise goals and IT-related goals and more than 100 indicators that can be reused. However, as different market situations and environments require different measures, COBIT recommends that each enterprise should build its own goals cascade, compare it with COBIT Goals Cascade and then refine it [4]. Balanced Scorecard (BSC) [6] is an approach that applies measurement concepts to verify whether organization activities meet its goals with respect to vision and strategy. BSC does not provide an explicit way to define goals, strategies and indicators related to different organizational levels, being more applicable at enterprise levels. GQM + Strategies [1] is an extension of GQM [10] and supports an organization in creating a model consisting of goals, strategies, and measures from the business level down to project and operational levels and back up. GQM + Strategies help to identify goals, strategies and indicators that are aligned with high-level business goals and also provide a mechanism to monitor success and failure of goals and strategies through measurement. The main GQM + Strategies components are [1]: Organizational Goals (what does organization want to achieve), Strategies (how to achieve goals), Context Factors (external and internal environments), Assumptions (unknown estimations), GQM graphs [10] (how to measure if a goal was reached and a strategy was succeeded or failed) and Interpretation Model (how to interpret indicators to verify measurement goal achievement and meet information need) [10].

3   The SINIS Method

SINIS (Select Indicators for IT Services) is a method to support indicators selection for IT Services measurement driving a top-down derivation of organization goals into IT services goals, strategies and indicators. SINIS can be used by managers and systems analysts with knowledge about organization's related IT services. SINIS was developed based on GQM + Strategies components [1], considering the conceptualization provided by Reference Software Measurement Ontology (RSMO) [13] and modeling critical processes. Besides, COBIT Goal Cascade catalog [4] and a list of measures for IT services defined in [11] are considered as databases for reuse and used as inputs to some SINIS activities. Figure 1 shows an overview of SINIS with four phases, represented by different colors. Activities' description for each phase is as follows.

(i) *Elicit IT Services Context Factors and Assumptions:* In this phase, context factors and assumptions describing the organizational scenario are identified. Context factors are aspects factually known (e.g., organization X needs to improve service availability) and assumptions are aspects believed to be true but have little or no evidence about (e.g., in organization X IT Services costs cannot be increase). Context factors and assumptions provide useful information to define the scope of IT services goals and strategies to be considered. Documents can be used as a source to context factors and assumptions identification, such as containing vision and mission statements, organizational goals, internal and external constraints, market trends, opportunities, staff competences and technological advances. If

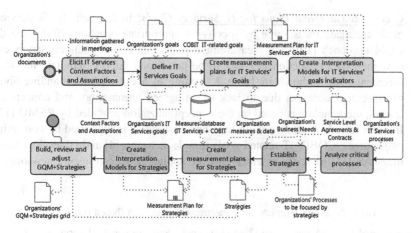

Fig. 1. Overview of SINIS.

documents are not available, meetings with organizational stakeholders can be used as a way to gather information.

(ii) *Define IT Service Goals, Indicators and Interpretation Models:* In this phase, IT Service goals are established, as well as a measurement plan to provide information for goals achievement analysis. It consists of three activities:

ii.1. *Define IT Services Goals:* During this activity, context factors and assumptions defined in the first phase are used to support definition of IT services goals. In order to reduce effort, saving cost and time, reuse is supported by consulting COBIT IT-related goals [4] to verify whether they are applicable or can inspire new ones. The identified goals must be recorded by using the template presented in Table 1. The template is based on GQM + Strategies [1] and also requires information regarding the BSC dimensions related to the recorded goal. BSC dimensions' were included in the template mainly because next SINIS activities involve searching for COBIT management practices and indicators, and COBIT Cascade Goals considers goal classification per BSC dimension.

Table 1. SINIS template for IT services goal (based on [1]).

IT services goal	<Name of the IT services goal>
Activity	<Is the goal to maintain, increase or reduce?>
Object	<What is the object the goal is related to?>
Magnitude	<What is the quantity of goal to be achieved?>
Time frame	<When should the goal be achieved?>
Responsible	<Who is the primary responsible for goal attainment?>
Constraints	<What relevant constraints may prevent goal achievement?>
COBIT IT-related goal	<One of 17 available IT-Related Goals from COBIT>
BSC dimension	<Finance, Customer, Internal or Learn and Growth>
IT service process	<Process that can impact goal achievement>

ii.2. *Create Measurement Plans for IT Services Goals:* In this activity, IT services goals are made measurable by specifying appropriate questions (following the GQM approach [10]) and measurement plans that define goals indicators and how their data collection is going to be performed. SINIS' template for Measurement Plan is shown in Table 2. Aiming to avoid misunderstanding about measurement concepts due to lack of an agreed terminology and conceptualization, the template is based on the conceptualization provided by RSMO [13]. In order to reduce effort, saving time and cost, reuse is supported by consulting two sources: COBIT IT-related goals sample measures [4] and IT services list of measures [11] to verify whether they are applicable or can inspire new ones.

Table 2. SINIS template for measurement plan item (based on [13]).

IT services goal	\<Name of the IT services goal - Same to match IT services goal\>
Measurement goal	\<What is going to be controlled: Maintain, Increase or Reduce?\>
Information need	\<What is the information need attended by the measurement?\>
Indicator	\<Name of the indicator to monitor the recorded goal\>
Measurable entity	\<What entity is being measured by the indicator?\>
Base measures	\<Measures from which the indicator is obtained (if applicable)\>
Calculation formula	\<Formula used to calculate the indicator (if applicable)\>
Measurement procedure	\<Procedure to be followed to collect and store data for the indicator\>
Measurement responsible	\<Role performed by people in charge of collect and store data or tool that collect and record data without manual intervention\>
Measurement unit	\<Measurement unit in which the indicator is expressed\>
Measurement moment	\<Activity on which measurement should be performed\>
Measurement periodicity	\<Frequency of measurement\>

ii.3. *Create Interpretation Models for IT Services' Indicators:* During this activity, interpretation models are defined to determine how data collected for the defined indicators should be interpreted in order to support informed decisions about the IT services goals achievement. Targets can be defined based on previous service level agreement contracts and reports or business's needs. Table 3 shows SINIS template for IT services' indicator interpretation model.

(iii) *Define Strategies, Indicators and Interpretation Models:* Strategies represent ways to achieve goals, which can be initiatives or projects. One or various strategies can be implemented to achieve the same goal. Strategies can be prioritized considering which are more effective and feasible according to the context of each organization. This means considering organization's constraints and capabilities.

Table 3. SINIS template for indicators interpretation model (based on [13]).

Indicator	<Name of indicator – same to match measurement plan>
Target	<Value expected (minimum or maximum) for the indicator in order to achieve the associated goal>
Interpretation model	<Procedure to be followed to analyze data collected for the indicator>
Interpretation responsible	< Role performed by people in charge of analyze data>
Interpretation moment	<Activity in which data analysis should be performed>
Interpretation periodicity	<Frequency in which data analysis should be performed>

In this phase, we need to know what is needed to do in order to achieve IT Service Goals, or in other words, how do we get there (Basili et al. 2005). GQM + Strategies does not provide specific directions about how to support strategies selection. SINIS considers that strategies to achieve IT Service goals must focus on processes that impact goals achievement, i.e., the critical processes. In this phase, the strategies to achieve the established IT Service goals are defined as well as indicators to evaluate if the strategies achieve the expected results. Strategies' indicators must be aligned to respective IT Goal indicator. This phase involves four activities:

iii.1. *Analyze Critical IT Service Processes:* The strategies to achieve IT Service goals must focus on processes that impact goals achievement, i.e., the critical processes. Thus, in this activity processes related to the established IT Service goals are analyzed (as well as relationships between them). By doing this, it is possible to identify where the strategies must be focused on. SINIS advocates that the processes should be modeled and the relationship among them should be investigated in order to identify critical cause-effect relations that need to be considered when establishing the strategies. For processes that generate activities log database (such as Incident Management), process mining can be used to find which part of the process is causing delay and possibly is a root cause that needs to be addressed by a strategy [17].

iii.2. *Establish Strategies to achieve IT Service Goals:* In this activity, considering the results of the processes analysis made in the previous activity, strategies are established aiming to achieve the IT Service goals. Service Level Agreements contracts and delivery reports also can be analyzed since they can provide information to help identifying root causes or blockers to attend IT services goals. The established strategies will be implemented in projects, initiatives or even simple activities. Table 4 presents the suggested template for recording the established strategies.

iii.3. *Create Measurement Plans for Strategies' Goals:* In this activity, similar to the activity *Create Measurement Plans for IT services goals*, strategies are made

Table 4. SINIS template for strategies.

IT services goal	<Name of associated IT services goal>
Strategy	<Strategy name>
Description	<Strategy description>

measurable by specifying appropriate questions and measurement plans to define indicators and data collection procedures. COBIT indicators [4] and IT services list of measures [11] can be used as a source to measurement plans definition. The template used to record the measurement plan items is the same presented in Table 2.

iii.4. *Create Interpretation Models for Strategies' Indicators:* This activity is similar to *Create Interpretation Models for IT Services' Indicators* described in previous phase. However, in this activity indicators related to strategies' goals are considered.

(iv) **Build, Review and Adjust GQM + Strategies Grid:** During this phase, context factors, assumptions, goals, strategies and indicators are organized in a GQM + Strategies grid aiming to provide an overview of IT services measurement. Ideally, the grid has to present the cleanest possible view. SINIS template for grid is shown in Fig. 2.

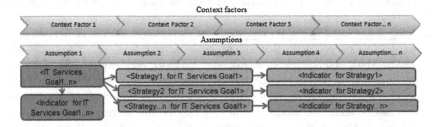

Fig. 2. SINIS template for GQM + Strategies grid (based on [1]).

The template was designed in a way to facilitate viewing in a single page different levels of goals, strategies and indicators. Also, general context factors and assumptions were disposed in this same single page, allowing to verify if they are current or have changed. If it is necessary to change context factors and assumptions, the grid provides an easy view of goals, strategies and indicators that are impacted by the changes and also might change.

GQM + Strategies grid and interpretation models must be presented to all stakeholders through meetings in which information sources, context factors and assumptions must be validated, and applicability, completeness and consistency of goals, strategies and indicators must be evaluated. Also, discussions can point out potential findings and improvement opportunities.

4   Case Study

Motivated by the research question "How to support selection of IT services indicators for different levels and aligned with organizational goals?" we developed SINIS. In order to verify if SINIS is useful to support selection of IT services indicators from business level to operational levels and aligned to organizational goals, we carried out a case study in which we analyzed if SINIS is suitable for an IT Services measurement initiative in a industrial setting and how can SINIS be further improved. We followed three steps, as follows.

Step 1: Select Organization for Case Study
In the first step, we selected a large global organization headquartered in Brazil (here, called Organization A due to confidentiality issues). It operates in over 30 countries and has offices, operations, exploration and joint ventures across five continents. The selected department to apply SINIS method was Infrastructure, which is part of IT Services Area, and responsible for application servers, databases, backup, storage, security and network. IT Services Area follows ITIL library practices [OGC 2011] and intends to improve the measurement process because much effort has been spent to select proper indicators and perform services measurement. Infrastructure members do not know how their projects and operational work results influence the department, area or organizational goals. Infrastructure manager does not participate in defining Organization A or IT Services strategic plan and goals. In the beginning of the year he receives a list of goals to be achieved by the Infrastructure and is free to define the department plans to achieve those goals. He derives lower level indicators to support goals monitoring, but he does not follow any specific method. Each department member defines by himself/herself a list of initiatives and keeps working on it during all year, expecting to contribute to indicators targets achievement. It is worth noticing that there is no clear connection between initiatives' and indicators' results.

Step 2: Execute SINIS method - SINIS was applied and main results are presented.

(i)   ***Elicit IT Services Context Factors and Assumptions:*** In this phase, we met with infrastructure manager and coordinators to identify relevant context factors and assumptions from organizational goals and other information about the organization. Table 5 shows the obtained results.

Table 5. Context factors and assumptions of infrastructure department of Organization A.

Context factors	Assumptions
CF1: Organization A first goal is to reduce costs	A1: IT Services cannot increase costs
CF2: IT Services Area has a subarea "ITIL Office" to manage service delivery and continuity, incidents, problems and changes	A2: Even having several subareas, ITIL Office works in an integrated way and cross serves all technical subareas of IT services area

(*Continued*)

Table 5. (*Continued*)

Context factors	Assumptions
CF3: Organization A has critical business processes based on IT Services that need high availability	A3: There is a service continuity team responsible for managing crisis situations that are opened for applications that support critical business processes
CF4: IT Services Area supports all business units of Organization A	A4: Evaluation of IT Service quality is driven by a Service Level Agreement

(ii) *Define IT Service Goals, Indicators and Interpretation Models*

ii.1. *Define IT Services Goals:* In this activity, together with Infrastructure manager, we analyzed elicited context factors and assumptions and COBIT IT-Related Goals. Due to space restrictions, in this paper we explore only one of the defined IT services goals. Context factor CF3 reveals that Organization A business requirements include service availability improvement. Considering the COBIT IT-Related Goal "Delivery of IT services in line with business requirements" and the context factor CF3 ("...service availability need to be increased"), we defined the IT services goal "Reduce time in Crisis". It is directly related to the Crisis process (a subprocess of Incidents Management) that is started in Organization A when a crisis situation (mentioned in the assumption A3) occurs, i.e., when an application classified as high critical for business is unavailable. In this case, a crisis room is opened by the service continuity team. When a crisis room is opened, all technical teams connect to a conference room and work together until the issue is solved and the application is back again. This process had been created to minimize service unavailability and to reduce impact to applications considered critical to business. Table 6 shows the IT service goal defined by using the SINIS template. We considered Assumption A1 to establish a constraint during IT service goal definition.

Table 6. IT services goal.

IT services goal	Reduce time in crisis
Guidance	Reduce
Object	Time in crisis
Magnitude	10 %
Time frame	Annual
Responsible	IT services infrastructure department
Constraints	Do not increase cost
COBIT IT-related goal	Delivery of IT services in line with business requirements
BSC dimension	Customer
IT service process	Incident management

ii.2. *Create Measurement Plans for IT Services Goals:* this activity was carried out with the infrastructure manager, department members and an expert in quality and measurement who knew about data available and possible to be collected. Analyzing the measures associated to the COBIT IT-Related goal "Delivery of IT services in line with business requirements", which was used as a basis to define the IT service goal considered, the measures suggested in the IT services list of measures [11] and data available in Organization A, we selected "number of crisis" and "number of hours in crisis" as the measures to be used. The first measure was based on "number of business disruptions due to IT service incidents" (from COBIT) and the second one on "service interruptions duration" (from IT services list of measures). "Number of hours in crisis" indicator was selected to monitor the IT service goal "Reduce Time in Crisis". Table 7 presents the defined measurement plan.

Table 7. Measurement Plan for IT services goal "Reduce Time in Crisis".

IT services goal	Reduce Time in Crisis
Measurement objective	Reduce
Information need	How many hours were spent in crisis?
Indicator	Number of hours in crisis (NHC)
Measurable entity	Crisis
Base measures	Time spent in each crisis (TSC) (being NHC the number of hours in crisis)
Calculation formula	$NHC = TSC_1 + TSC_2 + \ldots + TSC_{NC}$
Measurement procedure	TSC: Extract data from incident report and conference call report NC: Extract data from incident report
Measurement responsible	Service continuity analyst
Measurement unit	Hours
Measurement moment	Base measures must be collected after every crisis situation. Indicator must be collected before performance monitoring meetings
Measurement periodicity	Monthly (indicator)

ii.3. *Create Interpretation Models for IT Services' Indicators:* This activity was performed with the infrastructure manager. He defined targets for the indicator and how its data should be interpreted. IT Service goal is to reduce 10 % of time in crisis, to previous year. Reports for 2014 year informed that total time in crisis was 765 h. Thus, decreasing 10 % means to get a target of 688.5 h. Table 8 presents the interpretation model defined by using the SINIS template.

Table 8. Interpretation Model for IT services goal indicator "Number of hours in Crisis".

Indicator	Number of hours in Crisis
Target	Maximum 688.5 h (annual value)
Interpretation model	If total time in crisis is the target or less, IT services goal is achieved
Interpretation responsible	IT services continuity team
Interpretation moment	During managers performance meeting
Interpretation periodicity	Every month, accumulated data is analyzed and compared to goal taking same month in previous year as a reference. In the end of the year, total value is compared to total value in the previous year

(iii) *Define Strategies, Indicators and Interpretation Models*

iii.1. *Analyze Critical IT Service Processes:* In order to identify possible blockers that can prevent IT Services goals to be achieved and identify processes in which the strategies should be focused on, we accessed available documents for Incident Management process (including crisis), the IT service process related the "Reduce Time in Crisis" goal (see Table 6), modeled it (Fig. 3) and looked for relations with other processes. As a result, Change and Problem Management processes were identified.

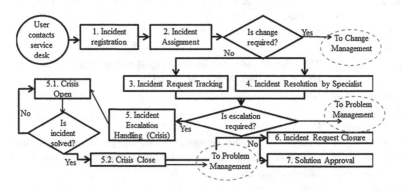

Fig. 3. Incident management process of Organization A.

iii.2: *Establish Strategies to achieve IT Service Goals:* We start this activity by investigating problems related to the processes identified in the previous activity that could impact goal achievement. We searched for root-cause crisis reports of service level agreement for last year and noticed that several root-causes were recurrent, i.e., several crises were caused by repeated problems. Problem Management is a process related to Incident Management and responsible for investigating root-causes. In this sense, when a crisis is closed, the root-cause that derived it must be found and definitive solution must be implemented aiming to avoid recurrences. Since we noticed that a same issue was causing several crises, we concluded that root-cause investigation was not working properly. By analyzing root-cause crisis reports we also found that many crises were caused by implemented changes. Infrastructure manager informed that Change Management should guarantee proper planning to prevent services being impacted, which means Change Management should not impact Incident Management. However, reports showed evidences that this was not happening, resulting in crisis caused by changes. After understanding possible reasons that are blockers to IT services goals achievement, strategies were defined to mitigate them. Table 9 presents three strategies defined using SINIS template.

Table 9. Strategies for IT services goal "Reduce Time in Crisis".

IT services goal	Reduce Time in Crisis		
Strategies	Reduce crisis caused by changes	Improve changes quality	Reduce crisis caused by repeated issues
Description	Reduce number of hours of crisis caused by changes	Improve quality of changes planning and execution	Reduce number of hours in crisis caused by issues that could have been avoided

iii.3. *Create Measurement Plans for Strategies' Goals:* This activity was done with infrastructure, services continuity, problem and change managers, and an expert in quality and measurement who knew about available and possible to be collected. Since we identified that the processes to be focused by the strategies were Problem Management, Change Management and Incident Management, we analyzed measures related to these processes in COBIT, the measures associated to these processes in the IT services list of measures [11] and data available in Organization A. Table 10 shows some of the measures identified in each source and the measures selected to be used, defined considering the identified measures and the available data.

Table 10. Measures investigated and measurement plan for strategies' goals.

Source	Measures found	Measures defined for Organization A
COBIT Indicators	Number of recurring incidents caused by unresolved problems	Percentage of crisis caused by recurrent issues
IT services list of measures	Successful/failed change requests	Number of changes executed with success
	Emergency/normal requests	Number of emergency changes
	Amount of time to find/solve root cause	Total number of hours to find problems root cause

After selecting measures, the measurement plans were defined. Table 11 presents the plans by using the SINIS template. Due to space limitation, some adaptations were done to present several measurement plans in the same table.

Table 11. Measurement plans for strategies' goals.

IT services goal	Reduce time in crisis	Reduce time in crisis	Reduce time in crisis
Strategy	Reduce crisis caused by changes	Improve changes quality	Reduce crisis caused by repeated issues
Measurement objective	Control and decrease	Control and increase	Control and decrease
Information need	How many hours in crisis were due to failed changes?	How many changes were closed on time, with success and not emergency?	How many hours in crisis were due to repeated issues?
Indicator	Percentage of hours in crisis caused by changes	Percentage of changes closed on time, with success, without rework and not emergency	Percentage of hours in crisis caused by recurrent issues
Measurable entity	Crisis	Changes	Crisis
Base measures	Hours in crisis caused by changes (HCCG); Total hours in crisis (THC)	Number of changes closed on time, with success, without rework and not emergency (NCTSRE); Total number of executed changes (TC)	Hours in crisis caused by recurrent issues (HCCRI); Total hours in crisis (THC)
Calculation formula	(HCCG/THC)*100	((NCTSRE)/TC)*100	(HCCRI/THC)*100
Measurement procedure	HCCG: extract data from problem report; THC: extract data from crisis report	NCTSRE: extract data from problem report; TC: extract data from change report	HCCRI: extract data from problem report; THC: extract data from crisis report
Measurement responsible	Problem management performance responsible	Change management performance responsible	Problem management performance responsible
Measurement moment	Before performance monitoring meetings	Before performance monitoring meetings	Before performance monitoring meetings
Measurement periodicity	Once a month	Once a month	Once a month

iii.4. _Create Interpretation Models for Strategies' Indicators:_ This activity was performed with the infrastructure manager, who defined targets for indicators and how results should be interpreted. IT Service goal is to reduce 10 % of time in crisis, compared to previous year. Table 12 presents the defined interpretation model.

(iv) **Build, review and adjust GQM + Strategies grid:** During this phase, we organized context factors, assumptions, goals, strategies and indicators in a GQM + Strategies grid and presented it to all infrastructure team to gather members' opinion and concerns. Figure 4 presents the resulting grid. As a feedback, infrastructure team commented that a lot of useless measures would be now abandoned. Moreover, infrastructure team will enhance focus on achieving strategies' indicators. Infrastructure manager stated now he will spend less time managing team activities to achieve IT Services indicators, since now the team knows how to support it.

Table 12. Interpretation model for IT services goal indicator "Number of Hours in Crisis".

Indicator	Percentage of crisis caused by changes	Percentage of changes closed on time, with success, without rework and not emergency	Percentage of crisis caused by recurrent issues
Target	Maximum 6 %	Minimum 90 %	Maximum 8 %
Interpretation model	If maximum 6 % hours in crisis had root-cause identified as related to changes, they are considered exceptions and target is reached.	If minimum 90 % of changes were closed on time, with success, without rework and not emergency, target is reached.	If maximum 8 % hours in crisis are related to recurrent issues, target is reached.
Interpretation responsible	Problem manager	Change manager	Problem manager
Interpretation moment	Before managers performance meeting		
Interpretation periodicity	Every month and once a year		

As examples of indicators usage, Fig. 5 shows data collected to "Number of hours in crisis", which has been monthly evaluated and compared to last years. Figure 6 presents data collected to the indicator "Percentage of crisis caused by changes", related to the strategy "Reduce crisis caused by changes", which has been monthly evaluated. Average of percentage is now 8.32 %, still not reaching the indicator target (6 %). Figure 6 also shows data collected to the indicator "Percentage of changes closed on time, with success, without rework and not emergency" related to the strategy "Improve changes quality".

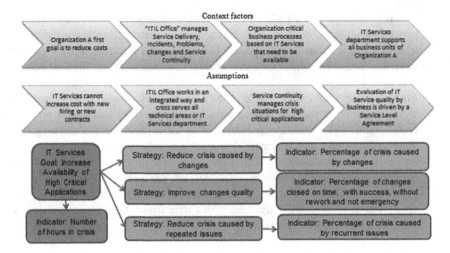

Fig. 4. GQM + Strategies grid.

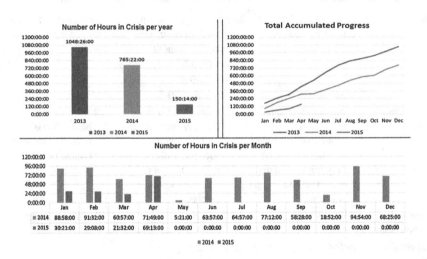

Fig. 5. Number of hours in crisis: indicator of achievement of the "Reduce time in crisis" goal.

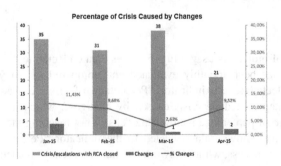

Fig. 6. Indicator for "Reduce crisis caused by changes" strategy.

Step 3: Collect Lessons Learned to improve SINIS
In the last step of the case study, we collected lessons learned (Table 13). The positive ones represent SINIS characteristics that could support successful results. The negative ones represent SINIS characteristics that need to be improved.

Table 13. Lessons learned.

	Impact	Lesson learned	Future work
1	Positive	Having available sources to read, support and reuse was good for having ideas and remembering goals, indicators and strategies	Create a unique catalog of IT services goals, strategies and indicators, using RMSO conceptualization and categorized by maturity models processes, COBIT and ITIL processes, aiming to make easier to directly search and reuse
2	Negative	Searching different sources for reuse was difficult because sources do not follow a common conceptualization and categorization	
3	Positive	Having numeric targets for strategies' indicators was good for having a way to measure if strategies are performing as expected	Start data collection and, after having enough data, submit processes to Statistical Process Control to evaluate if they are stable and able to attend expected targets
4	Negative	Targets for indicators were created based on past experiences and manager expectations; there is no information if processes are able to attend them	

5 Related Works

In the literature there are some proposals that help organizations to define IT services indicators. COBIT 5 Goals Cascade [4], for example, is a mechanism to translate stakeholder needs into specific, actionable and customized enterprise goals, IT-related goals and enabler goals, providing a set of goals and measures, which can be used as reference during indicators selection. COBIT recommends that each enterprise should build its own goals cascade, compare it with COBIT and refine it. Although COBIT provides a set of goals and measures to be reused, there is no procedure to be followed to do so.

Lepmets et al. [7] present a framework of measures for IT services, but only a catalog is provided, without a method to select and align measures to business goals. These authors state that alignment between the business goals and IT service quality measurement goals in industry needs to be studied and could provide additional support to their measurement framework. In [18], Jäntti et al. presented a system to support IT service measurement. During a case study they learned that besides a well designed and easy-to-use measurement tool, there is a need for a systematic measurement process, and measures need to be based on business objectives. To answer that need, authors suggest a resumed process framework based on ITIL, but they emphasize that the study was focused on the implementation of the measurement system and the framework was not validated in real cases.

There are some proposals that although not devoted to IT services, can be used in this context. GQM + Strategies [1] is an approach created based on software engineering experiences that has been applied in several domains. GQM + Strategies proposes deriving goals into strategies and measures for different organization levels. However, it does not detail how to identify critical processes to be considered in strategies or how to define proper strategies and measures. In [2, 5], lessons learned, results and experiences from applying GQM + Strategies approach are presented, but authors did not suggest a method to be used when applying GQM + Strategies to other cases.

Some proposals were not applied to IT services, but could be adapted to do that. For instance, Barreto and Rocha [8] suggest an approach to monitor goals using statistical process control. The approach is related to software processes and does not consider IT services processes.

SINIS reuses knowledge provided by other proposals (mainly COBIT and GQM + Strategies) and addresses some of the cited gaps. It defines a set of activities, guides about what should be done in order to select relevant indicators to goals monitoring, suggests templates and reuses goals and measures recorded in the literature.

6 Final Considerations

In this paper we presented a method to select indicators for IT Services at different levels and a case study in which the proposed method was used in a real company.

Motivation for this work was found in the literature and also in Organization A, which was not able to properly define an appropriate set of strategies aligned with IT Service goals in which teams could focus work on. Employees were wasting time in activities that were not related to IT services goals because they were not clearly informed about which strategies should be defined and related to IT services goals. By using SINIS method, Infrastructure department was able to define strategies for members to work on that could really help attending IT service goals, instead of working in several and unfocused initiatives. When defining strategies related to Changes and Problems to support Incidents (crisis), SINIS had also clarified how relevant is the relationship different IT services processes, as well as explicitly showed contributions of those activities to the achievement of top-level business goals.

There are some limitations in this study. SINIS was applied in only one IT Service department of only one company. Besides, SINIS application was conducted by one of the authors. We are aware that the case study results are not enough to evidence SINIS' applicability. However, results can be seen as a sign of that and can be used to improve SINIS for new applications. Moreover, results suggest that SINIS supported an aligned selection of indicators in different organizational levels. Organization A has already requested to apply SINIS in IT Security Department, which is also unable to align top level goals to lower levels strategies and indicators and is wasting time on measurement without knowing if collected data is really able to support business goals. We have started the use of SINIS in the IT Security Department and we expect to get new results soon. As future work, we intend to apply a survey aiming to get perceptions about SINIS use. We also intend to improve SINIS documentation in order to allow other people to use it without intervention of the authors.

Acknowledgments. We would like to thank FAPERJ (project E-26/110.438/2014) and CNPq (Process Number 461777/2014-2) for the financial support to this research.

References

1. Basili, V., Trendowicz, A., Kowalczyk, M., Heidrich, J., Heidrich, J., Seaman, C., Münch, J., Münch, J., Rombach, D.: Aligning organizations through measurement - the GQM + Strategies approach. The Fraunhofer IESE Series on Software and Systems Engineering, p. 225. Springer, Cham (2005). ISBN 978-3-319-05046-1
2. Basili, V., Lampasona, C., Ramírez, A.: Aligning corporate and IT goals and strategies in the oil and gas industry. In: 14th International Conference Product-Focused Software Process Improvement (PROFES), Paphos, Cyprus, vol. 7983, pp. 184–198 (2013)
3. Forrester, E., Buteau, B., Shrum, S.: CMMI for services, guidelines for superior service. CMMI-SVC Version 1.3 – SEI, 2nd edn. Addison-Wesley Professional, Boston (2010)
4. ISACA "COBIT 5 – Control Objectives Management Guidelines Maturity Models: A Business Framework for the Governance and Management of Enterprise IT. Information Systems Audit and Control. Association, USA (2012)
5. Kaneko, T., Katahira, M., Miyamoto, Y., Kowalczyk, M.: Application of GQM + Strategies in the Japanese Space Industry. In: 21st International Workshop on Software Measurement (IWSM), Nara, Japan, pp. 221–226 (2011)
6. Kaplan, R., Norton, D.P.: The Balanced Scorecard Translating Strategy into Action. Havard Business School Press, Boston (1996)
7. Lepmets, M., Ras, E., Renault, A.: A quality measurement framework for IT services. In: Annual SRII Global Conference, San Jose, California, vol. 1, pp. 767–774 (2011)
8. Barreto, A.O.S., Rocha, A.R.: Defining and monitoring strategically aligned software improvement goals. In: Ali Babar, M., Vierimaa, M., Oivo, M. (eds.) PROFES 2010. LNCS, vol. 6156, pp. 380–394. Springer, Heidelberg (2010)
9. Softex "MPS.BR – Guia Geral MPS de Serviços" (in Portuguese and Spanish) (2012). www.softex.br
10. Solingen, R., Berghout, E.: The Goal Question Indicator Method: A Practical Guide for Quality Improvement of Software Development. McGraw-Hill, New York (1999)
11. Trinkenreich, B., Santos, G., Barcellos, M.: Metrics to support IT service maturity models – a systematic mapping study. In: 17th International Conference on Enterprise Information Systems (ICEIS), Barcelona, Spain (2015)
12. Trinkenreich, B., Santos, G.: Metrics to support IT service maturity models – a case study. In: 17th International Conference on Enterprise Information Systems (ICEIS), Barcelona, Spain (2015)
13. Barcellos, M.P., Falbo, R.D., Rocha, A.R.: Using a reference domain ontology for developing a software measurement strategy for high maturity organizations. In: 16th IEEE International Enterprise Distributed Object Computing Conference. Beijing, China, pp. 114–123 (2012)
14. Eckerson, W.: Performance management strategies. Bus. Intell. J. **14**(1), 24–27 (2009)

15. Cases, M., Bodner, D.A., Mutnury, B.: Architecture of service organizations. In: Salvendy, G., Karwowski, W. (eds.) Introduction to Service Engineering, pp. 109–134. Wiley, Hoboken (2010)
16. Abdi, M., Dominic, P.D.: "Strategic IT alignment with business strategy: service oriented architecture approach. In: International Symposium on Information Technology. Kuala Lampur – Malaysia (2010)
17. Trinkenreich, B., Santos, G., Confort, V., Santoro, F.: Toward using business process intelligence to support incident management metrics selection and service improvement. In: 27th International Conference Software Engineering Knowledge Engineering, Pittsburg, USA (2015)
18. Jäntti, M., Lahtela, A., Kaukola, J.: Establishing a measurement system for IT service management processes: a case study. Int. J. Adv. Syst. Meas. **3**(3 and 4), 125–136 (2010)
19. Kilpi, T.: Implementing a software metrics program at Nokia. IEEE Softw. **18**(6), 72–77 (2001). ISSN:0740-7459
20. Parmenter, D.: Key Performance Indicators – Developing, Implementing and Using Winning KPIs, 3rd edn. Wiley, New York (2015)
21. OGC: "ITIL Service Operations" The Stationary Office – TSO. London, UK (2011)

Requirements, Features, and Release Management

Requirement Prioritization with Quantitative Data - A Case Study

Enrico Johansson[1]($\boxtimes$), Daniel Bergdahl[2], Jan Bosch[3], and Helena Holmström Olsson[1]

[1] Department of Computer Science, Malmö University, Malmö, Sweden
{Enrico.Johansson,Helena.Holmstrom.Olsson}@mah.se
[2] LINAF AB, Management Consulting, Lomma, Sweden
Daniel.Bergdahl@linaf.se
[3] Department of Computer Science and Engineering, Chalmers University of Technology,
Gothenburg, Sweden
Jan.Bosch@chalmers.se

Abstract. Feature content in system releases tends to be prioritized using limited amounts of qualitative user input and based on the opinions of those in product management. This leads to several problems including the wasteful allocation of R&D resources. In this paper, we present the results of our efforts to collect quantitative customer input before the start of development using a mock-up for a mobile application developed by Sony Mobile Communications Inc. Our research shows that (1) product managers change their prioritization when quantitative data is presented to them; (2) product managers change their prioritization which is converged to the prioritization indicated by the quantitative data (3) the quantitative data is regarded as beneficial by the product managers.

Keywords: Requirements engineering · Customer data · Survey · Mock-up · Data-driven development · Case study · Prioritization · Product management

1 Introduction

Companies use a range of techniques to collect customer feedback in the early stages of product development. In the pre-development phase, techniques such as customer interviews, customer observation and customer surveys are typically used to get an understanding for customer perceptions of new product functionality [2, 6–10]. Furthermore, mock-ups and different prototyping techniques are common to have customers try early versions of the product and for evaluating e.g. user interfaces. In addition, there exist a number of techniques that can be used to validate customer needs during the development process, e.g. the HYPEX model [1]. Inspired by the 'Build-Measure-Learn' loop as outlined in the Lean Startup literature [11], they emphasize the need to build smaller increments of features that can be frequently validated by customers to avoid developing features that are not appreciated. In a number of recent studies [1, 12, 13], the notion of frequent customer validation is described as 'innovation experiment systems' in which the R&D organization responds based on instant feedback from customers. Typically, these techniques

© Springer International Publishing Switzerland 2015
P. Abrahamsson et al. (Eds.): PROFES 2015, LNCS 9459, pp. 89–104, 2015.
DOI: 10.1007/978-3-319-26844-6_7

provide a limited set of qualitative data reflecting individual customer needs [2]. In this paper, we explore the value of mockups as a tool to collect consumer usage from a product management perspective when prioritizing requirements for future releases. Mockup techniques are widely used in software development to create user interfaces to show to the end consumer how the software will look like without having to develop the underlying functionality. From a consumer interaction perspective, one would only discover the missing functionality once the development of the application had started and the first interaction with the UI had been made. Populating the UI with a number of features that are the possible requirements for next release of the software gives the possibility to collect quantitative data [4] about the usage of the specific application. The question is how this data is valued by product managers when taking investment decision for future releases pre-development (e.g. before any funding are given to the development). In most software development companies, the pre-study is the phase in which decisions are taken on whether to develop a feature or not. In this phase, the expected value of a feature is estimated and if the outcome is positive the feature is developed no matter what happens in the later stages of development. However, there are a number of problems associated with this.

First, the estimated value of a feature is typically based on very limited data that can prove whether the estimation is correct. Instead, previous experience and opinions held by product management is what guide decision–making and feature prioritization processes [1]. Due to lack of mechanisms to validate feature value with customers also after development has started, the outcome of the pre–study phase is difficult to question and no continuous re-prioritizations of features and feature content occurs. As a result, feature prioritization becomes an opinion-based process leading to software companies investing in developing features that were considered value adding in the pre-study phase, but the opportunity to continuously validate if this is also true in later stages of development and close to release is not employed [1].

Second, the estimations that are done in the pre-study phase are typically based on limited amounts of qualitative feedback from customers. Data is collected by asking customers what they want and by observing what they do and the output is a limited set of individual customer opinions and experiences regarding system use. While this feedback is valuable, it does not represent a large customer base and it does not reveal actual system usage. Ideally, qualitative customer feedback in the pre–study phase should be complemented with quantitative data that confirm individual perceptions but this has proven difficult to accomplish [3].

Third, due to lack of mechanisms to measure feature usage, companies invest in developing features that have no proven customer value. Often, and as recognized in previous research the majority of features in a system are never, or only very seldom, used. This situation could be avoided if accurate data collection mechanisms were in place, allowing companies to allocate resources to development with proven customer value. In this paper, based on a case study conducted at Sony Mobile, we explore data collection techniques that allow for collection of quantitative data also in the pre-development phase, i.e. before development of a feature starts.

The remainder of this paper is organized as follows. The next section presents the problem our research addresses. Section 3 describes the research methodology and research question. Section 4 describes the case study and data collected. Section 5 contains final analysis and discussion of the result and possibilities for further work.

2   Problem Statement

Based on the research presented above as well as our own research [4], we have learned that three problems are likely to occur in companies developing software-intensive systems. Below we describe each problem in more detail.

2.1   Release Content Cast in Stone

Many companies use a release model [5] where the feature content for each release is decided upon before the start of development. If companies lack mechanisms to continuously validate feature content with customers, they would find it difficult to re-prioritize pre-study outcomes. This causes companies to complete the building of features even if during development it becomes obvious that the feature clearly doesn't provide value to customers. This causes a sizeable part of the R&D resources to be allocated to wasteful activities and deteriorates the competitive position of companies over time.

2.2   Featuritis

There is evidence that a majority of features are seldom or never used and that customers seldom use the full potential of the functionality they receive [3]. Often referred to as "featuritis" [15], this means half or more of the R&D effort of a company is wasted on non-value adding activities. Similar to the previous problem, if competitors manage to have less waste in their R&D activities, over time the market position of the company is affected negatively.

2.3   Everything and the Kitchen Sink

Although often treated as atomic in research, features can be implemented iteratively and to a lesser or greater extent. Engineers often have a tendency to build features such that all use cases, exceptions and special situations are taken into account. Often, however, the value of a feature to customers is already accomplished after building a small part of the feature that provides the greatest value. Further development does not lead to (much) more value for customers. However, there is a risk that companies find it difficult to decide on when and how to stop building a feature when further iterations fail to add value to customers due to a lack of mechanisms for collecting feedback before, during development and after deployment of functionality [2].

2.4   Summary of Problems

There is a need to overcome these problems to stay competitive. The one who makes the best prediction (by prioritizing the features with highest value) not only wins the market shares but also reduces waste in the development cycle. However, prioritization is a challenging part of the requirement engineering processes since it is trying to predict the future. This is especially true in a market driven context addressing end-users as customers. A number of qualitative prioritization methods are defined in requirement engineering processes. Qualitative prioritization methods are often by nature subjective and involve for example guessing or weighing requirements against each other. An alternative approach to find the requirement priority is to quantitatively measure usage by introducing mockups to collect what users find interesting. In [4] research shows that collecting quantitative feedback before development is feasible, the data collected deviates from the original feature prioritization, i.e. it is beneficial, and the data gives further insight in requirement prioritization than a qualitative method could have provided.

3   Research Methodology

3.1   The Case Company

A case study has been performed at Sony Mobile Communications Inc. (Sony Mobile). Sony Mobile is a wholly owned subsidiary of Tokyo-based Sony Corporation, a leading global innovator of audio, video, game, communications, key device and information technology products for both the consumer and professional markets.

3.2   The Research Questions

Three aspects of the requirement prioritization are within the scope of the study. The goal of the aspects is to capture if and how quantitative data have an impact on requirement prioritization. The questions are formulated as following.

1. What impact does quantitative data that measures customer usage via a mock-up have on prioritization made by product managers?
2. How does the prioritization made by product managers match the consumer usage customers measured via a mock-up?
3. How valuable do product managers believe that quantitative data is for prioritizing requirements?

3.3   Research Process

In our study, we focus on the data collection practices, and especially if quantitative data collected in the pre-development phase impacts the decision of senior product managers.

To study the described topic, we conducted a case study research [17, 20] based on the case company where two of the authors also have an assignment. As a research method, case study research is typically used to contribute to our knowledge of individual, group, organizational and social phenomena, and is typically used to explain 'how' and 'why' and questions that require an extensive and in-depth understanding of the phenomenon [17, 20]. The case study with an associated outcome from each step is described in the high level flowchart in Fig. 1 below. Each step is then further described more in detail.

STEP 1: Choice of Product and Application.
The first step is to select a product and application that meets requirements 1-4 shown below:
1. Possibility to change the feature set for selected users by showing a mock-up of a new feature set.
2. Large number of interactions with end consumers
3. Main assumption and statistics is that people using the app are first time users.
4. Senior product managers working with the feature set that are willing to do a prioritization with and without the quantitative data collected.

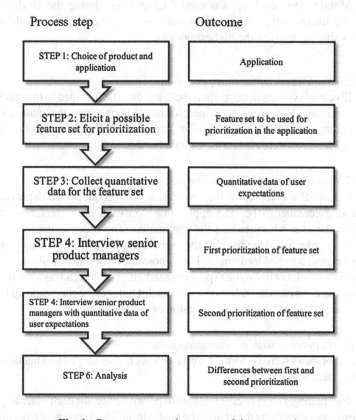

Process step   Outcome

STEP 1: Choice of product and
application   Application

STEP 2: Elicit a possible
feature set for prioritization   Feature set to be used for
                                      prioritization in the application

STEP 3: Collect quantitative
data for the feature set   Quantitative data of user
                                      expectations

STEP 4: Interview senior
product managers   First prioritization of feature set

STEP 4: Interview senior product
managers with quantitative data of   Second prioritization of feature set
user expectations

STEP 6: Analysis   Differences between first and
                                      second prioritization

Fig. 1. Process steps and outcome of the case study

Requirement 1 targets the technical aspects of the Android applications. It must be possible to create a mockup of an existing application and replace the application in the already deployed product. Requirements 2-4 address different aspects of the validity of the study and are further discussed in the validity threat section.

The choice of product landed on Sony Xperia™ phone and a specific Android application. This choice of product and application has been governed by compliance with all four requirements. Due to confidentiality reasons the nature and name of the application cannot be disclosed. However, we can provide the following base data: The application was first deployed to live users in January 2013 and at present it is available in approximately 40 million devices globally. With a few exceptions, the application is shipped with every mobile phone and tablets that Sony Mobile ships. Every month, the application is used approximately 3.5 million times where every use typically involves three main use cases. Based on collected data we know that the original application has approximately 9.5 million interactions per month. The use of the application is consistent over the year and does not show e.g. seasonal variations or variations due to product releases. The application is considered to be one of the base.line applications delivered with Sony Mobile. The mock-up was used 34,393 times during the 10 days it was published. The idea was that the user preference of different features should indicate what features should be given the highest priority.

STEP 2: Elicit a feature set for the application.
A competitive analysis was done to elicit the features to be included in the application. App store and Google play were scanned for either apps within the same domain or apps from competitive brands with similar functionality. Each app was then investigated and 12 features were chosen as suitable for the study.

STEP 3: Collect quantitative data for the feature set.
As described in [4] a mock-up of the application was produced and deployed to the user base in December 2014. The application consisted of 12 features that were displayed to the user when starting the application. The order of the features were randomized in order avoid the risk that the user selected e.g. the first or last option. To keep development cost and lead time as low as possible it was only available in English and hence only available in English speaking markets. The design was such that it was only shown once for each user. Returning users did not receive the mock-up behavior but was instead shown the actual first version of the application.

STEP 4: First interview with product managers.
Individual interviews were performed with five selected senior product managers from the case organization.

The product managers had twelve features to prioritize against each other to get most of their investment concerning the goal of the application. The duration of each interview was approximately 1 h and was conducted by two of the researchers. During the interviews, open questions were asked, related to the prioritization of selected features for the specific android application.

Also, in order to validate the feature set elicited by the researchers the interviewee had the possibility to add features both prior, during and after they set the prioritization.

STEP 5. Second interview adding result from the mockup.
In step 5 the product managers were once again presented with the purpose and context of the study. After that, the mockup result and prioritization of the first interview was presented. When having secured that the context was understood, the prioritization made earlier and the mock-up data was presented and acknowledge by the product managers. Now they were are asked to re-prioritize the order of the 12 features. A last question in the interview was an open question about the value of the data presented in their line of work.

STEP 6: Analysis.
The analysis was done by comparing the prioritization made in the first interview but the prioritization made in the second interview. A difference between prioritization before and after the data could be seen as an indication that the quantitative data presented impacts the decision making of the product managers. The difference is shown per feature and for each product manager. Also, the difference could show if the prioritization is aligned towards the usage of the mockup. For example, a high usage of a specific feature in the mockup would indicate that his feature is of high interest for the many users and thus be placed high (low number) in the prioritized list

3.4 Validity Threats

Requirement 2 in STEP 1 targets the external validity [16, 17] of the study. External validity refers to how well data and theories from one single case study can be generalized. Another aspect of the external validity regards whether the domain (mobile applications) of the case study can be generalized to other domains, as for example IT systems. This threat can be dealt with by doing multiple use cases and are not in scope for this paper.

Requirement 3 in STEP 1 targets the internal [16, 17] validity of the study. Internal validity refers to how well the case study is designed to avoid confounding factors. A confounding factor can be described as a possible independent variable causing the effect, rather than the variable concerned in the case study. Another aspect of the external validity regards whether the domain if the case study can be generalized to others such as for example IT systems.

Requirement 4 in STEP 1 targets the construct [16, 17] validity by making sure the senior product managers have experience within the same feature set as the application chosen. Another threat to the construct validity is the discourse of the interview. Since all participants are from the same company and project it is believed that the discourse in the interviews was the same for all interviews. However to further secure the discourse aspect the first part of the interview was used to explain the context for the prioritization. The context of the interview was explained as; (1) investment decisions of an existing application and the (2) AIDAS (Attention, Interest, Desire, Action and Satisfaction) is used to define the wanted effect of the investment [18, 19]. AIDAS is an acronym for a model that illustrates a theoretical consumer journey from the moment a brand or product attracted consumer attention to the point of action or purchase. This journey is often referred as a conversion funnel.

The following explanation was made in the first part of the interviews to further secure the context. During the interview the context of prioritization was described from three different angles:

1. The purpose of the list is to be used for prioritization of the investments that should be made in the next release of the application
2. The categories of the feature chosen and the investment should be made to impact the ACTION segment in the AIDAS model.
3. Finally the interviewers explained that the feature set chosen was related to the usage of the device itself (e.g. not controlling or concerning another device or service).

4   Results

4.1   Data Collected from Mock-up Application

The features, enumerated as FT01-FT05, FT07-FT13, The feature FT06 was excluded due to semantic and technical reasons (see [4] for a thorough explanation of why FT06 had to be excluded from the feature list). Based on the 34,393 interactions the relative selection distribution was as shown in and Fig. 2 below.

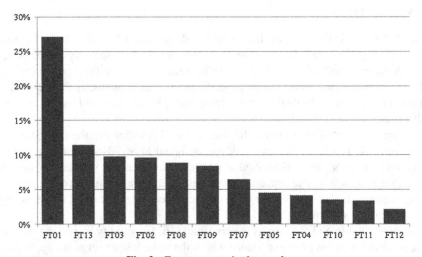

Fig. 2. Feature usage in the mockup

Looking at Fig. 2 it is clear that FT01 is by far the most used feature, FT13 also stands out and there seems to be a small preference for FT02, FT03, F08 and FT09.

4.2   Variation in Prioritization Between First and Second Interview

The five product managers were asked to prioritize the same twelve features that were used in the mock-up with and without information about result from the mockup. The features were shown to the product managers with the same text that was used in the application. Additional explanation was given on request though the features in this domain and context to a large degree are given for the product managers. No additional features were added during the interviews.

The different prioritizations are listed in Table 1. The prioritization based on usage of the mock-up is denoted Usage, S1-1 to S5-1 denotes each of the product managers and first interview and S1-2 to S5-2 denotes the second interview.

Table 1. Prioritization based on mock-up usage, first interview and second interview. Items in priority order top to bottom.

Use	S1-1	S2-1	S3-1	S4-1	S5-1	S1-2	S2-2	S3-2	S4-2	S5-2
FT01	FT13	FT03	FT02	FT03	FT02	FT01	FT03	FT02	FT01	FT02
FT13	FT02	FT01	FT03	FT04	FT04	FT13	FT01	FT01	FT03	FT04
FT03	FT01	FT09	FT08	FT01	FT07	FT02	FT02	FT03	FT04	FT13
FT02	FT05	FT11	FT09	FT12	FT05	FT03	FT09	FT08	FT02	FT08
FT08	FT08	FT05	FT05	FT13	FT10	FT05	FT08	FT09	FT12	FT09
FT09	FT10	FT04	FT12	FT02	FT08	FT08	FT05	FT05	FT07	FT03
FT07	FT04	FT02	FT01	FT09	FT09	FT10	FT04	FT10	FT13	FT11
FT05	FT07	FT08	FT10	FT08	FT01	FT04	FT10	FT12	FT05	FT07
FT04	FT09	FT10	FT04	FT10	FT11	FT07	FT11	FT04	FT09	FT05
FT10	FT03	FT12	FT07	FT05	FT12	FT09	FT12	FT07	FT08	FT10
FT11	FT12	FT13	FT11	FT07	FT03	FT12	FT07	FT11	FT10	FT01
FT12	FT11	FT07	FT13	FT11	FT13	FT11	FT13	FT13	FT11	FT12

Our hypothesis is that the priority of the features would be aligned to the feature usage of a mockup when that information is available to the product managers. To analyze and visualize this hypothesis the prioritization of the product managers have been compared to a prioritization constructed by taking into account the feature usage only. In Figs. 3 and 4 the rank of the prioritization made be the product managers has been compared to the rank (1–12) of the prioritized list constructed by mock-up data. For each feature (P) the difference in distance between the ranks is calculated as Rank (Prioritization by Product Managers) – Rank (Prioritization by feature usage). This is done for each of the product managers. The data is grouped per feature and is presented in Fig. 3 without information from the mock-up and Fig. 4 with information about the mock-up.

Product Manager Prioritization - First Interview. In Fig. 3 we see that the product managers had different opinions in 57 out of 60 possible prioritizations. Looking in more detail the differences are more than just small variations, as almost one third (19 items) differ more than 3 positions (see Table 2 for details).

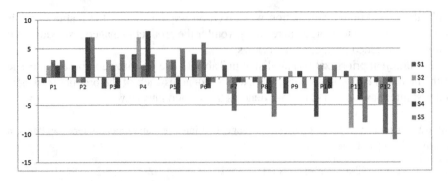

Fig. 3. Difference in prioritization of each feature without knowledge about feature usage from mock-up

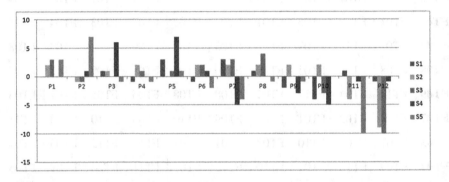

Fig. 4. Difference in prioritization of each feature with knowledge about feature usage from mock-up

Table 2. Difference in prioritization; number of items that differ per difference.

Difference	Count
>0	57
>1	45
>2	31
>3	19
>4	14
>5	12
>6	10
>7	5
>8	3
>9	2
>10	1

Visually it also appears that the product manager's low priority items differ a lot from the usage of mock-up. Giving low priority to consumer high priority, however investigating this further we see that the average change per priority is about 16,5 with a standard deviation close to 6, this variation is considered random, in spite of its visual appearance in Fig. 3.

Product Manager Prioritization – Second Interview. After reprioritization the difference is listed in Table 3 below.

Table 3. Number of items with difference > X.

Difference	Count	(change)
>0	49	−8
>1	29	−16
>2	19	−12
>3	12	−7
>4	8	−6
>5	6	−6
>6	5	−5
>7	3	−2
>8	3	0
>9	2	0
>10	0	−1

Visually the difference is smaller between the prioritization done by product managers and the prioritization constructed by the feature usage of the mock-up. After reprioritization the number of items that differs three or more positions have decreased from 19 to 12, the number of items with same priority as the user group has gone from 3 to 11. The average difference is approximately 11,33 (down from 16,5) with a standard deviation of 4,8.

4.3 Alignment Towards Consumer Data Between First and Second Interview

First Interview. To further investigate if the product managers prioritize differently we look at the prioritizations from a feature perspective. The total difference in prioritization is 180 with an average prioritization difference of 15. The difference can be illustrated as in Fig. 5 below. Largest difference is for FT13 (32) and smallest difference for FT08 (8). Noting that if all product managers had agreed with the consumer selection the difference would have been 0, if all product managers had prioritized with a priority 1 point above or below the difference would be 5. The maximum possible difference is 55, had all product managers prioritized differently with the maximum offset of 11 for that feature.

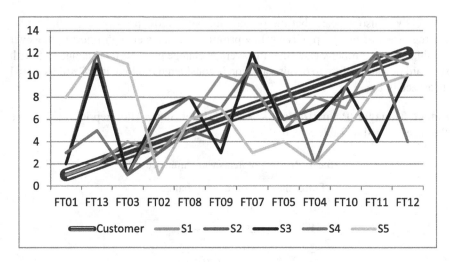

Fig. 5. Difference in prioritization per feature, first interview

Second Interview. Also in the second round of prioritization we compare the prioritization from a feature perspective. Producing the same graph as before the product managers had seen the customer prioritization we get the illustration shown in Fig. 6 below. Visually it appears that all product managers have aligned with the data and doing the same calculations as before we see that the total difference is 138 (was 180) with an average of 11,5 (was 15).

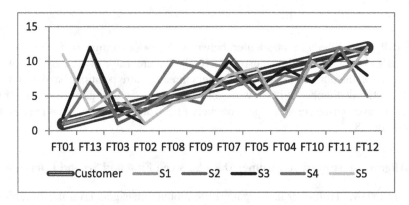

Fig. 6. Difference in prioritization per feature, second interview

There is still large disagreement on FT13 that differs 26 (was 32). FT02, FT03, FT05, FT08 and FT11 now have a difference of 8 or lower (FT03 has 7).

4.4 Answers to Open Questions About Value of the Mockup Data

As a response to the question "What is the basis for your new prioritization?" all of the product managers agreed that the consumer data made them re-prioritize. Some highlights of the responses are denoted below. For confidentiality reasons the complete responses cannot be reported in the paper, since they included the specific features and the nature of the features.

- "We have similar data from other sources that would be interested to compare"
- "Would have been interesting to understand the impact of changing the naming of the features"
- "Cannot prioritize solely on quantitative data, but gives valuable support when prioritizing"
- "Important data for pre-development decisions"
- "Did not know that this specific feature would be so popular"
- "As a strong product manager I need to set the direction and use this data for experimentation"
- "Important to understand what the consumer wants as presented by the data"
- "Small differences do not change my prioritization, need to see considerable differences to change my prioritization"
- "Triangulation with other data sources important"
- "Would try to use this method for pre-development decisions"
- "Need to consider the top usages but difficult who to interpret the rest"
- "Need to understand the cost of the feature before prioritizing, even if customer wants the feature there might be no business case to develop"

4.5 Summary

Looking at the numbers there seems to be a difference in prioritization before and after the product managers were shown the result of the mock-up. Looking at prioritization order and the different features we see that the product manager's prioritization is less different from consumers after the data was presented.

5 Discussion

5.1 Research Question 1: What Impact Does Quantitative Data that Measures Consumer Usage via a Mock-up Have on Prioritization Made by Product Managers?

According to Figs. 3 and 4 we see that there has been a re-prioritization of features when using the quantitative data. One could argue that the impact can be of a random nature or another factor impacted the prioritization. This threat has been handled during the interviews by direct question from the interviewers to re-prioritize based on input from the data. Thus our research indicates that this changes stems from the availability of the quantitative data collected.

Another insight is the variation between the product managers both in the first interview and second interview. An interpretation can be that product management is regarded an individual skill based on individual opinion. This makes it even more important to have something to align with and to get feedback from. Peers in product management would have their own opinion; we therefore see the quantitative data as a valuable feedback source for each individual product manager to use in their daily work.

5.2   Research Question 2: How Does the Prioritization Made by Product Managers Match the Consumer Usage Measured via a Mock-up?

This is a challenging question in light of the variation in the first prioritization by the product managers. However, a trend towards aligning with customer data can be seen in Fig. 5 by comparing to Fig. 6. Both visually and by measuring the discrete distance for all product managers it can be derived that prioritization is conforming to the quantitative data collected. There is however a not negligible difference between individual product managers prioritization. The difference is interesting, thus is indicates that there are more factors besides customer usage that impacts the decision making.

5.3   Research Question 3: How Valuable Do Product Managers Believe that Quantitative Data Is for Prioritizing Requirements?

As an open question in the end of the interview the senior product managers got a qualitative question about if the data present was beneficial in their prioritization and gave more insight. All of the product managers were positive to use the data in the prioritization, although many of them did not prioritize the features with most usage. This would indicate that product managers have multiple factors to consider. Other aspects could be that their accountability is not towards consumer's satisfaction only. Even if product managers decide not to follow the consumer data, they should be aware of the consequences of missing expectations [21]. The consequences are especially true within software services such as web and many smartphone applications that target a wide consumer base. You only get limited number of chances for consumer engagement. If the opportunities are missed the consumer will engage with a competitor or alternative service. Then the business opportunities are lost for this particular instantiation of the conversion funnel as for example described in the A, I and D steps in the AIDAS model. You would need a new investment to regain the consumer base and you need to start a new instance of the AID steps.

Using a mock-up to evaluate features should be an integrated part of the prioritization of features. The strength is to relatively cheaply (compared to a complete development cycle) collect information about consumer expectations about possible new features. The collection could also be in an iterative way to compare combination of features set of the product. Example of features-sets could be elicited by analyzing the scope in similar products or looking at new opportunities.

6   Conclusion and Further Study

Concluding, the contributions of the paper are threefold. First, product managers change their prioritization when quantitative data is presented to them. Second, product managers change their prioritization which is converged to the prioritization indicated by the quantitative data. Third, the quantitative data is regarded as beneficial by the product managers.

Finally, there are a number of opportunities for further study that we are considering, especially concerning the empirical design. Examples of further studies could be; expanding the analysis to more applications, other types of applications, consider the cost of value delivered for each features, other case companies and other domains as for example IT systems where doing a mock-up could more expensive.

Acknowledgments. The development work needed for of the case study has been funded and supported by Sony Mobile. This research was in part funded by Software Center (www.software-center.se). We thank the senior product managers that participated in the study for valuable input during the after the interviews.

References

1. Olsson, H.H., Bosch, J.: From opinions to data-driven software R&D: a multi-case study on how to close the 'open loop' problem. In: Proceedings of EUROMICRO, Software Engineering and Advanced Applications (SEAA), Verona, Italy, 27–29 August 2014
2. Bosch-Sijtsema, P., Bosch, J.: User involvement throughout the innovation process in high-tech industries. J. Prod. Innov. Manage (2014). doi:10.1111/jpim.12233
3. Backlund, E., Bolle, M., Tichy, M., Olsson, H.H., Bosch, J.: Automated user interaction analysis for workflow-based web portals. In: Lassenius, C., Smolander, K. (eds.) ICSOB 2014. LNBIP, vol. 182, pp. 148–162. Springer, Heidelberg (2014)
4. Johansson, E., Bergdahl, D., Bosch, J., Olsson, H.H.: Quantitative requirements prioritization from a pre-development perspective. In: Rout, T., O'Connor, R.V., Dorling, A. (eds.) SPICE 2015. CCIS, vol. 526, pp. 58–71. Springer, Heidelberg (2015)
5. Saliu, O., Ruhe, G.: Software release planning for evolving systems. Innovations Syst. Softw. Eng. **1**(2), 189–204 (2005)
6. Hofman, H.F., Lehner, F.: Requirements engineering as a success factor in software projects. IEEE Softw. **18**, 58–66 (2001)
7. Kabbedijk, J., Brinkkemper, S., Jansen, S., van der Veldt, B.: Customer involvement in requirements management: lessons from mass market software development. In: Requirements Engineering Conference (2009)
8. Yiyi Y., Rongqiu C.: Customer participation: co-creating knowledge with customers. In: Wireless Communications, Networking and Mobile Computing (2008)
9. Holmström Olsson, H., Bosch, J.: Towards data-driven product development: a multiple case study on post-deployment data usage in software-intensive embedded systems. In: Fitzgerald, B., Conboy, K., Power, K., Valerdi, R., Morgan, L., Stol, K.-J. (eds.) LESS 2013. LNBIP, vol. 167, pp. 152–164. Springer, Heidelberg (2013)
10. Holmström Olsson, H., Bosch, J.: Post-deployment data collection in software-intensive embedded products. In: Herzwurm, G., Margaria, T. (eds.) ICSOB 2013. LNBIP, vol. 150, pp. 79–89. Springer, Heidelberg (2013)
11. Ries, E.: The Lean Startup: How Constant Innovation Creates Radically Successful Businesses. Penguin Group, London (2011)
12. Olsson H.H., Alahyari H., Bosch, J.: Climbing the "Stairway to Heaven": a multiple-case study exploring barriers in the transition from agile development towards continuous

deployment of software. In: Proceedings of the 38th Euromicro Conference on Software Engineering and Advanced Applications, Cesme, Izmir, Turkey 5–7 September 2012
13. Bosch, J.: Building products as innovations experiment systems. In: Proceedings of 3rd International Conference on Software Business, Cambridge, Massachusetts 18–20 June 2012
14. Fagerholm, F., Sanchez G., Mäenpää, H., Münch, J.: Building blocks for continuous experimentation. In: The Proceedings of the RCoSE 2014 Workshop, Hyderabad, India, 3 June 2014
15. Wikipedia. http://en.wikipedia.org/wiki/Feature_creep
16. Campbell, D.T., Stanley, J.C.: Experimental and quasi-experimental designs for research, p. 1983. Houghton Mifflin Company. Clark, R. E, Boston (1966)
17. Robson, C.: Real World Research, 2nd edn. Blackwell, Oxford (2002)
18. Sheldon, F.: The Art of Selling. The Sheldon University, Libertyville (1911)
19. Ferrell, O.C., Michael, H.: Marketing Strategy. Thomson South-Western, Mason (2015)
20. Runesson, P., Höst, M.: Guidelines for conducting and reporting case study research in software engineering. Empirical Software Eng. 14, 131–164 (2009)
21. Grover, R., Vriens, M.: The Handbook of Marketing Research: Uses, Misuses, and Future Advances. Sage Publications Inc, Thousand Oaks (2006)

A Method for Requirements Capture and Specification Based on Disciplined Use Cases and Screen Mockups

Gianna Reggio, Maurizio Leotta[✉], and Filippo Ricca

DIBRIS, Università di Genova, Genoa, Italy
{gianna.reggio,maurizio.leotta,filippo.ricca}@unige.it

Abstract. We present a novel method for capturing and writing requirements specifications that enriches disciplined use cases with screen mockups. Disciplined use cases are characterized by a quite stringent template, which allows to impose a large number of constraints helping to prevent common mistakes and to increase the quality of the specifications. Disciplined use cases are expressed using natural language, but the strong structuring allows to reach a good level of precision without having to introduce new (and more complex) notations. Screen mockups associated with the steps of the scenarios present the corresponding GUIs as seen by the human actors before/after the step executions, improving the comprehension of the requirements, and allowing also to precisely present non-functional requirements of the user interface. The method has been successfully applied in an industrial project and the effectiveness of the screen mockups has been validated by means of controlled experiments.

1 Introduction

A number of methods, techniques and approaches have been proposed in literature for representing software requirements. Among them, use cases are a widely used technique to specify the purpose of a software system, and to produce its description in terms of interactions between actors and the subject system [5]. However, even presented by means of use cases, the requirements could be difficult to comprehend, incomplete, inconsistent, contradictory and may cause/provoke defects in the software system under development.

Screen mockups (also known as user interface sketches, user interface prototypes or wireframes) are used for prototyping the user interface of a subject system [7,9]. Mockups can be used in conjunction with use cases, associating them with the steps of the scenarios, to improve the comprehension of functional requirements and to achieve a shared understanding on them. Simultaneously, they allow to represent the non-functional requirements concerning the user interface [6]. However, *enriching the use cases with the screen mockups arises the problem of guaranteeing that the mockups are coherent with the textual part of the use cases*, and that they truly provide information on how to structure the GUIs supporting the functionalities presented by the use case.

© Springer International Publishing Switzerland 2015
P. Abrahamsson et al. (Eds.): PROFES 2015, LNCS 9459, pp. 105–113, 2015.
DOI: 10.1007/978-3-319-26844-6_8

As a matter of fact, the consistency between use cases and screen mock-ups cannot be guaranteed if the former are poorly structured and have a low level of *precision*. Requirements specifications based on use cases may have very different levels of precision from scarcely structured scenarios made by lists of freely formed natural language sentences, to use cases presented following quite detailed and structured templates, for example Cockburn [5], till to methods where the use cases are represented by means UML models [2] or even by formal specifications [4]. We believe that disciplined natural language specifications, i.e. where the text must follow very detailed and stringent patterns [8,10] and a glossary of terms is added to reduce ambiguity, are a good compromise. For this reason, we have conceived a method for capturing and describing requirements specifications based on *disciplined use cases* and screen mockups, taking the Cockburn guidelines as starting point. *Disciplined use cases* are: (1) character-ized by a high level of precision without having to introduce additional notations and the consequent effort required to learn and to use them, (2) suitable to be enriched in a consistent way with the screen mockups, and (3) able to help the requirements analyst to detect errors, incompleteness, bad smells (e.g. unused elements), and bad quality factors (e.g. too many extensions and too many steps in a scenario) in the requirements specification (thanks to many well-formedness constraints).

Even if Screen Mockups are quite common in many industries and several pro-posals are emerging to integrate/use them in conjunction with use cases (or more in general with requirements) [15,17], our method is the only one that allows to obtain consistent screen mockups that are fully integrated in the development process, and thus that are not just a bunch of drawings added to the use cases. To the best of our knowledge, this is the main novelty aspect of our work.

This paper extends our previous work [11], where we described the tem-plate of disciplined use cases and how to integrate screen mockups, with: (i) the description of a comprehensive method for capturing and writing requirements specifications (see Sect. 2), (ii) some details on the empirical assessment of the method (see Sect. 3), and (iii) the complete list of well-formedness constraints for the precise use cases integrated with screen mockups (see Appendix A).

2   Requirements Capture and Specification Using Disciplined Use Cases and Screen Mockups

The starting point of our method (see Fig. 1) is what we call a "free use case specification", i.e. a use case specification based on whatever template, in general allowing a lot of freedom to the specification writers. In case not yet available, the free specification may be easily produced by stakeholders or domain experts with or without the assistance of the analyst.

Once the free specification has reached a stable form, the analyst may start the task of making the use case disciplined and adding the screen mockups (i.e., as described in [11], and verifying that the well-formedness constraints shown in Appendix A hold). Obviously, the result of such activity is the detection of

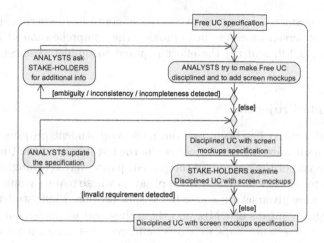

Fig. 1. Requirements capture and specification using disciplined use cases and screen mockups

inconsistencies (i.e. two different points of the specification express two contrasting statements about something), *ambiguities* (i.e. the specification uses words without stating their precise meaning relying on some common, but not always shared, understanding), and *incompleteness* (i.e. it is not possible to understand how the system should work in some specific cases). In these cases the analyst should ask the stakeholders and/or the domain experts additional information to be able to obtain a disciplined use case specification equipped with screen mockups; notice that also adding the screen mockups may generate many questions about the system under specification.

Once the analyst has terminated her/his work, the resulting disciplined specification augmented with screen mockups may be given to the stakeholders to get the final approving. They have no problem in reading and understanding it, since it is essentially structured natural language text; moreover the presence of the screen mockups offers a kind of paper prototyping, allowing them to validate also the user interface. Any change request may be easily processed by the analyst because the strong structuring of our use case specifications offers a good support to trace the influence on the whole specification of a change. This characteristic of our specifications will be valuable also on the case of future evolution of the requirements on the system.

3 Empirical Assessment

In this section we describe (1) how our method has been fine-tuned during several editions of a software engineering course at the University of Genoa [1], and (2) how we evaluated its applicability in the industry through a case study.

Moreover, we evaluated by means of a series of controlled experiments: (1) the effectiveness of screen mockups in improving the comprehension of functional requirements [12,14], and (2) the effort required to build the screen mockups [13,16].

3.1 Students Projects

The proposed method has been used during several student projects in several editions of the software engineering courses in the last decade at the University of Genoa, where two of the authors of the present paper were teaching. Each year, students had to realize a Java desktop application whose requirements, produced by ourselves, were given as a use case based specification. First, students had to model a design by means of UML, and then, they had to implement it in Java [1]. Initially, no screen mockups were used, and even if standard requirements on the GUIs were provided (i.e. usability requirements), the use cases often resulted difficult to understand and ambiguous for what concerns the user interaction. For example, a use case step for EasyCooking — a software helping to write recipes and diets — requiring "to list foods" was interpreted by all the students as "to list the complete nutritional details of foods" while the intention of the requirements authors was simply to list the names of such foods. We discovered that, after the introduction of screen mockups the number of misunderstanding about the required user interactions decreased, and moreover, we witnessed that the effort of producing the screen mockups had as a "side effect" that various ambiguities/incompleteness even mistakes were discovered during the writing of the requirements specification. Some examples of the disciplined requirements specification with screen mockups for the students projects may be found at http://sepl.dibris.unige.it/2015-UseCasesMockups.php.

3.2 Industrial Case Study

Our method has been applied with success during a joint project [3] involving the University of Genoa, Italy, and two local companies, having the goal of developing the EC2M system. Such system consists in an improved ECM making use of ontologies to better classify, retrieve and share documentation among different branches of the companies. The functionalities offered by EC2M can be classified as: interactive and non-interactive: the first allow the user(s) to interact with EC2M using GUIs (e.g. logging in and inserting/retrieving documents) while the latter focus on the interactions between software systems using specific protocols (e.g. exchanging information or documentation using SOAP and REST). Since our method has been devised for describing the requirements specification of interactive software systems, in this project we applied our method only for the portion of requirements describing the interaction between the EC2M system and the user(s).

Creating the Free UC Specification. As described in Sect. 2 our method takes a free UC specification as input. Using the information gained in the course of the first two meetings with our industrial partners, we developed a preliminary version of the UC specification, composed by 12 use cases and three primary actors. The free UC specification reflects the requirements as informally expressed by the industrial partners (i.e. the two local companies) during the meetings. For this reasons, later, we discovered that there were several problems, for instance: (1) the meaning of the terms reported in the use cases was not always agreed by all the partners (the glossary is missing in this phase), (2) the granularity of the actions described in the use cases steps was not uniform (some too abstract and others too detailed), and (3) only a few extensions to the main success scenarios were reported.

Making the UC Specification Precise. Starting from the free UC specification, we first developed a "precise UC specification" (i.e. complying with the Well-formedness constraints listed in Table 1) asking, when needed, the industrial partners some clarifications. In this way, we greatly improved the quality of the requirements specification. e.g. by adding the Glossary, leveling out the granularity of the steps (e.g. subdividing a single step in more steps), redefining some actors, and considering new scenarios. Once the "precise UC specification" was settled, we added to it the screen mockups verifying that they comply to the well-formedness constraints (see Table 2). We chose to associate the mockups with the most relevant steps whose subject was EC2M. In this phase, the Pencil tool has been used; it proved to have the capability to quickly create realistic screen mockups.

Verifying Stakeholders Requirements. Finally, we organized a meeting where the "precise UC with screen mockup specification" has been shown to the industrial partners. That occasion has been very useful for identifying some misunderstandings between our understanding of the EC2M system and what the industrial partners really desired. Moreover, the screen mockups have allowed to perform a sort of prototype verification helping the industrial partners to detect problems difficult to find inspecting only textual use cases. After the meeting we fixed the identified problems. The final specification was composed by 15 use cases with the relative descriptions, three primary actors, two secondary actors, 11 glossary entries, and 10 screen mockups.

During the project's meetings, the industrial partners found the screen mockups (and the glossary) very effective to improve the comprehensibility of the use cases and useful to find the ambiguities in the requirements specification. As an example, the EC2M system allows to semantically classify the documents by means of an ontology and at the same time the ontology allows to search documents using semantic tags. Since an ontology is a quite complex object, several ways can be chosen to graphically represent and use it. They are strongly different for what concerns, for instance, the usability perspective. The creation of screen mockups for the steps related to the usage of the ontology allowed to: (1) improve the understanding of the operations involving the ontology for non-experts, and (2) precisely define the kind of interactions required to the system users in order to complete the steps mentioned above. The professionals involved in the creation of the functional requirements specification for EC2M were satisfied of the method. One of them at the end of the project reported the following phrase: "discipline and mockups are two essential ingredients to improve the quality and comprehension of requirements!".

4   Conclusion and Future Work

In this work we have proposed a novel method for capturing and specify requirements of a software system. The novelty is the integration and synergy between screen mockups and use cases. In fact, the proposed method produces disciplined use cases and coherent screen mockups that are fully integrated in the development process. The positive aspects of the requirement specifications produced with our method are: – easier to comprehend (thanks to the screen mockups), – less prone to inconsistencies (thanks to the glossary), – less prone to incompleteness (thanks to the strong constrains on the form of the scenarios), – and in general of "good quality" since checking the many well-formedness constraints associated with our template results in a deep and strongly structured inspection.

It is important to note that differently from specifying use cases using formal languages or modelling notations our specifications may be read and understood also by non-experts. On the other side, the production of this kind of requirements specifications requires an extra effort compared to producing use case specifications adhering to a very loose template, and obviously the knowledge of our quite precise template.

The method has been successfully applied in an industrial project and used for many years in software engineering student's projects at the University of Genoa.

As future work, we intend to implement a supporting tool able to: (1) help in the creation and visualization of the requirements specifications using our format, and (2) automatically check the compliance of the requirements specifications to the various well-formedness constraints.

A   Precise Use Cases with Screen Mockups Specification Well-Formedness Constraints

See [11] for the definition of the form of the requirement specification based on disciplined use cases augmented with screen mockups.

Table 1. Well-formedness constraints for requirements specification

- A summary use case cannot be included in either a user-goal or a subfunction use case
- A user-goal use case cannot be included in a subfunction use case
- A summary use case must have the goal and the stakeholder parts
- If a use case C includes C1 in the use case diagram, then at least a line corresponding to "include C1" must appear in the description of C, and vice versa (i.e. every inclusion in the use case descriptions must appear in the use case diagram)
- If a use case C extends C1 in the use case diagram, then at least a line corresponding to an extension point for C must appear in the description of C1, and vice versa (i.e. every extension point in the use case descriptions must correspond to an extension relationship in the use case diagram)
- The actors listed in the use case descriptions should be in accord with those appearing in the use case diagram and vice versa
- Each listed actor of a use case must appear at least in one step of its scenarios
- The subject of a step of a scenario different from the system, must appear among the use case actors
- If a use case has no actors, then it must have a trigger[*]
- If a step has a condition *cond* different from true, then there should be some extensions starting from the same step with conditions $cond_1, \ldots, cond_n$ s.t. the logical disjunction of $cond, cond_1, \ldots, cond_n$ is true
- Each complete scenario must include at least a step where the subject is the system
- All the initial steps of a set of extensions starting from the same point must have the same subject
- Each data listed in the glossary must appear at least in one step of a use case
- Each system attribute listed in the glossary must at least
  - appear in the effect part of a step of a use case
  - appear either in the condition or in the interaction part of a step of a use case

[*] *(e.g. a use case describing a periodic activity made by the system each hour)*

Table 2. Well-formedness constraints for screen mockups

Actor as Subject and Initial Mockup (i.e., at the beginning of the step)

- Let $S_0, S_1, \ldots, S_n$ ($n \geq 0$) be some steps having an actor as subject s.t. $S_1, \ldots, S_n$ are the first steps of extensions starting from S_0, and let M be the initial mockup of $S_0, S_1, \ldots, S_n$
  - If the interaction part of S_i ($0 \leq i \leq n$) refers to some communication from the actor to system, then some means to represent it must appear in M (e.g. when $S_0 =$ "Client confirms", $S_1 =$ "Client refuses", and two buttons "Confirm" and "Refuse" appear in M)
  - If M contains some means for realizing some communication from the actor to system, then there should be S_i ($0 \leq i \leq n$) referring to such interaction

Actor as Subject and Final Mockup (i.e., at the end of the step)

- Let $S_1, \ldots, S_k$ ($k \geq 1$) be some steps having an actor as subject, and let M be the final mockup of $S_1, \ldots, S_k$ ($S_1, \ldots, S_k$ must be steps having the same interaction part appearing in different scenarios of even different use cases)
  - If the interaction part of S_1 (that it is coincident with those of $S_2, \ldots, S_k$) refers to some communication from the actor to system, then M should show how it is going to be realized (e.g. the step S_1 has the form "User confirms the deletion", and in M there is a button "Confirm Deletion"; notice that this step may represent the confirmation of different kinds of deletions)
  - If the interaction part of S_1 (that it is coincident with those of $S_2, \ldots, S_k$) includes a reference to some specific information (flowing from the actor to system), then such information must appear in some way in M (e.g. "Actor inserts the password" and "password" appears in M)
  - If M shows how some communication is going to be realized (from the actor to system), then the interaction part of step S_1 (that it is coincident with those of $S_2, \ldots, S_k$) should refer to it

System as Subject and Mockup

- Let $S_1, \ldots, S_m$ ($m \geq 1$) be some steps having the system as subject, and let M be the final mockup of $S_1, \ldots, S_m$ ($S_1, \ldots, S_m$ must be steps having the same interaction part appearing in different scenarios of even different use cases)
  - If some information appears in M, then it should be derived by the interaction parts of the previous steps or by the system attributes (e.g. in M appears "You are logged as John Doe", and the name of the current logged user "John Doe" is recoverable by the system attributes or it was provided by the user in some previous step)
  - If the interaction part of S_1 (that it is coincident with those of $S_2, \ldots, S_m$) refers to some communication from system to actor, then some means to represent such communication must appear in M (e.g. "System confirms the required deletion" and either a pop-up or a message box containing a sentence equivalent to "deletion confirmed" appears in M)

References

1. Astesiano, E., Cerioli, M., Reggio, G., Ricca, F.: A phased highly-interactive approach to teaching UML-based software development. In: Proceedings of Educators Symposium at MoDELS 2007, pp. 9–18. University of Goteborg (2007)
2. Astesiano, E., Reggio, G.: Knowledge structuring and representation in requirement specification. In: Proceedings of 14th International Conference on Software Engineering and Knowledge Engineering, SEKE 2002, pp. 143–150. ACM (2002)
3. Briola, D., Amicone, A., Laudisa, D.: Ontologies in industrial enterprise content management systems: the EC2M project. In: Proceedings of 5th International Conference on Advanced Cognitive Technologies and Applications, pp. 153–160. IARIA (2013)
4. Choppy, C., Reggio, G.: Improving use case based requirements using formally grounded specifications. In: Wermelinger, M., Margaria-Steffen, T. (eds.) FASE 2004. LNCS, vol. 2984, pp. 244–260. Springer, Heidelberg (2004)
5. Cockburn, A.: Writing Effective Use Cases. Addison Wesley, New York (2000)
6. Ferreira, J., Noble, J., Biddle, R.: Agile development iterations and UI design. In: Proceedings of Agile Conference, AGILE 2007, pp. 50–58 (2007)
7. Hartson, H.R., Smith, E.C.: Rapid prototyping in human-computer interface development. Interact. Comput. 3(1), 51–91 (1991)
8. Leotta, M., Reggio, G., Ricca, F., Astesiano, E.: Towards a lightweight model driven method for developing SOA systems using existing assets. In: Proceedings of 14th International Symposium on Web Systems Evolution, WSE 2012, pp. 51–60. IEEE (2012)
9. O'Docherty, M.: Object-Oriented Analysis and Design: Understanding System Development with UML 2.0. Wiley, Hoboken (2005)
10. Reggio, G., Leotta, M., Ricca, F., Astesiano, E.: Business process modelling: five styles and a method to choose the most suitable one. In: Proceedings of 2nd International Workshop on Experiences and Empirical Studies in Software Modelling, EESSMod 2012, pp. 8:1–8:6. ACM (2012)
11. Reggio, G., Ricca, F., Leotta, M.: Improving the quality and the comprehension of requirements: disciplined use cases and mockups. In: Proceedings of 40th Euromicro Conference on Software Engineering and Advanced Applications, SEAA 2014, pp. 262–266. IEEE (2014)
12. Ricca, F., Scanniello, G., Torchiano, M., Reggio, G., Astesiano, E.: On the effectiveness of screen mockups in requirements engineering: results from an internal replication. In: Proceedings of 4th International Symposium on Empirical Software Engineering and Measurement, ESEM 2010, pp. 17:1–17:10. ACM (2010)
13. Ricca, F., Scanniello, G., Torchiano, M., Reggio, G., Astesiano, E.: On the effort of augmenting use cases with screen mockups: results from a preliminary empirical study. In: Proceedings of 4th International Symposium on Empirical Software Engineering and Measurement, ESEM 2010, pp. 40:1–40:4. ACM (2010)
14. Ricca, F., Scanniello, G., Torchiano, M., Reggio, G., Astesiano, E.: Assessing the effect of screen mockups on the comprehension of functional requirements. ACM Trans. Softw. Eng. Methodol. 24(1), 1:1–1:38 (2014)
15. Rivero, J.M., Grigera, J., Rossi, G., Luna, E.R., Montero, F., Gaedke, M.: Mockup-driven development: providing agile support for model-driven web engineering. Inf. Softw. Technol. 56(6), 670–687 (2014)

16. Scanniello, G., Ricca, F., Torchiano, M., Gravino, C., Reggio, G.: Estimating the effort to develop screen mockups. In: Proceedings of 39th Euromicro Conference on Software Engineering and Advanced Applications, SEAA 2013, pp. 341–348 (2013)
17. Zhang, J., Chang, C., Chung, J.Y.: Mockup-driven fast-prototyping methodology for web requirements engineering. In: Proceedings of 27th International Computer Software and Applications Conference, COMPSAC 2003, pp. 263–268. IEEE (2003)

A Case Study on Artefact-Based RE Improvement in Practice

Daniel Méndez Fernández[1] and Stefan Wagner[2]([⊠])

[1] Technische Universität München, Munich, Germany
http://www4.in.tum.de/mendezfe
[2] University of Stuttgart, Stuttgart, Germany
stefan.wagner@informatik.uni-stuttgart.de
http://www.iste.uni-stuttgart.de/

Abstract. *Background:* Most requirements engineering (RE) process improvement approaches are solution-driven and activity-based. They focus on the assessment of the RE of a company against an external norm of best practices. A consequence is that practitioners often have to rely on an improvement approach that skips a profound problem analysis and that results in an RE approach that might be alien to the organisational needs. *Objective:* In recent years, we have developed an RE improvement approach (called *ArtREPI*) that guides a holistic RE improvement against individual goals of a company putting primary attention to the quality of the artefacts. In this paper, we aim at exploring ArtREPI's benefits and limitations. *Method:* We contribute an industrial evaluation of ArtREPI by relying on a case study research. *Results:* Our results suggest that ArtREPI is well-suited for the establishment of an RE that reflects a specific organisational culture but to some extent at the cost of efficiency resulting from intensive discussions on a terminology that suits all involved stakeholders. *Conclusions:* Our results reveal first benefits and limitations, but we can also conclude the need of longitudinal and independent investigations for which we herewith lay the foundation.

Keywords: Requirements engineering · Artefact orientation · Software process improvement · Case study research

1 Introduction

Requirements engineering (RE) constitutes an important success factor for software development projects since stakeholder-appropriate requirements are important determinants of quality. Its interdisciplinary nature, the uncertainty, and the complexity in the process, however, make the discipline difficult to investigate and to improve [1]. For an RE improvement, process engineers have to decide whether to opt for *problem orientation* or for *solution orientation* [2,3]. In a solution-driven improvement, the engineers assess and adapt their RE reference model, which provides a company-specific blueprint of RE practices and artefacts, against an external norm of best practices. The latter is meant to

© Springer International Publishing Switzerland 2015
P. Abrahamsson et al. (Eds.): PROFES 2015, LNCS 9459, pp. 114–130, 2015.
DOI: 10.1007/978-3-319-26844-6_9

lead to a high quality RE based on universal, external goals (see, e.g. CMMI for RE [4]). Solution-driven improvement approaches might thus serve the purpose of achieving externally predefined goals by implementing a set of best practices adhered by many organisations [2] (e.g. as part of a certification). They do not necessarily consider company-specific goals, however, that dictate the notion of RE quality within a particular socio-economic context (e.g. a company) and, thus, may result in an RE reference model that is alien to the organisational culture. In consequence, those RE improvement approaches encounter problems and are often rejected by practitioners [1,5]. A notion of RE quality where company-specific goals dictate the improvement is the core of problem-driven approaches.

Besides the improvement principles, the paradigm in which the targeted RE reference model is structured (and, thus, improved) plays an important role. A reference model can either be *activity-based* or *artefact-based* [6]. In short, an activity-based improvement approach focuses on improving the quality of the RE practices while an artefact-based one puts its focus on improving the quality of the RE artefacts.

Most available RE improvement approaches today are solution-driven [7]. Yet, RE is complex by nature, and we postulate that RE quality depends on the contribution of an RE reference model to context-specific goals. Therefore, improvements cannot be meaningfully implemented without a qualitative problem investigation that reveals which goals must be achieved [2,3] and which artefacts should be created in which way. In response to the lack of problem-driven and artefact-based RE improvement approaches, we elaborated such an approach [8] which we call *ArtREPI*. We further realised our approach using the EPF Composer[1] and made first experiences using ArtREPI in practice (see also Sect. 2).

Problem. Although we made first conceptual and empirical contributions to support a problem-driven and artefact-based RE improvement, we still have little evidence on its practical benefits and limitations.

Contribution. In this paper, we report on the first industrial case study to evaluate *ArtREPI* in comparison to solution-driven and activity-based REPI approaches previously used in the same contexts. The purpose, however, is not to evaluate only the particularities of our approach itself, but also

1. to reveal first qualitative insights into the benefits and limitations of a problem-driven and artefact-based RE improvement in general, and
2. to lay the foundation for future independent empirical investigations.

Based on our contribution and the disclosed material [9], practitioners can therefore already apply our RE improvement approach, and researchers can build their conceptual and empirical work on our results to further explore the full spectrum of an RE improvement.

Outline. In Sect. 2, we discuss fundamentals and related work. In Sect. 3, we introduce the artefact-based RE improvement approach. We provide our case

---

[1] http://www.eclipse.org/epf/.

study design in Sect. 4, the results in Sect. 5, and a critical reflection in Sect. 6, before concluding our paper in Sect. 7.

2   Fundamentals and Related Work

Requirements engineering process improvement, as software process improvement in general, is a cyclic approach to continuously analyse problems/the current situation in RE as part of an appraisal, plan an improvement, realise the improvement and evaluate the improvement before initiating the next iteration. We can distinguish solution-driven approaches and problem-driven approaches as well as artefact and activity orientation.

In literature, there exist mostly solution-driven contributions [3]. R-CMM, proposed by Beecham et al. [4], is a prominent representative of these approaches. It is based on CMMI and an empirical investigation in twelve companies [10]. The investigation revealed patterns and best practices based on problems experienced by practitioners. Therefore, it aimed at a generalised, external notion of RE quality. A technical validation using an expert panel [11] further illustrates selected success criteria, such as understandability. Approaches of this category focus on a solution-driven benchmarking of the maturity of RE according to a specific norm of best practices and may thus lead to the problems described in the introduction (see also [1,5] for richer investigations).

In response to their shortcoming, Pettersson et al. contributed an approach to problem-driven RE improvement [2] called the iFLAP approach. Same as in ArtREPI, they make use of qualitative methods for the problem analysis and postulate the importance of strong stakeholder involvement. Although their concepts are promising to conduct a problem-driven REPI, the consequential next steps, i.e. the actual improvement realisation by crafting a new RE reference model, was not in scope of their contribution.

To the best of our knowledge, there exists no holistic approach to a REPI covering all improvement phases in a seamless manner, let alone considering an improvement specifically directed at the RE artefacts. Recent work in this direction is made by Kuhrmann et al. [12], but taking more a perspective on the management of software process models. The focus is thereby set on how to manage an artefact-based improvement rather than on how to conduct it. They do not look at how to analyse, design, and evaluate a process in a problem-driven manner focusing on the quality of the artefacts which is in scope of ArtREPI.

Available validation and evaluation research, which would be directly related to the contributions of this paper, focuses on the evaluation of methods or metrics used in isolated REPI phases, such as the analysis, on experience reports, or on the analysis of general success factors and lessons learnt. In the case study we present here, we therefore do not discuss the relation to existing evidence taking into account particular approaches, but exclusively take a qualitative view and rely on the evaluation of ArtREPI against the general perceptions and the experiences of the participants with solution-driven, activity-based REPI in the same context. Further details on the publication landscape on REPI can be taken from our previously published mapping study [7].

Previously Published Material. In [8], we first introduced the basic concepts of ArtREPI and its design science principles. Since then, we realised our approach using the EPF Composer as a means of a technical validation and made all material (models, process documentation, document templates, and evaluation instruments) publicly available [9] to support the dissemination. In a previous short paper [13], we then briefly reported on initial experiences from an ongoing case study. In the paper at hands, we report on the by now completed case study in detail including the case study design, the results containing a second case, and the implications the results have.

3   ArtREPI: Artefact-Based RE Process Improvement

Figure 1 gives an overview of the basic structure of ArtREPI, which we use for our evaluation presented in this paper. As shown in the figure, we distinguish two contexts important to the notion of RE quality: an external context that contains norms of best practices and the socio-economic context where the notion of quality is dictated by individual demands. External norms of best practices are not only key to solution-driven RE improvement approaches but also important to a problem-driven improvement as one principle is to support technology transfer according to context-specific goals.

The socio-economic context is further characterised by a set of disciplines that aim at managing software processes. Of particular interest is that we have process owners who usually have the sovereignty over an RE reference model (although often underrepresented in practice [1]) and a set of project participants who work according to an (explicitly established or implicitly lived) RE reference model. The latter is subject to an improvement in case an organisational change is triggered. For reasons of complexity, we omit the discussion of further disciplines or roles, such as an improvement sponsor. A change is performed as part of an RE process improvement project which is in scope of ArtREPI. ArtREPI consists of four phases and yields a set of mandatory and optional results. The mandatory ones eventually serve a seamless improvement based on a unified underlying data model of the improvement results. The full model can be taken from our online sources [9] while in the following, we provide a brief overview of the single phases.

3.1   Improvement Preparation

In the preparation phase, we lay the groundwork for the improvement and aim at getting an understanding about the application domain, such as the chemical sector, typical constructs and rules followed therein, and the terminology used. We discuss contemporary problems and the primary improvement goals which, in collaboration with the process owners, we refine to concrete metrics and measurements to evaluate the success of the improvement after completion. Where possible and reasonable, we reuse metrics from previously conducted ArtREPI. The outcome of the preparation phase is an improvement plan that defines the concrete procedures and time schedules as well as resource allocations (cases and subjects) for subsequent steps including interviews or workshops.

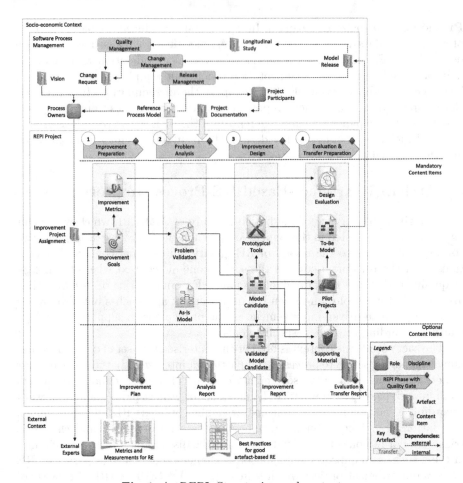

Fig. 1. ArtREPI: Structuring and context.

3.2 Problem Analysis

The second stage aims at discovering problems in the use of the current RE reference model independent of whether it is explicitly defined as a company standard or not. In case a company standard exists, we analyse it first to get an overview of the basic artefacts, roles, and activities. We then conduct a document analysis in selected exemplary development projects and abstract from the contents to build an as-is model of the RE artefacts, milestones, and roles. We complement this syntactic analysis with a semantic analysis where we analyse, for example, linguistic defects in document templates. We use the defined as-is model to conduct a gap analysis where we compare the current state of practice with an external standard which serves as a knowledge base. More precisely, we rely on *AMDiRE* (**a m**odel for **d**omain-**i**ndependent **RE**) that defines a best practice norm for artefact-based RE (see also [14]). We use potential gaps from our analysis as candidates for further validation which we do via semi-structured interviews. There, besides asking about experiences and expectations, we ask the participants why certain contents identified as incomplete in comparison to AMDiRE have or have not been specified in their projects. We take their reasoning as our primary input to establish later on a tailoring profile for the artefact-based RE reference model. The aim of the whole analysis is not to benchmark the process against an external standard. Instead and according to the problem-driven nature of ArtREPI, it aims at getting a better understanding on potential improvements which then can only be validated by project participants. To this end, we trigger a self-reflection via interviews by indicating only possibilities for changes that eventually only they can judge upon.

3.3 Improvement Design

In the third stage, we conduct the actual realisation of the improvement based on the candidates previously identified during the gap analysis. To this end, we conduct a series of action research workshops where we build a new model candidate by deciding which content items to consider in the candidate (e.g. "use case model") before we then subsequently define the actual content model that abstracts from concrete modelling concepts used to specify the content items in a project. The latter serves to build a prototypical (modelling) tool or document templates, and to establish content-related dependencies to the artefacts of further development phases, such as of testing, serving the purpose of a process integration into the overall software process model. We enrich the artefact model with process elements (roles, milestones) and a tailoring profile that emerges from the interviews and that defines under which project circumstances to document certain content items or not. Depending on the improvement project complexity or criticality, we may perform a validation of the model candidate before entering the last stage. In this validation step, we validate the model via feedback gathered by domain experts not involved in the improvement workshops.

3.4 Improvement Evaluation and Transfer Preparation

The success of a problem-driven improvement can eventually only be determined by the degree to which the improvement outcome satisfies the improvement goals. In the last step, we therefore conduct technical action research workshops with project participants in pilot projects where we apply the resulting RE reference model under realistic conditions. We specify a set of RE artefacts following the new RE reference model. Afterwards, we compare the outcomes and the followed process with the artefacts previously created in the same project environment by an interview. The participants rate the new model following the criteria agreed on in the preparation phase. In case of a positive rating, we release the new model complemented with supporting material.

4   Case Study Design

In [8], we introduced in detail how we inferred our ArtREPI approach presented in Sect. 3 from fundamental and applied research projects where we conducted an artefact-based and problem-oriented RE improvement. We argued so far that our approach is successful, because it emerged from successful RE improvements leading to new RE company standards. We were aware, however, that we need to better understand the benefits and limitations we can expect from ArtREPI and whether our approach can be used by others if we are not involved. This motivates the design for our empirical investigations:

1. We rely on *case study research* with action research components in an industrial environment as we are particularly interested in elaborating qualitative insights into benefits and shortcomings in applying an RE improvement approach that also depends on subjective (and social) factors. The design follows the guideline of Runeson and Höst [15].
2. We included *two* cases where the second one was conducted with little direct involvement of the ArtREPI authors. This should allow us to get an indication whether the success of an improvement depends on our influence, and it should provide a first step in scaling up to practice.

4.1   Objectives and Research Questions

The study has the general objective to understand the benefits and limitations of applying ArtREPI in practice. We formulate two research questions to steer the study design structured into the evaluation of the improvement tasks (ArtREPI stage 1-3) and of the resulting RE reference model (ArtREPI stage 4):

RQ 1 How well are process engineers supported in their RE improvement tasks?
RQ 2 How well are project participants supported by the resulting RE reference model?

4.2   Cases and Subjects

We applied ArtREPI as part of two improvement projects in two different contexts. For each project, we give a summary of the most important context information we are able to provide within the limits of existing non-disclosure agreements in Table 1. We chose the contexts because of their suitability to our research questions. We looked at two different settings (large versus small and agile). Furthermore, REPI project 2 has, in contrast to the first case, only little involvement of those researchers developing ArtREPI (see also the next section).

REPI 1: Large scale RE Process. The first improvement project was conducted as part of a research cooperation between Technische Universität München and Wacker Chemie and was described, in parts, as the intermediate evaluation

Table 1. Overview of cases (REPI 1 and REPI 2).

No.	Aspects	Descriptions
1	Improvement goal	Integration of RE into quality management
	REPI context	2 process engineers, 4 domain experts, 4 external improvement consultants
		Effort: 8 PM including 13 workshops
	Pilot projects	3 pilot projects, 8 participants
2	Improvement goal	Re-design of RE to support agility
	REPI context	2 main process engineers (previously coached by improvement consultants)
		Effort: approx. 6 PM
	Pilot projects	3 project participants to rate the reference model w/o pilot projects

in [8].[2] Wacker Chemie is a German company that works in the chemical business and develops custom software for their operation processes and their production sites. The improvement project aimed at defining a detailed artefact-based RE with a seamless integration into quality management.

REPI 2: Agile RE Process. The second improvement project was conducted as part of a Master's Thesis at the company SupplyOn AG which is a software as a service provider. The improvement project aimed at the re-design of the RE of the Rational Unified Process to an artefact-based agile RE approach. In contrast to project 1, where we evaluated the resulting RE reference model explicitly via pilot projects, we relied on informal reviews and expert opinion.

4.3 Data Collection and Analysis Procedures

We answer our research questions by collecting and analysing data from the application of ArtREPI and the assessments via questionnaires in both cases by improvement consultants who also authored ArtREPI. To this end, the improvement consultants coach the process engineers on ArtREPI, its underlying principles, and corresponding tools in a 3 h workshop. These process engineers then apply ArtREPI as described in Sect. 3 and conduct the last phase of ArtREPI (i.e. the evaluation) by applying the resulting RE reference model in pilot projects of the company. In REPI 1, the improvement consultants formed part of the improvement project team after the coaching. In REPI 2, they where not directly involved anymore after the coaching sessions.

We collect the data for both research questions using questionnaires with open and closed questions. Each closed question is formulated as a statement where the participants should state their agreement on a Likert scale defined on an ordinal scale from 0 (*"I strongly disagree"*) to a maximum of 7 (*"I strongly agree"*) to avoid that they choose the middle. They have, however, always the possibility to refuse an answer. The open questions give them the possibility to provide a rationale for their decision. The original questionnaires can also be found in our online material [9].

---

[2] In [8], we reported on first results from the first evaluation steps where the context-specific evaluation (ArtREPI stage 4) was still ongoing.

To answer RQ 1, we conduct an assessment by letting the involved process engineers rate ArtREPI on the basis of a questionnaire where they directly compare ArtREPI to previously followed solution-driven, activity-based improvement approaches. We summarise the questions in Table 2. At the end, we finally asked the process engineers three concluding questions about the overall suitability of the approach to cover the particularities of their context.

Table 2. Condensed RQ 1 instrument: Support of **process engineers** in improvement.

Criteria	Statements (closed question)
Structuredness	The approach was systematic
Simplicity	The approach was easy to use
Goal orientation	The approach considered problems and needs of all involved stakeholders
Experience orientation	The approach considered company culture and stakeholder experiences
Transparency	The decisions during the workshops were reproducible
Effectivity	The improvement has led to the desired results
Efficiency	I perceived the efficiency of the undertaking as high
Knowledge transfer	The approach actively supported knowledge transfer
Overall suitability (1)	ArtREPI was better suited than solution-driven approaches
Overall suitability (2)	I would apply ArtREPI again
Overall suitability (3)	I want to add following positive/negative aspects (open)

To answer RQ 2, we conduct an assessment by letting the involved project participants rate the outcome of ArtREPI using again a questionnaire. This evaluates the resulting RE reference model after application in the pilot projects in direct comparison with the one previously used in same context to evaluate whether the improvement goals have eventually been achieved. Table 3 summarises the questions for this RQ. In the questions, we use "model" as a reference to the RE reference model (upper part in the table) and "artefacts" as a short reference for the artefacts created using the model (lower part in the table).

For the analysis of our results, we rely on descriptive analysis and qualitative interpretation of our data. We intentionally refrain from summarising visual accumulations of the ratings (e.g. via radar charts) because of the heterogeneity in the data as providing answers to each criterion was not obligatory. We therefore report on every rating given by each subject. We additionally indicate to whether the participants experienced an improvement or deterioration of applying ArtREPI in direct comparison to previously used improvement approach which we assume to be present if the mean values differ by at least one point.

5   Case Study Results

In the following, we summarise the results from the rating given in the assessments, structured according to the research questions. For reasons of confidentiality, we cannot provide details about workshop contents, the company-specific RE reference model and the pilot projects, but we will report the rating results.

Table 3. Condensed RQ 2 instrument: Support of **project participants** by RE reference model (resulting from the improvement tasks).

Criteria	Statements (closed question)
Flexibility	The model allows for flexibility in the RE process
Ease of use	The model is easy to understand
Effectivity	The application of the model has led to the desired results
Efficiency	When applying the model, I perceived the efficiency as high
Customisation/Tailoring	The model can be tailored to project-specific situation of the company
Process integration	The model is integrated into further development activities and within the line organisation
Structuredness of artefacts	The artefacts are well structured and can be understood by people not involved in their creation
Syntactic artefact quality	The model supports a high syntactic artefact quality w.r.t. completeness and consistency
Traceability of artefact	The model supports traceability within RE and between RE and further disciplines
Semantic artefact quality	The model supports semantically consistent and complete artefacts
Testability of artefacts	The model supports the creation of testable artefacts

5.1   RQ 1: Support in RE Improvement Tasks

Table 4 summarises the ratings of the ArtREPI approach by the process engineers in direct comparison to previously used approaches which were based on CMMI. For each criterion, we show each subject's ratings. We had 6 subjects in context 1 and 2 subjects in context 2 (see Table 1). Furthermore, we give the mean and median as central tendencies and further show whether ArtREPI is clearly considered better $(+)$ or worse $(-)$. No clear comparison is indicated by a 0. At the bottom of the table, we show the results of the rating of whether ArtREPI was considered better suited for the respective context than previously used REPI approaches.

Overall, ArtREPI was rated as a structured improvement approach that tends to better support knowledge transfer than previously used approaches. Surprising to us, however, is the result of REPI 2 conducted by people not involved at all in the development of ArtREPI. Our assumption was that the rating would be worse than in REPI 1, but it was better regarding the goal orientation, the effectivity and efficiency, and the support for knowledge transfer. Qualitative statements from the open questions provide some explanations. The subjects in REPI 1 rated that the initial preparation phase was performed in a "too academic" fashion with "too many discussions to clarify the terminology", especially by those subjects with no REPI experience made before (S1 and S2). This might also be the reason for the negative comparison regarding the experience orientation. In contrast, REPI 2 was conducted solely by process engineers employed by the respective company and familiar with the culture and the domain.

Finally, the overall rating whether ArtREPI was better suited to achieve the company-specific improvement goals in comparison to previously used approaches were answered positively in both cases. The process engineers stated for both cases that they would apply ArtREPI in follow-up improvement cycles. The answers

Table 4. Results for RQ 1: Rating of improvement procedure by subjects S_x on a scale of 0 (*"I strongly disagree"*) to 7 (*"I strongly agree"*) from a **process engineering perspective**. See also Table 2 for details on the used instrument.

		REPI 1									REPI 2				
		S1	S2	S3	S4	S5	S6	Mean	Median	Comp.	S1	S2	Mean	Median	Comp.
Structuredness	Old	-	-	5	6	5	3	4.75	5	+	6	4	5	5	0
	New	6	5	6	7	7	5	6	6		6	5	5.5	5.5	
Simplicity	Old	-	-	5	5	5	5	5	5	0	6	5	5.5	5.5	0
	New	5	5	6	5	5	3	4.83	5		6	5	5.5	5.5	
Goal Orientation	Old	-	-	4	6	4	4	4.5	4	0	4	4	4	4	+
	New	3	3	5	6	6	4	4.5	4.5		6	6	6	6	
Experience Orientation	Old	-	-	4	-	3	6	4.33	4	–	6	6	6	6	–
	New	2	2	5	-	5	2	3.2	2		4	3	3.5	3.5	
Sustainability	Old	-	-	5	4	4	4	4.25	4	+	4	5	4.5	4.5	0
	New	6	5	6	4	7	4	5.33	5		4	5	4.5	4.5	
Effectivity	Old	-	-	5	5	6	3	4.75	5	0	3	4	3.5	3.5	+
	New	3	3	6	5	6	5	4.66	5		7	6	6.5	6.5	
Efficiency	Old	-	-	5	6	5	4	5	5	–	3	4	3.5	3.5	+
	New	1	2	6	6	5	4	4	4.5		7	5	6	6	
Knowledge Transfer	Old	-	-	4	6	4	4	4.5	4	0	3	4	3.5	3.5	+
	New	5	5	5	6	6	3	5	5		7	6	6.5	6.5	
Overall Suitability	New	-	-	5	-	-	5	5	5		7	6	6.5	6.5	

to the open questions showed for REPI 1, however, that the engineers expect an integration into the organisation as a prerequisite for a repetition. Another suggestion was to check in a follow-up study whether the efficiency of ArtREPI could be improved. Further informal statements included that:

1. the action research workshops, where the new artefact-based RE reference model was crafted by the process engineers, together with the group discussions, fostered discussions the engineers would otherwise not have, e.g. about roles and responsibilities in the RE that just seemed clear to everybody.
2. independent of the results from the pilot projects (described next), they would need additional longitudinal studies before declaring the new RE reference model as a new standard as too many changes have been made.

5.2   RQ 2: Support by resulting RE Reference Model

The success of an improvement eventually depends on whether the resulting RE reference model achieves the improvement goals. RQ 2 therefore focuses on evaluating the REPI outcome in pilot projects. Table 5 shows the rating of the artefact-based RE reference model resulting from the improvement cycle from the perspective of project participants. We distinguish criteria to rate the application of the reference model itself and criteria to evaluate the RE artefacts produced following the reference model. In REPI 1, we applied the model in three pilot projects (two with custom software development and one with standard software). In REPI 2, it was not possible to fully implement the new model immediately, but they included the artefacts created during the coaching sessions. Therefore, their rating is does not reflect the full experience with ArtREPI.

Table 5. Results for RQ 2: Rating of resulting RE reference model by subjects S_x on a scale of 0 (*"I strongly disagree"*) to 7 (*"I strongly agree"*) from a **project perspective**.

			REPI 1										REPI 2			
		S1	S2	S3	S4	S5	S6	S7	S8	Mean	Med.	Comp.	S1 S2 S3	Mean	Med.	Comp.
Process Quality Flexibility	Old	7	7	0	4	2	5	6	6	4.63	5.5	0	5 6 1	4	5	+
	New	4	4	6	6	5	2	6	5	4.75	5		6 6 7	6.33	6	
Ease of Use	Old	5	-	5	4	6	4	4	5	4.71	5	−	5 2 5	4	5	+
	New	3	-	5	3	5	2	4	4	3.71	4		5 5 5	5	5	
Effectivity	Old	4	-	5	6	-	5	5	5	5	5	0	5 - 1	3	3	+
	New	6	-	5	6	-	2	6	6	5.16	6		6 - 7	6.5	6.5	
Efficiency	Old	3	-	4	5	-	6	6	5	4.83	5	−	6 - 0	3	3	+
	New	1	-	5	6	-	2	6	3	3.83	4		5 - 7	6	6	
Customisation	Old	7	-	1	3	1	6	6	4	4	4	0	5 7 4	5.33	5	+
	New	6	-	6	6	4	1	6	5	4.86	6		6 7 7	6.67	7	
Process Integration	Old	3	-	2	3	3	6	5	3	3.75	3	+	5 3 5	4.33	5	+
	New	6	-	4	4	6	6	5	5	5.14	5		5 6 5	5.33	5	
Artefact Quality Structuredness	Old	2	5	3	5	3	2	5	2	3.38	3	0	3 4 2	3	3	+
	New	4	7	3	6	4	2	5	4	4.25	4		3 6 6	5	6	
Syntactic Quality	Old	0	5	4	4	0	2	6	3	3	3.5	+	- 2 2	2	2	+
	New	7	7	5	5	2	5	6	6	5.38	5.5		- 7 6	6.5	6.5	
Traceability	Old	4	4	1	3	2	2	6	3	3.13	3	+	1 3 0	1.33	2	+
	New	7	6	6	7	4	5	6	4	5.63	6		6 6 6	6	6	
Semantic Quality	Old	4	4	2	3	-	3	7	3	3.71	3	+	4 3 5	4	4	+
	New	6	6	5	4	-	5	7	6	5.57	6		6 6 5	5.67	6	
Testability	Old	1	2	3	4	5	2	6	3	3.25	3	+	5 3 3	3.67	3	+
	New	5	4	5	6	7	5	6	5	5.38	5		6 7 6	6.33	6	

The results indicate that ArtREPI supported the participants in achieving their improvement goals (see Sect. 4.2). For REPI 1, we could improve, e.g., the traceability, the testability, and the process integration of the RE reference model, thus, supporting the better integration into quality management which formed the improvement goal. The negative results in the comparison to the previously used RE reference model regarding the process quality might be explained from the complexity of the new (richer) model and the learning curve associated with all new methods in general. In contrast, the positive rating in REPI 2 might be explained by the new RE reference model to support agility due to its new (light weight) simplicity.

Overall, we observe that ArtREPI can show its strength especially in the artefact quality as expected, because it is oriented towards artefacts. In the process quality, the picture is, however, more mixed. Qualitative feedback to the open questions provides explanations:

- The success of a pilot study strongly depends, beyond political factors, on the quality of the prototypical implementation. Hence, project participants should be involved in the technical validation, too.
- Coaching sessions before the pilot studies should not only focus on the new RE reference models, but on the underlying principles, e.g. new levels of abstraction in the requirements or new roles and responsibilities.
- Although artefact-based RE reference models are inherently process agnostic, they should include suggestions for methods and modelling techniques (e.g. UML-based ones) project participants are familiar with. This should increase the organisational willingness to change.

5.3 Threats to Validity

There exist many threats to validity inherent to case study research [15]. Threats to the *internal validity* mainly arise from potential bias during the data collection, let alone because of our action research components, and because of the general subjective nature in the ratings. We applied selected techniques to reduce those threats, e.g. researcher and method triangulation, but to a certain extent we were particularly interested in gathering subjective opinions by the interviewees. Another mitigation strategy followed in advance was to apply ArtREPI in the second case with little influence of the approach authors. It provides a first indication towards scaling up to practice [16], thus, it provides a first step in strengthening the *external validity*. This generalisation, however, needs further attention in future work.

Finally, a more general problem is that many things remain (objectively) unmeasurable. As a matter of fact, we still have a limited understanding on how to reliably measure long-term improvement effects going beyond RE, because of the complexity of confounding variables in a software project ecosystem. In our studies, we therefore refrained from such measurements in advance. Measurements are still important to determine the success of an improvement given that (1) RE forms part of a larger context that needs to be taken into account, while (2) we consider problem orientation where we cannot rely on an external reference to determine a notion of software process quality (in the sense of an oracle).

Another facet important to an improvement is finally the question how much the notion of process quality is determinable by the quality of the artefacts and also how much project participants eventually rely on the created artefacts. We can observe first empirical investigations in that direction (e.g. [17]). Still, even if we can measure certain phenomena on basis of the artefacts, we still do not fully understand to which extend the notion of RE quality eventually manifests itself in the created artefacts. That is, the investigations are based on the critical assumption that the success of a project and, in particular, of an artefact-based improvement depends on the documented results on which project participants rely. To elaborate the extent to which the application of ArtREPI eventually leads to an improvement, and how to measure the success of an improvement (including subjective and cognitive facets), we first need a better understanding on the measurability of such an improvement. In [18], we provide a richer discussion on the limitations of measurements in RE.

6 Discussion

Our results indicate that ArtREPI is well suited to cover the needs of a structured improvement where problem and artefact orientation are important, while supporting knowledge transfer by continuous stakeholder involvement. The direct comparison of the two cases further indicates that the effectivity, efficiency, the knowledge transfer, and even the goal orientation are strengthened when the improvement is conducted by company members with no intervention from outside. The results from pilot projects further suggest that the improvement eventually achieved the local improvement goals. Our overall results therefore strengthen our confidence in the benefits of ArtREPI as a self-contained and holistic approach to a problem-driven RE improvement as long as the improvement goals are in tune with the (known) benefits of artefact orientation.

6.1 Limitations of ArtREPI

One benefit in case study research is that it gives us the possibility to get qualitative feedback, i.e. explanations for the particular ratings. We are particularly interested in revealing limitations of ArtREPI as this supports us steering the development and the evaluation of the discussed improvement principles, and it helps us fostering the discussions on RE improvement in general.

Limitations we could reveal by our second case concern more social aspects of a process improvement. For example, we, as researchers involved in the development of ArtREPI, seemed to lower the efficiency and effectivity of an improvement due to long preparation phases to increase our understanding of the domain and the terminology used. Our initial assumption that the success of ArtREPI depends on that we ourselves should conduct the improvement thus is wrong. However, the exact consequences of applying ArtREPI without any involvement of the authors at all (e.g. without coaching) remain still unknown.

Also, there exists a plethora of organisational factors, such as the support by the management, the support at project level (a champion), and general social as well as empirical skills that constitute success factor for an improvement. It might be possible to include some factors in the approach. For instance, one suggestion was to involve project participants earlier during technical validation stages to mitigate the threats arising from a missing organisational willingness to change. Other factors, however, might not be covered at all, because models abstracts, by nature, from desires, beliefs, experiences, and expectations, which all are important. To fully reveal those factors, and to fully explore to which extent they can eventually be influenced on a methodological layer, we need more (especially longitudinal) investigations in that direction.

6.2 Success Factors for ArtREPI

Besides the general focus of problem orientation, which is to emphasis context-specific goals over the possibility for an external certification of an RE, we found several factors that influence the success of an RE improvement:

- Improvement goals need to be in tune with the expected benefits of the chosen paradigms (in our case artefact orientation) known in advance.[3]
- Support by higher management, especially when communicating new roles and responsibilities.

---

[3] This implies that we need sufficient evidence on potential benefits of artefact orientation to the chosen context beforehand to justify the decision to conduct an organisational change.

- Backup by project environments, e.g. via the early involvement of project participants in the validation stages of a new RE reference model (before initiating the evaluation stages).
- Domain knowledge.
- Reflection of the organisational culture.
- Social and empirical skills.

Those factors might not be surprising in themselves but together in their extent. The success of a problem-driven improvement is determined by the reflection of the organisational culture of a company in every facet of the improvement approach. That is, all relevant stakeholders need to be involved in early stages to cover their needs, a backup by representative projects needs to be ensured (in the sense of champions), and project participants need to identify themselves with the resulting reference model. All those facets aim at supporting the willingness for a change in the way of working to reshape an existing organisation [19].

In our current understanding, this can only be achieved by applying exhaustive, qualitative empirical method that foster continuous stakeholder involvement but which also come themselves with limitations, e.g. regarding the measurability of improvement effects (see also our Sect. 5.3).

7   Conclusion

In this paper, we reported on our first steps to empirically evaluate the principles of an artefact-based and problem-driven RE improvement (ArtREPI). Our investigation should give a first qualitative impression of the general benefits and shortcomings in direct comparison to existing principles of solution-driven RE improvements that currently dominate the publication landscape [7]. The purpose was also to lay the foundation for independent empirical investigations to eventually explore the full spectrum of RE improvement.

To this end, we reported on two industrial case studies and analysed (1) how ArtREPI would support process engineers in achieving a problem-driven and artefact-based RE improvement, and (2) how well project participants were supported in their project environments by the resulting artefact-based RE reference model. We further conducted the second case with very little influence of the approach authors to investigate, in a first step, to what extent the results might be influenced by us researchers being involved in the RE improvement.

Our results strengthen our confidence that ArtREPI is suitable for a self-contained, problem-driven RE improvement where the improvement goals are in tune with the scope of artefact orientation. More important, we could also reveal first limitations and factors important to future work in RE improvement research. We need to further explore the measurability of an improvement and its long-term effects, and to further support scaling up to practice. To support the generalisation of our observations that, so far, are only valid for chosen local improvement contexts [16], we need to (1) foster independent replications of our case studies which we support by our contribution and our publicly accessible online material [9], and (2) we need to take new perspectives.

Rather than further investigating the technicalities of applying ArtREPI ourselves, we need to concentrate on exploring further social and cognitive facets and the long-term effects of an RE improvement for which our contribution has provided one foundation and sensitisation. We thereby encourage researchers and practitioners to join us in this endeavour to fully understand the broad spectrum of possibilities and limitations in an artefact-based and problem-driven RE improvement.

Acknowledgements. We want to thank R. Wieringa and M. Broy for the collaboration during the development of ArtREPI. We further want to thank R. Bossek and M. Kuhrmann for their support during the systematisation of ArtREPI, and S. Wiesi, J. Mund, J. Eckhardt, and H. Femmer for their support in the REPI projects. Finally, we are grateful to all subjects involved during the case studies and to B. Penzenstadler, M. Daneva, and A. Vetrò for their valuable feedback on previous versions of this manuscript.

References

1. Méndez Fernández, D., Wagner, S.: Naming the pain in requirments enginering: a design for a global family of surveys and first results from Germany. Inf. Softw. Technol. **57**, 616–643 (2014). doi:10.1016/j.infsof.2014.05.008
2. Pettersson, F., Ivarsson, M., Gorschek, T., Öhman, P.: A practitioner's guide to light weight software process assessment and improvement planning. JSS **81**, 972–995 (2008)
3. Napier, N., Mathiassen, L., Johnson, R.: Combining perceptions and prescriptions in requirements engineering process assessment: an industrial case study. TSE **35**, 593–606 (2009)
4. Beecham, S., Hall, T., Rainer, A.: Defining a requirements process improvement model. Softw. Qual. Control **13**(3), 247–279 (2005)
5. Staples, M., Niazi, M., Jeffery, R., Abrahams, A., Byatt, P., Murphy, R.: An exploratory study of why organizations do not adopt CMMI. JSS **80**, 883–895 (2007)
6. Méndez Fernández, D., Penzenstadler, B., Kuhrmann, M., Broy, M.: A meta model for artefact-orientation: fundamentals and lessons learned in requirements engineering. In: Petriu, D.C., Rouquette, N., Haugen, Ø. (eds.) MODELS 2010, Part II. LNCS, vol. 6395, pp. 183–197. Springer, Heidelberg (2010)
7. Méndez Fernández, D., Ognawala, S., Wagner, S., Daneva, M.: Where do we stand in requirements engineering improvement today? First results from a mapping study. In: ESEM (2014)
8. Méndez Fernández, D., Wieringa, R.: Improving requirements engineering by artefact orientation. In: Heidrich, J., Oivo, M., Jedlitschka, A., Baldassarre, M.T. (eds.) PROFES 2013. LNCS, vol. 7983, pp. 108–122. Springer, Heidelberg (2013)
9. Méndez Fernández, D.: ArtREPI online resources. https://goo.gl/8UfUee. doi:10.13140/RG.2.1.2165.5521
10. Beecham, S., Hall, T., Rainer, A.: Software process improvement problems in twelve software companies: an empirical analysis. EMSE **8**, 7–42 (2003)
11. Beecham, S., Hall, T., Britton, C., Cottee, M., Austen, R.: Using an expert panel to validate a requirements process improvement model. JSS **76**, 251–275 (2005)

12. Kuhrmann, M., Beecham, S.: Artifact-based software process improvement and management: a method proposal. In: ICSSP (2014)
13. Méndez Fernández, D.: Artefact-based requirements engineering improvement: learning to walk in practice. In: Jedlitschka, A., Kuvaja, P., Kuhrmann, M., Männistö, T., Münch, J., Raatikainen, M. (eds.) PROFES 2014. LNCS, vol. 8892, pp. 302–305. Springer, Heidelberg (2014)
14. Méndez Fernández, D., Penzenstadler, B.: Artefact-based requirements engineering: the AMDiRE approach. RE J. **20**, 405–434 (2014)
15. Runeson, P., Höst, M.: Guidelines for conducting and reporting case study research in software engineering. EMSE **14**, 131–164 (2009)
16. Wieringa, R.: Empirical research methods for technology validation: scaling up to practice. Softw. Syst. **95**, 19–31 (2014). doi:10.1016/j.jss.2013.11.1097
17. Liskin, O.: How artifacts support and impede requirements communication. In: Fricker, S.A., Schneider, K. (eds.) REFSQ 2015. LNCS, vol. 9013, pp. 132–147. Springer, Heidelberg (2015)
18. Méndez Fernández, D., Mund, J., Femmer, H., Vetrò, A.: In quest for requirements engineering oracles: dependent variables and measurements for (good) RE. In: EASE (2014)
19. Pfleeger, S.: Understanding and improving technology transfer in software engineering. JSS **47**(2–3), 111–124 (1999)

Practices of Modern Development Processes

Artefacts in Agile Software Development

Gerard Wagenaar[1](✉), Remko Helms[2], Daniela Damian[3], and Sjaak Brinkkemper[2]

[1] Avans University of Applied Science, Breda, The Netherlands
g.wagenaar@avans.nl
[2] Utrecht University, Utrecht, The Netherlands
{r.w.helms,s.brinkkemper}@uu.nl
[3] University of Victoria, Victoria, Canada
danielad@cs.uvic.ca

Abstract. Agile software development methods prefer limited use of artefacts. On the basis of existing artefact models and results from three case studies we present a Scrum artefact model. In this model we notice teams using Scrum artefacts, but they, in addition, decided to produce various non-Scrum artefacts, most notably design documents, test plans and user or release related materials.

Keywords: Agile software development · Artefacts · Case studies · Scrum

1 Introduction

The application of an agile software development method, for instance XP or Scrum, is common nowadays in delivering state-of-the-art software [6, 23]. All agile methods have in common a profound focus on communication, as articulated in one of the principles in the agile manifesto: *"The most efficient and effective method of conveying information to and within a development team is face-to-face conversation"* [4]. This emphasis on communication in software development does not come as a surprise. A field study on software design process for large systems [8] already indicated that developing large software systems must be treated, at least in part, as a learning, communication, and negotiation process.

Opposite, or complementary, to face-to-face communication is documentation through the use of artefacts. Most agile methods do not have artefacts as method of choice in communicating. Explicitly documenting (design) issues which are of little or no value to customers is not encouraged in agile thinking, but it is certainly not prohibited to produce and use artefacts. Citing another agile principle, *"The best architectures, requirements, and designs emerge from self-organizing teams"* [4], the use of artefacts is situational and a choice made by an agile team, dependent on the value it attaches to them. One agile method, DSDM [31], even defines deliverables which bear a great similarity to artefacts.

But the use of artefacts certainly has to be considered in agile methods, if only because face-to-face communication is simply not always feasible. In global software development direct face-to-face conversation is not possible and other mechanisms to support communication have to be applied [14]. And in co-located agile software

P. Abrahamsson et al. (Eds.): PROFES 2015, LNCS 9459, pp. 133–148, 2015.
DOI: 10.1007/978-3-319-26844-6_10

development projects the production of artefacts contributes to coordination mechanisms, such as synchronization and boundary spanning [33]. Knowing of such circumstances, agile artefacts have to be considered.

In our research we investigated the existence of artefacts as well as their use in three agile software development teams. We have focussed on Scrum teams, which is in fact not a major restriction, because Scrum certainly is an agile software development method [1, 2, 12]. Based on evidence from practice we will show for three Scrum teams their artefacts and we will provide a typology for their use. With this research we will on the one the hand provide another building block in the theory of artefacts within agile software development and on the other hand provide practitioners with a reference to mirror their own way of working relative to the context of use in the companies we studied.

The remainder of this paper is organised as follows. In the next section we will outline the theoretical background motivating our work. Then we will present our research method. The results will be presented for three case studies, followed by a discussion. A final section presents our main conclusions.

2   Theoretical Background

In this section we will first discuss artefacts and their use as a communication mean in (agile) software development. We will then describe existing artefact models to develop a preliminary Scrum artefact model thereafter.

2.1   Artefacts in Agile Software Development

A general description of an artefact is an object made by humans. In software development many definitions have been used, for example: "*A software artefact is understood to be a deliverable or an outcome of a software process*" [11], "*An artefact is a deliverable that is produced, modified, or used by a sequence of tasks that have value to a role*" [19]. For our purpose we define:

An artefact is a tangible deliverable produced during software development.

Tangible here means being easily seen or recognized rather than being restricted to only being touched or felt, thus including materials in both physical and electronic format.

Artefacts function as a mean of communication in software development [8], but most agile methods do not have artefacts as method of choice in communicating. Their importance is recognized nevertheless and the agile approach to artefacts may be compared with "*travelling light*": "*Create just enough models and documentation to get by*" [3, p. 29]. To emphasize their significance it has been shown that agile software development practitioners indeed perceive their internal documentation as important, whilst at the same time acknowledging that too little of it was available [32]. This result was partially confirmed in a case study on the impact of agile principles and practices on large-scale software development projects [17].

In a case study on knowledge management usage in agile software projects [35] it was seen that even outdated and inadequate documentation was used, because it provided a context for knowledge sought for. And it was used even instead of face-to-face communication: *"Despite the documentation be reduced and outdated the team uses [it] as a source of knowledge to ... reduce the direct communication"* [35, p. 634].

We conclude that 'working agile' and 'using artefacts' are no contradictory terms.

2.2   Artefact Models

As starting point for a Scrum artefact model we take the Scrum process framework, which distinguishes artefacts, people and events [26, 27]. Core Scrum artefacts are the Product Backlog, the Sprint Backlog and the Potentially Shippable Product Increment (or Increment for short). The Product Backlog lists all features, functions, requirements, enhancements, and fixes that constitute the future software product. The Sprint Backlog contains a subset of Product Backlog items selected for one Sprint. The Increment is the sum of all the Product Backlog items completed during a Sprint. Sometimes supplementary artefacts are associated with Scrum, although they are not labelled as such in Scrum's process framework. These are the 'Definition of Done' (DoD) which is a set of acceptance criteria, and the 'Burn down chart' which is a visualization of progress.

Existing research on artefact models had its foundation in modelling artefacts from a theoretical point of view to confront the model with some experiences from practice thereafter. As a first example, a theoretical Scrum Process-Deliverable Diagram[1] [5] served as foundation for a Scrum artefact class diagram (SACD) [9]. Using experiences from one project, the main components of the SACD became a Product Backlog, a Sprint Plan and a Build/Release (including a Build History). These are easily recognizable as the core Scrum artefacts model. In addition the model includes:

- Project management information, including a project initiation document (budget, resources) and a risk list.
- Architectural information, consisting of domain model and system architecture.
- Release-related materials, such as installation and maintenance guide, training materials.

As a second example a systematic literature study investigated the use of artefacts in agile methods and resulted in the development of an agile artefact class diagram (AACD) with 19 artefacts and relations between them [13]. This diagram was subsequently extended to a more generic model to abstract it from local, project-specific processes (Fig. 1) and process interfaces were added to support the model's use in distributed project settings, where a process interface is a mean to exchange data between software processes [16]. On the basis of experiences from practice the diagram was further refined [10].

---

[1] A Process-Deliverable Diagram describes both processes and deliverables in one diagram [34]; the interpretation of deliverable in a PDD is analogous to our artefact.

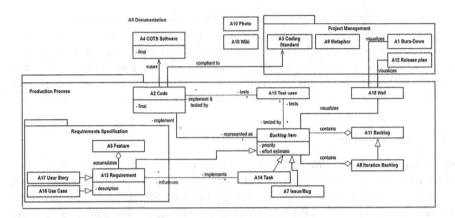

Fig. 1. Agile artefact class diagram (adapted from [16])

Although the diagram was not confronted with descriptions of agile methods themselves nor explicitly based on experimental data (with exception of later refinements), the AACD provides an overview of agile artefacts.

Both SACD and AACD contain agile and/or Scrum artefacts. But they also contain other artefacts, which are similar to an approach to software development which advocated program design first and documenting it thoroughly, using such artefacts as a design and a test document [24].

2.3 Use of Artefacts

The AACD also launches a typology with its clustering of artefacts to packages, such as 'Production process' or 'Project management' (Fig. 1). A well-known distinction separates process from product artefacts [30]. The former are used in the process of development (for instance project plans, risk assessments, schedules); the package 'Project management' in the AACD is an example. The latter supports the product that is being developed (for instance a requirements document or a user guide). We will make use of these categories to characterize agile artefacts.

But product and process artefacts do not suffice. In a later version of the AACD tools are introduced [16]. Other research also indicated the use of tools by agile teams, for instance story cards and the Wall [28, 29]. In fact, using Scrum leads to an absolute need for tools [15]. This need, found in the context of global software development, includes tools for communication and collaboration in general, but also, more specifically, to support project management, backlog management and visualization. Examples of such tools are wikis, electronic workspaces, whiteboards, et cetera.

Neither the physical artefacts (story cards, Wall) nor the tools adhere to our definition of artefact. This is a major reason to introduce a third category: Supporting tools. These are not tangible deliverables produced during software development, but they do support their production. In this line of thought a whiteboard (the wall) is a support tool, supporting an artefact like the Sprint Backlog. We do however, in the context of our current research, only include tools specifically aimed at supporting Scrum product or process artefacts, thus excluding some more general tools as, for instance, e-mail or a text processor. The SACD does not explicitly address supporting tools as a category, whereas the AACD does.

2.4 Towards a Scrum Artefact Model

When reflecting upon the core Scrum artefacts and the two class diagrams there is similarity up to a certain level. All address the core Scrum artefacts, although not always by the same name. But both diagrams reveal other, additional, artefacts. Combining them the contours of a Scrum artefact model arises (Fig. 2).

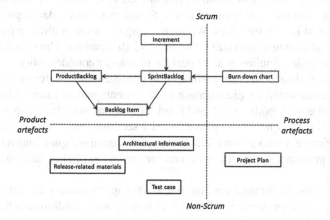

Fig. 2. Preliminary Scrum artefact model

In the upper half of Fig. 2 our preliminary model contains the core Scrum artefacts, supplemented with a Burn down chart. The situation for the non-Scrum artefacts is less clear. The two existing models differ from each other and for the moment we include in our preliminary model their non-Scrum artefacts, but they are by no means meant to be complete; they serve as example for future refinements, based on empirical evidence. In the composition of our preliminary model we mapped, and summarized, elements from the diagrams. For instance, project plan represents both the 'Project management' package from the AACD as well as the project management information from the SACD. Relations for the non-Scrum artefacts (lower half of Fig. 2) are deliberately left out, because there, again, is a need for validation.

3   Case Study Design

We are interested in artefacts in agile software development. Limiting ourselves to Scrum as the agile development method of choice, our goal is to collect evidence to revise and/or expand the elements of the preliminary model (Fig. 2). Our research method should be exploratory to allow for rich evidence from which elements and relationships in the model can be reasoned about. We selected an exploratory comparative case study approach as our method with as unit of analysis one iteration of Scrum software development in a co-located team. This approach is an accustomed way to investigate phenomena in a context where events cannot be controlled and where the focus is on contemporary events [37]. For the case study we operationalized our goal into the following research questions:

RQ1   Which artefacts do Scrum teams produce and how are they related to each other?
RQ2   How can those artefacts be characterized to designate their use in Scrum team practices?

A case study protocol was drawn up to guide the case study [18]. According to the protocol organizations were required to use Scrum as software development method with a team of at least 5 members. We found 3 organizations willing to participate in our research, all having a team size between 5 and 10 members. The organizations will be named Controller, Sunflower and Local for reasons of confidentiality.

The primary data collection method was semi-structured interviewing of team members, accompanied by examination of documents and/or information systems. A questionnaire with both level 1 and level 2 questions was drawn up to guide the interviews [37]. The questionnaire contained 2 sections, apart from some questions on the interviewee's background. The first section contained questions related to the use of agile practices within the team and the second explicitly addressed (the use of) artefacts.

Representatives of the team were interviewed for approximately 1 h each. Interviews comprised in total approximately 12 h with 13 interviewees. Additionally 6 more interviews were held either before the main series of interviews started to provide some general context, or afterwards, to clarify some remaining issues. Examples of artefacts, when available, were studied; they included, among others, contents of information systems and (design and test) artefacts.

Thirteen interviews were transcribed and coded. We used a combination of open and axial coding [21] on the basis of our preliminary Scrum artefact model, complemented with additional artefacts when necessary.

For each organization the results of the interviews and additional material were bundled in a case study report.

3.1   Validity

In terms of validity of our research method 4 criteria are widely used: construct validity, internal validity, external validity and reliability [37].

Construct validity identifies correct operational measures for the concepts being studied. To enhance construct validity (1) key informants should review draft case study reports, (2) multiple sources of evidence should be used, and (3) a chain of evidence should be established [37]. We applied all three: (1) each interviewee was provided with a summary for his or her approval and key informants commented on a draft case study report, (2) various team members were involved to complement viewpoints, and (3) there is a direct link from interviews (and other material) to conclusions by the use of the qualitative data analysis tool Nvivo[2].

Internal validity is mainly a concern for explanatory case studies [24, 37]. Our case studies are exploratory, but we did apply pattern matching, one of the analytical techniques to enhance internal validity, by consistently coding material on the basis of our preliminary Scrum artefact model.

External validity defines the domain to which a case study's findings can be generalized. The use of replication logic is listed as the main tactic to guarantee this validity [37]. Using a multiple-case study with a replication design on the basis of a questionnaire contributes to external validity, and thus to generalizability of results.

Reliability should demonstrate that the study can be repeated. The use of a case study protocol and the development of a case study database [37] were both applied in our study to increase reliability.

4 Results

The results from the case study will be described next. We will first give an impression of (the structure of) each organization. We will then list the results pertaining to RQ1, divided into core Scrum artefacts and non-Scrum artefacts. At the same time, to answer RQ2, we will, for each artefact, indicate its usage as product or process artefact and/or, if applicable, the use of a supporting tool.

4.1 Organizations

We start with a summary describing some key characteristics of the organizations/teams (Table 1). Most numbers are indicative; the size of the Scrum team is not.

Table 1. Key characteristics case study organizations/Scrum teams

Organiza-tion	Domain	Size		Scrum experience	Installed base	Number of users
		Company	Scrum team			
Controller	Manage-ment of objects	120	5	2 years	1500	n/a[a]
Sunflower	Floral industry	15	6	2½ year	125	750
Local	Govern-ment taxing	5.000	10	1½ year	50	1000

[a]Controller has no direct insight in the number of users.

---

[2] NVivo is a software package to aid qualitative data analysis designed by QSR (http://www.qsrinternational.com).

The organizations all deliver product software [35], where Controller and Local fabricate several software packages and Sunflower only one. The size of an organization relates to an organization as a whole. All other numbers refer to one software product, and its associated Scrum team. The installed base refers to the number of software packages in use with different customers (companies). Since one installation of a package may have any number of users, this number is significantly higher than the installed base.

Organization Controller is a company, providing the branch of management of (technical) objects, such as fleet management, with a software solution. Software development within Controller takes place in the Development department with circa 35 employees, half of them operating in 2 to 3 Scrum-teams with 5–6 members each. The other employees perform supporting tasks, from providing architectural building blocks of source code to database management. The composition of the team under study is: 1 Product Owner, 2 developers and 2 testers, one of whom functions as Scrum Master. A Sprint within Controller takes 2 weeks, occasionally 3 weeks.

Organization Sunflower is a small Dutch company with around 15 employees. It provides floral industry (trading of flowers, plants and bulbs) with its Enterprise Resource Planning product. The product is developed and maintained by a Scrum team of six employees: 3 developers and 3 consultants. One additional, junior, developer assists the team in the background. A Sprint within Sunflower takes one month.

Organization Local is a business unit of a larger organization and develops product software for the public sector, particularly local government. It has a range of products, among which is a taxing application. This product is developed by a Scrum-team of 10 persons: a Product Owner, a Scrum Master, 2 designers, 4 developers and 2 testers. A Sprint within Local takes 2 weeks, occasionally 3.

4.2   Scrum Artefacts

All teams use all core Scrum artefacts. **Product Backlog**, **Sprint Backlog** and **Backlog Items** are all registered with a supporting tool, whether commercially available (Scrumworks[3], in use with Controller) or developed within the organization itself. All tools are also used to register progress information, from project planning to actual status.

Furthermore all teams use a **Burn down chart** and the **Increment** as result of a Sprint. All source code is admitted to be sparsely commented, but Controller (GIT[4]) and Local (PVCS[5]) track information on versions and associated changes.

Sunflower and Local support the Sprint Backlog and its items with a whiteboard.

4.3   Non-Scrum Artefacts

There is one artefact all teams use in a similar way. This is progress information which is for the greater part available through their tools. Although minor details differ from one team to another we will use the term 'Project plan' for all of them, although it is not

---

[3] A description can be found at: www.collab.net.
[4] A description can be found at: www.git-scm.com.
[5] A description can be found at: www.serena.com.

always mentioned as such. We will now continue with a list of non-Scrum artefacts for each team.

Controller Controller uses (exhaustive list):

- *Test scripts* which are drawn up by the testers of the Development Team in a so-called GWT-structure: Given defines the initial situation, When defines actions, Then predicts the final situation. Test scripts are typically product artefacts and are related to backlog items as well as to the source code.
- An *implementation document,* which primary aim is to support consultants in the installation of software at a customer's site. Its contents include a description of the standard functions of a module, extended with instructions for the adjustment of parameters, user roles, et cetera. The implementation guide is a product artefact, accompanying the release.
- A *user guide* containing a description of the software to support customers in their use of the software. The user guide is also a product artefact; it relates to both sprint backlog and release.

Sunflower In addition to the core Scrum artefacts Sunflower produces a *Help file* accompanying the software; this file serves as a user guide. The *Fix-list* provides an overview of features in a release and is sent to customers at the date of a new release; it relates to both sprint backlog and release. Both are product artefacts.

Local In addition to the standard Scrum artefacts Local also uses (exhaustive list):

- A *functional design* with major chapters on: Assignment/Scope, Constraints, Current and future situation, Adjustments data model, Adjustments set-up and Functional Description; this is typically a product artefact. The design relates to backlog items on the one side and to source code on the other side.
- A *test plan* containing: Background information, Logical test cases, Physical test cases (description of test configuration and test scenarios) and Expected results & (screen prints showing) Actual result; this is again typically a product artefact, although it has an small and implicit aspect of a process artefact in the sense that from the availability of actual test results (or not), progress may be derived.
- A *user guide* accompanying the software; it is a product artefact.
- *Release notes* accompany every release, highlighting its new features. They are a product artefact.

5   Discussion

In the previous section we have presented all artefacts in use with the 3 case study organizations. We will now turn to a discussion of the results. In first instance we will integrate the results of individual organizations to constitute our extended Scrum artefact model. We will then specifically discuss the use of non-Scrum artefacts and explicitly relate them to previous models. We end our discussion with a paragraph on the use of supporting tools.

5.1   Artefact Model

We first summarize the artefacts found in the case studies (Table 2).

Table 2.   Summary team's artefacts

Artefacts	Artefacts		
	Controller	Sunflower	Local
Project plan	*Project plan*	*Project plan*	*Project plan*
Product Backlog	*Product Backlog*	*Product Backlog*	*Product Backlog*
Sprint Backlog	*Sprint Backlog*	*Sprint Backlog*	*Sprint Backlog*
Backlog item	*Backlog item*	*Backlog item*	*Backlog item*
Design	–	–	*Functional design*
Test	*Test script*	–	*Test plan*
Increment	*Source code*	*Source code*	*Source code*
	Release	*Release*	*Release*
Release notes	–	*Fix list*	*Release notes*
Implementation guide	*Implementation document*	–	*Implementation guide*
User guide	*User guide*	*Help file*	*User guide*
Burn down chart	*Burn down chart*	*Burn down chart*	*Burn down chart*

In the leftmost column of Table 2 we find ***Scrum artefacts*** as well as *non-Scrum artefacts*. The definition of 'Increment' in the Scrum process framework is somewhat ambiguous, i.e. it is not definite on whether the increment consists of either source or compiled code. For this reason, and because of the results from the case studies, we separated Increment into source code and release (compiled code). To incorporate non-Scrum artefacts in this column we introduced generic descriptions derived from a general software development life cycle. The leftmost column in this way also introduces a vocabulary for the artefacts encountered in the case study organizations, since their naming differs (slightly) from one organization to another.

The table, as a synthesis of results of the study, now contains building blocks to redraw the preliminary model as an extended Scrum artefact model (Fig. 3).

In comparison with our preliminary model (Fig. 2) we note that all Scrum artefacts were already included. For the non-Scrum artefacts Project plan and Test were already identified, Design was not and Release-related material has been refined.

Both our preliminary and our extended artefact model are rather reticent in its number of artefacts in comparison with the other diagrams. This is an explicit choice. We choose to nominate artefacts independent of their representation. Where, for instance, in the

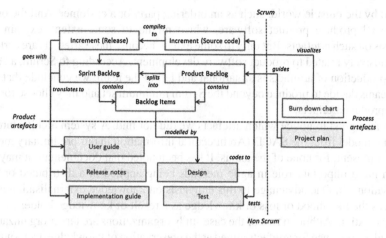

Fig. 3. Extended Scrum artefact model

AACD Backlog Item is a generalization of (all of) Requirement, Task and Issue/Bug, we restricted ourselves to Backlog Item.

5.2 Non-Scrum Artefacts: Design, Test and Release-Related Material

The extended Scrum model contains artefacts from both the Scrum artefact and the agile artefact class diagram. Both individual class diagrams do not cover the extended Scrum artefact model, but the class diagrams together make a fair prediction of most artefacts. However, they fail to include a 'design' artefact. The importance of functional documents for computer systems has been established for a long time: Inadequate documentation causes software quality to degrade over time [22]. And design is an artefact clearly identified in our research. The SACD in general lacks 'intermediate' results of software development, although it could be argued that the system architecture and the domain model represent (parts of) a design. But both system architecture and domain model cover a Sprint Backlog as a whole, perhaps even the Product Backlog. The design we found relates to one requirement, which makes it a new element in agile artefact models. Local explicitly decided to include designers in its Scrum team to draw up a design as an artefact. Local did so because a gap was experienced between the description of some Backlog items and their elaboration in source code by a developer. In addition, Scrum team members from Controller and Sunflower do not make a formal design, but they use whiteboard, computer or pencil and paper to make informal drawings or Visio-diagrams.

More generally we observe that the teams, while using Scrum and its artefacts, do not feel themselves limited in their production of additional, non-Scrum, artefacts. We already mentioned Local's design artefact. Both Controller and Local introduced testers in the team to write and execute test scripts/plans to assure software quality.

Furthermore, the Scrum teams produce 'final' results, other than an increment (release). We found quite some artefacts being in just this category: Implementation guide, user guide, release notes. One could argue that such artefacts are obligatory, dictated by the outside world, such as an ordering party or a customer. And the organizations all produce product software, which might, to some extent, explain their emphasis on such artefacts. But only to some extent, because these artefacts are certainly not exclusively related to product software development. According to Scrum, a choice on the production of artefacts is situational and left to the team; we conclude that most of the teams decide to produce beyond the Scrum minimum set and they choose for non-Scrum product artefacts.

It is also good to notice which artefacts we did not find. A system architecture and a domain model from the SACD (Architectural information in our preliminary model), were not present, for none of the teams. It has been noted that documentation may play a much more important role in agile methods being applied in a distributed or large organisation [7]. One advantage to this emphasis on knowledge externalisation is that it reduces the likelihood of loss of knowledge as a result of knowledge holders leaving the organization. Although two of the case study organizations are larger organizations, we found no evidence for artefacts aimed at the preservation of knowledge over a number of Sprints. Design and test artefacts play their role only in the current Sprint and may be considered as to apply to one item of the Sprint Backlog only. An overall architecture for the Product Backlog or even some design to bundle requirements in a Sprint was not encountered. This is in line with previous findings where it was found that internal documentation was perceived as lagging behind [17, 32]. Thus when interviewees were asked how teams would acquaint a new employee with the team's previous efforts and results, all answered: *"Training on the job"*, to admit thereafter that this was not a wise practice. Two teams provided some guidance as how to solve this problem. A user guide is not meant for internal use, but when an organization provides courses for (prospective) users, these courses are very often structured using this guide. And the teams admitted to send their new employees to just this course to give them an impression of the software they will be working on. Via a detour external documentation thus becomes internal documentation. But it is still somewhat disturbing that none of the software products is backed up by a sound explicit architecture, the more because the products have quite an extensive installed base and/or number of users. There seems to be a great trust in tacit rather than explicit knowledge [20].

5.3 Supporting Tools

All teams use electronic workspaces to support Product and Sprint Backlog with their individual items as well as the accompanying project plan. Version control was explicitly used by two of the teams (Controller and Local); the other team used some scripts to produce a release.

A need for tools when using Scrum in the context of global software development was already established [15]. We observed all teams using tools, although they were all co-located. Most tools have in common that they support both product and process artefacts, but the tools support Scrum rather than non-Scrum artefacts. We conclude that the co-located teams use integrative tools, perhaps as intensive as distributed teams.

6 Conclusions

Our paper presents a clear and empirical overview of the artefacts Scrum teams use and what they use them for. The value of our work lies in its thorough foundation in practice, which provides practitioners with a reference model to mirror their own choices, whilst at the same time improving abstract artefact models by introducing new (categories of) artefacts.

No existing individual agile artefact model included the artefacts we encountered in our research, although a majority of them was covered by the combination of SACD and AACD. Thus combining the models already was a step forward. But we also enriched the models by identifying a new artefact not yet included: A design artefact. We also made a clear distinction between product and process artefacts in our model; one that was lacking in the diagrams so far. And finally we abstracted our model by separating function from form in denominating our artefacts independent of their origin (Backlog Item instead of feature, bug, task) and separating supporting tools from artefacts themselves.

Dimensioning our Scrum artefact model in Scrum and non-Scrum as well as product and process artefacts shows that, apart from the core Scrum artefacts (Product and Sprint Backlog, Increment), Scrum teams produce many other artefacts, especially non-Scrum product artefacts: Design, test and release-related material. Despite the popularity of Scrum, elements from previous software development methods linger on.

All teams use support tools for the Product and Sprint Backlog, whether or not combined with a whiteboard, while at the same time including (Sprint) project management information as a process artefact. Albeit the fact that all teams are co-located they use supporting tools (and artefacts); this use is not exclusively reserved for distributed teams.

We did not find evidence for artefacts aiming at the preservation of knowledge over a number of Sprints. All non-Scrum product artefacts play a role only in one Sprint and may be considered even as to apply to one item of the Sprint Backlog only. An overall architecture or even a design bundling the requirements in a Sprint was not encountered.

6.1 Limitations

Limitations are inherent when a case study is selected as research method. We studied three teams using Scrum. We have taken measures to reinforce validity, and therefor feel that some generalization of results is justified, but the sample remains small.

We limited ourselves in our study to artefacts which were within the sphere of influence of the teams themselves. We did not explicitly investigate or verify whether artefacts followed general organizational standards, derived from, for instance, ISO/IEC 15504.

6.2 Future Work

Of course we would like to see our results confirmed with other organizations. To this extend we will continue working on our artefact model. We also feel that further research concerning the reasons for deciding, whether or not, to produce certain artefacts is motivated. To this extent the influence of context variables (for instance, organization or team size, Scrum maturity) on such decisions constitutes an interesting research topic.

We did not find extensive internal documentation, such as architectures, UML design or module descriptions. What still occupies us is the use of artefacts in knowledge management in the longer term; it would be interesting to consider artefacts in this broader perspective.

Acknowledgements. The results from this research would not have been possible without the generous cooperation from the three case study organizations. The (first) author also wants to express his gratitude to Avans University of Applied Sciences for facilitating and supporting this research.

References

1. Abrahamsson, P., Oza, N., Siponen, M.: Agile software development methods: a comparative review. In: Dingsøyr, T., Dybå, T., Moe, N.B. (eds.) Agile Software Development: Current Research and Future Directions, pp. 31–59. Springer, Berlin (2010)
2. Abrahamsson, P., Warsta, J., Siponen, M.T., Ronkainen, J.: New directions on agile methods: a comparative analysis. In: Proceedings of the 25th International Conference on Software Engineering, pp. 244–254, Portland (OR), USA. IEEE, 3–5 May 2003
3. Ambler, S.: Agile Modeling: Effective Practices for eXtreme Programming and the Unified Process. Wiley, New York (2002)
4. Beck, K., Beedle, M., Van Bennekum, A., Cockburn, A., Cunningham, W. et al.: Agile manifesto (2001). http://agilemanifesto.org/
5. Blijleven, V.: Scrum development process from a method engineering perspective (2012). http://foswiki.cs.uu.nl/foswiki/MethodEngineering/Scrumdevelopmentprocess20112012
6. Bustard, D., Wilkie, G., Greer, D.: The diffusion of agile software development: insights from a regional survey. In: Pooley, R., Coady, J., Schneider, C., Linger, H., Barry, C., Lang, M. (eds.) Information Systems Development: Reflections, Challenges and New Directions, pp. 219–230. Springer, New York (2013)
7. Chau, T., Maurer, F., Melnik, G.: Knowledge sharing: agile methods vs. Tayloristic methods. In: Proceedings of the Twelfth IEEE International Workshops on Enabling Technologies: Infrastructure for Collaborative Enterprises, pp. 302–307, Linz, Austria. IEEE, 9–11 June 2003
8. Curtis, B., Krasner, H., Iscoe, N.: A field study of the software design process for large systems. Commun. ACM **31**(11), 1268–1287 (1988)
9. Dijkstra, O.: Extending the agile development discipline to deployment - the need for a holistic approach (2013). http://dspace.library.uu.nl/handle/1874/279416
10. Femmer, H., Kuhrmann, M., Stimmer, J., Junge, J.: Experiences from the design of an artifact model for distributed agile project management. In: Proceedings of the IEEE 9th International Conference on Global Software Engineering, pp. 1–5, Sjanghai, China. IEEE, 18–21 August 2014
11. Georgiadou, E.: Software process and product improvement: a historical perspective. Cybern. Syst. Anal. **39**(1), 125–142 (2003)
12. Glaiel, F., Moulton, A., Madnick, S.: Agile project dynamics: a system dynamics investigation of agile software development methods. In: Proceedings of the 31st International Conference of the System Dynamics Society, Cambridge (MA), USA. System Dynamics Society, 21–25 July 2013
13. Gröber, M.: Investigation of the usage of artifacts in agile methods (2013). http://www4.in.tum.de/~kuhrmann/studworks/mg-thesis.pdf

14. Herbsleb, J.D., Moitra, D.: Global software development. IEEE Softw. **18**(2), 16–20 (2001)
15. Hossain, E., Babar, M.A., Paik, H.: Using scrum in global software development: a systematic literature review. In: Proceedings of the Fourth IEEE International Conference on Global Software Engineering, pp. 175–184, Limerick, Ireland. IEEE, 13–16 July 2009
16. Kuhrmann, M., Méndez Fernández, D., Gröber, M.: Towards artifact models as process interfaces in distributed software projects. In: Proceedings of the IEEE 8th International Conference on Global Software Engineering, pp. 11–20, Bari, Italy. IEEE, 26–29 August 2013
17. Lagerberg, L., Skude, T.: The impact of agile principles and practices on large-scale software development projects: a multiple-case study of two software development projects at Ericsson (2013). http://liu.diva-portal.org/smash/record.jsf?pid=diva2:608712
18. Maimbo, H.: Designing a case study protocol for application in IS research. In: Proceedings of the 9th Asia Conference on Information Systems, pp. 1281–1292, Bangkok, Thailand. PACIS, 7–10 July 2005
19. Méndez Fernández, D., Penzenstadler, B., Kuhrmann, M., Broy, M.: A meta model for artefact-orientation: fundamentals and lessons learned in requirements engineering. In: Petriu, D.C., Rouquette, N., Haugen, Ø. (eds.) MODELS 2010, Part II. LNCS, vol. 6395, pp. 183–197. Springer, Heidelberg (2010)
20. Nonaka, I.: A dynamic theory of organizational knowledge creation. Organ. Sci. **5**(1), 14–37 (1994)
21. Paasivaara, M., Lassenius, C.: Communities of practice in a large distributed agile software development organization - case Ericsson. Inf. Softw. Technol. **56**(12), 1556–1577 (2014)
22. Parnas, D.L., Madey, J.: Functional documents for computer systems. Sci. Comput. Program. **25**(1), 41–61 (1995)
23. Rodríguez, P., Markkula, J., Oivo, M., Turula, K.: Survey on agile and lean usage in finnish software industry. In: Proceedings of the ACM-IEEE 12th International Symposium on Empirical Software Engineering and Measurement, pp. 139–148, Lund, Sweden. ACM, 17–22 September 2012
24. Royce, W.: Managing the development of large software systems. In: Proceedings of IEEE WESCON, pp. 1–9 (1970)
25. Runeson, P., Höst, M.: Guidelines for conducting and reporting case study research in software engineering. Empirical Softw. Eng. **14**(2), 131–164 (2008)
26. Schwaber, K., Beedle, M.: Agile Software Development with Scrum, 1st edn. Prentice Hall, Englewood Cliffs (2002)
27. Schwaber, K., Sutherland, J.: The scrum guide – the definitive guide to scrum: the rules of the game (2013). http://www.scrumguides.org/docs/scrumguide/v1/Scrum-Guide-US
28. Sharp, H., Robinson, H.: Three "C"s of agile practice: collaboration, co-ordination and communication. In: Dingsøyr, T., Dybå, T., Moe, N.B. (eds.) Agile Software Development, pp. 61–85. Springer, Berlin (2010)
29. Sharp, H., Robinson, H., Petre, M.: The role of physical artefacts in agile software development: two complementary perspectives. Interact. Comput. **21**(1–2), 108–116 (2009)
30. Sommerville, I.: Software documentation (revised version) (2001). https://ifs.host.cs.st-andrews.ac.uk/Research/Publications/Papers-PDF/2000-04/Documentation.pdf
31. Stapleton, J.: DSDM, Dynamic Systems Development Method: The Method in Practice. Addison Wesley Publishing Company, Boston (1997)
32. Stettina, C.J., Heijstek, W.: Necessary and neglected? An empirical study of internal documentation in agile software development teams. In: Proceedings of the 29th ACM International Conference on Design of Communication, pp. 159–166, Pisa, Italy. ACM, 3–5 October 2011

33. Strode, D.E., Huff, S.L., Hope, B.G., Link, S.: Coordination in co-located agile software development projects. J. Syst. Softw. **85**(6), 1222–1238 (2012)
34. van de Weerd, I., Brinkkemper, S.: Meta-modeling for situational analysis and design methods. In: Syed, M.R., Syed, S.N. (eds.) Handbook of Research on Modern Systems Analysis and Design Technologies and Applications, pp. 35–54. IGI Global, Hershey (2008)
35. Xu, L., Brinkkemper, S.: Concepts of product software. Eur. J. Inf. Syst. **16**(5), 531–541 (2007)
36. Yanzer Cabral, A., Blois Ribeiro, M., Lemke, A.P., Silva, M.T., Cristal, M., Franco, C.: A case study of knowledge management usage in agile software projects. In: Filipe, J., Cordeiro, J. (eds.) Enterprise Information Systems. LNBIP, vol. 24, pp. 627–638. Springer, Heidelberg (2009)
37. Yin, R.K.: Case Study Research: Design and Methods, 4th edn. Sage Publications, Inc., Thousand Oaks (2009)

Is *Water-Scrum-Fall* Reality? On the Use of Agile and Traditional Development Practices

Georgios Theocharis[1], Marco Kuhrmann[1](✉), Jürgen Münch[2],
and Philipp Diebold[3]

[1] The Mærsk Mc-Kinney Møller Institute and Center for Energy Informatics,
University of Southern Denmark, Odense, Denmark
g.theoharis84@gmail.com, kuhrmann@mmmi.sdu.dk
[2] Department of Computer Science, University of Helsinki, Helsinki, Finland
Juergen.Muench@cs.helsinki.fi
[3] Fraunhofer Institute for Experimental Software Engineering,
Kaiserslautern, Germany
philipp.diebold@iese.fraunhofer.de

Abstract. For years, agile methods are considered the most promising route toward successful software development, and a considerable number of published studies the (successful) use of agile methods and reports on the benefits companies have from adopting agile methods. Yet, since the world is not black or white, the question for what happened to the traditional models arises. Are traditional models replaced by agile methods? How is the transformation toward Agile managed, and, moreover, where did it start? With this paper we close a gap in literature by studying the general process use over time to investigate how traditional and agile methods are used. Is there coexistence or do agile methods accelerate the traditional processes' extinction? The findings of our literature study comprise two major results: First, studies and reliable numbers on the general process model use are rare, i.e., we lack quantitative data on the actual process use and, thus, we often lack the ability to ground process-related research in practically relevant issues. Second, despite the assumed dominance of agile methods, our results clearly show that companies enact context-specific hybrid solutions in which traditional and agile development approaches are used in combination.

Keywords: Development practices · Agile methods · Software process · Systematic literature review · Comparative study · Scrum

1 Introduction

Software managers and developers are still on the quest for adequate methods to organize, plan, and direct software projects. Since the early 1970s, software processes are defined to capture and organize knowledge about software and systems development and, since then, a continuously growing number of software development approaches competes for the users' favor. The software process comes

© Springer International Publishing Switzerland 2015
P. Abrahamsson et al. (Eds.): PROFES 2015, LNCS 9459, pp. 149–166, 2015.
DOI: 10.1007/978-3-319-26844-6_11

in different shapes—be it as rigid plan-driven approach or as slim agile method, and since the 2000s, we find two basic streams. Traditional (or rich) processes aim to address the whole software project lifecycle, e.g., by providing comprehensive guidelines, standardized procedures, project planning templates, and interfaces to further organization processes, while agile methods aim at reducing the software process to its minimum to avoid "bureaucracy", and to provide users with only this amount of rules and guidelines that is required to perform a project. Over the past decades, we observed the "rise of agile methods" [8]. Apparently, agile methods provide a better way to address practitioners' needs, to accelerate software development, and to improve quality and customer satisfaction. Several studies provide evidence regarding the benefits of agile methods, e.g., [6,9]. Yet, practice shows the world not being fully "agilized", as there exist settings in which agile methods are either not (fully) applicable or cannot show their strengths. In such situations, the software process is usually adopted to the current context, which, for instance, is shown in our previously conducted study [21] in which we could identify different combination patterns showing a trend toward West's "Water-Scrum-Fall" [40]. In particular, we found combinations of traditional and agile software development approaches, which was also found in another independently conducted study [39]. Furthermore, surveys on the use of agile methods, such as [17,38], suggest that even the agile methods appear to be rarely used in their "pure" form. For instance, Diebold et al. [7] conducted a study in which they show how Scrum is used in practice (with a particular focus on variations and respective rationale).

Problem Statement. Available studies draw a picture of a diverse process ecosystem in which different development approaches are combined with each other. Therefore, knowledge of the project context, customization settings, and variability operators is required to efficiently assemble a company- or project-specific process. However, different studies reveal considerable gaps in the body of knowledge [4,24,25]. As mentioned by Dingsøyr et al. [8], current literature focuses on researching agile methods, yet ignoring the other processes to a large extent. To identify useful strategies to systematically and efficiently combine development approaches for a particular context, understanding of the state-of-the-practice is required. In particular, we miss empirical data on the process use in general, about common combinations, and trends over time.

Objective. To investigate the use of different software process models in practice, we analyze published studies that provide data on software processes, their use, potential/implemented combinations, and trends by analyzing how the use of software processes evolved over time. Our research aims to investigate practically applied processes and combinations to lay the foundation for developing appropriate process customization and configuration instruments.

Contribution. This paper presents our findings from a literature study on the use of process models in practice. In a set of 22 selected papers, only five provided quantitative data. Furthermore, data from the annually conducted VersionOne survey [38] were used for comparison. Our findings show software processes mainly used as hybrid approaches that either combine traditional and agile methods or compose project processes from different practices. However, our findings also show absence of detailed knowledge about which approaches are used in particular, how those are combined, and how they relate to the respective company context. Studies that investigate the whole process ecosystem are scarcely to find. Therefore, our study also concludes with the call for more research to generate more and better data on process use to pave the way for developing efficient instruments for process selection, tailoring, and combination.

Outline. The reminder of the paper is organized as follows: Sect. 2 discusses related work and gaps in the current body of knowledge. In Sect. 3, we describe our research approach, present the results of our study in Sect. 4, and provide a discussion on the results in Sect. 5. We conclude the paper in Sect. 6.

2   Related Work

Agile software development methods were introduced and used in the late 1990s. They gained attention and companies and developers worldwide increasingly adopted them. In February 2001, the *Agile Manifesto*, was published and described the principles of Agile Methods. Since then, agile methods gained increasing attention in practice as well as in research and, consequently, a number of agile methods was proposed. In 2014, Tripp and Armstrong [37] investigated the "most popular" agile methods and found, inter alia, Extreme Programming (XP), Scrum, Dynamic Systems Development Method (DSDM), Crystal, Feature Driven Development (FDD), and Lean development the most frequently used. Beyond such one-time studies, few studies investigate the development over time. For example, a comprehensive perspective on the use of agile methods is provided by Dingsøyr et al. [8], who summarized "a decade of agile software development", provided an overview of the publication body, and motivate further research toward a sound theoretical framework of agile software development. Dybå and Dingsøyr [9] conducted a literature review on empirical studies on agile software development. They summarized the major approaches, but found most of the research done in the context of XP (with immature teams) and concluded the strength of evidence (still) low. Furthermore, they vote for more rigorous research in the field of agile methods (especially on methods of particular relevance for industry). Such an industry perspective is given by the VersionOne survey [38] that investigates the use of agile methods over time and draws a slightly different picture[1]. Aggregating the VersionOne data, Scrum became the most popular agile method. However, this study also points to a certain trend toward using hybrid and customized approaches, which is also supported by Diebold et al. [7], who study how Scrum is actually implemented in practice.

---

[1] A similar study is available by the "Status Quo Agile 2014" study [17]. However, this study does not provide as comprehensive historical data as the VersionOne survey series.

Going beyond aforementioned agile-focused studies and reviewing the available scientific and "grey" literature on software processes in general, one may conclude that agile methods took over from traditional processes. In fact, literature reflects this trend. For instance, in their 1996-study, Khurana et al. [15] list more than 25 fine-grained "techniques" for software engineering (mapped to different software engineering activities), e.g., prototyping, Fagan inspections, and SSADM [32]. Studies conducted in the early 2000s, e.g., [3,11] show several of the mentioned techniques still in use, but also show them slowly disappearing and being replaced by (the new) agile methods.

However, within that diversity of traditional and agile methods, another trend came to light: just in 1997, Fitzgerald [10] found 6 out of 8 companies in Ireland using custom or non-formalized development processes—a trend that still can be observed over time (e.g., Reifer [31]) and also in recent studies, e.g., [18]. Among other things, those studies also show that the traditional process models are still of certain relevance. For example, Solinski and Petersen [36] found Scrum and XP the most popular and adopted methodologies. They also found combinations of the classic Waterfall/XP, and Scrum/XP the most common combinations. Recently published studies, e.g., [18,39] also indicate to a situation in which traditional and agile approaches coexist and make the majority of practically used (mixed/hybrid) approaches.

Therefore, current literature on software processes and their application (patterns) in practice leaves researchers and practitioners alone with a diffuse picture: agile methods gained popularity and the related (scientific) literature is dramatically increasing (cf. [8]), e.g., understanding of benefits of certain practices and analyzing the impact of agile methods. Traditional process models are seemingly vanished from the researchers' to-do lists and, if at all, appear only in the context of process modeling, in domains having special requirements to the software process, e.g., compliance, regulations, and norms (safety & security, medical devices, etc.), as part of surveys, and as subject to discussion why companies might be reluctant to buy-in agile methods (e.g., [26,37]). However, information about general software process use, local/global trends, and detailed information about combination patterns is missing in literature. The present paper thus aims to fill a gap in literature by providing first steps toward a more comprehensive picture of process use to lay the foundation for further research.

3   Research Design

In this curiosity-driven and exploratory study, we opted for a research design in which we applied instruments from *Systematic Literature Review* process [16]. The core study was conducted by stepwise collecting information starting from a small set of reference publications to form the basic knowledge (snowballing). Based on the harvested publications, we conducted an automatic search in different literature databases to find further publications, which then were used for another snowballing iteration. Finally, the VersionOne survey [38] was chosen for a broader analysis and discussion.

In subsequent section, we detail the research design and explain the different procedures to collect and analyze data.

3.1 Research Questions

To conduct the study, we defined the following research questions:

RQ 1 *Which development approaches are used in practice?* This research question aims at developing a catalog of practically used development approaches (processes, methods, or practices) and to investigate the approaches' use over time.

RQ 2 *Which development approaches are combined in practical use?* In order to answer this research question, we use the initial catalog to study how development approaches are combined in order to address specific software development contexts.

RQ 3 *Are there patterns and trends observable?* This research question aims to investigate patterns of process use to better support the adaptation of agile methods in non-agile environments and trends of process use, i.e., does the region affect the process selection (e.g., due to local standards), or is there any general trend to find.

3.2 Data Collection Procedures

To get information on the process use in general, we were especially interested into primary studies that we collected using a multi-staged search and selection procedure. The data collection procedure comprised the following steps:

1. Snowballing based on two manually selected reference publications [18,39].
2. Initial analysis of the found extra four publications: [3,11,14,30].
3. Automated search in five literature databases, complemented by a search using Scopus and Google Scholar as meta-search engines.
4. Snowballing of the publications obtained in the automated search.
5. Using the VersionOne survey [38] to add extra perspectives to the discussion.

The manual paper selection (following the snowballing procedures [16]) was conducted twice. The initial selection was performed on two reference publications [18,39] and aimed at extending the set of reference publications that built the foundation to construct search queries to support the automated search in different literature databases. The resulting six publications were read with the purpose of finding proper keywords to initiate the automatic search. The second iteration was performed on the publications obtained from the automated search with the purpose of completing the result set.

The automatic search was conduced using the following literature databases: *ACM, IEEE, Springer, Wiley,* and *Elsevier.* To obtain the data, based on the reference publications and the initial snowballing results, we developed different

Table 1. Inclusion and exclusion criteria for the study's SLR parts.

No.	Description
IC_1	The paper describes a longterm observation of the use of development methods
IC_2	The paper surveys practitioners for the use of development methods
IC_3	The paper reports on the use of development methods in general, e.g., as secondary study
IC_4	The paper is on tools implementing certain methods (infer information about method use)
EC_1	The paper is a proposal only
EC_2	The paper occurred multiple times in the result set
EC_3	The paper is not on the use of development methods (out of scope)
EC_4	The paper is a workshop-, tutorial-, or poster summary
EC_5	The paper is not in the domain of software engineering or computer science in general
EC_6	The paper reports on teaching experiences using development methods only
EC_7	The paper is not available in English (or German)
EC_8	The paper's full text is not available for download

search query candidates that we stepwise tested and refined. We conducted the automated search using the following simple search query: *((("method choice") or "method use") and "software development") and "survey")*[2].

In order to confirm the search results, *Scopus* and *Google Scholar* were used. The outcomes of the automatic search were treated in a rigorous and proven selection process, as described in detail in [19] applying the in-/exclusion criteria from Table 1.

3.3 Analysis Procedures

For the analysis procedure, we implemented two different approaches. In general all selected publications were included in a spreadsheet in which we classified the respective publications, e.g., for study type, applied instruments, context, and outcomes. We then boiled down all initially selected studies to their essence to prepare the qualitative analysis. For the primary studies (in which we were especially interested) we analyzed the publications for quantitative detailed data on processes, use, combinations, and so forth, and collected these data in a separate spreadsheet for an in-depth analysis.

Due to the low number of studies, we did not perform any statistical tests. Instead, we rely on simple data tables and charts on which we base our discussion and interpretation. Since we found a considerable number of process mentions, we also perform a clustering and a categorization.

3.4 Validity Procedures

To improve the validity of our results, we opted for different strategies. The initial data collection and study selection procedures were performed by two researchers

---

[2] We conducted several test runs finding this simple string producing the best results. Including/adding keywords like "process" just inflated the result set, yet no extra publication providing quantitative data on process use could be found in these tests.

adopting the schematic procedures from previously conducted studies [19,20]. That is, data collection and selection was initially performed independently using previously defined spreadsheet templates, followed by a series of workshops to perform the final selection and classification. The finally selected papers and initial analysis results were then given to another team of researchers to review, confirm and/or revise the results, and to develop a joint conclusion.

4   Study Results

In this section, we present the results of the study. In Sect. 4.1, we give an overview of the study population. Sections 4.2–4.4 present the results from the literature review and, finally, Sect. 5 presents a discussion.

4.1   Study Polulation

In this section, we summarize the study population. The different search procedures resulted into 473 papers from which 22 papers were selected for consideration. Finally, five of the 22 papers provided quantitative data, i.e., survey results on process use, and were selected for an in-depth analysis. These studies were conducted in Germany (2006, 2006, 2013), USA (2014), and Brunei (1998). The remaining papers were considered for the qualitative analysis only. Table 2 provides a summary of the final result set.

4.2   RQ1: Which Development Approaches Are Used in Practice?

In this section, we provide an overview of the review findings. The five selected papers mention 62 different development approaches in total[3]. Among the named methods, we find representatives of the traditional development models (e.g., Waterfall, RUP, V-Model), a number of agile methods (e.g., Scrum, Kanban, XP), and also a considerable share of non-standardized, very specific, and/or "legacy" approaches, such as SSADM [32] or Jackson's System Design [13].

As we found a large number of methods and also varying data presentation, we decided to classify the mentioned approaches as traditional process model, agile method, technique (self-contained method that is neither traditional nor agile, e.g., prototyping), unclassified (if an approach could not be assigned to one of the other classes, or if the paper just states "other", "custom", or "don't know"). Furthermore, due to the heterogeneous data formats, we normalized the data as relative numbers (percentage of mentions related to the respective n) that is shown in Table 3. This table shows that companies usually use multiple development approaches, which becomes obvious due to the percentage rate larger than 100 %. However, the SUCCESS study [3] has to be considered an

---

[3] Due to space limitations, the study data set including the full list of mentioned processes is available for download here: http://goo.gl/bUB3Tr.

Table 2. Overview of the papers obtained from the literature search (Instruments: "Q" – questionnaire, "I" – interview, "SLR" – systematic literature review, "M" – miscellaneous instruments).

Paper	Year	Scope in time		Study type		Instruments	Quantitative
		Snapshot	Trend	Primary	Secondary		Data
[39]	2014	✗		✗		Q	✓
[18]	2013	✗	(✗)	✗		Q	✓
[3]	2006	✗		✗		I, Q	✓
[11]	2006	✗		✗		Q	✓
[14]	2003	✗		✗		M	
[30]	2002	✗		✗		Q	
[35]	2014	✗		✗		Q	
[36]	2014	✗		✗		Q	
[27]	2014	✗		✗		Q	
[5]	2013	✗		✗		Q	
[26]	2013	✗		✗		Q	
[37]	2013	✗		✗		Q	
[22]	2013	✗		✗	✗	M	
[34]	2013	✗			✗	SLR	
[8]	2012		✗		✗	SLR	
[23]	2010	✗		✗	✗	Q, SLR	
[28]	2009	✗		✗		M	
[33]	2008	✗		✗		Q	
[9]	2008	✗			✗	SLR	
[12]	2003	✗			✗	SLR	
[29]	1998	✗			✗	SLR	✓
[2]	1983	✗		✗		Q	

outlier, as the total mentions are below 100 %. As we don't have access to the raw data, we cannot reproduce this phenomenon, yet, since 49 % of the mentions are categorized as "unclassified", we cannot conclude to what extent, e.g., agile and traditional approaches are used and/or combined. Especially the *3ProcSurvey* [18] and the IOSE-W^2 study [11] show that companies use multiple processes. For example, in the *3ProcSurvey*, agile methods account for 119 % of the mentions, i.e., even in one project different agile methods are used in combination.

The most frequently mentioned development models across all studies are: Scrum (61), the Waterfall (54), the Rational Unified Process (RUP; 44), and the Agile Unified Process (43). V-shaped processes are present in different variants and account for 105 mentions in total. However, these numbers present the mentions without paying attention to the development over time. For example, in recent studies, RUP accounts for 5.9 % [39] and 16.2 % [18], whereas for

Table 3. Mentions of categorized process types (*n*: number of participants, mentions: number of mentioned processes in total, *: incomplete/not available raw data).

Paper	Year	n	Mentions	Ratio	Traditional	Agile	Technique	Unclassified
[39]	2014	153	316*	2.07	66%	88%	52%	0%
[18]	2013	37	93	2.51	92%	119%	5%	35%
[11]	2006	65	199	3.06	109%	26%	103%	68%
[3]	2006	217*	180	0.83	28%	3%	3%	49%
[29]	1998	36	54	1.50	33%	0%	72%	44%

the German context [21] we found a certain trend: in 2006, RUP accounts for 41.5% of all mentions and in 2013, RUP made only 16.2%. Furthermore, and all mentions in 2013 referred to company-specific variants. That is, available studies indicate that—although RUP contributes a high number of mentions—the "classic" (standard/non-customized) RUP is losing its relevance. Further trends are discussed together with observed pattern in Sect. 4.4.

4.3 RQ2: Which Development Approaches Are Combined in Practical Use?

In this section, we analyze the combination of the different approaches. The numbers presented in Table 3 show that companies instrument different approaches and use them in combination. However, only one study [18] provides data of sufficient detail to present and discuss the combinations. Figure 1, based on [21], shows the combination of the different development approaches for Germany. It reveals two major clusters and, when analyzing these clusters, shows that the German standard software process V-Modell XT is often combined with Scrum, and Scrum itself is normally used in combination with Kanban and XP. Therefore, based on [21], we can name the following "standard" combination pattern for Germany: *V-Modell XT + (Scrum + (Kanban + XP))*.

In other words: companies use the national standard to provide a general management framework (and to comply with certain compliance requirements), and embody the generic process with concrete methods. Furthermore, as even Scrum is fairly generic thus requiring some embodiment [7], companies use Kanban and XP practices for this embodiment.

As mentioned before, we only have sufficient data from the *3ProcSurvey* [18] to allow for such a detailed analysis. However, the numbers from Table 3 suggest a similar picture for other regions, e.g., for USA [39], the "classic" Waterfall, Scrum, and the Agile Unified Process account for a high share of mentions thus suggesting a similar picture in which the V-Modell XT (Germany) is replaced

Left table (use of approaches per respondent):

Participant	Rational Unified Process (Standard)	Rational Unified Process (modified)	Open Unified Process	V-Modell XT (Standard)	V-Modell XT (modified)	V-Modell 97	W-Modell	Hermes	eXtreme Programming	Scrum	Kanban	Crystal	Feature Driven Development (FDD)	None	Other
1				x						x					
2										x	x				
3					x					x					
4															x
5				x	x				x	x					x
6															x
7				x	x					x	x				
8				x							x				
9	x			x	x	x			x	x					
10										x	x				
11					x	x				x					
12										x	x				
13				x						x					
14	x				x	x				x	x				
15									x	x					x
16					x					x					
17															x
18										x					
19															x
20								x						x	
21	x				x				x	x					
22										x	x	x			x
23									x	x					
24					x				x	x					x
25					x		x								
26		x			x								x		
27					x					x					
28									x	x	x	x			
29					x					x					
30									x	x	x				
31	x				x	x				x					
32					x										
33	x				x					x					
34														x	
35															x
36										x					x
37													x		x

Right table (combination of approaches within clusters):

	V-Modell XT (Standard)	V-Modell XT (modified)	V-Modell 97	eXtreme Programming	Scrum
V-Modell XT (Standard)					
V-Modell XT (modified)	3				
V-Modell 97	1	4			
Xtreme Programming	2	3	2		
Scrum	5	12	5	9	
Kanban	2	2	1	3	8

Fig. 1. Combination of development approaches (from [21]). The left part shows the use of approaches per respondent revealing two major clusters, and the right part illustrates the combination of the different approaches within these clusters.

by the Waterfall model as overall management framework in which Scrum is embedded (this situation is often referred to as the *Water-Scrum-Fall* [40])[4].

In a nutshell, although we lack detailed information and raw data about the actual combination of the different approaches, we find indication to a mixed application of traditional and agile approaches. Based on our findings from [18] and available numbers from the other studies, we hypothesize that companies, especially large ones, use a traditional process as reference model to define the basic management procedures and interfaces to the other company- and business processes, while particular project teams utilize a pool of (agile) methods and practices to run development projects. Yet, confirmation of this hypothesis remains subject to future work.

---

[4] Although [27] supports this assumption, this study was excluded from the quantitative analysis, as the authors rejected papers not explicitly dealing with agile methods, and summarized all non-agile approaches under "custom or other". We thus have insufficient information about what processes are eventually meant and how those could affect our study results.

4.4   RQ3: Are There Patterns and Trends Observable?

This research question aims at identifying trends in process use. Since software processes are proposed for decades, the question for the relevance occurs. Are approaches proposed in the mid 1990s still relevant? Or are those approaches dispensable, as they are increasingly replaced by agile methods. Again, due to the absence of longitudinal studies that monitor process use over time, we hardly can provide reliable conclusions. Only for Germany there are three independently conducted studies providing numbers for a period of seven years. In [21], the results from [3,11,18] were analyzed for trends in process use. The analysis revealed that although agile methods gained popularity, at the same time, traditional processes were increasingly used as well (Fig. 2).

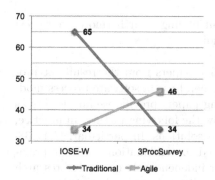 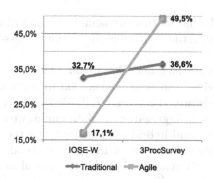

Fig. 2. In-/decrease in use of different process classes (based on the IOSE-W^2 study from 2006 and the *3ProcSurvey* from 2013). The left part shows the absolute numbers and shows the decreased mentions regarding traditional processes and the "rise" of agile methods. However, the right part shows that both kinds of processes are increasingly used (in combination).

Extending this discussion to the other papers analyzed in the present study, this picture is consistent with the finding that companies usually use mixed-method approaches to organize and operate their projects. For example, [18] showed that the RUP is—if at all—only used in tailored variants. That is, the standard RUP is not used anymore. Comparing this finding to the USA-based study [39], RUP accounts for only 5.9 % of all mentions (whereas we don't have information if this number refers to the standard RUP, tailored variants, or both). Nevertheless, we see "dinosaurs" like the Waterfall model still in use (because of its simplicity regarding general project organization). Furthermore, the combination of different approaches does not only happen between traditional and agile approaches. As, for example, the VersionOne survey [38] shows, even agile methods are used in combination (an in-depth analysis, also consistent with [17], shows that the building blocks used for combination are the individual practices). The VersionOne data shows Scrum champion the other agile methods (56 % in 2014), however, the data also shows a stable, yet slightly increasing, number of mixed approaches. Moreover and in line with Diebold et al. [7], we further hypothesize that even the majority of the Scrum users does not apply Scrum by the letter rather than in a customized fashion.

Therefore, we conclude that hybrid approaches that include traditional and agile approaches shape the today's "standard process ecosystem." The "traditional part" is given by a (national) standard, or by a domain- or context-specific standard, e.g., norms like ISO/IEC 26262. The remaining part is given by a context-specific combination of different agile methods or practices. And here, all studies show one trend: Today, Scrum, Kanban, and XP (practices) can be considered the dominating approaches.

5   Study Summary and Discussion

In this section, we summarize and discuss our findings. Furthermore, we review the study with regards to the threats of validity.

Summary and Discussion. Although only five papers from the result set provided sufficient information to analyze the general use of software process models over the years (cf. Table 2), the remaining papers provide useful insights as well. Aggregating all data found, we can draw the following picture: in practice, we find hybrid approaches to be the favored solutions. In particular, [7,17,38] showed that even the agile methods are used in combination, and our previously conducted study [18] as well as further independently conducted research [39] provided extra evidence that agile and traditional approaches are used in a mixed-method approach. Among all reviewed studies, we could find a clear trend toward adopting Scrum to the organization's software development [18,38,39]. However, we also found some indication that Scrum is often used in combination with further methods [17,38], and could provide a combination matrix (Fig. 1, cf. [21]). Other than expected, Lean Development and DevOps (so far) play no role. However, the current data does not allow for any conclusions thus requiring further research to integrate those new emerging movements into the analysis.

Several industry-related studies showed a certain reluctance of the management to buy-in agile methods [26,37], which we use as basis to assume that the use of hybrid approaches is, inter alia, caused by this reluctance. For example, Tripp and Armstrong [37] analyzed the motivation to adopt agile methods and found some relevant drivers. Furthermore, they analyzed the perceived impact of 12 selected project management and development-related practices finding those practices negatively correlating with (general) project management, but positively correlating with software development (factor: software quality). Murphy et al. [26] analyzed the use and perception of agile software development at Microsoft. Their major findings include that Scrum is considered the most favorite development approach. However, the study's respondents also considered the suitability of agile methods for large projects critical (substantial communication effort and overhead, reluctance of the management to accept the agile approach). On the other hand, Lagerberg et al. [22], and Solinski and Petersen [36] also found positive impacts of adopting agile practices in large companies, e.g., improved knowledge sharing, increased project visibility, and reduced need for other coordination instruments. Melo et al. [5] conducted a study in Brazil in which they analyzed the evolution of agile software development from the perspectives of education, research, and application in industry and found that the management-related agile practices are either adopted to a large extent or (completely) rejected, while the development-related practices made their way into the projects.

Therefore, we assume that managers prefer the structured planning-oriented way of working, which they need to perform estimation, planning, and controlling tasks, while developers prefer the freedom that agile methods offer the teams. Furthermore, we consider the often missing organizational interface of agile methods (e.g., procurement and contracting procedures, sub-contractor management, and enterprise resource planning) another reason for management's reluctance toward agile methods. Agile methods usually focus on the system under development, management of features or requirements, development and (code-related) quality assurance practices, and the management of change. Organizational interfaces to the company level are, often provided by the traditional approaches.

Hence, integrating traditional and agile approaches into a mixed-method or hybrid approach offers some benefits: managers get their "safe" environment and developers get their freedom and slim development methods. Our study reveals some indication [17, 38] that project teams increasingly compose a "best of" from different practices—quite often on a per-project basis [18]. That is, practices became the building blocks of assembling company- or project-specific software processes. However, information about particular practices used in combination, their linking to the hosting organization, or the exact way of performing those combinations is—if at all—barely available, and reveals a significant gap in the current publication body.

Threats to Validity. In the following, we critically discuss our study results regarding these threats. The major threat emerges from the low number of papers selected for the study, and the often low data quality (either due to blurry/reduced data presentation or due to absence of raw data) of the studies analyzed. Therefore, we could present precise data from only one region (Germany), but had to partially infer and normalize data from other studies. Furthermore, since we rely on independently conducted studies, we have no control about the respective data quality. We refer to studies that were conducted using surveys and interviews, i.e., these studies may introduce extra threats to validity by relying on subjective and potentially non-generalizable data. This situation results in an assumption-based line of argumentation that we, however, backed-up by referring to further independently conducted studies, and by performing data analysis and interpretation independently in two teams of researchers. Although we found similar trends, due to the eventually low number of analyzed studies, we therefore have to consider our findings—especially their generalizability—critical.

Another threat to validity is the study selection as such. Due to the blurry terminology that suffers from heterogeneity and massive overloading, after several test runs, we limited the automatic search to "method" and related terms. Yet, the term "development method" has to be considered of insufficient precision to address the entire field. Therefore, even as this term is common in the researched field, limiting the search this way introduces a threat that we addressed by manually conducted search and selection procedures. However, according to Badampudi et al. [1], who found the efficiency of snowballing comparable to automatic searches, we consider our result set suitable for this study. Still, the finally selected result set needs to be considered with care, as we have no knowledge about further publications not triggered by the search and selection procedures applied in this study, and non-scientific studies, e.g., blog posts and forum entries.

6 Conclusion

In this paper, we studied literature for the use of different software development approaches over time. For this, we conducted a literature study in which we applied different instruments from the SLR process to obtain relevant publications. From the different search and selection procedures, we selected 22 publications for inspection and, furthermore, collected quantitative data from five papers from out of this set.

Our findings show a diverse picture in which a variety of different development approaches is used that range from "old-fashioned" traditional approaches to agile methods. Furthermore, our findings show different approaches usually used in combination, i.e., mixed- or hybrid approaches represent the common model of use, and the combination includes "traditional-agile" as well as "agile-agile" approaches. Among the different combinations, Scrum, the classic Waterfall model, and V-shaped processes account for the majority of the mentions. Since we can rely our findings on a limited data basis only, we also extended our investigation to further independently conducted studies from the field of agile methods. In particular, we reviewed the VersionOne survey data and determined trends from the available data. These data confirm our findings that Scrum became the most popular agile method, and that agile methods are adapted and combined with other processes (traditional and agile) [7,38].

From our findings, we conclude that the *Water-Scrum-Fall* or similar combinations became reality. We discussed possible reasons and argue that the main driver for this kind of integration is the expectations of different stakeholder groups toward the "optimal" software development approach. Project managers require some stability to perform the usual project management tasks, such as estimation, planning, or controlling. Furthermore, project managers also have the responsibility to align projects with the respective company strategy, i.e., projects must interface further (business) processes like human resource management, sales, contracting, and so forth. Since agile methods usually address only system- or development-related tasks, such interfaces are missing often. Hence, traditional approaches are used to provide a basic structure and a framework for project organization and to provide interfaces to the respective company. Then again, developers ask for approaches that—on the one hand—support the development related tasks, but—on the other hand—provide extensive freedom to select the best practices for the respective situation. That is, the hybrid method in which traditional and agile approaches are combined seemingly provides the "win-win" situation.

However, our findings give only indication. Although we could find some trend, still, the limited data does not close the gap that we still miss a clear understanding of how to perform such integration in a structured manner. In particular, the available data does not allow for crafting detailed combination patterns, and the data does only partially allow for investigating the rational behind the approaches' combination, as for instance in [18] we found project managers making the decision based on experiences and preferences on a per-project base, but couldn't confirm nor generalize this finding by the other studies, as the required data was not available. Nonetheless, such an understanding is of *growing importance*, as current software development does not only include fast development and release cycles, but increasingly addresses cyber-physical systems that have high requirements, e.g., regarding safety and security. Thus, we must pay special attention to the respective norms and standards that are of similar complexity as traditional software process models. Therefore, discovering approaches to systematically, efficiently, and reliably integrating agile and traditional software development approaches, might also pave the way toward agile software development in critical domains[5].

Future Work. Although based on limited data, our findings have some impact and show some future research directions. The presented study reveals a gap in literature awaiting more work—we ourselves were not able to fully answer all our research questions to full extent. Therefore, our study is a call for action to conduct further research. For this purpose, our study provides initial findings and an initial combination matrix showing how different approaches are used in combination. Furthermore, our findings lay the foundation for further empirical research to gain better insights into the practical application and relevance of certain development approaches. Since we found some confirmation of the *Water-Scrum-Fall* combination pattern, we need to pay more attention to this customization setting that will, eventually, also affect the field of software process improvement (SPI). In [20], we could identify SPI in the context of small-to-medium enterprises and agile software development as "hot topics" (also supported by the more practitioner-oriented surveys on agile methods [17,38]). For this, a better understanding about the different strategies to assemble hybrid approaches for software development promises some benefits, e.g., better addressing and balancing stakeholder requirements, efficient process design, and so forth.

---

[5] This need is also supported by the just recently published GULP study (https://goo.gl/RciNpy) in which authors come to the conclusion that projects will be increasingly operated following a hybrid approach in future (population: 114 IT experts, mainly freelancers and project management consultants; study region: Germany).

In general the results of this exploratory study show that there is less material published on the combination of software development approaches than expected. Therefore, we would like to motivate the process community to start thinking of how to address this issue, to collect more knowledge, and to build a database that allows for theory development as well as for supporting practitioners in efficiently developing hybrid approaches best fitting their actual requirements. In addition, further data sources and studies have to be collected and analyzed to round out the big picture of process use and to collect more evidence.

Acknowledgements. This research was partially carried out and supported by a Software Campus project (BMBF 01IS12053) funded by the German Ministry of Education and Research.

References

1. Badampudi, D., Wohlin, C., Petersen, K.: Experiences from using snowballing and database searches in systematic literature studies. In: International Conference on Evaluation and Assessment in Software Engineering, pp. 17:1–17:10. ACM (2015)
2. Beck, L., Perkins, T.: A survey of software engineering practice: tools, methods, and results. IEEE Trans. Softw. Eng. **SE–9**(5), 541–561 (1983)
3. Buschermöhle, R., Eekhoff, H., Josko, B.: SUCCess and failurE of hard- and Software projectS (SUCCESS). BIS-Verlag der Carl von Ossietzky Universität Oldenburg (2006)
4. de Carvalho, D.D., Chagas, L.F., Lima, A.M., Reis, C.A.L.: Software process lines: a systematic literature review. In: Mitasiunas, A., Rout, T., O'Connor, R.V., Dorling, A. (eds.) SPICE 2014. CCIS, vol. 477, pp. 118–130. Springer, Heidelberg (2014)
5. de O. Melo, C., Santos, V., Katayama, E., Corbucci, H., Prikladnicki, R., Goldman, A., Kon, F.: The evolution of agile software development in Brazil. J. Braz. Comput. Soc. **19**(4), 523–552 (2013)
6. Diebold, P., Dahlem, M.: Agile practices in practice: a mapping study. In: International Conference on Evaluation and Assessment in Software Engineering, EASE 2014, pp. 30:1–30:10. ACM, New York (2014)
7. Diebold, P., Ostberg, J.-P., Wagner, S., Zendler, U.: What do practitioners vary in using scrum? In: Lassenius, C., Dingsøyr, T., Paasivaara, M. (eds.) XP 2015. LNBIP, vol. 212, pp. 40–51. Springer, Heidelberg (2015)
8. Dingsøyr, T., Nerur, S., Balijepally, V., Moe, N.B.: A decade of agile methodologies: towards explaining agile software development. J. Syst. Softw. **85**(6), 1213–1221 (2012). Special Issue: Agile Development
9. Dybå, T., Dingsøyr, T.: Empirical studies of agile software development: a systematic review. Inf. Softw. Technol. **50**(9–10), 833–859 (2008)
10. Fitzgerald, B.: The use of systems development methodologies in practice: a field study. Inf. Syst. J. **7**(3), 201–212 (1997)
11. Fritzsche, M., Keil, P.: Kategorisierung etablierter vorgehensmodelle und ihre verbreitung in der deutschen software-industrie. Research Report (in German) TUM-I0717, Technische Universität München (2007)
12. Georgiadou, E.: Software process and product improvement: a historical perspective. Cybern. Syst. Anal. **39**(1), 125–142 (2003)

13. Jackson, M.A.: A system development method. In: Tools and Notions for Program Construction: An Advanced Course, pp. 1–25. Cambridge University Press, Cambridge (1982)
14. Jones, C.: Variations in software development practices. IEEE Softw. **20**(6), 22–27 (2003)
15. Khurana, M., He, Z., Court, I., Ross, M., Staples, G., Wilson, D.: Software quality practices - an empirical study. Softw. Qual. J. **5**(2), 75–85 (1996)
16. Kitchenham, B., Charters, S.: Guidelines for performing systematic literature reviews in software engineering. Technical report EBSE-2007-01, Keele University (2007)
17. Komus, A., Kuberg, M., Atinc, C., Franner, L., Friedrich, F., Lang, T., Makarova, A., Reimer, D., Pabst, J.: Status quo agile 2014 (2014)
18. Kuhrmann, M., Fernández, D.M.: Systematic software development: a state of the practice report from germany. In: International Conference on Global Software Engineering. IEEE (2015)
19. Kuhrmann, M., Fernández, D.M., Tiessler, M.: A mapping study on the feasibility of method engineering. J. Softw. Evol. Process **26**(12), 1053–1073 (2014)
20. Kuhrmann, M., Konopka, C., Nellemann, P., Diebold, P., Münch, J.: Software process improvement: where is the evidence? In: International Conference on Software and Systems Process. ACM (2015)
21. Kuhrmann, M., Linssen, O.: Vorgehensmodelle in deutschland: Nutzung von 2006–2013 im überblick. MAW-Rundbrief **39**, 32–47 (2015)
22. Lagerberg, L., Skude, T., Emanuelsson, P., Sandahl, K., Stahl, D.: The impact of agile principles and practices on large-scale software development projects: a multiple-case study of two projects at ericsson. In: International Symposium on Empirical Software Engineering and Measurement, pp. 348–356. ACM (2013)
23. Lee, G., Xia, W.: Toward agile: an integrated analysis of quantitative and qualitative field data. MIS Q. **34**(1), 87–114 (2010)
24. Martínez-Ruiz, T., García, F., Piattini, M., Münch, J.: Modelling software process variability: an empirical study. IET Softw. **5**(2), 172–187 (2011)
25. Martínez-Ruiz, T., Münch, J., Piattini, M.: Requirements and constructors for tailoring software processes: a systematic literature rewview. Softw. Qual. J. **20**(1), 229–260 (2010)
26. Murphy, B., Bird, C., Zimmermann, T., Williams, L., Nagappan, N., Begel, A.: Have agile techniques been the silver bullet for software development at microsoft. In: International Symposium on Empirical Software Engineering and Measurement. ACM/IEEE (2013)
27. Papatheocharous, E., Andreou, A.S.: Empirical evidence and state of practice of software agile teams. J. Softw. Evol. Process **26**(9), 855–866 (2014)
28. Petersen, K., Wohlin, C.: A comparison of issues and advantages in agile and incremental development between state of the art and an industrial case. J. Syst. Softw. **82**(9), 1479–1490 (2009)
29. Rahim, M., Seyal, A.H., Rahman, M.A.: Use of software systems development methods an empirical study in brunei darussalam. Inf. Softw. Technol. **39**(14–15), 949–963 (1998)
30. Reifer, D.: How good are agile methods? IEEE Softw. **19**(4), 16–18 (2002)
31. Reifer, D.: Is the software engineering state of the practice getting closer to the of the art? IEEE Softw. **20**(6), 78–83 (2003)
32. Rose, G.B.: SSADM - the open methodology. In: IEE Colloquium on an Introduction to Software Design Methodologies, number Ref. No: 1991/181, pp. 6/1–6/5. IET, December 1991

33. Salo, O., Abrahamsson, P.: Agile methods in european embedded software development organisations: a survey on the actual use and usefulness of extreme programming and scrum. IET Softw. **2**(1), 58–64 (2008)
34. Senapathi, M., Srinivasan, A.: Sustained agile usage: a systematic literature review. In: International Conference on Evaluation and Assessment in Software Engineering, pp. 119–124. ACM (2013)
35. Senapathi, M., Srinivasan, A.: An empirical investigation of the factors affecting agile usage. In: International Conference on Evaluation and Assessment in Software Engineering, pp. 1–10. ACM (2014)
36. Solinski, A., Petersen, K.: Prioritizing agile benefits and limitations in relation to practice usage. Softw. Qual. J., 1–36 (2014)
37. Tripp, J., Armstrong, D.: Exploring the relationship between organizational adoption motives and the tailoring of agile methods. In: Hawaii International Conference on System Sciences (HICSS), pp. 4799–4806 (2014)
38. VersionOne. State of agile survey (2006–2014). http://www.versionone.com/agile-resources/more-resources/blogs/
39. Vijayasarathy, L., Butler, C.: Choice of software development methodologies - do project, team and organizational characteristics matter? IEEE Softw. (99), 1 (2015)
40. West, D.: Water-Scrum-Fall is the reality of agile for most organizations today. Technical report, Forrester (2011)

Tickets Without Fine

Artifact-Based Synchronization of Globally Distributed Software Development in Practice

Masud Fazal-Baqaie[✉], Marvin Grieger, and Stefan Sauer

s-lab – Software Quality Lab, University of Paderborn, Paderborn, Germany
{mfazal-baqaie,mgrieger,sauer}@s-lab.uni-paderborn.de

Abstract. Global software development projects are characterized by the collaboration of team members that are distributed among different locations and belong to different organizations. They bear their own specific challenges, especially if combined with an agile approach, so that established development processes might become inappropriate. Based on the experience with a real life industrial project involving organizations from India and Germany, we explain how the systematic design and implementation of an artifact-based and ticket-driven process can foster process conformance, transparency, and communication, and thus help to overcome these challenges.

Keywords: Global software development · Situational method engineering · Artifact-based development · Software development process · Ticket-driven development

1 Introduction

Distributed development projects become more and more important as even smaller and regionally oriented companies start to collaborate with near- and offshore companies due to cost pressure, lack of resources, or knowhow [1–4]. Often, the development cannot be completely outsourced to a single company, because onshore domain experts need to be involved or existing systems that are created and maintained by third party companies need to be extended and integrated [5]. This leads to situations, where virtual teams, spread over different locations, carry out projects on- and offshore [6].

Another trend that is gaining importance is the rise of agile development approaches, e.g., Scrum [7]. Agile development is characterized by stressing direct interaction and communication among team members and the customer. This is fostered, e.g., by creating only lightweight specifications on a "just in time" basis. In addition, the development is carried out in "sprints", which are development iterations of a few weeks duration, so that the working software can be demonstrated regularly. In fact, many companies strive to apply agile development, especially as it promises constant feedback in terms of runnable increments that assure the customer that the project is on the right track.

Continuous delivery and constant feedback makes agile approaches particularly appealing for distributed projects that quickly lack transparency and communication [8]. Especially for emerging development collaborations, where little to no previous

© Springer International Publishing Switzerland 2015
P. Abrahamsson et al. (Eds.): PROFES 2015, LNCS 9459, pp. 167–181, 2015.
DOI: 10.1007/978-3-319-26844-6_12

experience in working together exists, an agile approach appears to be highly beneficial to address the high degree of uncertainty [9].

However, successfully combining distributed and agile development is highly difficult. Due to their differences and distances in location, time, organization, language, culture, knowledge, and/or experience, virtual teams face a variety of challenges to communicate and coordinate their work [9–11]. To the contrary, in agile development good working communication and transparency is especially important and a key success factor. Co-location of the project members is often regarded as a prerequisite. As a result, project teams fail to adapt their conventional development process sufficiently to cater for the different situation. Often, the existing process is only changed slightly to accommodate the short development iterations of the agile approach, but the team then fails to implement bigger, more fundamental process improvements to address resulting issues [4, 12, 13]. Therefore, how can a project team systematically define and implement process improvements to come up with a "situational software engineering method" [14] for their project?

In this paper, we report on our experiences from an ongoing industrial project with distributed, agile development, where we implemented major improvements to address issues of the conventional process. Our contribution is four-fold: First, we provide insight into a real world example of a distributed agile development project. Secondly, we illustrate the challenges of such projects based on our example. Thirdly, we explain how an improved process is designed and implemented pragmatically, based on identified challenges. Finally, we present our experiences with the applied artifact-based, ticket-driven process. As we observed an improvement in process conformance, communication, and transparency, we assume it to be beneficial for projects with similar situations.

This paper is organized as follows: In Sect. 2, we provide background information about the project setup and explain the initial development process. In Sect. 3, we explain the issues of the initial process and the derived requirements for the new process. Thereafter, in Sect. 4, we illustrate the concepts of the new process, its implementation with a ticket system within the same project and the results. In Sect. 5, we conclude our paper with a summary and ideas for further research.

2 Background

In this section, we provide background information about the project, especially its organization and the initially used development process.

2.1 Project Organization

The development project is situated in the financial domain. The goal is to develop an online portal that provides self-service and reporting capabilities to end customers using a web application framework. Phase one of the project is scheduled for roughly one year of development and its goal is to deliver the initial version of the portal.

The organizations that are involved in the project are the client (a bank), the onshore partner (an IT company), us (the s-lab – Software Quality Lab), a design agency, and the offshore partner (an India-based company). The client, the onshore partner, the design agency, and we are all set up in different locations in Germany within half an hour to two hours of traveling. The offshore partner is situated in Bangalore, India. Table 1 provides an overview of the people and their tasks from the different organizations that are involved in this project and form the virtual team. As illustrated, there are about 15 team members that need to interact and to coordinate their activities, where most of the development is carried out by the Indian co-located team members.

Table 1. Project Organization

Person	Role	Tasks
Client Bank		
1 Department Manager	Business Owner	Provisioning and prioritizations of requirements
2 Department Members	Domain Experts	Answering of domain-related questions & provisioning of requirements; German user acceptance tests
1 IT Member	German Test Manager	German acceptance test management
Onshore Partner		
1 IT Project Manager	German Project Manager	Overall project management; management of German team members
1 IT Consultant	Architect / Infrastructure Manager	Integration of portal with the backend systems; Provisioning of development infrastructure
1-2 Developers	Backend-Developer	Backend system development based on our project requirements (external to our team)
s-lab – Software Quality Lab		
1 Researcher	German Requirements Engineer / Process Engineer	Analysis of requirements with client & communication of requirements to the offshore partner; Process monitoring & process adjustment
Design Agency		
1 Web Designer	Lead Designer	Design of look & feel
Indian Offshore Partner		
1 IT Project Manager	Indian Project Manager	Management of Indian team members
1 Business Analyst	Indian Requirements Engineer	Interface between Indian and German team members; Indian user acceptance tests
3 Developers	UI / Portal Developers	UI and portal development
1 Technical Expert	Portal Architect	Overall software architecture of Portal
1 Tester	Indian Tester	Indian thorough tests

2.2   Initial Process

Before the start of the development, the development process was discussed by the team. The German Project Manager requested the use of an agile approach with three-weeks-iterations for three reasons. First, the frequent deliveries should allow for constant feedback on the interpretation of the requirements. Secondly, going through all development phases quickly should unfold problems in the process and allow the team to learn based on previous iterations. Thirdly, being able to present results regularly should help to gain acceptance and reduce criticism in the involved project organization as well as outside the project team. The team agreed to the initial process that was proposed by the Indian Project Manager based on previous (agile) projects. The team agreed due to the following two reasons. First, the Indian company has the most exposure to and experience with distributed projects, so it seemed to be a good advice to follow its proposal. Secondly, the process minimized the adaption effort for the Indian team members who represented the biggest part of the team. It was also assumed that the German team members would be more capable of adapting to a new process.

Beside the process, the team agreed also on the use of two central specification artifacts demanded by the Indian team members: the *Functional Specification* and the *Technical Specification*. Both were described as "essential" by them. We will explain them in the following process discussion.

The initial process is depicted in Fig. 1. It shows the activities carried out to develop the features (where a feature is a coherent chunk of functionality) that are scheduled for a development iteration. Except for the first two activities (bordered gray), which are carried out in preparation of a sprint, all activities are carried out as part of the three-weeks-iteration. In the following, we briefly explain the activities in sequential order.

Creation of User Stories. The German Requirements Engineer (RE) creates *User Stories* based on requirements identified when discussing with the Business Owner and the Domain Experts. These are short functional requirement descriptions from the

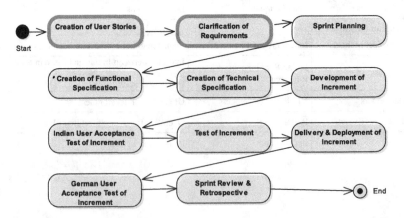

Fig. 1. The initial development process for the features developed in one development iteration.

perspective of a future system user that result in features of the system. For each *User Story*, a ticket is stored in the common ticket system available to the whole team.

Clarification of Requirements. The German RE explains the *User Stories* to the Indian RE via video conference or phone. The most important results are noted down as comments as part of the ticket.

Sprint Planning. During a video conference session, the team agrees on the *User Stories* that shall be in scope of a development iteration (called "sprint" according to agile terminology). This is driven by the effort estimation of the Indian team members for the different *User Story* tickets.

Creation of Functional Specification. The Indian RE creates a so-called *Functional Specification*, that covers all the *User Stories* that were scheduled for the sprint and that describes all user interfaces to the finest granularity, but without technical details. As part of this activity, clarification sessions take place between the Indian and German REs and, if not known to himself, the German RE gets the information from the Business Owner and the Domain Experts. The *Functional Specification* is a more or less structured text document (created with Microsoft Word) that has to be signed-off by the German RE and is attached in the ticket system.

Creation of Technical Specification. The Indian Developers create the *Technical Specification*, which is based on the *Functional Specification* and describes technical details of the solution design for all *User Stories* in scope of the sprint. It contains, e.g., database schemas and sketched components. This specification is created again as a text document, it has to be signed off by the German Architect, and it is attached to a ticket in the ticket system.

Development of Increment. The Developers develop and adapt features based on the Functional and *Technical Specifications*. We call the sum of all the implemented features "increment" according to agile terminology.

Indian UAT of Increment. The Indian RE tests the increment to check whether it conforms to the intention of the requirements (user acceptance test, UAT), i.e., that the requirements were understood correctly. He documents his results using a dedicated test management software.

Test of Increment. The Indian Tester tests the implementation for bugs, i.e., behavior unintended by the Developers like malfunctioning under certain conditions. He documents his results using a dedicated test management software.

Delivery and Deployment of Increment. The Developers prepare installation files containing the increment. With the help of the German Architect they send and deploy this delivery to the client-testing environment. They document the increment and its known issues in release notes that are attached to a ticket in the ticket system along with the delivery.

German UAT of Increment. The Domain Experts test the delivered increment under the supervision of the German Test Manager. The Business Owner also checks the delivery to get an impression of its quality. They document their results using spreadsheets that are attached to a ticket in the ticket system.

Sprint Review and Retrospective. In a video conference, the team discusses the results of the iteration and improvements of the development process for the following sprints.

3 Issues of the Initial Process

With the initial process, the team was able to successfully deliver a couple of increments. The frequent delivery helped to make results visible early on, even though there were challenges induced into the project from outside, e.g., contractual and infrastructural issues. The frequent deliveries helped the team to understand the goals of the project better. In addition, it helped to overcome initial doubts about the capability of the distributed team raised by some stakeholders.

However, over time, issues with the process became more and more visible, but could not be addressed sufficiently by local improvements to the process. In the following, we characterize the identified issues grouped by their causes. The issues are neither a direct consequence of the process alone nor caused by the distributed nature of the project alone. It is more the combination of both, process and situation, that caused the issues.

3.1 Specifications on Sprint-Level

The specification documents addressed a whole sprint instead of single features. This made it harder to handle them. For example, clarifications for a certain requirement *stalled the complete process*, as the documents were signed-off as a whole.

In addition, the team had the tendency to work with local copies, therefore they missed updates to the uploaded documents. In general, it was *difficult to accommodate changes*, as the documents were not very structured. Often it was not clear which parts needed to be updated and – more importantly – how updates of the *Functional Specification* needed to be propagated to the *Technical Specification*.

As a result, it was *difficult to postpone a scheduled requirement* and to replace it by another one, what became necessary, when scheduled requirements where blocked by technical dependencies that would not be resolved in that sprint.

3.2 Unsuitable Granularity of Specifications

The *Functional Specification* and the *Technical Specification* did not provide multiple levels of granularity. Therefore, it was not possible to agree on rough requirements, sign them off, and then work on the details. *Each clarification caused lots of rework on the details*. It was very *difficult to maintain the Functional Specification to keep up with the pace of changes and clarifications*.

Another issue, caused by the detailed *Functional Specification*, was the *tendency to overspecify* requirements. As it was unclear, what details would be important for the design and implementation, the Indian RE asked for as many details as possible. For example, the Indian RE requested details on the mechanism to notify the user about errors, without knowing whether there was a suitable mechanism already provided by the portal framework. He then precisely described that mechanism, so that the Developers did not know, whether there was a justified reason for the non-standard mechanism or whether they could use the built-in one.

Asking the German side for details also had the drawback that the Indian side would *stop thinking about the requirements and questioning the logic behind them*. For example, they implemented a table where two columns displayed the identical information to the user. Both columns were named "type", however supposed to show information for two different kinds of type. Not even the Indian Tester found it suspicious that they showed the identical information and no question was raised.

3.3 Missing Communication Cycles

The communication in the initial process was organized very sequentially from requirements over design and implementation to the testing. At the start of the sprint, only the selected *User Stories* were ready, but no design approach. Thus, it was *unclear what feature would be implemented and to which extend in the sprint*. Therefore, the Business Owner did not know what exactly to expect. This also caused that the *Developers had to make wild guesses for their effort estimation.*

Another issue was that the *Tester was not always able to test the implementation of a requirement*. For example, some functionality had to be triggered by the backend, but the Tester did not have means to trigger it manually. Thus, occasionally, the Developers missed to provide the means to test the implementation.

3.4 Missing Oversight and Transparency

With the initial process, it was very difficult to establish oversight and transparency. For example, the *sprint planning never really took place*, because *all* potential *User Stories* for a sprint were scheduled anyway, due to the bad effort estimation. On the contrary, *requirements had to be postponed regularly* to following sprints and the German team members were informed about that only at the end of the sprint. Postponing the specification for those requirements would have saved considerable effort during the sprint.

Sometimes, *activities were skipped* in order to hold the schedule, e.g., sometimes the development ended for some features, before the *Functional Specification* was delivered for sign-off. As a result, often there was a lot of uncertainty on whether the team was on track and what would be delivered at the end of the sprint.

Beside the issues for the current sprint, there was also *little transparency on what needed to be prepared* for future sprints, e.g. to integrate the backend system. Once the *Functional* and *Technical Specifications* where ready, there was only little time left for the German Architect to plan his activities, so the development stalled.

As it was not tracked explicitly, there was also *no overview on who was working on what or waiting for input from whom*. For example, there were contrary expectations on whether the Indian RE was waiting for the German RE or vice versa.

4 Improved Ticket-Driven Process

In the following, we describe the improved process that was designed to address the identified issues presented in Sect. 3. We first describe how we conceptualized our approach. Afterwards, we explain its implementation with a ticket system. We describe how we rolled-out the process within the same project and then explain our experiences with it.

4.1 Conceptualization

Our improved process focuses on reducing the early specification effort, while improving the transparency and communication. We base our redesign on an artifact-based software development methodology [15], where the process is driven by the created artifacts. This allows for a more fine-grained control over the specification of features. Specifications are split into artifacts per feature instead of artifacts per sprint. For this project, we defined features as functionality that can be implemented in a couple of days and that are mostly independent of each other.

Artifacts. Figure 2 shows a class diagram of our artifact types. As depicted, we defined a *Feature* artifact that contains three other sub-artifacts. When defining our artifacts, we focused on what is important in order to address the identified issues, therefore we omitted e.g. test-related sub-artifacts. Each artifact is structured in terms of its fields, which allows refining it stepwise by adding information field-wise. The feature-centric specification addresses the issues of the sprint-wide scope described in Sect. 3.1.

Artifact Lifecycles. Each artifact type has a defined lifecycle that allows us to differentiate several levels of maturity and/or granularity, i.e., control in detail, what part of the artifact needs to be described. In addition, for each state of an artifact, it is defined, which role is allowed to progress it from one state to another. Artifact lifecycles enable us to address the issues related to the unsuitable granularity described in Sect. 3.2 by controlling, which level of detail is provided.

We use the lifecycle of the *Requirements Specification* artifact to exemplify artifact lifecycles. This artifact replaces to some extent the purpose of the requirements artifacts of the initial process: *User Story* and *Functional Specification*. Figure 3 illustrates the states of a *Requirements Specification* artifact. The state "Sketched" is the initial state of a *Requirements Specification*. Once the German RE provided the "Summary/Story" and the "Functional Background", it is in state "Ready for Discussion" and can be reviewed by the Indian RE and discussed with the Indian team. Based on the discussion, the Indian RE refines the *Requirements Specification*'s description (and adds the "Key

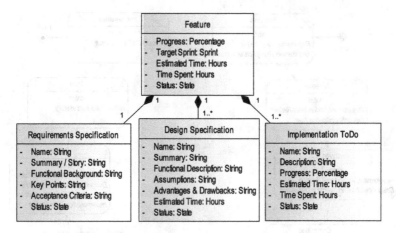

Fig. 2. The artifact model of the improved process.

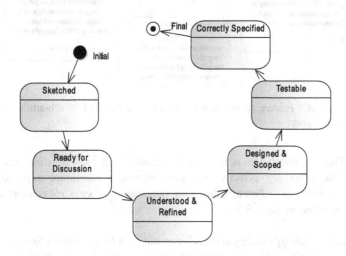

Fig. 3. The lifecycle of a Requirements Specification artifact.

Points"). Once the refinement is correct, the German RE sets it to "Understood & Refined". When the solution approach is determined, the *Requirements Specification* is extended with more details that reflect the design decisions and the scope of the *Feature* for the sprint ("Designed & Scoped"). This is reflected especially in the "Acceptance Criteria" that explain what should work from the user point of view after the requirement is implemented. In order to ensure Testability, the Indian Tester sets the *Requirements Specification* to "Testable", once he is convinced that it can be tested. This particularly addresses the testability issue described in Sect. 3.3. Finally, the German RE sets the *Requirements Specification* to "Correctly Specified" after a final check.

State-based Process Refinement. We use the introduced artifact states in order to define the improved process, where each artifact is only "barely good enough"

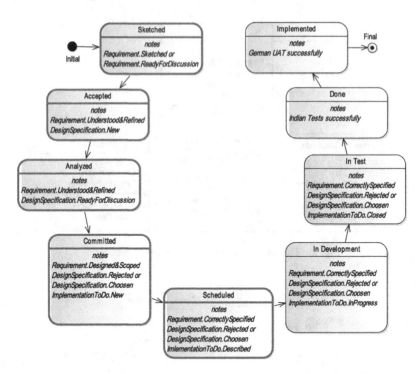

Fig. 4. Lifecycle of a Feature artifact that is based on the states of its sub-artifacts. Pre-sprint states are bordered gray.

described. That means that it is not overly detailed and too effort-intensive for the purpose of the following activity. We also introduce additional steps to enforce the interaction between different roles. Our state-based process refinement addresses the issues described in Sect. 3.3.

We exemplify this by looking at the relationship of a *Requirements Specification* and its *Design Specifications*. Figure 4 shows the lifecycle of a *Feature* that is based on the stepwise maturity and refinement of its sub-artifacts. Please note that it does not depict the process description for the new process (cmp. Figure 1 for process description of initial process). A process description defines the activities that need to be performed to progress a sub-artifact to the next state. As shown in Fig. 4, a *Feature* is in state "Accepted", if its *Requirements Specification* is understood and refined (as described before). It gets into the state "Analyzed", if design alternatives, which are created by the developers based on the *Requirements Specification*'s description, are ready for discussion. This involves that the necessary *Implementation ToDos* are created and estimated. A *Feature* is "Committed", once a *Design Specification* is picked for implementation and its *Requirements Specification* was designed and scoped. Only after this step, it can be "Scheduled" for a sprint. The example illustrates that requirements description and solution design are much more intervened in the improved process. This addresses the missing communication cycles of the former process (see Sect. 3.3).

Status-based Progress Measurement. As exemplified in the previous subsection, the progress of a *Feature* is based on the progress of its sub-artifacts and their status changes. This gives more transparency about the actual progress with a *Feature* and therefore with a sprint in general as the statuses are directly visible. It also speeds up communication as the status of a *Feature* and the status of its sub-artifacts have a defined meaning. This allows addressing the issues of missing oversight and transparency described in Sect. 3.4.

4.2   Implementation

Important for a pragmatic and applicable process is that it is properly integrated in the tools used as part of the project and that it is adopted to their capabilities [16]. We chose to use the ticket system Redmine[1] as our main tool, as it is the ticket system that has been already in use for the project and that is accessible by all team members from all involved organizations. Consequently, we had to implement a representation of the artifact types and their lifecycles.

Instead of representing all artifacts explicitly, we chose to combine *Features*, *Requirements*, and *Design Specifications* to a single ticket type. On the one hand, this simplifies the usage of the ticket system, because it reduces the number of different tickets to create and maintain. On the other hand, it makes it easier to ensure the consistency of the artifacts for one *Feature*, because all the information is located in one single ticket. However, this also means that artifacts are not shared among *Features*, e.g., *Implementation ToDos*. In addition, following the agile idea of backlog items, the specification of completed *Features* of former sprints is not updated. Therefore, the specification of *Features* might become outdated with changes in future sprints, but specification maintenance overhead is saved.

The different fields of the artifacts (e.g. Requirement summary or Design Specification functional description) were mainly converted into sections of the free-form text description field of a ticket. This implies that we had to standardize the description field for a ticket by providing a template containing the structure of the sections, as illustrated in Fig. 5. The sections of the description are filled in based on the progress of the *Feature*. For some fields (Feature target sprint or Feature estimated time) there exist dedicated fields in the ticket system that can be reused.

Regarding the lifecycle of the artifacts, we were not able to define all lifecycle states explicitly, due to the configuration of our ticket system. Therefore, we used and defined the meaning for the existing states of the ticket system to fit to our artifact lifecycles, e.g., we used the ticket status "New" for Feature sketched. In addition, we used the existing field "category" to reflect additional states, e.g. the state "Requirement testable" and the state "Requirement correctly specified". For *Implementation ToDos* we used the existing ticket type ToDo that provides all the required states and fields.

---

[1] www.redmine.org.

Status:	In progress		Start date:	01.04.2015
Priority:	8-normal		Due date:	
Assignee:			% Done:	10%
Category:	Correct/Specified		Estimated time:	34.00 hours
Target version:	DemonstrationSprint		Spent time:	0.30 hour
Cherwell Change Request:			Complexity:	
Description				

Requirement

Summary/story:

As a user I want to download monthly reports about my business. The company has to be able to push new reports to the reporting section, so that they appear in the reports download section of the user.

Functional Background:

A client receives various monthly reports on his business from the company. Currently the dealer is receiving these reports via mail and would like to have a download section on the portal where the client himself can download reports.

Key Points:

- The reports themselves are currently generated not by the backend system itself, but with another system using multiple information sources

Acceptance Criteria:

- I can upload a report using a mockup UI
- The uploaded report will show up accordingly in the users reports section
- The user can sort the reports by time and date

Design Specification

Summary:

[Brief summary of the approach that explains its core features to understand what is the difference to other solutions and what it comprises]

Functional Description of Solution:

The company pushes new reports to the portal via the integration component. Each user of a client can access the reports in a common download section. The entries will be shown dynamically based on the reports available in the database.

Assumptions:

- It is sufficient to refresh the reports section of a client every minute

Advantages & Drawbacks

- Reduce risk that reports cannot be created with data available to the portal

Fig. 5. A ticket of the ticket system combining a Requirement and Design Specification artifact.

4.3 Roll-Out

We rolled-out our improved process in the described project based on three elements. First, we documented the process using the wiki system of the ticket system. This ensures that the documentation is always available to the team and quickly accessible from the tool itself. In addition, we created a "Demonstration Sprint", where we created tickets that represent a *Feature* in its different lifecycle states. It serves as a practical example for what kind of description has to be provided for each state and for how a ticket evolves. Lastly, we taught the improved process using a webinar, where we used the wiki documentation and the Demonstration Sprint to illustrate the new process. To foster learning by doing, we then directly used the improved process for the preparation of the following sprint. Thereby we started with *User Stories* that were delayed from the earlier sprint and therefore already discussed and known. That allowed us to reduce the complexity of the transition and to focus more on the process than the actual clarification of the *Features*.

4.4 Results

The improved process is currently in use as the project is still ongoing. In the following, we want to report on our experience up to now and on what we have planned for the future.

Adoption and Process Conformance. Regarding its adoption, the process was adopted fairly well in a short period of time. Initially, we had some transition effort, mainly to encourage the team members to update the states accordingly. In contrast, the new structure of the ticket description seems to provide more precise guidance on *what* to describe and *how* to describe it and was adapted quickly. After a couple of days, the team started to understand the usage of ticket states and their importance. Since then, they made proper usage of the ticket system capabilities to reassign, comment, and change the status of tickets, such that the transparency improved a lot. However, even after several weeks, the proper usage of the ticket system has to be monitored and enforced, especially for the ToDos, where it is not always apparent that the status of a ticket was not updated. Some team members seem not to be aware of the importance of updated tickets for other people, such that we have to repeatedly communicate and stress this fact with the help of the project managers.

Transparency. Regarding the transparency, we were able to make a big step forward (cmp. issues in Sect. 3.4). The Business Owner and the Project Managers can utilize the ticket overview view of the ticket system to get an overview of the current sprint and the preparation of the following one. This is especially helpful during the weekly video conference between Germany and India, where the tickets serve as the basis for the discussion. In addition, every team member is able to drill down into individual tickets, where the ticket description provides a concise and consistent overview, especially of what functionality can be expected after its implementation. The German Architect, for example, stresses the improved transparency that allows him to get in touch early and proactively, if a Feature involves the integration of the portal and the backend system. Furthermore, everybody is able to see what needs to be done to bring a ticket to the next state.

Communication. Regarding the communication, the improved process also demonstrated its advantages. There is much more exchange between the German RE and the Indian teams already in early stages of requirements clarification and specification (cmp. issues in Sect. 3.3). Thus, early in the process, we discuss requirements in terms of technical solution approaches and their possible advantages and drawbacks. This allows to focus in the analysis of requirements on those details that, firstly, actually influence the later design decisions and, secondly, are important to limit the scope to what can be implemented in a few days (cmp. issues in Sect. 3.2). This accelerates the process overall. It also allows us to avoid overspecification and to postpone the discussion of details. If the functional and technical discussion of a ticket reveals that there are obstacles or open questions that do not allow to implement the ticket during a sprint, we are now also able to postpone it easily and prepone other tickets instead (cmp. issues in Sect. 3.1). In such cases, our ticket states allow us to keep track of the remaining steps to prepare postponed tickets.

Next Steps. For the following sprints, we want to further drive the ticket-driven idea and reduce the turnaround time of individual tickets. Currently, the team has the tendency to deploy and test tickets at the end of the sprint, even though they might have been implemented in the beginning. This is a habit from the initial process and obfuscates the actual progress. It also compromises the ability to demonstrate features to the Business Owner or Domain Experts already during the sprint, which would improve the transparency and communication even more.

5 Conclusions

In this paper, we presented an ongoing industrial project with a distributed, agile development process, where we implemented significant process improvements by adopting an artifact-based, ticket-driven process. As our first contribution, we provided background on the project and the decisions that let to its initial process and thus illustrated a real world example of a distributed agile development project. Afterwards, as our second contribution, we explained different process conformance-, transparency-, and communication-related issues that turned up with the initial agile approach, despite its advantages. These are very likely also relevant to other, similar projects. As our third contribution, we explained how we conceptionalized, implemented and rolled out process improvement in the context of a distributed project. Then, as our final contribution, we presented an improved artifact-based and ticket-driven process designed to address the discussed issues of distributed, agile projects. Based on the successful adoption and the improved process conformance, project transparency, and team communication, we believe it to be beneficial for similar distributed, agile project.

We will continue with our efforts to adopt a fully ticket-driven process by trying to reduce the ticket turnaround times. As connection point for future research in general, we see the use of a "ticket system 2.0" that allows defining sub-artifacts and their lifecycle states for a single ticket type. Further investigation is needed to find out, whether existing ticket systems from manufacturers like Atlassian, HP, or IBM already offer sufficient support. Such a system would allow replacing the manually structured and managed description text field of a ticket type (as in Fig. 5) with an automatically derived structure that is based on the defined sub-artifacts. In addition, the ticket states could be explicitly derived from sub-artifact states, based on defined rules. This would reduce the barrier to define an artifact-based, ticket-driven process and the manual management effort to use it. The system would need to allow the project team itself to perform the customizations for their project in order to ensure enough flexibility.

References

1. Conchúir, E.Ó., Ågerfalk, P.J., Olsson, H.H., Fitzgerald, B.: Global software development. Commun. ACM **52**(8), 127–131 (2009)
2. Kobitzsch, W., Rombach, D., Feldmann, R.L.: Outsourcing in India. IEEE Softw. **18**, 78–86 (2001)
3. Noll, J., Beecham, S., Richardson, I.: Global software development and collaboration: barriers and solutions. ACM Inroads **1**, 66–78 (2011)
4. Šmite, D., Wohlin, C., Gorschek, T., Feldt, R.: Empirical evidence in global software engineering: a systematic review. Empirical Softw. Eng. **15**, 91–118 (2010)
5. Damian, D.: Stakeholders in global requirements engineering: lessons learned from practice. IEEE Softw. **24**, 21–27 (2007)

6. Casey, V., Richardson, I.: Uncovering the reality within virtual software teams. In: Proceedings of the 2006 International Workshop on Global Software Development for the Practitioner, pp. 66–72. ACM (2006)
7. Schwaber, K., Sutherland, J.: The Scrum Guide (2013)
8. Herbsleb, J.D., Mockus, A.: An empirical study of speed and communication in globally distributed software development. IEEE Trans. Software Eng. **29**, 481–494 (2003)
9. Ramesh, B., Cao, L., Mohan, K., Xu, P.: Can distributed software development be agile? Commun. ACM **49**, 41–46 (2006)
10. Fazal-Baqaie, M., Sauer, S., Heuft, T.: Agile Entwicklung mit On- und Offshore-Partnern - Methodenverbesserung in der Praxis. In: Proceedings of Projektmanagement und Vorgehensmodelle 2014, pp. 59–69. GI, Köllen Druck+Verlag GmbH, Bonn (2014)
11. Nguyen-Duc, A., Cruzes, D.S.: Coordination of software development teams across organizational boundary - an exploratory study. In: ICGSE 2013, pp. 216–225 (2013)
12. Heijstek, W., Chaudron, M.R.V., Qiu, L., Schouten, C.C.: A comparison of industrial process descriptions for global custom software development. In: ICGSE 2010, pp. 277–284. IEEE (2010)
13. Fazal-Baqaie, M., Raninen, A.: Successfully initiating a global software project. In: Proceedings of the 22nd European & Asian System, Software & Service Process Improvement & Innovation Conference (EuroAsiaSPI2015). Publizon (to appear)
14. Fazal-Baqaie, M., Luckey, M., Engels, G.: Assembly-based method engineering with method patterns. In: Software Engineering 2013 Workshopband, pp. 435–444. GI, Köllen Druck+Verlag GmbH, Bonn (2013)
15. Engels, G., Sauer, S.: A meta-method for defining software engineering methods. In: Engels, G., Lewerentz, C., Schäfer, W., Schürr, A., Westfechtel, B. (eds.) Nagl Festschrift. LNCS, vol. 5765, pp. 411–440. Springer, Heidelberg (2010)
16. Fazal-Baqaie, M., Güldali, B., Luckey, M., Sauer, S., Spijkerman, M.: Maßgeschneidert und werkzeugunterstützt. Entwickeln angepasster Requirements Engineering-Methoden. OBJEKTspektrum (Online Themenspecials) RE/2013, 1–5 (2013)

Ontology-Based Identification of Commonalities and Variabilities Among Safety Processes

Barbara Gallina[1]([✉]) and Zoltán Szatmári[2]

[1] Mälardalen University, Västerås, Sweden
barbara.gallina@mdh.se
[2] Resiltech Srl, Pontedera, Italy
szatmari@mit.bme.hu

Abstract. Safety standards impose requirements on the process used to develop safety-critical systems. For certification purposes, manufacturers have to properly interpret and meet these requirements, which exhibit commonalities and variabilities. However, since different terms are used to state them, the comparative work aimed at manually identifying and managing these commonalities and variabilities is hard, time-consuming, and costly. In this paper, we propose to solve this problem by creating ontology-based models of safety standards and automate the comparative work. Then, we show how the result of this comparative study can be exploited to semi-automate the generation of safety-oriented process line models. To illustrate our solution, we apply it to portions of ISO 26262 and EN 50126. Finally, we draw our conclusions and future work.

1 Introduction

Safety standards impose requirements on the development process of safety-critical (software) systems. For certification/conformance purposes, manufacturers have to properly interpret and meet these requirements, which exhibit commonalities and variabilities. More specifically, commonalities and variabilities can be identified when comparing different criticality levels within the same version of a single standard, different versions of the same standards, or different standards within the same domain or even within different domains. The time and cost required for performing the comparative work increases when moving from one single version to different standards within different domains. This is due to the usage of different terms, which sometimes do not denote a different semantics. Irrelevant terminological differences are sometimes introduced for political reasons [1]. These differences slow down not only the provision of deliverables but also the audit of such deliverables. Identifying commonalities and variabilities is crucial to enable manufacturers to speed up the creation of process-related deliverables via systematic reuse. At the same time well-defined and managed reuse, speed up the audit process on the certification authority side. In the context of security-informed safety [2], irrelevant terminological differences contained within safety-specific and security-specific standards prevent cross-fertilization

© Springer International Publishing Switzerland 2015
P. Abrahamsson et al. (Eds.): PROFES 2015, LNCS 9459, pp. 182–189, 2015.
DOI: 10.1007/978-3-319-26844-6_13

as well as reuse. Authors state: The commonalities between safety and security are frequently obscured by the use of different concepts and terminologies. Indeed, there is considerable variation in terminology both within and between the safety and security communities. Thus, to achieve a shared understanding of the key concepts within each domain, there is a need to establish a lingua franca or even a common ontology [2]. In this paper, to ease the identification and systematization of commonalities and variabilities, we propose a new method called OPER, which stands of Ontology-based Process Elements Reuse. In our method, we propose to provide ontology-based models (given in compliance with OWL2.0) related to the safety processes mandated within the standards, then to semi-automate the identification of commonalities and variabilities. Finally, based on model-driven engineering principles, we propose to semi-automate the generation of Safety-oriented Process Line (SoPL) [3] models (given in compliance with SPEM (Software Process Engineering Meta-model) 2.0) based on the calculated commonalities and variabilities. OPER supports the creation of a lingua franca but at the same time allows certification bodies to preserve their specificities if this is required. The rationale behind OPER is that ontologies are able to capture domain knowledge in a precise way. Ontologies provide a natural formalism for representing domain knowledge and capturing constraints. In this paper, we use ontologies to capture the process (and SoPL) requirements. Then, we apply ontology-related reasoning to manipulate, validate the constructed models or transform them to a required representation. To show the usage and effectiveness of OPER, we apply it on small portions of safety standards. The rest of the paper is organized as follows. We present: essential background, in Sect. 2; OPER, in Sect. 3; OPER's application, in Sect. 4; finally, conclusion and future work, in Sect. 5.

2   Background and Related Work

Safety standards (focus on ISO 26262 [4] and EN 50126 [5]). Based on Gallina et al. [3], for both standards, we focus on a specific portion of the process that includes hazard analysis and risk assessment (HARA) activities. The portion is named Concept phase in ISO 26262 and Risk Analysis in EN 50126. For the HARA activities, we recall the required information that is necessary to understand our examples presented in Sect. 4. *ISO 26262-HARA clause* is aimed at: identifying and categorizing the hazards; formulating the safety goals related to the preventions/mitigations of the hazards. This clause consists of a number of tasks that need to be performed in a specific order: (1) Initiation of HARA, (2) Situation analysis, (3) Hazard identification, (4) Hazard classification, (5) ASIL determination, (6) Determination of safety goals, and (7) Verification of hazard analysis, risk assessment, and safety goals. *EN 50126-Risk Analysis Phase* is aimed at: empirically or creatively identifying the hazards associated with the system; estimating the risk associated with the hazards; developing a process for risk management. This phase consists of a number of tasks that need to be performed in a specific order: (1) Hazard identification, (2) Hazard classification,

(3) Risk evaluation, (4) Determination and classification of acceptability of the risk, (5) Establishment of the Hazard Log, (6) Assessment of all phase's tasks. **Safety-oriented Process Lines** -A *Safety-oriented Process Line* (SoPL) [3] is a family of highly related safety-oriented processes that are built from a set of core process assets in a pre-established fashion. Core assets can be classified as full or partial commonalities or variabilities [3]. A *partial commonality* denotes a composite process element (e.g., a task composed of steps) that contains a subset, which constitutes the commonality among all the composite process elements of the same type. For instance, two tasks represent a partial commonality if they contain a subset of equal steps. During the domain engineering phase [3], safety processes are compared to retrieve core assets: (partial) commonalities and variabilities. Once the core assets are defined, a safety process can be derived by performing two steps: (1) selection of all the (partial) commonalities plus the desired variants at variation points; (2) composition of the selected elements. **SPEM 2.0** -SPEM 2.0 [6] is the OMG's standard for systems and software process modelling. SPEM 2.0 offers support for modeling reusable process content as well as process variability. In SPEM 2.0, a process element (e.g. an activity) can be defined as a variability element and its variability type can be characterized. The *Variability Type* enumeration class defines the different types of variability. In this paper, we only recall one variability type, namely *contributes*, which logically replaces the original element (the base) with an augmented variant. In SPEM 2.0, the expected work can be broken down hierarchically via a series of elements (e.g., activities). **Ontology-related Concepts** -An *ontology* [7] is a model that represents a domain and is used to reason about the inter-related objects in that domain. An ontology generally includes: (1) Individuals (Objects) that are basic elements of the domain. (2) Classes that are sets of objects sharing certain characteristics. (3) Relations (properties) that are sets of pairs (tuples) of objects. Relations define ways in which objects can be associated to each other. (4) Attributes that are special relations where the class is related to a concrete domain (e.g. integer, string). To automate the analysis of an ontology (i.e., inference of logical consequences from a set of asserted facts or axioms and evaluation of model consistency), reasoners are used. Reasoners are also used to check whether a class is a subclass of another class(subsumption test). By performing such tests it is possible to compute the inferred ontology class-hierarchy, i.e., a class-hierarchy. Ontologies can be easily extended and combined. OWL2.0 (Web Ontology Language) [7] is an ontology language. An OWL2.0 ontology consists of a collection of facts, annotations, and axioms, which describe different items (individuals, concepts, relations and attributes). OWL2.0 can operate with different expression levels, called OWL2.0 profiles, which allow different sets of axioms. In this paper, we choose OWL2.0 EL, because it allows us to define: Subclass, Disjoint classes, Disjoint union and Equivalent Classes. A commonly used ontology development tool is Protégé [8] since it facilitates the use of several reasoners and provides application program interfaces (e.g., OWLAPI) for efficiently querying/manipulating the dataset, generated as the output of the reasoning. **Model-driven Engineering (MDE)** -MDE is a model-centric

software development methodology. Model transformations are used to refine models. A model transformation (e.g. Model-to-Model), defined as a set of rules, transforms a source model (compliant with one meta-model) into a target model compliant with the same or a different meta-model. **Related Work** -No related work exists on ontology-based identification of commonalities and variabilities among processes. As already extensively explained by Gallina et al. [3], SoPL is an extension of the *process line* notion.

3 OPER

OPER builds on top of previous work and combines principles related to ontologies, SoPL engineering, and MDE. OPER is constituted of three chained tasks, which are: T1 (Ontology-based safety process modeling), T2 (Ontology-based Commonalities & Variabilities Identification and Merging), and T3 (SPEM2.0-compliant SoPL model generation). **In T1**, a process engineer in cooperation with an ontology and a standards expert is responsible of modeling safety processes according to the best practices in ontology modeling (i.e., OWL2.0 EL). These models are also based on the SPEM 2.0-terminology. For instance, the structures that represent the breaking down of the work (e.g., process, phases, activities, tasks, etc.) are aligned. To model the processes, Protégé is used. To provide such models, we map SPEM 2.0 and OWL2.0 EL concepts. The mapping, shown in Table 1, focuses on concepts related to the process structure.

This structure describes a hierarchy of process elements, where phases are hierarchically broken down into activities/tasks/steps. Each process is represented as a tree (according to the graph theory terminology). We interpret the full and the partial commonality properties on two process elements in this hierarchy. The process elements are mapped to classes in the ontology, and the relations are expressed using object properties. For sake of clarity, we point out that we only consider a two-level hierarchy of work decomposition. **In T2**, the experts identify commonalities and variabilities in order to merge them within a single model representing an ontology-based SoPL. The trivial equivalences between corresponding process elements are defined. More precisely, an "equivalent of" axiom is added to the model (including the two safety process models) when two safety process elements are called in a different way in the different standards but they denote the same concept [9]. Based on the definition of full (or partial) commonality and the previously defined matching, our bottom-up algorithm identifies the safety process elements that have some type of commonality. Our algorithm is implemented in Java and uses OWLAPI. The first part

Table 1. Concepts mapping

SPEM2.0	BreakDownElement	Variability type	Equivalence relation	Composition of BreakDownElements
OWL2.0 EL	Class	ObjectProperty	EquivalentClasses Axiom	ObjectProperty

of our implementation consists of an algorithm aimed at constructing the common subtree, where the nodes are the process elements and the edges are the refinement relations between them. This algorithm traverses the safety process models (trees) and based on the defined equivalence relations the commonalities are identified. In order to get the SoPL model, the variabilities should be also added to the model. In the second phase the algorithm traverses each process model and identifies the variabilities and adds the required process elements to the process line model and connects them using the extends relation to the required model element. In our implementation the safety process-related trees are defined via a recursive data structure as presented in Table 2, column-1. Each node in the tree is an object that has a parent and that can be related to other nodes in the tree, via *composes* and *contributes* relations.

The pseudo code given in Table 2, column-2, represents a recursive function that is used to build a common subtree. The function is called with three process trees as parameters: the root elements (A and B) and a newly created root element of the common process tree (C). In each recursive call A, B, C logically represent the same node (same hierarchical level and process element). For each child tree nodes connected by a composes relation to the tree node represented by A we identify the equivalent pair in the set of child nodes of B. After a successful match, we add a new node (D) (based on the two equivalent nodes (nodeA and nodeB)) as a child node of C to the common subtree and start a new recursive iteration. **In T3**, the process engineer jointly with an ontology expert generates a SPEM2.0-compliant model representing the SoPL by using a model transformation implemented within a transformation engine. During this task, we define a transformation aimed at generating a SPEM 2.0-compliant SoPL model from an OWL2.0-compliant SoPL model. Our transformation (still part of an ongoing work) includes the following rules: (1) Identify the hierarchical levels of the process tree. The leaves in the ontology-based process tree are mapped onto the lowest level of the SPEM2.0 process structure. Then, by parsing the tree bottom-up, each parent node in the process tree is mapped to the next level of the SPEM2.0-compliant work breakdown structure. (2) Identify the base elements of the ontology-based SoPL: determine the root process element and by following the composes relation the common subtree can be identified. (3) Transform the base into SPEM 2.0 SoPL model: each process element in the common subtree should be transformed into a SPEM 2.0 work breakdown element based on the hierarchical level identified in the first rule. (4) Transform

Table 2. Pseudo code

Recursice data structure	Common subtree construction function
Structure TreeNode {	function buildCommonSubTree(TreeNode: A,B,C){
TreeNode: parent	foreach (nodeA=A->composes)
TreeNode[]: composes	if (hasEquivalent(nodeA,B->composes)
TreeNode[]: contributes }	nodeB=getEquivalent(nodeA,B->composes); D = new TreeNode(nodeA,nodeB);
	buildCommonSubTree(nodeA,nodeB,D) }

the variability-related part of the SoPL model. To do that, the following steps should be performed: (1) traverse the process tree by starting from the root process element; (2) follow both the composes and contributes relations. Every process element that is characterized by a contributes relation should be transformed into a variability element and its variability type attribute should be set to contributes.

4 Applying OPER

We construct the two ontologies that represent the safety processes. For each standard, we consider only one clause, see Sect. 2, (interpreted as SPEM2.0-task) and we only model one hierarchical level. The two safety process trees are depicted in Table 3, column-1, on the left-hand side, we can see the model of the EN 50126-*Risk Analysis* phase and on the right hand side the ISO 26262-*Concept phase*. Before executing the algorithm to create the SoPL model, we add the (partial) equivalence relations. In Table 3, column-1, these relations are shown by using dotted lines. After the execution of our algorithm, we obtain the SoPL ontology, depicted in Table 3, column-2. *HARA* represents a partial commonality. The naming of the new nodes is performed semi-automatically. First, if two nodes are merged into one single node, the names are concatenated automatically. Then, a manual post-processing performed in order to provide a human-readable name. For presentation purposes, in Table 3, column-2, we show the result of post-processing. Simplified names for the common process elements instead of the generated ones are given. In Table 3, column-2, we present the commonalities (via *composes*) and the variabilities (via *contributes*).

This ontology is built up from three parts using the ontology composition support: (1) the commonalities, the variabilities that are derived from (2) EN 50126 (marked in green) and from (3) ISO 26262 (marked in orange). By applying the transformation rules given in Sect. 3, we can manually create the SoPL model. Based on the model depicted in Table 3, column-2, the hierarchical level of the process elements can be specified and afterwards the base (common subtree) can

Table 3. Ontologies models

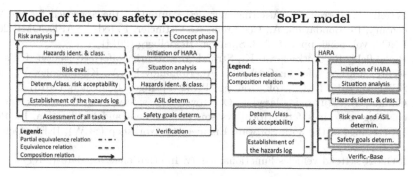

Fig. 1. Partial safety-oriented task line.

be mapped to SPEM 2.0 SoPL model. The variabilities (marked in orange and green) are mapped to work breakdown elements and the contributes relation is used to connect them to the required place in the model. The base, Base-Task in Fig. 1, can vary in an additive way via the contributes relationship to distinguish tasks that are compliant with either EN 50126 or ISO 26262.

5 Conclusion and Future Work

To reduce the complexity, cost, and time related to the interpretation and comparison of standards, in this paper, we presented OPER, a novel method that permits users to: (1) refer to a common process-related lingua franca, (2) semi-automate the standards comparison, and (3) generate SoPL models from safety process models represented via ontologies. The method was presented in the context of safety standards. However, more in general, it is applicable to normative documents that contain process-related requirements. In this paper, we focused on simple process structures. In a short-term future, we will tackle more complex structures. In cooperation with industry and assessors, we will properly define the concepts mapping that underlies the automated comparative work. In a medium/long-term future, we plan to provide a prototype of tool-chain (including THRUST [10]), aimed at providing evidence concerning the effectiveness in terms of time and cost reduction (manual vs. semi-automatic work).

Acknowledgments. This work is supported by the Swedish Foundation for Strategic Research (SSF) project SYNOPSIS-SSF-RIT10-0070.

References

1. Ferrell, T., Ferrell, U.: Assuring avionics – updating the approach for the 21st century. In: Bondavalli, A., Ceccarelli, A., Ortmeier, F. (eds.) SAFECOMP 2014. LNCS, vol. 8696, pp. 375–383. Springer, Heidelberg (2014)
2. Bloomfield, R., Netkachova, K., Stroud, R.: Security-informed safety: if it's not secure, it's not safe. In: Gorbenko, A., Romanovsky, A., Kharchenko, V. (eds.) SERENE 2013. LNCS, vol. 8166, pp. 17–32. Springer, Heidelberg (2013)
3. Gallina, B., Sljivo, I., Jaradat, O.: Towards a safety-oriented process line for enabling reuse in safety critical systems development and certification. In: Post-Proceedings of the 35th Software Engineering Workshop (SEW). IEEE, October 2012
4. ISO26262: Road vehicles Functional safety. International Standard (2011)

5. BS EN50126: Railway applications: The specification and demonstration of Reliability. Availability, Maintainability and Safety (RAMS) (1999)

6. Object Management Group: Software & Systems Process Engineering Meta-Model (SPEM), v2.0. Full Specification formal/08-04-01 (2008)

7. OWL 2 Web Ontology Language. http://www.w3.org/tr/owl2-syntax/

8. Protégé. http://protege.stanford.edu/

9. Pataricza, A., Gönczy, L., Kövi, A., Szatmári, Z.: A methodology for standards-driven metamodel fusion. In: Bellatreche, L., Mota Pinto, F. (eds.) MEDI 2011. LNCS, vol. 6918, pp. 270–277. Springer, Heidelberg (2011)

10. Gallina, B., Lundqvist, K., Forsberg, K.: THRUST: a method for speeding up the creation of process-related deliverables. In: Proceedings of the 33rd IEEE Digital Avionics Systems Conference, DASC (2014)

Human Factors in Modern Software Development

What Motivates Software Engineers Working in Global Software Development?

Sarah Beecham[⊠] and John Noll

Lero, The Irish Software Research Centre, University of Limerick, Limerick, Ireland
{Sarah.Beecham,John.Noll}@lero.ie

Abstract. Context: Working in a distributed environment poses new challenges to software engineer motivation.

Problem: Where should global project managers focus their efforts so that they have the best chance of motivating their teams, for higher staff retention, increased productivity and improved software quality?

Method: We asked a group of software engineers attending a workshop on global collaboration to complete a survey on software engineer motivation. We then identified motivation themes in the responses. Finally, we mapped these themes to software engineer motivators identified in previous research.

Results: Thirteen participants completed the survey. Analysis of the results yielded 27 motivation categories. The vast majority (23 of 27) were partially or wholly mapped to *Intrinsic* motivators.

Implications: We conclude that Global Software Development projects that relegate some teams to performing routine tasks (such as maintenance or testing) will experience lower productivity and quality due to demotivation. Finally, we hypothesize that GSD introduces new motivators, such as opportunities to travel and interact with different cultures.

Keywords: Global Software Development · GSD · Software engineer · Motivation · Empirical software engineering

1 Introduction

Highly motivated engineers working in distributed software development have a significant influence on project success [8]. Motivation can be viewed in terms of needs, and the key need for software engineers is to "identify with their task," which requires being given a task that is challenging, and understanding the purpose and significance of the task in relation to the complete system being developed. Software engineers' needs are complex: they also require regular feedback, trust, appreciation, rewards, a career path and sustainable working hours. Furthermore, among other fixed environmental factors, these motivators require sensitive tuning in line with a software engineer's personality and career stage [2].

Although motivation is a well-researched area, existing theories have not kept pace with today's fast changing software engineering environment [1]. The move

© Springer International Publishing Switzerland 2015
P. Abrahamsson et al. (Eds.): PROFES 2015, LNCS 9459, pp. 193–209, 2015.
DOI: 10.1007/978-3-319-26844-6_14

towards developing software globally places particular demands on software engineers, who are often required to work in globally distributed teams around the clock, communicate and collaborate with people with mixed values and cultural styles, and share code and development issues with team members they have never met in person. Global Software Development (GSD) is fast becoming the norm, regardless of the risk it poses to motivation [12].

Despite the depth of research conducted in GSD, there is a lack of understanding of motivational issues [8]. However before developing a model of motivation for GSD, we need a better understanding of how the software engineer's personal needs match the demands of the job [1]. For example, a mature and established strand of research based on the Job Characteristics Theory [5] is predicated on the belief that motivating software engineers depends on a good personality/job fit, where if you want an engineer to do a good job, "give them a good job to do [15]."

In this paper we conduct an empirical study to explore the characteristics and motivational needs of software engineers working in GSD. We particularly ask the question, "Do software engineers engaged in GSD share similar characteristics with the general population of software engineers?" Having some insight into the potential differences of the global software engineer is important, because if software engineers working in multi-site teams have different needs, then we need to re-think how they are managed. Alternatively, if the characteristics of software engineers working in GSD environments appear similar to those in the wider community of software engineers, then, we need to check whether their motivation is compromised by the environment. So the study we conduct here is a starting point to answering the wider question of how the global software engineer can survive and grow within a GSD environment.

2 Background

The power that motivation has on people in general and on the workplace in particular has given rise to many theories, that try to explain the conscious or unconscious decisions people make to expend effort or energy on a particular activity [22]. These theories inform techniques managers can adopt to motivate their software engineers to engage fully in their tasks, increase their commitment to the organization, improve their productivity, and produce higher quality software [2]. Creating the right conditions can also stimulate innovation [12]. Conversely, a demotivated workforce can lead to project failure [26].

Looking at motivation in a GSD context, we argue that some of the issues found in GSD can be addressed (even if partially) by meeting the motivational needs of software engineers [20]. For example, GSD is known to suffer from high staff turnover [7,16], and since motivation can in some instances have a positive effect on staff retention [14], ensuring that software engineers are motivated might be one way to reverse this trend.

So the question now remains, how can we motivate software engineers working in a distributed environment?

2.1 Software Engineer Characteristics

A review of the literature found that in nearly three-quarters (73%) of the cases software engineers form a distinct identifiable occupational group [2]. This finding indicates that studying motivation for software engineers as a separate profession could benefit managers of software engineers.

Of the many software engineer characteristics identified in the literature, "growth oriented", "introverted," and "need for independence" were the most cited, which indicates these occur across many different contexts (although not that they are the most important). However, some characteristics contradict each other, such as "introverted" (with a low need for social interaction), and "need to be sociable" and "identify with a group or organization." The view that software engineers are introverted reflects findings from the many studies coming from Couger and colleagues, that began in the 1980s, who measured the "Social Needs Strength" of engineers [5] in their Job Diagnostics Survey. This view is not universal as some studies characteristic software engineers as sociable people [2].

2.2 Software Engineer Motivation Factors

Table 1 presents an aggregation of the motivators from three motivation literature reviews covering over 150 empirical studies in software engineer motivation [2,9,11]. Since these reviews had many overlapping themes, we just give the original source in the right column. These distinct aspects are presented in Table 2, where Problem Solving, Team Working, Change, Challenge, and Benefit are some of the reasons people work in software engineering.

Examined chronologically, each review finds new factors. For example, França et al.'s 2011 review [11] found that software engineers are motivated by having fun, innovating, and even by punitive penalty policies. The importance of relationships with stakeholders outside the team is also new, suggesting that the task of developing software is enhanced if you know why and for whom the software is being developed. The most recent review included here, conducted in 2012 by De Farias et al. [9], looked at motivation of software engineers in a GSD context. They found that the GSD practitioner has specific and new needs, such as recognition of cultural differences and individuality. Clearly, new motivators are emerging, yet no work has been conducted to test whether all the historic motivators still apply.

Findings from Tables 1 and 2 are explored further in Sect. 4.

2.3 Demotivation and Herzberg's Two Factor Theory

Although motivation is important, managers of teams distributed across multiple sites need to be particularly concerned with factors known to demotivate, that are challenged by working in multi-site teams. According to Herzberg's two factor theory [15], Hygiene Factors (extrinsic motivators) have the power to demotivate if absent, but when present do not trigger the long term desired impetus and

Table 1. Software engineer motivators

ID.	Motivator	Type	Source	ID.	Motivator	Type	Source
M1	Rewards and incentives	Ext	[2]	M17	Identify with the task	Int	[2]
M2	Development/ training needs addressed	Int	[2]	M18	Autonomy	Int	[2]
				M19	Appropriate working conditions/infrastructure	Ext	[2]
M3	Variety of work	Int	[2]				
M4	Career Path	Int	[2]	M20	Making a contribution/task significance	Int	[2]
M5	Empowerment/ responsibility/ shared leadership	Int	[2]				
				M21	Sufficient resources	Ext	[2]
M6	Good Management	Ext	[2]	M22	Team quality	Ext	[11]
M7	Sense of belonging/team spirit	Ext	[2]	M23	Creativity/Innovation	Int	[11]
				M24	Fun (playing)	Int	[11]
M8	Work/life balance	Ext	[2]	M25	Professionalism/setting standards	Ext	[11]
M9	Working in successful company	Ext	[2]				
				M26	Having an ideology	Ext	[11]
M10	Employee participation	Int	[2]	M27	Non-financial benefits (availability of rewards)	Ext	[11]
M11	Feedback	Ext	[2]				
M12	Recognition	Int	[2]	M28	Penalty Policies	Ext	[11]
M13	Equity	Int	[2]	M29	Good relationship with users/customers	Int	[11]
M14	Trust/respect	Int	[2]				
M15	Technically challenging work	Int	[2]	M30	Recognition of cultural differences	Int	[9]
M16	Job security/stable environment	Ext	[2]	M31	Recognition of individuality	Int	[9]

positive energy of Motivator Factors (intrinsic motivators). Table 1 distinguishes these two factors in the 'Type' column.

Software engineers working in a multi-site team are likely to face many demotivating factors. These factors are discussed in full by the first author in [1], where a case study of an organization engaged in GSD found many instances where demotivators identified in a review of the literature [2] were causing problems. These demotivators are summarized in Table 3 and elaborated below.

Inequity. Remote working may mean the engineer misses out on training, growth, and promotion opportunities, may not share the same holiday allowances as colleagues, and may need to work anti-social hours or longer hours to communicate with colleagues in other locations.

Interesting Work Going to Other Parties. It is sometimes the case that complex tasks are retained at the "home" site, and that less motivating tasks such as testing or maintenance go to the remote teams.

Unfair Reward System. Performance may not be rewarded fairly if the remote software engineer is only noticed when there is a problem.

Poor Communication. Since these factors were identified outside of the GSD research, this demotivator is particularly significant, since many GSD related

Table 2. Motivating and demotivating aspects of software engineering [2,11]

ID	Motivating factor
Asp 1	Problem solving (process of understanding/solving a problem in programming terms)
Asp 2	Team working
Asp 3	Change
Asp 4	Challenge (Software Engineering as a challenging profession is in itself motivating)
Asp 5	Benefit (creating something to benefit others or enhances well-being)
Asp 6	Science (observing, identifying, describing, investigating, and explaining phenomena)
Asp 7	Experiment (trying something new, experimentation to gain experience)
Asp 8	Development practices (Object Oriented, XP and prototyping practices)
Asp 9	Lifecycle software development, project initiation and feasibility studies, maintenance
Asp 10	Creativity
ID	**Demotivating Factor**
De-asp. 1	Software process/lifecycle maintenance (also found to be a motivating activity)
De-asp. 2	Boredom (repetitive tasks)

issues can be traced back to poor communication. Poor feedback, and loss of direct contact with other team members and management can become a real barrier to motivation.

Bad Relationship with Users and Colleagues. The social side of working in a co-located environment is often lost when working remotely; this lack of face to face contact can result in mistrust and difficulty in building good relationships with colleagues. This factor was identified by Franca et al. [11] as an emerging issue.

Poor Working Environment. Being physically separated from the rest of the team, or the home site, is considered demotivating. This is often a pre-condition of working in multi-site teams, so very little can be done to change this despite the introduction of many GSD specific communication tools [23].

Role Ambiguity. Our previously published case study [1] showed that when working in remote teams, each member was expected to take on many different roles, and when asked to define his role; one person even admitted he had several business cards with different titles, one of which was left blank to be filled-in on-demand. While this ambiguity addresses the intrinsic need for variety and challenge, people can be overstretched, and also this ambiguity makes it difficult for team members to know where to go to for help and support.

Lack of Influence. Having no voice and being left out of decision making can easily occur when working in multi-site teams. In our case study [1], Project Managers working remotely with a client were clearly demotivated by head office interference when senior management discussed issues with the client without involving the on-site project manager.

Other demotivators specifically concerned with the software engineering task are listed in Table 2 as "De-asps." De-motivators are not necessarily the opposite of motivators, and so should be treated separately.

Table 3. Demotivation factors selected from [2, p. 869] fuelled by GSD

ID[a]	Demotivator factor fuelled by GSD (related motivator from Table 1)	Source
D3	Inequity (M13)	[1, 27]
D4	Interesting work going to other parties (M15)	[1, 27]
D5	Unfair reward system (M1)	[1]
D6	Lack of opportunities; stagnation; career plateau; monotony; poor job fit (M4, M17)	[1, 27]
D7	Poor communication (M11, M6)	[1]
D10	Bad relationship with users and colleagues (M22, M29)	[1]
D11	Poor working environment (M19)	[1]
D14	Poor cultural fit/stereotyping/role ambiguity (M30, M31)	[1]
D15	Lack of influence/not involved in decision making (M10)	[1]

[a] Beecham's [2, p. 869] original numbering retained.

2.4   GSD Environmental Impact on Motivation

Although some research suggests that the needs of a global software engineer are similar to those of the general population of engineers [8], we still do not understand how working in a distributed environment places specific challenges to these motivators.

To clarify the impact multi-site development has on software engineer motivation, we consider factors associated with GSD that may trigger discontent, as suggested in Šteinberga and Šmite [27], and our previous work [1], and summarized in Table 4.

Table 4 ignores factors from Table 1 that are similar in both collocated and GSD contexts. The factors are an aggregation of findings from Šteinberga and Šmite's theoretical study [27], and our previous empirical study [1]. For transparency, the source of the inhibitor is included in the table. Also, since the treatment and outcome of motivators are likely to be predicated on whether the motivator is a hygiene factor or a motivator, the table is also divided into Intrinsic and Extrinsic needs. We also add new factors introduced by De Farias [9], since these factors are all associated with GSD.

Table 4 contains twice as many intrinsic motivators as extrinsic motivators that are potentially compromised by working in GSD. This is extremely important, as intrinsic motivators have longer-term effects on motivation.

The research literature doesn't as yet explain whether GSD attracts a different type of engineer to the type of engineer who traditionally worked in a collocated team. Therefore, before we plan how to motivate our software engineers who work in multi-site teams, we need to establish who exactly we are dealing with. It could be that what we have learned about software engineer motivation previously needs to be revisited. The current state of practice in GSD motivation is unclear, leaving us asking:

"Do software engineers engaged in GSD share similar characteristics and needs to those engineers in the general population?"

To address this question, we conduct an empirical study, with a group of practitioners working in GSD, which we discuss next.

Table 4. Motivation factor inhibited by GSD (related motivators/aspects from Table 1/Table 2)

ID	Intrinsic motivators/aspects	Source
I1	Team work (Asp 2)	[27]
I2	Equity (M13)	[1]
I3	Development practices (Asp 8)	[1,27]
I4	Technically challenging work (M15)	[1,27]
I5	Identify with the task (M17)	[1]
I6	Autonomy (M18)	[27]
I7	Empowerment and responsibility (M5)	[1,27]
I8	Trust and respect (M14)	[1,27]
I9	Employee participation (M10)	[1,27]
I10	Career Path (M4)	[1]
I11	Making a contribution (M20)	[1]
I12	Recognition (for doing a good job) (M12)	[1]
I13	Recognition of cultural differences (M30)	[9]
I14	Recognition of individuality (M31)	[9]
ID	**Extrinsic motivators/aspects**	**Source**
I15	Sense of belonging (M7)	[1,27]
I16	Feedback (M11)	[27]
I17	Rewards and incentives (M1)	[1]
I18	Good Management (M6)	[1]
I19	Work/life balance (M8)	[1]
I20	Appropriate working conditions (M19)	[1]
I21	Sufficient resources (M21)	[1]

3 Method

We conducted an empirical study to investigate the research question posed in Sect. 2: RQ: "Do software engineers engaged in GSD share similar characteristics and needs to those engineers in the general population?"

Data Collection. We held a two day workshop on GSD with a diverse a group of practitioners who work in a multi-national organization, and are all involved in developing software in distributed teams across Europe. During a session dedicated to motivation, participants answered a survey on what motivates them.

The survey, as shown in Table 5, was an adaptation of a set of motivation questions created by Helen Sharp and Mark Dalgarno for use in industry motivation workshops [24], and was designed specifically to reveal what motivates practising software engineers. The survey comprised two parts: a set of questions about

Table 5. Motivation survey questions

Individual Background	What Motivates software engineers?
1. What role in software development are you aligned to?	1. What aspects of your work in software engineering do you get most satisfaction from?
2. What is your nationality?	2. What makes you stay working in software engineering?
3. How many years experience do you have in software development in your current role?	3. What factors attracted you to work in software engineering?
4. How many years experience in software engineering do you have? (If different roles, please list all and number of years for each).	4. What makes software development worthwhile to you?

the respondent's background and experience, and a series of questions about the respondent's motivation.

Note that we retained the word 'satisfaction' in our survey since it is often used to measure software engineer motivation. For example, satisfaction is considered in great detail in the Job Diagnostics Survey for Data Processing Personnel (JDS/DP) tool [4] that is used extensively to measure software engineer motivation.

This survey exercise was followed by an interactive presentation on software engineer Motivation that included a summary of what are considered typical characteristics and motivators of software engineers according to the systematic literature review on software engineer motivation [2].

Data Analysis. We aggregated the responses to four demographic questions to create a picture of the respondents background and experience as a group. We then analyzed the responses to the questions in part 2 of the survey, grouping the survey responses into themes (see Sect. 4) using content analysis [19].

Validation. At the end of the motivation session, two final questions were posed to the practitioners: "Do you think you form a distinct group of professionals, that are different to other professions?" and "Given the list of characteristics, do you think you are typical?" There was a unanimous agreement with both questions.

4 Results

Our sample represented practitioners from six different countries, who all participated in the global collaboration workshop held in Turkey (a venue chosen specifically as a neutral place since none of the participants were based in Turkey). The participants comprised a team of software engineers who were all working on the same software development project. Many of these engineers had not met face to face before the workshop (since they were based in different countries). This group had (on average) been working in their current roles for just under seven years with an average total software engineering experience of nearly twenty-seven years. The current roles of all participants require them to

Table 6. Demographics of survey respondents

Experience (years)				Min	Max	Avg
In current role				<1	20	6.5
Total Software Engineering				4	34	26.5
Nationalities	**France**	**Germany**	**Spain**	**UK**	**India**	**Argentina**
Num. respondents	1	4	3	3	1	1
Roles	**Developer**		**Project Mgr.**		**Senior Mgr.**	
Num. respondents	5		4		4	

develop software across globally distributed teams; we can therefore assume that this group have, on average, a minimum of seven years experience in GSD. These figures are summarized in Table 6.

As mentioned in Sect. 3, we assigned a category to each phrase or statement in a survey response. In total, 97 such statements or phrases were analyzed and grouped into 27 categories. In some cases, a phrase fell into more than one category; regardless, the majority of statements fell into the top seven categories.

Table 7 shows how the respondents answered each question in the survey; the results are presented as the number of respondents who responded in a given category, and the number of responses in each category. These results indicate that creating working software products (as represented by the "Construction/delivery/completion" category) is the aspect of software engineering that the most respondents mentioned (11 total), and is also mentioned most often (17 responses) overall, and the most often as the most satisfying aspect of software engineering (Question 1, 10 responses). This category comprises statements such as "Get things done (and working)," "Seeing product through to implementation," and "seeing disparate parts come together to complete a project." One respondent even identified "Construction" explicitly as the aspect from which he received the most satisfaction.

"Construction..." was followed by challenge and creativity ("Problem solving," "Technical innovation/novelty/creativity," and "Dynamic challenge/change/variety/flexibility"), "Impact", and "Familiarity with task/role/aptitude." Statements such as, "Solve problems, finding errors," "It allows me to show a creative side of me," and "Challenges: working in a dynamic environment" capture challenge and creativity; one respondent went so far as to say he found satisfaction in the fact that software engineering was "Unpredictable - never sure what you will be doing next year."

Extrinsic motivators, such as salary or other rewards, were mentioned rarely by this group. One respondent did mention that it "would be difficult to switch to something else at same pay level," and another said there was "Good money" in the profession; but overall, barely 5 % (5 responses total) mentioned monetary reward at all, and none identified this as the most satisfying.

Table 7. Response categories, motivators, and aspects relating to the task

Category	# Resp.	Q1	Q2	Q3	Q4	Tot	Motivators (Table 1)	Aspects (Table 2)	Ex-/Intrinsic
Construction/delivery/completion	11	10	3	3	1	17	New	New	Int
Problem solving	8	4	2	4	2	12	M15, 23	Asp 1	Int
Impact (economic/lasting)	7	2	2	1	5	10	M20	Asp 5	Int
Dynamic challenge/change/variety/flexib'y	7	2	3	2	3	10	M3, 15	Asp 3, 4	Int
Familiarity with task/role/aptitude	7		2	4	1	7	M17	–	Int
Technical innovation/novelty/creativity	6	4	3	3	3	13	M23	Asp 10, 7	Int
Vibrant market/profession/field/opp'nities	5	1	2	1	2	6	M1, 4, 9	Asp 3, 4	Both
Economic reward/necessity	5		2	2	1	5	M1, 16	–	Ext
Intellectual challenge/complexity	4		2	2	1	5	M15	Asp 4	Int
Sense of achievement	4			2	3	5	M17, 20	–	Int
Teamwork	4	1	1	1	1	4	–	Asp 2	Both
Intellectual curiosity	3	1	2	2	0	5	M23	Asp 6, 7, 10	Int
Tangible recognition of contribution	3	2			1	3	M1, 11, 12	–	Both
Sense of competency/knowledge sharing	3		2		1	3	M17	–	Int
Sense of belonging/friendship/community	3		1	1	1	3	M7, 10, 22	Asp 2	Both
Seeing the big picture	3	3				3	M17, 20	Asp 5	Int
Personal growth and development	3				3	3	M2, 4	–	Int
Customer/user satisfaction	3	3				3	M29	–	Int
Promoting teamwork	2	2	1			3	M7, 22	Asp 2	Both
Enjoyment/fun/play	2		1		2	3	M24	–	Int
Job stability	2		1		1	2	M16	–	Ext
Inertia	2		2			2	M16	De-asp 2	Ext
Travel	1		1			1	M27, 30	–	Both
Interaction	1	1				1	M1, 7, 10, 30,	Asp 2	Both
Goal oriented	1	1				1	M17	–	Int
Equity	1			1		1	M13	–	Int
Cultural mix	1		1			1	M30	–	Int

When asked, "what makes you stay working in software engineering?" extrinsic motivators were more commonly cited, but the majority still favored intrinsic motivators. Intrinsic motivators were also the majority reason for choosing the field in the first place (Question 3).

Question 3 elicited responses indicating an aptitude for thinking logically and problem solving, as represented by statements such as "Computers are not vague; there is an optimal solution," "Fits my logical way of thinking," and "Technical subjects were easy at school." Others seemed attracted by the opportunity to respond to challenge with creativity: "Build something that do[es] not exist before," "Challenge to overcome," and "Creativity" are examples.

In contrast to Question 1, when asked "What makes software development worthwhile to you?" (Question 4), "Impact" was the most common response category, as exemplified by statements like "Knowing that what I do has an economic impact" or "Solving problem[s] helping others." One respondent went so far as to claim, "The result is ageless..." Impact was followed by challenge and creativity, such as "Challenging yourself" and "Creating something new."

As with the other questions, intrinsic motivators dominate the responses to this question.

This effect is summarized in Table 7. This table shows, in descending order of frequency, the response category, number of respondents who made statements falling into that category, number of statements from all questions that fall into that category, and Motivators from Table 1 that apply to the category. Also shown is whether the category represents Intrinsic or Extrinsic motivation, or both; and Aspects from Table 2 that apply to the category. As can be seen from the last column ("Ex-/Intrinsic") in this table, the vast majority of categories seen in the survey responses represent intrinsic motivators, and only one of the top *twenty* response categories is wholly extrinsic.

5 Discussion

The motivation literature does not, as yet, include comprehensive guidelines for motivating software engineers engaged in Global Software Development. However, before going forward with specific guidelines, we need to know whether engineers who are engaged in GSD are similar to those engineers drawn from the general population. Our research question, "Do software engineers engaged in GSD share similar characteristics and needs to those engineers in the general population?" addresses this point.

The needs of software engineers are changing, as reflected in the new motivation factors found in reviews of motivation [9, 11] that update the initial study of software engineer motivation published in 2008 [2]. And in our empirical study here, we have found new motivators: "Construction, delivery and completion of the product," "travel" and "cultural mix." This growing list of motivators (see Table 1) suggests that there might be a shift in what today's software engineer needs. However, what isn't clear from this research is whether all those historical factors listed in Table 1 are still important to the global team member.

Results of our empirical study with a small, but experienced group of practitioners working in distributed teams, found many familiar factors were important, as shown in the mapping of survey responses to known motivators in Table 7. And indeed, the engineers themselves felt they fit the general software engineer profile. However, a closer inspection of their survey responses revealed some differences.

This group of developers are highly motivated by intrinsic factors (19 of the top 20 motivators were partly or entirely intrinsic). Also, they found 20 of the 31 factors in Table 1 as motivating. Of note is that most of the eleven motivators that they did not identify with are extrinsic (Table 8), such as having a work/life balance, working conditions, sufficient resources, and good management.

These results are consistent with Herzberg's two factor theory, which states that *lack* of extrinsic motivators can be demotivating, but their *presence* is not necessarily motivating over the long term. A typical extrinsic motivator is "right office conditions," where an excessively-noisy, over-heated office can demotivate, but having the right noise level and temperature won't be exciting long term (or

Table 8. Motivators not expressed in survey responses

ID	Motivator	Type
M5	Empowerment/responsibility/shared leadership	Intrinsic
M6	Good Management	Extrinsic
M8	Work/life balance	Extrinsic
M14	Trust/respect	Intrinsic
M18	Autonomy	Intrinsic
M19	Appropriate working conditions/infrastructure	Extrinsic
M21	Sufficient resources	Extrinsic
M25	Professionalism/setting standards	Extrinsic
M26	Having an ideology	Extrinsic
M28	Penalty Policies	Extrinsic
M31	Recognition of individuality	Intrinsic

perhaps even short term). It is clear that if an engineer has an excessively hot office, or too much noise (extrinsic demotivator) he or she many not be able to take advantage of the challenging job (the intrinsic motivator). A further concern is that a workforce that focuses on extrinsic motivators, such as salary, visiting exotic countries, and mixing with different cultures, may only be motivated in the short term. Travel and salary may attract a software engineer to a job, however it is the interest and engagement with the job itself that will keep the engineer in the job, and will excite him or her to produce better software. As such, those managers who can influence motivation not only need to ensure that extrinsic motivators are not acting as a barrier to motivation, but also need to promote intrinsic motivation.

Tapping into the intrinsic motivation needs of the software engineer – those motivators associated with the job itself – correlates to desirable outputs such as low staff turnover, higher productivity, and better quality software [2]. Even though motivation is just one of many complex factors that reduce software defects [8], the message is, "ensure the workforce have the right intrinsic motivators in place," such as the right level of challenge, variety, recognition, participation, etc. But beware: if the extrinsic motivators are not also addressed, intrinsic motivators, even if in place, will not have the power to motivate.

Of the areas we identified as potentially challenged by working in GSD (Table 4), a worrying nine of 14 intrinsic motivation factors (I1, I2, I4, I5, I9, I10, I11, I12, and I13) potentially inhibited by Global Software Development would be considered important by our survey respondents. However, there is no indication that factors such as I3 ("Development Practices"), I6 ("Autonomy"), I7 ("Empowerment and responsibility"), I8 ("Trust and respect"), and I14 ("Recognition of individuality"), were important intrinsic reasons for them to work in software engineering. This might be a reflection of the fact that the majority of respondents were highly experienced people in senior positions; as such, they would likely have a great deal of autonomy and command respect, and would not be so concerned with development practices themselves (although they might be concerned about which practices their teams use). Regardless, it's clear that in contrast, only I15 ("Sense of belonging"), I16 ("Feedback"), and I17 ("Rewards and incentives") were considered to be important extrinsic reasons to be in the field.

More importantly, only *one* demotivating factor (D11 "Poor working environment") would *not* be considered relevant to this group.

These results have important implications for project managers in charge of Global Software Development projects: to the extent that our respondents are representative of practitioners working in GSD, their motivational needs are not the kind that can be satisfied by "throwing money at the problem." Giving the teams fancy offices with powerful workstations and free food is not going to result in a lasting motivational effect. Rather, managers must understand and cater to each team's need for technically challenging work developing, in a team context, a product that has impact, with opportunities for career growth.

Returning to the research question posed in Sect. 2: "Do software engineers engaged in GSD share similar characteristics and needs to those engineers in the general population?" we find that our survey participants share many motivation factors with software engineers in general. However, two important differences are apparent.

First, our respondents appear to be more motivated by intrinsic factors than the general software engineer population, and seem to be less interested in hygiene factors: the bulk of factors (7 of 11) listed in Table 8 as not being present in the survey responses are extrinsic.

Second, there appears to be a new factor – "Construction/delivery/completion" – that is important to this group, but has not been identified by previous research.

These differences imply that, while the software engineer working in GSD looks very similar to the engineer working in the general population, he or she is even more interested in intrinsic factors, and less influenced by hygiene factors. Therefore, we need to think carefully about those intrinsic motivators that are challenged by GSD.

5.1 Hint at a Solution

To stimulate individual intrinsic motivation (and, in turn, a team's motivation), hygiene factors must be considered, since a lack of these factors can lead to demotivation. Motivation is a social process that defines how people join, remain part of, and perform adequately in, a human organization [17]. The global organization is a social arrangement comprising members who must be motivated to join, to stay, and to perform at acceptable levels. It is within a social context that teams working remotely are encouraged to work harder and more effectively. Some research suggests that social interaction itself can be motivating [22].

Developing software is essentially a human intellectual and social activity [3,10,13,18,25]. If the work is viewed as repetitive, boring, and fragmented, then the individual may not feel part of the overall organization and may perceive his or her work to be meaningless. It is important for engineers' motivation that they perceive that their contributions matter [6,13]. Research shows that monotony creates apathy, dissatisfaction and carelessness [6,21,25], especially when an individual does not develop new skills. However, an under-researched need is career advancement in GSD, which can be problematic. For example, if a programmer desires to become a software architect, he or she needs to see a career path and be given an opportunity to learn related new skills. Working remotely can mean the individual either doesn't have the scope to advance up the career ladder, or may be overlooked due to lack of visibility to upper management.

6 Conclusions

This paper attempted to answer the question, are software engineers who work in Global Software Development contexts motivated by different factors than software engineers working in a co-located setting?

We started with a list of thirty-two factors from the literature that have been shown to motivate software engineers in a co-located development environment. These are divided into intrinsic and extrinsic motivators. We then compared these factors to a set of motivators identified from a survey of software engineers engaged in Global Software Development.

What we discovered is that, whether working in a co-located or distributed environment, software engineers are motivated by the same factors, especially, a need for challenging, creative work with impact for customers and users. However, our results indicate software engineers working in Global Software Development are less interested in extrinsic than intrinsic factors. This has important implications for managers of distributed software development projects, as certain aspects of distributed software development can interfere with many intrinsic factors [1].

We also identified a new motivator having to do with building and delivering a working product. This was the most commonly cited factor, and means that managers need to ensure all teams contribute meaningfully to creating and delivering the product.

It appears that the global software engineer profile is changing; there is less interest in those environmental factors that can act as barriers to motivation. This research suggests, that those engineers that remain in globally distributed teams for the long term, are resilient to the demotivating factors that are inherent in GSD.

6.1 Limitations

As with any empirical study, the results presented in this paper are subject to certain limitations and threats to validity.

Construct Validity. The chief threat to construct validity involves how we determined what motivates this group: do the questions we asked actually reveal the motivators of our respondents?

Our survey is derived from a earlier survey used by Helen Sharp [24]; so, to the extent that the original survey is valid, ours is too. Further, the survey explores motivation from four perspectives using four different questions (satisfaction, remaining in post, attraction to post, and what make the job worthwhile), so we do not rely on a single construct to measure motivation.

Internal Validity. Two threats to internal validity are present in this study. The first is selection bias due to the fact that all participants were working for the same company. This could introduce a confounding factor due to some characteristic of the organizational culture or the domain in which it operates that are inherently motivating.

The second threat is researcher bias. The coding process relies heavily on researcher interpretation of statements written by the respondents; the researcher's background or experience could influence this interpretation. However, this bias is mitigated by having two researchers with different backgrounds and cultures independently analyze all statements; this increases the likelihood that the final agreed category for each statement is based on the statement's actual meaning.

External Validity. The participants in this study share certain characteristics that are different from the general population of software developers engaged in GSD. First, they were all male, highly experienced, and more than half were project managers or senior management (however all were involved in the software development). In addition, all but two were of European background, and all were currently working in Europe. As such, they are unlikely to be motivated by some of the things that might motivate junior developers, and may not share the same motivators as their counterparts in Asia or North America (although we have no reason to believe they do not). We should, therefore, be cautious about generalizing the results seen here.

We also note that the sample size of 13 participants is very small, and our future plans are to extend this short, easy to administer, survey to capture the motivators of the wider population of Global software engineers. Also, we need to add specific GSD questions in the new survey to include recognition of a) Development process applied, and b) Whether the participant is working at a central office or a remote/satellite location. Nevertheless, results from our small sample, allow us to form hypotheses for future research which we put forth below.

6.2 Future Directions

While this paper has focused on the factors in GSD that can demotivate software engineers, there are likely to be many aspects unique to GSD that can tap into both the intrinsic and extrinsic needs of software engineers. To motivate further research in this area, we propose the following hypotheses derived from our observations:

Global Software Development projects in which some teams are not directly engaged in creation of new products or significant new functionality will experience lower productivity due to lack of motivation. This hypothesis is based on the observation that "construction/delivery/completion" is the category with the most responses from our survey. It follows that teams who are not given a significant role in the development and delivery of the product will lack this important motivator, and as a result the project as a whole will experience lower productivity and quality.

Global Software Development projects in which some teams are allocated routine tasks will experience issues due to lack of motivation. This hypothesis stems from the frequency that intellectual challenge, innovation, and creativity were cited by respondents as important motivators. Teams who are solely responsible for routine maintenance or testing will not have the same intellectual challenges as teams involved in creating new products or significant new features. And, such teams may lack a sense of belonging to the core contributors, or even perceive the difference in task allocation to be implicit negative feedback on their performance. The absence of such extrinsic motivators can be *demotivating* [15].

Some team members may find aspects of Global Software Development to be motivating. Many of our respondents cited interacting with different teams and customers to be motivating. One specifically cited "... a chance to travel and work with colleagues from other countries" as a reason for *staying* in software engineering. Cultural differences and geographic separation are frequently cited as barriers to be overcome [20]. But these characteristics of global software development may also emerge as motivators, and therefore additional advantages of GSD.

References

1. Beecham, S.: Motivating software engineers working in virtual teams across the globe. In: Wohlin, C., Ruhe, G. (eds.) Software Project Management in a Changing World, pp. 255–282. Springer, Heidelberg (2014)
2. Beecham, S., Baddoo, N., Hall, T., Robinson, H., Sharp, H.: Motivation in software engineering: a systematic literature review. Inf. Softw. Technol. **50**(9), 860–878 (2008)
3. Burn, J.M., Couger, J.D., Ma, L.: Motivating IT professionals. The Hong Kong challenge. Inf. Manage. **22**(5), 269–280 (1992)
4. Couger, D., McIntyre, S.: Motivation norms of knowledge engineers compared to those of software engineers. J. Manage. Inf. Syst. **4**(3), 82–93 (1987)
5. Couger, J.D., Zawacki, R.A.: Motivating and Managing Computer Personnel. Wiley, New York (1980)
6. Crepeau, R., Crook, C., Goslar, M., McMurtrey, M.: Career anchors of information systems personnel. J. Manage. Inf. Syst. **9**(2), 145–160 (1992)
7. Ebert, C., Murthy, B.K., Jha, N.N.: Managing risks in global software engineering: principles and practices. In: IEEE International Conference on Global Software Engineering (ICGSE 2008), pp. 131–140. IEEE (2008)
8. El Khatib, V., Trang, S., Reimers, K., Kolbe, L.: The role of motivational factors in distributed software development teams: an empirical investigation. In: ECIS. paper 221 (2013)
9. de Farias Jr., I.H., Duarte, L., de Oliveira, J.P.N., Dantas, A.R.N., Barbosa, J.F., de Moura, H.P.: Motivational factors for distributed software development teams. In: 2012 IEEE Seventh International Conference on Global Software Engineering Workshops (ICGSEW), pp. 49–54. IEEE (2012)

10. Ferratt, T.W., Short, L.E.: Are information systems people different: an investigation of motivational differences. Manage. Inf. Syst. (MIS) Q. 10(4), 377–387 (1986)
11. França, A., Gouveia, T., Santos, P., Santana, C., da Silva, F.: Motivation in software engineering: a systematic review update. In: 15th Annual Conference on Evaluation Assessment in Software Engineering (EASE 2011), pp. 154–163, April 2011
12. Frey, B.S., Osterloh, M.: Successful Management by Motivation: Balancing Intrinsic and Extrinsic Incentives. Springer, Heidelberg (2002)
13. Garza, A.I., Lunce, S.E., Maniam, B.: Career anchors of Hispanic information systems professionals. In: Proceedings - Annual Meeting of the Decision Sciences Institute, pp. 1067–1072 (2003)
14. Hall, T., Beecham, S., Verner, J., Wilson, D.: The impact of staff turnover on software projects: the importance of understanding what makes software practitioners tick (refilling the pipeline: meeting the renewed demand for information technology workers). In: ACM-SIGMIS CPR 2008 Conference (2008)
15. Herzberg, F., Mausner, B., Snyderman, B.B.: Motivation to Work, 2nd edn. Wiley, New York (1959)
16. Holmstrom, H., Conchúir, E.Ó., Ågerfalk, P.J., Fitzgerald, B.: Global software development challenges: a case study on temporal, geographical and socio-cultural distance. In: 2006 International Conference on Global Software Engineering, ICGSE 2006, pp. 3–11. IEEE (2006)
17. Huczynski, A., Buchanan, D.: Organizational Behaviour: An Introductory Text, 2nd edn. Prentice Hall, London (1991)
18. Jordan, E., Whiteley, A.M.: HRM practices in information technology management. In: Computer Personnel Research Conference (SIGCPR) on Reinventing IS: Managing Information Technology in Changing Organizations, pp. 57–64. ACM Press (1994)
19. Krippendorff, K.: Content Analysis: An Introduction to its Methodology, 2nd edn. Sage Publications, Beverly Hills (2004)
20. Noll, J., Beecham, S., Richardson, I.: Global software development and collaboration: barriers and solutions. ACM Inroads 1(3), 66–78 (2010)
21. Peters, L.: Managing software professionals. In: 2003 Proceedings of Managing Technologically Driven Organizations: The Human Side of Innovation and Change (IEEE Cat. No.03CH37502), IEMC 2003, pp. 61–66. IEEE (2003)
22. Petri, H., Govern, J.: Motivation: Theory, Research, and Application, 6th edn. Wadsworth Publishing, Belmont (2012)
23. Portillo-Rodríguez, J., Vizcaíno, A., Piattini, M., Beecham, S.: Tools used in global software engineering: a systematic mapping review. Inf. Softw. Technol. 54(7), 663–685 (2012)
24. Sharp, H.: What motivates software engineers: a workshop report. Overload Project Management(99), October 2010. http://accu.org/index.php/journals/1703
25. Sumner, M., Yager, S., Franke, D.: Career orientation and organizational commitment of IT personnel. In: ACM SIGMIS CPR Conference on Computer Personnel Research (Atlanta, Georgia, USA, 14–16 April 2005), pp. 75–80 (2005)
26. Verner, J., Babar, M., Cerpa, N., Hall, T., Beecham, S.: Factors that motivate software engineering teams: a four country empirical study. J. Syst. Softw. 92(1), 115–127 (2014)
27. Šteinberga, L., Šmite, D.: Towards a contemporary understanding of motivation in distributed software projects: solution proposal. Scientific papers:15, University of Latvia (2011)

Empower a Team's Product Vision with LEGO® SERIOUS PLAY®

Danielle Pichlis[1]([⊠]), Stefanie Hofemann[1], Mikko Raatikainen[1],
Juho Sorvettula[2], and Calle Stenholm[2]

[1] Aalto University, Helsinki, Finland
{danielle.pichlis,stefanie.hofemann,mikko.raatikainen}@aalto.fi
[2] Steeri Oy, Helsinki, Finland
{juho.sorvettula,calle.stenholm}@steeri.fi

Abstract. This paper investigates how software development teams and their products can be influenced by the use of service design tools. More specifically, a case study incorporating LEGO® SERIOUS PLAY® workshops was conducted in collaboration with Steeri Oy, a company that develops customer relationship software. Two workshops were held with two different software development teams, with the aim of creating a shared vision of the product within the team. The workshops provided the teams with many new insights into their product's problems and opportunities, a common language of metaphors with which to communicate, and a holistic view of the product, including their role in the system. These LEGO SERIOUS PLAY workshops, as examples of a service design tool in use, illustrate their value in unlocking valuable insights and team potential.

1 Introduction

Over the past few decades, the field of software engineering has undergone several transformations with the advent of agile and lean methodologies. At the same time, the discipline of service design has emerged in response to the rising importance of the service sector [4]. At first, the focus of service design was on the development of traditional services, like hotels and banks although more recently it has been applied to digital products and services.

Despite the growing prevalence of digital services, the fields of software engineering and service design have rarely crossed paths. There exists many synergies between them as, for example, the first three stages of service design (exploration, creation and reflection [6]) share similarities with requirements elicitation. There is a difference, however in the ethos between these two approaches: for example, service design aims at the divergent exploration of the problem space and user needs. This is achieved through the use of *service design tools* (cf. [3,5,6]) which are the methods or practices that the service designer uses.

This paper investigates how software engineering teams respond to the use of LEGO® SERIOUS PLAY® as an example of a service design tool to create a shared vision. This topic is explored in an industrial setting in more detail

© Springer International Publishing Switzerland 2015
P. Abrahamsson et al. (Eds.): PROFES 2015, LNCS 9459, pp. 210–216, 2015.
DOI: 10.1007/978-3-319-26844-6_15

as *"What impact does a LEGO SERIOUS PLAY workshop have on a software development team?"*

The LEGO SERIOUS PLAY (LSP) method, while not specifically designed as a service design tool, works very well to achieve the goals of service design. It was developed internally by The LEGO Group itself, in an effort to inject more creativity and imagination into the way it developed new strategies and strategic direction [2]. The method, as described in the LSP Open Source Brochure [1], consists of a core process, a participant etiquette and a facilitator code of conduct. The success of the LSP method can be explained by the following two fundamental elements [2]: the core process and accompanying etiquette which creates leaning in; and that the LEGO® bricks are universally approachable, allowing thinking with your hands.

2   Research Design

This research followed the case study method [7] in which the LEGO SERIOUS PLAY method was applied as an *intervention* in an industrial context in a quasi experimental manner. That is, the objectives were to introduce and observe the intervention and effects rather than develop the intervention in an industrial setting. The case company, Steeri Oy, is a small-sized Finnish company that consults in, and develops customer relationship software. The study was conceived out of the company's desire to experiment with service design tools - and implemented in the form of two workshops with two different software development teams (one workshop each). Both of the teams develop and maintain a software solution that is currently available, and in the use of their customers.

During the planning of each workshop, the facilitators met with the product owners to determine the purpose of the workshop and plan the practicalities. The workshop involved all members of the product team, even the corresponding person from marketing. The time reserved for each workshop was 5 h, which included an hour-long lunch break and two small coffee breaks.

To begin the workshop, the participants were given a brief overview of the LSP method, the purpose of the workshop and what will be expected of them. The Core LSP Process consists of four steps that are repeated throughout the workshop [2]: (1) introduce the building task, (2) each participant constructs their own model (or a shared model in shared building tasks) with LEGO bricks, (3) participants take turns telling the story of their model, and (4) the facilitator and participants reflect on the model by asking questions about it. For more detailed instructions on facilitating an LSP workshop, please refer to the LSP Open Source Brochure [1].

The building tasks are illustrated in Fig. 1, where "A" and "B" denotes the first and second workshops, respectively. The tasks were tailored for each product team and their particular challenges, though they share the same general structure — starting from the user's point of view, and finishing with "what could be". The number of minutes indicated in the figure refer only to the building time allowed for each task, and don't include the time spent sharing and discussing the models. The final task was a longer team assignment.

Fig. 1. The structure of the workshops, as designed by the facilitators

The workshops were video and audio recorded, with the permission of the participants, by a non-participating observer, and all of the models were photographed. After each workshop, the facilitators reviewed the material and summarised the themes in a visual booklet. To understand what had happened since the workshops, the facilitators met with both product owners 4 months later for a follow-up discussion.

3   Results and Analysis

3.1   Building Tasks

The first building task for workshop A resulted in models that represented different aspects of the user's personality (*colourful, strong personality*), moods (*sometimes demanding* = crocodile, *sometimes happy* = *giraffe*, see Fig. 2a), and working situation (*isolated, hectic work life, limited by environment and responsibilites, not the decision maker*). The same building task in workshop B was formulated slightly differently and focussed the participants on the customer's problem. They identified personnel issues such as *frustrated employees* and *chaotic environment*, as well as technical issues such as *fragile, unstable, isolated and incompatible systems*.

The second building task aimed to explore the user's problems arising from their daily work, or with the team's product. Workshop A resulted in everyday issues such as *lack of time, difficult decisions* and *ad hoc approaches*, as well as specific issues with the product, such as *learnability, navigability, stability*

(a)   (b)

Fig. 2. (a) The changing moods of the customer, and (b) the UI "maze"

and *trust*. The issues of learnability and navigability were represented in one model as a maze the user was trying to navigate through (see Fig. 2b). In workshop B, the resulting models and stories focussed even more heavily on the product and its issues, such as *difficulties in deployment, potential deadlocks in the architecture, needing to integrate additional systems* and *an unpolished solution*. Only two models focussed specifically on the user's point of view, highlighting that the *user doesn't understand what happens inside* and *receives unexpected output*. The participants that built these particular customer-related issues had been dealing directly with those customers experiencing them earlier that week.

For the third building task, the participants were asked to consider the user's problem that they built in the previous task, and build a solution. The fourth building task also invited the participants to build ideas for a new and improved solution. The wording of the task however, prompted a wider scope of possibilities and encouraged the participants to temporarily disregard technical constraints.

The fifth and final building task required the whole team to collaborate, and build a single, shared model, based on the previous building challenge.

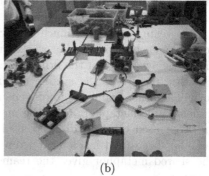

(a)   (b)

Fig. 3. (a) The stakeholder map, and (b) the architectural model

In workshop A, the first piece placed in the middle of the table was a representation of the solution — a kind of a black box. Around that, they placed the different stakeholders and their relationships using metaphors (Fig. 3a). In workshop B, most participants assigned themselves, or were assigned those aspects of the software they are most familiar with. As the pieces became ready, they were assembled in the middle of the table and connected to each other to symbolise the flow of data. The resulting group model, as pictured in Fig. 3b, was a 3D architectural model of the current product, which as it was pointed out, makes a very useful architectural document.

3.2 Intangible Results

Overall, the LSP method delivered on its promise to create *highly engaged* participants, a phenomenon remarked upon by both product owners. The participants of both workshops were eager to build their models, collaborate and share their stories. Of course, some participants were more engaged than others. When the participants experienced difficulties, the facilitators reminded them that there's no such thing as a "bad" model, and encouraged them to just start building something — to think with their hands. The facilitators observed an *open atmosphere*, in which participants were not afraid to voice their opinions. Any concerns that were raised, such as frustrations with certain technologies, were brought out into a positive, non-toxic environment. The *team building* effect of the workshops was a surprisingly powerful outcome. Though the workshops were not specifically designed as team building exercises, the camaraderie effect was so pronounced that one participant remarked that the workshop was better than any other team building event he had attended. Finally, and perhaps most crucially, the participants *had fun*.

3.3 Life After LEGO Serious Play

Perhaps unsurprisingly, the teams had resumed their normal work, and due to slightly smaller team sizes, efforts were now quite focussed on keeping up with customer projects. However, both teams were still experiencing the positive, long-lasting effects of the workshop.

One team reported a much better *coherence* within the team. Before the workshop, each team member worked mostly on their own part of the software, with little awareness of the other parts. The workshop provided the team with a holistic picture of the system and the importance of their team members' work. The other team saw improvements in how they *communicated*. A couple of memorable metaphors from the models remained in the minds of the team, and were used often in discussions. For example, the metaphor of the maze has often been used inside that team to describe the confusing user interface. The shared metaphor gives the team a common understanding of important concepts.

4 Discussion

The LSP workshops allowed the teams to uncover a number of important insights related to the solution. For one team, multiple models depicting the user interface as a confusing maze highlighted the importance of this issue — raising its priority in future development tasks. For the other team, the better understanding of the solution's core value had positive ramifications in marketing and sales activities. By starting from the customer's perspective, the participants were encouraged to step outside of the scope of their everyday work. Even those participants who had no direct contact with the customers of their product, were able to articulate certain traits and concerns of the customer via their tacit knowledge. Ultimately, the workshops enabled the teams to study their product from a different perspective and in a different environment, uncovering insights related to its strengths and weaknesses.

After the completion of the workshops, the benefits of the shared visions did not dissipate immediately. Both teams reported long-lasting benefits in the form of team coherence related to the holistic view of the system, and team communication due to common metaphors.

Evident in the workshops were the two hallmarks of the LSP method, the "leaning in" (or 100 % engagement) as well as the "thinking with their hands" phenomenon. The open, non-judgemental atmosphere created by the method allowed the workshop to function very effectively as a team building exercise. One of the teams in particular benefited greatly from communicating with their colleagues in a different kind of setting, hearing the concerns and wishes of team members and gaining a new perspective. The element of play, provided by the bricks, worked as the secret ingredient to encourage a fun, relaxed atmosphere, and enable the aforementioned benefits.

While the LSP method was used in this study to create a shared vision, many alternative service design tools could also have been used, such as stakeholder mapping, customer journey mapping and storyboarding, to name a few. The strength of the LSP method however, and an essential ingredient in shared visions, is the 100 % engagement of the team. The LEGO bricks, along with the method's core process, enabled the highly-engaging, non-judgemental and positive atmosphere that was conducive to creating shared visions.

5 Conclusions

In this study, the LSP method enabled two software development teams to create their own shared vision of their product. While the resulting LEGO models represented the product visions in different ways, both teams gained long-lasting benefits from its creation, in the areas of team coherence and communication. The workshops enabled the teams to uncover valuable insights about their products, and work together in a way they hadn't done before.

Service design tools, such as LSP, offer software development teams an exciting alternative for enhancing their product and team development. In the case of the LEGO bricks, they enabled the teams to step back from the software and view it through the metaphors as a kind of black-box. This freed them from having to deal with daily issues, such as bugs or detailed design decisions. The fun, playful element of the bricks and the high level of engagement provided by the methodology sets it apart from other methods, as a reliable tool for achieving the desired results — the participants can't help but be absorbed by the activity.

Further research and experimentation at the intersection of service design tools and software engineering has the potential to shed more light on how they may benefit from each other. LSP, while it promises a large payoff in terms of benefits, is quite an intensive, resource-heavy process and other service design tools may also be used for similar purposes. There is certainly no shortage of tools in the service designer's toolkit to choose from and experiment with. For the software engineering field, there are many wonderful benefits to gain from trying out a service design approach to supplement, or even overhaul routine development.

Acknowledgement. The authors would like to extend their gratitude to the articipants of the workshops and Steeri itself for the willingness to experiment with new approaches. They also acknowledge the financial support of TEKES as part of the Need for Speed (N4S) program. LEGO® SERIOUS PLAY® is a registered trademark of The LEGO Group.

References

1. Open-source: Introduction to LEGO SERIOUS PLAY (2010)
2. Kristiansen, P., Rasmussen, R.: Building a Better Business Using the LEGO Serious Play Method. Wiley, New Jersey (2014)
3. Kumar, V.: 101 Design Methods: A Structured Approach for Driving Innovation in Your Organization, 1st edn. Wiley, New Jersey (2012)
4. Mager, B.: Service design as an emerging field. In: Miettinen, S., Koivisto, M. (eds.) Designing Services with Innovative Methods, pp. 28–42. Taik Publications, Helsinki (2009)
5. Service design tools (2014). http://www.servicedesigntools.org/
6. Stickdorn, M., Schneider, J.: This is Service Design Thinking: Basics, Tools, Cases, 1st edn. Wiley, New Jersey (2011)
7. Yin, R.K.: Case Study Research, 3rd edn. Sage, Thousand Oaks (2003)

Early Product Design in Startups: Towards a UX Strategy

Laura Hokkanen[✉], Kati Kuusinen, and Kaisa Väänänen

Department of Pervasive Computing, Tampere University of Technology,
Korkeakoulunkatu 1, 33720 Tampere, Finland
{laura.hokkanen,kati.kuusinen,kaisa.vaananen}@tut.fi

Abstract. Startups often begin with minimal product versions to test and validate their product ideas as early as possible. Therefore, the first versions of the product need to be able to communicate the product idea to users in order to receive meaningful feedback. However, if user experience (UX) of the product is poor, users tend to concentrate on the disturbing user interface instead of the actual product idea. Thus, we suggest that startups should have a UX strategy from the beginning in order to understand their goals related to UX at different stages of product maturity. To this end, we conducted an interview study with eight Finland-based startups and 13 participants. Our results contribute towards understanding both needs for early UX design in startups as well as the restrictions for UX work that the scarce resources of startups induce. This work contributes to creating a UX strategy model for startups.

Keywords: User experience · Startup · Lean · User interface · Design

1 Introduction

Startups are known for their small resources and highly innovative products. The possibility to create software products for global markets seems to be open to everyone who has ideas and perseverance. Customer development model [1] as well as Lean startup method [10] have been introduced to help startups to find scalable business models. Aforementioned approaches suggest having close co-operation with potential customers while experimenting rapidly. Such practices aim at ensuring that the resulting product is profitable instead of building a product first and then trying to sell it. For design and development of products, processes and ways of working need to be adapted to the startup context which is characterized by scarce resources, time pressure and uncertainty [9].

The ability of delivering good user experience (UX) from the earliest product version can enable positive word of mouth advertisement [3] and keep interested people as users for longer. Regarding the UX design, the traditional major upfront user research and design that aims at a complete product design is not suited to the needs of startups: Due to the scarce resources, startups need to do "just enough" to test their idea without creating waste in the process. A startup might change the product drastically based on an experiment with end-users. This means that also the targeted user group can change which can make the conducted user research and other upfront work futile. While

P. Abrahamsson et al. (Eds.): PROFES 2015, LNCS 9459, pp. 217–224, 2015.
DOI: 10.1007/978-3-319-26844-6_16

startups should minimize the time invested in the design work for early product versions, the UX design of the product still needs to have an adequate quality level to enable testing of the product idea [5].

In this paper, we present results of an interview study conducted to gain understanding of how startups approach UX design in their early product versions in eight startups in Finland. All the startups were building, or had recently built, first versions of their products. Through the interviews, we answered the following two research questions: (1) how startups start the UX design of their early product versions, and (2) which skills and resources help startups in achieving the desired UX in the first publicly launched products.

The rest of this paper is structured as follows. Section 2 presents related work considering startups, their development styles, and UX practices. In Sect. 3 we describe our study context and methods. Section 4 presents results including approaches, practices and resources for early UX design in startups. Section 5 gives discussion over the results and presents the final remarks for the paper.

2   Related Work

Software startups are characterized by both engineering and business concerns to a more extensive degree than established companies [11]. Those concerns include being young and immature, having scarce resources, operating with novel technologies in dynamic markets, and being influenced by divergent stakeholders such as investors, customers, partners, and competitors [11].

Customer development [1] and a continuation of it, Lean startup method [10] have been gaining attention as new entrepreneurial practices. Academic research on how well Customer development and the Lean startup method work is scarce but they have been widely adopted by incubators, accelerators and university entrepreneurship courses [12]. The Lean startup [10] suggests that by validating hypotheses of customer's problems startups find a problem/solution fit. After this the startup should validate what product would suite to the solution. Validation should be done by building minimum viable products (MVP) and measuring the key performance indicators when "getting out of the building" with the MVPs. This means validating with real potential customers.

UX, defined as "*a person's perceptions and responses that result from the use or anticipated use of a product, system or service*" [6], has become an important competitive advantage in e-commerce [2]. UX is commonly divided into practical-oriented and hedonic dimensions [4]. Basically, UX development consists of activities related to gaining understanding of the user and the context of use, designing and developing for good UX, and evaluating the resulting outcome [6]. UX design has roots in human-centered design (HCD) [6]. HCD starts with thorough user research and design activities which are followed by design iterations. Similarly to software processes, startups generally do not afford to follow rigorous methods for UX development. However, little is known about UX development in startups. May [8] describes lessons learned from applying lean methodology in a startup and recommends planning the UX activities from early on. Klein [7] presents lean startups light weight methods for UX work. Finally,

Hokkanen and Väänänen-Vainio-Mattila [5] reports that lack of UX expertise hinders the startup from collecting useful feedback from users.

3 Methods, Research Context, and Participants

To gain insights of startups' approaches on UX design for early product versions, we conducted a semi-structured interview study with eight startups. One to three entrepreneurs from each startup took part in the interview. The eight interviews were conducted by one researcher and they lasted between 50–90 min. Each interview session consisted of questions aiming to understand the state of the startup after which their current goals and work practices were discussed. The focus of interviews was on UX related practices and motivations. However, activities such as product and business development were also covered on a high level to understand their effects on UX design. The interview data was analyzed from written transcripts of voice records. The analysis was done by iterative thematic coding. Main themes were first established based on interview questions. Sub-themes emerged from the data.

All the eight startups were small, employing one to six persons, and creating one single software product. Table 1 presents characteristics of both the startups and the interviewees. The startups are numbered from ST11 to ST18, to differentiate them from the startups in our previous study [5].

The interviewees were all working full time in their startups. The majority of them (H04, H05, H07, H08, H09, H10, H13) had a university degree in ICT related subjects. H04 and H13 had majored in Human-Computer Interaction (HCI). Two of the interviewees had their educational background in design, H01 in visual arts and H06 in visual design. H11 and H12 were finishing their bachelor's degree in mechanical engineering at the moment of the interview. H02 had a bachelor's degree in international business. H03 had not continued studies after the secondary school. Regarding the gender of the interviews, all were males except H01.

All the startups except ST15 were currently actively developing a product version. ST15 had completed a pilot project with a customer. ST14 had launched their first product version over a year ago and it was building a renewed version of their product for which they were redesigning the UX. Other startups were in more similar states. Startups ST13, ST16, ST17 and ST18 were preparing a release of an early product version for users. Startups ST11, ST12 and ST14 were currently collecting user feedback of their early product versions. Two startups (ST15, ST17) currently had no UX related expertise in their team. Other startups had at least one person with expertise on HCI or design. Despite all the startups had found people interested in their product, none of the companies had steady revenue streams. Proof of scalability of the business model was still unestablished.

Table 1. Summary of the participated startups and interviewees. CEO = Chief Executive Officer, UXD = User Experience Designer, B2B = Business to Business, B2C = Business to Consumer, SaaS = Software as a Service.

Startup	Interviewees	Company established (year)	Size of startup (persons)	Product	Market
ST11	H01 (CEO)	2013	1	Online marketplace	B2B, B2C
ST12	H02 (CEO), H03	2014	6	Online marketplace	B2C
ST13	H04 (UXD)	2014	4	Online community and marketplace	B2B, B2C
ST14	H05, H06 (CEO)	2014	2	SaaS for pet owners	B2C
ST15	H07 (CEO), H08	2011	2	Automation software	B2B
ST16	H09 (CEO)	2014	5	Mobile sports application	B2B, B2C
ST17	H10, H11, H12	-	3	Mobile personal finances application	B2C
ST18	H13 (UXD)	2015	3	Mobile social application	B2C

4 Findings

4.1 Approaches to Early Product Versions

All interviewees described that they had started with an early product version that was minimal and restricted or very restricted on functionality compared to their vision of the product. Startups were familiar with the Lean startup concept of MVP but only ST16 used the term to describe the product version they were currently building. All the startups approached product development in a lean way: They implemented only the core functionalities to gain feedback instead of building the complete product at once.

ST14 had built a product version first for their own use only. ST15 developed a safety critical product that needed a certain level of quality to be usable and they had started with building a simulation of their product. At the time of interviews, startups ST13 and ST16 were preparing for a closed trial of their product with invited users. Startups ST11, ST12, ST17 and ST18 were building or currently had a version accessible to anyone.

All the startups were endeavoring towards achieving various goals with their early product versions. Via early product versions startups expected to receive overall feedback (ST11, ST16, ST17), get better understanding of their potential customers or users (ST16, ST18), and see how users would use their product (ST18). Startup ST14, which was replacing the underlying technology mainly for improving UX, considered it very important to test the technical viability of the product. Other goals were to get a proof of interest in the product to convince potential partners or customers (ST15, ST16) or to start receiving revenue (ST14). Testing the product idea was the major concern for startups when building the early product versions. Startups looked for validation of the product idea but also for specific features and visual design.

4.2 Design Practices for Early Product Versions

Decision-Making Process. The question of what to include and what to exclude when building an early product version is crucial. Startup team's vision combined with their skillset defined what was done. ST12 had made a feature list for the whole product. Priorities where decided together with the whole startup team by choosing "*the minimum ones so [that] this service can work*" (H02). Also, in ST14, ST15, ST16, and ST17, the interviewees described using their own vision while deciding on the contents of the early product version. In ST14 and ST17, the startup team iterated user interface (UI) ideas by exchanging ideas and sketching them, after which one of the members implemented the sketches as working software. ST16 had approached the design decision by what they need to communicate with the product and then thinking of how to realize it. ST11 consisted only of one person (H01) and she alone designed and implemented the early product version based on her ideas and skills.

The products of ST11, ST12 and ST13 had customers in B2B and B2C markets. All of them prioritized the B2B customers' needs in the early product versions and wanted to get feedback from them. H07 showed images of UI to their pilot customer to gain feedback on their UI design and then developed it further. ST18 had an idea of what their product would be in five years and H13 described the first early version to be the smallest possible core part of it: "*Well, this [product version] that we are building now is as simple as it can be. Basically you can't even do anything with it.*"(H13). ST17 was mainly concerned about the functionality at the time of the interview and the plan was to make the product visually more attractive later.

Practices for Understanding Users. Talking with people was the most common way to gain feedback for product improvements but it required finding the right people to talk with. Four of the startups (ST12, ST13, ST15 and ST16) had contacted potential customers and users face-to-face to show the UI design and ask questions of it. H13 had conducted a major user research study on their product as part of his thesis work, and the startup had utilized those results in their product development. ST11 and ST17 had little or no contact with end users. H01 had discussed with her acquaintances about the product idea but she mainly trusted on her own experiences on working with people who are potential users. In ST17, the team had discussed with their friends but they had not gained much value for product development from these discussions since their idea seemed to be too vague for their friends to relate to it. ST12 had eight test users that they contacted directly to get feedback on improvements in the early product version. ST14, that had had the first product version available for users for some years, had received feedback by asking their customers and web page visitors to answer surveys. ST12 had recently been contacted directly by people who had difficulties using their product.

Interviewees from startups ST11 and ST12 said that the quality of UX had an effect on collecting user feedback: If UX was poor, each user had to be explained that the product is incomplete. In such cases startups gained feedback mostly by asking feedback and comments from users personally, which required plenty of resources. Startups ST13, ST17 and ST18 considered that UX is important when validating the product idea. Startup ST14 believed that good UX would create competitive edge and that they should put effort on it before investing on marketing.

4.3   Relevant Skills and Resources in UX Work in Startups

Table 2 presents skills and practices that had helped the startups to design and implement UX of their current or earlier product versions. Finding the minimal implementation that would communicate the product idea and provide value to users was seen to be most important. This included choosing only what was necessary for the early product version.

Table 2. Skills and practices that startups found useful in creating UX for first product versions

Skill or practice	Startups
Graphic design skills	ST11, ST12, ST13, ST15
Feedback collection	ST12, ST15, ST17
Producing minimal implementation that brings value to users	ST12, ST13, ST15, ST16
User testing	ST12, ST13, ST14
Usability theories or heuristics	ST12, ST13, ST14
Recognizing good UI solutions from other products and mimicking them	ST13, ST14, ST17, ST18
Social skills	ST17
Iterative process	ST16

Startups ST13 and ST18 had all the necessary skills and resources to do UX work so far since they both had UX experts in the founding teams (H04,013). H02 would have acquired services to evaluate and improve UX if they had had money for it (H2). Interviewees from ST14 believed that having had skills to do user tests would have helped them. In ST17, they considered that their team had coped with UX so far but they were not prepared to analyze and utilize user feedback they would receive in the future. In ST11 the lack of implementation skills caused problems in providing desired UX.

5 Discussion and Conclusions

All the startups had adopted an approach of starting with a limited product version based on some studies and own hypotheses, and then iterating the version with real users and customers. Good UX was considered important for the product's success. None of the interviewees said that the innovation and uniqueness of the product alone would make the startup successful. Instead, the way in which the startup was able to deliver the solution was what mattered. The process of getting from an idea to a great product was perceived to require experimentation and feedback outside of the company. Of the interviewees, only H04 and H13 who had background in HCI were able to compare different means of gaining understanding of users and evaluating the UX.

As our study is based on interviews of 13 entrepreneurs from eight small software startups based in Finland, it naturally is limited to a narrow part of startups. However, considering that the related research on startups in general – and especially on UX work in startups – is very limited, our study offers new insight both for the academia and for startups. Future work on the topic of UX work in startups is required to build better practices for startups to design UX for early product versions.

Creating good UX from early on enables startups to collect meaningful feedback and gain positive attention even with restricted implementations. In addition to this, startups need some expertise for collecting and utilizing feedback. The limitations in resources and skills in a startup could be overcome by developing a feasible strategy to understand users and design UX that communicates the product idea and desired UX from early on. Based on our results we will start to form a UX strategy model to guide startups in gaining user information and designing UX.

References

1. Blank, S.: Why the lean start-up changes everything. Harv. Bus. Rev. **91**, 63–72 (2013)
2. Cyr, D., Head, M., Ivanov, A.: Design aesthetics leading to m-loyalty in mobile commerce. Inf. Manag. **43**(8), 950–963 (2006)
3. Füller, J., Schroll, R., von Hippel, E.: User generated brands and their contribution to the diffusion of user innovations. Res. Policy **42**, 1197–1209 (2013)
4. Hassenzahl, M.: the interplay of beauty, goodness and usability in interactive products. In: Proceedings of HCI. Lawrence Erlbaum Associates, vol. 19, no. 4, pp. 319–349 (2004)
5. Hokkanen, L., Väänänen-Vainio-Mattila, K.: UX work in startups: current practices and future needs. In: Lassenius, C., Dingsøyr, T., Paasivaara, M. (eds.) XP 2015. LNBIP, vol. 212, pp. 81–92. Springer, Heidelberg (2015)

6. ISO: 9241-210:2010. Ergonomics of human system interaction-part 210: human-centred design for interactive systems. International Standardization Organization (ISO). Switzerland (2009)
7. Klein, L.: UX for Lean Startups: Faster, Smarter User Experience Research and Design. O'Reilly Media, Inc., Newton (2013)
8. May, B.: Applying lean startup: an experience report: lessons learned in creating & launching a complex consumer app. In: Agile Conference (AGILE), pp. 141–147. IEEE (2012)
9. Paternoster, N., Giardino, C., Unterkalmsteiner, M., et al.: Software development in startup companies: a systematic mapping study. Inf. Softw. Technol. **56**, 1200–1218 (2014)
10. Ries, E.: The Lean Startup: How Today's Entrepreneurs Use Continuous Innovation to Create Radically Successful Businesses. Random House LLC, New York (2011)
11. Sutton, S.M.: The role of process in a software start-up. IEEE Softw. **17**, 33–39 (2000)
12. York, J.L., Danes, J.E.: Customer development, innovation, and decision-making biases in the lean startup. J. Small Bus. Strateg. **24**, 21 (2014)

Effort and Size Estimation Validated by Professionals

An Empirical Study on Memory Bias Situations and Correction Strategies in ERP Effort Estimation

Pierre Erasmus[1] and Maya Daneva[2(✉)]

[1] SAP-Netherlands, 's-Hertogenbosch, The Netherlands
[2] University of Twente, Enschede, The Netherlands
m.daneva@utwente.nl

Abstract. An Enterprise Resource Planning (ERP) project estimation process often relies on experts of various backgrounds to contribute judgments based on their professional experience. Such expert judgments however may not be bias-free. De-biasing techniques therefore have been proposed in the software estimation literature to counter various problems of expert bias. Yet, most studies on de-biasing focus on systematic bias types such as bias due to interdependence, improper comparisons, presence of irrelevant information, and awareness of clients' expectations. Little has been done to address bias due to experts' memory. This is surprising, knowing that memory bias retrieval and encoding errors are likely to affect the estimation process outcome. This qualitative exploratory study investigates the memory bias situations encountered by ERP professionals, and the possible coping strategies to problems pertaining to those situations. Using interviews with 11 practitioners in a global ERP vendor's organization, we explicate how experts retrieve and encode stored memory, what kind of errors they experience along the way, and what correction techniques they were using. We found that both errors due to memory retrieval and due to memory encoding seemed to lead to project effort underestimation. We also found that the most common memory correction strategy was the use of mnemonics.

Keywords: Memory bias · Expert judgments · Project effort estimation · Empirical study · Exploratory qualitative research method · Grounded theory

1 Introduction

Experts-judgement-based estimation plays an important role in Enterprise Resource Planning (ERP) project management [1]. If an ERP implementation project happens in a client organization that has been collecting data on their ERP projects, then expert-judgment-based methods complement quantitative approaches to sizing and estimating projects (e.g. such as in [2]). If client organizations and consultants find themselves in situations where historical data from past projects are unavailable or are irrelevant (e.g. if the projects differ significantly), then expert-judgment-based methods are the only viable option for the project team to come up with an estimate. Unfortunately, using expert-judgment based methods is far from straightforward, due to various biases that interfere with the experts' willingness to provide a fair and well-grounded judgment. The 2012 systematic review of Halkjelsvik and Jørgensen on expert-judgement-based

© Springer International Publishing Switzerland 2015
P. Abrahamsson et al. (Eds.): PROFES 2015, LNCS 9459, pp. 227–242, 2015.
DOI: 10.1007/978-3-319-26844-6_17

predictions of performance time [3] indicates a number of examples of estimation bias reported in software engineering (SE), in engineering in general, and in psychology. An important bias in expert judgment estimation is due to memory errors [4] that the expert is unaware of at estimation time. While in the field of empirical SE, techniques for de-biasing software estimates have been proposed to counter various problems of expert bias, most studies on bias and on de-biasing focused on systematic bias types e.g. bias due to interdependence [5], due to improper comparisons [6], due to presence of irrelevant information [7], due to awareness of clients' expectations [8]. To the best of our knowledge, we could find no study that dealt with de-biasing of estimates due to memory errors. This seems surprising, knowing that memory retrieval errors as well as memory encoding errors are likely to affect the estimation process outcome [4].

We felt motivated to make a step towards better understanding the project estimation situations in which memory errors may occur and the actions (if any) that experts might take if they recognize that they might have injected memory bias into their estimates. Therefore, this paper sets out to answer the following research questions (RQs): **RQ1:** What memory retrieval errors do ERP experts experience in ERP project effort estimation? **RQ2:** What memory encoding errors do ERP experts experience in ERP project effort estimation? **RQ3:** What memory correction techniques do ERP experts use in ERP project estimation?

We answer these RQs by carrying out an exploratory interview-based multiple case study [9] with 11 practitioners involved in the estimation process of ERP projects. The results of our effort are three conceptual models that are independent from any particular expert-judgment-based estimation technique and that describe on an abstract level situations in which memory bias occurs and the coping strategies that could help with it, according to our case study participants.

The paper is organized as follows: Sect. 2 presents background, related work and our motivation. Section 3 presents our research process and Sect. 4 – our results. Section 5 provides a discussion on the results, comparing them with findings from previously published studies. Section 6 evaluates validity threats and Sect. 7 concludes.

2   Background, Related Work and Motivation

The following streams of related work provide the background to this paper: (1) empirical studies on expert consciousness [10], on expert reconstructive memory [11], on the misinformation paradigm [12], and (2) empirical studies from the area of expert judgement based estimation, in particular, on estimation biases [13–33].

Expert consciousness. Kessel [10] suggests that the consciousness of an expert plays an important role in estimating effort of work activities. It could both increase and decrease the accurateness of an estimate. The consciousness of the expert increases the richness and details of objective awareness and includes both the perceiver and the surrounding environment. Moreover, flexibility of anticipation and memory enable the expert to imagine situations other than the logical ones determined by the project scope. The cumulative result of social perception and interpersonal communication leads to developing an emotional self-consciousness [10]. It is this self-evaluation of the expert's self-consciousness that is vital for accurate effort estimates. Experts may deviate from their logical projections due to their consciousness. The unfavorable consciousness of the expert could be obscured in situations like: (i) Self-doubt about their own situation and skill may lead to overestimation; (ii) Resource scarcity may cause experts to adopt the pressure on them to provide an underestimated version of the desired outcome; (iii) Experts might make a judgment reflecting on a situation where they could imagine the most skilled person to carry out the task, therefore result in underestimations; (iv) Intimidation by external parties (or even colleagues that take part in the estimation process) could have an impact on an expert's judgment to adjust a logical defined value to satisfy certain stakeholders; (v) Oversimplification might result in the underestimation.

In contrast, the favorable consciousness of experts could be in the form of: (i) insights of typical cause and effects situations in certain conditions – might it be technology-specific or environment-specific; (ii) insight of scalability issues concerning specific technologies; (iii) insight of integration challenges concerning specific technologies and within certain environments; (iv) understanding of customer or industry specific challenges such as the complexity of customer's (or industries) business processes or organizational structure.

Kessel [10] suspects a possible correlation between the accurateness of estimates and the ability to control the consciousness of an expert. Even though it might be very difficult to control the consciousness of an expert, it is more realistic to set the conditions to promote the favorable consciousness where the expert can consider conditions logically and explicitly mention them with the possible effect they might have. Appropriate approaches or techniques can potentially decrease (or eliminate) the unfavorable consciousness which often obscure an estimate from a logical outcome which might contain less bias.

Expert's Reconstructive Memory. This terms refers to the idea that remembering the past reflects our attempts to reconstruct the events experienced previously [11]. These attempts are based partly on traces of past events and might affect the memory of the scope and effort incurred of a specific task carried out in the past. Moreover it can also affect our general knowledge, our expectations, and our assumptions about what must have happened. Therefore reconstructive memory might influence an estimates task duration and scope. As such, recollections may include errors when our assumptions and inferences, rather than traces of the original events, determine our recollections. Errors or false memories, constitute the prime evidence for reconstructive processes in remembering. As stated in [11], reconstructive memory refers to the idea that retrieval of memories does not occur in completely accurate form. Memory of past events does not appear like a video might replay a scene, but rather that recollection of memories involves a process of trying to reconstruct (rather than replay) past events. The reconstructive memory is the effect when the mind fills in the gaps of our memory with a reconstructive version of past events, therefore reconstructing the original event or task. The implication for the design of an expert-judgment-based estimation method is that it will need to include a mechanism to reduce imprecisions due to reconstructive memory.

230 P. Erasmus and M. Daneva

The Misinformation Paradigm. The misinformation effect [12] refers to a case where the memory for an event is not encapsulated in time in the way the event itself is. Information provided after the event can modify our memories for the event itself. The misinformation effect happens when incorrect information received after an event gets incorporated into one's memory for the event. In light of this situation, Burt and Kemp indicate that consistent information improves our later reconstruction, whereas conflicting or misleading information is harmful [11].

Effort Estimation Tendencies Using Expert Judgment. First, studies (e.g. [13–15]), on experts' overestimation and underestimation found that duration of tasks lasting fewer than 5 min tended to be overestimated, while duration of longer tasks (e.g. taking hours/days/weeks to complete) tended to be underestimated. A possible reason for this tendency to make biased predictions of future task durations is that, in making such predictions, people use memories of past durations, and those memories are systematically biased. That is, memories of previous task duration are incorrect; therefore, predictions of future duration for similar tasks are also incorrect. The memory bias account of Christenfield and McKenzie [15] suggests that it is error in memory that causes a corresponding error in prediction.

Second, empirical evidence indicates a person's overall tendency to underestimate task duration in retrospect, remembering tasks that they have completed as having taken less time than they actually did [16–19]. In support of the memory bias account, research has indicated that tasks that are likely to be remembered as taking longer than they actually did, such as novel tasks [20] or short tasks [21], are also likely to be predicted to take longer than they actually will.

Third, an expert's past experience could refer to performing the task directly or observing others completing the task. A prediction then could be made by using this general representation as an anchor and adjusting the prediction up or down on the basis of the specific task at hand. In this way, the process of predicting task duration may be similar to that of remembering task duration using reconstructive memory.

Fourth, empirical research [22–24] has also suggested that people using a top-down approach to planning, do predict for the task as a whole but fail to sufficiently weight the various components of the task. On the other hand, underestimation may result from people using a bottom-up process to planning, so that, when listing the individual components of a task, they neglect key subcomponents in the process [24, 25]. Moreover, it has been suggested that people may, in making their predictions, disregard their memories of how long similar tasks have taken in the past, and so ignore relevant prognostic information [26–28]. For example, Buehler et al. [26] explain that people continue to underestimate how long it will take them to complete future tasks, even though they are aware that similar tasks have taken longer than planned in the past. This narrow focus causes people to disregard their memories of how long similar tasks have taken previously, as well as leading them to discount the possibility of surprises or interruptions that may delay completion.

Solutions to the above problems have also been suggested. E.g. Kahneman and Tversky [28] argue that prediction would be improved if memories of past completion times were fully consulted during the prediction process. Other solutions are: to reflect on past completion times [27, 29], to break down tasks into their individual components [22, 23, 30], to list possible surprises that could arise during the task [22, 27], to form alternative scenarios of how the task might be completed [22, 23], and to examine the problem as observers instead of as actors [22, 29, 31]. However, evidence from empirical studies on the effectiveness of these solutions is inconclusive. There are studies suggesting that these solutions alone shown little improvement of the overall accuracy of prediction altering behavior subsequent to prediction using implementation intentions [31, 32]. Moreover, in the case of novel tasks, even if experts are supplied someone else's experience with the task [14], they are extremely resistant to using this information [33].

Furthermore, other authors (e.g. [24, 34] found that the most accurate estimations that stood out above the rest, were in situations when estimators receive accurate feedback of past completion times on prediction. These studies indicate that supplying feedback of actual task duration before making a new prediction may be a viable way of increasing predictions. Use of feedback has also been found to improve judgment accuracy for a number of tasks, and forecasting outcomes of time series [35].

We note that with very few exceptions (e.g. [24]) most of the work comes from the sub-fields of psychology (e.g. social psychology, cognitive psychology) and the tasks studied are not in the context of SE. Although there is extensive work on the phenomenon of expert bias in software estimation [5–8], we could find no study dealing with bias due to memory errors. In the context of ERP, projects are usually large, multiple stakeholders often come with incomplete or imprecise requirements [1, 2, 36], all of which is conductive to a situation in which an expert may not be in the position to remember every project implementation detail from the past. Moreover, most project organizations do not have the practice to document experts' assumptions while estimating. Being involved in a variety of ERP projects, we thought we could collect possible experiences from practitioners to help understand what is going on in the field. If we understand the possible ways in which memory errors are experienced, project teams could think of mitigation strategies to de-bias their estimates.

3 Research Plan and Execution

The objective of the present study is to understand how ERP experts participating in project effort estimation, experience memory bias and what they do to cope. Our research plan was to conduct an exploratory case study inspired by Yin's guidelines [9]. We used semi-structured open-end in-depth interviews with 11 practitioners from a global ERP consulting company. Our research process included these steps: (1) Compose an interview guide following the guidelines in [37]; (2) Do a pilot interview to check the applicability of the guide to real-life context; (3) Carry out interviews with practitioners according to the finalized interview script; (4) Sample and follow-up with those participants that possess deeper knowledge or a specific perspective. We note that our interview protocol was not changed after the pilot interview. For this reason, we included the data of this interview to our analysis. The interview guide is receivable from the authors upon request.

Each interview lasted between one and two hours. All took place face-to-face. The interviews included 4 consultants 3 project managers, 2 technology architects and 2 solution architects. A consultant is an individual responsible for the implementation of specific solutions. A project manager is an individual that is responsible for managing a certain project, with a predefined scope, delivered within a specified budget, ensuring a specific quality is delivered within a specified time period. A technology architect is responsible for the high level design and integration across a group of solutions or platforms. A solution architect is an individual that is responsible for the detailed architecture and design for a specific solution or product. These experts had ten to twenty years' ERP experience in their own sub-field of ERP expertise. The experts are based in Germany, Netherland, USA and South Africa. The business domains for which these practitioners implemented the ERP solutions were automotive, banking, health care, and telecom.

At the interview meeting, one researcher (Erasmus) and the interviewee walked through the questionnaire which served to guide the interviews. The questionnaire consisted of three parts: (i) questions referring to the estimation practice in one concrete ERP project of the interviewee; (ii) questions about the general estimation practice in the company, based on the interviewees' experience; and (iii) questions about the role of memory bias in estimation. Examples of the questions asked are: "What roles are involved in the estimation process?", "What information do you provide and to whom?".

For determining the number of practitioners to be interviewed, we followed Charmaz [38], according to whom this number was dependent on the level of 'saturation'. This meant, we had to analyze our data immediately after each interview by using coding practices [38], and compare the codes of one interview with the codes of the previously

Table 1. Interviews and numbers of newly generated codes.

Interview	Number of new codes
Interview 1	63
Interview 2	22
Interview 3	8
Interview 4	12
Interview 5	6
Interview 6	4
Interview 7	5
Interview 8	3
Interview 9	0
Interview 10	1
Interview 11	0

done interviews. As soon as no more new codes were determined during the interview process, we accepted that saturation has been reached. Table 1 illustrates the process of code discovery. As it could be seen from the table, Interview 1 helped us find out 63 codes, Interview 2 revealed 22 more codes, Interview 3 brought 8 new codes to what we already had in Interview 1 and Interview 2. As the interviewing and the coding was progressing, the number of newly identified codes became less and less. In Interview 9, zero new codes were added, in Interview 10 only one new code was added, and in Interview 11 – again zero new codes. At this point we stopped the data collection process.

Our data analysis used the Grounded Theory (GT) practices according to Charmaz [38]. GT is a qualitative approach applied broadly in social sciences to construct general propositions (called a "theory" in this approach) from verbal data. GT is exploratory and recommendable in research contexts where the researcher has no pre-conceived ideas, and instead is driven by the desire to capture all facets of the collected data and to allow the theory to emerge from the data. In essence, this was a process of making analytic sense of the interview data by means of coding and constant comparison of pieces of data that were collected in the case study. Constant comparison means that the data from an interview is constantly compared to the data already collected from previously held interviews, until a point of saturation is reached, i.e., where new sources of data don't lead to a change in the emerging theory (or conceptual model). We first read the interview transcripts and attached a coding word to a portion of the text – a phrase or a paragraph. The 'codes' were selected to reflect the meaning of the respective portion of the interview text to a specific part of the RQ. This could be a concept (e.g. 'bias', 'de-biasing action'), or an activity (e.g. 'feedback-giving'). We clustered all pieces of text that relate to the same code in order to analyze it in a consistent and systematic way. The results of the data analysis are presented in Figs. 1, 2 and 3 and discussed in Sect. 5.

4   Results

Our multiple iterations of coding, constant comparing of information from the interviews, and conceptual modeling in our GT process yielded the models presented in Figs. 1, 2 and 3. Their overall purpose is to explicate and bring insights into the situations in which memory bias and errors occur and the coping actions that the practitioners use. The models take the perspective of the ERP vendor's organization and are to help the vendor's architects, consultants and project managers see those concepts that are important to consider when attempting to de-bias early ERP project estimates, including context. The models describe what happens in all those estimation processes about which we learnt from the participants in the case study. We make the note that in all the three models we take a generic perspective of ERP estimation that is, it abstracts from the use of a specific estimation approach.

In the models in Figs. 1, 2 and 3, we used a dark-colored ellipse to mean an effect of an undesired outcome, a light-colored ellipse to mean a research domain (among those mentioned in our Related Work, Sect. 2), a cloud to mean a cause of undesired outcome, an arrow to mean the relationship between causes, activities, and domains, a hexagon to mean a root cause/problem and a tab note to mean a reason for a problem, respectively.

In what follows, we structure our analysis according to the topics included in our research questions.

RQ1. What memory retrieval errors do ERP experts experience in ERP project effort estimation?

Our case study results (Fig. 1) suggest that there is a consensus among the practitioners that *Memory Bias Retrieval Error* occurs in certain situations while trying to retrieve stored memory by an expert. Retrieval error situations documented in the observations include:

(1) Failure to retrieve or remember a certain scenario which occurred in the past. There is a general tendency to underestimate in these situations.
(2) Failure to retrieve or remember details or deeper insights of certain scenarios. There is a general tendency to underestimate in these situations.
(3) Only remember most important & interesting information. There is a general tendency to underestimate in these situations.
(4) Knowledge or information that has not been used in the short term is often been forgotten in the long-term. There is a general tendency to underestimate in these situations.
(5) Deviations or issues that occurred during a certain scenario is often forgotten or not took into account during estimation or prediction. There is a general tendency to underestimate in these situations.

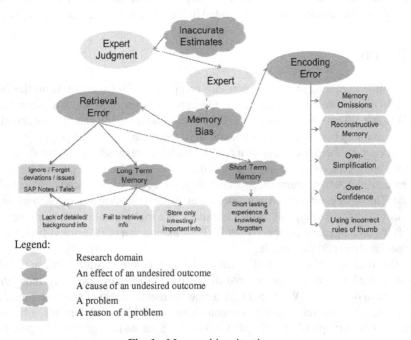

Legend:

Research domain
An effect of an undesired outcome
A cause of an undesired outcome
A problem
A reason of a problem

Fig. 1. Memory bias situations.

RQ2. What memory encoding errors do ERP experts experience in ERP project effort estimation?

Memory Bias Encoding Error occurs while trying to encode stored memory. Encoding error situations documented in the observations include (Fig. 2):

(1) Memory Omissions: Difficult to understand or complex activities were left out during estimation. There is a general tendency to underestimate in these situations reported by all (11) interviewees.
(2) Reconstructive memory: Tendency to add incorrect memories not related to a certain scenario. There is a general tendency to overestimate in these situations, as reported by eight interviewees.
(3) Oversimplification: Experts tend to oversimplify the memories of certain scenarios. There is a general tendency to underestimate in these situations, as reported by seven interviewees.
(4) Overconfidence: Expert tends to be overconfident in general while encoding the memories of certain situations and imagine the best case scenario or the most skilled person caring out this task. There is a general tendency to underestimate in these situations, as reported by five interviewees.
(5) Using incorrect rules of thumb: Experts often estimate using rules of thumb based on past experience, some of these rules of thumb might never been validated while the expert continuous to rely on an incorrect rule of thumb. There is a general tendency to underestimate in these situations, but there were also cases where experts overestimate in these situations, as reported by three interviewees.

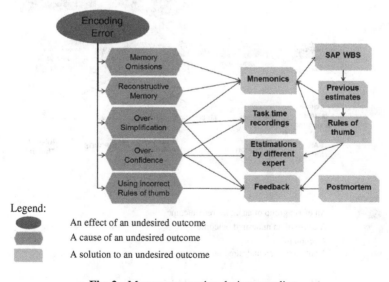

Fig. 2. Memory correction during encoding.

RQ3. What memory correction techniques do ERP experts use in ERP project estimation?

Our case study found that in the experiences of our participants, memory correction techniques could be used to reduce memory bias during both memory retrieval (Fig. 3) and memory encoding (Fig. 2).

In particular, we found five memory correction techniques:

(1) Producing mnemonics could aid our memory, which acts as memorable anchor points. Mnemonics could be delivered in retrieval schematics, which helps to fill gaps in our memory. In the case of SAP projects, the following material were used to produce mnemonics: SAP Work Breakdown Structures which is delivered by the ERP vendor for each of its solutions, SAP Notes (which is created for most issues identified) and general rules of thumb provided by experts.
(2) Actual time recordings per task would benefit and correct most cases where memory bias occur, but shown to be in short supply and infrequently available.
(3) A task estimated and provided by an expert and validated by a second expert shown to reduce some of the memory bias.
(4) Experts who get general feedback (via postmortem reports) about estimated project durations and overall completed status seems to deliver more accurate estimates with a lower degree of memory bias.

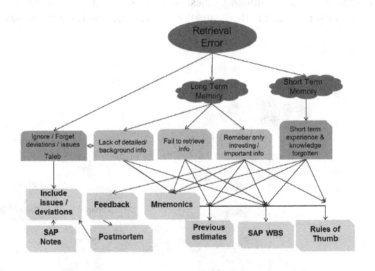

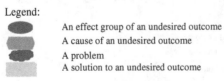

Legend:

An effect group of an undesired outcome
A cause of an undesired outcome
A problem
A solution to an undesired outcome

Fig. 3. Memory correction during memory retrieval

(5) Estimates which include possible issues found during previous project (via searching for SAP Notes associated with a certain solution) enable a lower degree of memory bias and helps reminding an expert of the expected deviations which reduce memory bias.

As indicated earlier, the resulting models are compatible with any estimation technique that employs expert judgments. The models are not prescriptive in the sense that we do not suggest any process or propose a new method, but instead just describes what we found in the case study. This means that an ERP professional could use our conceptual models as a framework for reasoning about his/her own estimation process independently of his/her concrete context. Clearly, not all of the possible biases or error types that are described in Figs. 1, 2 and 3 are necessarily present in each estimation process that an ERP professional can get engaged into. In other words, some biases might be traceable to the project context. For example, one can use the concepts of the models to depict the estimation situation of a specific professionals, be it an architect, a project manager, a consultant, in a specific project, in a specific client organization and, thus, take into account the bases and errors important in his/her own case. The model's completeness still should be validated empirically, e.g. by new case studies in our case study organization or in other ERP vendors' organizations.

An interesting observation we made while creating the models, was that the consultants and the solution architects talked about memory errors when thinking of project scope, while technical architects thought of experiencing more errors when thinking of particular tasks. Also, the consultants and the solution architects were more certain in their estimates regarding tasks, while technical architects felt more certain when estimating scope.

5 Discussion

This section discusses our finding in the light of prior publications that were included in Sect. 2. First, our results (Fig. 1) are consistent with the findings in [3, 24] regarding the inaccurate estimates coming out of experts due to bias. Our findings agree with the findings of Jørgensen regarding the planning fallacy phenomenon – which happens regardless of a software engineering professional's knowledge that past tasks of a similar nature have taken longer to finish than generally planned [24]. According to Jørgensen, this is an indication of optimist's bias. Our findings support this claim. However, we contributed to what is already published on expert bias but in a different domain, the result are similar to studies from other domains such as medical studies focus on experts such as doctors or surgeons retrieving how long an operation took or in criminology, remember the events and appearances of an crime scene. This all add to our understanding of memory bias documented in psychology literature studies [22, 27, 30, 40] by including descriptions of biased situations that occur due to memory retrieval error and memory encoding error. We clearly observed that experts had coping strategies in those situations (Figs. 2 and 3). However the strategies were implicit and specific to experts, and were not organization-wide established practices. The coping strategies (Figs. 2 and 3) were common sense and experts were willing to discuss them with each other, however each expert seemed to have preference for some techniques over others. Investigating why these preferences exist and if the preferences indicate that some strategies are better choices in some contexts than in others would be an interesting line for future research.

Second, we observed that our practitioners did use the feedback-giving solution similarly to [24, 34]. However, they did not think of other solutions that we found mentioned in literature (such as e.g. controlling the consciousness of experts [10] and leveraging the use of consistent information [12]).

Third, our results agree with the findings in the planning fallacy studies of Roy et al. [40]. Their memory bias explanation for why experts are incorrect in estimating future tasks holds that this is due to experts having incorrect memories of how long previous tasks have taken, and that these biased memories cause biased predictions. The coping strategies in Figs. 2 and 3 converge with the ideas proposed by these authors, particularly the ways of using feedback by colleagues to correct an expert's memory in order to increase predictive accuracy in estimation. Another related or similar memory correction technique used in criminology and phycology that detectives and phycologist often used is to ask victims or patient to go back to certain moment in time, to focus on the surroundings and different senses of what they experienced before and after the event they trying to recall. This assists the memory to recall finer details that might help cycle through the actual event.

However, we found two strategies which were not previously discussed: the use of rules of thumbs embedded in Work Breakdown Structures and SAP Notes (a special tool within the SAP's implementation toolbox).

6 Limitations

We note that in this paper we propose conceptual models only. Such models, as suggested by Charmaz [38], are not supposed to be validated against the data that has been used for the development of the model. We used the checklist in [38] to evaluate the possible threats to validity of the observations and conclusions in this research. Because our research is exploratory interview-based case study, the key question to address when evaluating the validity of its results, is [9]: to what extent can the practitioners' experiences in memory bias and bias correction could be considered representative for a broader range of projects and project organizations. We cannot deem our interviewees' settings representative for all the possible ways in which experts could inject errors and counter memory bias in ERP project estimation. However, following [39], we think that it could be possible to observe similar experiences in projects and companies which have contexts similar to those in our study, e.g. where (i) technical and non-technical experts collaborate, (ii) the projects are global and large scale, and (iii) experts are pressured to finish the estimation tasks quickly and have no time to review, re-think, and possibly revise their estimates.

We also acknowledge the inherent weaknesses of interview techniques [9, 37]. A threat is the extent to which the practitioners answered our question truthfully. We took two steps to minimize this threat by (i) recruiting colleagues of the first author who were willing to have a conversation on our topic of research and to whom the first author had good work relationship; (ii) that we ensured no project or expert identity-revealing data will be used in the study. Next, a well-known threat in interview studies is that an interviewee has not understood a question. However, we think that in our study, this threat was nearly non-existent because: (i) the first author is a contributor to some of the interviewee's projects and shared the work context of the interviewees, the domain knowledge and the vocabulary used to talk about project concepts. Next, we accounted for the possibility that the first researcher might instil his bias in the data collection process. We implemented Yin's recommendations [6] in this respect, by establishing a chain of findings: (i) we included participants with diverse backgrounds (i.e. type of ERP projects being delivered), and this allowed the same phenomenon to be evaluated from diverse perspectives (data triangulation [37]).

7   Conclusions and Future Work

This exploratory study contributes to increasing our understanding of expert-judgment based processes in estimation of ERP projects. Using a qualitative research method, we explored memory bias situations that ERP practitioners experienced during their processes of estimating their ERP projects. We also explored the correction/de-biasing strategies those experts were using in their estimation. The results of our effort are, respectively, three conceptual models which describe on a generic level the concepts that ERP project implementation experts use when reasoning about situations in which they witness memory bias to occur. These models came out of applying a GT approach. As such, the models present the state of practice described by concepts which we discerned from our interviews with 11 practitioners. Of course, these models should be subjected to further empirical studies in order to improve their generality. More work in the future is necessary to include at least these steps: (1) an empirical study to evaluate the three models with ERP practitioners in other roles, and (2) an evaluation study of the utilization of the coping strategies in other non-ERP software projects. This research included four roles of experts: consultants, technology architects, solution architects and project management. Another type of expert which plays an important role in effort estimation is key account managers. They understand the specific customer organizational structure, skill and resources available, and are able to adjust effort estimations accordingly, removing or improving assumptions made about a specific customer.

7.1   Implications for Research, Practice and Teaching

Our results have some implications. First, being aware of the limitation of our work, we think the results of this first exploratory study could be of value in at least two ways: (a) it could possibly serve as a roadmap for further empirical studies on bias due to memory errors and on de-biasing techniques that can possibly help in ERP context, and (b) it could be used as a conceptual framework [39] to provide explicit guidance to practitioners and allow for better-checked discourse-based process.

Second, the study has some implications for practice. Perhaps, the most important implication is that memory correction techniques could and should be deployed as part of project estimation processes in the ERP industry, because of the impact they may have on the resulting estimates. While expert judgment had shown to be the predominant method for deriving estimates by practitioners in the ERP domain, this study signals that memory bias seems to be problematic during the estimation and scoping process. Furthermore, we also found that the different types of experts seem to have an impact on the accuracy of the estimates depending on where and how a project lead assigns them to provide estimates: technology architects have shown to be more accurate than solution consultants to determine the initial scope. Solution architects and consultants have shown to be more accurate then technology architect to derive the estimates for certain tasks. Based on these observations, we could recommended ERP project managers to invite technology architects to derive the estimation scope and rely on the solution architects and consultants to provide the estimates for the individual tasks.

Third, our exploration into memory bias in ERP project estimation has some implications for teaching. Most project management courses in Computer Science schools are designed with the software measurement discipline in mind, and in turn place a heavy accent on the use of functional size estimation and of algorithmic models for project estimation. While these textbooks are indispensable, students might benefit also by developing awareness of the bias-injecting circumstances in their project estimates and the possible range of de-biasing strategies at their disposal in a particular context. Students who would consider a career in the consulting sector (e.g. in ERP in particular) would certainly be better off if could have acquired deeper knowledge on expert judgment based techniques, and the role of de-biasing therein.

References

1. Erasmus, P., Daneva, M.: ERP effort estimation based on expert judgments. In: 2013 International Conference on Software Process and Product Measurement, Mensura 2013, LNCS, pp. 104–109 (2013)
2. Erasmus, P., Daneva, M.: ERP services effort estimation strategies based on early requirements. In: REFSQ Workshops 2015, pp. 83–99 (2015)
3. Halkjelsvik, T., Jørgensen, M.: From origami to software development: a review of studies on judgment-based predictions of performance time. Psychol. Bull. 138(2), 238–271 (2012)
4. Roy, M.M., Christenfeld, N.J.S.: Bias in memory predicts bias in estimation of future task duration. Mem. Cogn. 35, 557–564 (2007)
5. Jørgensen, M., Grimstad, S.: Software development estimation biases: the role of interdependence. IEEE Trans. Software Eng. 38(3), 677–693 (2012)
6. Jørgensen, M.: Relative estimation of software development effort: it matters with what and how you compare. IEEE Softw. 30(2), 74–79 (2013)
7. Jørgensen, M., Grimstad, S.: Avoiding irrelevant and misleading information when estimating development effort. IEEE Softw. 25(3), 78–83 (2008)
8. Jørgensen, M., Sjøberg, D.I.K.: The impact of customer expectation on software development effort estimates. Int. J. Project Manage. 22, 317–325 (2004)
9. Yin, R.: Case Study Research Methods. Sage, Thousand Oaks (2012)

10. Kessel, S.: Self and Consciousness: Multiple Perspectives. Lawrence Erlbaum, New Jersey (1992)

11. Roediger, H.L.: Reconstructive Memory. In: Smelser, N.J., Baltes, P.B. (eds.) International Encyclopedia of the Social and Behavioral Sciences. Elsevier, Oxford (2002)

12. Burt, C.D.B., Kemp, S.: Construction of activity duration and time management potential. Appl. Cogn. Psychol. **8**, 155–168 (1994)

13. Handley, S.J., Thomas, K.E., Newstead, S.E.: The effect of prior experience on estimating the duration of simple tasks. Current Psychol. Cogn. **22**, 83–100 (2004)

14. Thomas, K.E., Newstead, S.E., Handley, S.J.: Exploring the time prediction process: the effect of task experience and complexity on prediction accuracy. Appl. Cogn. Psychol. **17**, 655–673 (2007)

15. Christenfeld, R.M., McKenzie, C.: The broad applicability of memory bias and its coexistence with the planning fallacy: reply to Griffin and Buehler (2005). Psychol. Bull. **131**, 761–762 (2005)

16. Block, R.A., Zakay, D.: Prospective and retrospective durations judgments: a meta-analytic review. Psychon. Bull. Rev. **4**, 184–197 (1997)

17. Fraisse, P.: On the relationship between time management and time estimation. Br. J. Psychol. **90**, 33–347 (1963)

18. Poynter, D.: Judging the duration of time intervals: a process of remembering segments of experience. In: A Life-Span Perspective, pp. 305–322 (1989)

19. Wallace, M., Rabin, A.I.: Temporal experience. Psychol. Bull. **57**, 213–236 (1960)

20. Koole, S., Van't Spijker, M.: Overcoming the planning fallacy through willpower: effects of implementation intentions on actual and predicted task-completion times. Eur. J. Soc. Psychol. **30**, 873–888 (2000)

21. Christenfeld, N.J.S., Roy, M.M.: Effect of task length on remembered and predicted duration. Psychon. Bull. Rev. **16**, 202–207 (2008)

22. Byram, S.J.: Cognitive and motivational factors influencing time predictions. J. Exp. Psychol. 216–239 (1997)

23. Connolly, T., Dean, D.: Decomposed versus holistic estimates of effort required for software writing tasks. Manage. Sci. **43**, 1029–1045 (1997)

24. Jørgensen, M.: Top-down and bottom-up expert estimation of software development effort. Inf. Softw. Technol. **46**, 3–16 (2004)

25. Molokken-Ostvold, K., Jørgensen, M.: Expert estimation of web-development projects: are software professionals in technical roles more optimistic than those in non-technical roles? Empirical Softw. Eng. **10**, 7–29 (2005)

26. Buehler, R., Griffin, D., Ross, M.: Inside the planning fallacy: the causes and consequences of optimistic time prediction. In: Heuristics and Biases: The Psychology of Intuitive Judgment, pp. 250–270 (2002)

27. Hinds, P.J.: The curse of expertise: the effects of expertise and debiasing methods on predictions of novice performance. J. Exp. Psychol. 205–221 (1999)

28. Kahneman, D., Tversky, A.: Intuitive prediction: biases and corrective procedures. In: Judgments Under Uncertainty: Heuristics and Biases, pp. 414–421 (1982)

29. Buehler, R., Griffin, D., Ross, M.: Exploring the "Planning Fallacy": why people underestimate their task completion times. J. Pers. Soc. Psychol. **67**, 366–381 (1994)

30. Kruger, J., Evans, M.: If you don't want to be late, enumerate: unpacking reduces the planning fallacy. J. Exp. Soc. Psychol. **40**, 586–598 (2004)

31. Newby-Clark, I.R., Ross, M., Buehler, R., Koehler, D.J., Griffin, D.: People focus on optimistic scenarios and disregard pessimistic scenarios while predicting task completion times. J. Exp. Psychol. Appl. **6**, 171–182 (2000)

32. Taylor, S.E., Pham, L.B., Rivkin, I.D., Armor, D.A.: Harnessing the imagination. Am. Psychol. **53**, 429–439 (1998)
33. Griffin, D., Buehler, R.: Biases and fallacies, memories and predictions: comment on Roy, Christenfeld, and McKenzie (2005). Psychol. Bull. **131**, 757–760 (2005)
34. Buehler, R., Griffin, D., MacDonald, H.: The role of motivated reasoning in optimistic time predictions. Pers. Soc. Psychol. Bull. **23**, 238–247 (1997)
35. Remus, W., O'Connor, M., Griggs, K.: Does feedback improve the accuracy of recurrent judgment forecasts? Organ. Behav. Hum. Decis. Process. **66**, 22–30 (1996)
36. Daneva, M.: ERP requirements engineering practice: lessons learned. IEEE Softw. **21**(2), 26–33 (2004)
37. King, N., Horrock, C.: Interviews in Qualitative Research. Sage, London (2010)
38. Charmaz, K.: Constructing Grounded Theory. Sage, London (2007)
39. Wieringa, R.J., Daneva, M.: Six strategies for generalizing software engineering theories. Sci. Comput. Program. **100** (2015)
40. Roy, M., Mitten, S., Christenfield, J.: Correcting memory improves accuracy of predicted task duration. J. Exp. Psychol. **14**(3) 266

Applying a Verification Protocol to Evaluate the Accuracy of Functional Size Measurement Procedures: An Empirical Approach

Christian Quesada-López[✉] and Marcelo Jenkins

Center for ICT Research (CITIC), University of Costa Rica,
San Pedro Montes de Oca, Costa Rica
{cristian.quesadalopez,marcelo.jenkins}@ucr.ac.cr

Abstract. This paper presents a verification protocol for analyzing the source of inaccuracy in measurement activities of Function Points Analysis (FPA) and Automated Function Point (AFP). An empirical study was conducted with the protocol to determine the accuracy of FPA and AFP, and common differences during their application. The empirical study was conducted and differences between the measurement process regarding accuracy, reproducibility, and protocol adoption properties were reported. Effectiveness of the verification protocol to evaluate functional size measurement procedures was provided. The application of the protocol enabled participants to identify differences and their causes between counting results in a systematic way. Many participants had a favorable opinion regarding the usefulness of the protocol, and most of them agreed that the application of this protocol improved their understanding of measurement methods.

Keywords: Functional size measures · Function point analysis · Automated function points · Accuracy verification protocol · Empirical procedure

1 Introduction

Function Point Analysis (FPA) was originally proposed by Albrecht to size software from the end user point of view to estimate development effort [1, 2]. FPA is one of the mostly used functional size measurement methods (FSM) in the software industry. FSM generates a variety of productivity, financial and quality indicators in different phases of the software development process [3]. Several studies have proposed automated measurement procedures for FPA from specific input artifacts in different phases of the software life cycle (requirements, design, and source code). The aim is to reduce the cost of counting and the inconsistency of manual counts [4]. FSM automation could help the process of regularly updating the baseline counts during development [5]. This might allow the size comparison for the same product in different phases [6], tracking progress, and sizing deliveries [7]. The effectiveness of automated counting has been rigorously tested by few studies. Besides, very few works had been conducted on verifying measurement results in detail [8]. The analysis has been limited to evaluating total count

© Springer International Publishing Switzerland 2015
P. Abrahamsson et al. (Eds.): PROFES 2015, LNCS 9459, pp. 243–250, 2015.
DOI: 10.1007/978-3-319-26844-6_18

variations between manual and automated measurements [9]. None of these studies reported the use of a systematic verification protocol. Reporting the accuracy of the results in different levels of the counting process, and understanding the nature of the differences between these results, has become significant in order to improve the accuracy and calibrate the counting procedures and tools. FSM automation is an attractive approach but to ensure that the counting process produces accurate results, standard verification protocols have to be used [8]. The absence of systematic evaluation could explain the low adoption rate of FSM methods [10]. The Object Management Group (OMG) proposed a standard for the automated measurement of function points from source code (AFP) [4]. Lavazza states that empirical evidence is needed concerning the relationships between FPA and AFP measures [11]. Currently, automated counting tools do not provide automated function point counts that are within an acceptable accuracy with FPA [12]. This paper is organized as follows: Sect. 2 presents the related work on accuracy verification protocols. In Sect. 3 the accuracy verification protocol is presented, Sect. 4 describes the experimental design, and Sect. 5 present and discusses the results of the empirical study. Finally, Sect. 6 outlines conclusions and future work.

2   Related Work

Jacquet and Abran proposed a process model for FSM that states the measurement results must be documented and audited [13]. The results should be audited according to different methods to ascertain their quality. An accuracy verification protocol permits to report measurement results from different procedures and tools in the software life cycle and compare accuracy results between them. Soubra et al. state that very little work has been conducted on verifying measurement results produced by FSM automation. They proposed a verification protocol designed to provide evidence of the accuracy of an automated FSM tool using COSMIC Full Function Points. The protocol states that all the details of the measurement steps must be kept for traceability purposes [8]. The verification protocol presented in this study was adapted from Soubra protocol where general phases were used and adapted according to the counting guidelines of IFPUG FPA, and recommendations in [4, 14]. Morris and Desharnais proposed a method for checking the validity of the data collected using FPA [15]. This method identifies common errors during the counting process based on historical data that highlight exceptions from the norm. Our approach is similar to [15], however, in our case, we analyze and evaluate all detailed measurements of the measurement process.

3   Verification Protocol

In a previous study [16] FPA and AFP overall results were compared, but to understand the sources of inaccuracy, a systematic and detailed analysis about basic functional components (BFC) relationships should be conducted. This accuracy verification protocol proposes a top down evaluation of measurement results in order to identify differences reported by applying one or more measurement processes (through measurement procedures and automated counting tools). The protocol could be used to compare measurements results from different procedures applied to specific software artifacts for the same application through the software life cycle. Based on the comparison of measurement results, counting differences through the measurement process could be identified and FSM procedures could be calibrated. The aim of this protocol is to report differences between the measurement results and point out specific flags in the measurement process where differences have been identified. The protocol looks for consistency comparing measurement results differences against a "true value" reported by an expert. Due to space limitations protocol is briefly described, details about the protocol model is available online at https://goo.gl/uu0WTn.

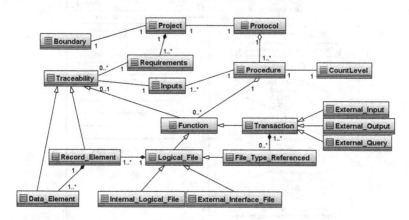

Fig. 1. Data collection model. Adapted from [11, 17].

The data collection model is shown in Fig. 1. This model describes the level of detail for the data to be collected in a counting process for the application of the protocol. According to [14], this protocol is level of detail 1: 'Detailed Linked and Flagged Count'. This model stored the specific data levels extracted in the process. All user identifiable functions are recognized, linked to a specific application requirement, and related to any basic data element representing the dependencies in the different object types that are counted. The protocol allows kept traceability for all measurement results in the process and storages and analyses the outputs. The verification protocol is conducted in 3 main phases as shown in Fig. 2. *Phase 1: Overall UFP result comparison.* The overall measurement results for each counting process are compared against the "true value" (by an expert). If the protocol stops in this phase, only the overall FP results will be verified. *Phase 2: Accuracy detailed comparison.* The measurement results for each step in the process are compared against the "true value". This phase is conducted to identify the place where a difference in the counting process is presented. When an error is identified, Phase 3 is triggered. Each step in this phase represents a deep analysis of the measurement process for each procedure. At the end of this phase, any assignable cause responsible for an error is isolated, linked, and reported. *Phase 3: Error identification and recovery.* This phase determines the reason for a difference in any measurement result for any counting process. An inspection about the quality of requirements, input artifacts, and process for each procedure is conducted to identify from where the error comes from. Differences are recorded and reported, and a revision to attempt to correct the differences is done. If the error can be fixed, the measurement results are updated and the verification process is conducted again.

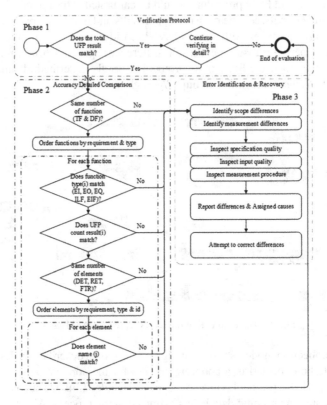

Fig. 2. Accuracy verification protocol. Adapted from [9].

4   Description of the Empirical Study

The objective written in GQM [18] form is: Analyze an accuracy verification protocol with the purpose of evaluating measurement results effectiveness from the point of view of software engineers in the context of a graduate metrics course applying the FPA and AFP measurement process. We report the empirical study according to [16, 19]. The empirical study was developed in a graduate metrics course with 14 professionals from the same background in software engineering. Practitioners applied the IFPUG FPA and OMG AFP methods to measure the same software application, a web site for a fictional university (a small transactional registry system). Subjects reported and compared all measurement details according to the verification protocol. The subjects were mainly analysts (53 %), and developers (40 %). They were not experts in functional size measurement. The broad research questions addressed by this experiment were: (1) what are the FPA and AFP measurement process performance in terms of accuracy and reproducibility? (2) Is the verification protocol an effective procedure to identify measurement differences and sources of inaccuracy between FPA and AFP process?

The experimental objects included: application requirements specification and source code. "True value" size in FPA based on requirements (144 UFP). "True value" size in AFP based on source code (115 AFP). Differences in size response to the requirements documented were not fully implemented in the application that were injected on purpose. The experiment included 3 tasks: the FSM counting process task (for each procedure), the application of the verification protocol, and a post-measurement survey to evaluate perception about the protocol. Subjects were not aware of the broad research questions. They were informed that the researchers wanted to study the measurement process of the FPA and AFP methods and an accuracy verification protocol, and completed tasks as a course exercise. All professionals were guaranteed anonymity. The survey material was prepared in advance. The experiment was performed over a 9-week period, and the students were graded on the exercise. In total, 28 detailed measurement processes and 14 applications of the protocol were conducted by professionals.

Threats to Validity. Two researchers applied FPA and AFP to count functional size used as a "true value", but they were not CFPS certified. The application is small, but requirements and source code were a very similar example of the practices in a real case in the industry. The subjects were not counting experts; however, they are familiar with software engineering practices. Although subjects' lack of experience could cause variances in counting, we expected similar performance among participants.

5 Analysis and Interpretation

The analysis for unadjusted function points (UFP) and automated function points (AFP), standard deviation (Std. Dev.), accuracy (MRE), and reproducibility (REP) was conducted. FPA presented a higher standard deviation size (33.87) than AFP (17.96). Accuracy for FPA (21 %) was lower than AFP (14 %). The same is presented with reproducibility; FPA (23 %) and AFP (15 %). The main causes (factors of influence) of measurement differences between counting procedures using FPA and AFP were reported applying the verification protocol after the measurement phase. All verification protocol reports were carefully analyzed and tabulated to obtain the summary of differences between FPA and AFP methods. In this empirical study, all participants were able to identify differences between measurement procedures applying the protocol in a systematic way. Most of the participants reported the same differences and found common reasons for these differences. All differences reported can be categorized into: (1) different function points counted and/or different number of functions identified by new or not implemented functionality, (2) different classification of function type (external queries as external outputs). AFP, rules seems to work well when transactions have to be classified in inputs or outputs and files have to be classified as internal logic files, (3) different files referenced or record elements identified because AFP identified different logical files than FPA, in some cases, AFP separate database tables that are joined in a FPA logical file, inherence implementation affects the detection of logical files in AFP and convention names rules should affect the identification of logical files, and (4) different number of data elements identified because AFP rules and convention names applied did not identified error messages counted as a data elements in FPA and in some cases technical fields were not detected (see details at https://goo.gl/uu0WTn).

The perceived usefulness, and the intention to use were analyzed according to a post tasks survey (n = 13). Regarding *perceived usefulness*, many participants (70 %) had a favorable opinion about the usefulness of the verification protocol to validate and improve the quality of measurements results of functional size in software systems. In their opinion, the protocol verified the accuracy and identified common causes in measurement results. In addition, with the implementation of the protocol in different phases of the software life cycle, they would trace the implementation of functional requirements and the growth of the software. Main concerns about the protocol were the necessity of a "true value" of reference in order to compare the results. In general, they agreed that if a company uses function points, the protocol would be a powerful tool to improve the measurement process. Participants expressed that the detailed analysis of the procedures in order to report measurements, and the analysis to identify common causes of differences helped them to understand many details of the procedures that otherwise would had been misunderstood or simply omitted. Most participants (92.3 %) agreed that the application of the protocol improved their understanding about FPA and AFP processes. Regarding *intention to use*, most participants (92.3 %) would recommend the use of the verification protocol in the process of learning measurement methods, 61.5 % of the participants will use the protocol, if they adopted function points as a part of their processes. Half of the participants think that the automation of the verification protocol could be complex, the process of identifying and tagging for requirement traceability between inputs seems to be difficult and time consuming. They agreed that if measurement results are collected, the process of verification would be easy to conduct.

6   Conclusions and Future Work

This study reported on a verification protocol for analyzing the source of inaccuracy in FSM activities of IFPUG FPA and AFP. An empirical study was conducted with the protocol to investigate the accuracy of FPA and AFP and common differences during their application. With the application of the protocol participants were able to identify counting differences and their causes in a systematic way. Most participants had a favorable opinion regarding the usefulness of the protocol, and agreed that the application of the protocol improved their understanding of measurement methods. From a research perspective, our study adds insight about the effectiveness of the verification protocol to evaluate FSM procedures. Further research is needed to corroborate the usefulness of the verification protocol and to draw more conclusions on the perceived adoption properties. Replications should be conducted using more complex applications, using a bigger sample of subjects, and more than one counting expert in order to consider the variation interval for the functional size of the application. For future works, more examination with automated measurement procedures is needed, case studies based on the protocol to investigate the accuracy of FPA and AFP and common differences during their application could improve the understanding regarding BFCs relationships between FPA and AFP. The verification protocol could be improved adding detailed specifications about how to trace the software inputs and requirements. Apart from conducting replication studies, verification protocol should be automated to be analyzed in real environments. From a practical perspective, the protocol could be used to calibrate measurement procedures and automated counting tools.

Acknowledgments. This research was supported by VI at University of Costa Rica No. 834-B5-A18, and Ministry of Science, Technology & Telecommunications (MICITT).

References

1. Albrecht, A.J.: Measuring application development productivity. In: Proceedings of the Joint SHARE/GUIDE/IBM Application Development Symposium, vol. 10, pp. 83–92, October 1979
2. ISO: ISO/IEC 20926, Software and systems engineering - Software measurement – IFPUG functional size measurement method (2009)
3. Garmus, D., Herron, D.: Function Point Analysis: Measurement Practices for Successful Software Projects. Addison-Wesley Longman Publishing Co., Inc., Boston (2001)
4. Object Management Group, Automated Function Points (AFP) Version 1.0, January 2014, OMG Document Number: formal/2014-01-03, http://www.omg.org/spec/AFP
5. Ellafi, R., Meli, R.: A source code analysis-based function point estimation method integrated with a logic driven estimation method. In: SMEF 2006, Roma, Italy (May 2006)
6. Sag, M.A., Tarhan, A.: Measuring COSMIC software size from functional execution traces of Java business applications. In: 2014 Joint Conference of the International Workshop on Software Measurement and the International Conference on Software Process and Product Measurement (IWSM-MENSURA), pp. 272–281. IEEE, October 2014
7. ISO: ISO/IEC 14143-1- Information Technology - Software measurement - Functional Size Measurement. Part 1: Definition of Concepts (2007)
8. Soubra, H., Abran, A., Ramdane-Cherif, A.: Verifying the accuracy of automation tools for the measurement of software with COSMIC–ISO 19761 including an AUTOSAR-based example and a case study. In: 2014 Joint Conference of the International Workshop on Software Measurement and the International Conference on Software Process and Product Measurement (IWSM-MENSURA), pp. 23–31. IEEE, October 2014
9. Özkan, B., Demirörs, O.: Formalization studies in functional size measurement. In: Modern Software Engineering Concepts and Practices: Advanced Approaches: Advanced Approaches, vol. 242 (2010)
10. Abrahao, S., Poels, G., Pastor, O.: Assessing the reproducibility and accuracy of functional size measurement methods through experimentation. In: Proceedings of the 2004 International Symposium on Empirical Software Engineering, ISESE 2004, pp. 189–198. IEEE, August 2004
11. Lavazza, L.: Automated function points: critical evaluation and discussion. In: 2015 IEEE/ACM 6th International on Emerging Trends in Software Metrics (WETSoM), pp. 35–43. IEEE, May 2015
12. Heller, R.: Automated function point counting–a fact based analysis. Q/P Management Group, Inc. www.qpmg.com/Library/confirm_download.php?id=49&pid=1

13. Jacquet, J.P., Abran, A.: From software metrics to software measurement methods: a process model. In: The Third IEEE International Software Engineering Standards Symposium and Forum, ISESS 1997, Emerging International Standards, pp. 128–135. IEEE, June 1997
14. Total Metrics: Total metrics-levels of counting. Version 1.3, January 2004. http://www.totalmetrics.com/function-point-resources/downloads/Levels-of-Function-Point-Counting.pdf (2001)
15. Desharnais, J.M., Morris, P.: Post measurement validation procedure for function point counts. In: Position Paper Forum on Software Engineering Standards Issues, October 1996
16. Quesada-López, C., Jenkins, M.: An evaluation of functional size measurement methods. In: Paper Presented at the CIBSE 2015 - XVIII Ibero-American Conference on SE, pp. 151–165 (2015)
17. Abrahao, S.M., Director-Lopez, O.P.: On the functional size measurement of object-oriented conceptual schemas: design and evaluation Issues, Universidad Politecnica de Valencia (Spain) (2004)
18. Basili, V.R., Rombach, H.D.: The TAME project: Towards improvement-oriented software environments. IEEE Trans. Software Eng. 14(6), 758–773 (1988)
19. Runeson, P., Höst, M.: Guidelines for conducting and reporting case study research in software engineering. Empirical Softw. Eng. 14(2), 131–164 (2009)

From Function Points to COSMIC - A Transfer Learning Approach for Effort Estimation

Anna Corazza[1], Sergio Di Martino[1]($\boxtimes$), Filomena Ferrucci[2],
Carmine Gravino[2], and Federica Sarro[3]

[1] Dipartimento di Ingegneria Elettrica e delle Tecnologie dell'Informazione,
Università di Napoli "Federico II", Naples, Italy
{anna.corazza,sergio.dimartino}@unina.it
[2] Dipartimento di Informatica, Università di Salerno, Fisciano, Italy
{fferrucci,gravino}@unisa.it
[3] CREST, Department of Computer Science, University College London,
London, UK
f.sarro@ucl.ac.uk

Abstract. Software companies exploit data about completed projects to estimate the development effort required for new projects. Software size is one of the most important information used to this end. However, different methods for sizing software exist and companies may require to migrate to a new method at a certain point. In this case, in order to exploit historical data they need to resize the past projects with the new method. Besides to be expensive, resizing is also often not possible due to the lack of adequate documentation. To support size measurement migration, we propose a transfer learning approach that allows to avoid resizing and is able to estimate the effort of new projects based on the combined use of data about past projects measured with the previous measurement method and projects measured with the new one. To assess our proposal, an empirical analysis is carried out using an industrial dataset of 25 projects. Function Point Analysis and COSMIC are the measurement methods taken into account in the study.

Keywords: Effort estimation · COSMIC · Function points · Transfer learning

1 Introduction

Software development effort estimation represents a crucial management activity. Software companies exploit data about completed projects to estimate the effort required to develop new projects. Besides the actual effort needed to develop past projects, software size is one of the most important information employed to this end. In this context, Functional Size Measurement (FSM) methods are especially important since they are meant to provide an early software size estimation based on the Functional User Requirements (FURs). Several FSMs exist that differ in several aspects. Function Point Analysis (FPA) [1] was the first FSM method;

© Springer International Publishing Switzerland 2015
P. Abrahamsson et al. (Eds.): PROFES 2015, LNCS 9459, pp. 251–267, 2015.
DOI: 10.1007/978-3-319-26844-6_19

conceived in the era of transactional systems, it is meant to size a software product by identifying the set of "features" it provides. COSMIC, initially conceived for real time systems, sizes a software depending on the data movements from/to persistent storage and users, that can be deducted from FURs [2] needed to realize each requirement. COSMIC is considered a 2nd generation FSM method to distinguish it from other previous FSM methods (including FPA) that represent 1st generation FSM. Software companies choose an FSM method based on several criteria, e.g., know-how, customers measurement requirements, organizational policies or also effectiveness. So, the migration from a method to another might be motivated by the changes in one or more of those criteria. Nevertheless, a company that wants to migrate from a measurement method to another and use the new method for effort estimation needs to face the lack of historical data in terms of the new measure. This happens for example to the software companies that would like to migrate from a 1st generation FSM method (e.g., FPA) to a 2nd generation FSM method (COSMIC).

To address the problem, a company could re-measure the past projects with the new measurement method. Besides being expensive, often resizing is also not possible due to the lack of adequate documentation. Another solution could be sizing only the new projects and use public data from other companies (i.e., without-company) until the company builds its own database (i.e., within-company) to predict software development effort. However, there is no evidence in literature that without-company models perform as well as within-company models to predict the effort of new projects [3]. Therefore, the use of statistical conversion equations from FPA to COSMIC has been proposed to automatically re-size past projects (e.g. [4,5]). Several conversion equations have been proposed, based on the use of different datasets and regression methods. Nevertheless, the effectiveness of this approach strongly depends on the employed conversion equations [6], especially when the conversion equation is obtained from without-company data [7].

In this paper we propose a different approach, based on *transfer learning* and able to estimate the effort of new projects exploiting and adjusting the information gathered about past projects over the time. The approach proposed herein builds adaptive regression models based on the combined use of data on past projects sized with the previous measurement method (source domain) and incoming data about new projects sized with the new measurement method (target domain). In particular, to estimate the effort of new projects sized with COSMIC, we start by applying Least Squares Regression (LSR) to the projects measured with FPA. Then we apply the LSR on the (few) COSMIC points, in combination with a regularization factor that allows the estimator to start from the source initial solution and smoothly adapt to the target domain, until enough information is available in terms of projects measured with COSMIC. In other words, we exploit the knowledge acquired from the source domain as long as we do not have enough points in the target domain.

To assess the effectiveness of the proposal, we carried out an empirical study using an industrial dataset of 25 projects. We use as baseline the predictions obtained with the LSR estimation model based only on FPA sizes. Furthermore, we compare the predictions provided by the proposed approach with respect to those obtained by using only COSMIC sizes. Finally, we also perform a comparison with the predictions obtained by a simple conversion equation.

In the remainder of the paper, Sect. 2 provides background information on the employed FSM methods and on the conversion equations from FPA to COSMIC. Section 3 introduces the proposed transfer learning approach. Section 4 explains the design of the empirical study and reports its results, while Sect. 5 discusses the threats to its validity. Related work are presented in Sect. 6. Section 7 concludes the paper.

2 Functional Size Measures: 1st and 2nd Generation

In the following, we first provide a brief history of FSM methods and then the main notions of FPA and COSMIC methods. We also present the related work on the migration from FPA to COSMIC.

2.1 Functional Measurement Methods

In our investigation we focused on Functional Size Measures, because, differently from dimensional measures, such as Lines of Code, they are particularly suitable to be applied in the early phases of the development lifecycle, when only Functional User Requirements (FURs) are available, being the typical choice for tasks such as estimating a project development effort.

The first FSM method proposed in the literature was FPA, introduced by Albrecht in 1979 [1] as a measure to quantify the functionalities provided by a software from the end-user point of view. Since 1986 FPA is managed by the International Function Point Users Group (IFPUG) [8] and it is named IFPUG FPA (or IFPUG, for short), which has been standardized by ISO as ISO/IEC 20926:2009. FPA has evolved in many different ways (e.g., MkII Function Point, the Boeing 3D Function Points, or the Full Function Point (FFP) [9]). Since these methods are all based on the original formulation by Albrecht, they are also known as 1st generation FSM methods.

At the end of the 90's a group of software measurers formed the *Common Software Measurement International Consortium* (COSMIC) to define a new FSM method to overcome some limitations of the original formulation. The result was the COSMIC-FFP method, which is considered the first "2nd generation FSM method". To highlight this concept, the first version of the method is the 2.0. Important refinements were introduced in 2007 in the version 3.0, named simply COSMIC and standardized as ISO/IEC 19761:2011. The current version of COSMIC is 4.0.1, introduced in April 2015.

In the following we describe the main concepts underlying the IFPUG and COSMIC methods. Among the 1st generation methods, we analyze IFPUG since it is still the most widely used by software practitioners.

2.2   The IFPUG Method

IFPUG sizes an application usually using its FURs. Indeed, to identify the set of "features" provided by the software, each FUR is functionally decomposed into Base Functional Components (BFC), and each BFC is categorized into one of the five *Data* or *Transactional* BFC Types. The Data BFC are defined as follows:

- Internal Logical Files (ILF) are logical, persistent entities maintained by the application to store information of interest.
- External Interface Files (EIF) are logical, persistent entities referenced by the application, but are maintained by another software application.

While the Transactional BFC are defined as follows:

- External Inputs (EI) are logical, elementary business processes crossing the application boundary to maintain the data on an Internal Logical File.
- External Outputs (EO) are logical, elementary business processes that result in data leaving the application boundary to meet a user requirements (e.g., reports, screens).
- External Inquires (EQ) are logical, elementary business processes that consist of a data trigger followed by a retrieval of data that leaves the application boundary (e.g., browsing of data).

Then, the "complexity" of each BFC is assessed through the identification of further attributes (such as the number of data fields to be processed). Once derived this information, a table provided in the IFPUG method [8] specifies the complexity of each function, in terms of Unadjusted Function Points (UFP). The sum of all these UFPs gives the functional size of the application. Subsequently, a Value Adjustment Factor (VAF) can be computed to take into account some non-functional requirements, such as Performances, Reusability, and so on. The final size of the application in terms of Function Points is given by $FP = UFP \cdot VAF$. For more details on the IFPUG method, readers may refer to the counting manual [8].

2.3   The COSMIC Method

The basic idea underlying the COSMIC method is that, for many types of software, most of the development effort is devoted to handle data movements from/to persistent storage and users. Thus, the number of these data movements can provide a meaningful sight of the system size [2]. To identify and count these data movements, the measurement process consists of three phases [2]:

1. The *Measurement Strategy* phase is meant to define, among others, the *purpose* of the measurement, the *scope* (i.e. the set of FUR to be included in the measurement), and the *functional users* of each piece of software.

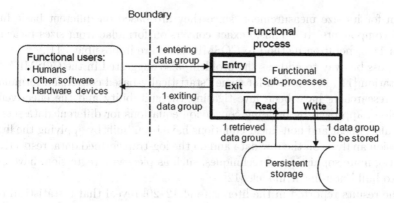

Fig. 1. The four types of COSMIC Data Movements, and their relationship with a Functional Process [2]

2. The *Mapping Phase* requires to express each FUR in the form required by the *COSMIC Generic Software Model*. This model, necessary to identify the key elements to be measured, assumes that (*i*) each FUR can be mapped into a unique *functional process*, meant as a cohesive and independently executable set of data movements, (*ii*) each functional process consists of *sub-processes*, and (*iii*) each sub-process may be either a *data movement* or a data manipulation.

   As depicted in Fig. 1, data movements are defined as follows:
   - An Entry (E) moves a data group from a functional user across the boundary into the functional process where it is required.
   - An Exit (X) moves a data group from a functional process across the boundary to the functional user that requires it.
   - A Read (R) moves a data group from persistent storage within each of the functional process that requires it.
   - A Write (W) moves a data group lying inside a functional process to persistent storage.
3. The *Measurement Phase*, where the data movements of each functional process have to be identified and counted. Each of them is counted as 1 COSMIC Function Point (CFP) that is the COSMIC measurement unit. Thus, the size of an application within a defined scope is obtained by summing the sizes of all the functional processes within the scope.

For more details about the COSMIC method, readers are referred to the COSMIC Measurement Manual [2].

2.4 Converting Function Points into COSMIC

From the brief descriptions of the two FSM methods reported in the previous sections, we can see that FPA and COSMIC consider different aspects of a software system for its size measurement, since they are based on different basic functional components [10]. Thus, "exact conversion formulae from sizes measured with a 1st generation method to COSMIC sizes are impossible" [11].

A possible way to address the problem, also suggested in the COSMIC documentation [11], is to search for some "statistically-based conversion formulae". Some researchers have been investigating the suitability and the effectiveness of such an approach by building conversion equations for different data sets. In particular, linear and non-linear equations have been built by applying the linear regression analysis on the raw data and on the log-transformed data, respectively [4]. Also, more sophisticated techniques, such as piecewise regression, have been used to build non-linear models [12].

The results reported in the literature [4,12–20] reveal that a statistical conversion is possible, thus supporting the suggestions provided in the COSMIC documentation [11]. The studies also showed that both linear and non-linear models should be analyzed to identify the best correlation. Furthermore, more complex techniques, such as piecewise regression [12], did not provide significantly better results, being at the same time hardly applicable.

As results of these investigations different conversion equations have been proposed, that might be exploited to convert historical FP based data sets into COSMIC based data sets. Among them, empirical evidence seem to suggest that a trivial 1 CFP $\cong$ 1 FP conversion could be applied to have a quick and dirty approximation of the size in terms of COSMIC [4], even if authors pointed out that "1 to 1 conversion cannot be attributed to anything other than an influential coincidence" [4], as FPA and COSMIC are meant to measure different attributes of the software.

In [6] we analyzed the effectiveness of all the conversion equations proposed in the literature for effort estimation purposes. The obtained results revealed that the effectiveness depends on the employed conversion equations. No guidelines can be provided to the software company on how to carry out the selection. Furthermore, the use of without-company conversion equations resulted to be worse than within-company conversion equations [7].

For this reason, we decided to investigate a different strategy based on the idea of *transfer learning* that has been successfully applied in other contexts [21].

3   The Proposed Transfer Learning Approach

To support a company in the migration from a size measure to another, we would like to find a solution aiming at transferring the knowledge about the relationship between software size and development effort, extracted from a *Source Domain* (SD), where each past project is sized in terms of Function Points, to a *Target Domain* (TD), where the size measure is COSMIC. Let us note that, given this problem definition, the SD and the TD have different feature space and distribution. As a consequence, the most of the traditional machine learning methods cannot be applied [21].

Since this is a kind of problem arising in many scenarios, also outside software engineering, the research community has provided a new family of approaches, known as *transfer learning* [21]. Indeed, transfer learning is a general framework including several techniques to bring some knowledge from an SD into a TD on a given task that could be classification, regression or clustering. More formally, given an SD with a *Source Task* (ST) and a TD with a *Target Task* (TT), a transfer learner is aimed at improving the effectiveness of the prediction function in the TD using the knowledge of SD and ST [21].

Given the combinations of differences among Domains and among Tasks, there is a taxonomy of transfer learning approaches, as extensively discussed in [21]. In our case, like the most of transfer learning problems in software engineering [22], we are in the so-called *transductive transfer learning* scenario, where ST and TT are the same (to build an effort estimation model), while SD and TD are different [23]. Moreover, in our case, also the feature spaces between the SD and TD are different, since based on different size measures (Function Points in the SD and COSMIC in the TD).

The goal of our proposal is to transfer the knowledge from an SD based on FP to a TS based on COSMIC, to build an effort estimation model in the TD. This model will be built incrementally, using any new project developed by the company during the migration, and sized only with the new measure. More in details, as we want to learn from both the domains SD and TD, we consider a training set composed by two parts, the source training set T_{FP}, whose points are expressed in terms of FP, and the target training set T_{CFP}, in terms of CFP. The former is composed by $m_{FP} = |T_{FP}|$ points represented by a feature vector x_{FP}, the latter by $m_{CFP} = |T_{CFP}|$ points in the target domain, corresponding to the feature vector x_{CFP}. Clearly, since FPA and COSMIC are able to express the size of a software with one number, the dimension of feature vectors in both domains is equal to 1. Furthermore, in both domains a real number y is associated to each item, representing the actual development effort, expressed in person/hours. In conclusion, we adopt the following notation: $T_{FP} = \{(x_{FP}^i, y^i), 1 \le i \le m_{FP}\}$ and $T_{CFP} = \{(x_{CFP}^i, y^i), 1 \le i \le m_{CFP}\}$.

In the proposed approach we use as estimation technique the Least Square Regression (LSR), since it is a simple but effective technique widely and successfully employed in the industrial context and in several researches to estimate development effort (see e.g., [24–26]). If we had enough previous projects measured with COSMIC, we could simply disregard the dataset based on Function Point and apply LSR to construct an effort estimation equation directly in the target domain. In this case, the LSR equation can be written as follows:

$$(a_{CFP}^*, b_{CFP}^*) = \arg \min_{a,b} \sum_{x_{CFP}^i \in T_{CFP}} \left(a x_{CFP}^i + b - y^i\right)^2 \tag{1}$$

where a_{CFP}^* and b_{CFP}^* represent the coefficient and the intercept of the linear equation minimizing the sum of the squares of the errors.

However, since the proposed approach is meant to support a company at the beginning of the migration when the number of examples in T_{CFP} (i.e. completed projects whose size is measured in CFP) is not sufficient for an effective learning of the relationship between software size and development effort, we extract as much information as possible from the source domain to improve regression in the target domain.

To this aim, we apply LSR to estimate the solution in the source domain:

$$(a_{\text{FP}}^*, b_{\text{FP}}^*) = \arg\min_{a,b} \sum_{x_{\text{FP}}^i \in T_{\text{FP}}} \left(a x_{\text{FP}}^i + b - y^i\right)^2. \tag{2}$$

Parameters $(a_{\text{FP}}^*, b_{\text{FP}}^*)$ represent the information that we extract from the SD and will inject in the final estimator.

Now, starting from the observation that a relationship 1 to 1 between FP and COMSIC could be a basic approximation [4], we want that this estimator considers these parameters as a good approximation until enough information is available in terms of projects measured with COSMIC. Better than that, we want that, starting from this initial estimation, it smoothly adapts to the new COSMIC-based domain.

Regularization factors are often used in machine learning to minimize the value of parameters. In our case, however, the introduction of such a factor aims to pushing the parameters of the LSR models we are trying to learn in the TD to be as similar as possible to the ones trained in the SD. A similar idea is considered in [27] to generalize an approach proposed by [28] for maximum entropy classification. In that case, the approach is considered among the baselines and more complex approaches outperform it. However, in the natural language processing field both the number of features and the source domain training set are much larger than in the case of effort estimation. On the other hand, a crucial aspect of the effort estimation domain is the usual scarcity of past information: in fact usually a software company has just a limited number of both points (past projects) and features (software size) with respect to most machine learning problems, and such approaches would risk overfitting. Therefore, we need to find a good compromise between the effectiveness of the approach and the risk of overfitting.

Thus, we propose a modification of the LSR equation in the TD by introducing a regularization factor that has the effect of favoring the solution which is as similar as possible to the parameters $(a_{\text{FP}}^*, b_{\text{FP}}^*)$ found in the SD:

$$(a_C^*, b_C^*) = \arg\min_{a,b}$$

$$\left((1 - \lambda) \sum_{x_{\text{CFP}}^i \in T_{\text{CFP}}} \left(a x_{\text{CFP}}^i + b - y^i\right)^2 + \lambda \left((a - a_{\text{FP}}^*)^2 + (b - b_{\text{FP}}^*)^2\right)\right). \tag{3}$$

The weight of the regularization factor is controlled by the value of λ: when its value is large, the resulting parameters will be more similar to the optimal SD solution, due to the effect of the regularization factor. On the contrary, when its value is lower, the resulting parameters will depend more on the new projects in the target training set. At the limit, for a null value of λ, the estimation will be only based on the projects measured with COSMIC, which is the ideal situation when enough observations with the new measures have been collected.

After some experiments, we found that a simple way to define this factor is $\lambda = \frac{1}{m_{CFP}+\epsilon}$, where ϵ is a small number which avoids that λ goes to infinity in the initial situation, that is when m_{CFP} approaches to zero. The rationale behind this definition of λ is that the more CFP points we get, the less is the importance of the knowledge extracted from the FP source domain.

4   Empirical Study

In this section we present the design and the results of the empirical study we performed to assess the effectiveness of our transfer learning based approach for effort estimation. To this aim, we defined the following research question:

RQ: Is the proposed transfer learning based approach good for effort estimation when migrating from Function Points to COSMIC?

4.1   Data Set

The data set considered in our study includes information about 25 Web applications developed by an Italian medium-sized software company, whose core business is the development of enterprise information systems, mainly for local and central government. In particular, the set of Web applications includes e-government, e-banking, Web portals, and Intranet applications. All the projects were developed with SUN J2EE or Microsoft .NET technologies. Oracle has been the most commonly adopted DBMS, but also SQL Server, Access and MySQL were employed in some of these projects.

As for the collection of the information, the software company used timesheets to keep track of the Web application development effort. In particular, each team member annotated the information about his/her development effort on each project every day, and weekly each project manager stored the sum of the efforts for the team. Furthermore, to collect all the significant information to calculate the values of the size measure in terms of COSMIC, we defined a template to be filled in by the project managers. All the project managers were trained on the use of the questionnaires. One of the authors analyzed the filled templates and the analysis and design documents, in order to cross-check the provided information. The same author calculated the values of the size measure. As for the calculation of the size in terms of IFPUG, the company has always applied this FSM method to measure its past applications.

Table 1 reports on some summary statistics related to the 25 Web applications employed in our study[1]. The variables are EFF, i.e., the actual effort expressed in terms of person-hours, CFP, expressed in terms of number of COSMIC Function Points, and FP, expressed in terms of number of Function Points.

---

[1] Raw data cannot be revealed because of a Non Disclosure Agreement with the software company.

Table 1. Descriptive statistics of EFF, CFP and FP

Var	Obs	Min	Max	Mean	Median	Std Dev
EFF	25	782	4537	2577.00	2686	988.14
CFP	25	163	1090	602.04	611	268.47
FP	25	89	915	366.76	304	208.65

4.2   Validation Method

To assess the prediction models we performed a cross validation, by considering a training set made of N points for which we have both Function Points and COSMIC measures (i.e., FP and CFP variables). We wanted to evaluate the performance of the proposed approach as a function of the dimension of the source training set m_{FP}: that is, we took the FP for m_{FP} points, and the CFP for the remaining training points, which formed the target training set.

Although the dimension of our data set is reasonable for the task, it is quite small for evaluation. In order to exploit it as much as possible, for each value of m_{FP}, we adopted the Leave-One-Out (LOO) protocol: at each iteration we kept a point for testing, while we split the remaining $N - 1$ points in source and target training sets, built the estimator and applied it to the test point. All in all, as the dimension of the source training set is m_{FP}, the target training set had size $m_{CFP} = N - m_{FP} - 1$. The performance on the single test points was then merged to obtain the performance on the complete data set.

In the proposed solution, the sequence in which projects are considered (being in m_{FP} or in m_{CFP}) may strongly impact the results. In order to avoid the chance of obtaining an extremely favorable or unfavorable disposition of points between the two training sets, we randomized the experiment by repeating the LOO procedure on 100 random permutations of the data set for each value of m_{FP}, and then considering the average of the performance. Furthermore, on the basis of the standard deviation of performance, we can also estimate its confidence interval.

4.3   Employed Benchmarks

Since we wanted to verify whether the proposed transfer learning approach can support the companies in the migration from FPA to COSMIC for development effort estimation, as baseline we considered the predictions obtained with the estimation model obtained from the Function Points sizes (named *FP model* in the following). The rationale is that the company should achieve effort predictions that are at least not significantly worse than those it would obtain going on with FPA. Furthermore, we compared the predictions obtained by the model built with the transfer learning based approach (named CFP_{TL} *model* in the following) with those obtained by exploiting the estimation model based on the measured COSMIC sizes (named *CFP model* in the following). Indeed, this represent the accuracy the company could obtain by a dataset whose points are all measured in COSMIC. Finally, we consider also the 1 CFP $\cong$ 1 FP conversion, since it is the starting point of our transfer learner. In the following we denote by CFP_{FP} this model. It is important to note that the FP and CFP_{FP} models provide different size predictions because in the application of the LOO for the former we measured the observations in the training and test sets in terms of FP while for the latter the observation in the test set is measured in terms of CFP.

The three estimation models for the three baselines were built using LSR employing FP, CFP, and CFP_{FP} as independent variables, respectively. The dependent variable was EFF for all the three models.

4.4 Evaluation Criteria

The accuracy of the obtained prediction was evaluated exploiting Absolute Residuals (AR), i.e., $|Actual - Predicted|$, where $Actual$ and $Predicted$ are the actual and the estimated efforts, respectively. To have a summary measure for comparing the different estimation approaches we employed Mean of AR (MAR) [29]. In particular the results are presented through a graphical representation, namely a simple plot. A method X is better than another method Y if the MAR value obtained with X is less than the one of obtained with Y.

Moreover, we tested whether there was a statistically significant difference between the absolute residuals achieved with the CFP_{TL} model and those obtained with the FP, CFP, and CFP_{FP} models. The results were intended as statistically significant at $\alpha = 0.05$. In order to have also an indication of the practical/managerial significance of the results, we verified the effect size, which is a simple way of quantifying the standardized difference between two groups. In particular, we employed the Cliffs d non-parametric effect size measure because it is suitable to compute the magnitude of the difference when a non parametric test is used. In the empirical software engineering field, the magnitude of the effect sizes measured using the Cliffs d can be classified as follows: negligible ($d < 0.147$), small (0.147 to 0.33), medium (0.33 to 0.474), and large ($d > 0.474$) [30].

4.5 Results

Figure 2 shows the main results we obtained in the study. In particular, we have reported the MAR values plus the standard deviation we got over 100 random sequences of projects using the CFP_{TL} estimation model. This is done on a range from 2 to 24 projects measured with COSMIC. This because we cannot perform LSR on less than 2 points. The figure also shows the MAR values we obtained using the FP, CFP_{FP}, and CFP models. For these three models, we exploited the leave-one-out cross validation on the entire data set of 25 projects to obtain the effort predictions and the corresponding mean of the absolute residuals.

We can observe that the MAR values achieved with the CFP_{TL} estimation model are lower than those obtained with the FP and CFP_{FP} models. Thus, the effort predictions obtained with the proposed transfer learning based approach

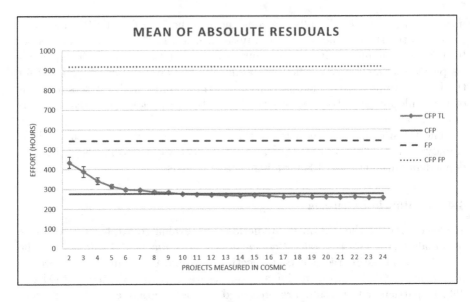

Fig. 2. Results of the study in terms of MAR

are better than those obtained with the model based on Function Points sizes and those achieved using the estimated COSMIC sizes (i.e., those considering the assumption 1 CFP $\cong$ 1 FP). In particular, the MAR value achieved with the CFP$_{FP}$ model is about three times higher than the one obtained with the CFP$_{TL}$ model, thus highlighting much better results with the transfer learning approach. The values of MAR achieved with the CFP$_{TL}$ model are about two times lower than the MAR value obtained with the FP model.

The results achieved in terms of MAR are confirmed by the performed statistical tests. Indeed, the performed Mann-Whitney test revealed that the absolute residuals obtained with the CFP$_{TL}$ models are significantly lower than those obtained with the FP model (p-value = 0.008) with a medium effect size (d = 0.443). Similarly, the predictions obtained with the CFP$_{TL}$ model are significantly better than those obtained with the CFP$_{FP}$ model (p-value < 0.001) with a large effect size (d = 0.917).

These results clearly reveal that the company involved in our study can abandon the FP based model and employ the CFP$_{TL}$ model for effort estimation during the migration (from Function Points) to COSMIC as method for sizing their applications since their second project in COSMIC.

To further highlight the potential of the proposed transfer learning based approach we have also compared the effort predictions obtained with the CFP$_{TL}$ model with those achieved using the CFP model. The results reported in Fig. 2 show that after measuring 8–9 Web applications with COSMIC and using the obtained sizes in the proposed transfer learning based approach the obtained effort predictions are very close to the ones achieved using the model based only on the measured COSMIC sizes.

The results in Fig. 2 also show that for several points (i.e., from 13 to 24) the effort predictions obtained with CFP_{TL} model are even slightly better that those achieved with the CFP model, since the corresponding MAR values are lower than those achieved with CFP model. This is a rather surpising results that can be justified as follows. While usually the Absolute Residuals with COSMIC are by far lower than those with FPA, on one specific project the Absolute Residuals with COSMIC are much higher, being almost double of FPA. This of course has a strong impact on the cumulative measure MAR. Probably, when using the transfer learner equation, this problem is mitigated by the 100 runs. However, the difference achieved in the predictions is not statistically significant (p-value $= 0.122$) with a small effect size ($d = 0.267$). We think that this point deserves further investigation in the future.

The results presented and discussed above allow us to positively answer our research question: *the proposed transfer learning based approach is good for effort estimation when migrating from Function Points to COSMIC.*

5 Threats to Validity

It is widely recognized that several factors can bias the construct, internal, external, and conclusion validity of empirical studies [31].

As for the construct validity, how to collect information to determine size measures and actual effort represents a crucial aspect [32]. As described in Sect. 4, we have supervised the procedure employed by the involved software company to carefully collect the information we needed for the empirical analysis. In particular, we tried to perform the data collection task in a controlled and uniform fashion. Of course we have to take into account that empirical studies do not ensure the level of confidence achieved with controlled experiments.

Some factors should be taken into account for the internal validity: subjects' authoring and reliability of the data and lack of standardization [31,33,34]. The managers involved in the study were professionals who worked in the software company. No initial selection of the subjects was carried out, so no bias has been apparently introduced. Moreover, the software applications were developed with technologies and methodologies that subjects had experienced. Consequently, confounding effects from the employed methods and tools should be excluded. As for the reliability of the data and lack of standardization, the used questionnaires were the same for all the Web applications, and the project managers were instructed on how to fill them in, to correctly provide the required information. Instrumentation effects in general did not occur in this kind of studies.

As for the conclusion validity, we carefully applied the estimation methods and the statistical tests, verifying all the required assumptions (e.g., the hypotheses underlying the application of linear regression analysis).

With regard to the external validity, we are confident that the type of the analyzed Web applications did not bias the validity of the achieved results, since for their functionalities, target platforms, and complexity they can be considered representative samples of typical current Web applications. Another threat could be the fact that we exploited only applications from one company. To the best of our knowledge, there is only one data set that contains (Web and non-Web) applications from different company, i.e., ISBSG. However, in our analysis we were interested in analyzing the experience and the possibilities for the migration among size measures for a single company developing Web applications. Nevertheless, it is recognized that the results obtained for a given company might not hold for others. Indeed, each development context might be characterized by some specific project and human factors, such as development process, developer experience, application domain, tools, technologies used, time, and budget constraints that could influence the results [35].

6   Related Work on Transfer Learning in Software Engineering

Transfer learning techniques have been already applied in software engineering in the last years, showing their potential. Some studies applied them in the field of defect prediction. Among them, Zimmermann et al. [36] found that defect predictors performed worse when trained on cross-application data than from within-application data. Other recent studies on the use of TL for defect predictions are those by Ma et al. [37] and Nam et al. [38].

Focusing in the field of effort estimation, some studies have been done in the past to migrate estimation models among companies. A survey can be found in [3,24]. More recently, transfer learning approaches have also been proposed for effort estimation [22,39–41], as a suitable way to integrate data from different companies and different time frames (which is a different problem from the one we are willing to address). To the best of our knowledge, no one has ever proposed a migration strategy from a size measure to another, using transfer learning approaches.

7   Conclusion

We have investigated the problem of migrating from a measurement method to another and use the new size measure for effort estimation purposes. The subject of our study was a company that decided to migrate from FPA [1] to COSMIC [2], which represents one of the most recent and common transitions we are observing in the context of software measurement. The problem for a company mainly consists in the lack of enough data (in terms of the new measurement method) to build an estimation model. A simple way to overcome this problem could be re-sizing the past projects with the new measurement method. However, besides to be expensive, resizing is also not always possible due to the lack of adequate documentation. As alternative, in the paper we propose to exploit a transfer learning approach able to estimate the effort of new projects exploiting and adjusting the information gathered about past projects over the time. In particular, we aimed at transferring the knowledge extracted from a source domain, in this case represented by projects for which we have the Function Points metrics, to the target domain, where points are represented by COSMIC.

As estimation technique we applied the LSR, adapted by using a regularization factor that allows the estimator to start from an initial estimation in terms of Function Points sizes and smoothly adapt to the new COSMIC domain, until enough information is available in terms of projects measured with COSMIC.

To assess the proposed transfer learning approach, we have performed an empirical study using an industrial dataset of 25 projects and employing leave-one-out cross validation as validation strategy. The results have revealed that the effort estimations obtained with the proposed transfer learning approach are significant better than those achieved with a Function Points based estimation model. Furthermore, the predictions achieved with the proposed approach are quite close with those achieved by employing an estimation model exploiting only COSMIC sizes. Thus, the proposed transfer learning based approach is good for effort estimation and the company involved in our study can employ it for effort estimation purposes during for migration from a 1st generation FSM method (i.e., Function Points Analysis) to a 2nd generation FSM method (i.e., COSMIC).

Concerning future work, several directions could be consider for our research. First of all, we intend to replicate the study with further datasets, also considering different types of software projects and a larger number of points. Moreover, we intend to verify whether conversion equations built on external datasets could be employed in the application of the method to perform the adaptation towards the COSMIC domain more rapidly. Besides the COSMIC and Functions Points based measurement methods, the migration problem could regard other size measurement approaches, e.g., extension of Function Points [9]. So, in the future we could consider the applicability of the proposed transfer learning approaches in other measurement contexts.

References

1. Albrecht, A.: Measuring application development productivity. In: Proceedings of the Joint SHARE/GUIDE/IBM Application Development Symposium, pp. 83–92 (1979)
2. Abran, A., Desharnais, J., Lesterhuis, A., Londeix, B., Meli, R., Morris, P., Oligny, S., O'Neill, M., Rollo, T., Rule, G., Santillo, L., Symons, C., Toivonen, H.: The COSMIC Functional Size Measurement Method Measurement Manual, version 4.0.1 (2015)
3. Mendes, E., Kalinowski, M., Martins, D., Ferrucci, F., Sarro, F.: Cross- vs. within-company cost estimation studies revisited: an extended systematic review. In: Proceedings of the 18th International Conference on Evaluation and Assessment in Software Engineering, EASE 2014, pp. 12:1–12:10 (2014)
4. Cuadrado-Gallego, J.J., Buglione, L., Domínguez-Alda, M.J., Sevilla, M.F., de Mesa, J.A.G., Demirors, O.: An experimental study on the conversion between IFPUG and COSMIC functional size measurement units. Inf. Softw. Technol. **52**, 347–357 (2010)
5. Lavazza, L.: An evaluation of the statistical convertibility of function points into cosmic function points. Empir. Softw. Eng. **19**, 1075–1110 (2014)
6. Di Martino, S., Ferrucci, F., Gravino, C., Sarro, F.: Web Effort Estimation: Function Points Analysis vs COSMIC (submitted to an International Journal for review)

7. Ferrucci, F., Gravino, C., Sarro, F.: Conversion from IFPUG FPA to COSMIC: within-vs without-company equations. In: 2014 40th EUROMICRO Conference on Software Engineering and Advanced Applications, pp. 293–300 (2014)
8. IFPUG: International Function Point Users Group. www.ifpug.org
9. Gencel, Ç., Demirörs, O.: Functional size measurement revisited. ACM Trans. Softw. Engi. Methodol. **17**(3), 71–106 (2008)
10. Van Heeringen, H.: Changing from FPA to COSMIC- a transition framework. In: Software Measurement European Forum (2007)
11. Abran, A., Londeix, B., O'Neill, M., Santillo, L., Vogelezang, F., Desharnais, J.M., Morris, P., Rollo, T., Symons, C., Lesterhuis, A., Oligny, S., Rule, G., Toivonen, H.: The COSMIC Functional Size Measurement Method, Version 3.0, Advanced and Related Topics (2007)
12. Lavazza, L., Morasca, S.: Convertibility of function points into COSMIC function points: a study using piecewise linear regression. Inf. Softw. Technol. **53**(8), 874–884 (2011)
13. Ferrucci, F., Gravino, C., Sarro, F.: A case study on the conversion of function points into cosmic. In: The Proceedings of the 37th EUROMICRO Conference on Software Engineering and Advanced Applications (SEAA), pp. 461–464 (2011)
14. Abran, A.: Convertibility Across Measurement Methods, pp. 269–280. Wiley, New York (2010)
15. Ho, V., Abran, A., Fetcke, T.: A comparative study case of COSMIC, full function Point and IFPUG methods. Technical report, Département dinformatique, Université du Quebec á Montréal, Canada (1999)
16. Desharnais, J., Abran, A., Cuadrado-Gallego, J.: Convertibility of function points to COSMIC: identification and analysis of functional outliers. In: Proceedings of the International Workshop on Software Measurement, pp. 130–146. Shaker-Verlag (2007)
17. Abran, A., Desharnais, J., Azziz, F.: Measurement convertibility: from function points to COSMIC. In: Proceedings of the International Workshop on Software Measurement, pp. 227–240. Shaker-Verlag (2005)
18. Abualkishik, A.Z., Desharnais, J.M., Khelifi, A., Ghani, A.A.A., Atan, R.B., Selamat, M.H.: An exploratory study on the accuracy of FPA to COSMIC measurement method conversion types. Inf. Softw. Technol. **54**, 1250–1264 (2012)
19. Gencel, Ç., Bideau, C.: Exploring the convertibility between IFPUG and COSMIC function points: preliminary findings. In: Proceedings of International Conference on Software Process and Product Measurement, pp. 170–177 (2012)
20. Lavazza, L., Bianco, V.D., Liu, G.: Analytical convertibility of functional size measures: a tool-based approach. In: Proceedings of International Conference on Software Process and Product Measurement, pp. 160–169 (2012)
21. Pan, S.J., Yang, Q.: A survey on transfer learning. IEEE Trans. Knowl. Data Eng. **22**, 1345–1359 (2010)
22. Kocaguneli, E., Menzies, T., Mendes, E.: Transfer learning in effort estimation. Empir. Softw. Engg. **20**, 813–843 (2015)
23. Arnold, A., Nallapati, R., Cohen, W.W.: A comparative study of methods for transductive transfer learning. In: Seventh IEEE International Conference on Data Mining Workshops, ICDM Workshops 2007, pp. 77–82. IEEE (2007)
24. Kitchenham, B., Mendes, E., Travassos, G.: Cross versus within-company cost estimation studies: a systematic review. IEEE Trans. Softw. Eng. **33**, 316–329 (2007)

25. Mendes, E., Di Martino, S., Ferrucci, F., Gravino, C.: Effort estimation: how valuable is it for a Web company to use a cross-company data set, compared to using its own single-company data set? In: Proceedings of the 6th International World Wide Web Conference, pp. 83–93. ACM press (2007)
26. Menzies, T., Chen, Z., Hihn, J., Lum, K.: Selecting best practices for effort estimation. IEEE Trans. Softw. Eng. **32**, 883–895 (2006)
27. Daumé, H.: Frustratingly easy domain adaptation. In: Proceedings of ACL 2007 (2007)
28. Chelba, C., Acero, A.: Adaptation of maximum entropy capitalizer: Little data can help a lot. In: Lin, D., Wu, D. (eds.) Proceedings of EMNLP 2004, pp. 285–292. Association for Computational Linguistics, Barcelona, Spain (2004)
29. Shepperd, M.J., MacDonell, S.G.: Evaluating prediction systems in software project estimation. Inf. Softw. Technol. **54**, 820–827 (2012)
30. Kampenes, V., Dyba, T., Hannay, J., Sjoberg, I.: A systematic review of effect size in software engineering experiments. Inf. Softw. Technol. **4**, 1073–1086 (2007)
31. Mendes, E., Counsell, S., Mosley, N., Triggs, C., Watson, I.: A comparative study of cost estimation models for web hypermedia applications. Empir. Softw. Eng. **8**, 163–196 (2003)
32. Kaner, C., Bond, W.: Software engineering metrics: what do they measure and how do we know? In: Proceedings of the International Software Metrics Symposium. IEEE press (2004)
33. Mendes, E., Counsell, S., Mosley, N.: Comparison of Web size measures for predicting Web design and authoring effort. IEE Proc. Softw. **149**, 86–92 (2002)
34. Kitchenham, B., Pickard, L., MacDonell, S., Shepperd, M.: What accuracy statistics really measure. IEE Proc. Softw. **148**, 81–85 (2001)
35. Briand, L.C., Wüst, J.: Modeling development effort in object-oriented systems using design properties. IEEE Trans. Softw. Eng. **27**, 963–986 (2001)
36. Zimmermann, T., Nagappan, N., Gall, H., Giger, E., Murphy, B.: Cross-project defect prediction: a large scale experiment on data vs. domain vs. process. In: Proceedings of the 7th Joint Meeting of the European Software Engineering Conference and the ACM SIGSOFT Symposium on the Foundations of Software Engineering, ESEC/FSE 2009, pp. 91–100 (2009)
37. Ma, Y., Luo, G., Zeng, X., Chen, A.: Transfer learning for cross-company software defect prediction. Inf. Softw. Technol. **54**, 248–256 (2012)
38. Nam, J., Pan, S.J., Kim, S.: Transfer defect learning. In: Proceedings of the 2013 International Conference on Software Engineering, pp. 382–391. IEEE Press (2013)
39. Ferrucci, F., Mendes, E., Sarro, F.: Web effort estimation: the value of cross-company data set compared to single-company data set. In: Proceedings of the 8th International Conference on Predictive Models in Software Engineering, PROMISE 2012, pp. 29–38 (2012)
40. Minku, L.L., Yao, X.: How to make best use of cross-company data in software effort estimation? In: Proceedings of the 36th International Conference on Software Engineering, ICSE 2014, pp. 446–456 (2014)
41. Minku, L.L., Sarro, F., Mendes, E., Ferrucci, F.: How to make best use of cross-company data for web effort estimation? In: Proceedings of the 9th ACM/IEEE International Symposium on Empirical Software Engineering and Measurement, ESEM 2015 (2015)

Empirical Generalization

Investigating Functional and Code Size Measures for Mobile Applications: A Replicated Study

Filomena Ferrucci[1], Carmine Gravino[1](✉), Pasquale Salza[1],
and Federica Sarro[2]

[1] Department of Computer Science, University of Salerno, Fisciano, Italy
{fferrucci,gravino,psalza}@unisa.it
[2] Department of Computer Science, University College London, London, UK
f.sarro@ucl.ac.uk

Abstract. In this paper we apply a measurement procedure proposed by van Heeringen and van Gorp to approximate the COSMIC size of mobile applications. We compare this procedure with the one introduced by D'Avanzo et al. We also replicate an empirical study recently carried out to assess whether the COSMIC functional size of mobile applications can be used to estimate the size of the final applications in terms of lines of code, number of bytes of the source code and bytecode. The results showed that the COSMIC functional size evaluated with van Heeringen and van Gorp's method was well correlated to all the size measures taken into account. Nevertheless, the prediction accuracy did not satisfy the evaluation criteria and turned out ot be slightly worse than the one obtained in the original study and based on the approach proposed by D'Avanzo et al.

Keywords: Functional size measurement · COSMIC · Android mobile applications · Code size measure · LOC · Empirical study

1 Introduction

Software sizing is used in software engineering to estimate the size of a software application or component in order to implement other software project management activities, such as effort estimation and productivity benchmarking.

Lines of Code (LOCs) represent one of the most extensively used code size measure and the main input to parametric software cost and effort estimation tools. Nevertheless, LOCs as well as other code size measures are not available early in the development process when effort/cost estimations are needed.

Functional Size Measurement (FSM) methods have been introduced to overcome the limitations of LOCs. They have been widely investigated in software engineering research and also applied in industry for sizing software systems in terms of the functionality provided to the users [14]. The obtained functional size can be used to estimate LOCs using backfiring FSM/LOCs ratios based on earlier projects. Then, the calculated LOCs can be used in the parametric software cost models, e.g., COCOMO [4].

© Springer International Publishing Switzerland 2015
P. Abrahamsson et al. (Eds.): PROFES 2015, LNCS 9459, pp. 271–287, 2015.
DOI: 10.1007/978-3-319-26844-6_20

The Function Point Analysis (FPA), was the first FSM method to be introduced in 1979. Several variants have been then proposed (known as 1st generation FSM methods) to improve the size measurement or extend its application domain. COSMIC [2] is a 2nd generation FSM method, being the first to comply to the standard ISO/IEC14143/1 [14]. It is based on fundamental principles of software engineering and measurement theory, and conceived to be applicable to business, real-time, and infrastructure software (or hybrids of these) [2].

Recent studies have investigated the applicability of 1st and 2nd generation FSM methods to mobile applications [1,8,13,23–26]. This domain is rapidly growing and new software engineering processes, including functional size measurement and estimation methods [23], might be required to improve the quality of these applications. The International Function Point User Groups (IFPUG) has proposed guidelines for the application of IFPUG FPA to mobile applications [24,25] and some software companies have used them [26]. As for COSMIC, at the best of our knowledge, three proposals to size mobile applications have been reported in the literature [1,8,13]. A proposal focused on the measurement of mobile games apps [1], while the other two [8,13] proposed some guidelines for an approximate and quick sizing of mobile apps. In particular, D'Avanzo et al. [8] focused on apps that use internal data storage, while different basic assumptions where made by van Heeringen and van Gorp [13]. The approach proposed by D'Avanzo et al. has been recently applied by Ferrucci et al. [11] to size 13 Android applications, while no study has been reported in the literature on the use of the other existing approaches so far.

In this paper, we apply the measurement approach proposed by van Heeringen and van Gorp [13] to compute the COSMIC size of 13 mobile Android applications. In particular, we replicate the empirical study proposed by Ferrucci et al. [11] to assess (1) how this size relates to some size measures of the source and compiled code, (2) if it can be used to predict the final application code size in terms of LOCs or number of bytes of the source code and bytecode, (3) which approach between [13] and [8] provides better estimates of code size measures for mobile applications?

It is worth noting that the idea of estimating code size in terms of bytes has been recently proposed by Lind and Heldal [19] that presented a practical approach to estimate the size of compiled C code of embedded applications. Their study highlighted a better correlation between bytecode and COSMIC size with respect to LOCs. They argued that this was due to the fact that the compiler behaves always in the same way by filtering differences in programming style (like 'condensed' programs with many operations per line, few comments vs. only one operation per line, many comments). They also encouraged further studies considering different types of applications and from other domains in order to conclude that bytes can be used as code size measure [18].

To carry out the empirical study we employed the same applications and methodology used in our previous work [11] and the measurement method proposed by van Heeringen and van Gorp [13].

The rest of the paper is organised as follows. Section 2 provides background information on COSMIC. Section 3 introduces and compares the two COS-MIC measurement approaches proposed in literature to size mobile applications. Section 4 explains the design of the empirical study and reports its results. Section 5 discusses future work and concludes the paper.

2 COSMIC

Functional size is defined as the size of the software derived by quantifying the Functional User Requirements (FURs) [2]. FURs describe what the software is expected to do for its users. COSMIC defines a standardised measure of software functional size expressed in COSMIC Function Point (CFP) units.

A functional process is one of the main concepts underlying COSMIC. It is defined as a set of data movements representing an elementary part of the FURs. A functional user is defined as a (type of) user that is a sender and/or an intended recipient of data in the FURs. Thus, a functional user can be a human or, for instance, an external device as well. A boundary is a conceptual interface between the software being measured and its functional users. With these definitions, it is possible to focus on four different data movement types: an Entry (E) moves data from a functional user to a functional process; an Exit (X) moves data from a functional process to a functional user; a Write (W) moves data from a functional process to persistent storage; a Read (R): moves data from persistent storage to a functional process.

1 CFP unit is given per each data movement and their sum represents the measured size. COSMIC defines a measurement process that consists of three phases: the Measurement Strategy Phase, the Mapping Phase, and the Measurement Phase. Each of them is explained in the following.

Measurement Strategy Pattern is a concept introduced in the last current version (4.0) of COSMIC [2]. Previous versions do not refer to any strategy patterns. The Measurement Strategy Phase sets the key parameters of the measurement: the purpose, defining what the measurement result will be used for; the scope defining which pieces of software (in terms of FURs) have to be measured; the level of granularity which describes how much detailed the documentation about the software is (e.g., in terms of the requirements description or also the structure description). The complete list of parameters can be found in the COSMIC Context Software Model and it is necessary to carefully define them.

In the *Mapping phase* the measurer extrapolates the functional processes from the available FURs of the software being measured. This is a technical work in which the principles and, above all, the rules of the COSMIC method (reported in the COSMIC Generic Software Model [2]) have to be carefully followed. The measurer identifies the potential functional processes inside the FURs by looking for each functional process that is started by a triggering Entry and comprises at least two data movements: an Entry plus either an Exit or a Write. The triggering Entry is the Entry of the functional user that starts the functional process. Data manipulations inside a functional process are not counted as CFP

[2], i.e., they are considered associated to the corresponding data movements. The object of interest is defined as any 'thing' that is identified from the point of view of the FURs; it may be any physical thing, as well as any conceptual object or part of a conceptual object in the world of the functional user about which the software is required to process and/or store data. Each Entry, Exit, Read, or Write is a movement of data group of a single object of interest. There are only two exceptions: the triggering Entry which can start a functional process without data movement, e.g., in specific enquiry for a list of items; the error/confirmation message which is defined as an Exit for the attention of a human user that either confirms only that entered data is accepted, or only that there is an error in the entered data.

The Measurement Phase defines how to count data movements, consisting in associating a CFP to each data movement. The amount of all data movements represents the functional value of the measurement. It is worth noting that in cases (differently from our work) of aggregating measurement sizes (software stratified into different layers) or when measuring the size of software changes, this phase may become more complex [2].

The COSMIC community has also proposed approaches for counting the size of software in terms of COSMIC by exploiting approximate countings. There are a couple of situations when a need arises in practice to measure a functional size approximately [3]: it can happen either early in the life of a project before the Functional User Requirements (FURs) have been specified in detail ('early sizing'), or when a measurement is needed but there is insufficient time or resources to apply the standard detailed method ('rapid sizing'). These motivations are not mutually exclusive and contribute to reach a trade-off between a correct measurement and time and budget available.

There exist some proposals for a quick and approximate COSMIC sizing (e.g., [3,9,10]). The use of COSMIC approximate methods has also been suggested recently in the context of mobile apps [8,13], with the aim of helping measurers to size mobile apps in a fast and accurate way.

3   Towards Applying COSMIC to Mobile Applications

In this section we summarize the approach proposed by van Heeringen and van Gorp to size mobile apps in terms of COSMIC. We also compare this approach with the one presented by D'Avanzo et al. [8] and experimented in our previous work [11] for code size estimation purposes. The comparison is made in this section in terms of the guidelines of the two approaches applied on a set of functional requirements of a mobile application.

3.1   van Heeringen and van Gorp Approach

The approach proposed by van Heeringen and van Gorp [13] is based on a set of assumptions: (i) A mobile app is considered to be an application layer that is developed on top of one or more data layers; (ii) No persistent data is stored in the application layer because they consider storing data on the device as a technical solution. Thus, no Reads and Writes are expected; (iii) Because mobile apps are considered to be business applications, they include possible error messages in every functional process as 1 Exit, together with 1 Entry when the messages come from a data layer.

The proposed measurement phase consists in identifying the type of each functional process and quantifying the parameters involved for the identified type of functional process. Five different functional process types ($\mathcal{A}1$–$\mathcal{A}5$) can be identified as follows.

$\mathcal{A}1$. *View Functionality.* Data is presented to at least one of the functional users, with a minimum of 6 COSMIC Functional Points (CFPs): 1 triggering (start) Entry; 1 question for information Exit to the data layer; a couple of 1 Entry and 1 Exit for reception and show of data respectively; a couple of 1 Entry and 1 Exit for reception and show of error messages. The ability of changing the view of the displayed data does not afflict any data movement but other additional data groups add 2 CFPs (1 Entry to receive data and 1 Exit to show). In this case, a separate data movement for the question for information to the data layer is not necessary because it can be included in the previous one. For each data group which shows calculated or derived data, another 1 Exit for showing data is added to the functional size.

$\mathcal{A}2$. *Data Manipulation Functionality.* It is used to manipulate information (add/change/delete) about a data layer, with a minimum of 4 CFPs: 1 start Entry; 1 Exit to provide information to data layer; a couple of 1 Entry and 1 Exit for reception and show of error messages. Further 2 CFPs for any other data group manipulated are considered (1 Entry for entering data by the user and 1 Exit to provide them to the data layer). When the manipulated data is also shown to the functional user, the size is increased of 3 CFPs: 1 question Exit to data layer, 1 Entry for receiving data and 1 Exit for data showing. Furthermore, if there is a validation process involving the data layer, 1 Entry for questioning the data layer and 1 Exit for receiving data are also added.

$\mathcal{A}3$. *Enquiry Functionality.* It shows the data that can be manipulated and it is considered equal to the view functionality ($\mathcal{A}1$).

$\mathcal{A}4$. *User Supporting Functionality.* If it is mandatory in order to complete a manipulation process, it is reduced to $\mathcal{A}2$. On the other hand, when it can be avoided but the user can exploit it, e.g. a calendar view to simplify the insertion of a date, it is considered as a separate functionality and it is reduced to $\mathcal{A}1$.

$\mathcal{A}5$. *Special Functionality.* It includes some special cases:

- Dynamically generated menus, when the view of the menu depends on the information from the data layer. $\mathcal{A}1$ is applied;
- Log in, with a total of 5 CFPs: 1 start Entry, 1 Exit for credentials providing to the data layer, 1 Entry for log status and a couple Exit/Entry for error messages. The log out functionality has only a couple of Entry/Exit for messages showed from the application layer. If the log out is recorded into the data layer, another 1 Exit to provide credentials and 1 Entry to receive error messages are expected;

- Help functionality, $\mathcal{A}1$ is applied;
- Invoking External Functionality, it is outside the scope of the app being measured. Therefore, no CFPs are considered.

3.2 D'Avanzo et al. Approach

D'Avanzo et al. [8] propose guidelines to measure business mobile applications where the persistent storage is considered as an internal database, so it is accessible by Read and Write data movements. Moreover, differently from van Heeringen and van Gorp [13], in the case of external applications, these guidelines consider only the data movements between the application being measured and the external one. The guidelines can be summarised as follow:

$\mathcal{B}1$. *Open the application and see info on home screen.* Data movements are: 1 triggering Entry, by opening the application; 1 Read from persistent storage; 1 Exit to show data. If other data is expected an additional 1 Read and 1 Exit are counted, or only 1 Exit is counted in case the data shown is the result of a calculation.

$\mathcal{B}2$. *See details.* Same as $\mathcal{B}1$ except for the additional data movements.

$\mathcal{B}3$. *Create/set/delete data.* Data movements are: 1 triggering Entry; 1 Write to persistent storage; 1 Exit for error/confirmation messages.

$\mathcal{B}4$. *Update data.* It is a combination of the functional process to enquiry the data ($\mathcal{B}2$) and the one to update them ($\mathcal{B}3$), with at least 6 CFPs expected.

$\mathcal{B}5$. *Process input and stored data to provide an output.* Data movements are: 1 triggering Entry; 1 Read from persistent storage; 1 Exit to show the result. Further couples of Entry/Exit are added for each further data visualisation, not read from the database, and 1 Exit if error/confirmation messages are expected.

$\mathcal{B}6$. *Share data with an external application.* Data movements are: 1 triggering Entry; 1 Read from persistent storage; 1 Exit towards external application. Any possible error/confirmation messages are considered associated to the external application functional process and they are not measured.

$\mathcal{B}7$. *Import data from an SD card to the database.* Data movements are: 1 triggering Entry; 1 Entry from an SD card; 1 Exit for error/confirmation messages; 1 Write to persistent storage; 1 Exit for error/confirmation messages. Another Exit is counted if the data is also shown to the user.

$\mathcal{B}8$. *Export data from the database to an SD card.* Data movements are: 1 triggering Entry; 1 Read from persistent storage; 1 Exit to SD card; 1 Exit for error/confirmation messages. Another Exit if the data is shown to the user.

3.3 Example of Application and Discussion

To better understand the differences between the two considered approaches, an example of application is given. We considered an app realising an academic transcript manageable by the user, whose FURs are described in Table 1. From here on we will refer to the van Heeringen and van Gorp approach as $\mathcal{A}$, while $\mathcal{B}$ will denote the D'Avanzo et al. approach.

Table 1. Functional user requirements.

FUR	Description
R1	User opens the application to see on home screen the principal info included in his transcript, i.e., the list of exams, the number of exams, the number of credits and the average mark
R2	User clicks on the icon button 'new' to insert data about a new exam in the database. The system provides error/confirmation messages
R3	User selects an exam from the list in the home screen and clicks on the button 'delete' to delete it from the database. The system provides error/confirmation messages
R4	User clicks on the button 'delete all' to delete all the exams data from the database. The system provides error/confirmation messages
R5	User selects an exam from the list in the home screen and clicks on the button 'update' to update its data in the database. The system provides error/confirmation messages
R6	User selects an exam from the list in the home screen and clicks on the button 'details' to see detailed info
R7	User clicks on the icon button 'projection average' and the system shows a new box containing the current average mark and a form to specify the number of future exams, their credits and the expected mark. The system provides the expected average mark given by the input data values and the current exams
R8	User clicks on the button 'export exams' to export exams from database to SD. The system provides error/confirmation messages
R9	User clicks on the button 'import exams' to import exams from SD to the database. The system provides two error/confirmation messages, one for the input from SD and another for the writing on the database. The system shows the list of exams after importing
R10	User sets the lode value for the statistics $(30+0, 30+1$ etc.$)$. The system provides error/confirmation messages
R11	User sets maximum credits value. The system provides error/confirmation messages
R12	User clicks on the button to read change log
R13	User clicks on the button to read FAQ
R14	User clicks on the button to read application license
R15	User clicks on the button to read info to donate a payment to the developer

Since R1 is an opening functionality which lies on data visualisation, $\mathcal{A}$ suggests to apply rule $\mathcal{A}1$ with 6 basic CFPs and 1 additional Exit for calculated and shown statistic data, with a total of 7 CFPs. $\mathcal{B}$ applies rule $\mathcal{B}1$ with 4 CFPs, which also include 1 Exit for calculated data. The main difference in this case regards the different point of views about the role of the persistent storage, considered as a distinct functional user in $\mathcal{A}$ and as belonging to the application boundary in $\mathcal{B}$. This means that every Read in $\mathcal{B}$ matches a couple Exit/Entry in $\mathcal{A}$. Moreover, $\mathcal{A}$ expects always the presence of error messages movements, then a couple Entry/Exit is needed to read/show the messages.

R2, R3, R4, R10, R11 refer to data manipulation functionality, then $\mathcal{A}$ applies rule $\mathcal{A}2$ with a total of 4 CFPs while $\mathcal{B}3$ is applied for $\mathcal{B}$ obtaining 3 CFPs. Thus, $\mathcal{A}$ and $\mathcal{B}$ behave in a similar ways because 1 Write of $\mathcal{B}$ matches 1 Exit of $\mathcal{A}$ towards persistent storage and 1 Exit to show error messages is considered for both. $\mathcal{A}$ includes an additional Entry to read error messages from data layer.

$\mathcal{A}$ and $\mathcal{B}$ interpret R5 in different ways. The FUR is an update activity based on data already present into the persistent storage. $\mathcal{A}$ applies rule $\mathcal{A}2$ for data manipulation. On the other hand, $\mathcal{B}$ applies $\mathcal{B}4$ which is a mix of $\mathcal{B}2$ and $\mathcal{B}3$, relying on the fact that the data has to be read before writing the modification. This difference brings $\mathcal{A}$ to count 4 CFPs against the 6 CFPs obtained with $\mathcal{B}$.

R6 is treated as a visualisation functionality in both the approaches. Because there is just data extrapolation from persistent storage, without any calculation, $\mathcal{A}$ applies rule $\mathcal{A}1$ with a score of 6 CFPs. $\mathcal{B}$ identifies a specific rule (i.e., $\mathcal{B}2$) for this kind of FUR, where the main intent is to show details about a selected item, with a score of 3.

In R7, the data are first shown after user's triggering button. Thus, $\mathcal{A}$ requires to apply rule $\mathcal{A}1$ with a score of 6 CFPs. After this, the user can edit 3 different boxes and enquiry the persistent storage on any change. Rule $\mathcal{A}1$ states that for each new enquiry, other 2 CFPs has to be considered. This leads to a total of 12 CFPs. In the case of $\mathcal{B}$, rule $\mathcal{B}5$ is applied adding 3 Entry/Read couples to a base of 4 CFPs, with a total of 9.

R8 and R9 are respectively the FURs for exporting to and importing from the SD card. In $\mathcal{A}$, two different rules are applied: view functionality ($\mathcal{A}1$) and manipulation data functionality ($\mathcal{A}2$). The data is moved from persistent storage to the SD card and vice versa by first reading (i.e., $\mathcal{A}1$), with a total of 5 CFPs. Then, $\mathcal{A}2$ provides the writing functionality with a score of 3 CFPs, excluding the starting Entry expected for the rule. In the case of import, R9 expects data to be also shown on the screen. So, 9 CFPs are counted for R9 and 8 CFPs for R8. As for data direction, for $\mathcal{B}$ there are two different rules: for R8 is applied rule $\mathcal{B}8$ obtaining 4 CFPs while for R9 6 CFPs are obtained by applying rule $\mathcal{B}7$ and considering an extra Exit to show data on the screen.

R12, R13, R14 and R15 belong to the type of help functionalities which are considered equivalent to the view functionality. Thus, $\mathcal{A}$ applies rule $\mathcal{A}5$ (equal to $\mathcal{A}1$ in this case) with a total of 6 CFPs. $\mathcal{B}$ applies $\mathcal{B}2$ with a score of 3 CFPs.

3.4 Discussion

Taking into account the measurement performed on a set of 13 mobile apps, including the above-mentioned example, we were able to perform a comparison of the approach $\mathcal{A}$ and $\mathcal{B}$ in terms of guideline applicability. The achieved outcomes and some insights originated from the analysis are summarised in the following.

$\mathcal{A}$ defines the boundary of the application layer in a more strict way than $\mathcal{B}$: the persistent storage is considered as a separate functional user and any interaction with it is measured as Entries or Exits rather than Writes or Reads as done by $\mathcal{B}$. This is reflected also on the constant presence of error messages in $\mathcal{A}$. In our opinion, persistent storage needs a proper definition and it might be associated to every simple data structure as key/value maps or stored files. In that case, the use of Read/Write, as $\mathcal{B}$ does, could be more appropriate. In the presence of more complex structures as SQLite database, requiring a standardised SQL communication, even if it is stored as a normal file, considering them as separate data layers (as done in $\mathcal{A}$) matches better.

$\mathcal{A}$ expects the presence of error messages in any rule. As far as we are concerned, it regards also confirmation messages, but only for communication with the data layer and not with the persistent storage. However, possible error messages due to the persistent storage are external to the functional processes since they are generally handled by the mobile operating system.

Moreover, $\mathcal{A}$ lacks of any interaction between different data layers. For instance, in many cases we observed some operations of import/export data from/to an SD card. While $\mathcal{B}$ has its proper guidelines facing this kind of situation, to cover this case with $\mathcal{A}$ a combination of rules has to be considered with a risk of introducing redundant data movements. On the other hand, $\mathcal{B}$ does not consider communication with a remote data storage (e.g., a web service). Even if not explicitly mentioned, in $\mathcal{A}$ this can be seen as a data layer. Communication with a remote data storage is generally included in mobile apps, thanks to the mobility feature of devices, so it should be carefully considered in the data layer way.

Both $\mathcal{A}$ and $\mathcal{B}$ also address the situation in which there is an interaction with an external application. $\mathcal{A}$ considers it as an external application. However, excluding any data movement from the application being measured might be misleading. Let us consider a generic app which shares a list of items with an external e-mail app. Because the e-mail app handles only textual input, the shared data needs to be converted in a text form in the first place. The conversion as well as sending the data to the e-mail app are in charge of the generic app itself. The example and the derived discussion suggest that some effort is needed to elaborate a more flexible approach for measuring the functional size of mobile apps. In particular, the simplicity of $\mathcal{A}$ in the definition of its rules and the readiness of $\mathcal{B}$ with persistent storage interaction might inspire a future and improved version of the measurement process.

4 Empirical Study

In this section we present a replication of our previous work [11] where we empirically analysed whether the COSMIC functional size of mobile applications obtained by following the guidelines provided by D'Avanzo et al. (approach $\mathcal{B}$) [8] can be exploited to estimate the size of the final applications in terms of lines of code and number of bytes of the source code and bytecode. Differently from the original study, in this replication we have exploited the measurement approach proposed by van Heeringen and van Gorp (approach $\mathcal{A}$) [13] to size the mobile apps in terms of COSMIC. In the following we first describe the design of the replication and then the results we achieved. With the aim of the comparison with the original study, we also reported the results we achieved in our previous work [11] (approach $\mathcal{B}$).

4.1   Design

As in the original study, the research questions we investigate are:

- **RQ1:** Does COSMIC measure relate with code size measures for mobile applications?
- **RQ2:** Can COSMIC measure be used to estimate code size measures for mobile applications?

Since we want to compare the results achieved by employing the functional sizes obtained with the two measurement approaches proposed in [13] (i.e., $\mathcal{A}$) and [8] (i.e., $\mathcal{B}$), in the present study we also investigate a new research question:

- **RQ3:** Which approach between $\mathcal{A}$ and $\mathcal{B}$ provides better estimates of code size measures for mobile applications?

In the following, we provide details about the employed data set, the estimation technique, the validation method, and the evaluation criteria. Threats that could affect the validity of the empirical study are also discussed.

Data Set and Variables. We have employed a data set including information[1] on 13 Android mobile applications randomly downloaded from Google Play Store. For each application one of the authors collected the requirements in a Functional User Requirements (FURs) document. Then, following the guidelines proposed by van Heeringen and van Gorp [13], COSMIC was applied to the FURs document obtaining the results reported in Table 2. In particular, $CFP_{\mathcal{A}}$ is the independent variable of our study denoting the number of COSMIC Function Points (CFP) obtained by applying the guidelines proposed by van Heeringen and van Gorp [13]. $CFP_{\mathcal{B}}$ denotes the number of CFP obtained by applying the guidelines proposed by D'Avanzo et al. [8].

Table 2 also shows the information about the 13 mobile application code sizes. Since in Android the Java code is mainly used to develop functionalities, while XML is used to design the user interfaces, we considered both Java and XML size, to analyse apart the components constituting the interface of the mobile apps. We did not measure any other raw asset files, such as images or local database files, because they do not directly relate to the application functionalities. We considered each Java class involved (except for external libraries) and only the XML layouts that are needed to visualize the application. For example, we

---

[1] Requirements and CFPs data are publicly available on https://goo.gl/Nj6mAO.

Table 2. Descriptive statistics of mobile app code sizes and COSMIC sizes.

Descriptive statistics	Java		XML		Bytecode	CFP_A	CFP_B
	kB	LOC	kB	LOC	kB		
Min	19.00	473.00	12.00	167.00	23663.00	18.00	15.00
Max	322.00	7514.00	94.00	1695.00	272775.00	220.00	145.00
Mean	122.50	2786.60	42.30	590.70	111892.30	70.62	49.30
Median	91.50	2295.50	38.00	487.50	94298.50	58.00	40.00
Std Dev	96.85	2157.30	23.20	427.40	73823.36	51.79	35.03

discarded those XML files that describe additional resolutions for other devices, such as tablets, since these are optimisations and do not describe functionalities. As for the LOC, the variables $Java_{LOC}$, XML_{LOC}, and $Total_{LOC}$ represent the lines of code for the Java code, XML code, and their sum, respectively. As for number of bytes, we considered both the source and the compiled code. The variables $Java_{kB}$, XML_{kB}, and $Total_{kB}$ represent the Java size, XML size, and their sum in terms of kilobytes, respectively. The variable $Bytecode_{kB}$ denotes the size of the compiled code in terms of kilobytes. These variables represent the dependent variables of our empirical study. The information about these variable were collected by using the apps APK files downloaded from the official store. The code size was measured with the 'du' UNIX command and the lines of code with the 'CLOC' tool.

Correlation Test and Estimation Technique. To assess (RQ1) the relationship among the independent variable (i.e., CFP_A) and the dependent variables (i.e., $Java_{kB}$, $Java_{LOC}$, XML_{kB}, XML_{LOC}, $Total_{kB}$, $Total_{LOC}$, and $Bytecode_{kB}$) we applied the nonparametric association statistics Spearman's rho [12], which is widely employed in the literature. This statistic ranges from $+1$ to -1, where $+1$ indicates perfect correlation and -1 indicates a perfect inverse correlation, while 0 indicates no correlation.

To verify whether or not the functional size of a mobile application can be exploited to predict the corresponding code size (RQ2), expressed both in terms of bytes and lines of code, we built a prediction model for each dependent variable (e.g., $Total_{LOC}$) using CFP_A as independent variable, by applying the Linear Regression (LR) analysis. To evaluate the goodness of fit of a regression model, we exploited the square of the linear correlation coefficient, R^2, that shows the amount of the variance of the dependent variable explained by the model related to the independent variable. Other useful indicators are the F value and the corresponding p-value (denoted by Sign F), which high and low values, respectively, denote a high degree of confidence for the prediction.

To answer RQ3, i.e., to compare the accuracy of CFP_A and CFP_B in predicting code sizes, we employed the results of the original study [11].

Validation Method and Evaluation Criteria. To validate the built estimation models we carried out a cross validation, meaning that the original data set was divided into different subsets of training and validation sets. Training sets were used to build models with LR and validation sets were used to validate the obtained models. In particular, we applied a leave-one-out cross validation, i.e., the original data set was divided into $n = 13$ different subsets of training and validation sets, where each validation set has one observation.

As for evaluation criteria, we applied the Spearman's rho test to verify whether the predicted size is a useful estimation of the actual size. Furthermore, we employed some summary measures to assess the accuracy of the obtained estimations, namely MMRE, MdMRE and Pred (l) [7], which have been widely used in empirical studies similar to ours (see e.g., [16]). In the context of effort estimation, where these measures were proposed [7], l is widely set to 0.25 and a good estimation model should have a MMRE ≤ 0.25 and Pred $(0.25) \geq 0.75$, that is, the mean estimation error should be less than 25 %, and at least 75 % of the estimated values should fall within 25 % of their actual values [7]. In this study we used $l = 0.25$. In the future, we will further analyse this point. We employed summary measures also to compare the results achieved herein with those obtained in the original study. Moreover, we tested the statistical significance of the results by using absolute residuals, i.e., to establish whether one approach provided significantly better code size estimations than the other employed [15]. Absolute Residuals (AR) is defined as $|Actual - Predicted|$, where *Actual* is the actual code size (e.g., Java$_{\text{LOC}}$) and *Predicted* is the estimated code size. In particular, we performed the Wilcoxon signed rank test [6] to verify the following null hypothesis 'the two considered populations of absolute residuals have identical distributions'. For all the statistical tests, we accept a probability of 5 % of committing a Type-I-Error [12].

Threats to Validity. Reliability of the data and lack of standardisation should be taken into account for the internal validity [17,20]. We did our best to collect information in a uniform fashion. The construct validity can be biased by the collection of the information used to determine the size measures. The measurement task of the functional size is crucial. One of the authors, with previous experiences in measuring software in terms of COSMIC, performed the measurement task. Another author cross-checked the information obtained. As for the measurement of the code sizes, we manually inspect Java classes and XML files to remove noisy content (e.g., third part libraries). As for the conclusion validity, we carefully applied the estimation method and the statistical tests, verifying all the required assumptions. Another threat to conclusion validity could be the few number of applications composing the data set. However, observe that 'a rule of thumb in regression analysis is that 5 to 10 observations are required for every variable in the model' [22]. Furthermore, this kind of studies can contribute to provide useful indications that can be further validated in subsequent studies.

4.2 Results and Discussion

The results of the Spearman's rho test revealed that all the considered code size measures were positively associated with the independent variable CFP_A, with a statistics greater than 0.8. Furthermore, the results of the performed tests were statistical significant as the p-values of the statistics were less than 0.05. This means that when the value of the CFP_A increases, the value of the code size measures (e.g., $Java_{kB}$) increases as well. The dependent variables having the highest association with independent variable were XML_{LOC} and $Total_{kB}$ that were characterised by a statistics grater than 0.9.

According to these results we can positively answer RQ1: for the considered mobile apps COSMIC sizes obtained with the measurement approach A well relates to the considered code size measures.

To answer RQ2 we built size estimation models by exploiting LR. To this aim, we first verified the assumptions underlying its application: linearity (i.e., the existence of a linear relationship between the independent variable and the dependent variable); homoscedasticity (i.e., the constant variance of the error terms for all the values of the independent variable); residual normality (i.e., the normal distribution of the error terms), and residual uncorrelation (i.e., error terms are uncorrelated for consecutive observations).

It is worth noting that we also verified the presence of influential observations (i.e., extreme values which might influence the models obtained from the regression analysis) by using the residuals plot and Cook's distance and performing a stability analysis as suggested by Mendes and Kitchenham [21]. According to this analysis no transformation of the original data was performed and no observation was removed.

Table 3. Results of the linear regression using CFP_A as dependent variable.

Dependent variable	R^2	F	Sign. F (p-value)
$Java_{kB}$	0.777	38.22	<0.001
$Java_{LOC}$	0.759	40.35	<0.001
XML_{kB}	0.895	94.13	<0.001
XML_{LOC}	0.840	57.86	<0.001
$Total_{kB}$	0.896	94.78	<0.001
$Total_{LOC}$	0.845	60.07	<0.001
$Bytecode_{kB}$	0.813	47.82	<0.001

Table 3 shows the results of the LR analysis. We can observe that the models are characterised by a high R^2 value, i.e., greater than 0.8 except for the models having $Java_{LOC}$ and $Java_{kB}$ as dependent variables for which the value is very close to 0.8 (i.e., 0.777 and 0.759, respectively). Furthermore, a high F value and a p-value (Sign. F) less than 0.001 were obtained, indicating that the prediction is possible with a high degree of confidence.

We have performed a leave-one-out cross validation to evaluate the accuracy of the obtained estimates of the code sizes with respect to the actual code sizes. Again, we applied a Spearman's rho test to establish whether the predicted size is a useful estimation of the actual size.

The results revealed that the predicted size is always statistically positively correlated with the actual size for all the considered code size measures, with statistics greater than 0.8, except for XML_{kB}. Thus, the obtained size predictions can provide a good indication of the actual sizes. To quantify the accuracy of the obtained estimates, we computed the summary measures MMRE, MdMRE, and Pred (0.25) (see Table 4, results using $CFP_{\mathcal{A}}$). We can observe that no model was characterised by values satisfying the thresholds of Conte et al. [7]. The best result in terms of summary measures was obtained with $Bytecode_{kB}$, having MdMRE equals to 0.25 and Pred (0.25) equals to 0.54. On the other hand, the worst result was obtained for the models predicting $Java_{kB}$. Thus, as answer to RQ2 we can state that $CFP_{\mathcal{A}}$ did not provide quite good estimations of the source code sizes for the considered mobile apps.

Table 4. Results of cross validation in terms of summary measures.

Dependent variable	Using $CFP_{\mathcal{A}}$			Using $CFP_{\mathcal{B}}$		
	MMRE	MdMRE	Pred (0.25)	MMRE	MdMRE	Pred (0.25)
$Java_{kB}$	0.61	0.36	0.31	0.46	0.46	0.54
$Java_{LOC}$	0.56	0.30	0.46	0.43	0.24	0.54
XML_{kB}	0.38	0.34	0.31	0.43	0.29	0.31
XML_{LOC}	0.31	0.28	0.38	0.32	0.28	0.46
$Total_{kB}$	0.36	0.25	0.46	0.29	0.19	0.77
$Total_{LOC}$	0.46	0.27	0.46	0.35	0.20	0.62
$Bytecode_{kB}$	0.44	0.23	0.54	0.33	0.21	0.54

We also compared the results achieved in the replication study presented here with those obtained in the original study. For this reason in Table 4 we also reported results obtained using $CFP_{\mathcal{B}}$. The comparison suggested that better code size predictions were obtained with $CFP_{\mathcal{B}}$, for all the considered code size measures. However, the performed Wilcoxon test revealed that the differences were not statistically significant. To conclude, we can answer RQ3 saying that $\mathcal{B}$ [8] provided slightly better (not statistically significant) code size estimations than $\mathcal{A}$ [13].

5   Conclusions and Future Work

In this paper we presented a replication of our previos study [11] that exploited functional sizes in terms of COSMIC to estimate code size measures about 13 mobile applications. The two studies differ in the independent variable, representing the functional size in terms of COSMIC, since two different measurement approaches have been employed. In the replication we applied the approach proposed by van Heeringen and van Gorp [13], while the original study used the approach proposed by D'Avanzo et al. [8]. On the other hand, the original and the replication studies share the research questions RQ1 and RQ2, the set of mobile applications, the set of dependent variables, the estimation technique, the validation method, and the evaluation criteria. In the replication we considered a further research question (RQ3) to investigate which of the analysed approaches provided better code size estimations.

The results of the replication highlighted that, for the considered mobile apps, the COSMIC functional size was well correlated to all the size measures taken into account, thus, confirming the results of the original study and the findings by Lind and Heldal [18,19]. Nevertheless, the prediction accuracy did not satisfy the evaluation criteria and turned out to be slightly worse than the one obtained in the original study based on the approach proposed by D'Avanzo et al. [8].

The results of our study should encourage the use of functional size measurement methods, in particular COSMIC, to size mobile applications and employ the obtained measure for implementing other software project management activities, such as effort estimation and productivity benchmarking.

In the future we intend to apply the considered approaches on larger data sets and different kinds of mobile applications to confirm/contradict the results obtained so far also to understand the reasons for the low prediction accuracy. In particular we would like to analyse if it depends on the approximated methods of COSMIC measurement or on other factors. We will also investigate whether a unique/unified approach is suitable to measure different kinds of apps, or different approaches are needed. The contribution of single BFCs could be also investigated [5] to provide a better comparison with the approach proposed by van Heeringen and van Gorp [13].

Finally, the collection of effort data could be useful to derive effort/cost estimation models.

References

1. Abdullah, N.A.S., Rusli, N.I.A., Ibrahim, M.F.: Mobile game size estimation: COSMIC FSM rules, uml mapping model and unity3d game engine. In: 25th IEEE Conference on Open Systems (ICOS), pp. 42–47 (2014)
2. Abran, A., Baklizky, D., Desharnais, J., Fagg, P., Gencel, C., Symons, C., Jayakumar, K.R., Lesterhuis, A., Londeix, B., Nagano, S.I., Santillo, L., Soubra, H., Trudel, S., Vogelezang, F., Woddward, C.: The COSMIC Functional Size Measurement Method, Measurement Manual, Version 4.0.1 (2015)
3. Abran, A., Londeix, B., O'Neill, M., Santillo, L., Vogelezang, F., Desharnais, J., Morris, P., Rollo, T., Symons, C., Lesterhuis, A., Oligny, S., Rule, G., Toivonen, H.: The COSMIC Functional Size Measurement Method, Advanced and Related Topics, Version 3.0 (2007)

4. Boehm, B.W., Abts, C., Brown, A.W., Chulani, S., Clark, B.K., Horowitz, E., Madachy, R., Reifer, D.J., Steece, B.: Software Cost Estimation with COCOMO II. Prentice Hall Press, Upper Saddle River (2009)
5. Buglione, L., Gencel, Ç.: Impact of base functional component types on software functional size based effort estimation. In: Jedlitschka, A., Salo, O. (eds.) PROFES 2008. LNCS, vol. 5089, pp. 75–89. Springer, Heidelberg (2008)
6. Conover, W.J.: Practical Nonparametric Statistics, 3rd edn. Wiley, New York (1998)
7. Conte, S.D., Dunsmore, H.E., Shen, V.Y.: Software Engineering Metrics and Models. Benjamin-Cummings Publishing Co., Inc., Redwood City (1986)
8. D'Avanzo, L., Ferrucci, F., Gravino, C., Salza, P.: Cosmic functional measurement of mobile applications and code size estimation. In: 30th ACM/SIGAPP Symposium on Applied Computing (SAC), pp. 1631–1636 (2015)
9. De Marco, L., Ferrucci, F., Gravino, C.: Approximate cosmic size to early estimate web application development effort. In: 39th EUROMICRO Conference on Software Engineering and Advanced Applications (SEAA), pp. 349–356 (2013)
10. De Vito, G., Ferrucci, F.: Approximate cosmic size: the quick/early method. In: 40th EUROMICRO Conference on Software Engineering and Advanced Applications (SEAA), pp. 69–76 (2014)
11. Ferrucci, F., Gravino, C., Salza, P., Sarro, F.: Investigating functional and code size measures for mobile applications. In: 41st EUROMICRO Conference on Software Engineering and Advanced Applications (SEAA), pp. 365–368 (2015)
12. Gibbons, J.D.: Nonparametric Statistical Inference. Marcel Dekker Inc., New York (1986)
13. van Heeringen, H., van Gorp, E.: Measure the functional size of a mobile app: using the cosmic functional size measurement method. In: 24th International Workshop on Software Measurement (IWSM) and the 9th International Conference on Software Process and Product Measurement (MENSURA), pp. 11–16 (2014)
14. ISO/IEC: ISO/IEC 14143–1:2007: Information technology - Software measurement - Functional size measurement - Part 1: Definition of concepts (2007)
15. Kitchenham, B., Pickard, L., MacDonell, S., Shepperd, M.: What accuracy statistics really measure. IEE Proc. Softw. **148**(3), 81–85 (2001)
16. Kitchenham, B., Mendes, E.: Software productivity measurement using multiple size measures. IEEE Trans. Softw. Eng. **30**(12), 1023–1035 (2004)
17. Kitchenham, B., Pickard, L., Pfleeger, S.L.: Case studies for method and tool evaluation. IEEE Softw. **12**(4), 52–62 (1995)
18. Lind, K., Heldal, R.: On the relationship between functional size and software code size. In: Workshop on Emerging Trends in Software Metrics (WETSoM), pp. 47–52 (2010)
19. Lind, K., Heldal, R.: A practical approach to size estimation of embedded software components. IEEE Trans. Softw. Eng. **38**(5), 993–1007 (2012)
20. Martin, W., Harman, M., Jia, Y., Sarro, F., Zhang, Y.: The app sampling problem for app store mining. In: 12th Working Conference on Mining Software Repositories (MSR), pp. 123–133 (2015)
21. Mendes, E., Kitchenham, B.: Further comparison of cross-company and within-company effort estimation models for web applications. In: 10th International Software Metrics Symposium (METRICS), pp. 348–357. IEEE Press (2004)
22. Menzies, T., Chen, Z., Hihn, J., Lum, K.: Selecting best practices for effort estimation. IEEE Trans. Softw. Eng. **32**(11), 883–895 (2006)

23. Nitze, A., Schmietendorf, A., Dumke, R.: An analogy-based effort estimation approach for mobile application development projects. In: 24th International Workshop on Software Measurement (IWSM) and the 9th International Conference on
Software Process and Product Measurement (MENSURA), pp. 99–103 (2014)
24. Preuss, T.: Mobile Applications, Functional Analysis, and the Customer Experience, chap. 22. Auerbach Publications (2012)
25. Preuss, T.: Mobile applications, function points and cost estimating. In: International Conference on Cost Estimation and Analysis Association (ICEAA) (2013)
26. Sethumadhavan, G.: Sizing android mobile applications. In: 6th IFPUG International Software Measurement and Analysis Conference (ISMA) (2011)

Defining Continuous Planning Through a Multiple-Case Study

Tanja Suomalainen[(⊠)]

VTT Technical Research Centre of Finland Ltd., Kaitoväylä 1, P.O. Box 1100,
90571 Oulu, Finland
tanja.suomalainen@vtt.fi

Abstract. New and innovative approaches that support continuous development
and planning throughout organisations are needed. Continuity is required in all
levels of an organisation, from business strategy and planning to software development and operational deployment, as well as between these levels. Continuous
planning is one of these activities. However, continuous planning is not
commonly adopted and applied throughout organisations and currently involves
only a certain level of planning, e.g., release planning. Based on the current literature, continuous planning is a relatively new and not yet fully studied field of
research. To augment the knowledge relating to continuous planning, this paper
presents a multiple-case study in which the various levels of planning, along with
their timeframes, are explored. The research results point out the key activities,
as well as the bottlenecks, of continuous planning.

Keywords: Continuous planning · Continuous deployment · Levels of planning

1 Introduction

Given that the current business environment of information systems and technology
(ICT) organisations is very unstable and constantly changing, organisations are increasingly adopting agile and lean development practices [1, 2]. Even though many software
development companies have already succeeded in adopting these practices, this is not
the end of the process [3]. Olsson et al. [3] argue that software development companies
must move beyond the concept of agile development toward a situation in which software functionality is continuously deployed and customer feedback is the main driver
of innovation. "Continuous deployment" (CD) is a term used to refer to this phenomenon. Although the concept of deploying software to customers as soon as new code is
developed is not new and is based on agile and lean principles, CD expands upon these
agile and lean principals by moving from cyclic to continuous value delivery. CD is
about developing the ability to deliver the smallest possible added value to the customer,
which requires automating all processes that must be executed to deliver software to the
customers [4]. New and innovative approaches that support continuous practices
throughout organisations are needed, continuous planning being one of them, in order
to remove the disconnection between an organisation's important activities [5, 6].

P. Abrahamsson et al. (Eds.): PROFES 2015, LNCS 9459, pp. 288–294, 2015.
DOI: 10.1007/978-3-319-26844-6_21

Continuous planning is about implementing planning practices continuously in rapid parallel cycles, instead of only on predefined, regular planning occasions. Thus, planning is not conducted only as part of a top-down annual event [7]. However, environmental changes, instead of the predefined and regular planning cycle (e.g. financial year), trigger planning, and thus, plans are adjusted according to internal and external events [8]. Furthermore, planning should be performed continuously so that at any time, the full scale of the development can be presented [9]. Based on the current literature, continuous planning is not commonly adopted and applied throughout the organisation and currently involves only a certain level of planning, e.g., release planning (e.g. using Scrum) [5, 6]. Hence, continuous planning requires a wider perspective than that currently considered. To start filling this gap in the empirical research, a multiple-case study was conducted in three large information and communications technology (ICT) organisations. The specific research questions were defined as follows:

RQ1: What are the main levels of planning?
RQ2: How planning is conducted?
RQ3: How does continuous planning emerge through these levels of planning?

Thus, the main contribution of this paper is to present and analyse the current state of the art in continuous planning. The paper sheds light on the poorly studied research area of continuous planning by defining the main levels of planning, along with their timeframes. The remainder of this paper is structured as follows: In Sect. 2, we define continuous planning based on the current literature. In Sect. 3, the research design of this paper is presented. Then, in Sect. 4, the case study findings are presented and summarised. Finally, Sect. 5 presents the conclusions.

2 Continuous Planning

Continuous planning involves implementing planning practices continuously, not just as part of a top-down annual event [7]. Planning should be performed continuously so that the full scope of development can be presented at any time [9]. Fitzgerald and Stol [6] define continuous planning as a holistic attempt involving multiple stakeholders from business and software functions whereby plans conceived of as dynamic open-ended artifacts that evolve in response to changes in the business environment and thus involve a tighter integration between planning and execution. In terms of software development, continuous planning refers to the organisational capacity to conduct planning in rapid parallel cycles (in hours, days, weeks, or months) depending on the level of planning.

The current problem in planning is that time is divided into a number of planning horizons, each lasting a significant period of time [6]. The only form of continuous planning is what is emerging from agile and lean software development practices and is related to sprint iterations or software releases, and this is not widespread throughout the organization [5, 6]. Furthermore, with the traditional planning model, a failure within the plan may require additional cycles of planning before the problems can be solved, and the typical cadence of annual planning is not adequate in this regard [6]. It has only been recently realised that planning should be examined from a broader, even more continuous perspective [5, 6]. Continuous planning is not only a project- or team-level activity, as presented, e.g., by [10]. Rather, it involves higher-level planning as well, e.g., strategy-level planning. Fitzgerald and Stol [6] define a umbrella term called 'Continuous *' (continuous star) for a number of initiatives that are termed continuous in the context of software development, continuous planning being one of these initiatives. However, they do not define in detail how continuous planning should be conducted or what the mechanisms of continuous strategic planning are, for instance.

3   Research Design

In this section, the research design, along with the research method and the main data collection methods, is described. Thereafter, the case companies are presented.

3.1   Research Method and Data Collection

This research builds on a multiple-case study [11] with a timeframe of October 2014–June 2015. The main data collection method used was interviews, which were either narrative or semi-structured with open-ended questions [12]. The interviews involved the vital themes of the research, which were the same for all the interviewees, but the questions varied between the various interview sessions. In total, 24 interviews were conducted. In Company A, we conducted nine interviews involving people in the following roles: scrum master, team leader/project manager, sales directors, quality managers, business developer, and the president and vice president of a business area. In Company B, we conducted twelve interviews involving product marketing managers, the chief strategy officer, product managers, persons from product marketing management, directors of product management, and the executive vice president, and vice president of research and development (R&D). In Company C, we conducted three interviews involving the line manager, domain manager, and product owner. The interviews were held either in English or Finnish, and each interview lasted around 1 h. All the interviews were recorded and transcribed. During the data analysis, all transcribed interviews were carefully read and analysed with the help of a qualitative data analysis tool called NVivo. The data analysis proceeded according to a generic data analysis process presented by Creswell [13].

3.2   Case Companies

All the case companies were relative large ICT companies with several levels of planning. Also, all the companies had adopted agile and lean development practices and were moving towards continuous deployment and planning practices.

Case Company A is a global company with roughly 1,800 employees that operates in eight countries, providing cutting-edge technological solutions to the automotive and wireless industries. In the wireless business segment (the case context) the company offers products and solutions based on their own platforms for defence, public safety and other authorities markets and Internet of Things (IoT) markets, as well as for industrial use.

Case Company B is an online security and privacy company from Finland with approximately 1,000 employees in 20 offices around the world. The company offers millions of people around the globe the ability to surf invisibly and store and share information in a way that is safe from online threats. The company has partnerships with more than 200 operators, and it operates 22 wholly owned subsidiaries.

Case Company C is a multinational provider of communications technology and services. It operates in the environment of communications technology by providing equipment, software, and services to its customers. The company employs more than 110,000 people and works with customers all over the world.

4   Multiple-Case Study Findings

The following levels of planning were identified in all the case companies: strategic, financial, business, product, and team-level planning. Figure 1 summarises the findings from the multiple-case study. The figure reveals all the timeframes presented in the data and presents the various levels of continuous planning activities along these timeframes.

	Strategic	Financial	Business	Product	Team
3 years	Strategy period (A, B, C)		Business area strategy period (A)		
2 years			Tentative business area strategy (A)		
1 year	Strategy planning (A, B, C)	Budget period (A, B, C) Budget planning (A, B, C) Budget review (B)	Accurate business area strategy (A) Product domain plan period (based on product roadmaps) (B) Product domain strategy plan period (C) Product portfolio plan period (C)	Product roadmap period (A, B)	
6 months		Budget review (B)	Accurate product domain plan (B) Tentative product domain plan (B)	Accurate product roadmap (B) Tentative product roadmap (B) Product roadmap (C)	
3 months	Strategy review (A)	Budget review (C)	Product domain strategy review (C)	Product roadmap review (B, C)	
2 months					Feature roadmap period (A, B) Release plan period (C)
1 month			Business area strategy review (A)		Feature roadmap period (A)
2 weeks				Product roadmap review (A, B)	Release plan review (C)
1 week			Business area steering group reviews (B) Product portfolio review (C)	Product roadmap review (B)	Feature roadmap review (B)
Today	Strategy review (A) – if needed	Financial forecast (A) – if needed		Product roadmap review (B) – if needed	Feature roadmap review (A, B)

Fig. 1. Summary of the case study findings

The timeframe for long-term planning, <u>strategic planning</u>, was commonly three years plus the current year. In case A, strategic plans were reviewed quarterly and monthly. Thus, it was pointed out that the strategy process is constantly rolling, which means that the strategy is continuously planned. In contrast, in cases B and C, the strategic plan was reviewed and updated annually. Currently, their strategic planning practices are considered to be more traditionally project-based than continuous strategy practices because they were performed annually, management approved them and thereafter, they were implemented for the rest of the year. However, in case B, the goal was to have a continuous strategy with strategic themes that would be reviewed quarterly. It was acknowledged that these issues might be relevant to the company in ten years. Thus, they should be reviewed now.

Financial planning was conducted once a year in all the case companies. In case A, the budget and financial planning was considered continuous. The case company changed its financial planning practices, moving them toward continuous financial planning, in the beginning of 2012, and there has not been bi-annual budgeting since then. One of the main reasons for this change was that the bi-annual budgeting was too heavy and time-consuming, and it requires a great deal of effort to get it done and approved. Thus, the case company realised that creating a yearly budgeting frame with a rolling review process would be much more convenient than bi-annual budgeting. In cases B and C, the financial planning was reviewed and validated annually. In case B, some business areas reviewed their financial plans bi-annually to check their current status, and in similar way, the budgeting frame was reviewed quarterly within the product areas in case C. Similarly to case A, it was realised in case C that the yearly planning was quite inflexible and that it was difficult to make large changes. Thus, one of the interviewees in case C pointed out *"Relating to the product domain and its markets, the need to be more agile and able to change direction during the year will certainly increase in the future."* It was realised that one year is too long a timeframe in which to plan ahead and make, e.g., financial estimates, and thus, a half a year would be a more ideal and accurate timeframe in which to make financial plans.

The business planning was conducted inside the business area in case A. Then, the timeframe for the business plan was around three years. The first year was more accurate than the other two years, and it was updated with a monthly review cycle. In cases B and C, the business-level planning was performed via the product domain function. Then, the business planning had a one-year timeframe. In case B, the first half of the year was more accurate and the rest of the year, which involved more tentative content. Furthermore, in case B, the business plans were discussed in weekly business-area-steering group meetings. Instead, in case C, the business plan was updated, and input was collected through a quarterly product domain strategy meeting and weekly product portfolio meetings.

The product planning was conducted at the product management level by creating a product roadmap in all cases. In case A, it was pointed out that the product roadmap relates to the business area strategy, and the strategy was being implemented with the help of technology. In contrast, in case C, product roadmapping was seen more as a collaborative effort between product management and development. In case A, the product roadmaps were created within the timeframe of one year, and they were revised with biweekly review cycles. In case C, the timeframe was half a year, and the product roadmaps were reviewed at least quarterly. In case B, the product roadmaps had a one-year planning timeframe, which was divided into four quarters. The first two quarters are more clearly visible (i.e., high-confidence plan), and the last two quarters are more tentative. The product roadmaps are reviewed and updated weekly, biweekly or quarterly depending on the product. Inside the case company, the practices relating to product roadmapping varied between the various products because they were different by nature (e.g., due to product maturity, the legacy and complexity of the product and the customers and sales channels). Despite these various practices, planning relating to product roadmapping is considered continuous because of the tight review cycle, and the content is kept as tentative as possible. The tentative content helps to reduce external linkages needed for following and implementing the roadmap. Then, for example, changing interest points, dropping something out of the roadmap or dramatically changing the focus areas of the roadmap is easier. As one of the product managers in case B described, *"One of the worst cases is that you need to sell the future commitment of your business, and in that sense, you lose your flexibility to make changes in that business area, to start new investment areas, for instance."* The content of the roadmap may even change radically every quarter, so the rolling forecast for the next year was considered the most practical way of planning.

The team-level planning was commonly conducted by the R&D team that was involved in release planning. In all of the cases, release planning was conducted within a timeframe of two months. In cases A and B, at the team level, the product roadmap was divided into a feature roadmap. The feature roadmapping commonly involved practices relating to requirement management and prioritisation. In case A, the feature roadmaps were reviewed within a daily review cycle because they focused on implementation and verification issues in daily work. In contrast, in case B, the feature roadmap was reviewed continuously instead of on a predefined and scheduled date. In case A, features were implemented and verified with two-, four- or six-week release cycles, depending on the team. Similarly, in case C, the team could decide the sprint length; three weeks was optimal, but weekly releases are suitable in situations with many changes.

5 Conclusions

The paper presents the current state of art regarding continuous planning through a multiple-case study. The research described how planning is currently conducted in organisations by defining the main levels of planning: strategic, financial, business, product and team, as well as their timeframes. None of the case companies utilised the practices of continuous planning throughout the organisation. The continuity of the activities was often based on the conditionality, e.g., whether the circumstances forced companies to update and review their plans. The continuity of the activities could be explained by both internal and external changes in the companies. External changes, e.g., in the turbulent business environment, forced the case companies to adopt continuous strategic and financial planning practices. Internal changes, e.g., the adoption of agile and lean development practices, forced all the case companies to shorten their product planning review cycles to months and to shorten team-level planning to weeks or days. Business planning, in contrast, was the only activity that was not seen as continuous in any of the case companies. In a similar way, regarding strategic planning, continuity could also be needed in business planning in order to respond and react to changes in the business environment. Both business and product planning should be continuous and proactive, rather than reactive, by nature. With the help of continuous business and product planning, companies may be able to influence the markets by inventing and developing new products and services, as well as being able to react to changing market requirements. The research will be continued by defining the main benefits and challenges of continuous planning, as well as identifying the main drawbacks of continuous planning practices.

References

1. Papatheocharous, E., Andreou, A.S.: Empirical evidence and state of practice of software agile teams. J. Softw. Evol. Process **26**, 855–866 (2014)
2. Kurapati, N., Manyam, V.S.C., Petersen, K.: Agile software development practice adoption survey. In: Wohlin, C. (ed.) XP 2012. LNBIP, vol. 111, pp. 16–30. Springer, Heidelberg (2012)
3. Olsson, H.H., Bosch, J., Alahyari, H.: Towards R&D as innovation experiment systems: a framework for moving beyond agile software development. In: Proceedings of the IASTED International Conference on Software Engineering, SE 2013, pp. 798–805 (2013)
4. Järvinen, J., Huomo, T., Mikkonen, T., Tyrväinen, P.: From agile software development to mercury business. In: Lassenius, C., Smolander, K. (eds.) ICSOB 2014. LNBIP, vol. 182, pp. 58–71. Springer, Heidelberg (2014)
5. Suomalainen, T., Kuusela, R., Tihinen, M.: Continuous planning: an important aspect of agile and lean development. Int. J. Agile Syst. Manag. **8**, 132–162 (2015)
6. Fitzgerald, B., Stol, K.: Continuous software engineering and beyond: trends and challenges. In: Proceedings of the 1st International Workshop on Rapid Continuous Software Engineering, pp. 1–9. ACM (2014)
7. Hope, J., Fraser, R.: Beyond Budgeting: How Managers can Break Free from the Annual Performance Trap. Harvard Business School Press, Boston (2003)
8. Rickards, R.C., Ritsert, R.: Rediscovering rolling planning: controller's roadmap for implementing rolling instruments in SMEs. In: Procedia Economics and Finance of 2nd Annual International Conference on Accounting and Finance (AF 2012) and Qualitative and Quantitative Economics Research (QQE 2012), pp. 135–144. Elsevier (2012)
9. Westkamper, E., Von Briel, R.: Continuous improvement and participative factory planning by computer systems. CIRP Ann. Manufact. Technol. **50**, 347–352 (2001)
10. Shalloway, A., Beaver, G., Trott, J.R.: Lean-Agile Software Development: Achieving Enterprise Agility. Addison-Wesley Professional, Upper Saddle River (2009)
11. Yin, R.K.: Case Study Research: Design and Methods. 3rd edn. Sage Publications, Thousand Oaks (2003)
12. Runeson, P., Höst, M.: Guidelines for conducting and reporting case study research in software engineering. Empirical Softw. Eng. **14**, 131–164 (2009)
13. Creswell, J.W.: Research Design: Qualitative, Quantitative, and Mixed Method Approaches, 2nd edn. Sage Publications, Thousand Oaks (2003)

Issue Dynamics in Github Projects

Riivo Kikas$^{(\boxtimes)}$, Marlon Dumas, and Dietmar Pfahl

Institute of Computer Science, University of Tartu, Tartu, Estonia
{riivokik,marlon.dumas,dietmar.pfahl}@ut.ee

Abstract. Issue repositories are used to keep of track of bugs, development tasks and feature requests in software development projects. In the case of open source projects, everyone can submit a new issue in the tracker. This practice can lead to situations where more issues are created than what can be effectively handled by the project members, raising the question of how issues are treated as the capacity of the project members is exceeded. In this paper, we study the temporal dynamics of issues in a popular open source development platform, namely Github, based on a sample of 4000 projects. We specifically analyze how the rate of issue creation, the amount of pending issues, and their average lifetime evolve over the course of time. The results show that more issues are opened shortly after the creation of a project repository and that the amount of pending issues increases inexorably due to forgotten (unclosed) issues. Yet, the average issue lifetime (for issues that do get closed) is relatively stable over time. These observations suggest that Github projects have implicit mechanisms for handling issues perceived to be important to the project, while neglecting those that exceed the project's capacity.

1 Introduction

Issue trackers have become essential collaboration instruments in modern software development projects [1]. They are used for registering and tracking new feature requests, development tasks and bugs for example. In closed-source projects, usage of issue trackers is generally restricted and sometimes codified, so that new issues can only be opened by development team members, managers and a reduced set of stakeholders and may need to comply with established norms and minimum requirements [1].

On the other hand, in open source projects, for example in Github projects, it is common practice that everyone can open a new issue in the issue tracker of a project with basically no requirements placed on the content and quality of new issues [2,4]. This practice can lead to a potentially large and continuous inflow of issues exceeding the project's development team capacity, including low-quality issues or issues that are only marginally relevant to the project. As the inflow of issues exceeds the capacity of the project members, it is natural to conjecture that not all issues are effectively handled, and are either closed without resolution or implicitly ignored.

This paper aims to shed light into the extent to which open source projects, particularly those hosted in Github, cope with the inflow of issues they are

© Springer International Publishing Switzerland 2015
P. Abrahamsson et al. (Eds.): PROFES 2015, LNCS 9459, pp. 295–310, 2015.
DOI: 10.1007/978-3-319-26844-6_22

subjected to throughout their lifetime. Based on a sample of more than 4000 Github projects, we analyze the temporal dynamics of issues in terms of how often they are created (arrival rate), the amount of pending issues, and their lifetime. Specifically, the paper addresses the following research questions:

- RQ1: What is the issue arrival rate and how does it change over time?
- RQ2: How do opened and pending issue numbers evolve over time?
- RQ3: What is the average issue lifetime and how does it change over time?

The rest of the paper is structured as follows. The next section presents related work. Then, Sect. 3 describes the dataset employed and the concepts used in the analysis. In Sect. 4 we present and discuss the results of our analysis with respect to the above research questions. Finally, Sects. 5 and 6 respectively provide an analysis of threats to validity and present conclusions and opportunities for future work.

2   Related Work

There are several previous studies that focus explicitly on the analysis of issue in Github datasets. Closest to our research is a study by Bissyande et al. [2], giving a basic overview of issue tracker usage in 100,000 Github projects. Their work explores how many issues are tracked on average, labels and tags usage, who enters issues (developer or not), issue tracker usage and project success (number of watchers), and user community size and issue fix time. Compared to our work, they do not analyze the evolution of pending issues and their lifetimes. Cabot et al. [3] studies how tagging is used in Github issue trackers. Their results show that only small sets of projects use labels, and usage of labels correlates with a higher number of closed issues. Related to this, Izquierdo et al. [9] have presented a tool demo to explore issue label usage in projects.

The question of issue lifetime has been studied from different perspectives both in open source and closed source projects. Marks et al. [12] studied issue lifetimes in Mozilla and Eclipse. They found that 46 % of bug reports in the Mozilla project and 76 % of bug reports in the Eclipse project are closed within three months of their creation. Grammel et al. [8] study community involvement in closed source IBM Jazz projects. Their findings suggest that community created issues can be valuable, but they are handled differently than those created by project members. The average issue lifetime for community created issues is 39 days, whereas for the team issues it is 5.9 days.

Ko and Chilana [11] study why some issues in the Mozilla tracker are left open for long periods. Their findings suggest that issues resulting in fixes or code changes are proposed by a "group of experienced, frequent reporters". They conclude that open source projects benefit most from this group of experts.

Garousi [5] studies three open source projects with a focus on issue creation and resolution times. Their findings show that bugs and critical issues are handled faster than other issue types. For the jEdit and DrPython projects, the fractions of issues that are closed within the first day is 23 % and 42 % percent, respectively. Garousi also concludes that more bugs are submitted in the beginning of a project's lifetime. In addition, he shows that issues pile up over time and then are closed in batches.

Compared to these previous studies on issue lifetime, we employ a larger volume of projects and we consider not only issue lifetime, but also arrival rate and number of pending issues. The latter variable ("number of pending issues") has been studied separately by Kenmei et al. [10], who use a time-series modeling to analyze how the number of opened issues changes over time.

Other studies have considered how the arrival rate of new issues in a project and their resolution time can be used to plan future work [10] and to predict the lifetime of pending issues [6,13]. These latter studies are orthogonal to ours.

3   Dataset and Terminology

Github is an online platform for hosting git source code repositories. It offers a web interface for repositories, an issue tracker, and a mechanism for pull based software development and code review. Github has been gaining popularity in recent years, with usages from single-person projects to major companies such as Google and Microsoft using Github for hosting their open source projects.

We use a dataset from Github, collected by the GHTorrent project team [7]. Github provides a public stream of actions such as creation of new pull requests, commits, issues, but does not, for example, provide issue content text. GHTorrent project is augmenting this data by crawling the Github API to retrieve past data and consolidates the data from both sources into a single database.

3.1   Data Extraction and Filtering

Our GHTorrent data extraction is from April 2, 2015 and contains more than seven million projects (not counting forked projects). In order to exclude special cases and anomalies, we selected a subset of the extracted data, applying following filtering criteria.

- Projects must have been created between January 2012 and December 2014. We limited our observation period to this interval, because older data is often not fully available due to the crawling behavior of GHTorrent.
- Projects must have at least 100 opened issues and one closed issue. This criterion gives us projects that actually use the issue tracking capabilities.
- Projects must have at least five commits to the main repository. This criterion gives us projects where some issues generated development activity.
- Projects must not show any activity before repository creation date. In Github, it is possible to fork a repository and therefore inherit an already existing codebase which technically shows up as code committed before the project creation.

An examination of the selected data revealed projects with unexpectedly high issue tracker activity in short periods, such as several thousands of newly

298   R. Kikas et al.

created issues during a single day. This can be caused by a data import from
old tracking system or automatically created issues by using the Github API.
To get rid of possible import behavior, we additionally filtered out projects that
created or closed more than 2000 issues in a single month or created more than
500 issues during a single day.

3.2 Descriptive Statistics

After filtering, 4452 projects met our criteria. Figure 1a shows the distribution
of the projects' observation time lengths. Our sample contains projects with
observation times ranging from 0 to 35 months. We observed that there were
relatively few projects with a short observation time. We wanted to have at
least 100 projects within each observation time interval. This resulted in the
removal of all projects with observation less than eight months, i.e., projects
created after April 2014. In Fig. 1a, projects that were filtered out due to their
observation time are marked in gray color.

The final dataset contains of 4024 projects, with 967,037 total issues, of
which 675,970 (69.9 %) have been closed at least once and 291,067 (30.1 %) have
not been closed during the observation period. The mean number of issues per
project is 240.3. Issues can be re-opened and re-closed, and this affects 27376
(4.0 %) issues.

The number of issues per project (Fig. 1b) varies almost two orders of
magnitude with the largest project having 4885 issues in total.

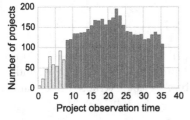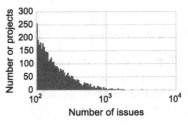

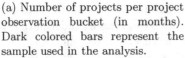

(a) Number of projects per project observation bucket (in months). Dark colored bars represent the sample used in the analysis.

(b) Number of projects per number of opened issues bucket (logarithmic scale).

Fig. 1. Basic properties of the dataset.

3.3 Terminology

The centerpiece of our analysis are issues, i.e., bug reports, new feature requests,
and development related changes such as refactoring. In Github, issues are typically free text, can be submitted by anyone, support commenting, and can be

referenced from other issues. The dataset does not give any information about issue text or content, but it records when an issue was created and by whom, and a set of events associated such as closing, reopening, being commented, being referenced from another issue. All these events are accompanied with the time of the action and which user is responsible for it.

In this paper we distinguish the following issue states:

- **Opened Issue** - Newly created issue. Each issue is opened only once during its lifetime.
- **Pending Issue** - Issue that has been opened but not yet closed. These issues denote unresolved cases that need attention or actual work.
- **Sticky Issue** - Issue that does not get closed during our observation period. Sticky issues are a subset of pending issues.
- **Closed Issue** - Issue that is marked closed in the issue tracking system. In practice an issue might be reopened and closed again, but here we use only the first closing event. We do not distinguish closed issues based on the resolution type, meaning that a closed issue might have been closed after the bug was fixed or closed without any activity.

One might consider our notion of pending issue as too simplistic since we do not take into account reopening and re-closing. The justification for this is the fact that reopening and re-closing affects only 4 % of all issues.

Our dataset contains projects that are created at different points in time during our observation period and therefore have varying time periods during which we could observe project behavior. Below we list our time related terminology:

- **Issue Lifetime** - Time from the first opening of the issue to the first closing of the issue.
- **Project Observation Time** - Number of months between project creation and the end of observation period (December 31, 2014). This number is obtained by calculating the number of days between the two dates, dividing by 30.4 (the average number of days in a month), and rounding down to the nearest integer.
- **Relative Time** - Each project is transformed into a relative timescale. The relative timescale starts from repository creation, and after each 30.4 days, a new relative month starts. This results in the last month typically not being a full month, as projects can start on any day during a month, but our observation period ends with the 31st day of a month. Relative time 'zero' represents the first month of the project observation time, relative time month 'one' represents the second month of the project observation time.
- **Observation Period** - From January 2012 until end of December 2014. This is the period we have data about projects and we can use for the analysis.

3.4 Notations

In our analysis, we focus on the following metrics over time: opened issued, sticky issues, and pending issues. In the following, we give the definitions of these metrics.

Let N be the set of projects and $\mathcal{T}$ the set of all possible project observation times. Each project $i \in N$ has observation time of $T_i \in \mathcal{T}$.

We denote a single issue as a tuple (a_j, b_j) where j is a unique issue identifier, and a_j and b_j denote opening and closing times since project creation (measured in minute resolution). For each issue, it must hold $(a_j \leq b_j) \vee (a_j \leq T_i \wedge b_t = nil)$. Let PI_i denote the set of issues associated with project i. Even though T_i has discrete values, we assume that a_j and b_j are continuous and have minute level resolution in order to be able to derive exact ordering between closing and opening. Let $m(a_j)$ denote the corresponding relative month of a_j and $m^{-1}(t)$ the value in minutes for the corresponding month end date.

Let $o_{i,t}$ denote the number of total newly opened issues for a project i at a relative time $t \in \mathcal{T}$, then

$$o_{i,t} = |\{(a_j, b_j)|(a_j, b_j) \in PI_i, m(a_j) = t\}|.$$

We use $s_{i,t}$ to denote sticky issues, i.e.,

$$s_{i,t} = |\{(a_j, b_j)|(a_j, b_j) \in PI_i, m(a_j) \leq t \wedge b_j = nil\}|.$$

It represents sticky issues as total number of sticky issues by the end of month t.

Let $p_{i,t}$ denote the number of pending issues at time t. The number of pending issues is the number of opened - but not yet closed - issues at a certain point of time (measured in minute resolution).

Thus, we devise the number of pending issues $p_{i,t}$ for a project i during a month t as follows:

$$p_{i,t} = \frac{1}{m^{-1}(t-1) + 1 - m^{-1}(t)} \sum_{d=m^{-1}(t-1)+1}^{d \leq m^{-1}(t)} \delta_{i,d}$$

where $\delta_{i,d}$ denotes the number of open issues for project i at minute resolution d, i.e.

$$\delta_{i,d} = |\{(a_j, b_j)|(a_j, b_j) \in PI_i, a_j \leq d \wedge (b_j = nil \vee b_j > d)\}|.$$

Finally, issue lifetime for issue j, denoted by LT_j, is the amount of days between issue creation and closing and can be calculated only for closed issues, i.e., $b_j \neq nil$:

$$LT_j = (b_j - a_j)/(60 * 24).$$

3.5   Examples

We illustrate our concepts with the help of an example project, Bootstrap[1], a front-end framework for creating user-interfaces in browsers.

Figure 2a shows the numbers of opened and sticky issues observed per month. Note that here we only show the share of sticky issues that correspond to issues opened in the month of observation. Each bar on the plot corresponds to $o_{i,t}$

---

[1] https://github.com/twbs/bootstrap.

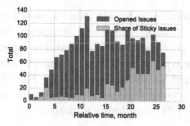
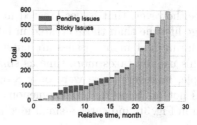

(a) Opened issues for Bootstrap. (b) Pending issues for Bootstrap.

Fig. 2. Opened, pending, and sticky issues for Bootstrap.

and $s_{i,t} - s_{i,t-1}$ (except for the case $t = 0$, the sticky issues is equal to $s_{i,t}$). We see that Bootstrap had increasing numbers of opened issues during the first year of observation, then the number of opened issues leveled off. The monthly share of sticky issues started to rise around month 20. One reason for this could be that our observation period limits the available time for observing issues opened after month 20 being closed. Figure 2b plots the number of pending and sticky issues observed over time. We see that the number of pending issues increases and the majority of pending issues is made up by sticky issues. When comparing the relative share of sticky issues with opened issue per month, we observe that the majority of opened issues get closed, but the amount of work still to be done, represented by the amount of pending issues, is continuously increasing due to the amount of sticky issues.

Figure 3a shows issue lifetime distributions as boxplots for groups of issues opened in a specific month of the project observation time (relative time in months). Note that in Fig. 3a month $= 0$ is an abbreviation for the time up to the beginning of month $= 1$, i.e., representing the observation time interval $[0, 1)$ months. Issue lifetimes remain stable on average over the project observation time (mean lifetime equals 12.9 days, median lifetime equals 0.78 days).

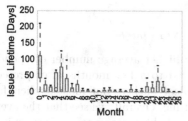
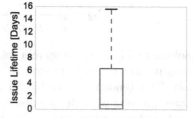

(a) Issue lifetime distributions over time for Bootstrap. (b) Issue lifetime distribution for Bootstrap (all issues).

Fig. 3. Issue lifetime for Bootstrap. For both figures, outliers are removed. The maximums correspond to $1.5 * (75p - 25p) + 75p$, where 25p and 75p denote corresponding percentiles.

We see, however, that issues created in month = 0 have a considerably higher average lifetime than those created in later months. One possible explanation is that during first month issues are entered that require additional development and this usually takes more time as simply correcting a bug. In this particular example, however, there were only 8 opened issues in month = 0. Therefore, this is not an important phenomenon. The overall issue lifetime distribution, shown in Fig. 3b, indicates a small median (0.78 considering all issues) but large variation.

4   Results

In the following subsections we answer the research questions outlined in the introduction. First, we look at the opened issues rates, then we analyze the pending issues, and finally we analyze the issue lifetime distributions.

4.1   Issue Arrival Rate (RQ1)

To answer RQ1 we investigate the arrival rates of opened issues in our set of Github projects. We analyze projects with different project observation times separately, because we suppose that the length of the observation time has an effect on the opened issues. For example, projects with short observation times might (on average) have different numbers of opened issues during the first months of the observation time due to increased popularity of Github and the size and type of projects hosted in Github.

We classify projects based on observation times into buckets and calculate the average number of opened issues per month for all projects in a bucket separately. Figure 4 shows a line for each group of projects in the same bucket. There are T buckets in total and for each line l representing a bucket, a point t on the line represents the average number of opened issues at relative time since creation of the projects in the bucket (i.e., the start of the project observation time), given by the following formula:

$$\mathcal{O}_{t,l} = \frac{1}{\sum_{i \in N \wedge T_i = l \wedge t \leq l} 1} \sum_{i \in N \wedge T_i = l \wedge t \leq l} o_{i,t}$$

Looking at Fig. 4, we observe a relatively higher average number of opened issues right after project creation as compared to a few months after project creation. This tendency is visible for all project buckets but most explicit for buckets of projects with shorter observation time. Overall, we see that the average number of opened issues is stable or shows slight negative trend over project observation time. For the first month, a project in Github receives on average 19.7 new issues, but one year later, during the 12th month, it receives 10.3 opened issues. The relative decline of opened issues after the first few months might be explained as a start-up effect, i.e., at the beginning many issues are submitted but never worked on because they represent wishful thinking regarding features to be included in the project. Furthermore, we observe that projects

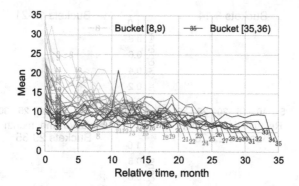

Fig. 4. Opened issues for projects with different lifetime. Color intensity varies with observation period length (Color figure online).

in buckets with shorter observation time seem to have significantly higher numbers of opened issues than those in buckets with longer observation times. For example, in the first month after project creation, projects in buckets with the shortest observation time have on average more than five times more opened issues than projects with the longest observation time. This might be explained by the relative growth of Github and the increasing size of projects in recent time. The drop-offs in the last months are caused due to a technical artifact. Namely, our relative time line starts with repository creation, and due to this, the last month is probably not a full month, as the observation period still ends during the end of a month. In addition, we observe that for some groups, there are outlier months, for example the outlier at month 12. We observe stable average numbers of opened issues for all buckets with relative times after month 28.

To understand what is the ratio of (the share of) sticky issues to opened issues for projects with different observation times, we calculated the ratio of sticky to opened issues for different buckets. In Fig. 5, we display the ratios for each bucket and display the corresponding lines in four different graphs, each graph containing a subset of buckets. The purpose is to make patterns between groups of buckets more visible. The ratio of sticky to opened issues varies mostly between 0.2-0.6, meaning that still more issues get closed than stay open during observation time. We observe that the ratio of sticky issues is higher for early months, then levels off and finally starts to rise due to the technical effect that project observation time ends. The exception is the set of recent projects with short observation times. Compared to other buckets, projects in buckets with observation times 8–14 have less sticky issues in the early months followed by a steady growth of the ratio. One possible explanation for this phenomenon might be that issue submitters in recent projects are more realistic in their issue management and do not fill the issue tracker with issues that will never be worked on or are resolved only after a long time. Another explanation could be that due to the growth of the projects maintained in Github, more development capacity is available to work on issues and thus issues receive more attention and

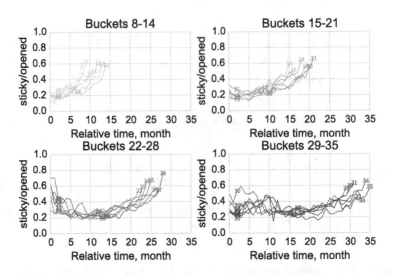

Fig. 5. Ratio of (shares of) sticky issues to opened issues.

are resolved more quickly. This explanation, however, would not explain why the ratio for projects with short observation time strongly grows after a few months.

To answer RQ1, we can conclude that the monthly rate of opened issues for projects in our data set decreases over time on average. During first 12 months, the average number of issues opened drops roughly by a factor of two. The ratio of sticky issues to opened issues changes differently over time for projects with shorter observation time as compared to projects with longer observation time.

4.2 Pending Issue Growth (RQ2)

To answer RQ2 we analysed the dynamics of pending issues and sticky issues over time. Again, we consider projects with different observation times separately. In Fig. 6a, displaying the average numbers of pending issues over time, we classified projects with different observation times into buckets. For each bucket we show the average of pending issues over time as different lines T_i, the values of each line defined as:

$$P_{t,l} = \frac{1}{\sum_{i \in N \wedge T_i = l \wedge t \leq l} 1} \sum_{i \in N \wedge T_i = l \wedge t \leq l} p_{i,t}$$

where l denotes the project observation time and t is the relative time for projects with observation time l, thus also it must always hold that $t \leq l$. Similarly, in Fig. 6b we plot the total number of sticky issues over time for each bucket.

One can see that pending issues are growing at approximately constant rates for all buckets. This phenomenon is underpinned by the growth pattern of sticky issues, issues that have not been resolved within our observation period.

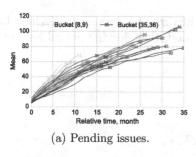

(a) Pending issues.

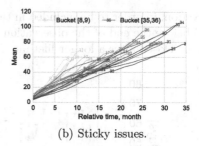

(b) Sticky issues.

Fig. 6. Pending and sticky issues. Even though, sticky issues are a subset of pending issues, we have plotted them on separate Figures for clarity.

The growth rates for both pending and sticky issues are different between buckets. Generally, there seems to be a tendency that more recent projects (shorter project observation time) have on average higher growth rates in the early months of observation time. On the other hand, there exist strong differences between growth rates of buckets with just one month difference of project observation time. For example projects in bucket 34 have in time interval [34, 35) 25 percent more pending (and sticky) issues than projects in bucket 35 in the same time interval.

As an answer to RQ2, we can say that pending issues are growing constantly and this comes mostly from the sticky issues, that do not get resolved during our observation period.

4.3   Issue Lifetime (RQ3)

So far, we observed that there is a steady arrival of new issues and an increasing number of pending (and sticky) issues. Although the amount of pending issues grows, most opened issues actually get resolved (closed) during project observation time. In this section, we answer RQ3 by analyzing issue lifetimes in Github projects.

Figure 7 shows issue lifetime distributions for issues opened during each month (relative time from the start of project observation time) of all projects in our data set, i.e., we do not classify data into buckets with the same project observation times. We consider all issues that are not sticky. Each boxplot represents issue lifetimes for corresponding ILT_t group, defined as $ILT_t = \{LT_j | (a_j, b_j) \in PI_i, i \in N, b_j \neq nil, m(a_j) = t\}$.

In Fig. 7 one sees variation in maximum values but medians vary little over time. The median issue lifetime is 3.1 days for issues opened in month 0 (time interval [0, 1)), 4.1 days for issues opened in month 10 (time interval [9, 10)), 2.89 for issues opened in month 20 (time interval [19, 20)), and 1.78 for issues opened in month 30 (time interval [29, 30)). Thus, one can observe a slight increase from month zero until month 10 in the median value, and then a slight decrease. Around month 20, the median starts to drop more, but this might be a technical effect, caused by the fact that issued opened towards the end of our observation, in order to be included in the lifetime measurement must have been closed before the end of the observation period, thus, leaving out all issues that might be closed after a longer lifetime.

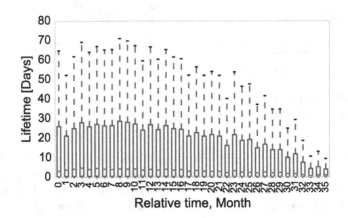

Fig. 7. Issue lifetime distribution depending on issue creation month, each month t lists distribution lifetime of ILT_t. Outliers have been removed.

Figure 8 shows distributions of issue lifetimes for groups of projects with the same project observation times l. Each boxplot represents the issue lifetime distribution for the set ILL_l, defined as $ILL_l = \{LT_j | (a_j, b_j) \in PI_i, i \in N, b_j \neq nil, T_i = l\}$. The observation that variation of issue lifetimes is growing for projects with longer observation time is not surprising, as in projects with longer observation time there is more time available to solve an issue. On the other hand, the median values seem to be stable. The median for projects with observation time 8 months is 2.64 days, for projects with observation time 20 months it is 3.4 days, and for projects with observation time 30 months it is 3.61 days. The variation over all projects is small, considering that the theoretical maximum difference can be more than four times for projects with observation time 8 months and projects with observation time 35 months.

As in the previous section, we also analyzed different project buckets separately. In Fig. 9, we show median issue lifetimes for each group of projects with different observation times. Formally, there are again T lines in total and for each line l, we calculate a median for set of issues $MLT_{l,t}$, defined as $MLT_{l,t} = \{LT_j | (a_j, b_j) \in PI_i, i \in N, b_j \neq nil, T_i = l, m(a_j) = t\}$. We observe few outliers distort the big picture. Ignoring those outliers, we observe that medians are stable. The drop in the last months of the observation times results to some extent from the fact that issues requiring longer time for closing are excluded from the analysis. Interestingly, median values for projects in different buckets are very similar, especially true for projects with observation times between 15 and 35.

To answer RQ3, we can conclude that issue lifetimes are stable over project observation times.

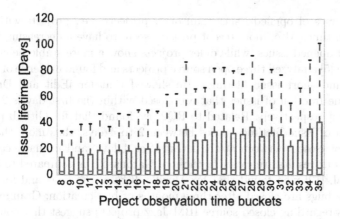

Fig. 8. Issue lifetime distribution depending on the project lifetime, each lifetime bucket l lists distribution of lifetime for issues in ILL_l.

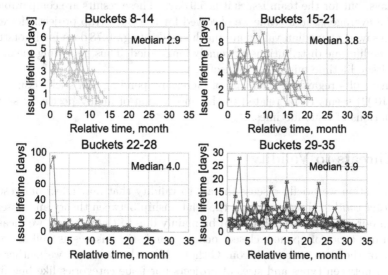

Fig. 9. Median issue lifetimes. For each group, we have calculated the median issue lifetimes over all issues over all months in that group.

4.4   Discussion

Our results partly confirm and partly extend published research. For example, our results related to RQ1 confirm results of Kenmei et al. [10] who studied trends of newly opened issues. They found for some systems (e.g., JBoss) that there is an increasing trend and for others (e.g., Mozilla) that there is not. Similarly, our results, which are averages over large numbers of projects do not show a trend of increasing numbers of opened issues over time for projects with comparable observation time. However, we found that more recent projects, i.e., projects with a shorter observation time in our study period, tend to have generally higher volumes of opened issues than older projects, i.e., projects with longer observation time. Also, more recent projects seem to have a decreasing trend in numbers of opened issues, while older projects show a more stable behavior.

Garousi [5] analyzed three open source projects and found evidence of increasing work and short issue lifetimes. He showed that for jEdit and DrPython projects, the fraction of issues that are closed within the first day is 23 % and 42 % percent respectively. Related to RQ2, we found that for Github projects, the median of issue lifetimes varies between 2 to 4 days, thus more than 50 % of issues get closed between at the latest after 4 days, and in many cases earlier. Thus, our results are closer to those of Garousi [5] as compared to those of Marks et al. [12] who found that for Mozilla 46 % of the bugs and for Eclipse 76 % of the bugs are closed after three months of bug creation. Grammel et al. [8] findings regarding closed source IBM Jazz projects suggest that community created issues can be valuable, but they are handled differently than those created by project members. The average issue lifetime for community created issues is 39 days, but for the team issues it is 5.9 days. These results are comparable to the 12.9 average issue lifetime we observed for the Bootstrap project. However, we also saw that median values are much smaller (e.g., 0.78 days for Bootstrap) and issue lifetime distributions extremely long-tailed. Thus, reporting mean values of issue lifetime might not be useful.

Our results regarding the trend of increasing pending and sticky issues over time (RQ2) seems to be related to the observation of highly positively skewed distributions of issue lifetimes.

5 Threats to Validity

In this section we briefly discuss threats to validity that may affect our results. *Construct validity* threats concern the relationship between theory and observation. In our study, these threats can be mainly due to the way how we measure the various types of opened, closed, pending, and sticky issues as well as to the quality of the data extracted from Github. Also, the fact that we neither distinguish between types and sizes of projects nor issue categories like bug fixes, enhancements, refactoring, and so on. We tried to address the issue of data quality by defining exclusion criteria that filter out projects with certain data anomalies, e.g., low activity, too small size, issue imports due to changes in issue tracker system used.

External validity concerns the generalization of the findings. Different to most of the studies presented in related work, our results rely on the analysis of more than 4000 Github projects from a time period of three years. We believe that our results are to some degree representative for open source projects in general. However, we noticed that there is some variation between projects depending on the length of the observation time. Also, we do not distinguish between types of projects and application domains. Finally, we would like to point out that closed source projects might have different issue behaviors due to the more controlled environment in which those projects are conducted.

Internal validity concerns external factors that may affect an independent variable. *Conlusion validity* concerns the correct application and interpretation of statistical methods. Both validity aspects are less relevant for our study since we neither conduct experiments nor statistical tests.

6 Conclusion and Future Work

Issue trackers are important for software projects to manage bugs and as a general task list indicating development actions needed to be done.

We analyzed issue dynamics of more than 4000 Github projects. Understanding issue volumes and issue lifetimes can be a source for understanding project performance and planning project resources. Once typical evolution patterns for issues are better understood, they might become an indicator for the state of a project and its future outlook.

We identified the following areas for future work. First, future work should look more into the semantics behind issues and distinguish between issue categories such as bugs or feature requests. The next step would be to study how issue growth actually impacts projects in terms of code changes, new releases or even project popularity.

Acknowledgement. This research was supported by the Estonian Research Council and by ERDF via the Software Technology and Applications Competence Centre - STACC.

References

1. Bertram, D., Voida, A., Greenberg, S., Walker, R.: Communication, collaboration, and bugs: the social nature of issue tracking in small, collocated teams. In: Proceedings of the ACM Conference on Computer Supported Cooperative Work, CSCW, pp. 291–300. ACM, Savannah (2010)
2. Bissyande, T.F., Lo, D., Jiang, L., Reveillere, L., Klein, J., Le Traon, Y.: Got issues? Who cares about it? A large scale investigation of issue trackers from github. In: 2013 IEEE 24th International Symposium on Software Reliability Engineering (ISSRE), pp. 188–197. IEEE (2013)
3. Cabot, J., Canovas Izquierdo, J.L., Cosentino, V., Rolandi, B.: Exploring the use of labels to categorize issues in open-source software projects. In: 2015 IEEE 22nd International Conference on Software Analysis, Evolution and Reengineering (SANER), pp. 550–554. IEEE (2015)
4. Crowston, K., Annabi, H., Howison, J.: Defining open source software project success. In: ICIS 2003 Proceedings, p. 28 (2003)
5. Garousi, V.: Evidence-based insights about issue management processes: an exploratory study. In: Wang, Q., Garousi, V., Madachy, R., Pfahl, D. (eds.) ICSP 2009. LNCS, vol. 5543, pp. 112–123. Springer, Heidelberg (2009)
6. Giger, E., Pinzger, M., Gall, H.: Predicting the fix time of bugs. In: Proceedings of the 2nd International Workshop on Recommendation Systems for Software Engineering, pp. 52–56. ACM (2010)

7. Gousios, G., Spinellis, D.: Ghtorrent: Github's data from a firehose. In: 2012 9th IEEE Working Conference on Mining Software Repositories (MSR), pp. 12–21. IEEE (2012)
8. Grammel, L., Schackmann, H., Schröter, A., Treude, C., Storey, M.A.: Attracting the community's many eyes: an exploration of user involvement in issue tracking. In: Human Aspects of Software Engineering, p. 3. ACM (2010)
9. Izquierdo, J.L.C., Cosentino, V., Rolandi, B., Bergel, A., Cabot, J.: Gila: Github label analyzer. In: 2015 IEEE 22nd International Conference on Software Analysis, Evolution and Reengineering (SANER), pp. 479–483. IEEE (2015)
10. Kenmei, B., Antoniol, G., Di Penta, M.: Trend analysis and issue prediction in large-scale open source systems. In: 2008 12th European Conference on Software Maintenance and Reengineering, CSMR 2008, pp. 73–82. IEEE (2008)
11. Ko, A.J., Chilana, P.K.: How power users help and hinder open bug reporting. In: Proceedings of the SIGCHI Conference on Human Factors in Computing Systems, pp. 1665–1674. ACM (2010)
12. Marks, L., Zou, Y., Hassan, A.E.: Studying the fix-time for bugs in large open source projects. In: Proceedings of the 7th International Conference on Predictive Models in Software Engineering, p. 11. ACM (2011)
13. Weiss, C., Premraj, R., Zimmermann, T., Zeller, A.: How long will it take to fix this bug? In: Proceedings of the Fourth International Workshop on Mining Software Repositories, p. 1. IEEE Computer Society (2007)

Studying the Effect of UML-Based Models on Source-Code Comprehensibility: Results from a Long-Term Investigation

Giuseppe Scanniello[1], Carmine Gravino[2]([✉]), Genoveffa Tortora[2], Marcela Genero[3], Michele Risi[2], José A. Cruz-Lemus[3], and Gabriella Dodero[4]

[1] University of Basilicata, Potenza, Italy
giuseppe.scanniello@unibas.it
[2] University of Salerno, Fisciano, Italy
{gravino,tortora,mrisi}@unisa.it
[3] University of Castilla-La Mancha, Ciudad Real, Spain
{Marcela.Genero,JoseAntonio.Cruz}@uclm.es
[4] Free University of Bozen, Bolzano, Italy
Gabriella.Dodero@unibz.it

Abstract. In this paper, we present final results of our long-term investigation whose goal was to study the contribution of software models on source-code comprehensibility. In this investigation we considered unified modeling language (UML) models produced in the analysis and design phases, and we conducted 12 controlled experiments in different contexts with different kinds of participants (e.g., PhD students and software practitioners). The total number of observations from these experiments was 333. We considered both source-code comprehensibility and the time to complete comprehension tasks. We use a meta-analysis to integrate gathered data and to obtain a global effect of analysis and design models on source-code comprehensibility. Results suggest that the use of UML models affects source-code comprehensibility, but in two opposite directions. In particular, models produced in the analysis phase reduce source-code comprehensibility and increase the time to complete comprehension tasks, while models produced in the design phase improve source-code comprehensibility and reduce the time to complete comprehension tasks.

Keywords: UML · Controlled experiments · Replications · Meta-analysis · Software models · Empirical studies

1 Introduction

In the context of object-oriented software analysis and design modeling, the unified modeling language (UML) [1] is considered the de-facto standard [2,3]. However, in many software companies there is still a resistance to the UML model-based development because it is perceived to be difficult to learn and use for professional software developers [4]. Many companies also believe that

© Springer International Publishing Switzerland 2015
P. Abrahamsson et al. (Eds.): PROFES 2015, LNCS 9459, pp. 311–327, 2015.
DOI: 10.1007/978-3-319-26844-6_23

the UML is expensive and not necessarily cost-effective [5]. This resistance is even stronger for organizations that use lean software development processes (e.g., test driven development and XP programming) [6]. Therefore, it may be important, if not crucial, to investigate whether the use of the UML in the analysis and design phases makes (or does not make) a practical difference in software development and evolution. Positive results from such an empirical investigation should further promote the adoption of the UML in the software industry.

Although the UML has been the subject of a number of empirical studies [7], only a few evaluations of its benefits in the whole software development life cycle have been reported [8]. This lack is even more evident in software maintenance with respect to the possible benefits of UML models produced in either the analysis or design phases (referred to in what follows as analysis and design models, respectively) on source-code comprehensibility.

Scanniello et al. [9] conducted an industrial survey on the use of the UML in Italian software companies. Results showed that very often software engineers have at their disposal only UML models produced in the analysis phase and, in a few cases, those produced in the design one. Based on these findings, we started a long term investigation, whose main goal was to study the contribution of analysis and design models given in terms of UML on source-code comprehensibility. We performed 12 controlled experiments with different kinds of human participants from different contexts [10–14] with the goal of verifying the following research question:

– *Do software models produced in the analysis and design phases aid in source-code comprehensibility, and do they affect the time to accomplish a comprehension task?*

In this paper, we present the results of a meta-analysis we have performed to integrate data gathered from our 12 experiments to obtain a global effect of analysis and design models on source-code comprehensibility.

This paper is organized as follows. Our long-term investigation is highlighted in Sect. 2 while the meta-analysis and its results are presented and discussed in Sect. 3. Section 4 summarizes related work. We conclude the paper with final remarks.

2   Our Long-Term Investigation

In the survey we conducted in 2009 [9], the main results suggested that many of the interviewed companies use UML diagrams produced in both analysis and design phases. The most used diagrams were: use case, class, and sequence diagrams. Another result of this survey was: maintenance operations were performed by practitioners with few years of experience in software development and maintenance. In particular, companies generally employ developers with a Bachelor or a Master degree in Computer Science and with experience in between 1 and 5 years.

On the basis of the main results of that industrial survey, we started a long-term investigation. We quantitatively studied source-code comprehensibility that developers achieved when they were provided with source code alone, or with source code and UML software models together. The models considered in our investigation were those produced in the analysis and design phases. In particular, we took into consideration the following UML diagrams: use case, class, and sequence. Use case narratives (or simply use case, from here on) were also taken into consideration. Our investigation followed two main directions:

- The first direction regards the comprehension of source code when it was complemented with analysis models based on the UML notation. In particular, use case diagrams and use cases were employed to represent functional requirements. Class diagrams were used to abstract the objects from the problem domain (i.e., the object or conceptual model), while sequence diagrams to model the dynamic and/or functional behavior. First, we conducted a pilot study with Bachelor students in Computer Science at the University of Basilicata. Results of this pilot were presented in [10] and can be summarized as follows: the use of analysis models does not significantly improve the comprehension of source-code. On this subject, we conducted (together with other researchers) a family of four controlled experiments [11]. The goal was to strengthen the findings obtained in the pilot study. The experiments were carried out with students and practitioners from Italy and Spain having different abilities and levels of experience with the UML. The achieved results indicated that UML analysis models seemed not to improve source-code comprehensibility, so confirming results from the pilot.
- We have conducted two kinds of controlled experiments. As for the first kind of experiments, our goal was to assess potential benefits deriving from the use of UML class and sequence diagrams (both produced in the design phase) on the comprehension of object-oriented source-code [12]. Two experiments with Bachelor and Master students in Computer Science were conducted. The data analysis revealed that participants having more experience on the UML and computer programming (i.e., Master students) benefited from the use of UML design models. As for the second kind of experiments, we conducted an experiment with Master students to investigate if providing source code with the graphically documentation of the design-pattern instances improves source-code comprehensibility [13]. These instances were documented by class diagrams. The control group comprised students who were given source code alone without any reference to the contained design-pattern instances. Successively, we carried out four controlled experiments with participants having different experience with programming and software modeling (i.e., Bachelor, Master, and PhD students and practitioners) [14]. The effect of textually documented design-pattern instances was also studied. Data regarding such a kind of documentation was not considered in the study presented in this paper.

All 12 experiments sketched before and summarized in Table 1. They were carried out by following the recommendations have been provided in [19–21].

In the following, we summarize the planning and the operation phases of these experiments, mainly presenting the information most salient for the meta analysis.

The experiments are reported according to the guidelines suggested by Jedlitschka et al. [22]. For replication purposes, we made available on the web[1] the raw data of all our experiments.

2.1 Goal

According to the Goal Question Metrics template [23] the goal of each experiment of our long-term investigation is: *analyze* the use of UML models *for the purpose of* understanding their utility *with respect to* the comprehensibility of object-oriented source code *from the point of view of* the software engineer *in the context of* students/practitioners.

2.2 Context Selection

We used different software systems in the performed experiments. The systems used were those described in the fourth column of Table 1. All the experimental objects were desktop applications and were implemented in Java. Music Shop and Theater Ticket Reservation as well as their models were created within a course on advanced object-oriented programming (AOOP). The lecturer of this course was not involved in the study presented here. The documentation and the models were originally devised to be provided to groups of 4 or 5 students for the implementation of the corresponding software as a laboratory activity of the AOOP course. We used the source code that the lecturer selected from among the software systems developed by student teams and that he considered the best. We did not have any control on the selection process. However, we reviewed the documentation and models to find possible issues. No remarkable modifications were needed. We only removed typographical errors and indented source code when needed. Source-code comments were removed to avoid that their effect was confused with the main factor understudy, namely the use of software models on source-code comprehensibility. The students that developed the software in the AOOP course and that we used as experimental objects did not participate in the experiments. We also used open-source software. In particular, we selected a chunk (i.e., vertical slice) of JHotDraw v5.1. This chunk included: (i) a nontrivial number of design-pattern instances and (ii) instances of well-known and widely adopted design patterns. We documented design-pattern instances present in the source code using both the JHotDraw documentation and the PMARt dataset [24]. This allowed us to document both intentional and unintentional design-pattern instances.

We conducted all the experiments except DePra (see Table 1) in research laboratories. All the experiments were conducted under controlled conditions. The most salient characteristics of participants are summarized in Table 1. Prior

---

[1] www2.unibas.it/gscanniello/SourceCodeComprMetaAnalysis/data.xlsx.

Table 1. Summary of the experiments*

Experiment	Number of Participants and Kind	Design	Exp. Objects	Results	
				Comprehension	Completion time
AnBsc [10]	16 3rd year Bachelor students	- One-factor-with more treatments - Randomized	A chunk of a system Music Shop software implemented in Java	The difference is not statistically significant	Time analysis not presented
DeBscExp1 [12]	16 2nd year Bachelor students	- Within-participants counterbalanced - Randomized	A chunk of a Theater Ticket Reservation system implemented in Java	The difference is not statistically significant	The difference is statistically significant. More time when models used
DeMscExp1 [12]	16 second year Master students			The difference is statistically significant. Better comprehension when models used	The difference is not statistically significant
AnMscExp1 [11]	24 1st year Master students	- Within-participants counterbalanced - Ability as blocking factor		The difference is not statistically significant	Time analysis not presented
AnMscExp2 [11]	22 2nd year Master students			The difference is not statistically significant	
AnMscExp3 [11]	22 1st year Master students			The difference is statistically significant. Better comprehension when models not used	
AnPra [11]	18 Practitioners			The difference is not statistically significant	
DeMscExp2 [13]	24 1st year Master students	-One-factor-with more treatments - Ability as blocking factor for students	JHotDraw: a two-dimensional graphics framework for structured drawing editors implemented in Java. A chunk (i.e., vertical slice) of the entire software was selected	Analysis on comprehension not presented	The difference is statistically significant. Less time when models used
DePra [14]	16 Professionals	- Years of working experience as blocking factor for practitioners		The difference is statistically significant. Better comprehension when models used	The difference is not statistically significant
DeMscExp3 [14]	16 1st year Master students			The difference is not statistically significant	
DeBscExp2 [14]	15 3rd year Bachelor students				
DePhd [14]	10 Ph.D students			The difference is statistically significant. Better comprehension when models used	

*The labels of the experiments are expressed using the upper-camel case notation. Each compound word has a specific meaning. The first word suggests the kind of UML-based documentation: (An) stands for those documents produced in the analysis phase and (De) stands for those documents produced in the design phase. The second word indicates the kind of participant. For example, Pra and Msc stand for practitioner and master student, respectively. The third word is a progressive id for the experiment. We used this compound id to better discern each experiment that was based on the same kind of documentation and involved the same kind of participants.

knowledge and experience of students participating in the experiments with students can be considered rather homogeneous. Participation in the experiments was on a voluntary basis. Participants were not paid. Each participant took part in only one experiment. Further information on the experimental objects and their selection process as well as the characteristics of participants in the experiments can be found in [10–14].

2.3 Variable Selection

In each experiment, we considered participants who were given source code alone as comprising the *control group*, while the *treatment group* comprised students who were given source code with software models based on the UML. Thus, method was the independent variable (manipulated factor or the main factor, from here on) considered in our study. It was a nominal variable that assumes the following two values: *models* (software models plus source code without comment) and *source code* (source code without comments).

The effect of the manipulated factor was analyzed on the following chosen dependent variables:

- *Comprehension.* This denotes the comprehension level of the source code achieved by a software engineer.
- *Completion time.* This denotes the time a software engineer spends to accomplish a comprehension task.

We used questionnaires to assess source-code comprehensibility. The correctness and completeness of the answers for these questionnaires were quantitatively evaluated by using an information-retrieval-based approach. Each answer was provided as string items (e.g., a sequence of method/class names and/or the text messages shown to a user), which were compared with the expected items. The correctness of the obtained answers was measured with the precision measure, while the completeness with the recall measure. To obtain a single measure to all the questions of a questionnaire, we computed the overall average of the F-measure values (i.e., a balanced harmonic mean of precision and recall). F-measure was used to estimate the comprehension variable. F-measure values range in between 0 and 1. The higher the value, the greater source-code comprehensibility was.

To determine completion time, we used the overall time (expressed in minutes) to answer a comprehension questionnaire. The higher the value of time, the greater the effort[2] to accomplish a comprehension task.

2.4 Design

We used different kinds of design in the experiments. As shown in Table 1, we used the within-participants counterbalanced experimental design in DeMscExp1,

---

[2] Time was an approximation of comprehension effort. This is compliant with the ISO/IEC 9126 standard [25], where effort is the productive time associated with a specific project task.

AnMscExp1, AnMscExp2, AnMscExp3, and AnPra. In the remaining experiments we adopted the one-factor-with more treatments design [21]. We used these kinds of experimental designs to mitigate the presence of a possible carry-over effect.[3] It is worth noting that the design of some experiments was randomized, while in others we used participants' ability as blocking factor (see Table 1 for details).

2.5 Experimental Tasks and Operation

Some differences among experiments in terms of experimental tasks and procedures were present. However, all participants were asked to fill in a comprehension questionnaire and a post-experiment survey questionnaire. The composition of both questionnaires depends on the experiment and the tasks. We formulated questions in the comprehension questionnaires using a similar form/schema. In addition, these questions were formulated to assess comprehension on the part of the source code we believed to be more relevant and related with understanding concepts in this source code that involved multiple relationships and software entities. Further details on the experimental tasks and the experimental procedure can be found in [10–14]. Differences in the experiments, with respect to these aspects, should not be a major issue in this paper because we used a meta-analysis to integrate and synthesize experimental data.

3 Meta Analysis

3.1 Motivations and Analysis Procedure

As the number of empirical studies grow, the need for aggregating evidences from multiple empirical studies increases [21]. There are two main reasons for aggregating evidences. Firstly, new research should always take existing knowledge into consideration as its starting point. That is, reviews summarizing the outcomes of various intervention trials are an efficient method for obtaining the "bottom line" about what works and what does not. Secondly, empirical studies may together give answers to certain research questions. Individual studies in isolation are not sufficient to answer these questions.

The collection, synthesis, and review of empirical evidence must meet scientific standards in itself. There are several strategies to summarize and synthesize outcomes from different empirical studies/experiments. Syntheses based on statistical methods are referred to as meta-analysis [21]. It can be applied to analyze the outcomes of several dependent and/or independent studies/experiments. The most important advantage in using a meta-analysis is that such a kind of secondary study allows achieving a higher statistical power than primary studies (i.e., the studies to be synthesized) for the variable of interest. There is no

---

[3] If a participant is tested first under experimental condition A and then under experimental condition B, she/he could potentially exhibit better or worse performance under condition B.

accepted minimum number of studies that are required for a meta-analysis, but a minimum of 10 is considered acceptable [26].

When conducting a meta-analysis, we have to verify whether the studies/experiments to be synthesized are homogenous or not [26]. I-squared and tau-squared are measures of heterogeneity that are used in meta-analysis. I-squared is the percentage of total variation across experiments that is due to heterogeneity rather than chance. On the other hand, tau-squared is an absolute measure of heterogeneity. It is a measure of the standard deviation of effect sizes across experiments. Values greater than 1 indicate that experiments are heterogeneous [26]. To test the presence of statistical heterogeneity the Cochran's Q test can be also used [26]. This test measures deviation of observed effect sizes from an underlying overall effect size. The widely used cut-off point is 0.1. If the value is inferior to this threshold we can reject the null hypothesis and assume that experiments are heterogeneous.

If experiments are not heterogeneous, they should be combined in a meta-analysis using a fixed-effect model. This model assumes that the size of treatment effect is the same (fixed) across all the experiments. To deal with heterogeneity, different strategies to combine experiments in a meta-analysis are possible: (i) ignore heterogeneity and apply a fixed-effect model, (ii) apply a random-effects model, or (iii) find the reasons of heterogeneity and perform sub-group analyses. In case our experiments are heterogeneous, we will go through the application of the second and third strategies. The second strategy will give indications on the global effect of analysis and design models with respect to comprehension and completion time, while the third will provide deeper insights under which conditions these kinds of models can make the difference with respect to the dependent variables. Each sub-group should have a minimum of 4 studies/experiments [27].

Meta-analysis results are commonly displayed graphically as "forest plots" [28]. This kind of pictorial representation provides a quick and easy way to illustrate the relative strength of treatment effects. Forest plots display point estimates and confidence intervals for individual experiments as well as an estimate of the overall summary effect size. It also shows the extent to which each experiment contributes to the overall result.

3.2 Results

To summarize the results of each experiment, we undertook the descriptive statistics of the measures of the dependent variables, that is, comprehension and completion time. The descriptive statistics for comprehension (i.e., mean, standard deviation, and number of observations) grouped by method are shown in the forest plot in Fig. 1 (on the left side). The same descriptive statistics for completion time are reported in Fig. 2.

Comprehension. On average, participants achieved mostly the same results when employing source code and source code plus analysis models. This was not completely true in AnMscExp3 and AnPra, where participants achieved better comprehension when using such a kind of models. As for design models, participants achieved a better source code comprehension when they were provided with models. Only in case of less experienced participants there was no difference between treatment and control groups.

Completion Time. There was no clear trend in the descriptive statistics on this dependent variable. Indeed, in many experiments participants spent slightly less time when accomplishing the comprehension task without software models (independently from the phase where the models were produced).

The results were synthesized by the Mean Differences (MDs) of the outcome measures of the experiments. This was possible because the experiments had the same outcome measures for comprehension and for completion time, respectively. On the bottom of the forest plots (left side) results for testing heterogeneity are also shown. As far as comprehension is concerned, I-squared indicates a moderate heterogeneity, while the Cochran's Q test suggests that experiments were heterogeneous ($p = 0.0001$). To be as much conservative as possible, we applied a random-effects model. As the squares in Fig. 1 suggest, experiments equally contributed to the overall result, that is, the use of models slightly improved source-code comprehensibility (MD = 0.01). Indeed, source-code comprehensibility was not statistically different when using or not using models in comprehension tasks. In fact, a plotted effect size is statistically different from the overall effect if the diamond (on the bottom of the forest plot) does not intersect the vertical line. This result was also confirmed by the overall 95 % confidence interval[4] (IC) whose value was $[-0.04; 0.06]$.

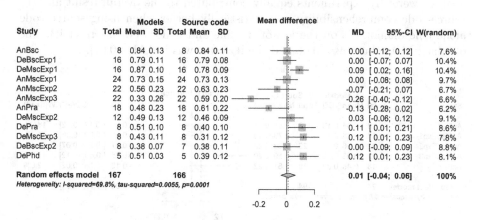

Fig. 1. Forest plot for Comprehension

We applied a random-effects model also on completion time since the experiments were heterogenous (see Fig. 2). Unlike comprehension, the squares were

---

[4] It is a range of values for which we are 95 % certain that it contains the true mean value.

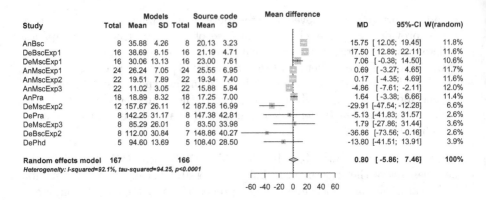

Fig. 2. Forest plot for Completion Time

not proportional in size, when studying completion time (see Fig. 2). This indicates that some experiments contributed more than others to the overall result. The forest plot suggests that completion time was not statistically different when using or not using models in comprehension tasks. The obtained MD value was 0.8.

We performed sub-group analyses for both the dependent variables since the experiments were heterogeneous. In particular, we grouped experiments according to the kind of models used in, namely An and De. The forest plot for An and comprehension is shown in Fig. 3. In this case we used a fixed-effect model because of the results of the heterogeneous tests. The main results of our meta-analysis were: (i) experiments equally contributed to the overall result and (ii) source-code comprehensibility was statistically better when using source code alone (the diamond is on the left of the line and it does not intersect it). The obtained MD value was -0.06 and the IC value was $[-0.11; -0.01]$.

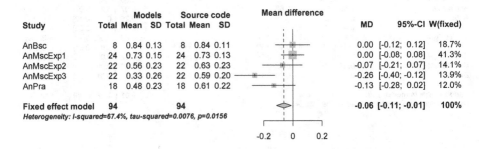

Fig. 3. Forest plot for Comprehension on the sub-group An

Figure 4 shows the forest plot for comprehension on the experiments where participants were administered with design models. Some experiments contributed more than others to the overall result. The most remarkable outcome was that the difference between using or not using models was statistically significant. Participants provided with design documents obtained a better comprehension of source code because the diamond is on the right side of the vertical line. On the basis of the possible values of comprehension MD was large enough (i.e., 0.06).

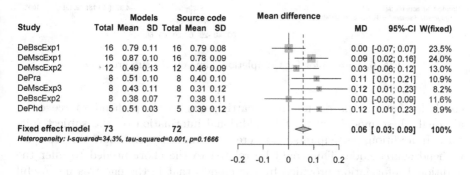

Study		Models			Source code		Mean difference	MD	95%-CI	W(fixed)
	Total	Mean	SD	Total	Mean	SD				
DeBscExp1	16	0.79	0.11	16	0.79	0.08		0.00	[-0.07; 0.07]	23.5%
DeMscExp1	16	0.87	0.10	16	0.78	0.09		0.09	[0.02; 0.16]	24.0%
DeMscExp2	12	0.49	0.13	12	0.46	0.09		0.03	[-0.06; 0.12]	13.0%
DePra	8	0.51	0.10	8	0.40	0.10		0.11	[0.01; 0.21]	10.9%
DeMscExp3	8	0.43	0.11	8	0.31	0.12		0.12	[0.01; 0.23]	8.2%
DeBscExp2	8	0.38	0.07	7	0.38	0.11		0.00	[-0.09; 0.09]	11.6%
DePhd	5	0.51	0.03	5	0.39	0.12		0.12	[0.01; 0.23]	8.9%
Fixed effect model	73			72				0.06	[0.03; 0.09]	100%

Heterogeneity: I-squared=34.3%, tau-squared=0.001, p=0.1666

-0.2 -0.1 0 0.1 0.2

Fig. 4. Forest plot for Comprehension on the sub-group De

The meta-analysis results for completion time on An and De are summarized in Figs. 5 and 6, respectively. Both these plots suggest that the time to complete a comprehension task was not statistically different when using or not using models. This was true independently from the kind of models administered to participants. In more details, participants administered with analysis models spent slightly more time to accomplish the comprehension task (see Fig. 5). Participants in the other experiments spent less time when accomplishing the task with models (Fig. 6).

Study		Models			Source code		Mean difference	MD	95%-CI	W(random)
	Total	Mean	SD	Total	Mean	SD				
AnBsc	8	35.88	4.26	8	20.13	3.23		15.75	[12.05; 19.45]	20.2%
AnMscExp1	24	26.24	7.05	24	25.55	6.95		0.69	[-3.27; 4.65]	20.0%
AnMscExp2	22	19.51	7.89	22	19.34	7.40		0.17	[-4.35; 4.69]	19.7%
AnMscExp3	22	11.02	3.05	22	15.88	5.84		-4.86	[-7.61; -2.11]	20.6%
AnPra	18	18.89	8.32	18	17.25	7.00		1.64	[-3.38; 6.66]	19.4%
Random effects model	94			94				2.67	[-4.93; 10.26]	100%

Heterogeneity: I-squared=94.9%, tau-squared=70.84, p<0.0001

-10 0 10

Fig. 5. Forest plot for Completion Time on the sub-group An

3.3 Discussion

The meta-analysis highlighted that participants obtained slightly better scores for comprehension when using analysis and design models. Therefore, we could

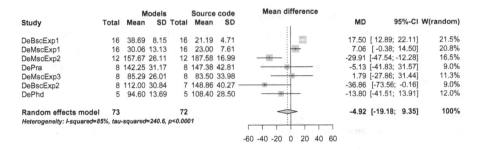

Fig. 6. Forest plot for Completion Time on the sub-group De

conclude that models do not help participants to comprehend source code, although these models do provide additional information on the subject software. In addition, participants who were given models spend more time to comprehend source code. This could be related to the effort needed to infer the additional information provided by the models that in the end was not useful to get an improved comprehension of source code. We further investigate on this point performing sub-group analyses. We looked at possible reasons why experiments were heterogeneous. The most plausible justification was: analysis models referred to objects (or entities) in the problem domain, while design models referred to objects in the solution domain and therefore better supported source-code comprehensibility. We made this assumption on the basis of results from our individual experiments. Results from meta-analyses on the two chosen sub-groups gave credit to our assumption. In particular, results indicated that the use of models affects source-code comprehensibility, but in two opposite directions. The use of analysis models reduces source-code comprehensibility and increases the time to complete comprehension tasks, while the use of models produced in the design phase improves source-code comprehensibility and reduces task completion time. Even though our results improved the findings for the individual experiments conducted in our long-term investigation, meta-analysis could not provide conclusive findings on whether analysis and design models helped in comprehending source code in the context of graduate, undergraduate, PhD students, and novice practitioners with respect to systems related to well-known domains.

We also judged the implications of our study. To this end, we adopted a perspective-based approach [29] and based our discussion on the practitioner/consultant (simply practitioner, from here on) and researcher perspectives [30]. Since our long-term investigation may have several implications, we restrict our discussion to those implications we believed more relevant with respect to the goal of our study:

- UML-based modeling is important to let software engineers get an improved comprehension of source code. These models should focus on aspects related to the solution domain of a subject software. Therefore, models produced in the analysis phase have less importance if they are only intended to support the comprehension of source code. On the other hand, these models are of primary importance in case we found the subsequent development phases on them. We can speculate on this point because we used in some of experiments the same software, but models produced in either the analysis or the design phases (e.g., AnBsc and DeMscExp1). From the practitioner perspective, this result is relevant because it gives a strong motivation in favor of the adoption of a development process based on the use of the UML. In addition, it could be useless to give UML-based analysis models to the software engineer when he/she has to perform small maintenance operations on source code. That is, this kind of models should be only used to support the subsequent phases of the development or to improve the comprehension of functional requirements [31]. From the researcher perspective, it is interesting to investigate whether variations in the context (e.g., larger systems and more or less experienced software engineers) might lead to different results.

- UML analysis models seem to uselessly overload participants while performing comprehension tasks. This result is relevant for the researcher because it is interesting to investigate more on this point and in which context it holds. Our study poses the basis for future work in this direction.
- Although we are not sure that our findings scale up to real projects, the obtained results could be true in all cases where models are concerned with a part of the entire software (e.g., in lean development processes) and maintenance operations are performed on a chunk of the source code of the entire system.
- We focussed on desktop applications. Models of these systems were realistic enough for small-sized in-house software and subcontracting development projects. From the researcher perspective, the effect of analysis and design models on different types of systems (e.g., smartphone and web apps) represents a possible future direction for our research. This point is clearly relevant for the researcher.

3.4   Threats to Validity

Internal Validity. This kind of threat to the results validity was diminished by the design of the experiments, adopted in all the experiments in our meta-analysis. Each group of participants either worked on two different tasks with and without models or worked on a single task. Another possible threat concerns the fact that we did not impose any time limit to perform tasks. We opted for this design choice because this is quite common in experiments similar to ours and because participants could have difficulty in performing tasks under time constraints [32,33].

External Validity. Performing experiments with students could be questioned concerning their representativeness with regard to software professionals. To deal with this concern, we performed several replications with professionals and highly experienced participants (i.e., PhD students). Another threat to external validity regards experimental objects, e.g., artifacts and tasks.

G. Scanniello et al.

Construct Validity. This kind of validity may be influenced by the measures used to obtain a quantitative evaluation of source-code comprehensibility. Construct validity might be also affected by the used comprehension and post-experiment survey questionnaires as well as social threats. We used post-experiment survey questionnaires designed with standard approaches and scales [34]. Responses to such a kind of questionnaire were used to explain quantitative results. To mitigate construct validity, we also conducted external replications.

Conclusion Validity. It concerns issues that affect the ability to draw a correct conclusion. To deal with conclusion validity, we performed statistical analysis on gathered data. Regarding the selection of populations, we drew fair samples and conducted our experiments with participants belonging to these samples. Another threat to conclusion validity could be related to the number of participants. This kind of threat was mitigated because our study was based on 333 observations.

4 Related Work

deSouza et al. [15] presented the results of a survey of 76 software engineers in Brazil. The goal was to establish which kind of software artifact was most useful when performing maintenance operations. Results of this survey suggested that source code and comments were considered the most important artifacts to source-code comprehension. Data model and requirements description were other important artifacts. Tryggeseth [16] reported an experiment with 34 participants in Norway. The used experimental object was a software of 2.7 K lines of code and around 100 pages of textual documentation including requirements specification, design documentation, a test report, and a user's manual. The gathered data suggested the following results: (i) having documentation while performing software maintenance reduces the time to understand both software and changes to implement a change request and (ii) documentation also enables a software engineer with more time and better knowledge to implement more detailed changes. The results of our long term investigation, from one side, confirm the results by Tryggeseth [16] (i.e., software models/documentation aid in source-code comprehensibility) with stronger evidence (e.g., [12,14]). On the other side, we contradict the Tryggeseth findings that time to execute maintenance tasks decreases when providing a software engineer with documentation (e.g., [12]).

With respect to the usefulness of design documentation, only a few studies have been reported in the literature. For example, Prechelt et al. [17] presented two experiments to investigate the support that the documentation of design-pattern instances provides to source-code comprehensibility. In particular, the authors compared the comprehension achieved by participants when design-pattern instances are (or are not) explicitly documented. The experiment was performed on Java source code by 74 German graduate students. The experiment was then replicated on C++ source code using 22 American undergraduate students. The most important result that researchers observed was: maintenance tasks are completed faster and with fewer errors if design pattern instances are explicitly documented. Successively, Scanniello et al. [14] presented the results of a family of controlled experiments to investigate the effect of documenting design-patter instances textually (i.e., by source-code comments) and graphically (i.e., by UML class diagrams). The most important result suggested that documenting design-pattern instances (independently from the kind of documentation) yields an improvement in correctness of understanding source code for those participants with an adequate level of experience. In the study presented in this paper, we used data gathered from participants who employed graphically documented design pattern instances and source code alone to accomplish comprehension tasks.

Budgen et al. [7] collected and analyzed empirical investigations on widely used UML notations and their usefulness, while Fernández-Saez [18] focussed on the existing literature on the quality of UML models. Both systematic literature reviews show that source-code comprehensibility and modifiability are the major concern. In addition, results suggested that there are few evaluations on how UML models support software engineers in the whole software development life cycle. A deeper discussion on research work on the use of the UML in the maintenance of source code is not possible for space reason. The interested reader can find more details in the two systematic literature reviews highlighted before.

5   Conclusion

In this paper, we presented results of a long-term investigation on the effect of using UML-based modeling in software maintenance and source-code comprehensibility, in particular. This investigation started in 2009 with an industrial survey and then on the basis of the results of this survey, we conducted a number of controlled experiments with students and practitioners from Italy and Spain. Results of individual experiments were synthesized through meta-analyses and presented in this paper for the first time. The most important outcome is: the use of UML models is important to let software engineers get an improved comprehension of source code given that these models focus on aspects related to objects (or entities) of the solution domain of a subject software. Models produced in the analysis phase are of less importance if we use them only to comprehend source code. On the other hand, analysis models are of primary importance in case they are the basis of the subsequent phases of the development process.

References

1. OMG: Unified modeling language (UML) specification, version 2.0. Technical report, Object Management Group, July 2005

2. Erickson, J., Siau, K.: Theoretical and practical complexity of modeling methods. Commun. ACM **50**(8), 46–51 (2007)
3. Grossman, M., Aronson, J.E., McCarthy, R.V.: Does UML make the grade? Insights from the software development community. Inf. Softw. Technol. **47**(6), 383–397 (2005)
4. Agarwal, R., Sinha, A.P.: Object-oriented modeling with uml: a study of developers' perceptions. Commun. ACM **46**(9), 248–256 (2003)
5. Arisholm, E., Briand, L.C., Hove, S.E., Labiche, Y.: The impact of UML documentation on software maintenance: an experimental evaluation. IEEE Trans. Softw. Eng. **32**(6), 365–381 (2006)
6. Cohen, D., Lindvall, M., Costa, P.: An introduction to Agile methods. Adv. Comput. **62**, 1–66 (2004)
7. Budgen, D., Burn, A.J., Brereton, O.P., Kitchenham, B.A., Pretorius, R.: Empirical evidence about the UML: a systematic literature review. Softw. Pract. Experience **41**(4), 363–392 (2011)
8. Anda, B., Hansen, K., Gullesen, I., Thorsen, H.K.: Experiences from introducing UML-based development in a large safety-critical project. Empirical Softw. Eng. **11**(4), 555–581 (2006)
9. Scanniello, G., Gravino, C., Tortora, G.: Investigating the role of UML in the software modeling and maintenance - a preliminary industrial survey. In: Proceedings of International Conference on Enterprise Information Systems, pp. 141–148 (2010)
10. Gravino, C., Tortora, G., Scanniello, G.: An empirical investigation on the relation between analysis models and source code comprehension. In: Proceeding of the International Symposium on Applied Computing, pp. 2365–2366. ACM (2010)
11. Scanniello, G., Gravino, C., Genero, M., Cruz-Lemus, J.A., Tortora, G.: On the impact of UML analysis models on source code comprehensibility and modifiability. ACM Trans. Software Eng. Methodol. **23**(2), 13 (2014)
12. Gravino, C., Scanniello, G., Tortora, G.: Source-code comprehension tasks supported by UML design models: results from a controlled experiment and a differentiated replication. J. Vis. Lang. Comput. **28**, 23–38 (2015)
13. Scanniello, G., Gravino, C., Risi, M., Tortora, G.: A controlled experiment for assessing the contribution of design pattern documentation on software maintenance. In: Proceeding of the Symposium on Empirical Software Engineering and Measurement. ACM (2010)
14. Scanniello, G., Gravino, C., Risi, M., Tortora, G., Dodero, G.: Documenting design-pattern instances: a family of experiments on source-code comprehensibility. ACM Trans. Softw. Eng. Methodol. **24**(3), 14 (2015)
15. de Souza, S.C.B., Anquetil, N., de Oliveira, K.M.: A study of the documentation essential to software maintenance. In: Proc. of the International Conference on Design of communication: documenting & designing for pervasive information, pp. 68–75. ACM, New York (2005)
16. Tryggeseth, E.: Report from an experiment: impact of documentation on maintenance. Empirical Softw. Eng. **2**(2), 201–207 (1997)
17. Prechelt, L., Unger-Lamprecht, B., Philippsen, M., Tichy, W.F.: Two controlled experiments assessing the usefulness of design pattern documentation in program maintenance. IEEE Trans. Softw. Eng. **28**(6), 595–606 (2002)
18. Fernández-Saez, A., Genero, M., Nelson, J., Poels, G., Piattini, M.: A systematic literature review on the quality of UML models. J. Database Manag. **22**(3), 46–70 (2012)
19. Juristo, N., Moreno, A.: Basics of Software Engineering Experimentation. Kluwer Academic Publishers (2001)

20. Kitchenham, B., Pfleeger, S., Pickard, L., Jones, P., Hoaglin, D., El Emam, K., Rosenberg, J.: Preliminary guidelines for empirical research in software engineering. IEEE Trans. Softw. Eng. **28**(8), 721–734 (2002)
21. Wohlin, C., Runeson, P., Höst, M., Ohlsson, M., Regnell, B., Wesslén, A.: Experimentation in Software Engineering. Springer, Heidelberg (2012)
22. Jedlitschka, A., Ciolkowski, M., Pfahl, D.: Reporting experiments in software engineering. In: Shull, F., Singer, J., Sjoberg, D. (eds.) Guide to Advanced Empirical Software Engineering, pp. 201–228. Springer, London (2008)
23. Basili, V.R., Rombach, H.D.: The TAME project: towards improvement-oriented software environments. IEEE Trans. Softw. Eng. **14**(6), 758–773 (1988)
24. Guéhéneuc, Y.G.: P-MARt: pattern-like micro architecture repository. In: Proceeding of EuroPLoP Focus Group on Pattern Repositories (2007)
25. ISO: Information Technology-Software Product Evaluation: Quality Characteristics and Guidelines for their Use, ISO/IEC IS 9126. ISO, Geneva (1991)
26. Pickard, L., Kitchenham, B.A., Jones, P.: Combining empirical results in software engineering. Inf. Softw. Technol. **40**(14), 811–821 (1998)
27. Fu, R., Gartlehner, G., Grant, M., Shamliyan, T., Sedrakyan, A., Wilt, T.J., Griffith, L., Oremus, M., Raina, P., Ismaila, A., Santaguida, P., Lau, J., Trikalinos, T.A.: Conducting quantitative synthesis when comparing medical interventions: AHRQ and the effective health care program. J. Clin. Epidemiol. **64**(11), 1187–1197 (2011)
28. Ried, K.: Interpreting and understanding meta-analysis graphs - a practical guide. Australian College of General Practitioners, vol. 35, August 2008
29. Basili, V.R., Green, S., Laitenberger, O., Lanubile, F., Shull, F., Sørumgård, L.S., Zelkowitz, M.V.: The empirical investigation of perspective-based reading. Empirical Softw. Eng. **1**(2), 133–164 (1996)
30. Kitchenham, B., Al-Khilidar, H., Babar, M., Berry, M., Cox, K., Keung, J., Kurniawati, F., Staples, M., Zhang, H., Zhu, L.: Evaluating guidelines for reporting empirical software engineering studies. Empirical Softw. Eng. **13**, 97–121 (2008)
31. Abrahão, S.M., Gravino, C., Pelozo, E.I., Scanniello, G., Tortora, G.: Assessing the effectiveness of sequence diagrams in the comprehension of functional requirements: results from a family of five experiments. IEEE Trans. Softw. Eng. **39**(3), 327–342 (2013)
32. Sjøberg, D.I.K., Hannay, J.E., Hansen, O., Kampenes, V.B., Karahasanovic, A., Liborg, N., Rekdal, A.C.: A survey of controlled experiments in software engineering. IEEE Trans. Softw. Eng. **31**(9), 733–753 (2005)
33. Mendonça, M.G., Maldonado, J.C., de Oliveira, M.C.F., Carver, J., Fabbri, S.C.P.F., Shull, F., Travassos, G.H., Höhn, E.N., Basili, V.R.: A framework for software engineering experimental replications. In: Proceedings of International Conference on Engineering of Complex Computer Systems, pp. 203–212. IEEE Computer Society (2008)
34. Oppenheim, A.N.: Questionnaire Design, Interviewing and Attitude Measurement. Pinter, London (1992)

Source Code Driven Decomposition
of Object-Oriented Legacy Systems

A Systemic Literature Review and Research Outlook

Inese Supulniece[1(✉)], Solvita Berzisa[1], Inese Polaka[1], Janis Grabis[1],
Egils Meiers[2], and Edgars Ozolins[2]

[1] Institute of Information Technology, Riga Technical University, Riga, Latvia
{Inese.Supulniece,Solvita.Berzisa,
Inese.Polaka,Grabis}@rtu.lv
[2] Visma Enterprise, Riga, Latvia
{Egils.Meiers,Edgars.Ozolins}@visma.lv

Abstract. Many enterprise applications have been developed over the last three decades therefore known as legacy systems. Usually they are monolith, inflexible, poorly documented and hard to maintain, however they are important to enterprises. The evolution of these systems depends on their decomposability. The purpose of this paper is to summarize existing knowledge, requirements and limitations for object-oriented legacy system decomposition based on systematic literature review. The investigation is performed as a part of the university-industry collaboration research project.

Keywords: Decomposition · Object-oriented · Legacy system · Literature review · Software clustering · Reverse engineering · Component identification

1 Introduction

Enterprise applications are business critical systems, mainly developed over the last three decades or more therefore also known as legacy systems. Despite the well-known disadvantages, such as being inflexible and hard to maintain, legacy systems are still vitally important to enterprises as they support complex core business processes; they cannot simply be removed as they implement and store critical business logic. On the other hand, proper documentation, skilled manpower and resources to evolve these legacy systems are scarce [1]. The need to preserve legacy applications is motivated by multiple aspects commonly associated with the advantages of reuse: taking advantage of software that has been extensively tested in real life, reducing risk, preserving domain knowledge, and speeding up the process for reaching current business objectives. It becomes vital for the enterprises to reuse their legacy systems as application front-ends and back-ends and do it in a gradual manner [2].

Maintainability and reuse of the legacy applications can be improved by decomposing them into modules. Modularization re-organizes a software system so that the related parts are collected together [3].

© Springer International Publishing Switzerland 2015
P. Abrahamsson et al. (Eds.): PROFES 2015, LNCS 9459, pp. 328–334, 2015.
DOI: 10.1007/978-3-319-26844-6_24

In this paper we provide a systematic literature review of decomposition of object-oriented legacy applications. We take a process improvement perspective by attempting to identify all key parts of the decomposition process including identification of phases, activities, techniques, methods and tools.

The systematic literature review is an initial stage of the university-industry collaboration research project. The industry partner is an IT company developing and supporting a legacy enterprise resource planning system over 20 years. This enterprise application is developed in the Delphi environment, has around 4 million lines of code and around 10,000 classes. It is used by many customers from different business domains. The main problems are: (1) complex maintenance and exponentially growing maintenance costs; (2) difficulties to analyze and calculate change impact; (3) increasing amount of bugs; (4) none of the employees understands the whole system – management would like to create a set of teams, where each team would own one or more modules and would be responsible for its development. The literature review sets the stage for further research on developing a methodology for decomposition of large-scale enterprise applications by taking into account both business consulting and application development perspectives.

The rest of the paper is structured as follows: Sect. 2 describes the research method. Section 3 presents our findings, best practices and limitations. Conclusion and future work is presented at the end of the paper.

2   Research Method

Guidelines for performing a systematic literature review in software engineering [4] are applied for our research to summarize the existing contributions, identify the gaps in the current research and avenues for future research. Items of the review protocol are listed in Table 1. The review process is presented in Fig. 1a. It also shows a number of papers analyzed in each step. The evaluation framework is presented in Fig. 1b.

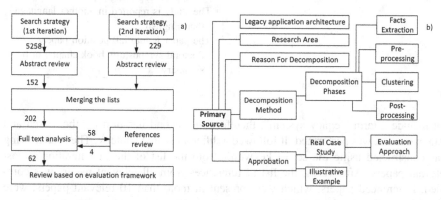

Fig. 1. The review process: (a) number of papers; (b) evaluation framework.

During the first search iteration, some papers describing a method for application decomposition, but were not in the set of relevant papers were found. These papers did

Table 1. Review protocol

Research Questions: What methods and techniques are used for decomposition of large monolith application? What are the existing research issues and what should be the future research agenda in the area decomposition of the large monolith legacy systems?

Search Strategy: The search string is constructed using terms "legacy system" and "decomposition" as main keywords, synonyms and related terms are also included. It is applied to titles, abstracts and meta data

Search String: ("legacy system" OR monolith OR "legacy code" OR "existing system" OR "legacy component" OR "legacy software" OR "monolithic system" OR "existing software" OR "pre-existing software" OR "legacy information system" OR "legacy program" OR "pre-existing assets") AND (decomposition OR reengineering OR re-engineering OR reuse OR "service identification" OR "candidate service identification" OR "service extraction" OR decomposing OR "service mining" OR "code clustering" OR "code segmentation" OR "feature extraction" OR "clustering" OR "remodularisation")

Data Sources: ACM Digital Library, IEEE Xplore, ISI Web of Knowledge, ScienceDirect, Scopus and Wiley Online Library and Google Scholar

Data Extraction and Study Selection

Inclusion Criteria:	*Exclusion Criteria:*
• A study is focused on legacy system source code driven decomposition or is described at least one step of it • The objective of the study is to present/propose a solution(s) to legacy system decomposition • The legacy system has an object-oriented architecture	• A study is from another field than computer science • A study that is not about legacy system source code driven decomposition • A study that has other objective(s) than providing a solution(s) to legacy system decomposition • The goal of a study is a migration from procedural to object oriented programming language • A study is about legacy system decomposition alternatives (e.g., wrapping, replacing) • The study is reported in another language than English • The paper is tutorial, position paper, doctoral symposium, book chapter or brief summary

not include a term "legacy system", therefore the second iteration for the search and data extraction was performed. It followed a different search strategy. The search string was constructed using the set of keywords from the list of the first iteration's most relevant papers. Afterwards, the list of references from all relevant papers was compiled. Referenced papers, which were present in more than 10 relevant papers, were added to the list of relevant studies.

3 Results

Literature review results indicate that decomposition methods are spread over several research domains, e.g., software clustering, migration to service-oriented architecture or product lines, reverse engineering/reusability and component based system engineering. Figure 2a shows the distribution of primary studies published per year along with the trend-line. The frequency of publications in journals is relatively low compared to conferences or workshops (see Fig. 2b). This might be due to the reason that the decomposition problem originates from the industry. The overview of the used keywords (Fig. 2c) indicates that application decomposition is mainly researched in the area of reverse engineering and software clustering.

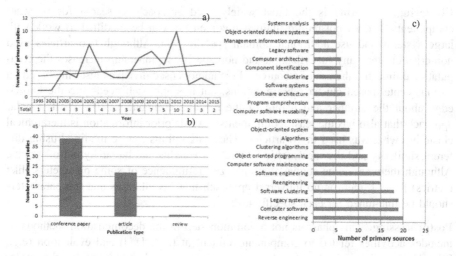

Fig. 2. Descriptive statistics: (a) number of primary studies per year; (b) number of primary studies by type; and (c) number of primary sources by keywords used.

3.1 Decomposition Method

Analyses of the identified methods according to the ISO/IEC 24744 [5] framework yields four main stages or phases: facts extraction, preprocessing, component identification and postprocessing.

Facts Extraction. Facts are data used as input for software decomposition. The most popular input data for object-oriented system decomposition is a system class/entity/object dependency model. It consists of classes/entities/objects and their relationships. It might include also relationship weights and features. Relationships might be aggregated on the class level. Usually this model is created in the form of graph, which can be directed or undirected. The nodes are classes/entities/objects and edges are their relationships.

Preprocessing. The data preprocessing step is not as much motivated by reduction of search space (number of objects that are to be merged into components) as by improving quality of the initial data. The approaches that are not framework/language dependent and are mentioned in multiple articles are the following:

- Exclusion of omnipresent classes or utilities – classes that are heavily used by other classes can be misinterpreted by decomposition algorithms and create noise as being important members of several components, e.g. [6].
- Incorporation of non-structural information from file names, comments etc. [7].
- Dividing classes into layers based on their functionality, e.g. [8].
- Using software system metamodel to assign class functionality according to business processes, e.g. [9].

Clustering. Clustering is the most widely used approach to search for software components. It does not require human involvement, can be modified to work with large systems and use additional domain specific data. Although two articles used non-crisp clusters, any fuzzyfication and non-specific membership increases the computational time and the use of resources. Five authors used divisive clustering based on various center-based cluster representations, but this approach needs specific knowledge about the number and nature of the existing components. The most popular approach that also has the least requirements towards prior information is hierarchical clustering what was used in 16 articles. These algorithms can be modified using different similarity and distance metrics as well as weights and hierarchy cut-off points. Although there are some studies that analyze the influence of some parameters (like metrics) [7, 10], there is no universal approach that fits all cases and the parameters should be fine-tuned for each specific task.

Postprocessing. This phase is not a common step in the decomposition methods. It includes activities related to component refinement (e.g., [11]) and evaluation (e.g., [8]). During refinement, the identified components are modified by moving the border classes to other components with target to improve component quality. That is done manually (e.g., [11]) or automatically (e.g., [12]). In the postprocessing phase, layers identification, component interface identification, outliner class processing and cluster merge also can be performed.

3.2 Approbation and Evaluation

In total studies report approbation on 187 software systems. 13 of them are business systems; the rest are IT development related and scientific applications. Decomposition is mainly performed for systems written in Java (see Fig. 3). Most of the studies have tested one system. Mostly are tested small (10 K-100 KLOC) and micro systems (<10 KLOC). There are only 8 large systems (>1 million LOC) tested in the studies.

The most popular evaluation measurements are authorativeness, stability, extremity of module size distribution and execution time.

Comparative evaluation of multiple methods using the same criteria is performed only in few papers (e.g., [10, 13, 14]). The most popular benchmarks are BUNCH [15],

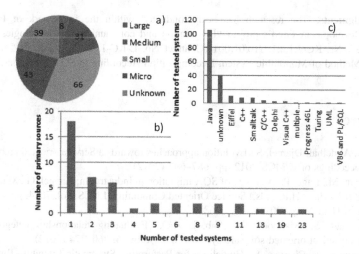

Fig. 3. Approbation statistics: (a) number of systems per system size; (b) number of primary sources per number of tested systems; (c) number of tested systems per programming language.

ACDC [16] and LIMBO [7]. The statistical significance of improvements achieved is evaluated in three papers. An interesting observation is that only one paper reports negative results [17]. This paper presents industry experience and the authors use decomposition approaches created by other researchers.

4   Conclusion and Future Research

This paper reports a systematic literature review on source code driven decomposition of object-oriented legacy systems. We will use the obtained results in the collaboration project between industrial partner and the university to create a decomposition method for large enterprise applications. Application of the decomposition methods is expected to lead towards an application design, which is easier to maintain, and development process suitable for autonomous teams.

The literature review provides the research framework and the review protocol other researchers can use in analyzing maintenance and improvement of legacy applications. It specifically emphasizes applied aspects of the application decomposition research. The main findings are that there is a need for clear benchmarks for comparing various decomposition methods and empirical evaluation of benefits brought by decomposition should be performed. The link between implementing decomposition results and improvements achieved in development and maintenance processes should be demonstrated.

The main requirements for enterprise application decomposition method are: (1) scalable and computationally feasible for large applications (several million LOC and >10000 classes); (2) a source code driven; (3) considers business domain knowledge (4) automatically produces the list of loosely coupled modules; (5) tractable for software architects; (6) parameterized process.

Acknowledgments. The research has been conducted within the framework of European Regional Development Fund's project "Information and communication technologies competence center" Nr. KC/2.1.2.1.1/10/01/001 (Contract No. L-KC-11-0003, www.itkc.lv) activity 1.3. "The Method of Monolithic System Decomposition According to SOA Principles."

References

1. Ali, S., Abdelhak-Djamel, S.: Evolution approaches towards a Service oriented architecture. In: Proceedings of ICMCS 2012, pp. 687–692 (2012)
2. Razavian, M., Lago, P.: A survey of SOA migration in industry. In: Kappel, G., Maamar, Z., Motahari-Nezhad, H.R. (eds.) Service Oriented Computing. LNCS, vol. 7084, pp. 618–626. Springer, Heidelberg (2011)
3. Muhammad, S., Maqbool, O., Abbasi, A.Q.: Evaluating relationship categories for clustering object-oriented software systems. IET Softw. **6**, 260–274 (2012)
4. Kitchenham, B., Charters, S.: Guidelines for Performing Systematic Literature Reviews in Software Engineering. Technical report (2007)
5. International Organization for Standardization. ISO/IEC 24744 :2014, Software Engineering: Metamodel for Development Methodologies (2014)
6. Zhang, Q., Qiu, D., Tian, Q., Sun, L.: Object-oriented software architecture recovery using a new hybrid clustering algorithm. In: Proceedings of FSKD 2010, pp. 2546–2550 (2010)
7. Andritsos, P., Tzerpos, V.: Information-theoretic software clustering. IEEE Trans. Softw. Eng. **31**, 150–165 (2005)
8. Erdemir, U., Tekin, U., Buzluca, F.: Object oriented software clustering based on community structure. In: Proceedings of APSEC 2011, pp. 315–321 (2011)
9. Wang, L., Han, Z., He, J., Wang, H., Li, X.: Recovering design patterns to support program comprehension. In: EAST 2012, pp. 49–54 (2012)
10. Cui, J.F., Chae, H.S.: Applying agglomerative hierarchical clustering algorithms to component identification for legacy systems. Inf. Softw. Technol. **53**, 601–614 (2011)
11. Boussaidi, G.E., Belle, A.B., Vaucher, S., Mili, H.: Reconstructing architectural views from legacy systems. In: Proceedings of WCRE 2012, pp. 345–354 (2012)
12. Belle, A.B., Boussaidi, G.E., Mili, H.: Recovering software layers from object oriented systems. In: Proceedings of ENASE 2014, pp. 78–89 (2014)
13. Andreopoulos, B., An, A., Tzerpos, V., Wang, X.: Multiple layer clustering of large software systems. In: Proceedings of WCRE 2005, pp. 79–88 (2005)
14. Erdemir, U., Buzluca, F.: A learning-based module extraction method for object-oriented systems. J. Syst. Softw. **97**, 156–177 (2014)
15. Mitchell, B.S., Mancoridis, S.: On the automatic modularization of software systems using the bunch tool. IEEE Trans. Softw. Eng. **32**(3), 193–208 (2006)
16. Tzerpos, V., Holt, R.C.: On the stability of software clustering algorithms. In: Proceedings of IWPC 2000, pp. 211–218 (2000)
17. Glorie, M., Zaidman, A., van Deursen, A., Hofland, L.: Splitting a large software repository for easing future software evolution—an industrial experience report. J. Softw. Maint. Evol. Res. Pract. **21**, 113–141 (2009)

On the Use of Safety Certification Practices in Autonomous Field Robot Software Development: A Systematic Mapping Study

Johann Thor Mogensen Ingibergsson, Ulrik Pagh Schultz,
and Marco Kuhrmann[✉]

Mærsk Mc-Kinney Møller Institute, University of Southern Denmark,
Campusvej 55, 5230 Odense M, Denmark
{jomo,ups,kuhrmann}@mmmi.sdu.dk

Abstract. Robotics has recently seen an increasing development, and
the areas addressed within robotics has extended into domains we consider safety-critical, fostering the development of standards that facilitate the development of safe robots. Safety standards describe concepts
to maintain desired reactions or performance in malfunctioning systems,
and influence industry regarding software development and project management. However, academia seemingly did not reach the same degree of
utilisation of standards. This paper presents the findings from a systematic mapping study in which we study the state-of-the-art in developing software for safety-critical software for autonomous field robots. The
purpose of the study is to identify practices used for the development
of autonomous field robots and how these practices relate to available
safety standards. Our findings from reviewing 49 papers show that standards, if at all, are barely used. The majority of the papers propose
various solutions to achieve safety, and about half of the papers refer to
non-standardised approaches that mainly address the methodical rather
than the development level. The present study thus shows an emerging
field still on the quest for suitable approaches to develop safety-critical
software, awaiting appropriate standards for this support.

Keywords: Autonomous field robots · Safety · Standards · Development practices · Systematic mapping study

1 Introduction

The domain of robotics is continuously expanding from large industrial machines
in cages to free-moving consumer products. This expansion is reflected by the
current market and projected increase in the future [16,28]. Robotics is a diverse
field with a variety of required skills including mechanical- and software engineering, which, due to the complexity of robotic systems, challenges researchers
and practitioners [7]. For instance, mobile outdoor robots fail up to 10 times
more often than other types of robots [7]. This increased risk of failure emerges

© Springer International Publishing Switzerland 2015
P. Abrahamsson et al. (Eds.): PROFES 2015, LNCS 9459, pp. 335–352, 2015.
DOI: 10.1007/978-3-319-26844-6_25

from the large number of different interacting hard- and software components, e.g., control, power, communication, and sensing. All these components incorporate software, such as navigation or computer vision software, and all these components can be considered safety-critical when a robot acts autonomously. Therefore, in order to improve software quality in general and safety-critical software in particular, different practices are applied to software development for robotic systems [1].

A subclass of mobile outdoor robots is given by *field robots*, and refers to machinery applied for outdoor tasks, e.g., in construction, forestry, and agriculture [45]. Field robots (Fig. 1) range from small research robots to large industrial agricultural robots. These robots work in a dynamically changing environment that results in challenging quality requirements regarding the software, and introduces constraints regarding perception systems, like identifying obstacles and determining the actual location [44].

(a) Research field robot.   (b) Research field robot.   (c) Industrial field robot.

Fig. 1. Exemplarily selected field robots developed at University of Southern Denmark in different research and collaboration projects [12].

Several standards aim to address the aforementioned issues to pave the way towards improved safety and quality in the respective areas by addressing hazards, functional safety, and performance alongside the development process. Despite the availability of such standards, it is still argued oftentimes that "a safe robot" is not enough and that a robot needs to be ethical for trustworthiness [43]. Nonetheless, trustworthiness of robots relies on modeling the robot as well as the environment, which is an issue notably in dynamic environments in which field robots operate.

Problem Statement. Safety is considered a "hot topic" in robot development, yet missing a link to the respective standards, e.g., [2,10,31,35]. Furthermore, we miss a comprehensive picture of how certification is done in practice, what (software development) practices are utilised in the development processes, and how safety is maintained in the whole ecosystem that comprises the robot and its environment.

Objective. Our goal is to understand how safety-critical robot software is developed in general, and how different practices contribute to the development process—given the constraint that such a software (system) is potentially subject to certification.

Contribution. In this paper, we present findings from a systematic mapping study in which we collected and structured the current body of knowledge regarding (software development) practices and standards applied to the development of safety-critical robotic software. We analysed 49 papers that were obtained in a rigorous selection procedure. Our findings show that standards are barely—if at all—used. A majority of 35 papers propose various solutions to achieve safety, and about half of the papers refer to non-standardised approaches to maintain safety, that mainly address the methodical rather than the development level. The present study thus shows an emerging field still on the quest for suitable approaches to develop and certify safety-critical software.

Outline. The remainder of this paper is organised as follows: Sect. 2 presents the fundamentals and discusses related work. In Sect. 3, we present the research design, followed by the presentation and discussion of our findings in Sect. 4. Finally, Sect. 5 concludes the paper.

2 Fundamentals and Related Work

Robots depend on knowledge from many domains, which results in robotics being a multi-faceted research area. Due to the central role of software for robots, different coding practices have been tested to improve safety and quality within robotics [1]. Software quality in general and quality of robotic software in particular has received much attention over the years. From the perspective of general quality, Kitchenham et al. [23], discuss standards, quality, and their impact. Notably, considerations regarding software languages and quality have also reached the robotics domain, e.g., in control [34] and vision [15]. Issues with software quality have been reported for years, e.g., unit mismatches crashing space probes [5], overdosed drug treatments in medicine [25], and a series of problems in the automotive domain [30]. Those (representatively selected and further) problems fostered the development of safety standards. At the one end of the spectrum, recommendations based on best practices, such as MISRA [29], were developed. At the other end of the spectrum, formal standards were developed, e.g., on functional safety ISO 25119 [39] (agriculture) and ISO 26262 [38] (automotive). Such standards aim at improving the systems' quality by verifying all hazards being covered, and that the system still can be trusted when the system is malfunction.

For robotic systems in particular, some research was conducted to analyse potential hazards and how to address them appropriately, e.g., [9,37]. Such hazard analyses usually refer to ISO 13482 [20], which is a standard for personal and mobile robots and provides a characterisation by mentioning the attributes: "multiple passengers" or "non-standing passengers" or "outdoor" or "uneven surfaces" or "not slow" or "not lightweight" or "autonomous" (ISO 13482 [20], Sect. 6.1.2.3, Person

Carrier Robots, Type 3.2). The type 3.2 robot, inter alia, covers agricultural robots, mobile robots, professional and domestic service robots, and so forth—as long as the robot moves slower than 20 km/h and is not for medical, military, water-borne, or flying use. That is, the type 3.2 categorisation properly addresses autonomous field robots as well [45].

Apart from safety in general, computer vision is crucial for autonomous field robots, as it adds further requirements regarding software quality for robotic software. Computer vision is used for sensing the environment, and the standard IEC/EN 61496 [41] defines specific requirements regarding quality and functional safety of perception systems. Given the requirements regarding safe operation of robots and the complexity of sensing and recognising the operation environment, functional safety and performance have to be considered critical quality attributes. Especially performance is covered in a new upcoming standard ISO/DIS 18497 [40] that puts emphasis on quantifying the performance requirements for perception systems. However, this and other standards on functional safety only refer to human damage as a critical factor. Nevertheless, for autonomous robots, it is also of importance to detect other machines and animals to keep the robot operating.

In summary, related work on safety regarding the development of software for autonomous field robots is, in current literature, only indirectly addressed by few standards and individual studies investigating selected quality attributes. However, little is known about how software quality manifests in the software development process of robotic software. The paper at hand thus closes a gap in literature by providing a big picture and detailed information about practices used in software development and safety certification, and how available standards relate to robotic software development.

3 Research Design

In this study, we used the *Systematic Literature Review* (SLR; [22]) process to collect papers that we used in a *Systematic Mapping Study* (SMS; [32]). The core study was conducted by initially reviewing a small set of manually selected publications to form the basic knowledge (snowballing). Based on these publications, we conducted an automatic search in different literature databases to collect further publications used to perform the mapping study. The mapping study in particular aims to cover standards and development practices for robots that are autonomous, mobile, and used outdoor to address a wide range of robotics including *autonomous field robots*, *autonomous mobile robots*, and *mobile outdoor robots*.

In the subsequent sections, we detail the research method by presenting the research questions and explaining the different steps for data collection and analysis.

3.1 Research Questions

In order to investigate the state-of-the-art of safety certification practices for autonomous field robots, we formulate the following research questions:

RQ 1. *What is the current state-of-the-art of developing safety-critical software for robotic systems?* This research question aims to gather information about those (general) aspects that are considered relevant for the development of robots. Hence, this research question is purposed to lay the foundation for the development of a map of relevant topics to capture and present the entire field.

RQ 2. *What (coding) practices are used for the development of safety-critical software for robotic systems?* This research question aims at understanding the practices that are used to develop robots in safety-critical contexts. The question addresses fine-grained coding-related practices, such as code generation or code reuse, as well as methodical process-related practices, i.e., traditional or agile software development.

RQ 3. *Which certification standards are relevant for certifying software for autonomous mobile robots?* This research question aims to collect those standards that have to be considered relevant for robot development. The purpose of this question is not to only collect standards and norms relevant for autonomous field robots, but also for the domain of robot development in general (for identifying transferable knowledge).

3.2 Data Collection Procedures

The data collection procedure comprised a snowballing and an automatic search in different literature databases, and included the following steps:

- Manual selection of relevant reference publications, using snowballing.
- Construction of search strings based on the reference publications.
- Automatic search in different literature in databases.
- Definition of in-/exclusion criteria for the paper selection.

Reference Publications. The study is based on a few manually selected reference publications, which are listed in Table 1. These papers served for construction of the search queries, and also served as quality assurance of the final result set as control values.

Query Construction. Based on the reference publications, we iteratively constructed the search strings to query the different literature databases (Table 2). The initial search query construction resulted in S_1, however, to achieve a larger margin of perception and results in relation to safety and safety standards with human interactions, the additional alterations were created. The context selector C_1 was created to remove results from areas that were not fitting with the overall objective of the study. Each database was queried thrice and utilising

Table 1. Reference publications used for query construction.

	Title	Subject/Contribution
[36]	Guaranteeing Functional Safety: Design for Provability and Computer-Aided Verification	Certification of safety zones for vehicles and robots
[1]	Towards Rule-Based Dynamic Safety Monitoring for Mobile Robots	Domain-specific language for robot control systems
[44]	Human detection for a robot tractor using omni-directional stereo vision	Vision methods for safe operation
[20]	ISO 13482 - The new safety standard for personal care robots	Analysing ISO 13482, which also is relevant for field robots

Table 2. Overview of the final search queries.

	Search String
S_1	((Robot **or** Robots **or** Robotics **or** Robotic) **near** (Autonomous **or** Mobile **or** Field **or** Automated **or** Wheeled)) **and** (Safety **or** Safe) **and** (Standard **or** Standards **or** ISO **or** IEC) **and** (Perception **or** Vision **or** Software)
S_2	((Robot **or** Robots **or** Robotics **or** Robotic) **near** (Autonomous **or** Mobile **or** Field **or** Automated **or** Wheeled **or** Human)) **and** (Safety **or** Safe) **and** (Perception **or** Vision **or** Software)
S_3	((Robot **or** Robots **or** Robotics **or** Robotic) **near** (Autonomous **or** Mobile **or** Field **or** Automated **or** Wheeled **or** Human)) **and** (Safety **or** Safe) **and** (ISO **or** IEC)
C_1	(Chem* **or** Surg* **or** train **or** water **or** medicin*)
Final	(S_1 **or** S_2 **or** S_3) **and** **not** C_1

C_1 in all searches. The queries from Table 2 were used to search the following databases[1], which have a certain focus on software development: *ACM Digital Library*, *SpringerLink*, *IEEE Digital Library* (XPlore), *Wiley InterScience*, and *ScienceDirect* (Elsevier). As the initially conducted test runs delivered a large number of hits and a considerable overhead, we decided to only include the top-50 results per search, which results in a maximum of 150 hits per database (cf. Table 6).

---

[1] **Note:** For technical reasons, we decided to define multiple search queries. For example, Wiley did not have the NEAR operator which was changed to and AND. ScienceDirect used W/n instead of the NEAR operator. IEEE had limitations on the search string length resulting in the asterisk (*) was used, further the NEAR operator could not be used if an asterisk was used resulting in NEAR was changed to an AND operator. In addition S_1 in connection with C_1 was too long, resulting in only surg* and medicin* from C_1 was used.

Table 3. Inclusion and exclusion criteria for the study.

No.	Description
IC_1	Title, keyword list or abstract make it explicit that the paper is related to safety in field robotics
IC_2	The paper is on tools, procedures or development methods
IC_3	The paper is in a journal, proceedings, conference or magazine (Special case for Springer Link to include chapters)
IC_4	The paper describes a long term observation of the use of development methods in relation to safety-critical development
IC_5	The paper surveys practitioners for the use of development methods
IC_6	The paper reports on the use of development methods in general, e.g., as secondary study
IC_7	The paper is on tools implementing certain methods (infer information about method use), for development of safety-critical software
IC_8	The paper describes the use of perception and sensor information for safe operation (e.g., navigation, control, obstacle avoidance etc.)
IC_9	The paper is about important aspects for environment sensing (e.g., transversal of rough terrain, stability monitoring, etc.)
EC_1	The paper is a proposal only
EC_2	The paper is not within safety or field robotics
EC_3	The paper occurred multiple times in the result set
EC_4	The paper is a workshop-, tutorial-, Ph.D. summary or poster summary
EC_5	The paper does not touch the domain of software engineering, computer science or robotics in general
EC_6	The paper is not in English
EC_7	The paper's full text is not available for download

3.3   Analysis Procedures

In this section, we describe the analysis preparation steps and the procedures used for the in-depth analysis of the final result set.

Analysis Preparations. To prepare the data analysis, we applied a proven procedure (cf. [24]) in which we (1) harmonised the result set by merging the individual search results and by removing the multiple occurrences, and (2) conducted a multi-staged voting procedure. In the voting procedure, two researchers performed an independent voting. The relevance of a paper was determined by applying the in-/exclusion criteria from Table 3. Based on the publication's title and abstract, each researcher voted a paper "in" (value 1) or "out" (value 0). If both researchers agreed, a paper was in the final result set (2 points), or a paper was excluded from further investigation (0 points). For those papers that were not finally decided in this stage, a third reviewer was called in to provide his votes and to make the final decision.

In-Depth Analysis. Having prepared the result set, we conducted the in-depth analysis to answer the research questions. In the following, we describe the applied procedures and link them to the research questions.

Schema Construction. Following the steps of conducting a systematic mapping study [32], as a first step, we select standard classification schemas to provide an overview of the publications, and develop study-specific classification schemas from the result set. As standard classification schemas, we opt for the *research type facet* and the *contribution type facet* as used by Wieringa et al. [42] and Petersen et al. [32]. These standard schemas are mainly used to answer RQ_1 and to draw a big picture of the maturity and the contributions provided by the studied result set.

Specific to the study, we developed further schemas, notably, to address RQ_2 and RQ_3. Table 4 presents the classification schema that was used to categorise the publications according the practices used in the software development (RQ_2). In particular, based on the different aspects of software development, we included methodical as well as technical practices, such as formal specification or simulation. In order to answer RQ_3, we collected information about norms and standards used in safety-critical systems. Table 5 presents the respective categories, but respects situations in which standards are not applied or available.

Data Presentation. To present the data, we visualise our data using systematic maps. Furthermore and due to the limited number of papers in the result set, we only use simple tables and charts to provide the data and a (tentative) interpretation of the results.

Table 4. Categories to capture development practices used in software development.

Criterion	Description
Simulation	Code or application is tested/proven using simulation
Formal Implementation Verification	System/code is described using a formal language that facilitates analysis, to guarantee/prove system properties
Mathematical Modeling and Algorithms	Using mathematics to prove/guarantee system properties
Behaviour Modeling	System models, Fault tolerant models and decision theory, e.g. to make diagnosis of systems and/or reconfiguration of the system
Formal Specification Deriving Implementation	Based on formal specification, e.g. Domain Specific Language (DSL), utilising code generation for implementation
Misc	Papers that either encompasses many of the above methods, or do not clearly define which method is used
Not in Software Development	Papers that does not focus on software or development practices

Table 5. Categories to capture standards used in safety-critical software development.

Criterion	Description
IEC 61508	Functional Safety of Electrical/Electronic/Programmable Electronic Safety-related Systems (E/E/PE, or E/E/PES)
ISO 13482	limited primarily to human care related hazards but, where appropriate, it includes domestic animals or property
ISO 26262	Road vehicles Functional safety
ISO 10218	Robots and robotic devices Safety requirements for industrial robots
IEC 61499	open standard for distributed control and automation
Guaranteeing safety	Not necessarily using a standard approach
Non-Standard Approach	When it is specifically mentioned that there is no standards available for the domain

3.4   Validity Procedures

To increase the validity of our study, we apply different techniques. Prior to the actual study, we analyse the domain of interest and select few reference publications, which are used to develop the search queries for the automated search. The developed search queries were tested in several dry-runs, and iteratively refined. To overcome subjectivity in the study selection, the study selection process is based on a proven procedure that relies on multi-staged voting procedures and researcher triangulation [24]. Furthermore, the classification of the result set is performed using standardised classification schemas [32,42]. The study-specific schemas were either grounded in standard schemas or crafted from common/observed terms and practices in the found publications.

4   Study Results

In this section, we present and discuss the results of the study. We provide an overview of the study population in Sect. 4.1, before answering the research questions in Sects. 4.2–4.4. Finally, we briefly discuss our findings and provide a (tentative) interpretation in Sect. 4.5.

4.1   Study Population

Table 6 provides an overview of the number of publications obtained from the different search steps. The initial search resulted in more than 63,000 hits. After applying the different in-/exclusion criteria (Table 3), eventually, 49 papers were selected for further investigation.

Table 6. Overview of the publication numbers obtained from the literature search (per database, per data collection step, cf. Sects. 3.2 and 3.3).

Step	IEEE	ACM	Springer	Elsevier	Wiley	Total
Step 1: Search (S_1 **OR** S_2 **OR** S_3)	1,298	2,892	15,509	37,114	6,585	63,398
Step 2: Filtering						
Apply F_1 and limit on results set (50)	150	88	150	149	150	687
Remove duplicates	42	0	42	46	43	187
Result Set (before the voting):	80	107	108	104	101	500
Final result set	10	2	26	8	3	**49**

Figure 2 visualises the result set according to the publication frequency over time (the result set contains publications from 1987 to 2015). Furthermore, the figure includes the classification according to the research type facets to illustrate the development of the considered domain over time.

From this information, we see safety-critical software development for autonomous field robots being a still emerging discipline, which gained more interest in the early 2000s. Since then, we observe the majority of the published papers of type *solution proposal* (35 out of 49), complemented by a few papers of type *evaluation research* (4 out of 49). However, in the result set, we find only seven papers of type *philosophical*, which indicates a gap of structuring/synthesising research activities, such as literature studies.

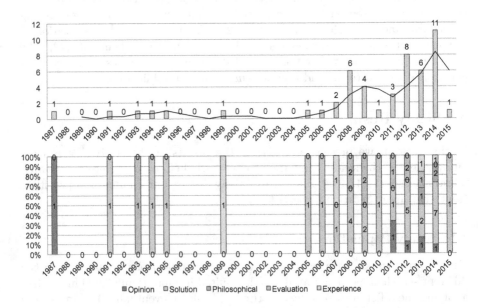

Fig. 2. Number of papers per year and distribution over the research type facets.

4.2 RQ 1: State-of-the-Art of Developing Safety-Critical Robotic Software

To present the state-of-the-art and the practices used for development (Sect. 4.3), we provide an integrated systematic map (Fig. 3). The right part of Fig. 3 illustrates the research- and contribution type facets and shows the majority of the papers proposing models (9 out of 49) or frameworks (22 out of 49). That is, the current publication body is focused on proposing new approaches to deal with the challenges coming along with developing safety-critical software for autonomous field robots. However, the map also shows eight papers presenting lessons learned. Nonetheless, the map clearly points to an emerging field.

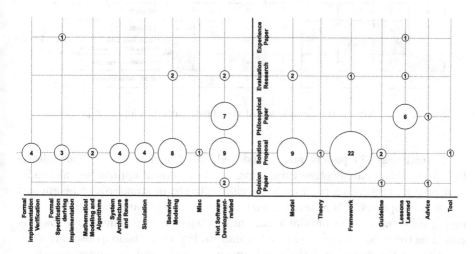

Fig. 3. Systematic map illustrating research type facets, contribution type facets, and software development practices.

Key-wording the abstracts of the selected papers reveals the focus points of these studies. Here, the focus lays on mobile and autonomous robots, and emphasis is put on software/system development (in general), control, environment, interaction with humans, modeling, and standards. Among all selected publications, the term "standards" was mentioned 32 times in the abstracts, also indicating the increasing interest in standards supporting the development of safe and performant robotic software.

4.3 RQ 2: Practices for the Development of Safety-Critical Robotic Software

The left part of Fig. 3 provides an overview of the publication classification regarding the practices applied to the development of safe robotic software (Table 4). The chart shows that, given that the majority of the papers is categorised as *solution proposal*, many different aspects are covered and that many different practices are addressed. However, regarding those practices that are close to software development, formal verification, software architecture and reuse, simulation, and behaviour modeling are the flourishing areas.

Simulation	Formal implementation verification	Mathematical modeling and algorithms	System architecture and reuse	Misc	Behavior modeling	Formal specification deriving implementation	Not SW dev-related	
0	1	1	1	0	0	1	1	IEC 61508
0	0	0	1	0	0	0	2	ISO 13482
0	0	0	0	1	0	0	0	ISO 26262
0	0	0	0	0	0	0	0	ISO 10218
0	0	0	0	0	0	1	0	IEC 61499
0	3	2	0	0	1	0	2	Guranteeing safety - Not necessarily using a Standard approach
4	1	0	2	1	9	2	15	Non-Standard Approach
0	0	0	0	0	0	1	0	No standards available

Fig. 4. Heat-map on the connection of standards with development practices.

Nevertheless, 20 papers are categorised into the non-development-related practices, which, among other things, include development approaches/methods, best practices regarding the way to develop software, or standards to be applied in the development. Therefore, the map indicates this research field still investigating different ways of obtaining safe field robots, with a slight trend towards modeling the robot as such and its environment. However, the map also raises the question for the maturity of the development approach and the underlying theories. For instance, only five papers deal with formal specification, mathematical models, and algorithms, while the majority of the development-related practices looks for modeling, design, and simulation. From the available data, we cannot conclude whether or not the theoretical parts are already in place. Furthermore, the studied papers do not allow for concluding to what extent those practices that improve software reliability are adopted for the development of robotic software. So far, we can only conclude that—at least for the development-related practices—the community is on the quest for pragmatic approaches to design and develop safe robotics software.

4.4 RQ 3: Certification Standards for Robotic Software

The third research question aims at investigating the role currently available standards for safety play in the development of software for autonomous field robots. Therefore, we collected the major standards addressing this topic for general software development as well as for related/specialised domains (cf. Table 5). Due to the scarcely available studies explicitly investigating the use and impact of standards in domain under consideration and due to the observation that available papers usually refer to multiple standards, we decided against creating a systematic map. Instead, we provide a heat-map in Fig. 4 to visualise the connections between the standards and the development practices (Table 4).

The heat-map shows—if at all—an only loose connection between development practices and available standards. Only the IEC 61508 (general functional safety) was mentioned in connection to different practices. However, the figure shows that safety seems to be mainly addressed by non-standardised approaches. At the same time, safety is aimed to be achieved by not-development-related practices, i.e., at the level of methods and approaches to develop the software/system. Although closely related to autonomous field robots, the standard ISO 10218 (industrial robots) was not referred at all. The overall picture drawn by the heat-map, however, shows a low involvement of standards in the robotic software development.

4.5 Discussion and Interpretation

Our findings indicate a trend toward developing new methods and processes to facilitate development of safety-critical robots (Fig. 2). Nevertheless, the current utilisation of standards is very limited (Fig. 4), and non-standardised approaches are used to ensure safety. So far, our findings present a snapshot and a baseline, as a new standard that explicitly addresses field robots ISO 13482 was recently released (September 2014); this standard is already mentioned thrice by independent studies [13,19,20]. That is, although we could not obtain much information on the use of standards in robot software development now, we expect an increasing number of projects and companies utilising this standard, an increasing number of studies and, thus, more evidence regarding the standard's suitability in future. This observation is also supported by an article in which authors specifically stated that they were missing a standard for their development [4], which should be available now.

RQ$_2$ uncovered that the majority of the results were solution proposals focusing on behaviour modeling, with a lower focus on reliable software development (categories: formal implementation verification [3,8,11,33], formal specification deriving implementation [1,4,14,26], and mathematical modeling and algorithms [6,27]). From our perspective these categories would give the highest confidence in safety-critical software. The limited use of these categories within robotic software development puts high constraints on the certification authorities, because the assessors need to be methodical and stringent when manually evaluating the code.

This issue is increased in magnitude when computer vision is introduced. As mentioned before, field robots have to sense and react to a dynamically changing environment. Looking into those papers dealing with computer vision, our findings show the main focus of vision-related software development instrumenting the *Non-standard approach* (Fig. 4) to provide safety. We also found these papers having a very limited use of formal methods or guarantees to uphold the safety in the vision system. This knowledge uncovers that within field robotics, guaranteeing safety in relation to perception and software by using certification is an area that has been neglected. Looking at vision in connection with the research type facet categorisation, it shows that the vision papers are solution driven, as was also the case for software.

5   Conclusion

This study presents the findings from a systematic mapping study on the use of safety certification practices in autonomous field robot software development. In a rigorous search and selection procedure, 49 papers were considered for investigation.

Our findings show the majority of the papers proposing new solutions addressing various aspects of safety and related software development practices. However, available standards are neglected, and more than a half of the papers shows non-standardised approaches used to develop safe robots. Nevertheless the limited use of standards limits the credibility of the achieved safety, and limits the usability.

A reason could be the relatively fresh standard ISO 13482 for this domain. Nonetheless, the minimal use of formal specification and verification in combination with guaranteeing safety might point to a significant focus on solution approaches for an emerging field thus not yet facing the need to fulfil stringent requirements by standards. For this, improved tool support could help researchers to facilitate the use of standards for safety-critical robotic software.

Finally, the domain of field robotics has been primarily focused on solutions. The absence of secondary studies shows a need for more research to structure and uncover the best way of achieving safe autonomous field robots. Furthermore, although standards were contributed to the community, those are neglected to a large extent. The community thus needs to foster a critical discourse on the availability and appropriateness of the available standards and complementing support tools, and to work out actionable approaches, as for instance proposed in [17, 18].

Threats to Validity and Limitations. As a literature study, this study suffers from potential incompleteness of the search results and a general publication bias, i.e., positive results are more likely published than failed attempts. That is, our study encounters the risk to draw an incomplete and potentially too positive picture. Beyond that general threat, the validity of the study could be biased by personal ratings of the participating researchers. To address this risk, we relied on a proven procedure [24] that utilises different supporting tools and researcher triangulation to support dataset cleaning, study selection, and classification. Another threat to validity is the study selection as such. As we faced a fairly unstructured domain for which no other structuring secondary studies are available, we had to iteratively develop and test the search queries. Furthermore, due to the terminology that suffers heterogeneity and massive overloading, e.g., the term "Standard" or (potentially) different meanings of the studied concepts like "Simulation", we received more than 63,000 hits, and we decided to limit the number of hits to be considered for the investigation to 50 (max.) per query run. Although we found this approach sufficient in previously conducted studies, such as [21], the final result set investigated in the present study needs to be considered with care, as we have no knowledge about publications not triggered by the search and selection procedures applied in this study.

Our contribution aims at creating a big picture of the research field thus having some limitations. Deeper insights and analyses regarding conceptual, methodical, and technical aspects of safety-certification practices are not part of this study. Furthermore, our study does not aim at creating taxonomies or generalised concepts. However, we could provide the basis to support such next steps and further discussion.

Future Work. The present study is a first step toward a deeper understanding of safety certification in autonomous field robot development. In this instance of the study, we primarily looked for "robots", but, in future, need to extend our work to "Automated Ground Vehicles (AGV)" to provide a more comprehensive picture and to develop appropriate process improvement proposals. Furthermore, standards in general and those mentioned in Table 5 have to be revisited to improve understanding about their relevance within the investigated domain. Given the domain's requirements, in-depth investigation, e.g., of IEC 61508 and other relevant standards, and the relation to development practices is necessary. That is, it is crucial to understand whether coding practices can be evaluated homogeneously across the standards or if an evaluation of those standards against the MISRA [29] software guidelines better contributes to the general understanding.

A second important facet is the extension of our study: So far, due to absence of respective structuring studies, our purpose was to initially generate a big picture of the domain. That is, the present study provides an overview and an initial domain structure proposal, which is grounded in reviewing scientific literature only. Continuing, the study needs to be refined and updated, e.g., by improving the search queries and classification schemes. Furthermore, practitioners need to be surveyed to (1) bring more practically relevant problems and experience into the study, to (2) confirm our tentative findings, and (3) to improve the data quality thus allowing for steering future research, such as supporting certification process improvement, improvement of (agile) software development in regulated environments, or to support tool development. This also helps improving the situation that notably many SMEs face: the push for showing new solutions limits the applicability of standards, because they are large and cumbersome to work with. For example, a formal specification tool for vision pipelines, such as proposed by Hochgeschwender et al. [15] and our recent contributions [17,18] focusing on safety and how to improve the development within computer vision, as is for example seen within control of robotics [1,3,4,8,26]. Providing a formal specification tool for safety-critical vision applications would greatly improve the possibility of complying with ISO 13482.

References

1. Adam, S., Larsen, M., Jensen, K., Schultz, U.P.: Towards rule-based dynamic safety monitoring for mobile robots. In: Brugali, D., Broenink, J.F., Kroeger, T., MacDonald, B.A. (eds.) SIMPAR 2014. LNCS, vol. 8810, pp. 207–218. Springer, Heidelberg (2014)
2. Biber, P., Weiss, U., Dorna, M., Albert, A.: Navigation system of the autonomous agricultural robot Bonirob. In: Workshop on Agricultural Robotics: Enabling Safe, Efficient, and Affordable Robots for Food Production (2012)
3. Biggs, G., Fujiwara, K., Anada, K.: Modelling and analysis of a redundant mobile robot architecture using AADL. In: Brugali, D., Broenink, J.F., Kroeger, T., MacDonald, B.A. (eds.) SIMPAR 2014. LNCS, vol. 8810, pp. 146–157. Springer, Heidelberg (2014)
4. Biggs, G., Sakamoto, T., Fujiwara, K., Anada, K.: Experiences with model-centred design methods and tools in safe robotics. In: International Conference on Intelligent Robots and Systems, pp. 3915–3922. IEEE (2013)
5. Board, M.I.: Mars Climate Orbiter Mishap Investigation Board Phase I Report, 10 November 1999
6. Bouraine, S., Fraichard, T., Salhi, H.: Provably safe navigation for mobile robots with limited field-of-views in dynamic environments. Auton. Robots 32(3), 267–283 (2012)
7. Carlson, J., Murphy, R.R., Nelson, A.: Follow-up analysis of mobile robot failures. In: IEEE International Conference on Robotics and Automation, vol. 5, pp. 4987–4994. IEEE (2004)
8. de Silva, L., Yan, R., Ingrand, F., Alami, R., Bensalem, S.: A verifiable and correct-by-construction controller for robots in human environments. In: International Conference on Human-Robot Interaction Extended Abstracts, pp. 281–281. ACM (2015)
9. Dogramadzi, S., Giannaccini, M.E., Harper, C., Sobhani, M., Woodman, R., Choung, J.: Environmental hazard analysis - a variant of preliminary hazard analysis for autonomous mobile robots. J. Intell. Rob. Syst. 76(1), 73–117 (2014)
10. Emmi, L., Gonzalez-de-Soto, M., Pajares, G., Gonzalez-de Santos, P.: New trends in robotics for agriculture: integration and assessment of a real fleet of robots. Sci. World J. 2014, 1–21 (2014)
11. Frese, U., Hausmann, D., Lüth, C., Täubig, H., Walter, D.: The importance of being formal. Electron. Notes Theoret. Comput. Sci. 238(4), 57–70 (2009)
12. Frobomind. http://www.frobomind.org
13. Gribov, V., Voos, H.: Safety oriented software engineering process for autonomous robots. In: Conference on Emerging Technologies & Factory Automation, pp. 1–8. IEEE (2013)
14. Hanai, R., Saito, H., Nakabo, Y., Fujiwara, K., Ogure, T., Mizuguchi, D., Homma, K., Ohba, K.: RT-component based integration for IEC 61508 ready system using SysML and IEC 61499 function blocks. In: IEEE/SICE International Symposium on System Integration, pp. 105–110. IEEE (2012)
15. Hochgeschwender, N., Schneider, S., Voos, H., Kraetzschmar, G.K.: Declarative specification of robot perception architectures. In: Brugali, D., Broenink, J.F., Kroeger, T., MacDonald, B.A. (eds.) SIMPAR 2014. LNCS, vol. 8810, pp. 291–302. Springer, Heidelberg (2014)
16. IFR: World Robotics 2014 Industrial Robots (2014)

17. Ingibergsson, J.T.M., Schultz, U.P., Kraft, D.: Towards declarative safety rules for perception specification architectures. In: International Workshop on Domain-Specific Languages and models for ROBotic systems (DSLRob 2015) (2015, in press)
18. Ingibergsson, J.T.M., Suvei, S.-D., Hansen, M.K., Christiansen, P., Schultz, U.P.: Towards a DSL for perception-based safety systems. In: International Workshop on Domain-Specific Languages and models for ROBotic systems (DSLRob 2015) (2015, in press)
19. Jacobs, T., Reiser, U., Haegele, M., Verl, A.: Development of validation methods for the safety of mobile service robots with manipulator. In: German Conference on Robotics (ROBOTIK 2012), pp. 1–5. VDE-Verl (2012)
20. Jacobs, T., Virk, G.S.: ISO 13482 - the new safety standard for personal care robots. In: International Symposium on Robotics (ROBOTIK 2014), pp. 1–6. VDE-Verl (2014)
21. Kalus, G., Kuhrmann, M.: Criteria for software process tailoring: a systematic review. In: Proceedings of the 2013 International Conference on Software and System Process, pp. 171–180. ACM (2013)
22. Kitchenham, B.: Procedures for performing systematic reviews, vol. 33, pp. 1–26. Keele University, Keele, UK (2004)
23. Kitchenham, B., Pfleeger, S.L.: Software quality: the elusive target. IEEE Softw. 13(1), 12–21 (1996)
24. Kuhrmann, M., Fernández, D.M., Tiessler, M.: A mapping study on the feasibility of method engineering. J. Softw. Evol. Process 26(12), 1053–1073 (2014)
25. Leveson, N., Turner, C.: An investigation of the Therac-25 accidents. Computer 26(7), 18–41 (1993)
26. Machin, M., Dufossé, F., Blanquart, J.-P., Guiochet, J., Powell, D., Waeselynck, H.: Specifying safety monitors for autonomous systems using model-checking. In: Bondavalli, A., Di Giandomenico, F. (eds.) SAFECOMP 2014. LNCS, vol. 8666, pp. 262–277. Springer, Heidelberg (2014)
27. Masehian, E., Katebi, Y.: Sensor-based motion planning of wheeled mobile robots in unknown dynamic environments. J. Int. Rob. Syst. 74(3–4), 893–914 (2014)
28. METI: Trends in the Market for the Robot Industry in 2012, July 2013
29. MISRA: MISRA-C Guidelines for the Use of the C Language in Critical Systems (2012)
30. Mitchell, R.L.: Toyota's lesson: software can be unsafe at any speed, February 2010
31. Moorehead, S.J., Kise, M., Reid, J.F.: Autonomous tractors for citrus grove operations. In: International Conference on Machine Control & Guidance, pp. 309–313 (2010)
32. Petersen, K., Feldt, R., Mujtaba, S., Mattsson, M.: Systematic mapping studies in software engineering. In: International Conference on Evaluation and Assessment in Software Engineering, pp. 68–77. British Computer Society (2008)
33. Rahimi, M., Xiadong, X.: A framework for software safety verification of industrial robot operations. Comput. Ind. Eng. 20(2), 279–287 (1991)
34. Reichardt, M., Föhst, T., Berns, K.: On software quality-motivated design of a real-time framework for complex robot control systems. In: International Workshop on Software Quality and Maintainability (2013)
35. Rovira-Más, F.: Sensor architecture and task classification for agricultural vehicles and environments. Sensors 10(12), 11226–11247 (2010)
36. Täubig, H., Frese, U., Hertzberg, C., Lüth, C., Mohr, S., Vorobev, E., Walter, D.: Guaranteeing functional safety: design for provability and computer-aided verification. Auton. Robots 32(3), 303–331 (2012)

37. TC 184: Robots and robotic devices - Safety requirements for personal care robots. International Standard ISO 13482:2014, International Organization for Standardization (2014)
38. TC 22: Road Vehicles Functional Safety. International Standard ISO 26262:2011, International Organization for Standardization (2011)
39. TC 23: Tractors and machinery for agriculture and forestry - safety-related parts of control systems. International Standard ISO 25119-2010, International Organization for Standardization (2010)
40. TC 23: Agricultural machinery and tractors - Safety of highly automated machinery. International Standard ISO/DIS 18497, International Organization for Standardization (2014)
41. TC 44: Safety of machinery - electro-sensitive protective equipment. International Standard IEC 61496-2012, International Electronical Commission (2012)
42. Wieringa, R., Maiden, N., Mead, N., Rolland, C.: Requirements engineering paper classification and evaluation criteria: a proposal and a discussion. Requirements Eng. **11**(1), 102–107 (2006)
43. Winfield, A.F.T., Blum, C., Liu, W.: Towards an ethical robot: internal models, consequences and ethical action selection. In: Mistry, M., Leonardis, A., Witkowski, M., Melhuish, C. (eds.) TAROS 2014. LNCS, vol. 8717, pp. 85–96. Springer, Heidelberg (2014)
44. Yang, L., Noguchi, N.: Human detection for a robot tractor using omni-directional stereo vision. Comput. Electron. Agric. **89**, 116–125 (2012)
45. Yang, S.-Y., Jin, S.-M., Kwon, S.-K.: Remote control system of industrial field robot. In: IEEE International Conference on Industrial Informatics, pp. 442–447. IEEE (2008)

Software Reliability and Testing in Industry

A Process for Risk-Based Test Strategy Development and Its Industrial Evaluation

Rudolf Ramler[1]([✉]) and Michael Felderer[2]

[1] Software Competence Center Hagenberg GmbH, Softwarepark 21, 4232 Hagenberg, Austria
rudolf.ramler@scch.at
[2] Institute of Computer Science, University of Innsbruck, Technikerstrasse 21a, 6020 Innsbruck, Austria
michael.felderer@uibk.ac.at

Abstract. Risk-based testing has a high potential to improve the software test process as it helps to optimize the allocation of resources and provides decision support for the management. But for many organizations the integration of risk-based testing into an existing test process is a challenging task. An essential first step when introducing risk-based testing in an organization is to establish a risk-based test strategy which considers risks as the guiding factor to support all testing activities in the entire software lifecycle. In this paper we address this issue by defining a process for risk-based test strategy development and refinement. The process has been created as part of a research transfer project on risk-based testing that provided the opportunity to get direct feedback from industry and to evaluate the ease of use, usefulness and representativeness of each process step together with five software development companies. The findings are that the process is perceived as useful and moderately easy to use, i.e., some steps involve noticeable effort. For example, the effort for impact estimation is considered high, whereas steps that can be based on existing information are perceived as easy, e.g., deriving probability estimates from established defect classifications. The practical application of the process in real-world settings supports the representativeness of the outcome.

Keywords: Test management · Software risk management · Software testing · Risk-based testing · Test process improvement · Multiple case study

1 Introduction

Software testing is an essential and widely practiced measure for assuring software quality. It is, however, also a costly and time-intensive activity in the development software products and services. An adequate test strategy plays a key role in balancing product quality with cost and time-to-market. Ideally this balance is approximated by considering the risks associated with the consequences of poor quality caused by software defects, which leads to a risk-based approach for software testing.

In many cases software testing is risk-based [2] – either implicitly or explicitly. However, making the underlying risks explicit helps to focus the testing activities on

© Springer International Publishing Switzerland 2015
P. Abrahamsson et al. (Eds.): PROFES 2015, LNCS 9459, pp. 355–371, 2015.
DOI: 10.1007/978-3-319-26844-6_26

the most critical issues first and, in addition, to optimally adjust the effort invested in software testing. Several risk-based testing approaches have therefore been proposed that consider the risks of the software product as the guiding factor to support decisions in all phases of the test process [4, 9]. Furthermore, also the recently published international standard for software testing, ISO/IEC/IEEE 29119 [11], explicitly involves risks as an integral part of the testing process.

An essential first step when introducing risk-based testing in an organization [7] is to establish a risk-based test strategy that anchors risk-orientation as basis for all testing activities in the entire software lifecycle. In this paper we describe a process that addresses the development and refinement of a risk-based test strategy. The process has been developed as part of a research transfer project on risk-based testing that provided the opportunity to get direct feedback from industry and to evaluate the process together with five software development companies.

The main contribution of the paper is a process for risk-based test strategy development that consists of seven steps, i.e., (1) definition of risk items, (2) probability estimation, (3) impact estimation, (4) computation of risk values, (5) determination of risk levels, (6) definition of test strategy, and (7) refinement of test strategy. The process has been developed in close collaboration with industry and is based on our previous work on introducing and integrating risk-based testing in industrial test processes [6, 7]. A further part of the contribution is the evaluation of the acceptance and use of a risk-based testing process in the context of five real-world cases.

The remainder of this paper is structured as follows. Section 2 presents our process for risk-based test strategy development. Section 3 describes the procedure used for the evaluation of the process. Section 4 presents and discusses the evaluation results. Section 5 provides an overview of related work. Finally, Sect. 6 summarizes and concludes our work and points out directions for future work.

2   Description of the Test Strategy Development Process

Risk-based testing (RBT) is a testing approach which considers risks of the software product as the guiding factor to support decisions in all phases of the test process [9]. A *risk* is a factor that could result in future negative consequences and is usually expressed by its likelihood and impact [12]. In software testing, the *likelihood* is typically determined by the probability that a failure assigned to a risk occurs, and the *impact* is determined by the cost or severity of a failure if it occurs in operation. The resulting *risk value* or *risk exposure* is assigned to a *risk item*. In context of testing, a risk item is anything of value (i.e., an asset) under test, for instance, a requirement, a feature, or a component. Based on the risk exposure values, the risk items are typically prioritized and assigned to *risk levels* defining a *risk profile*. The information collected in the risk profile can be used to support decisions in all phases of the test process, spanning over the core activities from *test planning*, *test design*, *test implementation* to *test execution* and *test evaluation* [12].

This section introduces a process for developing a risk-based test strategy that serves as basis for establishing and executing such a risk-based testing approach. A *test strategy* describes how testing is organized and performed on the different test levels [12]. The usually rather generic strategy has to be refined for its implementation in context of a specific project or product iteration. The refinement results in a concrete *test approach* that defines the different types of testing that need to be performed, the test and quality assurance techniques to be applied, and the coverage and exit criteria used for tacking the progress and determining test completion.

Figure 1 provides an overview of the overall process. It consists of different steps, which are either directly related to the risk-based test strategy development (shown in bold font) or which are used to establish the preconditions (shown in normal font) for the process by linking test strategy development to the related processes (drawn with dashed lines) of defect management, requirements management and quality management. The different steps are described in detail in the following subsections.

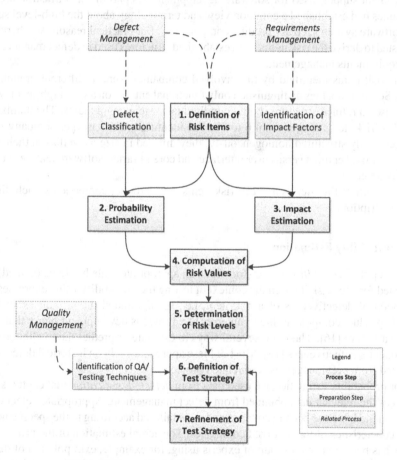

Fig. 1. Process for risk-based test strategy development.

2.1 Definition of Risk Items

In a first step, the *risk items* are identified and defined. The risk items are the basic elements of a software product that can be associated with risks. Risk items are typically derived from the functional structure of the software system, but they can also represent non-functional aspects or system properties. In the context of testing it should be taken into account that the risk items need to be mapped to test objects [12], i.e., testable objects such as sub-systems, features, components, modules or functional as well as non-functional requirements.

When we analyzed the development processes and the tool infrastructure of the involved companies we found that most of them had an elaborated workflow for reporting and tracking defects, often linked to a service or helpdesk system and task management support used for software development. As part of this infrastructure the companies had established a common view and terminology about the high-level structure software system such as "product components". For practical reasons we therefore suggested to derive the risk items from established structures used in defect management and requirements management.

The risk items identified by the involved companies were at different granularity levels. Some companies distinguished only functional entities on a very high-level while others used a refined structure showing individual system components. The number of identified risk items ranged from 6 to 17. The identified risk items per company were not necessarily structured homogeneously; they differed in size as well as in their type (e.g., functional entities versus user interface and core libraries, software features versus user documentation).

The result of this step is a list of risk items, e.g., product components, including a short description.

2.2 Probability Estimation

In this step the *probability values* (for which an appropriate scale has to be defined) are estimated for each risk item. In the context of testing the probability value expresses the likelihood of defectiveness of a risk item, i.e., the likelihood that a fault exists in a specific product component due to an error in a previous development phase that may lead to a failure [16]. There are several ways to estimate or predict the likelihood of a component's defectiveness [18]. Most of these approaches rely on historical defect data collected from previous releases or related projects.

For probability estimation we used data from *defect classification* that captures and enhances the relevant data obtained from defect management. Appropriate defect classification models have been introduced and were tailored according to the specific needs and characteristics of the involved companies. The actual estimation of the probability values has been done by a group of experts using, for example, extrapolation of defect trends and Wideband Delphi estimation techniques. The estimated values included the number of defects and the severity of the defects. These values were aggregated to a final probability value by summing up the number of defects weighted according their expected severity.

As result of this step, risk probability values are assigned to the risk items indicating their likelihood of defectiveness.

2.3 Impact Estimation

In this step the *impact values* are estimated for each risk item. The impact values express the consequences of risk items being defective, i.e., the negative effect that a defect in a specific component has on the user or customer and, ultimately, on the company's business success. The impact is often associated with the cost of failures. The impact is closely related to the expected value of the components for the user or customer. The value is usually determined in requirements engineering when eliciting and prioritizing the system's requirements. Thus, requirements management may be identified as main source of data for impact estimation.

The impact values were estimated similarly to probability values in the previous step. The group of estimators first identified possible impact factors by jointly developing a fishbone diagram showing which causes may trigger failures. The (business) values were determined by analyzing the available information associated with existing requirements. The use of requirements prioritization techniques was suggested for estimating the value of items for which related requirements information was not available. For each risk item the associated impact factors were aggregated weighted, for example, by the business value. The actual way of conducting the estimation and aggregation differed widely between the involved companies as it was found to be highly dependent on the available information. For example, an interesting approach proposed for a product that supports individual licensing of software components was to directly derive the impact values from the components' projected license revenues.

As result of this step, impact values are assigned to the risk items expressing the consequences of being defective.

2.4 Computation of Risk Values

In this step *risk values* are computed from the estimated probability and impact values. Risk values can be computed according to the definition of risk as $R = P \times I$ where P is the probability value and I is the impact value. Aggregating the available information to a single risk value per risk item allows the prioritization of the risk items according to their associated risk values or ranks. Furthermore, the computed risk values can be used to group risk items, for example, according high, medium and low risk. Nevertheless, for identifying risk levels it is recommended to consider probability and impact as two separate dimensions of risk.

Figure 2 shows a simplified and anonymized example of risk values computed from the estimated probability and impact values for the software system of one of the involved companies. The software system was structured into six high-level product components – at the level of functional areas or sub-systems – providing functionality for different user groups. The estimated probability values follow an exponential distribution due to the applied weighting while the estimated impact values can be separated in two main classes, i.e., high and low. Hence, the impact values of the class high lead to three risk items with high computed risk values.

Component	Estimated Probability	Estimated Impact	Computed Risk (= P * I)	Rank
A	5	21	105	6
B	29	50	1.450	1
C	25	10	250	4
D	18	46	828	2
E	14	8	112	5
F	13	50	650	3

Fig. 2. Example risk values from one of the involved companies.

As shown, the result of this step is mainly the combination of the probability and impact values to an aggregated risk value assigned to the risk items.

2.5 Determination of Risk Levels

In this step the spectrum of risk values is partitioned into *risk levels*. Risk levels are a further level of aggregation. The purpose of distinguishing different risk levels is to define classes of risks such that all risk items associated to a particular class are considered equally risky. As a consequence, all risk items of the same class are subject to the same intensity of quality assurance and test measures.

As suggested in the previous step, probability and impact were treated as two different dimensions. They represent the axes of a risk matrix used to support the definition of risk levels derived by subdividing each dimension into classes and by visualizing the associated clusters of risk items. Figure 3 shows the 2 × 2 matrix used to visualize the risks in terms of the estimated probability and impact values associated to the six components listed in Fig. 2. The fields of the matrix correspond to four risk levels, i.e., *level I* (low probability and low impact) to *level IV* (high probability and high impact). As indicated by the numbering of the levels, risk items with high impact and low probability (*level III*) were considered more critical and were therefore given higher priority than those with high probability and low impact (*level II*).

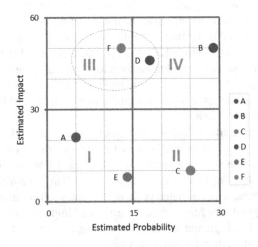

Fig. 3. Example risk levels from one of the involved companies.

Determining the appropriate risk levels has been conducted as a manual step in addition to computing aggregated risk values. It was used to review and adjust the initially derived classification. For example, special cases such as risk items located on or close to the border between two risk levels were discussed individually and assigned to the most appropriate level. *Component D* in Fig. 3 shows such a special case. Although the classification schema would suggest classifying *component D* as *level IV*, it has finally been decided to reclassify it as *level III* to build a cluster together with *component F* (indicated by the dashed circle).

The result of this step is the distinction of risk levels with risk items associated the different levels.

2.6 Definition of Test Strategy

In this step the *test strategy* is defined on the basis of the different risk levels. For each risk level the test strategy describes how testing is organized and performed. Distinguishing different levels allows to perform testing with different rigorousness in order to adequately address the expected risks. This can either be by achieved by applying specific testing techniques (e.g., unit testing, use case testing, beta testing, reviews) or by applying these techniques with more or less intensity according to different coverage criteria (e.g., unit testing at the level of 100 % branch coverage or use case testing for basic flows and/or alternative flows).

The basis for selecting appropriate testing techniques was a list of applicable quality assurance and testing techniques, i.e., techniques for which sufficient knowledge, experience and tool support is available in the company or the project. Such a list should be provided by the company-wide quality management. We supported this step by compiling an overview of common testing and QA techniques [11, 12] to encourage the discussion about what techniques are already part of the daily practice and what techniques may be included in future work.

Figure 4 shows an example of a selection of testing techniques made by one of the involved companies and their mapping to risk levels. This mapping, thus, allows relating the selected testing techniques to components as basis for a further refinement.

The result of this step is a list of testing techniques including application or coverage criteria for each of the different risk levels.

Testing techniques	Risk level I	Risk level II	Risk level III	Risk level IV	Components Risk level	A I	B IV	C II	D III	E I	F III
Unit testing (100% branch coverage)				X		X					
Code reviews		X	X	X		X	X	X			X
Manual testing of use cases (base flow)		X					X				
Manual testing of use cases (base + alternative flows)			X	X		X		X			X
Exploratory testing	X			X		X	X		X		
Automated smoke/regression tests			X	X		X		X			X
Beta test phase at selected customers		X	X	X		X	X	X			X

Fig. 4. Example catalogue of testing techniques of one of the involved companies.

2.7 Refinement of Test Strategy

In the last step the *test strategy* is *refined* to match the characteristics of the individual components of the software system (i.e., risk items). As shown in Fig. 4, the testing techniques and criteria that have been specified in the testing strategy for a particular risk level can be directly mapped to the components associated with that risk level. However, the test strategy is usually rather generic. It does not describe the technical and organizational details that are necessary for applying the specified techniques to a concrete software component. For each component, thus, a test approach has to be developed that clarifies how the test strategy should be implemented.

The degree of formality of the resulting test approaches varied between the involved companies. Companies with strict requirements for process documentation created and maintained a written document while others kept the strategy implementation an informal task assigned to the component owner, i.e., the responsible principal developer. The aspects included in most of the testing approaches were technology related decisions such as tools and frameworks to be used, guidelines for setting up the test environment and for creating and maintaining test data, responsibilities and involved roles, test end criteria as well as measurement rules for tacking the progress and determining test completion (definitions of done).

The detailed mapping was also used as basis for a quick, bottom-up effort estimation to cross-check that the testing approaches derived from a risk-based perspective are compatible with the organizational reality in terms of available time and resources. For each intersection point in the matrix of testing techniques and components (see Fig. 4) the expected effort was estimated. Subtotals per component, technique and risk level as well as the grand total were calculated. The outcome was compared to the availability of the assigned personnel and the planned testing budgets. This step led to discussions about how to balance the required testing effort under the light of the risk exposure, e.g., by adjusting the development plans or by revising the testing strategy, which is shown as feedback loop in the overall process.

The result of this final step is a testing approach describing the implementation of the strategy down to the level of risk items and in alignment with time budgets and available resources.

3 Evaluation Design

The test strategy development process has been evaluated together with five software development companies in context of a research transfer project on risk-based testing. This section provides an overview of the evaluation design. It is based on the guidelines for conducting and reporting case study research [16].

3.1 Research Questions

The goal of the evaluation is to analyze the applicability of the risk-based test strategy development process proposed in the last section. The analysis has been inspired by the Technology Acceptance Model (TAM) [3], one of the most prominent theories in Information Systems for explaining how users come to accept and use new technologies. TAM proposes two constructs that capture the relevant beliefs in information technology acceptance and usage [3]: *perceived usefulness*, defined as "the degree to which a person believes that using a particular system would enhance his or her job performance", and *perceived ease of use*, defined as "the degree to which a person believes that using a particular system would be free of effort".

The research transfer project provided the opportunity to practically apply the process in context of the involved companies as part of a main software project or in the company's product development cycle. Despite having a realistic real-world setting, the analysis has been extended towards investigating also the perceived *representativeness* of the results produced by the process, i.e., how closely they are perceived to match the genuine situation of the application context.

The following three research questions (RQ) were defined for the evaluation of the proposed risk-based test strategy development process and for each of its steps.

RQ1: Is the outcome of the process useful (*perceived usefulness*)?
RQ2: Is conducting the process easy (*perceived ease of use*)?
RQ3: Is the outcome of the process representative (*perceived representativeness*)?

3.2 Case Selection

Five software development companies provided the application contexts for developing and evaluating the described risk-based strategy development process. They were selected to participate in the research transfer project due to their interest in risk-based testing. The five companies are SMEs and represent typical cases from the Austrian software industry: Case A develops a commercial off-the-shelf software product for enterprise resource planning, Case B develops and manufactures biometric access

Table 1. Overview of case companies.

	Case A	Case B	Case C	Case D	Case E
Domain	ERP software	Access systems	Document manage- ment	Training and recruit- ment	Payment systems
Core business	Software product and service	Hardware incl. embedded software	Software product and custom develop- ment	Service including software platform and opera- tion	Solution develop- ment incl. software and hard- ware
Employees	15	40	10	40	15
Software Releases	2 to 4 releases per year; service releases on demand	Adjusted to hardware product cycles (years)	New releases every one and four weeks	On demand	Delivery as custom projects

systems, Case C develops a commercial off-the-shelf software product for document management, Case D provides recruitment and training services as well as a software platform to support these, and finally Case E is a solution provider offering billing and cash-less payment systems for restaurants and canteens. Their key characteristics are summarized in Table 1.

3.3 Data Collection Procedure

As a first step, basic information was collected about the company context and the state of the practice with respect to the organizations, products, software development and test processes as well as risk management practices. The actual development and evaluation of the test strategy development process advanced in an iterative way. All iterations included (1) a joint workshop involving all participating companies to discuss and prepare the steps of the process, (2) the application of selected steps to create tangible practical results supporting the daily work of the companies, and (3) a questionnaire to collect the feedback from each company. The questionnaire was designed according to TAM, which served as basis for the evaluation. Notes were recorded as part of the discussions that took place in the workshops. The outcome of the process steps were retrieved from filled spreadsheet templates prepared as "tool support" for the practical application as well as from the documents and material produced. In addition, (4) semi-structured interviews were conducted with key members from the different companies.

3.4 Analysis Procedure

The analysis of the collected data from the five cases was conducted by two researchers using a mix of quantitative and qualitative methods. In every iteration the outcome from the practical applications, i.e., the filled spreadsheet templates and any additional documents or material, was examined by the researchers. The results were prepared for presentation in the following workshops where they were discussed in groups and together with all workshop participants. The discussion notes were transcribed and linked to the referenced process steps as well as the companies to keep a complete chain of evidence. The recorded interviews with individual persons and any additional notes were processed in the same way. The answers to the questionnaires were analyzed from the viewpoint of the steps as well as from the viewpoint of the companies using basic descriptive statistics. The results were interpreted in combination with the transcribed notes. Besides the technology acceptance model TAM [3], a taxonomy for risk-based testing [9] was used as reference framework and to guide the analysis in comparing the risk-based testing approaches. The findings are the basis for the description of the results and discussion presented in the following section.

3.5 Validity Procedure

Based on the guidelines of Runeson et al. [16], validity threats were analyzed according to construct validity, reliability, internal validity, and external validity. Selected countermeasures against threats to validity were then taken. For example, data extracted from discussion notes was triangulated with interviews and all analysis steps were conducted by two researchers. Furthermore, it was seen as important that sufficient time was spent in collaborating with the companies in the course of the development, application and evaluation of the process. The research transfer project gave the researchers the opportunity to observe and discuss the processes, methods and tools applied as part of the daily work and to gain a good understanding of the context in which the companies operate.

4 Results and Discussion

In this section, we present the evaluation results according to the three research questions addressing the *perceived usefulness* (RQ1), the *perceived ease of use* (RQ2) and the *perceived representativeness* (RQ3) of the proposed process for risk-based test strategy development. For each of the three questions, we summarize the results for all companies and process steps using radar charts. Observable deviations and special cases are discussed in further detail.

4.1 Usefulness (RQ1)

Figure 5 shows the *perceived usefulness* per process step for each of the five companies. Overall the level of perceived usefulness is rather high (on average from 1.2 to 2.0), only one step (4. Computation of Risk Values) was perceived to have low usefulness by company B. As remarked by company B, the reason for this is that they used limited data and therefore were not able to obtain useful results; the step is considered valuable if more data would have been used. Nevertheless, the computation of risk values can be seen as an intermediate step with results superseded when the risk levels are defined visually using a risk matrix. Overall the results indicate that the process is useful for practitioners when developing a risk-based test strategy.

Usefulness of ...	A	B	C	D	E	Avg	sdev
1. Definition of Risk Items	2	1	1	1	2	1.4	0.49
2. Probability Estimation	2	2	1	1	1	1.4	0.49
3. Impact Estimation	1	2	1	1	1	1.2	0.40
4. Computation of Risk Values	1	5	1	2	1	2.0	1.55
5. Determination of Risk Levels	1	1	1	2	1	1.2	0.40
6. Definition of Test Strategy	1	1	1	3	1	1.4	0.80
7. Refinement of Test Strategy	1	2	3	2	2	2.0	0.63

Fig. 5. Perceived Usefulness per process step for each case (Avg = *average*, sdev = *standard deviation*, values are 1 = *high*, 2 = *rather high*, 3 = *medium*, 4 = *rather low*, 5 = *low*).

4.2 Ease of Use (RQ2)

Figure 5 shows the *perceived ease of use* per process step for each of the five companies. The overall the level of perceived ease of use is between moderate and rather high (average values range from 1.4 to 3.0), which is notably less than the perceived usefulness. One can also observe a greater variance in the ratings of the steps between the different companies (standard deviations ranging from 0.80 to 1.41). Steps perceived as easy were *2. Probability Estimation* and *4. Computation of Risk Values*. The steps that caused most effort were *3. Impact Estimation, 6. Definition of Test Strategy* and *1. Definition of Risk Items*. These were also the steps that required input from many different roles to make appropriate decisions and which sometimes triggered discussions within the companies about established structures and workflows.

The two estimation steps (2. and 3.) are in strong contrast to each other, which shows that deriving probability values from defect classifications helped to reduce the effort – with one exception; company C identified issues in their structuring of software components, which affected the effort of the steps 1 to 3.

For step 3 we observed that the actual way of how companies conducted impact estimation differed widely between the involved companies, mainly due to differences in the availability of relevant information (see Sect. 2.3). While company A was able to leverage existing information, others were required first to dig up such information by analyzing historical data or by conducting internal workshops. The range of necessary preparation activities and the varying effort is shown by the diverse ratings for ease of use; every single one of the involved companies perceived the ease of use differently. In the related discussions all companies supported the view that impact estimation is generally an activity that requires more methodical support.

On average, ease of use has been perceived as moderate to rather high. Although this can be interpreted as a largely positive result, it should be noted that the perceived effort (i.e., low ease of use) is a major blocker for the acceptance of risk-based testing in practice (Fig. 6).

Ease of Use of ...	A	B	C	D	E	Avg	sdev
1. Definition of Risk Items	1	2	3	5	2	**2.6**	1.36
2. Probability Estimation	2	1	3	1	1	**1.6**	0.80
3. Impact Estimation	1	5	3	4	2	**3.0**	1.41
4. Computation of Risk Values	1	1	1	3	1	**1.4**	0.80
5. Determination of Risk Levels	1	4	1	1	1	**1.6**	1.20
6. Definition of Test Strategy	2	4	2	2	4	**2.8**	0.98
7. Refinement of Test Strategy	1	1	3	2	4	**2.2**	1.17

Fig. 6. Perceived Ease of Use per process step for each case (Avg = *average*, sdev = *standard deviation*, values are 1 = *high*, 2 = *rather high*, 3 = *medium*, 4 = *rather low*, 5 = *low*).

4.3 Representativeness (RQ3)

Figure 7 shows the *perceived representativeness* per process step for each of the five companies. Overall representativeness is between medium and rather high (average values ranging from 1.6 to 2.5), which is however a consequence of the ratings of company B and partly due to company D. As indicated earlier, the reason for this is that the data used by company B to apply the process was very limited and therefore the representative was mostly perceived as low. Company D perceived the representativeness of the computed risk values and the resulting risk levels as low. In this particular case, the reasons are due to the fact that the focus of the company is actually not on software development but on operation issues. In future, when the focus shifts back to software development, the representativeness is considered to increase.

Representativeness of ...	A	B	C	D	E	Avg	sdev
1. Definition of Risk Items	1	4	1	1	1	**1.6**	1.20
2. Probability Estimation	1	5	1	2	2	**2.2**	1.47
3. Impact Estimation	1	5	1	1	2	**2.0**	1.55
4. Computation of Risk Values	1	5	1	4	1	**2.4**	1.74
5. Determination of Risk Levels	1	2	1	4	3	**2.2**	1.17
6. Definition of Test Strategy	1	4	1	3	1	**2.0**	1.26
7. Refinement of Test Strategy		4	2	2	2	**2.5**	0.87

Fig. 7. Representativeness per process step for each case (Avg = *average*, sdev = *standard deviation*, values are 1 = *high*, 2 = *rather high*, 3 = *medium*, 4 = *rather low*, 5 = *low*).

Taking the special situations of company B and C into account and considering the high level of representativeness in the other three cases, the results from applying the process for test strategy development can be stated as generally representative.

4.4 Threats to Validity

In this section we present the threats to validity of our results and the applied counter-measures taken to reduce the threats. Referring to Runeson et al. [16], we discuss threats to the construct validity, reliability, internal validity, and external validity.

Construct validity reflects to what extent the phenomenon under study really represents what the researchers have in mind and what is investigated according to the research questions. Of specific interest are the definitions of terms and concepts in the case context versus the research context. We defined all relevant terms and concepts of risk-based testing in Sect. 2. The process steps as well as the research questions are formulated based on these terms and in alignment with the taxonomy of risk-based testing [9], which has also been used in previous work.

Reliability focuses on whether the data are collected and the analysis is conducted in a way that it can be repeated by others with the same results; a threat in any data-centric study. The observations are of course filtered through the perception and knowledge profile of the researchers. Counteractions are that two researchers are involved in the study, the data collection and analysis procedures are well documented, and the data extracted from documents and tools is triangulated with interviews.

Internal validity is of concern when causal relations are examined. When the researcher is investigating whether one factor affects an investigated factor there is a risk that the investigated factor is also affected by a third factor. In our case, only few quantitative data is available, the quantitative analysis is not interpreted in isolation, and it is not even feasible to infer statistical analysis, due to the number of cases. The analyses about casual relationships are instead based on qualitative analysis. Feeding back the analysis results to the workshop participants and having multiple cycles of applications and discussions are action taken to reduce internal validity threats.

External validity is concerned with to what extent it is possible to generalize the findings, and to what extent the findings are of interest to other people outside the investigated cases. As the participating companies can been considered typical examples of the Austrian as well as the European software industry, the presented results are relevant for other contexts as well. Each case of course has its own specifics, and in that sense there is no general case. However, some key characteristics of the companies may be general and, for other companies with similar contexts, the results may be used as a reference. Replications may further strengthen the external validity of our work.

5   Related Work

Recently, risk-based testing attracted considerable interest in research [9], a taxonomy on it has been defined [10], and several risk-based testing approaches have been published as shown in a current systematic literature review on risk-based testing [4]. The taxonomy defines the risk drivers functionality, safety and security. As risk items are typically derived from the functional structure of software systems (see Sect. 2.1), we only discuss related risk-based testing approaches derived from the functional structure in the following. In the literature review a total of 22 risk-based testing approaches were identified, amongst them some risk-based testing approaches addressing the integration of risk analysis into test processes on a general level [1, 5, 14].

Amland [1] defines a risk-based testing approach that is based on the generic risk management process of Karolak [11] comprising the steps planning, identification of risk indicators, identification of the cost of a failure, identification of critical elements, test execution, and estimation and completion. *Felderer et al.* [5] take the standard test process of the ISTQB [12] as a starting point, integrate risk identification and risk analysis into this process and extend the activities of the standard test process by risk-specific elements. *Redmill* [14, 15] addresses the loose integration of risk analysis and testing to make testing more effective. The author proposes a single factor risk analysis, either based on probability or impact, or a two factor risk analysis, in which probability and impact are combined.

Although several risk-based testing approaches have been proposed [4], only a few empirical studies on risk-based testing are available [7, 8, 17, 19]. *Yoon and Choi* [19] propose a test case prioritization strategy for risk-based testing and evaluate its effectiveness on the basis of data from a traffic conflict avoidance system. *Souza et al.* [17] indicate in a small case study that risk-based testing focuses on the parts of a software that are more likely to fail. The risk-based testing approach is based on their risk-based test process, which consists of the phases risk identification, risk analysis, test planning, test design, test execution as well as test evaluation and risk control. *Felderer and Ramler* [7] provide an empirical case study on introducing risk-based testing into established test processes. In a retrospective analysis the authors investigate the applicability and the potential benefits from introducing risk-based testing in an industrial project. Finally, *Felderer and Ramler* [8] provide a multiple case study on risk-based testing in industry. The article analyzes how risk is defined, assessed, and applied to support testing activities in three industrial cases.

However, in related approaches on risk-based testing the aspect of test strategy development is only covered on a high level and without providing the guidance of a process for the application in practice. Furthermore, none of the related approaches further explores probability estimation based on defect classification. Finally, the process for risk-based test strategy development defined in this paper is the first work in which acceptance and use of a risk-based testing process are evaluated in an industrial context with five cases on the basis of the technology acceptance model.

6   Summary and Conclusions

In this paper we presented a process for risk-based test strategy development and refinement. It consists of seven steps, i.e., (1) definition of risk items, (2) probability estimation, (3) impact estimation, (4) computation of risk values, (5) determination of risk levels, (6) definition of test strategy, and (7) refinement of test strategy. The proposed process has been established as part of a research transfer project on risk-based testing that provided the opportunity to get direct feedback from industry and to evaluate the ease of use, usefulness and representativeness of each process step together with five software development companies.

The analysis for each process step based on feedback of the five participating companies showed an *overall positive result for the usefulness of the process*; average values for the different steps were in the range from 1.2 (close to high usefulness) to 2.0 (rather high usefulness). The *overall ease of use is perceived as moderate*; average ratings for the different process steps range from 1.4 (leaning towards high ease of use) to 3.0 (medium ease of use) with a great variance in the ratings of the different companies. The *overall representativeness is high with one notable exception*, company B. The average ratings are between high and medium (values ranging from 1.6 to 2.5), which is mainly a consequence of the negative ratings from company B using limited data when performing the process steps.

The definition of *Ease of Use* is related to "free of effort". The evaluation clearly indicated that despite the usefulness of the process, in the end, its acceptance and use is a matter of the involved effort. The three steps that caused most effort were *Impact Estimation, Definition of Test Strategy* and *Definition of Risk Items*. The effort was usually a result of these steps requiring information that was not readily available and which sometimes triggered time-consuming discussion involving several people. In contrast, the step *Probability Estimation* is a good example showing that deriving probability estimates from defect classification data generates useful and representative results and, at the same time, it reduces the involved effort.

Finally, the feedback from the companies confirmed that making risks explicit is valuable for many of the hard decisions that have to be taken in software development and testing. Balancing the time and resources needed for testing under the light of the risk exposure is one of them. The proposed process has been found to reveal discrepancies between available testing budgets and estimated risks early on, at a time when it is still possible to react adequately by adopting the test strategy.

In future, we plan to further disseminate the process for risk-based test strategy development and to accompany this by process refinement and additional evaluations. Especially the process steps impact estimation and definition of test strategy could benefit from refinement and derived guidelines. Furthermore, we plan to analyze the defect classification models generated during the application of the process and to identify typical patterns of defect management in practice.

Acknowledgments. This work has been supported by the research project Smart Testing funded by the Austrian Research Promotion Agency (FFG), the COMET Competence Center program of the Austrian Research Promotion Agency (FFG), and the project QE LaB – Living Models for Open Systems funded by the Austrian Federal Ministry of Science, Research and Economy.

References

1. Amland, S.: Risk-based testing: risk analysis fundamentals and metrics for software testing including a financial application case study. J. Syst. Softw. **53**(3), 287–295 (2000)
2. Bach, J.: Heuristic risk-based testing. STQE Mag. **11**(99), 96–98 (1999)
3. Davis, F.D.: Perceived usefulness, perceived ease of use, and user acceptance of information technology. MIS Q. **13**(3), 319–340 (1990)
4. Erdogan, G., Li, Y., Runde, R.K., Seehusen, F., Stølen, K.: Approaches for the combined use of risk analysis and testing: a systematic literature review. Int. J. Softw. Tools Technol. Transf. **16**(5), 627–642 (2014)
5. Felderer, M., Haisjackl, C., Breu, R., Motz, J.: Integrating manual and automatic risk assessment for risk-based testing. In: Biffl, S., Winkler, D., Bergsmann, J. (eds.) SWQD 2012. LNBIP, vol. 94, pp. 159–180. Springer, Heidelberg (2012)
6. Felderer, M., Ramler, R.: Experiences and challenges of introducing risk-based testing in an industrial project. In: Winkler, D., Biffl, S., Bergsmann, J. (eds.) SWQD 2013. LNBIP, vol. 133, pp. 10–29. Springer, Heidelberg (2013)
7. Felderer, M., Ramler, R.: Integrating risk-based testing in industrial test processes. Softw. Qual. J. **22**(3), 543–575 (2014)
8. Felderer, M., Ramler, R.: A multiple case study on risk-based testing in industry. Int. J. Softw. Tools Technol. Transf. **16**(5), 609–625 (2014)
9. Felderer, M., Schieferdecker, I.: A taxonomy of risk-based testing. Int. J. Softw. Tools Technol. Transf. **16**(5), 559–568 (2014)

10. Felderer, M., Wendland, M.-F., Schieferdecker, I.: Risk-based testing. In: Margaria, T., Steffen, B. (eds.) ISoLA 2014, Part II. LNCS, vol. 8803, pp. 274–276. Springer, Heidelberg (2014)
11. ISO/IEC/IEEE: ISO/IEC/IEEE 29119 Software Testing Standard. Draft. http://www.softwaretestingstandard.org/ (2013). Accessed 25 June 2015
12. ISTQB: Standard glossary of terms used in software testing. Version 2.1. (2010)
13. Karolak, D.W.: Software Engineering Risk Management. Wiley, Hoboken (1995)
14. Redmill, F.: Exploring risk-based testing and its implications. Softw. Test. Verif. Reliab. **14**(1), 3–15 (2004)
15. Redmill, F.: Theory and practice of risk-based testing: research articles. Softw. Test. Verif. Reliab. **15**(1), 3–20 (2005)
16. Runeson, P., Höst, M., Rainer, A., Regnell, B.: Case Study Research in Software Engineering: Guidelines and examples. Wiley, Hoboken (2012)
17. Souza, E., Gusmão, C., Venâncio, J.: Risk-based testing: a case study. In: Seventh International Conference on Information Technology: New Generations (ITNG), pp. 1032–1037 (2010)
18. Tian, J.: Software Quality Engineering - Testing, Quality Assurance, and Quantifiable Improvement. Wiley-Interscience, Hoboken (2005)
19. Yoon, H., Choi, B.: A test case prioritization based on degree of risk exposure and its empirical evaluation. Int. J. Softw. Eng. Knowl. Eng. **21**(02), 191–209 (2011)

Focused Inspections to Support Defect Detection in Automation Systems Engineering Environments

Dietmar Winkler[✉] and Stefan Biffl

Vienna University of Technology, Institute of Software Technology, CDL-Flex,
Favoritenstr. 9/188, 1040 Vienna, Austria
{dietmar.winkler,stefan.biffl}@tuwien.ac.at

Abstract. **[Context]** In Automation Systems Engineering (ASE) Environments, engineers coming from different disciplines, have to collaborate. Individual engineers, e.g., from electrical, mechanical, or software domains, apply domain-specific tools and related data models that hinder efficient collaboration due to limited capabilities for interaction and data exchange on technical and semantic level. Manual activities are required to synchronize planning data from different disciplines and can raise additional risks caused by defects and/or changes that cannot be identified efficiently. **[Objective]** Main objective is to improve (a) engineering processes by providing efficient data exchange mechanism and to support (b) defect detection performance in ASE environments. **[Method]** Software inspections (SI) are commonly used by engineers in Software Engineering (SE) by applying well-defined approaches to systematically identify defects early in the development process. In this paper we adapt the traditional SI process for application in ASE environments and provide a software tool to support frequent synchronization and focused reviews. We evaluate and discuss the adapted process in an industry context. **[Results]** Main results were that the adapted process and the software tool can be useful in the application context in order to identify defects early, increase overall product quality, and improve engineering processes in the ASE domain. **[Conclusion]** The proposed adapted inspection approach showed promising results to improve ASE projects.

Keywords: Inspection · Defect detection · Tool-support · Automation systems engineering environments · Feasibility study

1 Introduction

In Automation Systems Engineering (ASE) projects, e.g., developing hydro power plants, manufacturing systems, or steel mills, several engineers have to collaborate and exchange data within the project [4]. In industry practice, engineers work in parallel using individual highly specific engineering tools with heterogeneous and distributed data, e.g., for electrical planning, software planning and construction, process modeling, or simulation. Engineering tools are typically loosely coupled with strong limitations regarding collaboration, data exchange, and defect detection [5]. Experts have to handle a high number of data sets in large-scale engineering projects, e.g., up to 30 k data entities

© Springer International Publishing Switzerland 2015
P. Abrahamsson et al. (Eds.): PROFES 2015, LNCS 9459, pp. 372–379, 2015.
DOI: 10.1007/978-3-319-26844-6_27

in hydro power plants or several million of data points in steel mill construction projects. Typically, synchronization of data and defect detection across disciplines is executed manually by experts, who are familiar in at least two related disciplines [6]. In practice experts apply various approaches to identify deviations, e.g., by manually comparing lists of data objects or by using local expert-tools based on spreadsheet solutions (e.g., macros) or data bases. These solutions can be error prone and require a high effort for application and maintenance. Software Inspection (SI) variants have been developed and evaluated to support experts or groups of experts in Software Engineering (SE) to efficiently find defects systematically [2, 7]. Reading Techniques (RT) [1] support the inspection process by providing checklists and guidelines for defect detection. Thus, best-practices from SE might also help experts in the ASE domain to identify defects systematically.

Goal of this paper is to provide a best practice SI process (aligned with ASE engineering processes) supported by a synchronization tool that helps ASE experts in detecting defects in ASE environments. We initially evaluate the adapted process with focused inspections in a project at a hydro power plant systems development organization. The remainder of this paper is structured as follows: Sect. 2 provides related work on ASE and inspections. Section 3 presents research issues. We describe the solution approach in Sect. 4 and the prototype implementation/initial evaluation in Sect. 5. Finally, Sect. 6 discusses results, concludes and describes future work.

2 Related Work

This section summarizes related work on automation systems engineering environments (2.1) and inspections and reading techniques (2.2).

2.1 Automation Systems Engineering Environments

The variety and heterogeneity of stakeholders, engineering plans, and engineering tools [3] in ASE projects make collaboration in engineering projects more difficult [5], risky, and error prone [4]. Common information sets (i.e., common concepts) are available in ASE projects [9], where experts link heterogeneous data sources manually or by using individual expert solutions, discuss open issues at interfaces of two or more disciplines, and identify defects at defined milestones or quality gates. Thus, these common concepts represent an important glue between heterogeneous and distributed engineering disciplines. For instance, in hydro power plant engineering projects, experts use the term "signal" as common concept approach: signals represent software variables in the software domain or electrical connection points in the electrical domain. These common concepts represent the foundation for linking individual disciplines and for enabling efficient data exchange and defect detection across disciplines [6, 9].

2.2 Inspections and Reading Techniques

Inspections are well-established methods in Software Engineering (SE) to efficiently identify defects and assess the quality of software artifacts [1]. Several studies investigated team effects, inspection efficiency, inspection effectiveness, and false positives in academia [10] and industry. Laitenberger *et al.* provide a framework to describe the technical dimension of software inspection and impact factors along the project course including inspection processes, roles (e.g., moderator, inspectors, readers, and authors), products, and reading techniques [7]. Biffl presents a framework for inspection planning and control [2] on different levels, i.e., on management level (project quality planning and reporting), on inspection level (inspection planning and defect detection), and on inspection object level (defect detection and defect collection).

To support defect detection, the SI process follow a sequence of steps [7]: (a) *Preparation* of the inspection process; (b) *Individual Defect Detection* by inspectors; (c) *Defect Collection* by the inspection team based on individual candidate defect lists; and (d) *Defect Correction* by the author; and (e) *Follow-up* activities managed by the moderator. However, the main task of inspections is to find defects. Reading technique (RT) support inspectors in finding defects more efficient and effective by guiding inspectors through the inspection process. Several studies investigated different RTs and reported on benefits/weaknesses in different contexts (e.g., [1, 2], or [10]). Example RTs are *Ad-Hoc Reading* without any specific guideline, *Checklist-Based Reading (CBR)*, where inspectors apply domain-specific checklists, *Usage-Based Reading (UBR)* with focus on prioritized application use cases [11], or *Perspective-Based Reading (PBR)* [10] where artifacts are investigated from different viewpoints comparable to expert knowledge in related disciplines [2]. In the ASE domain inspections are mainly executed on an ad-hoc basis without any systematic RT support. Thus, we see benefits of adapting best-practice SI approaches in ASE.

3 Research Issues

Based on the related work and ASE needs we derive two main research issues:

RI.1. How can we support defect detection in ASE Environments? This research issue includes two important steps to enable efficient inspections in ASE environments: (a) efficient data exchange in environments with loosely-coupled tools and semantically heterogeneous data models and (b) apply a SI process to support effective and efficient defect detection.

RI.2. How can we show the feasibility of the adapted inspection approach in the ASE domain? The second research issue focuses on the evaluation of the defect detection process in an ASE environment in an industry-related application.

4 Solution Approach

This section presents the solution approach for applying SI processes in ASE projects.

4.1 Common Concepts in the Automation Service Bus

The Engineering Service Bus (EngSB) provides an integration platform to overcome technical heterogeneity of tools and the semantic heterogeneity of data models [3].

To address special needs of ASE, the Automation Service Bus (ASB) has been introduced as the technical foundation for efficient data exchange in ASE environments. To
overcome semantic heterogeneity of local (and isolated) data models we introduced
common concepts [9], i.e., information sets that hold common data relevant for related
disciplines, e.g., signals in the hydro power plant domain. See [3, 9, 12] for a detailed
description of the common concept approach. By using semantic technologies, risks of
incompatible data models across disciplines and domain borders are minimized [4].
Thus, common concepts represent the basis for inspecting engineering plans in order to
find changes, inconsistencies, and defects.

4.2 Inspection Process in the ASE Domain

Based on semantically integrated data models an inspection process can be implemented
to identify changes, candidate defects and inconsistencies efficiently. Following the
traditional SI process (see Sect. 2.2 and Fig. 1) the defect detection process can be
improved by applying semantic technologies for tool-supported difference checks
(Fig. 1, step 3').

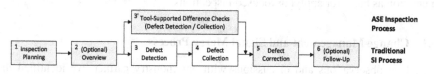

Fig. 1. Adapted inspection process.

In detail, the individual steps of the ASE defect detection approach consists of:

- *Step 1 "Inspection Planning"*. Similar to SI, the ASE inspection process has to be
  scheduled according to project needs by project and/or quality managers.
- *Step 2 "(Optional) Overview"*. This optional step can be used to introduce the overall
  project to the inspection team. The inspection team might include experts from
  different fields or even non-experts.
- *Step 3 "Tool-Supported Difference Checks"*. In contrast to traditional SI, step 3´
  bundles traditional activities from step 3 (individual defect detection) and step 4
  (defect collection). Because of the automation-supported merge process deviations
  (i.e., changes and candidate defects) are available to the inspection team, e.g., in a
  dashboard provided by the tool [8], as input for discussions in the team meeting.
  Result of this step is a set of agreed changes and a list of defects.
- *Step 5 "Defect Correction"*. Similar to traditional SI, the author receives a list of
  agreed defects (notifications) to be fixed.
- *Step 6 "(Optional) Follow-Up"*. In traditional SI processes the moderator checks
  the implementation of corrective actions and plan a follow-up meeting if needed.
  In the ASE inspection approach, changes will be merged and can be checked
  easily via the dashboard without high additional effort.

4.3   Reading Techniques in ASE Projects

RTs support inspectors in efficiently guiding individual inspectors in their inspection process. Following the heterogeneity of ASE project stakeholders, perspectives seem to be the most promising candidate RT for application in ASE projects: *Electrical Engineers* focus on electrical planning, power consumption, and wiring; *Mechanical Engineers* focus on the physical setting of the automation system by using CAD systems; *Software Engineers* are responsible for control applications by using function blocks or structured text approaches; finally *Project and Quality Managers* are not interested in individual disciplines but need to keep an overview on the phases, gates, and the project. According to this heterogeneous team, the inspection team can be seen as comparable to a SI team applying PBR RTs [10]. In our initial approach domain/discipline experts represent and perspectives and apply their domain/discipline specific expertise.

5   Implementation and Concept Evaluation

This section presents results of a pilot study of a change management process implementation as basis for applying focused inspections.

5.1   Change Management and Signal Merge Process

Based on observations and discussions with our industry partner, we identified the *change management process* as most critical process in the ASE environment [12]. For instance, changes are executed by a defined discipline (e.g., electrical engineer) in a local environment and should be merged with a central engineering database (EDB) that holds the current version of the overall project. The comparison of two different data models, i.e., the common integrated data model (EDB) and the modified version of the local data model (local change by electrical engineers), leads to a *"merge-view"* presenting the differences between these two data model versions. A deviation can be a real change or a candidate defect (inconsistency). This view is the basis for focused inspection where a team of experts inspect these deviations. After completing the inspection process, deviations are accepted (data elements are transferred to the EDB) or rejected (data elements are not transferred into the EDB). In parallel, a notification mechanism informs engineers on the outcome of the inspection process.

5.2   Focused Inspection

The adapted SI process in the ASE domain (see Fig. 1) includes similar roles compared to the SI process [7]. In our evaluation context the inspection team consists of engineers coming from different disciplines, related to ASE project stakeholders, i.e., basic engineering roles (electrical, mechanical, and software engineers) and management roles (systems integrator, project and quality manager).

- *Inspection Planning.* At our industry partner synchronization and inspection processes are planned on a bi-weekly basis. The inspection artifact is the changed engineering plan/data model (e.g., the electrical plan) represented by a signal list provided by the electrical engineer. The inspection team represents different perspectives that focus on different related disciplines, similar to the PBR RT.

- *Systems Overview.* In context of our evaluation example, all team members are familiar with the project, thus a system overview meeting has been skipped.
- *Tool-Supported Difference Checks.* During the change management process a list of deviations (generated during the merge process) represent the main input for the focused inspection approach (see Fig. 2). In our evaluation example we had an overall number of 152 signals in the EDB before starting a new synchronization/inspection process. The merge view showed three new signals, one signal has been changed, and 151 removed signals (see [12] for details). During the inspection process the inspectors can focus on these different categories of changes and can accept or reject them. Notifications will be sent.

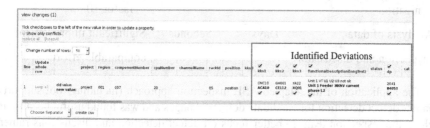

Fig. 2. Focus on changed signals during the merge-process.

- *Defect Correction.* Related individual engineers receive notifications on the acceptance/rejection of the change/defect and can check-out the current and accepted version of the engineering data for his discipline.
- *Follow-up.* Based on synchronization and inspection reports, generated during the notification mechanism, quality and project managers can decide on follow-up actions. At our industry partner no follow-up activities are planned as synchronization and inspection are embedded within the engineering process.

6 Conclusion

In this paper we presented an automation-supported change management process in the ASE domain including an adapted SI approach that supports engineers and managers in ASE environments: (a) efficient synchronization and data exchange based on integrated data and (b) efficient defect detection with focused reviews. Table 1 summarizes results from discussions with our industry partner on the improvements of ASB application after a year of testing and application in selected real-world contexts. In contrast manual synchronization steps, the effort for synchronization and inspection decreases significantly because of automation-supported data merging. We consider a comparable discussion effort (per signal deviation) but significant benefits in preparation and data handling. For instance, in the manual approach experts have to spend effort for identifying the deviation while there is no effort for identifying deviations in the ASB approach. As a consequence the frequency of synchronization increases and the overall project, process, and product quality increases due to defects that can be found early and more efficient in the engineering process.

Table 1. Comparison of manual and ASB synchronization processes.

	Manual	ASB	Change
Individual synchronization effort (without inspection and discussion)	30 min	5 min	Effort improvement (-83 %)
Avg. frequency of synchronization	2/month	20/month	Frequency increased: factor 10
Analysis of data	Days	Seconds	Significant improvement
Inspection and discussion	–	–	comparable effort

The application of the adapted ASE inspection approach (including tool support) enables defect detection for candidate defects/changes and was found useful because it helped the inspection team to better focus on defect detection and discussions rather than focusing on identifying deviations in different engineering plans.

Limitations. The nature of automation systems development projects includes a heterogeneous group of stakeholders (i.e., engineers from different disciplines and with different perspectives). Thus, inspection teams can be seen as group of experts applying different perspectives. However, in the first application of focused inspection in the ASE domain we did not provide any formal guidelines for different reading technique approaches but we rely on the expertise from different experts. Test data, used in the evaluation, represent a small snapshot of a large-scale real-world project. We decided to use this small sample to demonstrate the feasibility of the approach; more detailed evaluation and larger sets of data remain for future work.

Future Work will also focus on (a) providing discipline-specific guidelines and checklist to increase defect detection performance; and (b) in-depth evaluation of different RT approaches in larger industry contexts.

Acknowledgements. This work was supported by the Christian Doppler Forschungs gesellschaft, the Federal Ministry of Economy, Family and Youth, and the National Foundation for Research, Technology and Development, Austria.

References

1. Aurum, A., Petersson, H., Wohlin, C.: State-of-the-Art: software inspection after 25 years. J. Softw. Test. Verification Reliab. **12**(3), 133–154 (2002)

2. Biffl, S.: Inspection Techniques to Support Project and Quality Management, Habilitation, Shaker. ISBN: 3-8265-8512-7 (2001)
3. Biffl, S., Schatten, A., Zoitl, A.: Integration of heterogeneous engineering environments for the automation systems lifecycle. In: Proceedings of the 7th ETFA, pp. 576–581 (2009)
4. Biffl, S., Moser, T., Winkler, D.: Risk assessment in multi-disciplinary (Software+) engineering projects. IJSEKE SI SW Risk Assess. 21(2), 211–236 (2011)
5. Fay, A., Biffl, S., Winkler, D., Drath, R., Barth, M.: A method to evaluate the openness of automation tools for increased interoperability. In: Proceedings of the 39th Annual Conference of the IEEE Industrial Electronics Society (IECON), pp. 6842–6847 (2013)
6. Kovalenko, O., Winkler, D., Kalinowski, M., Serral, E., Biffl, S.: Engineering process improvement in heterogeneous multi-disciplinary environments with defect causal analysis. In: Barafort, B., O'Connor, R.V., Poth, A., Messnarz, R. (eds.) EuroSPI 2014. CCIS, vol. 425, pp. 73–85. Springer, Heidelberg (2014)
7. Laitenberger, O., DeBaud, J.-M.: An encompassing life cycle centric survey of software inspection. J. Syst. Softw. (JSS) 50(1), 5–31 (2000)
8. Moser, T., Mordinyi, R., Winkler, D., Biffl, S.: Engineering project management using the engineering cockpit: a collaboration platform for project managers and engineers. In: Proceedings of the 9th International Conference on Industrial Informatics (INDIN) (2011)
9. Moser, T., Biffl, S., Sunindyo, W.D., Winkler, D.: Integrating production automation expert knowledge across engineering domains. IJDST SI Emerg. Trends Challenges Large-Scale Networking Distrib. Syst. 2(3), 88–103 (2011)
10. Shull, F., Rus, I., Basili, V.: How perspective-based reading can improve requirements inspection. IEEE Comput. 33(7), 73–79 (2002)
11. Thelin, T., Andersson, C., Runeson, P., Dzamashvili-Fogelstrom, M.: A replicated experiment of usage-based and checklist-based reading. In: Proceedings of the 10th International Symposium on Software Metrics, pp. 246–256 (2004)
12. Winkler, D., Biffl, S.: Focused Inspection to Support Defect Detection in Automation Systems Engineering Environments. Technical Report, TU Wien, IFS-CDL 15-02. http://qse.ifs.tuwien.ac.at/publication/IFS-CDL-15-02.pdf. Accessed Sep 2015

A Field Study on the Elicitation
and Classification of Defects for Defect Models

Dominik Holling[(✉)], Daniel Méndez Fernández, and Alexander Pretschner

Technische Universität München, Munich, Germany
{holling,mendezfe,pretschn}@cs.tum.edu

Abstract. Background: Defect models capture faults and methods to provoke failures. To integrate such defect models into existing quality assurance processes, we developed a defect model lifecycle framework, in which the elicitation and classification of context-specific defects forms a crucial step. Although we could gather first insights from its practical application, we still have little knowledge about its benefits and limitations. **Objective:** We aim at qualitatively analyzing the context-specific elicitation and classification of defects to explore the suitability of our approach for practical application. **Method:** We apply case study research in multiple contexts and analyze (1) what kind of defects we can elicit and the degree to which the defects matter to a context only, (2) the extent to which it leads to results useful enough for describing and operationalizing defect models, and (3) if there is a perceived additional immediate benefit from a practitioner's perspective. **Results:** Our results strengthen our confidence on the suitability of our approach to elicit defects that are context-specific as well as context-independent. **Conclusions:** We conclude so far that our approach is suitable to provide a blueprint on how to elicit and classify defects for specific contexts to be used for the improvement of quality assurance techniques.

1 Introduction

Defect models capture faults and methods to provoke failures [1,2] and describe them formally. By operationalization, formal defect models can be used as a basis to create (semi-)automatic defect detection tools. On the one hand, such tools include (semi-)automatic test case generators to detect smells and gather evidence for described faults or execute certain test strategies for methods to provoke failures. On the other hand, they also include checklist generators or reading technique organizers to detect defects in non-executable, and therefore, non-testable artifacts. Since operationalizations directly target the described defects, they support systematic fault-based testing and yield good test cases [1].

In our definition, a *defect* is an umbrella term including all faults, errors, failures, bugs, and mistakes made when designing or implementing a system. Similar to the notion of quality in general, which constitutes a multifaceted topic with different views and interpretations [3,4], defects and especially their relevance, too, are something relative to their context. That is, a defect that might be

© Springer International Publishing Switzerland 2015
P. Abrahamsson et al. (Eds.): PROFES 2015, LNCS 9459, pp. 380–396, 2015.
DOI: 10.1007/978-3-319-26844-6_28

critical to one project might be without relevance to the next. The systematic integration of (domain-specific) defect detection and prevention mechanisms into the quality assurance (QA) of particular socio-economic contexts, e.g. a company or a business unit is therefore crucial.

To integrate defect models into existing quality assurance processes, we developed and previously published a defect model lifecycle framework [5]. This framework can be embedded into established quality improvement lifecycle models and provides a blueprint of steps and artifacts to plan, employ, and control defect models. A planning step comprehends the elicitation and classification of defects (or defect classes respectively) in order to later on describe their defect models formally and operationalize them in an employment step.

The construction of formalized defect models and their operationalization in tools is very expensive. Eliciting and classifying the "relevant" defects for specific contexts is thus crucial for taking the context-specific decision whether to invest this effort. Defect elicitation and classification methods hence needed to be comprehensive and to allow for frequency, and possibly severity, assessments. Based on these assessments, the effectiveness of defect models can be anticipated and the investment decision can be rationalized.

The subject of this paper is our Defect ELIcitation and CLAssification approach (DELICLA). We aim at understanding the effectiveness of DELICLA by means of qualitative methods with particular focus on interviews for the data collection and Grounded Theory for the analysis. One reason for relying on Grounded Theory coding principles is the categorization as well as the possible elaboration of cause-effect relations for defects. Once the defects are identified, they are integrated in a taxonomy: technical or process-related. The qualitative nature makes the approach agnostic to specific contexts/domains while, at the same time, always yielding context-specific results. By relying on an adaptable defect taxonomy, we follow the baseline of Card [6] and Kalinowski et al. [7], who note that it is beneficial to "tailor it to our [...] specific needs".

Problem Statement. Although we had gathered first insights from applying DELICLA in practice, we have yet little knowledge about its appropriateness to (1) elicit and classify defects in specific contexts of different application domains; (2) the extent to which it leads to results useful enough for describing and operationalizing defect models; and (3) if there are immediate additional benefits as perceived by practitioners. These problems are reflected by the research questions in Sect. 4.

Contribution. We contribute a field study where we apply our DELICLA approach to four cases provided by different companies. In each case, we conduct a case study to elicit and classify context-specific defect classes. The goal of our study is to get insights into advantages and limitations of our approach; this knowledge supports us in its further development.

Researchers as well as practitioners can directly apply our approach and the resulting defect taxonomies which include common and recurring defects. In addition to the defect-based perspective, we explicitly provide tacit knowledge about defects useful to organizations in order to advance in organizational learning [8]. By evaluating our approach in different contexts, we lay the foundation for its adoption in research and practice.

2   Related Work

In the classification step of our approach, we provide a basic defect taxonomy/classification. Efforts to create a standardized defect classification for the collection of empirical knowledge have been made in the past [9]. However, there has not yet been a general agreement as defects may be very specific to a context, domain or artifact. This leads to a plethora of taxonomies and classifications techniques in literature and practice. In the area of taxonomies, Beizer [10] provides a well-known example for a taxonomy of defects. Avizienis et al. [11,12] provide a three-dimensional taxonomy based on the type of defect, the affected attribute and the means by which their aim of dependability and security was attained. IEEE standard 1044 provides a basic taxonomy of defects and attributes that should be recorded along with the defects. Orthogonal Defect Classification (ODC) [13] is a defect classification technique using multiple classification dimensions. These dimensions span over cause and effect of a defect enabling the analysis of its root cause. Thus, defect trends and their root causes can be measured in-process. Apart from these general classification approaches, there are approaches specifically targeting non-functional software attributes such as security [14,15] or, based upon ODC, maintenance [16,17]. Leszac et al. [18] even derive their classification aiming to improve multiple attributes (i.e. reliability and maintainability). Our approach, presented next, deliberately chooses to employ a minimalistic/basic defect taxonomy to stay flexible for seamless adaptation to specific contexts and domains. This lightweight taxonomy enables the approach to be in tune with the expectations/prerequisites of our project partners (see RQ3 in Sect. 4). In contrast to ODC, we are not generalizing our taxonomy to be "independent of the specifics of a product or organization" [13], but rather require adaptability to context. In addition, we do not aim to capture the effects of defects (other than the severity where possible) as it is not required for the elicitation and classification of defects for defect models. However, our taxonomy can be mapped to ODC's cause measures by (1) refining the categories of technical and process-related defects into defect types and (2) using the associated tasks of the role of the interview partner as defect trigger. The severity can directly be taken in ODC's effect measures, but other required measures such as impact areas, "reliability growth, defect density, etc." [13] must be elicited in addition.

3   DELICLA: Eliciting and Classifying Defects

A first decision in the design of DELICLA was to use a qualitative approach for defect elicitation and classification. The central aspect of our approach is further its inductive nature where the focus is on generating theories rather than testing given ones. That is, the approach makes no a-priori assumptions about which defects might be relevant in a specific context, yet our hypothesis is that common and recurring defects exist in the context. In addition, we rely on circularity yielding further defects, if the approach is repeatedly used in the same or similar contexts.

There exists a multitude of techniques employable in qualitative explorative approaches with the ability to take a defect-based viewpoint. These established techniques have been explored with respect to three goals: (1) cost-effectiveness in their application, (2) comprehensiveness in the obtained results, and (3) ability to establish a trust relationship during the data collection.

Trust is important because humans generally are reluctant to disclose potential problems in individual project environments [7,19]. The assessed techniques include techniques for document analyses, interview research, participant observation, and creativity techniques such as brainstorming.

Due to their comprehensiveness and the possibility to establish a trust relationship [19,20], personal interviews were chosen as technique in the DELICLA approach. This allows to fully explore the participants' perspectives in their context while adopting their vocabulary. Using this technique in a semi-structured form yields the ability to guide the interview [19] along predefined questions without interrupting their flow of words.

For the analysis of the collected data, we employed Grounded Theory [21] and code the answers as described by Charmaz [22]. In a manual coding step, we code all mentioned defects including their cause and effect. These codes are then organized in a hierarchy representing a defect taxonomy. Following this form of open coding, we apply axial coding to the results to explicitly capture relationships between defects as well as possible causes and effects. In some cases, we apply selective coding to capture possible causalities between defects. Our DELICLA approach consists of the three steps explained next: (1) *Preparation*, (2) *Execution*, and (3) *Analysis*.

Preparation. The first activity in the preparation step is to create a pool of potential interview candidates (i.e. the participants). Candidates are identified with the project partner by focusing on their projects or domains of expertise. The selection of interview candidates is performed by the interviewer or project partner yielding a variation point. In case the interviewer is able to select the candidates, the context of the study (e.g. the projects and teams focused on) and the expenditure of time for the project partner must be exactly defined. Key aspects to consider before selecting any interview partners are the organizational chart and the assessment of their potential contributions by their managers. The order of interviews was from best to least contributing according to the executives' opinions; and lowest to highest branch in the organizational charts [19]. When interviewing the best performing, the interviewer is able to assess the maximum capabilities of team or project members thereby gaining a perspective of what can be achieved. Subsequent to interviewing executives on higher branches, defects collected in lower branches can be discussed and used to devise first indications towards future measures. Thus, even if the project partner selects the

Table 1. Instrument used for the interview preparation sheet.

ID	Question
Q1	What are the classical faults in the software you review/test?
Q2	What does frequently/always go wrong? With which stakeholder?
Q3	What was the "worst" fault you have ever seen? Which one had the "worst" consequences?
Q4	Which faults are the most difficult ones to spot/remove?
Q5	What faults were you unaware of before working in your context?
Q6	What faults do you find most trivial/annoying?
Q7	What faults do engineers new to your area make?

interview partners, the interviewer should be able to get an overview using an organizational chart and set the order of the interview partners.

After the interview partners have been selected, they are informed about the upcoming interview and their required preparation. An interview preparation sheet is given to them detailing the purpose of the interviews and the questions to be prepared. In our studies, we used the open questions seen in Table 1 for preparation similar to those presented by Charmaz [22]. An extension point are additional questions. Depending of the context, questions such as "How meticulously is the SCRUM methodology followed?" may be added. When informing the interview partners, the responsibles on the project partner's side must also be named for potential inquiries of interview partners about internal procedures. Interviews are not part of the everyday working life of the interview partners and may cause feelings of nervousness to anxiousness. To mitigate these feelings, the description of the purpose of the interviews is very detailed and emphasizes the defect-based view on tools, processes and people in defect models for quality assurance.

Each interview requires 30 min for the preparation by the interview partner and 30 min for the actual interview; usually a negligible amount of time. This lets interview partners prepare so that they "can be prepared to speak directly to the issues of interest" [19]. When planning the concrete times for the interviews, every two interviews include a 30 min break at the end. In case any interview takes more time than expected, this break is used to prevent the accumulation of delay for the following interviews.

The interviewer must also prepare w.r.t. the processes and tools employed by the interview partners and their roles at the project partner. To establish the trust relationship, an address of reassurance is prepared to be given before the interview. In addition, the room is small and any distractions are removed. All technology used during the interviews is tested beforehand and interviews are recorded as suggested by Warren [19].

Execution. With trust and comprehensiveness of results our main objectives, we follow the basic principles of interview research: At the beginning of the interview, the interview partner and interviewer agree on a first name basis. This basis takes down psychological walls and is a key enabler of an open discussion later in the interview. When sitting down, the interviewer never faces the interview partner as it creates the sense of an interrogation [19]. The interview starts with a short introduction consisting of a description of the survey, its goals and the reasons for personal interviews. This introduction aims to mitigate any fears and allows the interview partners to get used to the interview situation. The interviewer can display knowledge and emotional intelligence at this point by stating that elicited defects will be used rather than judged for example. At the end of the introduction the way of documenting the interview results is agreed upon. There, a trade-off might be necessary between recording the interview results and manually documenting them; we experienced recordings to threaten the validity by potentially influencing the behavior of the participants while manual documentation might be prone to bias. In any case, the anonymity of the analysis is guaranteed before the interview.

Following the introduction is the description of the context by the interview partners. This includes the tasks, activities and processes they are involved in. This part of the interview is individual and helps the interviewer later in the classification of the discussed defects. Questions such as "What are your inputs and outputs?" help the interview partners to express their role, constraints, tasks and results toward the interviewer. The semi-structured approach of the interview helps the interviewer in this part as it allows for inquiries by the interviewers in case of unfamiliar terms and concepts. This part is not described on the questionnaire as interview partners are typically able to elaborate their work context. This also helps them to get into a flow of words as "at a basic level, people like to talk about themselves" [19].

The core part of the interview is the discussion of defects including their description, frequency and severity. Also the resulting failures and possible detection and/or prevention techniques are discussed. Again, this part is individual, but is guided by the questions on the interview preparation sheet. This guidance exploits the order in the heads of the interview partners as they likely prepared the questions in the order they were on the preparation sheet. At the end of the interview, an agreement of future contact has to be reached.

In general, it is the interviewer's job to keep up an objective atmosphere and tone. It is hard for humans to admit defects and discuss them, but it is in fact the decisive point of the presented approach. Thus, the interviewer must cater to the interview partner using emotional intelligence. Additionally, "whatever the training and intentions of the interviewer, the social interaction of the qualitative interview may unfold in unexpected ways" [19].

Analysis. The analysis of the interviews is used for the classifications of the collected defects. Defects interesting for the description and operationalization of defect models are common and recurring defects and defects with a high severity. To perform the classification and go from defects to defect classes, the first step of Grounded Theory [21] is employed. In that step, the recordings are coded in chronological order whereas the codes are iteratively abstracted to categories eventually leading to a basic defect taxonomy. Codes may also include contexts, roles and distinctions of the employed quality assurance process. This helps the interviewer to capture "what is happening in the data" [19]. After coding, all excerpts of the recordings are grouped by code and reheard to focus on one particular defect and its context, origination and consequences.

In the classification, the basic taxonomy of defects contains two basic families of defects: technical and process-related defects. Process-related defects concern all methodological, organizational and process aspects (as defined by the defect causal analysis [23]) and contain defects causing technical defects. Technical defects are directly attributable to the product and are detectable by measures of quality assurance. These two families of defects yield extension points. An exemplary extension could be tool-related defects or defects rooted in the behavior of humans. These can be added dynamically and defects may belong to multiple classes depending on the context. Recall that, we deliberately chose to "tailor [the taxonomy] to our [...] specific needs" [6, 7] to stay flexible for seamless adaptation to specific contexts and domains w.r.t. the creation of defect models.

After the analysis, we created a report summarizing the results to the project partners and used it as basis for discussion in a concluding workshop. In this workshop, we presented the results and the discussion yielded a last validation of the results w.r.t. the expectations of the project partners. Afterwards, eligible defects for the creation and operationalization of defect models were discussed and selected constituting a last contact with the project partners to potentially initiate the development of tools based on the defect models.

4   Field Study Design

We conducted our field study by relying in total on four cases. In each case, we follow the same study design. In the following, we report on the design which we organize according to Runeson et al. [24].

4.1   Research Questions

The goal is to investigate the advantages and limitations in the elicitation and classification of defects for defect models using our DELICLA approach described in Sect. 3. To this end, we formulate three research questions.

RQ 1 (Suitability): What (kind of) defects can be elicited with the approach; what is the degree of sensitivity to their context; and how comprehensive is the approach?

The core idea behind the approach is to elicit and classify common and recurring/severe defects independent of the context it is used in while preserving the context-dependent usefulness to adapt QA techniques to those defects. Hence, our first research question targets the adaptability of the approach to different employment contexts and its ability to always elicit and classify defects relevant to quality assurance independent of context. In particular, it should not be affected by changes of domains (information and cyber-physical), test/quality assurance levels (review, inspection, unit, integration and system test) and project partner. Finally, we rate a defect as context-independent if we find a relation to existing evidence in a given baseline. This means, if we find a study that indicates to the same defect in a different context, we may assume that the defect is context independent.

RQ 2 (Operationalizability): Can the results of the approach be used for the description and operationalization of defect models?

The classification and elicitation of defects for defect models aims at their later description and operationalization. Thus, the results of the approach must yield a basis for decision-making to make the effort to describe and operationalize the respective defect models and yield starting points for their description and operationalization. This research question therefore aims at analyzing whether the basis of decision-making and starting points are retrievable by the approach, thereby manifesting a direct usefulness to project partners. We do not have a clear oracle to answer this question. To answer the research question, we will therefore point to indicators for successful description and operationalization of defect models based on our approach.

RQ 3 (Indirect Short-Term Benefit): Besides potential defect models and their operationalization, how valuable are our results to the project partners?

When our approach has been applied, project partners are given a final report to inform them about the results. This report contains all elicited and classified defects as well as possible proposals for action. In addition to the value for defect models. This research question targets the usefulness of the report in the eyes of those project partners considering the time invested on the project partner's side, thereby manifesting the indirect benefit of the approach. Again, we do not have an oracle. However, the quality of the results w.r.t. sufficiency and the cost-effectiveness can be rated by the project partners based on subjective expert judgement and feedback gathered during a concluding workshop.

4.2 Case and Subject Selection

We apply our process for the elicitation and classification of defect models to four software development projects of different industry project partners. We do not change our process throughout the field study to gain comparable results, although this affects internal validity. The four projects were chosen on an opportunistic basis. As we required real-world development projects and project managers/members to agree, the process was performed when possible. However, the chosen cases are suitable to answer our research questions if the selected projects are distributed across different companies working in different application domains.

4.3 Data Collection and Analysis Procedures

To collect and analyze the data, we use our DELICLA approach for the elicitation and classification of defects as described in Sect. 3.

To answer *RQ 1*, we list the top 14 defects (i.e. all defects mentioned in at least two interviews within the same context) we elicited and classified and evaluate their commonality in contrast with their context sensitivity. That is, for each defect, we analyze whether it is context-dependent or context-independent if we find a relation to existing evidence. As a baseline, we use the defects reported by Kalinowski et al. [7] and Leszak et al. [18].

We also quantify the number of defects elicited and give an assessment as to if the interviews allow for a comprehensive defect-based perspective on projects or organizations. There is no clear agreement on a sufficient number of interviews in general, but indicators toward sufficient numbers may be given [25]. For our cases, we agree on the sufficiency of the number of interviews when we observe a saturation in the answers given, i.e. when no new defects arise. Saturation is taken as a sign of comprehensiveness.

To answer *RQ 2*, we list indicators of tools and methods created from defects classified and elicited with our approach. These tools and methods may not have a fully formulated formal defect model description, but are able to demonstrate whether (and how) results may be operationalized.

To answer *RQ 3*, we describe indicators of the quality of the results and the involved costs by gathering expert feedback from project partners after performing our approach. This feedback is a direct external grading of our approach by industry experts and yields an assessment of its cost-effectiveness.

5   Case Study Results

We performed the case study in four different industry projects (settings) with different industry partners. For reasons of non-disclosure agreements, we cannot give detailed information on project-specifics and the particularities of context-specific defects. However, we can state their domain, the number of interviews conducted and the classes of defects.

The top 14 defects independent of their setting are shown in Table 2. The settings and their respectively elicited and classified defects are shown in Fig. 1. They are grouped by our basic taxonomy defined in Sect. 3 into technical (Fig. 1a) and process-related defects (Fig. 1b) and ordered each according to their context-sensitivity. Interestingly, we have found existing evidence for defects identified as context dependent as the existing evidence provided an extensive, and thereby, fitting defect description.

5.1   Case Description

Setting A is a medium size cyber-physical software supplier. 24 subjects were interviewed with the aim to draw a organization-wide picture of common and recurring (mentioned in at least 2 interviews) defects. These systems primarily targeted the automotive domain, but also were in the domain of aerospace, railway and medical. The predominant development process was the V-model.

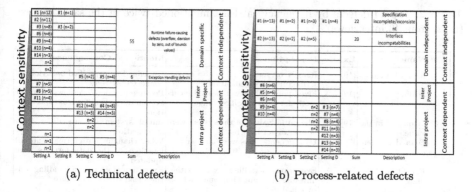

(a) Technical defects   (b) Process-related defects

Fig. 1. Defects with applicable ID (#, if number in top 14) and frequency (n) in the classification by setting, domain and context specificity

Setting B is a department of a large German car manufacturer. 3 subjects were interviewed to try out the approach and enable a first glance at a defect-based perspective in this department using the V-model as development process. Note that, this low number of interviews is discusses in threats to validity.

Setting C is a project of medium size in an information system developing company. 6 subjects were interviewed to give the company an introduction to the approach. The interviews were performed in a large scale website front end project developed using the SCRUM methodology.

Setting D was an information system project of a railway company. 10 subjects were interviewed to show process deficiencies and give a defect-based perspective on currently employed development and quality assurance measures. The project was a graphical rail monitoring application project developed using the SCRUM methodology.

5.2 Subject Description

As described in the subject selection, we chose our project partners and projects in an opportunistic manner. All interview participants had an engineering or computer science background and at least one year of experience. The first author applied the approach in the case studies.

In setting A, the majority of participants had a background in mechanical or electrical engineering and developed system using Matlab Simulink with either automatic code generation or using Matlab Simulink models as specification for their manually implemented systems.

In setting B, the interview partners were developing and/or testing the functional software for an electronic control unit developed in C++ and integrated into AUTOSAR.

In setting C, the interview partners included a broad selection of roles including architects, developers, testers, test managers, and scrum masters.

Table 2. Top 14 defects by frequency (at least mentioned twice in the same context (n>2) from 43 interviews)

	#	Name	Ex. Ev.	Description	Mentioned Consequences
Top 15 Technical Defects	1	Signal Range	[19]	Ranges of signals were not as described in the specification	Undefined / unspecified behaviour of connected systems
	2	Scaling	[19]	Fixed-point values were scaled incorrectly for their specified range	Possible under-/overflows and/or system outputs differ from specification
	3	Wrong initial value	[19]	The initial values of the system were not set or set incorrectly	Initial system outputs differ from specification
	4	Data dependencies	[7] [19]	Data dependencies were unclear	When changing data formats, not all locations of the data formats were updated
	5	Exception Handling	[19]	Exception handling was either untested or not implemented as specified	Execution of exception handling routines lead to system failure
	6	Dead code due to safeguards	[19]	Dead superfluous safeguards were implemented	Degraded system performance and/or real-time requirements not met
	7	Linkage of Components	[19]	Interfaces of components were not connected as specified	System outputs differ from specification
	8	Variable re-use	[19]	Mandatory re-use of variables and developers assumed incorrect current values	System outputs differ from specification
	9	Different base	[19]	Calculations switched base (10 to 2 and vice versa)	System outputs differ from specification
	10	State chart defects	[19]	Defects related state charts	System outputs differ from specification
	11	Transposed characters	[19]	Characters in user interfaces and framework configurations were transposed	Mapping of code to user interface does not work
	12	Web browser incompatibilities		Web browsers had different interpretations of JavaScript and HTML	Browser-dependent rendering of web pages
	13	Validation of input		Inputs were either not or not validated according to specification	Ability to input arbitrary or malicious data
	14	Concurrency		Concurrency measures were not used as specified	Deadlocks and atomicity violations
Top 14 Process-related Defects	1	Specification incomplete/inconsistent	[7] [19]	The specification was either inconsistent, lacking information or inexistent	Thorough verification of implementation impossible and testing deferred
	2	Interface incompatibilities	[19]	Agreed interfaces of components were not designed as discussed / specified	Rework for interfaces required after deadline for implementation
	3	Missing domain knowledge	[7]	Engineers lacked the concrete domain knowledge to implement a requirement	Delivery delayed and project time exceeded
	4	Cloning		Engineers used cloning as a way to add functionality to systems	Cloned parts provide functionality not required by the system in development
	5	Static Analysis runtime	[19]	Static analysis of the implementation was started too late in the process	Delivery delayed and project time exceeded
	6	Quality assurance deemed unnecessary		Engineers did not see the necessity for quality assurance	Review / Testing not performed according to specified process
	7	Late involvement of users	[19]	Users were involved late or not at all in a SCRUM-based process	Requirements not according to user problem statement
	8	Misestimating of costs	[19]	Inability to estimate cost for requirements in a SCRUM-based process	Delivery delayed and project time exceeded
	9	Call order dependencies	[19]	Call orders were switched without informing engineers	Extra testing effort required with difficult fault localization
	10	Misunderstood instructions		New engineers did not understand given documentation	Delivery delayed and project time exceeded
	11	Distributed development	[19]	Development and test team were at different locations	Communication deficiencies yielded untested components with runtime failures
	12	Insufficient test environment	[19]	The test environment did not contain all components to be tested	Some defects could only be detected in production environment
	13	Development by single person		A single person was developing a large part of the system	Incomprehensible implementation of components
	14	Overloaded employees		Engineers were overwhelmed with the amount of work requested from them	Careless misateks due to stress

In setting D, the interview partners were from several different teams defined in SCRUM to also gain a comprehensive view on synergy effects and defects missed by their managers.

RQ 1: Suitability. In all studies performed, the results always yielded technical and process-related defects. The top 14 defects of each category are shown in Table 2. For each defect, we additionally show whether we could find a relation to existing evidence (see column 4 in Table 2). Figure 1 further illustrates each defect (via its identifier provided in Table 2) in relation to its degree of sensitivity to the context. Remember from the introduction that "context" here refers to a specific company or business unit of a company.

In setting A, the interviews revealed 15 technical and 7 process-related defects. The technical defects were mainly run-time failures such as overflow due to the abstraction from the underlying computational model in Matlab Simulink. These failures were caused by wrong signal ranges of units, wrong scaling of fixed-point types and wrong initial values. The process-related defects were interface incompatibilities and incomplete/incorrect specifications. We performed 24 interviews in total. However, the top most common and recurring faults were named in 12, 11 and 8 interviews respectively. Since this was a cross-project company wide survey, the diversity of developers and testers interviewed introduced differences in the defects common and recurring in their respective fields. Baker and Edwards [25] hint at 12 interviews to be sufficient. In our setting, saturation was indeed achieved with even fewer interviews; the revealed common and recurring defects can be assumed to be comprehensive.

In setting B, the interviews revealed 3 technical and 1 process-related defect. The technical defects were related to initial values in C++ (2) and overflows (1). The process-related defect were due to interfaces (2) and incomplete specifications (2). Contrary to all other settings, this setting was only to give a first glance as described in the case description. Thus, comprehensiveness was intentionally neglected, but to provide a first glance 3 interviews were sufficient.

In setting C, the interviews revealed 5 technical defects and 6 process-related defects. The technical defects were related to web browser incompatibilities (4), validation of input data (3) and exception handling (2). The most prominent process-related defects were incomplete specification (5) and interface incompatibilities (3). With only 6 interviews, we did not perform a sufficient number of interviews per se. However, the project's size was only 10 persons and effects of saturation were quickly observable. This saturation yields an indication towards comprehensiveness, albeit inconclusive.

In setting D, the interviews revealed 3 technical defects and 7 process-related defects. The top technical defects were related to data dependencies (8), exception handling (4), concurrency (3). The prominent process-related defects were incomplete specifications (7), interface incompatibilities (4) and late involvement of the customers (4). Again, 10 interviews are below the sufficiency baseline, but the project's size was only 18 persons. Once again, saturation yields an indication towards comprehensiveness, albeit inconclusive.

392 D. Holling et al.

Although the aim of the DELICLA approach was only to elicit and classify technical defects, process-related defects were mentioned by interview partners and were classified as well. Many interview partners stated process-related defects as causes for technical defects, yielding a causal relation between some defects. For instance, in the cyber-physical settings, the inconsistent/incomplete specification was described to lead to incorrect signal ranges and wrong initial values. In the information system domain, the format of user stories as use cases without exceptions was described to lead to untested/incorrect exception handling. We did not believe in advance these causalities or process-related defects to be important at first. However, we later realized their potential for deciding whether to (1) employ defect models for quality assurance to detect or (2) make organizational, methodological or process adjustments to prevent these defects. Many project partners were intrigued about the causalities and estimated the effort to change their processes lower than to employ defect models for some technical defect. In particular, since process improvement by using elicited defects has been described in literature [7,23].

An interesting observation was the presence of domain independent defects of technical as well as process-related nature (see Fig. 1). Domain independent technical defects were run time failure causing defects in embedded systems in setting A and B as well as untested exception handling defects in information systems in settings C and D. Moreover, interface incompatibilities and incomplete/inconsistent specifications/requirements were process-related defects present in all settings.

We therefore conclude so far that our approach is suitable to elicit a broad spectrum of defects which cover the particularities of the envisioned context as well as context-independent defects.

RQ 2: Operationalizability. In all settings, we were able to derive possible solution proposals for handling each elicited and classified defect. These solution proposals do not necessarily include formal descriptions of defect models, but rather are indicators for operationalization possibilities. However, we or our project partners were able to design tools or methods that have an underlying defect model, and in some cases described next, we were able to operationalize the defects via tools.

Setting A resulted in a testing tool called 8CAGE [26]. 8Cage is a lightweight testing tool for Matlab Simulink systems based on defect models. The employed defect models target overflow/underflow, division by zero run time failures as well as signal range and scaling problems.

Setting B yielded an internal testing tool for the testing of the interfaces of the software to the AUTOSAR Runtime Environment (RTE) developed by the project partner. Due to frequent changes in the communication between each electronic control unit, the RTE had to be recreated for each change. Sometimes changes were not implemented leading to unusual failure message and large efforts spent in fault localizations. The internal testing tool can now be run to show these unimplemented changes automatically.

Settings C and D did not result in any tools as of now. However, they yielded requirements to specifically test exception handling functionality in Java systems. The task of the tool is to explicitly throw exceptions at applicable points in the code as to deliberately test the developed exception handling. We currently have collected these requirements and tool development is imminent. In addition, quality standards for SCRUM user story standards as a method of early defect detection have been proposed and partially implemented in setting C and B. These methods include perspective-based reading [27] of user stories before accepting them and explicit definitions of acceptance criteria including a specification for exception handling.

Overall, the tools and methods developed enable front-loading of quality assurance activities. This allows developers and testers to focus on common and recurring defects in specification and implementation and either makes them aware of the defects or allows the (semi-)automatic detection. Thus, the defect-based perspective may be able to increase the potential to avoid these defects in the future.

We therefore conclude so far that we could elicit defects suitable for operationalization in the chosen context.

RQ 3: Indirect Short-Term Benefit. After presenting the results in the workshop meeting of DELICLA, we asked the responsibles to assess the usefulness of our approach in terms of (1) being aware of the elicited and classified defects, (2) future actions based on the report, and (3) cost-effectiveness.

In setting A, the responsibles deemed the results satisfying. The defects were mostly known to them, but they were content to have written results in hand for justification towards their management. Using the results, they could convince their management and customers to invest into consulting regarding specific defects. The efficiency of only one hour per interview while leading to sufficiently comprehensive results was perceived positively. They agreed to perform further interviews in the future. However, they remarked that our approach did not reveal many defects previously unknown to them, but were now able to gain an essential understanding of their frequency. They also commented on the difficulty to select distinct projects for the proposed measures in this inter-project setting.

In setting B, the project responsibles only gave us a limited feedback. They stated all defects to be known and saw the advantage in now having a thorough documentation. We did not create defect models or develop operationalizations for them after applying the approach. However, they developed a tool without our involvement based on one reported defect.

In setting C, the project responsibles were surprised how non-intruding and conciliatory our approach is and how professionally it can be handled. They were aware of most of the defects, but not that 20 % of their test cases were already defect-based. The project was already in a late stage when we applied the approach and future actions could not be taken due to the time left. They also perceived the efficiency of one hour per interview partner as positive and described the comprehensiveness of results as given. When discussing further interviews, they questioned the application towards a whole organization as measure to find organization-wide defects with a small number of interviews.

In setting D, the project responsibles were aware of most defects elicited and classified and satisfied with the application of the approach in general. They said the approach "yields good results with little effort" and it provides "a view" on the defects in the project from "a different side". In addition, they stated that "nothing is missing [from the results] and [results are] diagnostically conclusive". Concerning the possible solution approaches presented, they "may not be the way to go", but "give a first idea for discussion in project meetings". Again, further interviews were discussed, but the time required to interview the complete project with more than 50 employees was deemed to much. The project partner rather wanted to use other techniques such as observation or focus groups to minimize time required on their side. However, qualitative interviews were deemed "a good starting point".

5.3   Threats to Validity

There is a plethora of threats to the validity, let alone those inherent to case study research. To start with, the qualitative nature of the approach as well as the qualitative nature of the evaluation technique rely to a large extent on subjective expert judgment. First and foremost, the approach was applied by the same person evaluating it. The *internal validity* is particularly threatened by the subjectivity in the interviews and especially in their interpretation. Coding used to classify the defects, for example, is an inherently creative task. However, our aim was to explore the potential of such qualitative methods, to reveal subjective opinions by the study participants, and to elaborate – despite the inherent threats – the suitability of the chosen approach.

The *construct validity* is threatened in two ways. First, the research questions were answered via qualitative methods only and we cannot guarantee that we could fully answer the questions based on our data. We compensated the threat, especially for research question 1, by taking an external baseline as an orientation. Second, we cannot guarantee that we have a sufficient number of interviews to reliably decide on the completeness of the data to elaborate comprehensive defects. We compensated this threat by applying the principles of Grounded Theory where we explicitly considered a saturation of the answers if no new codes arose. Also, we believe the number of interviews to be less important than the coverage of roles within (different) teams and superordinate roles. This is hinted at by setting B, C and D in particular.

Finally, the *external validity* is threatened by the nature of the approach and the evaluation as well. Our intention was, however, not to generalize from our findings but to evaluate the extent to which our approach is suitable to cover the particularities of contexts whereby the results hold specifically for those contexts. Yet, by comparing the results with an external baseline, we could determine context-independent defects which potential for generalization.

6   Conclusion

We have evaluated our DELICLA approach to elicit and classify defects for their eventual description and operationalization as defect models. DELICLA is entirely based on existing elicitation and analysis approaches [19]. Our approach uses a qualitative explorative method with personal interviews as elicitation and grounded theory as classification technique. We have evaluated the approach in a field study with four different companies. The chosen settings varied in their domains. Using our approach, we were able to elicit and classify defects having both a context-dependent and -independent relevance while providing indicators to the extent to which they relate to existing evidence. The approach was applicable in different contexts/domains due to the employment of qualitative approaches. We could use the elaborated defects to derive requirements for their (semi-)automatic detection by tools and create possible solution proposals in all settings. The feedback given to us by project partner executives was positive yielding "informative results with little effort". Thus, the results strengthen our confidence that the studies are representative and the approach is suitable to elicit context-specific defects without being too specific for a context. However, we are lacking a study with negative results.

Using DELICLA, we have gained an insight of existing defects in different contexts and domains. For some defects, we have built and operationalized respective fault models. Moreover, for some defects we were able to find cause effect relationships to other defects. This yields the question about the ability of the method to extensively find cause effect relationships for all defects. To answer this question, further work and maybe a higher level portrayal of defects as provided by the methodology of Kalinowski et al. [7] is required.

References

1. Pretschner, A., Holling, D., Eschbach, R., Gemmar, M.: A generic fault model for quality assurance. In: Proceedings of the MODELS, pp. 87–103 (2013)
2. Pretschner, A.: Defect-based testing. In: Dependable Software Systems Engineering. IOS Press (2015). (to appear)
3. Garvin, D.: What does product quality really mean? MIT Sloan Manage. Rev. **26**(1), 25–43 (1984)
4. Kitchenham, B., Pfleeger, S.: Software quality: the elusive target. IEEE Softw. **13**(1), 12–21 (1996)
5. Holling, D.: A fault model framework for quality assurance. In: International Conference on Software Testing, Verification and Validation (2014)
6. Card, D.N.: Defect analysis: basic techniques for management and learning. In: Advances in Computers (2005)
7. Kalinowski, M., Mendes, E., Card, D.N., Travassos, G.H.: Applying DPPI: a defect causal analysis approach using bayesian networks. In: Ali Babar, M., Vierimaa, M., Oivo, M. (eds.) PROFES 2010. LNCS, vol. 6156, pp. 92–106. Springer, Heidelberg (2010)
8. Schneider, K.: Experience and Knowledge Management in Software Engineering, 1st edn. Springer Publishing Company, Incorporated, Heidelberg (2009)

9. Wagner, S.: Defect classification and defect types revisited. In: Defects in Large Software Systems. ACM (2008)

10. Beizer, B.: Software Testing Techniques, 2nd edn. Van Nostrand Reinhold Co., New York (1990)

11. Avizienis, A., Laprie, J.C., Randell, B., Landwehr, C.: Basic concepts and taxonomy of dependable and secure computing. IEEE Trans. Dependable Secur. Comput. 1, 11–35 (2004)

12. Avižienis, A., Laprie, J.C., Randell, B.: Dependability and its threats: a taxonomy. In: Jacquart, R. (ed.) Building the Information Society. IFIP, vol. 156, pp. 91–120. Springer, Heidelberg (2004)

13. Chillarege, R., Bhandari, I.S., Chaar, J.K., Halliday, M.J., Moebus, D.S., Ray, B.K., Wong, M.Y.: Orthogonal defect classification-a concept for in-process measurements. IEEE Trans. SE 18, 943–956 (1992)

14. Aslam, T., Krsul, I., Spafford, E.H.: Use of a taxonomy of security faults. In: NIST-NCSC, pp. 551–560, July 1996

15. Landwehr, C.E., Bull, A.R., Mcdermott, J.P., Choi, W.S.: A taxonomy of computer program security flaws. ACM Comput. Surv. 26, 211–254 (1994)

16. Ma, L., Tian, J.: Analyzing errors and referral pairs to characterize common problems and improve web reliability. In: ICWE (2003)

17. Ma, L., Tian, J.: Web error classification and analysis for reliability improvement. J. Syst. Softw. 80, 795–804 (2007)

18. Leszak, M., Perry, D.E., Stoll, D.: Classification and evaluation of defects in a project retrospective. J. Syst. Softw. 61, 173–187 (2002)

19. Gubrium, J., Holstein, J.: Handbook of Interview Research: Context and Method. SAGE Publications, Thousand Oaks (2001)

20. Hove, S., Anda, B.: Experiences from conducting semi-structured interviews in empirical software engineering research. In: Software Metrics, September 2005

21. Glaser, B., Strauss, A.: The Discovery of Grounded Theory: Strategies for Qualitative Research. Aldine Publishing Company, Chicago (1967)

22. Charmaz, K.: Constructing Grounded Theory: A Practical Guide Through Qualitative Analysis. Sage, Los Angeles (2006)

23. Kalinowski, M., Travassos, G.H., Card, D.N.: Towards a defect prevention based process improvement approach. In: SE&AA (2008)

24. Runeson, P., Höst, M.: Guidelines for conducting and reporting case study research in software engineering. EMSE 14, 131–164 (2009)

25. Baker, S., Edwards, R.: How many qualitative interviews is enough? March 2012

26. Holling, D., Pretschner, A., Gemmar, M.: 8cage: lightweight fault-based test generation for simulink. ASE 2014, 859–862 (2014)

27. Shull, F., Rus, I., Basili, V.: How perspective-based reading can improve requirements inspections. Computer 33, 73–79 (2000)

Workshop on Processes, Methods and Tools for Engineering Embedded Systems

Performance Engineering for Industrial Embedded Data-Processing Systems

Martijn Hendriks[1]([✉]), Jacques Verriet[1], Twan Basten[1,3], Marco Brassé[2],
Reinier Dankers[2], René Laan[2], Alexander Lint[2], Hristina Moneva[1],
Lou Somers[2,3], and Marc Willekens[1]

[1] Embedded Systems Innovation by TNO, Eindhoven, The Netherlands
martijn.hendriks@tno.nl
[2] Océ Technologies B.V., Venlo, The Netherlands
[3] Eindhoven University of Technology, Eindhoven, The Netherlands

Abstract. Performance is a key aspect of many embedded systems, embedded data processing systems in particular. System performance can typically only be measured in the later stages of system development. To avoid expensive re-work in the final stages of development, it is essential to have accurate performance estimations in the early stages. For this purpose, we present a model-based approach to performance engineering that is integrated with the well-known V-model for system development. Our approach emphasizes model accuracy and is demonstrated using five embedded data-processing cases from the digital printing domain. We show how lightweight models can be used in the early stages of system development to estimate the influence of design changes on system performance.

1 Introduction

Performance metrics such as throughput and latency are key to many (embedded) systems. Typically, however, system-level performance tests only are available late in the development process, because they require an assembled system. It is well known that late changes are more expensive to make than earlier changes [21]. Therefore, if these tests show problems, then repairing these is expensive, if possible at all without major re-design. Having early insight in system-level performance metrics therefore is beneficial: it can decrease time-to-market, reduce development cost and improve quality of the product.

Architectural models such as the 4+1 architectural view model [12] and the CAFCR model [14] usually include performance engineering activities in order to obtain early insight in system-level performance. Nevertheless, these activities are not always done in practice. A recent study [15] identifies a number of major current problems in the wider scope of model-driven engineering. These also apply to model-based performance engineering and include the following issues:

This work is partially supported by the ITEA2 project 11013 PROMES.

P. Abrahamsson et al. (Eds.): PROFES 2015, LNCS 9459, pp. 399–414, 2015.
DOI: 10.1007/978-3-319-26844-6_29

(i) limited tool usability, (ii) inconsistencies between artifacts (e.g., between model and realization), (iii) lack of fundamentals/body of knowledge, (iv) lack of industrial evidence of benefits. Not explicitly mentioned in [15] and more specific for performance engineering is (v) the difficulty of building *sufficiently accurate* predictive models. This often is an implicit but important assumption, because non-accurate models can turn model-based performance engineering into a hazard instead of a benefit. Issues (i), (ii), (iii) and (v) are obstructions that increase the cost of performance engineering, and issue (iv) directly addresses the lack of evidence that performance engineering is beneficial. Our interpretation of this is that in practice it is often felt that the difficulties and cost of applying performance engineering outweigh the potential benefits: there is no business case. Making a business case for performance engineering such as described, e.g., in [22] is hard, because it is very difficult to quantify both the tangible and the non-tangible benefits without extensive empirical studies. Our work tries to solidify the business case in the particular domain of embedded data-processing systems by a description of how we have applied a process, techniques and tools to five industrial cases, and by a discussion of the costs and benefits.

Contribution. The paper has two contributions. Firstly, we couple a model-based performance engineering process to the well-known V-model development process [9]. We address model consistency (issue (ii)) and accuracy (issue (v)) by explicit calibration and validation steps, and by assuming evolutionary development. The performance engineering process allows arbitrary modeling tools, and is not part of the critical path in the development process; it can be applied when deemed necessary. There is much work on performance engineering, see, e.g., the survey [3]. Although the process, calibration, and validation ingredients are described by others as well, see, e.g., [16,18–20], we believe that our description makes an extra step in bringing these ingredients together in the full engineering scope. Secondly, we present how we have used two well-established techniques (discrete-event simulation and regression analysis) with the earlier described process in five industrial cases. The techniques and tools have been selected because they are relatively easy to use (issue (i)). The ideas in these cases add to the body of knowledge (issue (iii)), and their results to the evidence of the benefits of model-based performance engineering (issue (iv)).

Outline. We describe the process that we use in Sect. 2. Section 3 describes the techniques and tools that we have applied in the cases, which are consequently described in Sect. 4. Finally, Sect. 5 concludes.

2   Performance Models and the Development Process

Figure 1 shows a view which generalizes our way of working in several industrial cases (see Sect. 4). It relates the performance engineering process to the regular V-model development process [9]. The precondition of this hybrid process is that there is an existing system that is being evolved with a V-model iteration. The definition of existing system and iteration can be very broad. We distinguish the following steps:

1. Requirements analysis for a new system Y, the successor of an existing system X, leads to a number of performance-related questions. For instance, system Y might be required to have a higher throughput than X. A typical question then is how much the bottleneck components must be improved in order to achieve the new requirements.
2. An initial model of system X is built based on the initial questions.
3. The model of system X is calibrated and validated with respect to the requirements: we *predict the past*. This is a key step as it builds a certain degree of trust in the model and its predictions.
4. The envisioned changes of system Y compared to system X are incorporated in the calibrated and validated model. This step gives a predictive model, or a set of models (one for each design alternative), for system Y.
5. We use model analysis to explore the design alternatives: we *explore the future*[1]. The analysis results are input for the architecture and design steps.
6. After system Y has been realized, the predictive models can be validated against the actual realization. This retrospective validation builds experience, and allows us to reconcile the model with reality. This completes the iteration and brings us in the position where we might be able to re-use the models for a new V-model iteration.

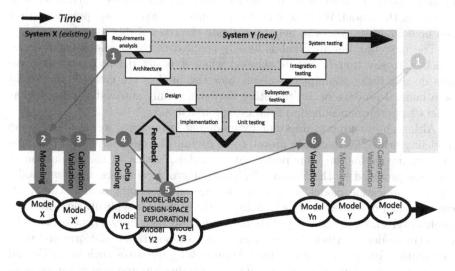

Fig. 1. Performance models in an iterative V-model development process.

The value of predictive models is mainly determined by their accuracy, and reasonably accurate models are a necessary precondition for model-based performance engineering. The sketched approach assumes a rather gradual development process with relatively small iterative steps. This enables us to take

---

[1] The phrase "predict the past, explore the future" originates from [16].

advantage of the existing system: calibration and validation on the existing system builds trust in the modeling approach and gives an indication of the accuracy of the models. Predictions in step 5, however, come from unvalidated models (due to changes introduced in step 4), and therefore always have an unknown accuracy. The development-validation-gap thus bears the risk of significantly wrong model predictions. We distinguish two cases to discuss this problem based on the *cost-to-validation*, which is the cost of the development process that is needed after step 5 to enable step 6. Firstly, we can have the situation with a small cost-to-validation, i.e., the model predictions of step 5 can relatively easily be validated. An example is the optimization of software parameters such as buffer sizes by model-based analysis. Insufficiently accurate model predictions only waste some time in this case, and the validation results can be used for additional calibration. The authors of [4] identify easy validation as one of the success factors of their model of the paper path inside a printer that nowadays is used by industry. Secondly, we can have the situation in which validation of the model prediction can be done only after further development steps (e.g., after several weeks of development and integration), or is not possible at all (e.g., when model predictions lead to the choice to *not* follow a certain design). Insufficiently accurate model predictions can then lead to significant waste of time and engineering resources or a suboptimal design. Thus, using model predictions in the situation with a non-negligible cost-to-validation implies a certain amount of trust in the model. We believe that experience and a set of best practices (that can be domain-specific) can help to mitigate the risks of this situation.

The modeling line in Fig. 1 is loosely coupled to the development process, which is to say that it can be skipped when it is not deemed necessary. We also do not make assumptions about how the models are created; this could be a manual process, or, on the other extreme, a fully automated process that generates performance models from design artifacts.

Although our process does not fix modeling formalisms, we do follow some modeling principles that have proved to be useful. The most important principle that we use in building our performance models, is that of the separation of concerns provided by the Y-chart [2]. This pattern decomposes a system model into an application model, a platform model, and a mapping model. The application model describes the functionality of the system; it typically describes the application's tasks, their computational loads, and their interdependencies. The platform model describes the resources of the computational platform and their capabilities. Platform resources include processing resources such as CPUs and storage resources such as memories, but also bandwidths and energy can be platform resources. The mapping model describes the deployment of the application tasks onto the platform resources.

To successfully apply the modeling process described above, it is essential to define models that accurately describe a system's performance. However, models should also be as simple as possible, because simple models require less effort to develop and to maintain. Simple models typically require little analysis time, which is beneficial for design-space exploration. On the other hand, the models must be sufficiently accurate for the purpose they serve. If a high accuracy is required, then typically a high model complexity is required. For instance, a cycle-accurate simulation is very accurate, but also very complex. In this paper, we will focus on simpler models that are accurate enough to *predict the past* and *explore the future*.

We distinguish three types of performance models with a varying degree of system knowledge and therefore with a different level of complexity. *Black-box models* are system models that do not use any a priori knowledge of internal behavior of the system. These models typically only consider the system's input and output behavior and are derived using experimental data [5]. *White-box models* are models that have all a priori knowledge about the internal workings of a system. As the structure of a white-box model is known, it is simpler to calibrate them. On the other hand, having system behavior knowledge typically results in more complex models. We distinguish a third model type, which combines both system knowledge and experimental data: *gray-box models* are created using high-level information about a system's internal behavior and corresponding experimental data. In this paper, we only use white-box and gray-box models, as we always have application knowledge and using this knowledge simplifies performance engineering.

3 Techniques and Tools

3.1 Discrete-Event Simulation and Execution Visualization

Discrete-event simulation is a methodology that discretizes the evolution of systems through a sequence of time-stamped events [8]. It allows the user to estimate all kinds of properties such as system throughput and processing latency. Discrete-event simulation is widely applicable, and often discrete-event simulation models are easier to manipulate and experiment with than the system under study. Another key benefit is that discrete-event simulation creates additional insight in the system dynamics.

In [10] we have presented the OctoSim framework, a discrete-event simulation approach for software-intensive embedded systems on a high level of abstraction that is based on a piecewise-linear notion of progress of computational tasks. The Y-chart based approach separates application, platform and mapping, and additionally separates the *execution* of tasks from the *application structure*. This results in models consisting of loosely coupled components with excellent opportunities for re-use. The OctoSim framework is available as a Java library, and can be classified as an embedded domain-specific language. The use of a general-purpose programming language has the advantage that all existing and often highly mature tooling for this language can be used. For instance, the Eclipse Integrated Development Environment (IDE) for Java developers can be used as a modeling environment [6]. This IDE includes a plethora of functionality, e.g., debugging, which in particular is useful during model development. The fact that the OctoSim library is based on Java interfaces makes the modeling language very flexible and powerful.

The OctoSim discrete-event simulation provides a simulation run (or a set of runs) which can be analyzed for key performance metrics. In addition to

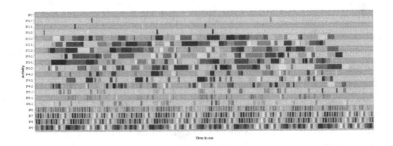

Fig. 2. A sample TRACE view which shows a system's activity over time.

these system-level numbers, we have experienced that detailed insight in the dynamics of the system is highly valued for both model validation, and to understand system-level numbers that are not expected. Therefore, we have coupled the TRACE tool, a Gantt chart viewer and analyzer, to our OCTOSIM tool [7]. Figure 2 shows an example of an OCTOSIM simulation run in the TRACE tool. TRACE enables us to zoom into the details of the behavior, and enables analysis methods to, e.g., compute and show differences in behavior or to compute and visualize the critical activities and resources [11]. TRACE is available as an ECLIPSE plug-in and therefore the full discrete-event simulation tool chain is available in a single, mature and widely-used IDE.

3.2 Regression Analysis

Regression analysis is a statistical technique for investigating and modeling the relationship between variables [13]. It involves *response variables* y_i and (independent) *predictor* or *regressor variables* $x_{i,j}$. The goal of regression is finding a regression model, i.e., a model that relates response variables y_i and regressor variables $x_{i,j}$. This is a function f, such that $y_i = f(x_{i,1}, \ldots, x_{i,m}) + \epsilon_i$, where ϵ_i is a zero-mean *error* or *residual*.

There are several types of regression depending on the structure regression function f. The most common type is linear regression, which finds *regression coefficients* $\beta_0, \beta_1, \ldots, \beta_m$, such that $y_i = \beta_0 + \sum_{j=1}^{m} \beta_j \cdot x_{i,j} + \epsilon_i$. Linear regression uses *least-squares estimation* to compute *intercept* β_0 and *slopes* $\beta_1, \ldots, \beta_m$. Besides estimations for the intercept and the slopes, linear regression also provides information on the quality of the found fit. Examples are the *coefficient of determination* R^2, which is the proportion of variation explained by regressors $x_{i,j}$, and an assessment of the significance of the intercept and slopes. Details about these and other supported techniques can be found in the textbook by Montgomery et al. [13].

In this paper, we use regression to create parameterized (white-box or graybox) models that are used for performance prediction. Using system knowledge, we first determine a model template, i.e., a function f describing the relation between input parameter values and system performance. For linear models, the template equals $y_i = \beta_0 + \sum_{j=1}^{m} \beta_j \cdot x_{i,j}$, where $x_{i,j}$ represents input parameters that can be controlled and β_i are constants. We use regression to calibrate the identified models. For the example of linear regression, this corresponds to determining the constants β_i using measurements of y_i for different values of input parameters $x_{i,j}$. Section 4 describes two cases, in which regression is used for model calibration; one case uses linear regression, the other non-linear regression.

4   Cases

In this section we describe five cases from industrial practice in which we have applied performance engineering techniques to aid the development process. The design questions span all three parts of the Y-chart: Sects. 4.1, 4.3, and 4.5 describe choices with respect to the application, Sect. 4.2 analyzes platform design alternatives, and Sect. 4.4 considers mapping alternatives.

4.1   Predicting the Effect of Application Changes

Problem Description. The first case involves the data paths of a family of wide-format printing systems. These printers can print images of over one meter in width. These images are printed by an ink-jet carriage that moves over the medium, e.g., a paper role. An image is printed in bands, called *swaths*; the height of these swaths equals the number of nozzles in the printer carriage and their width equals the image width. The corresponding data paths have to handle a huge amount of data. They take a bitmap as input and transform this bitmap into sequences of firing moments for the (thousands of) nozzles of the printers' ink-jet carriage. The data paths of the wide-format printers are different for each printer in the product family, but they are all built from a single library of generic image processing steps. Examples of these steps are copying, masking, re-sampling, and transposition.

We would like to quickly and accurately predict the performance of the data path of future wide-format printing systems. For instance, in an early development phase, we would like to assess the influence of different printer configurations on the data path performance. Examples of these configuration changes include a larger number of ink-jet nozzles or different printer dimensions. Similarly, we would like to accurately predict the performance of different sequences of image processing steps.

Performance Engineering. As we have access to the code of all image processing steps of an existing prototype, a white-box modeling approach has been used to address this challenge. The modeling step (step 2 in Fig. 1) mainly consisted of code analysis, which was used to determine the (nested) loops in the data path code and the corresponding loop bounds. This loop structure determines a template for the performance model. For instance, if the implementation contains a single loop iterating over the pixels of a swath, then this operation's latency can be expressed as $\beta_0 + \beta_1 \cdot n$, where n is the number of pixels in the swath and β_0 and β_1 are unknown constants. This determines the model structure, which is later used for calibration using (linear) regression.

Calibration and validation (step 3 in Fig. 1) has started with code instrumentation and systematic measurements. Code instrumentation has been applied to record the start and end times of image processing steps using an accurate clock. This additional code disturbs the measurements. However, the measurement overhead is very small compared to the execution times of the image processing steps. Measurements have been performed using different inputs; the inputs are selected using information of the loop bounds found during code analysis. Measurements with varying loop bounds were performed. For instance, if an image processing steps has an expected latency of $\beta_0 + \beta_1 \cdot n$, where n is the number of pixels in the swath and β_0 and β_1 are unknown constants, then the set of measurements should cover different values of n. Finally, linear regression was used to calibrate a performance model for each image processing step separately. The regressors are the loop bounds found using code analysis. For the example of an expected latency of $\beta_0 + \beta_1 \cdot n$, n is used as the only regressor. Linear regression will determine the values of intercept β_0 and slope β_1. We have validated the model by comparing model predictions for a new input (with a different number of pixels in the swath) with measurements. The differences are approximately 1 %.

A simplified and anonymized version of the resulting performance model is shown in Fig. 3. This model takes only one regressor, the input size. It is a simple model in EXCEL with a single input parameter, i.e., the size of the input of image processing step IP1. The input sizes of the subsequent steps are determined by the preceding steps, as for each step it is known how much output it produces for a given input size. By varying the sequence of image processing steps or the size of the input of the first step, different printer configurations can be evaluated and used for exploring the future (steps 4 and 5 in Fig. 1).

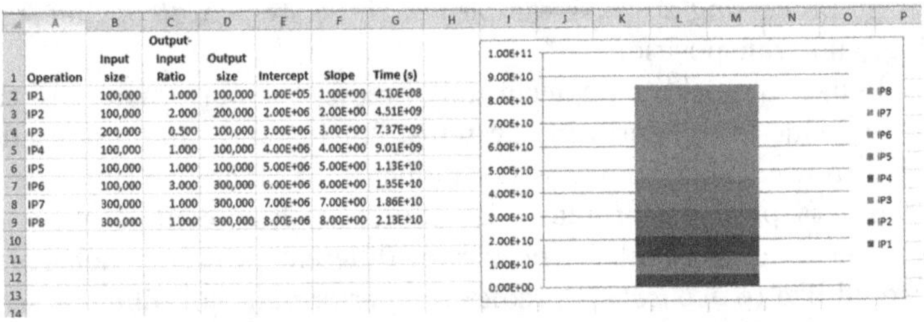

	Operation	Input size	Output-Input Ratio	Output size	Intercept	Slope	Time (s)
1	Operation	Input size	Output-Input Ratio	Output size	Intercept	Slope	Time (s)
2	IP1	100,000	1.000	100,000	1.00E+05	1.00E+00	4.10E+08
3	IP2	100,000	2.000	200,000	2.00E+06	2.00E+00	4.51E+09
4	IP3	200,000	0.500	100,000	3.00E+06	3.00E+00	7.37E+09
5	IP4	100,000	1.000	100,000	4.00E+06	4.00E+00	9.01E+09
6	IP5	100,000	1.000	100,000	5.00E+06	5.00E+00	1.13E+10
7	IP6	100,000	3.000	300,000	6.00E+06	6.00E+00	1.35E+10
8	IP7	300,000	1.000	300,000	7.00E+06	7.00E+00	1.86E+10
9	IP8	300,000	1.000	300,000	8.00E+06	8.00E+00	2.13E+10

Fig. 3. Simplified EXCEL performance model.

Costs and Benefits. The procedure used to estimate the performance of wide-format printers is a simple process, which allows a large degree of automation. The following benefits have been observed from using the data path performance model, both during data path development and for design-space exploration.

First, bottleneck identification. The performance model identifies which of the image processing steps are most expensive. This allows the data path designers to focus their attention in optimizing the data path performance on those image processing steps that contribute most to the execution time. Second, hardware scaling analysis. The input size is the main regressor of most of the image processing models. This allows exploration beyond the dimensions of existing wide-format printers. If there are plans for a printer that allows larger input widths or larger ink-jet carriages, then the model provides first predictions of the future data path performance. This gives an early impression whether the data path performance will be sufficient for the new printer configuration. Third, sequence optimization. A typical data path contains a number of re-sampling steps; these change the resolution of the image. Having the optimal sequence of image processing steps is essential in optimizing data path performance; the most expensive steps should be executed on as little data as possible. The predictive model allows all sequences to be specified and analyzed separately; the data path designer does not need to implement and test all sequences individually. Instead, the optimal sequence can be derived using the model and data path designers can implement this sequence. Fourth, detection of unexpected performance behavior. During code analysis, the loop structure of the image processing steps is identified. This is used as input for calibration using linear regression. In principle, each of the loop bounds should appear as a significant regressor in the corresponding model. However, we have unexpectedly identified an operation for which the input size was not considered a significant regressor. This has led to special attention to analyze and correct the unexpected behavior.

4.2 Predicting the Effect of Platform Scaling

Problem Description. The second case involves the data path of a high-production cut-sheet printer. Like the wide-format data path, this data path transforms an input bitmap into firing moments. The data path takes the input image, e.g., of A4 size, and divides it into a number of bands. These bands are processed in parallel individually by separate threads of the data path; each thread runs on a dedicated processor core. When there are more bands than processor cores, then bands are processed sequentially. This case involves a platform-scaling question: we would like to estimate the performance of the data path on different hardware platforms without individually purchasing and testing all of them. Using these estimations, discussions are fed to select the computational hardware of the printer being developed with the best balance between cost and performance.

Performance Engineering. We applied a gray-box modeling approach in which we use the information that a large part of the application is parallelized over the available processor cores of the platform. Estimating the performance of an application on a (multi-core) computer platform is very challenging, because (i) there are many platform parameters that influence system performance (e.g., the number and type of CPU cores, bus capacities, cache sizes and cache line sizes), and (ii) it is generally not possible to vary only one of the parameters to isolate its effect on performance. To create a simple, yet accurate, predictive performance model, it is essential to identify the parameters that have the highest influence on data path performance. Experiments have, unsurprisingly, identified the number of CPU cores as the most important platform parameter.

Our performance model that predicts application performance on a new platform consists of three parts (step 2 in Fig. 1). Amdahl's law [1], which estimates the maximum possible speed-up of an application running on parallel processors has been used for the first part of our model. It divides the computational load of the application into two parts: a sequential part, which cannot be parallelized, and a parallel part, which can be ideally parallelized. Amdahl's law can be formulated as $T(n) = T(1) \cdot (s + \frac{1}{n} \cdot (1 - s))$, where $T(n)$ is an application's execution time on n processors and $s \in [0, 1]$ is the sequential fraction of the application. Changing the platform, however, will affect both $T(1)$ and s (where we assume that Amdahl's law still applies on the new platform). The second part of our performance model therefore consists of a method to estimate $T(1)$ for an unknown platform. A first attempt to use the CPU clock frequency as a means to relate processors did not provide an accurate model: model predictions deviated greatly from measurements on the available platforms. A more suitable means to relate processors was found in an on-line performance benchmark [17]. This benchmark quantifies the performance of a single core of (multi-core) CPUs. The third and final part of our model consists of a relation between $T(1)$ and s, such that we can estimate s for the new platform from our estimation of $T(1)$ on the new platform that follows from the second part of the model.

Calibration and validation (step 3 in Fig. 1) has been based on measurements on several available homogeneous multi-core platforms. Regression has been used to identify model parameters $T(1)$ and s. The non-linear regression resulted in a good fit, and the sequential fraction s proved to be small; around five percent of the application cannot be parallelized. This sequential fraction involves mainly the parts at the beginning where the bitmaps are divided into bands and at the end where the band results are accumulated. This validates our use of Amdahl's law. Next, we have validated our method to estimate $T(1)$ using the benchmark data and the available platforms. It has proven to be sufficiently accurate for practical usage: the single-threaded data path performance of an unknown platform can be derived from the single-threaded data path performance of a known platform by scaling with the corresponding benchmark values. This has proven accurate within circa 10 %. By taking into account additional platform characteristics, an even better accuracy has been achieved. Finally, we have fitted a relation between $T(1)$ and s based on the measurements on the available platforms.

Costs and Benefits. Using little effort and simple means, a simple, yet accurate, predictive performance model has been created. The model can be used to estimate the data path performance on many different computational platforms without having to purchase all of them. The model is being used to trade off platform cost and performance to select promising candidate platforms for further investigation (steps 4 and 5 in Fig. 1). Note that when a new platform has been acquired for evaluation, it can be used to further calibrate and validate the model (steps 6 and 3 in Fig. 1) to improve the accuracy.

4.3   Optimization of Application Structure for Bitmap Processing

Problem Description. We consider a prototype data path for a second type of cut-sheet printer. The data path functionality that is the subject of this case converts Page Description Language (PDL) data (e.g., PostScript) to bitmap images that are suitable for the print engine. This conversion has been implemented in three functional image processing steps IP1 – IP3, and a step, IP4, that writes the bitmap data to a hard disk. Because often there are no data dependencies between PDL items (i.e., pages of the document to print), these steps can be parallelized. Furthermore, the steps allow pipelining. Figure 4 shows a schematic of the situation with three instances of the processing pipeline. The configuration question we face is how many copies of the processing pipeline IP1 – IP4 should be used. There is a trade-off between the memory usage (each pipeline instance statically allocates a significant amount of RAM) and throughput. The latter is hard to estimate based on static calculations because of (i) resource sharing (the steps IP1 – IP3 all are mapped to a 4-core CPU), (ii) pipelining behavior and (iii) the variation in the duration of the processing steps (which heavily depends on the PDL data).

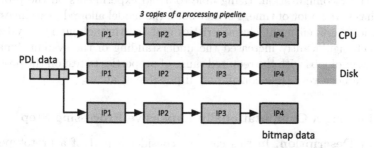

Fig. 4. Three parallel processing pipelines to convert PDL data to bitmap data.

Performance Engineering. In the modeling step (step 2 in Fig. 1) we have built a gray-box discrete-event simulation model using the OCTOSIM tool (see Sect. 3 and [10]). The model consists of a number of dependent tasks (as in Fig. 4), each with a parameter for the nominal execution time. It also includes details about data granularity and buffering. Resource interaction, e.g., when multiple tasks run on the CPU, is modeled by extrapolation of the nominal execution times by the platform model; see [10].

Calibration and validation (step 3 in Fig. 1) has been enabled by code instrumentation (as in Sect. 4.1) and systematic measurements using a small number of representative jobs. This gave us the nominal execution times of the processing steps IP1 – IP4 on the target platform, which have been used for model calibration. In order to validate our OCTOSIM model, we have measured the throughput of the system for the representative jobs for one, two and three copies of the pipeline. We then have compared these numbers with the predictions of our model (we predict the past). This has shown that the model is quite accurate given the high level of abstraction: the predictions are all within 10 % of the measured values.

Next, we have explored the future (steps 4–5 of Fig. 1) by using the model to predict the throughput of a number of fictive jobs and a varying number of pipeline copies. This has shown us that the ratios of the nominal execution times of IP1 – IP3 per PDL data item play an important role. If IP1 – IP3 have a similar duration, then the system does not scale well. In that case IP1, IP2 and IP3 of a single processing pipeline all are active more or less continuously (with different PDL data items). A single pipeline instance therefore already claims three of the four CPU cores. Using workloads derived from practical job sets, we were able to optimize the number of parallel pipelines for the expected use patterns of the printer.

Costs and Benefits. We estimate that modeling, calibration and validation, and analysis took approximately one full working week, starting from the basic OCTOSIM building blocks. The model has allowed us to experiment with different types of input and varying the number of pipeline copies, and this has led to a satisfactory configuration. Being able to avoid experiments on the prototype system has saved a lot of time. Furthermore, the model allowed us to investigate the relation between input characteristics and the throughput in a systematic way, which significantly increased the understanding of the system dynamics. Finding a set of jobs with the required range of properties to test on the prototype would have been very time-consuming, if possible at all.

4.4   Mapping a Computationally Expensive Processing Step

Problem Description. In this case we consider a part of a prototype data path that consists of three copies of a pipeline consisting of image processing steps IP5 – IP10. The current prototype implementation does not meet the performance requirements on throughput. Measurements show that the 4-core CPU is heavily loaded. Mapping a computationally expensive step (IP7, which uses three threads) to the GPU might improve the throughput. This, however, is not obvious due to the complex dynamic behavior of the system (pipelining, parallel processing, task interactions on the CPU, etc.). Furthermore, the three copies of the processing pipeline cannot use the GPU in parallel which might create a new bottleneck. The current situation and the design alternative are shown schematically in Fig. 5. Building a prototype of the design alternative would imply that the functionality of IP7 should be re-implemented for the GPU, which would require a lot of engineering effort. Instead of embarking on this directly, we have decided to first employ a model-based analysis.

Performance Engineering. We have created, calibrated and validated a gray-box OCTOSIM discrete-event simulation model for the current situation in a similar way as described in Sect. 4.3 (steps 2–3 in Fig. 1). The validation consisted of a manual inspection of the execution trace of the model using the TRACE tool, and

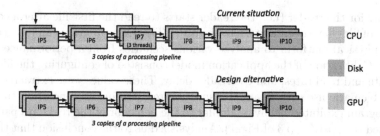

Fig. 5. The current situation and a possible new design which maps IP7 to the GPU.

of a comparison of the measured throughput with the modeled throughput (within
5 %). The delta-modeling (step 4 in Fig. 1) adjusted the mapping of IP7 and made
some additional minor structural changes. Our design-space exploration (step 5 in
Fig. 1) consisted of a systematic analysis of the throughput for a range of durations
of IP7, since we have no implementation of IP7 on the GPU and therefore no measurements. This led to the insight that even an efficient implementation of IP7 on
the GPU only leads to a small increase in system throughput.

Costs and Benefits. An experienced modeler used approximately two working
days to create the models from the basic building blocks in the OCTOSIM library
and to analyze them. This includes several meetings with the team that worked
on the system to create, calibrate and validate the model. The combination of the
model-based analysis results with the estimation of effort for the implementation
of IP7 on the GPU led to the decision to not pursue this solution direction. Note
that step 6 in Fig. 1 is not possible because of this decision. Performance engineering thus has provided insights that are at the basis of a significant design decision.

4.5   Combining an Application Model with a Real Platform

Problem Description. A prototype data path running on a regular desktop
PC with a standard operating system suffered a severe performance degradation
in some use cases: the throughput could unpredictably drop to less than 10 % of
the required value. Initial analysis led us to the insight that in these cases the
hard disk was the bottleneck. A critical step that reads data from the hard disk
became extremely slow. Modeling the behavior of the hard disk under the load
that the data path imposed on it, however, would require detailed knowledge of
OS and hard disk internals. This information simply was not available to us.

Performance Engineering. Instead of creating a model of the application, the
mapping and the platform, we created a model of the application and mapping
only that we could execute on the real platform (step 2 in Fig. 1). In other words,
we created a JAVA program that mimics the load that the data path imposes on the
hard disk. The program has three threads that each write a number of files to the
disk at a certain rate, and it has one thread that reads those files from the disk at a
certain rate. Configuration parameters of the model are the file size, the rates, and

the delay for the reader (i.e., the reader starts to read the first file after a certain number of files have been written to the disk). The JAVA program can be executed on the physical platform to analyze various scenarios from a performance point of view. Calibration of the application model consisted of configuring the file size, the write and read rates, and the reader delay. These values were extracted from the problematic use case. Manual inspection resulted in the conclusion that the test program exhibited behavior similar to the behavior of the real data path: we predicted the past (step 3 of Fig. 1). Analysis led us to the conclusion that the OS gives reading a lower priority than writing, which has the effect that in high load scenarios reading almost completely stops. We used this qualitatively validated model to experiment with two mechanisms to control the concurrency of the writers and reader in order to make the hard disk performance more predictable (we did not succeed in influencing the OS scheduling in a more direct way; step 4 in Fig. 1). The model predicted that a semaphore that prevents concurrent API calls to the file system from the writer and reader threads solves the problematic behavior: we have explored the future (step 5 in Fig. 1).

Costs and Benefits. Creation of the test program cost little effort; JAVA provides ample means for I/O and concurrency. The experiments that the test program allowed us to do would have been tedious using the actual system. The reason is that we then would have needed an appropriate set of jobs that imposes the required load on the disk. It is non-trivial to obtain such a set. The model-based experiments have provided more insight in the dynamic behavior of the hard disk and the implications for the data path performance. Furthermore, they have provided support for the envisioned semaphore solution which requires non-trivial implementation efforts.

5 Conclusion

We have introduced a model-based performance engineering approach that is coupled to the V-model. We have discussed the role of accuracy of model predictions and trust issues that can play a role, especially if the cost-to-validation is significant. Furthermore, we have applied model-based performance engineering with lightweight techniques and tools to five industrial cases from the digital printing domain. Y-chart separation of concerns (application, platform, mapping) and a high level of abstraction ensure simple but accurate models that enable design-space exploration. We have made several observations from these cases.

First, building the models, especially the discrete-event simulation models which require an explicit Y-chart application graph, is a useful exercise in itself. It stimulates *performance thinking* in the team, and documents and clarifies the design in a way that is often lacking. These models (or informal drawings representing the models) are good means for communication and facilitate knowledge transfer between team members. A next step in our process is validation of the constructed performance models to build trust and to quantify predictive accuracy. Usually, we take the system as the leading artifact to which the model must conform, but the roles could also be reversed. An example is given in Sect. 4.1 in which the system exhibits behavior that differs from the model prediction. In this case, we regard the regression model as leading and expect a software bug in the system that causes the difference.

Second, as already observed in [3,20], automation is an important factor for the acceptance of performance engineering. In the five cases that we have described above, the foundational parts of the gray- and white-box models have been relatively easy to obtain, i.e., the regression formulas (Sect. 4.1), Amdahl's law (Sect. 4.2), the application graphs (Sects. 4.3 and 4.4), and the application and mapping (Sect. 4.5). The data that is needed to calibrate and validate the models, however, was much harder to obtain (except for the case in Sect. 4.5). We believe that a systematic way of storing fine-grained performance-related system events will alleviate this. Furthermore, this would enable systematic access to information that can directly be used by architects and engineers to identify and diagnose performance problems, and to get more insight in the system dynamics. For instance, in the cases described in Sects. 4.1 and 4.3 we have added performance logging to the system that enabled us to immediately visualize a Gantt chart of the system's execution after a test run (Fig. 2 is an example of this). Architects and engineers acknowledge that this kind of visualization is very useful. Furthermore, the performance logging output is directly applicable for calibration and validation of performance models.

Third, there are various models for implementing performance engineering. Two extremes are (i) to hire a third party to do performance engineering, and (ii) to change the way of working of the development team to do performance engineering internally. Both have their strengths and weaknesses and both impose different requirements on the tools, processes and, last but not least, the people involved. The five cases have used the former model, and our conclusion is that the cost has been low and we believe that the benefits have been substantial.

To summarize our conclusions, the V-model based performance engineering method, where models are calibrated using existing products or prototypes and then used to explore design alternatives for new products, works in the presented cases from the digital printing domain. Although some of the modeling techniques that we have applied may be regarded as domain-specific, we believe that the process in which they are applied, is not. Other domains which also employ an evolutionary (in contrast to revolutionary) approach with respect to development can use the process of Fig. 1, but may need to apply different, possibly domain-specific, modeling and analysis techniques.

References

1. Amdahl, G.M.: Validity of the single processor approach to achieving large scale computing capabilities. In: AFIPS spring joint computer conference (1967)
2. Balarin, F., et al.: Hardware-Software Co-design of Embedded Systems: The POLIS Approach. Kluwer, Norwell (1997)
3. Balsamo, S., di Marco, A., Inverardi, P., Simeoni, M.: Model-based performance prediction in software development: a survey. IEEE Trans. Softw. Eng. 30(5), 295–310 (2004)

4. Beckers, J.M.J., Muller, G.J., Heemels, W.P.H., Bukkems, B.H.M.: Effective industrial modeling for high-tech systems: the example of happy flow. In: INCOSE International Symposium, vol. 17, issue 1 (2007)
5. Bohlin, T.P.: Practical Grey-box Process Identification: Theory and Applications. Springer, Berlin (2015)
6. Eclipse Foundation: Eclipse website (2015). http://www.eclipse.org/
7. Embedded Systems Innovation by TNO: Trace website (2015). http://trace.esi.nl
8. Fishman, G.S.: Discrete-Event Simulation: Modeling, Programming, and Analysis. Springer, New York (2001)
9. Forsberg, K., Mooz, H.: The relationship of system engineering to the project cycle. In: INCOSE International Symposium, vol. 1, issue 1 (1991)
10. Hendriks, M., et al.: A blueprint for system-level performance modeling of software-intensive embedded systems. Int. J. Softw. Tools Technol, Transfer (2014)
11. Hendriks, M. et al.: Analyzing execution traces - critical-path analysis and distance analysis. Submitted to STTT (2015)
12. Kruchten, P.B.: The 4 + 1 view model of architecture. IEEE Softw. **12**(6), 42–50 (1995)
13. Montgomery, D.C., Peck, E.A., Vining, G.G.: Introduction to Linear Regression Analysis, 3rd edn. Wiley, New York (2001)
14. Muller, G.J.: CAFCR: a multi-view method for embedded systems architecting; balancing genericity and specificity. Ph.D. thesis, Delft University of Technology (2004)
15. Mussbacher, G., Amyot, D., Breu, R., Bruel, J.-M., Cheng, B.H.C., Collet, P., Combemale, B., France, R.B., Heldal, R., Hill, J., Kienzle, J., Schöttle, M., Steimann, F., Stikkolorum, D., Whittle, J.: The Relevance of Model-Driven Engineering Thirty Years from Now. In: Dingel, J., Schulte, W., Ramos, I., Abrahão, S., Insfran, E. (eds.) MODELS 2014. LNCS, vol. 8767, pp. 183–200. Springer, Heidelberg (2014)
16. Parappurath, V.V., Voeten, J.P.M., Kotterink, K.C.: Calibration error bound estimation in performance modeling. In: Euromicro Conference on Digital System Design (2013)
17. PassMark Software: CPU Mark - Single Thread Performance (2015). https://www.cpubenchmark.net/singleThread.html
18. Pimentel, A.D., Thompson, M., Polstra, S., Erbas, C.: Calibration of abstract performance models for system-level design space exploration. J. Signal Process. Syst. **50**(2), 99–114 (2008)
19. Smith, C.U., Williams, L.G.: Software performance engineering. In: Lavagno, L., Martin, G., Selic, B. (eds.) UML for Real: Design of Embedded Real-Time Systems, pp. 343–365. Springer, Heidelberg (2003)
20. Voeten, J. et al.: Predicting timing performance of advanced mechatronics control systems. In: IEEE 35th Annual Computer Software and Applications Conference Workshops (COMPSACW) (2011)
21. Westland, J.C.: The cost of errors in software development: evidence from industry. J. Syst. Softw. **62**, 1–9 (2002)
22. Williams, L.G., Smith, C.U.: Making the business case for software performance engineering. In: 29th International Computer Measurement Group Conference. pp. 349–358. Computer Measurement Group (2003)

Fault-Prone Byte-Code Detection Using Text Classifier

Tsuyoshi Fujiwara[1]([✉]), Osamu Mizuno[1]([✉]), and Pattara Leelaprute[2]

[1] Software Engineering Laboratory, Graduate School of Science
and Technology, Kyoto Institute of Technology, Kyoto, Japan
t-fujiwara@se.is.kit.ac.jp, o-mizuno@kit.ac.jp
[2] Department of Computer Engineering, Faculty of Engineering,
Kasetsart University, Bangkok, Thailand
pattara.l@ku.ac.th

Abstract. Researchers have studied approaches to detect fault-prone modules for a long time. As one of these approaches, we proposed an approach using a text filtering technique. In this approach, we assume that faults relate to words and contexts in a software module. Our technique accepts inputs as a text information. Based on a dictionary that was learned by classifying modules that induce faults, the fault inducing probability over a target module is calculated, and it judges whether the given module is a fault-prone module.

Although our approach targeted the source code of software, especially in embedded software, the analysis of byte-code is also required. The source code based fault detection suffered from noises such as the way of writing, the used name of identifiers, and so on. Eliminating such noises may improve the accuracy of prediction. In this study, we aimed at fault detection from the byte-code of Java. Specifically, we tried to detect faults from the dis-assembled intermediate code of Java class file. To show the effectiveness of our approach, we conducted an experiment and compared our approach with source code based approach.

1 Introduction

In software development, it is expected that we can remove faults efficiently, and we can reduce the cost of development. If we can detect hidden faults in the software module by a filter, we can easily find faults before they appear in the operational use. Fault-prone module detection is one approach [12]. As for the measures for fault-prone module detection, various metrics have been proposed so far. For example, CK metrics in Object-oriented code [1,4], process metrics [10], software structures [3], and the metrics from static analysis [9,14].

We have proposed an approach to detect faults in source code modules in software by using the text classification technique [7,8]. In this approach, we decompose source code files into tokens and learn the correspondence between faults and tokens in the source code. By learning, we can make corpuses of faulty and non-faulty tokens for detection. Finally, we apply a new source code file to

© Springer International Publishing Switzerland 2015
P. Abrahamsson et al. (Eds.): PROFES 2015, LNCS 9459, pp. 415–430, 2015.
DOI: 10.1007/978-3-319-26844-6_30

the text classifier using these corpuses; then we obtain the probability to be faulty for a new source code.

However, source code based approach has some weaknesses as follow:

- The source code has noises such as writing formats and the name of identifiers. The difference between formats theoretically does not affect the fault-proneness of the code, but text classification based approach *can* detect the difference of formatting and *can* learn such difference as a cause of faults.
- Specifically in the embedded software, the same source code for various platforms may cause faults. For example, different assignment of GPIOs for pins will cause a fault in different platforms with the same code.

To tackle this problem, we develop an approach to detect faults in binary modules based on the text classifier. In this approach, the byte-code is disassembled to the assembly code and is applied to the text classifier. By doing so, the format of the code is standardized by the disassembler. On the other hand, the code depends on the platforms are extracted by the compiler.

To see the effectiveness, we applied this technique to the Java-based OSS projects. The result of experiment shows that our approach displays difference between source code based approach and also shows that the possibility of finding new faults that cannot be detected by source code based approach.

Furthermore, we applied our approach to cross-project fault prediction [5]. The predictive ability of the cross project prediction depends on characteristics between training project and target project (i.e. similar characteristics lead good result). For this reason, Jureczko et al. conducted to perform clustering on software projects in order to identify groups of software projects with similar characteristic [5]. Rahman et al. reported that cross-project prediction performance is no worse than within-project performance, and substantially better than random prediction [11]. We expect that the byte-code module based fault prediction is more robust than source code module based ones since we can ignore the effect of the specific identifiers or languages.

The rest of this paper is organized as follows: Sect. 2 describes systems, algorithm, and tools which we used for experiments. The objective of this paper is shown in Sect. 3. Targets, preparations and procedure of experiments are shown in Sect. 4. Section 5 describes experimental conditions, evaluation measures and the result of experiments. Section 6 discusses the result of experiments. Finally, Sect. 7 summarizes this study and also addresses future work.

2   Preliminaries

2.1   Fault-Prone Filtering

Basic Idea. The basic idea of fault-prone filtering is inspired by spam mail filtering [8]. In spam mail filtering, the spam filter first trains both spam and ham (non-spam) e-mail messages from the training data set. Then, an incoming e-mail is classified as either spam or ham by the spam filter.

This framework is based on the fact that spam e-mails usually include particular patterns of words or sentences. We applied a spam filter for fault-prone module prediction. We named this approach, "fault-prone filtering" [8]. Fault-prone filtering generates a dictionary like a process of SPAM filter and classifies fault-prone modules and non-fault-prone modules by using the dictionary.

Text Discriminator: CRM114. In our tool, we used CRM114 [13] text filtering software for its versatility and accuracy. Although CRM114 is for a SPAM filter, it is used for general-purpose uses, such as log surveillance of computers, and network traffic surveillance.

The classification techniques implemented in CRM114 are based mainly on Markov random field model. In these experiments, we used Orthogonal Sparse Bigrams Markov model (OSB) which is the classification strategies built-in the CRM114 to evaluate the effectiveness of our proposed approach. OSB consider tokens as combinations of exactly two words in a text file.

Procedure of Filtering (Training Only Errors). The typical procedure of fault-prone filtering is summarized as follows [7]:

1. We apply text classification to a newly created software module (for example, a class in Java), M_i, and obtain the probability to be fault-prone.
2. By the pre-determined threshold $t_{FP}(0 < t_{FP} < 1)$, we classify the module M_i into fault-prone or non-fault-prone.
3. When a fault report reveals the actual fault-proneness of M_i, we investigate whether the predicted result for M_i was correct or not.
4. If the predicted result was correct, we go to Step 1; otherwise, we apply text learning to M_i to learn actual fault-proneness and go to Step 1.

This procedure is called "Training Only Errors (TOE)" procedure because training process is invoked only when classification errors happen. The TOE procedure is quite similar to actual classification procedure in practice. For example, in actual e-mail filtering, e-mail messages are classified when they arrived. If some of them are misclassified, actual results (spam or non-spam) should be trained.

3   Research Question

In the past studies of fault-prone filtering, we obtained good results from the viewpoints of fault detection accuracy. However, source code based approach has some weakness as follows:

- The source code has noises such as writing formats and the name of identifiers. The difference between formats theoretically does not affect the fault-proneness of the code, but text classification based approach *can* detect the difference of formatting and *can* learn such difference as a cause of faults.
- Specifically in the embedded software, the same source code for various platforms may cause faults. For example, different assignment of GPIOs for pins will cause faults in different platforms with the same code.

We then propose an approach to using byte-code modules for fault-prone prediction. In this study, the following two approaches are used:

1. Fault-prone source code modules detection by using fault-prone filtering as the conventional technique.
2. Fault-prone byte-code modules prediction by using fault-prone filtering as the proposed technique.

By comparing these approaches, we state the following research questions for our purpose.

RQ1. Is there a difference in the accuracy of fault detection between the source code based and the byte-code based approaches?
RQ2. In the cross-platform application, is the accuracy of fault-prone module rediction improved by using byte-code modules?

4   Experiments

In this section, we show the target, the preparations and the procedure of our experiments. In our experiments, we detect fault-prone modules by setting the input of fault-prone filtering to byte-code. Then, we also detect by setting the input to source code and compare two cases. Hereafter, we treat a class as a module.

4.1   Target Project

Our experiments target an OSS project stated as below.

- **Apache Ant.** Apache Ant[1] is a build tool written in Java that is not much to depend on a specific environment, and can say a Java version of GNU make. In these experiments, we use three revisions of this project: rev. 1.5, rev. 1.6 and rev. 1.7. We obtained the fault data in Apache Ant by Jureczko and Madeyski [5] from PROMISE data repository [6].
- **Apache Tomcat.** Apache Tomcat[2] is a servlet container for Java Servlet, JavaServer Pages, Java Expression Language and Java WebSocket technologies written in Java.
  In these experiments, we use revision 1.6.0.39 of this project. We also obtained the fault data in Apache Tomcat from PROMISE data repository.

4.2   Preparations

Before conducting our experiments, we must get the byte-code files and the source code files every revision from the Apache Ant project and the Apache Tomcat project. Then, we obtain the data sets of all revisions related to Apache Ant and Tomcat from PROMISE.

---

[1] http://ant.apache.org/.

[2] http://tomcat.apache.org/.

Expand Jar Files. We need to expand the jar files because the byte-code files are compressed in the form of the jar (Java archive). JDK (Java Development Kit) provides the way to expand a jar file. We can obtain the class files written in Java byte-code by only applying the jar files to the `jar` command with `-x` and `-f` options.

Disassembling. We need to obtain the op-codes because we do not use class files for the learning. However, to extract the op-codes from binary data manually is too difficult, so we disassemble the class files. JDK also provides the way to disassemble class file. We can obtain assembly code by only applying the class files to the `javap` command with `-c` option.

Dividing Source Code Files. We can define many classes in a single source code file. When we treat a class as a module, it is too inconvenient to conduct our experiments because a single source code file can have many modules. Therefore, we must divide the source codes files into pieces each of which has only one module.

Tagging Modules with Labels. Based on data sets, we tag each of the modules with the label that the module is faulty or non-faulty. In our experiments, a faulty module is defined as the module that contains at least one bug, and a non-faulty module is defined as the module that contains no bugs. As a result, we obtained 291 of faulty modules and 1,096 of not fault-prone modules for Ant, and 96 of faulty modules and 733 of not fault-prone modules.

Making Tokenizers. When we perform fault-prone filtering, we need tokenizer that divide text information into tokens. In our experiments, we make lexical analysis programs using Lex as tokenizers. To tell the details, we make two tokenizers; one extract mnemonics[3] from assembly code, another extract words[4] from source code.

4.3   Method 1 (Ex. 1)

In our experiments, when we use fault-prone filtering, we adopt TOE as a learning algorithm. We show the specific processes by using TOE as follows.

(1) Sort the module group of the said project by revisions in ascending order.
(2) Apply one of the sorted modules to the proper tokenizer, and predict whether the module is fault-prone or not using the spam filter.

---

[3] Mnemonic means human-readable character string that have a one-to-one relation with op-codes.
[4] This "word" means an element that composes source code except ";"; variable names, operands, and keywords.

(3) Compare the prediction result and the label. Then if the prediction is correct, do nothing and return (2).

(4) If the prediction is incorrect, make the dictionary of spam filter learn the correct result and return (2).

By applying each of the assembly code and source code modules to the above processes, we conduct our experiments. At this time, we set the threshold that decide the detection that the module is fault-prone or non-fault-prone to 0.5. In this experiment, we applied all revisions of two projects, Apache Ant and Apache Tomcat.

4.4　Method 2 (Ex. 2)

To more specifically compare, we detect them changing the threshold and estimate the results. When we conduct this method, we also use the fault-prone filtering processes by using TOE showed in Method 1. Then, we conduct our experiments changing the threshold from 0.05 to 0.95 at intervals of 0.05. When we change the threshold and predict them again, we must take care not to amend the order of modules, because TOE greatly depend on the prediction order. In this experiment, we applied all revisions of two projects, Apache Ant and Apache Tomcat.

4.5　Method 3 (Ex. 3)

We expect that the byte-code module based fault prediction is more robust than source code module based ones since we can ignore the effect of the specific identifiers or languages. To investigate this assumption, we conducted the following experiment.

In this experiment, we prepare two projects, one for training and one for prediction. We used the resultant corpus of TOE application with 0.5 threshold for training. By applying this corpus for prediction project with 0.5 threshold, we get the result of cross-project prediction. We used Ant revision 1.7 and Tomcat revision 1.6.0.39 for this experiment.

5　Result of Experiments

In this section, we show the results of our experiments.

5.1　Conditions of Experiment

We show the conditions when we conduct our experiments.

Spam Filter. In our experiments, we use CRM114 for the spam filter, and Orthogonal Sparse Bigrams Markov model (OSB) as the algorithm of classification.

Threshold. When we apply the target modules to CRM114, we gain the values from 0 to 1. These values are probabilities that the modules are fault-prone, and are obtained by Bayesian discrimination. The threshold is a border value to decide the detection that the module is fault-prone or non-fault-prone. When the probability that the module is fault-prone is larger than the threshold, the module is fault-prone or else the module is non-fault-prone.

5.2 Evaluation Measure

Table 1 displays a classification result matrix. True negative (tn) indicates the number of modules that are classified as non-fault-prone and are observed as non-faulty. False positive (fp) indicates the number of modules that are classified as fault-prone but are observed as non-faulty. On the contrary, false negative (fn) indicates the number of modules that are classified as non-fault-prone but are observed as faulty. Finally, true positive (tp) indicates the number of modules that are classified as fault-prone and are observed as faulty.

To evaluate the results, we prepare three measures: recall, precision, and accuracy. The recall is the ratio of modules correctly classified as fault-prone to the number of entire faulty modules. Equation (1) defines the recall.

$$\text{Recall} = \frac{tp}{tp + fn} \tag{1}$$

Intuitively speaking, the recall shows the ratio of actual faults that can be detected by the detection methods.

The precision is the ratio of modules correctly classified as fault-prone to the number of entire modules classified fault-prone. Equation (2) defines the precision.

$$\text{Precision} = \frac{tp}{tp + fp} \tag{2}$$

Accuracy is the ratio of correctly classified modules to the entire modules. Equation (3) defines the accuracy.

$$\text{Accuracy} = \frac{tp + tn}{tn + tp + fp + fn} \tag{3}$$

The recall and the precision have a relation of a trade-off. It is easily possible to lower another value, instead of raising one of value. Thus, we calculate F_1

Table 1. Classification results matrix

		Prediction	
		fault-prone	non-fault-prone
Observed	faulty	True positive (tp)	False negative (fn)
	non-faulty	False positive (fp)	True negative (tn)

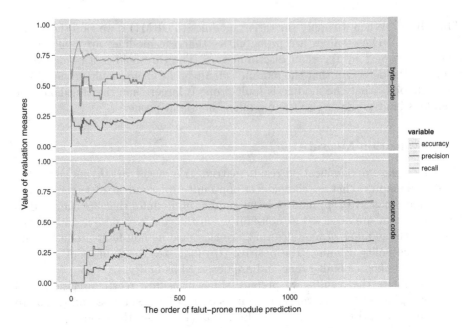

Fig. 1. Transition of each measure with byte-code and source code in Ant

value that is a harmonic average of recall and precision. Equation (4) defines the F_1 value.

$$F_1 = \frac{2 \times Recall \times Precision}{Recall + Precision} \tag{4}$$

F_1 value is a measure for evaluating recall and precision synthetically. It is calculated as a harmonic mean of the precision and the recall.

5.3   Result of Ex. 1

We show the progress graphs of fault-prone filtering under TOE experiments in Figs. 1 and 2, and the overall prediction results obtained by conducting Ex. 1 in Tables 2, 3, 4, and 5.

First, we explain about the graphs in Figs. 1 and 2. The upper graph in Fig. 1 shows the transition progresses of evaluation measures when we apply the byte-code modules fault-prone filtering to Apache Ant. The bottom graph in Fig. 1 shows the transition progresses of measures with source code modules. Concerning TOE, classifier first detects modules one by one in a no-learning state, and then it learns when the detection result is incorrect. Therefore, the detection performance varies according to the number of modules of which prediction is completed. These graphs show the results of the recall, the accuracy, and the precision measured when the detection of n-th modules is completed. Their vertical axis shows the value of accuracy or precision or recall. Then their horizontal axis shows the number of modules finished detecting at the time when we calculate

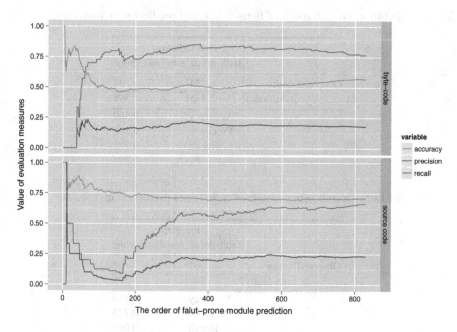

Fig. 2. Transition of each measure with byte-code and source code in Tomcat

Table 2. Overall result of byte-code based prediction in Ant

		Prediction	
		fault-prone	non-fault-prone
Observed	faulty	248	43
	non-faulty	686	410
	Accuracy	0.474	
	Precision	0.266	
	Recall	0.852	
	F_1	0.405	

Table 3. Overall result of source code based prediction in Ant

		Prediction	
		fault-prone	non-fault-prone
Observed	faulty	192	99
	non-faulty	388	708
	Accuracy	0.649	
	Precision	0.331	
	Recall	0.660	
	F_1	0.441	

Table 4. Overall result of byte-code based prediction in Tomcat

		Prediction	
		fault-prone	non-fault-prone
Observed	faulty	74	22
	non-faulty	335	398

Accuracy	0.569
Precision	0.181
Recall	0.771
F_1	0.293

Table 5. Overall result of source code based prediction in Tomcat

		Prediction	
		fault-prone	non-fault-prone
Observed	faulty	64	32
	non-faulty	208	525

Accuracy	0.710
Precision	0.235
Recall	0.667
F_1	0.348

the value of accuracy, precision, and recall. Similarly, the application result to Tomcat project is shown in Fig. 2.

Next, we explain about Tables 2 and 3. Table 2 represents the prediction result when the byte-code modules were predicted, and Table 3 represents the prediction result when the source code modules were predicted. We can confirm that the byte-code module prediction with fault-prone filtering has lower accuracy and precision than the source code module prediction. In particular, when the value of precision is 0.266, then we must check up three more extra modules to find one fault-prone module. However, the recall is greatly high, and it shows that we found 85 % faulty modules as fault-prone.

5.4 Result of Ex. 2

We show the result graphs of fault-prone filtering changing the threshold obtained by conducting Ex. 2 in Figs. 3 and 4.

These Figures show the transition of the precision and the recall of fault-prone filtering in the case that threshold value is manipulated. The left graph in Fig. 3 shows the precision, the right one shows the recall for both byte-code and source code based prediction in Ant project. Then, the horizontal axis of both of graphs shows the threshold.

Now, a point to notice is that increasing the threshold value results in increasing the recall in Fig. 3. Normally, when all of the data is used for learning,

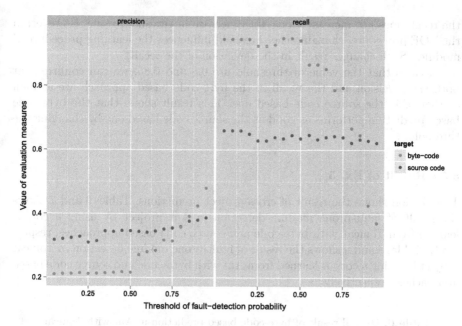

Fig. 3. Transition of precision and recall by changing threshold value in Ant

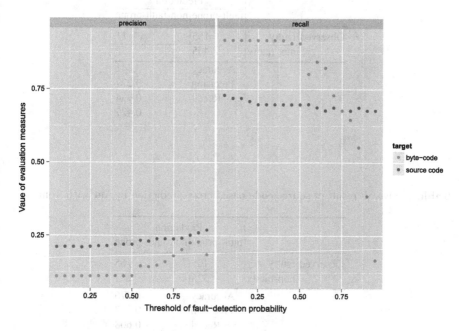

Fig. 4. Transition of precision and recall by changing threshold value in Tomcat

the recall does not increase along with increase in threshold value. However, in the TOE procedure, changing the threshold influences the learning procedure of modules. Such changes result in the deviation of the recall.

In cases that the value of threshold are 0.8 and 0.85, we can confirm that both the precision and the recall in the byte-code based approach are as high as that of in the source code based one. This result shows that the byte-code based prediction performs as good as the source code based one by changing the threshold.

5.5   Result of Ex. 3

This section shows the result of cross-project predictions. Tables 6 and 7 shows the result of fault-prone module detection in Ant project by using a corpus learned from Tomcat with byte-code and source code based approaches, respectively. Tables 8 and 9 shows the result of fault-prone module detection in Tomcat project by using a corpus learned from Ant with byte-code and source code based approaches, respectively.

Table 6. Overall result of byte-code based prediction in Ant with Tomcat

| | | Prediction | |
		fault-prone	non-fault-prone
Observed	faulty	155	11
	non-faulty	405	173

Accuracy	0.441
Precision	0.277
Recall	0.934
F_1	0.427

Table 7. Overall result of source code based cross-prediction in Ant with Tomcat

| | | Prediction | |
		fault-prone	non-fault-prone
Observed	faulty	101	65
	non-faulty	325	253

Accuracy	0.476
Precision	0.237
Recall	0.608
F_1	0.341

Table 8. Overall result of byte-code based prediction in Tomcat with Ant

		Prediction	
		fault-prone	non-fault-prone
Observed	faulty	69	7
	non-faulty	537	216
	Accuracy	0.344	
	Precision	0.114	
	Recall	0.908	
	F_1	0.202	

Table 9. Overall result of source code based cross-prediction in Tomcat with Ant

		Prediction	
		fault-prone	non-fault-prone
Observed	faulty	76	0
	non-faulty	699	54
	Accuracy	0.157	
	Precision	0.098	
	Recall	1.000	
	F_1	0.179	

6 Discussions

In Sect. 3, we have research questions as follows:

> **RQ1.** Is there a difference in the accuracy of fault detection between the source code based and the byte-code based approaches?
> **RQ2.** In the cross-platform application, is the accuracy of fault-prone module prediction improved by using byte-code modules?

From the result of experiments, we can say that the answer to the research question RQ1 is clearly yes.

In this section, we should investigate the result in more detail.

6.1 Byte-Code vs Source Code

First, we investigate the result of Ex. 1. Figure 1 shows the transition of evaluation measures for byte-code based and source code based prediction, respectively. Tables 2 and 3 show the overall evaluation measures for byte-code based and source code based prediction, respectively.

From Fig. 1 and Table 2, we can see the result of fault-prone module detection for byte-code modules. The accuracy and the precision are not high, but the recall is high. It is because the byte-code based method detects more modules as fault-prone. Especially, for the actual non-fault-prone modules, 686 modules out of 1,096 are wrongly detected as "fault-prone". On the other hand, for the actual fault-prone modules, 248 modules out of 291 modules are detected correctly as fault-prone. We consider that the characteristics of faulty code are emphasized too much in the byte-code based approach, and thus the characteristics of non-faulty code are missed. As for the results of source code modules based approach in Fig. 1 and Table 3, we can see the features of this approach. Comparing the F_1 values of both byte-code based and source code based approaches, we find that the source code based approach has balanced result. This result suggests that byte-code based approach has high capability to detect actual faults but requires more cost.

Next, we investigate the result of Ex. 2. Figures 3 and 4 show the transition of the precision and the recall for byte-code based and source code based predictions, by changing the threshold value for Ant and Tomcat projects, respectively. A point to notice is that the values of precision and recall in the source code based detect prediction hardly move, whereas those in the byte-code based one move largely according to the changing threshold value. This shows that in comparing with the source code based method, the byte-code based method generates more ambiguous prediction results whether a module is fault-prone or non-fault-prone. On the other hand, the most of the probabilities to be fault-prone in the source code based method is close to 1, as the recall hardly moves according to the changing the threshold value. It is because source code tokens tend to be unique by the identifiers, whereas byte-code tokens(mnemonic) have less variety than source code tokens.

As mentioned through the results of Ex. 1 and Ex. 2, the probabilities that module is fault-prone in byte-code module based prediction is ambiguous, and it might not suit to the empirical application. However, there must be a powerful determinant factor, as byte-code based prediction has the large value of recall when the value of threshold is set to 0.5, shown in Fig. 1 and Table 2. As a reason for that, the performance of the byte-code based prediction can be superior to the source code based one with a proper value of threshold that is shown in Fig. 1 and Table 3.

6.2   Cross-Project Prediction

Finally, we investigate the result of Ex. 3. Comparing Tables 6 and 7, the cross-project prediction using byte-code achieves relatively higher recall than that of using source code. However, from this table, other measures but recall shows similar values between Tables 6 and 7. On the other hand, Tables 8 and Table 9 show major difference between byte-code based and source code based predictions. We can see that the prediction does not work well by the source code based approach in Table 9, but the byte-code based approach can predict fault-prone modules in Table 8.

From this results, we can say that the byte-code based fault-prone module prediction works as well as that of the source code based prediction, or sometimes works in more accurate. Therefore, we expect that byte-code based prediction greatly contributes to the cross-project prediction in the future.

6.3   Threats to Validity

- **The number of target projects**
  It is a concern for the internal validity. In the experiments, we obtained results from Apache Ant project and Apache Tomcat project. Therefore, it may be a specific result for these two projects only. Furthermore, since they are open source software, we do not have confidence that we can obtain similar results from commercial projects.
- **The order of applying modules**
  In the experiment, we used a random order of modules when applying TOE procedure in a revision. The reason is that we cannot find detailed time-stamps from the byte-code and source code in a revision. Since the result of TOE procedure is affected by the order of application of module, there may be a difference in evaluation measures between the best and worst orders of modules.
- **Bugs in scripts**
  In the experiment, we developed scripts to execute the procedure. The bugs in the script may change the result of the experiment although the current result of the experiment seems reasonable.

7   Conclusion

In this paper, we proposed a fault-prone module detection approach for byte-code modules in Java using a text classification technique. We then conducted experiments using two OSS projects to show the detection accuracy of the proposed approach.

By comparing the accuracy measures of byte-code modules detection with that of source code modules, we can conclude that the byte-code modules detection has slightly higher accuracy measures.

In the future work, we need to apply more projects to generalize the result of this experiment.

We can see that the compiling procedure is a mapping process from the source code to the byte-code. When we got the different fault-proneness between the source code and the byte-code, we can say that the source code has an extra factor to disturb the analysis of fault-proneness. To clarify such issues, we can use the notion of metamorphic testing [2], and this is an important future issue for our research.

Acknowledgment. This work was supported by JSPS KAKENHI Grant Number 15K00096.

References

1. Briand, L.C., Melo, W.L., Wust, J.: Assessing the applicability of fault-proneness models across object-oriented software projects. IEEE Trans. Softw. Eng. **28**(7), 706–720 (2002)
2. Chen, T., Feng, J., Tse, T.: Metamorphic testing of programs on partial differential equations: a case study. In: Proceedings of the 26th Annual International Computer Software and Applications Conference (COMPSAC 2002), pp. 327–333. IEEE Computer Society, Los Alamitos, CA (2002)
3. Graves, T.L., Karr, A.F., Marron, J., Siy, H.: Predicting fault incidence using software change history. IEEE Trans. Softw. Eng. **26**(7), 653–661 (2000)
4. Gyimóthy, T., Ferenc, R., Siket, I.: Empirical validation of object-oriented metrics on open source software for fault prediction. IEEE Trans. Softw. Eng. **31**(10), 897–910 (2005)
5. Jureczko, M., Madeyski, L.: Towards identifying software project clusters with regard to defect prediction. In: Proceedings of the 6th International Conference on Predictive Models in Software Engineering (PROMISE 2010), p. 10, Article no. 9. ACM, New York, NY, USA (2010)
6. Menzies, T., Rees-Jones, M., Krishna, R., Pape, C.: The promise repository of empirical software engineering data (2015). http://openscience.us/repo
7. Mizuno, O., Ikami, S., Nakaichi, S., Kikuno, T.: Fault-prone filtering: detection of fault-prone modules using spam filtering technique. In: Proceedings of 1st International Symposium on Empirical Software Engineering and Measurement, Madrid, Spain (2007)
8. Mizuno, O., Kikuno, T.: Training on errors experiment to detect fault-prone software modules by spam filter. In: Proceedings of 6th Joint Meeting of the European Software Engineering Conference and the ACM SIGSOFT Symposium on the Foundations of Software Engineering, pp. 405–414 (2007)
9. Nagappan, N., Ball, T.: Static analysis tools as early indicators of pre-release defect density. In: Proceedings of 27th International Conference on Software Engineering, pp. 580–586. ACM, New York, NY, USA (2005)
10. Ostrand, T., Weyuker, E., Bell, R.: Predicting the location and number of faults in large software systems. IEEE Trans. Softw. Eng. **31**(4), 340–355 (2005)
11. Rahman, F., Posnett, D., Devanbu, P.: Recalling the "imprecision" of cross-project defect prediction. In: Proceedings of the ACM SIGSOFT 20th International Symposium on the Foundations of Software Engineering, FSE 2012, pp. 61:1–61:11. ACM, New York, NY, USA (2012). http://doi.acm.org/10.1145/2393596.2393669
12. Seliya, N., Khoshgoftaar, T.M., Zhong, S.: Analyzing software quality with limited fault-proneness defect data. In: Proceedings of 9th IEEE International Symposium on High-Assurance Systems Engineering, pp. 89–98 (2005)
13. Yerazunis, W.S.: CRM114 - the Controllable Regex Mutilator. http://crm114.sourceforge.net/
14. Zheng, J., Williams, L., Nagappan, N., Snipes, W., Hudepohl, J.P., Vouk, M.A.: On the value of static analysis for fault detection in software. IEEE Trans. Softw. Eng. **32**(4), 240–253 (2006). doi:10.1109/TSE.2006.38

Variability Management Strategies to Support Efficient Delivery and Maintenance of Embedded Systems

Susanna Teppola[1]([✉]), Päivi Parviainen[1], Jari Partanen[2],
and Petri Kettunen[3]

[1] VTT Ltd., Kaitoväylä 1, Oulu, Finland
{susanna.teppola,paivi.parviainen}@vtt.fi
[2] Bittium Wireless Ltd., Tutkijantie 8, Oulu, Finland
jari.partanen@bittium.com
[3] Department of Computer Science, University of Helsinki,
P.O Box 68, Helsinki, Finland
petri.kettunen@cs.helsinki.fi

Abstract. Software intensive organisations that are able to efficiently handle product variability can reach competitive advantage by shorter development lead times, improved customer satisfaction, and reduced costs of product management. Improved reusability and flexibility, combined with variability strategies can provide companies mechanisms to offer new product variants fast to customers. Especially for long living embedded systems, it is essential to effectively maintain the delivered systems and keep maintenance costs at reasonable level. This paper describes a case study in which three industrial product development projects were studied in order to understand which variability strategies were implemented in their specific variability context. Results indicate that variability challenges and selected variability strategies depend both on the product platform maturity, as well as, the project development model. However, variability strategy needs continuous evaluation during the product lifecycle.

Keywords: Variability management · Variability strategy

1 Introduction

Today's tight, customer-oriented markets companies have to continuously look for ways how to effectively produce new appealing products to various customers. Development of embedded products is typically performed by a multi-disciplinary team, which constantly has to make decisions and trade-offs to realize the desired functionality with reasonable costs. At the same time companies must be ready to adapt to new business opportunities, and therefore the products must be designed in a way that they can adapt to various changes appearing during the product lifetime [1]. These factors; fast product delivery and product upgrades to customers with appealing new features and dealing with increasing technical complexity of products requires a way to efficiently manage variants developed and delivered to customers. This has brought a

© Springer International Publishing Switzerland 2015
P. Abrahamsson et al. (Eds.): PROFES 2015, LNCS 9459, pp. 431–438, 2015.
DOI: 10.1007/978-3-319-26844-6_31

need for more lightweight but still efficient variability management tools and practices in companies.

However, it can be seen that there are still many challenges in adopting lightweight variability management practices in companies. Kratochvíl and Carson [2] have found that as many as half of software intensive companies face variability challenges:

- Companies lack software architectures that support continuous variability management taking into account the changes occurring during the product lifetime [3].
- Companies are struggling how to assess and understand implications of changes to different requirements and features on the software system [4].
- Making successful variability decisions is difficult and requires both a considerable amount of information and systematic working practices which are often difficult for companies to arrange [1, 5].

This paper presents a case study in which three embedded product development projects were studied in order to better understand which variability strategies companies targeted in their specific variability contexts. The case company works in highly competed B2B market, in which continuous changes take place both in technological and market side. The structure of the paper is the following. First we discuss of the variability decisions and variability management based on the related literature, after that the results of the case study are presented, and finally the conclusions are made.

2   Product Variability Decisions and Variability Management

Variability decisions are the design decisions how variability is built in the products. How variability is implemented and managed during product lifecycle depends on the product context, and on the drivers causing variation during product lifetime. This section discusses the variability strategies, drivers, and variability management practices based on related literature.

Drivers Causing Variability and Variability Strategy. For a product variability management the decision how much to customize for a single customer has big impact on the product complexity and reuse, but also, on the business potential the product has. This together with the lifetime expectancy ever increases the complexity and the amount of dependencies that is needed to be managed during the product lifecycle. Depending on the case the optimal level between commonalities and variability must be reached. Variability strategy means the implementation how flexible and variable the product is, i.e. how much the product shares common components, what is variable and how much is tailored [6].

The variability strategy typically links to the maturity of a product platform, and the project model of the delivered products. Codenie et al. [6] classifies the project models in the four types. Project-based development is a model that is used when products are developed on a per-contract basis for specific demands set by a single customer.

Technology-platform development deals with building a dedicated platform that solves a specific technological problem and aim to provide building blocks for a larger product. Customized product development is about developing products that need to be further adapted to suit the specific needs of customers, and out-of-the-box product development means generic products that can suit the needs of many customers. Thus, this classification comes from the ratio of domain engineering (commonalities) and application engineering (variability) they require. Typically, a product that is still young and emerging the platform is a collection of reusable assets where variability points are still unclear. In a mature platform, such as in software product line, the reuse is systematic and variability points are well identified [4].

Commonality and Variability Analysis. Commonality and variability analysis aims to develop common features that form the basis for reuse [7]. In domain engineering, commonality and variability analysis is used to identify, formalize, and document commonalities and variability. The analysis includes business and technical viewpoint and both previous and coming products/needs. During domain analysis, analysing and identifying needs for variability in the domain is carried out. This happens by identifying potential reuse applications and analysing their similarities and differences and then identifying possibilities (variation mechanisms) to support each of the variation need. This involves e.g. analyzing of HW and SW interfaces, and possibilities to capsulate or hide dependencies, and documenting all dependencies including description of the dependency and explanation of how to make the necessary variations or modifications.

Configuration and Deployment Reasoning. With long lifespan of products, maintenance is considered significant. The customers typically require that the updated modules work with the older deliveries and changes are not preferred in the current functionality of the system. In case of embedded products with long replacement cycles, backwards compatibility may be as important as pure functionality [8]. For these reasons the system has to be built backwards compatible and tested extensively with all HW variations every time released to customers. This requires good understanding of the system evolution, as well as perfect knowledge of the installed base [9]. Installed base information has high value for a company, because it serves input for immediate product sales and service but also product marketing and future product planning [8]. From the embedded product development point of view installed base information serves an input for HW and SW compatibility and manageability issues.

Transparency to Support Informed Variability Decisions. As variability decisions have long impact on the product lifetime costs, they must be based on the best multidiscipline knowledge and comprehensive background information. Therefore information available for all stakeholders to see, can support variability and design decisions, provide rationales, and indicate impacts even beforehand. For instance, the study by Ihme et al. [10] indicates that the most difficult challenge in variability management in today's small and medium sized organisations is the lack of transparency of variability and design decisions between R&D and business and customer interfaces, and within R&D. As the most important goal of improvement the study mentions the better variability management via transparency of variability and better product platform's support for variability. This indicates that transparency of variability and design decisions for each stakeholder is an important enabler for flexible and variable product platform development.

3 Research Methods

This paper presents a case study in which three embedded product development projects were studied in order to identify which variability strategies were implemented in their specific variability context. The topics that were studied were the following:

- What was the product development context concerning; product, lifetime, development team, platform maturity, development model and main variability drivers?
- What was the variability challenge in that particular product development context?
- What variability management strategies the case company targeted concerning: commonality and variability, configuration and deployment, and transparency?

The research methods included literature study, personal interviews (5) and workshops (3). Literature study provided the background information for preparing the interview questions and workshops. Personal semi-structured interviews were arranged for each case; the interviewees included program manager (1), project manager (2), product manager (1) and configuration manager (1). The interviewees were selected on the basis that they were the ones knowing best of variability challenges and implementations related to the particular case. Interview analyses were presented in separate workshops, in which 2–3 business case representatives were present. Next section describes the results of the cases.

4 Research Results

The following Table 1 describes the product development contexts and related variability challenges in three different projects delivering embedded products.

Table 1. Product development contexts and variability challenges in three projects.

	Case A	Case B	Case C
Product	Device platform with Android operating system (e.g. for smartphones, tablets, wearables)	Tactical communication device (IP clients and network extension units)	Radio channel emulator (with different number of channel units)
Lifetime	3–7 years	10–20 years	10–15 years
Development team	50–100 persons, distributed	20 persons, one-site	50 persons, one-site

(Continued)

Table 1. (*Continued*)

	Case A	Case B	Case C
Platform maturity	Early stages of development. Some reusable technology assets are identified	Product platform reaching a stable phase. Clearly identifiable generic part with variable application layer	Mature product platform with well-defined HW and SW interfaces, and variable application layer
Development model	Technology platform development in customer driven projects	Customized product development with a roadmap and in customer projects	Out-of-the-box product development with own product roadmap
Main drivers causing variation	Frequent changes in 3rd party technologies New customers with specific needs affecting strongly both HW and SW	Replacements of broken HW components Changes in 3rd party technologies Compliance to emerging standards New customer needs	Replacements of broken HW components Changes in 3rd party technologies. Compliance to emerging standards New customer needs
Variability challenge	How to identify which features in the technology platform should be kept fixed and which remain variable. How to stay aware of the evolving external components, and realize what their evolution might mean to the existing technology assets	Transition towards out-of-the-box development model; but how to maintain the delivered, often customized products, and ensure their backwards-forwards compatibility during the updates. Pressure for new HW variations	How to effectively maintain and provide new services/features for delivered systems, and ensure their backwards/forwards compatibility. How to make sure that all important HW and SW dependencies are supported in updates

The following Table 2 describes which variability strategies and practices the case company implemented in order to improve the flexibility and variability of their products.

Table 2. Variability strategies and related variability management practices in the products.

	Case A	Case B	Case C
Variability strategy	Generic technology platform providing building blocks for many variants. Next step is to identify business driven assets	Generic SW platform ensuring backwards compatibility to all existing HW configurations. Hidden SW variations	Generic SW platform ensuring backwards compatibility to all existing HW configurations. Hidden SW variations
Commonality and variability	A better understanding of the vertical business domains was needed in order to realise better, which parts of the product could be kept constant and which variable Reuse practices between many projects were established	A new generic SW architecture was developed, that could fit in all HW configurations. SW variability isolated in the application side and configurable during runtime (toggle able)	The SW variability was isolated in the application side; and all HW variants shared the generic SW platform Toggle able features which were configurable during runtime
Configuration and deployment	Maintenance did not play a pivotal role at the moment of the platform development	Better installed base information was still needed for managing release compatibilities. Also customers could benefit from the information related to future update needs	Installed base information was collected in device cards in order to better realise different customer configurations vs. HW and SW compatibilities
Transparency	Continuous design practice for identifying assets for reuse between projects. Variability design decisions were made by multidiscipline responsibilities and design information was saved in tools. Design decisions and rationales were traceable and shared to stakeholders	Practices were developed for making a product design and its evolution more visible for all stakeholders, including customers The knowledge of critical system architectures and design decisions was documented and continuously updated in wikis	For better compatibility management a tool for managing HW&SW release dependencies was developed. Tool included release level dependencies and time aspect (roadmap) A practice supporting managed and up-to-date dependency data was taken in use

5   Discussion and Conclusions

This paper describes a case in which three projects delivering embedded systems for business customers were studied in order to better understand which variability strategies were used in different industrial product variability contexts. The study was conducted in one company, and interviews and workshops were used as the main research methods.

The products represented different maturity levels of embedded product platforms; from an emerging device platform with ad hoc reuse to more mature platforms with more systematic reuse practices. Each case suffered different types of variability challenges. The emerging device platform was struggling mostly with commonality-variability issues, while the more mature product platforms had challenges with release compatibilities and HW&SW dependence management. These challenges caused a need for improved reuse practices, as well as better management of HW and SW component end-of-life information. As a variability strategy, the company focused on implementing more business driven technology assets and developing generic SW platform that could adapt to all HW configurations. This way the company could avoid several HW&SW branches to be maintained separately, and could improve the reusability across business domains. The perceived benefits for the company were the cost savings when all HW configurations could always be maintained with the same SW baseline, and better efficiency through improved reusability. Furthermore, management of installed base, HW&SW release dependencies, synchronization of separate application and platform roadmaps, an overall management of roadmaps, releases, and assets was expected to be improved.

The study indicates that variability challenges and suitable variability strategies depend strongly on the development model and on the maturity of a product platform. Also, different types of drivers causing variation are impacting differently during the product lifecycle. Thus, the selected variability strategy is not working for years, instead, the drivers that cause variability has to be re-evaluated repeatedly against the variability strategy. In order to support flexible and variable platform development, continuous transparency between R&D, business and customer interfaces are needed with clear, measurable objectives. This is a topic that we propose as the future research for this study.

References

1. Myllärniemi, V., Savolainen, J., Raatikainen, M., Männistö, T.: Performance variability in software product lines: proposing theories from a case study. Empir. Softw. Eng. 1–47, 24 February 2015
2. Kratochvíl, M., Carson, C.: Growing Modular: Mass Customization of Complex Products, Services and Software. Springer, Berlin (2005)
3. Chen, L., Babar, M.A.: Variability management in software product lines: an investigation of contemporary industrial challenges. In: Bosch, J., Lee, J. (eds.) SPLC 2010. LNCS, vol. 6287, pp. 166–180. Springer, Heidelberg (2010)

4. Bosch, J.: The challenges of broadening the scope of software product families. Commun. ACM **49**(12), 41–44 (2006)
5. Stallinger, F., Neumann, R., Schossleitner, R., Stephan Kriener, S.: Migrating towards evolving software product lines: challenges of an SME in a core customer-driven industrial systems engineering context. In: Proceedings of PLEASE 2011, pp. 20–24. Waikiki, Honolulu, 22–23 May 2011
6. Codenie, W., Gonzalez-Deleito, N., Deleu, J., Blagojevic, V., Kuvaja, P., Similä, J.: Managing flexibility and variability: a road to competitive advantage. In: Kang, K., Sugumaran, V., Park, S. (eds.) Applied Software Product Line Engineering, pp. 269–313. CRC Press, New York (2010)
7. Coplien, J., Hoffman, D., Weiss, D.: Commonality and variability in software engineering. IEEE Softw. **1998**, 37–45 (1998)
8. Borchers, H.W., Karandikar, H.: A data warehouse approach for estimating and characterizing the installed base of industrial products. In: International Conference on Service System and Service Management, pp. 53–59 (2006)
9. Rajlich, V., Bennett, K.: A staged model for the software life cycle. Computer **33**(7), 66–71 (2000)
10. Ihme, T., Parviainen, P., Teppola, S.: Variability management challenges in SMEs. ACSIJ **4**(5), 118–126 (2015)

Using Cross-Dependencies During Configuration of System Families

Christopher Brink[1], Philipp Heisig[2]([⊠]), and Sabine Sachweh[2]

[1] Software Engineering Group, Heinz Nixdorf Institute,
University of Paderborn, Paderborn, Germany
christopher.brink@uni-paderborn.de
[2] Smart Environments Engineering Laboratory,
University of Applied Sciences and Arts Dortmund, Dortmund, Germany
{philipp.heisig,sabine.sachweh}@fh-dortmund.de

Abstract. Nowadays, the automotive industry uses software product lines to support the management and maintenance of software variants. However, the development of mechatronic systems includes not merely software, but also other system parts like operating system, hardware or even mechanical parts. We call a combination of these system parts a system family (SF). This combination raises the question how different variable system parts can be modeled and used for a combined configuration in a flexible way. We argue that a modeling process should combine all of these system parts, while the product configuration has to consider dependencies between them. Based on our previous work, we address this question and discuss dependencies between different system parts.

Keywords: Product lines · Feature models · Hardware/software · Systems · System families · Dependencies

1 Introduction

While developing mechatronic systems a combination of different engineering disciplines like mechanical engineering, electrical engineering and software engineering is necessary [27]. Combining system parts of different engineering disciplines is a common and complex task in different domains like automotive or telecommunication industry [33]. Due to the complexity of such systems, they are often realized as system families so that commonalities can be reused. Like in [9,19], we use the term *system families* for a combination of different systems, which have a common basis and variable parts. In contrast to (software) product lines [11], system families consider not only one system part of one discipline, but also different system parts and variants.

To develop such variable systems, automotive suppliers usually use *feature models* [20] to describe common and variable parts of the software. A feature model consists of a hierarchically arranged set of features connected through different types of associations. During the product configuration (e.g. described

© Springer International Publishing Switzerland 2015
P. Abrahamsson et al. (Eds.): PROFES 2015, LNCS 9459, pp. 439–452, 2015.
DOI: 10.1007/978-3-319-26844-6_32

in [1, 8, 14]), the model can be used for creating valid combinations of features. Therefore, features are connected to software development artifacts, but they do not cover other system parts like hardware or operating systems as well as the dependencies between them which are necessary for a combined configuration. The challenge to consider different system parts together in product lines or system families has been described several times in the telecommunication and in the automotive domain [10, 15, 23, 25]. Even if some approaches already dealt with this challenge through consideration of hardware aspects in feature models [24], they do not sufficiently cover other system parts like hardware platforms or operating systems, which also may have variants [7]. The problem is that system parts may have different life cycles so that parts need to be replaced at certain development stages. Thereby dependencies between system parts have to be checked again, which is an error-prone process when doing it manually. Therefore it is necessary that all parts as well as the dependencies are modeled in a holistic way to support a combined system configuration.

Based on our previous research, we discuss dependencies between system parts and propose an approach to model system families which consist of different system parts in a flexible way. Each system part is represented by a variability model which may define dependencies to others. To support the exchange of parts, we further define a language to specify dependencies without specifying explicit relation between system parts and their elements. In addition, we present the combined configuration of system families including different tool-based algorithms, e.g. resolution of dependencies or detection of mismatches.

To illustrate our approach, we use an automotive case study from our European research project AMALTHEA[1], which is described in Sect. 2. In Sect. 3 we discuss the modeling of *multi variability models* as well as dependencies between different system parts. The following Sect. 4 will introduce the combined configuration of multi variability models including different tool-based algorithms to support the configuration process. Afterwards we discuss our approach (Sect. 5) as well as related work in Sect. 6. Finally we conclude our work.

2   Use Case - HVAC

To validate our approach, we use an industrial system family of an HVAC-System (**H**eating, **V**entilation, and **A**ir **C**onditioning) of the project partner Behr-Hella Thermocontrol (BHTC). The HVAC includes a fan and a number of flaps to control the airflow. Additionally, it has several elements to control the system, e.g. controller for airflow distribution, fan speed and the fresh air inlet. The system consists of different variants so that it can be either controlled via a tablet (*Display*) or a control display (*HMI_external*), which is the default within vehicles. In addition, the mechanism can be either controlled directly via the used electronic control unit (ECU) or via another external ECU. The control unit in this use case is a *Freescale MPC5668G* board, which has two heterogeneous cores to serve both, the control of the airflow as well as the control of the servomotors.

---

[1] www.amalthea-project.org.

In this variant, the user makes inputs via a tablet that forwards the signals by a wireless gateway through an SPI interface to the board. On the software side, the system has different mandatory features which all HVAC systems have in common, such as the control for the ventilation (*Blower*). Furthermore, the software part contains an alternative for the airflow control, which can be calculated either on the ECU of the HVAC (*internal*) or on an external one (*Air_external*). A second alternative specifies the possible user interfaces (*HMI*). The feature model in the upper left part of Fig. 1 summarizes all software variants of the HVAC. To realize the HVAC ECU, different kinds of hardware platforms (*Freescale MPC5668G* or *Freescale i.MX6*) and their variants are expedient. Thereby the selection of a platform or variant may depend on the software variant selection, e.g. the *MPC5668G* needs a variant which adds an additional bus type SPI in case a tablet should control the system. Besides the software and hardware a real-time operating system (RTOS) is further necessary to run and manage the software on the ECU. For this purpose, the HVAC uses ERIKA Enterprise[2], which is an open-source OSEK[3] compliant real-time kernel.

3   Multi Variability Models

Embedded systems consists of different system parts like application software, electrical hardware, operating system, a case and so on. Thereby these parts may have dependencies to each other and may be exchanged due to different life-cycles, like software and hardware in the automotive industry [23,26]. We used the HVAC to analyze the different dependencies between system parts. In addition, we use different variability models to capture specific needs of the respective system parts. To allow an exchange of them, we extend our technique to specify dependencies between different system parts.

3.1   Dependencies Between System Parts

During modeling the HVAC system and other use cases of our project, we observed various functional and extra-functional (cf. [28]) dependencies between the software, hardware, operating system and mechanics. Therefore, we collected and grouped these dependencies in the list below:

Functional Dependencies. Based on the HVAC use case an example for such a dependency would be a multi-core hardware platform which requires an operating system that supports multi-core systems.

Extra-Functional Dependencies. These dependencies focus mainly on resource constraints ([34]) that define the capabilities of a hardware platform on which the software will run. For instance, the HVAC requires a certain amount of memory to run the operating system.

---

[2] http://erika.tuxfamily.org/drupal/.
[3] http://osek-vdx.org.

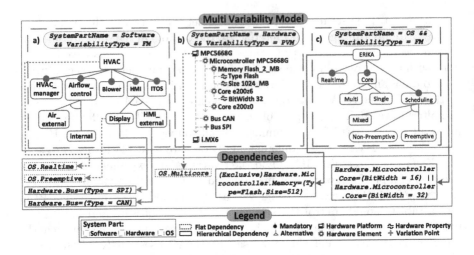

Fig. 1. Modeling multi variability models with cross-dependencies

Exclusive Dependencies. As a special kind of extra-functional dependencies we observed several dependencies that require a specific value of a property (e.g. a specific bandwidth) exclusively. To ensure the availability of these property values, the dependency target has to reserve the required amount for every exclusive dependency. This make them additive as the configuration process has to add up each required property value.

Combined Dependencies. Further dependencies between system parts that contain a combination of properties to clearly specify a requirement (e.g. memory size and memory type).

Alternative Dependencies. Dependencies that can be satisfied through disjunctive properties, such as a dependency to the bitwidth of a core which can either be 16 or 32 bit.

In addition to the different kinds of dependencies we were also able to observe different dependency directions. Thereby, we noticed a strong connection between the hardware and the mechanics that showed up in both directions. Furthermore, we observed in our use cases that no dependencies towards the software exists. One reason for this could be that we started the development with the software variant model and used it as a starting model.

3.2   Variability Models

In order to take the characteristics of different system parts into account, our approach uses multi variability models, which consist of two different model types (*VariabilityType*). As a suitable model type describes each part of the system, a system family can combine both types. The two types differ in their focus: pure feature models can be used for variant-rich parts of the system, whereas the *Property Focused Variability Model* (PVM), a specialized feature model, is convenient when only a small number of variants are available for a system part and the description of existing properties/capabilities should be focused, which is common for hardware platforms [7].

Feature Models. To model variant-rich system parts our approach makes use of feature models [20] as shown in Fig. 1a or c with feature models for the HVACs software and operating system side. Feature models realize dependencies within system parts on the one hand over the tree structure and on the other hand through *require* and *exclude* constraints [12, 21]. These dependencies have already been described many times before [3, 12, 13, 22] and are not the focus of our work. To make a feature within a feature model identifiable, element types can further attribute a feature. For example, in Fig. 1c the feature *Multi* refers to the element type *Multicore*. Using element types is due to the reason that referencing feature names can be error-prone (e.g. *Multi* do not necessary refer to a multi-core processor), whereas assigning an element type makes a feature clearly addressable and supports a further description of dependencies.

Property Focused Variability Model. In contrast to a feature model, a PVM [7] is a specialized feature model and allows the definition of an element type hierarchy for a system part (e.g. *Microcontroller.Core.Memory*). The model focuses on the description of available properties and the corresponding hierarchical structure and is intended for system parts with few variants like hardware platforms. System parts defined in this way contain an arbitrary number of possible realizations to enable an exchange of them. Figure 1b shows two realizations for the system part *Hardware*. First, the platform *MPC5668G* and in addition the platform *i.MX6*. Each realization may contain variants to allow the extension or change of existing properties as well as the hierarchical structure. For this purpose, each variant defines the element which should be changed and in addition the structure and properties that must be added or removed. For instance, in Fig. 1b the variant *Bus SPI* extends the hardware platform with an SPI bus. Within a PVM realization, dependencies can be defined between variants by means of require and exclude constraints, while Properties captures distinct system characteristics, like the clock rate of a CPU, in a standardized way. As a PVM consists of a typed hierarchical structure, properties are clearly identifiable. For example, a property *Size 8 KB* can refer to a distinct hardware element, such as a *Flash* memory, of a superior microcontroller, which again is part of a hardware platform.

3.3   Modeling Dependencies in SF

A common way to describe dependencies within or between feature models and their elements are direct require and exclude dependencies as well as complex dependencies that are bound to feature names [6, 22]. In case elements or models are exchanged, these dependencies are not valid anymore. For direct dependencies it is also possible that sufficient hardware variants cannot be chosen. One example for this is a variant which increases the hardware property *Size* of a hardware element *Memory* with the value *32* KB to *64* KB (cf. [7]). Here a *require* dependency to the *32* KB variant prevents the selection of the variant with *64* KB, although it would also satisfy the requirement. This problem also occurs when multiple system part realizations (e.g. hardware platforms) should be taken into account during configuration.

In order to allow the exchange of system part realizations while preserving the dependencies, our approach uses property-based dependencies to describe requirements between system parts. Therefore, required properties annotate feature models as well as PVMs. While dependencies towards feature models consist of a flat structure, dependencies against PVMs can be hierarchically structured. To cover these different types of dependencies, we define our property-based dependencies by means of an EBNF grammar:

```
Dependency = FlatDependency || (HierarchicalDependency, {'||',
HierarchicalDependency});

FlatDependency = SystemPart, '.', Property;
HierarchicalDependency = ['(Exclusive)'], SystemPart, {'.',
StructureElement}, '=(' Property, {',', Property}, ')';

SystemPart = Name;
StructureElement = Name;
Property =  Name, [ComparismOperator, Value], [Description];

ComparismOperator = ('=' | '>' | '<'| '<='| '>=');
Name = {(Lowercase | Uppercase | Numbers)};
Value = {(Lowercase | Uppercase | Numbers)};
Description = '(', {(Lowercase | Uppercase | Numbers)}, ')';
```

The grammar makes use of two different types to describe dependencies: On the one hand *FlatDependency* (dependencies towards feature models) an on the other hand *HierarchicalDependency*, which is suitable to describe requirements towards PVMs. Both definitions start with the intended system part, whereby logical operators (disjunction) can further connect hierarchical dependencies. This allows the description of **alternative dependencies** (e.g. the operating system in Fig. 1c needs either a bitwidth of 16 or 32). Furthermore, it is possible to annotate a *HierarchicalDependency* with an '*(Exclusive)*' with the result that properties of such dependencies are exclusively available for one source. Figure 1c gives an example for an **exclusive dependency** where the operating system needs at least 512 KB of memory size on its own. As the target has to reserve this properties, they become additive properties, which means that they are summed up during configuration.

As mentioned previously, element types realizes dependencies towards features. In contrast to a *FlatDependency*, a *HierarchicalDependency* can describe a hierarchical structure for required properties. This structure verifies during the configuration process the compatibility between different system part realizations. For this purpose, an algorithm matches the generic defined property type hierarchy (e.g. *Microcontroller.Memory*) against a specific realizations (e.g. *MPC5668G.Memory Flash_2_MB*).

Both dependency types can consist of an arbitrary number of required properties, which have a name and optionally a comparison operator, a value, and a description. These properties specify the requirements towards a system part as shown in Fig. 1a, where the HVAC software needs an operating system of type *Realtime*. A **combined dependency** aggregates several properties into one dependency and is common to describe requirements towards hardware platforms (e.g. the operating system in Fig. 1c needs a <u>flash</u> memory of <u>512 KB</u> memory size). Using combined dependencies instead of splitting such a requirement into two dependencies (e.g. *Hardware.Microcontroller.Memory=(size=64)* and *Hardware.Microcontroller.Memory=(type=flash)*) can be crucial as otherwise properties could be assigned to a wrong element. For instance, if a microcontroller has several memory types but the memory size should be assigned to the flash memory.

4   Combined Configuration of Multi Variability Models

For the purpose of product derivation, selecting desired product features resolves all variability of all existing system parts. Furthermore, a compatibility check between the product configuration and dependencies is necessary to ensure that particular system parts fulfill the requirements. In case of mismatches an algorithm supports an additional error analysis. Figure 2 gives an overview about this approach.

4.1   Product and System Part Configuration

The main objective of the configuration process is to bind all variation points to clearly describe an instance (product) of the system family. For this purpose a product configuration (PC) stores all configuration details to allow further analyses and a later product generation. We define a PC as non-empty set $SPC = (spc_1, spc_2, \ldots, spc_n)$ of system part configurations (SPC), whereby the PC covers all existing system parts (SP) within the multi variability model. As the name suggests, an SPC configures a system part independently of other system parts. Furthermore, SPCs can be characterized as *exclusive-or*, which means that exactly one system part realization (SPR), e.g. *MPC5669G* or *i.MX6* for the SP *Hardware*, has to be selected. This restriction is due to the fact that each SPR has different requirements which would otherwise be mixed up. As a result, this would prevent a compability check between requirements and a current PC. Depending on the underlying variability model, an SPC is either composed out

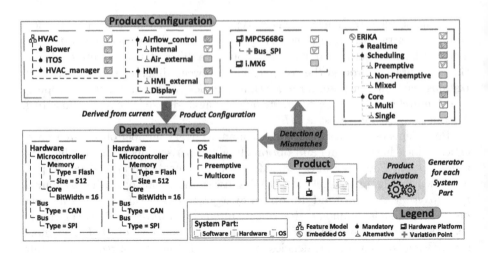

Fig. 2. Resolving cross-dependencies, detecting mismatches and derivating products for a combined configuration

of a finite set $F = (f_1, f_2, \ldots, f_n)$ of features (Feature Model) or relies on a SPR with bound variation points (PVM).

4.2   Restrictions Within the Selection Phase

Defined relationships and constraints within the variability models subjects the selection phase for a PC as shown in the top of Fig. 2. A PC is only consistent if none of the restrictions are violated. The configuration of feature models (as well as the specialized PVMs) has been described several times in literature [5] and will not treated further here.

4.3   Transformation of Requirements into Comparable Tree Structures

After the selection phase all SPs are configured and the question arises whether there are SPCs which meet the requirements (described through dependencies) of Fig. 1. In order to allow such a compatibility check, an algorithm collects all relevant cross-dependencies between the system parts and transform them into a comparable tree structure, which will be further denoted as Dependency Tree (DT). A DT covers all requirements which have been defined for a system part (e.g. software) by transforming particular dependencies into Dependency Tree Paths (DTP) and merge them together afterwards. As displayed in Fig. 2, DTs summarized requirements regarding the SPs *Hardware* and *OS*, while no requirements towards the SP *Software* have been defined. The reason for having two hardware DTs is due to the fact that either a 16- or 32-bit processor architecture is sufficient for the OSEK RTOS (cf. combined dependency in Fig. 1). In case a dependency consists of disjunction operators (||), it is necessary to split the logical expression at every disjunction to get the according tree paths. Note that the number of resulting DTs for a dependency can be calculated with $q \cdot (n+1)$ where q is the quantity of already existing DTs for an SP with $q \in \mathbb{N}_{>0}$ and n is the number of disjunction operators within a logical expression. To give an idea about this process, Fig. 3 shows an UML activity diagram for the derivation of the DTs. As displayed in Fig. 2, dependencies towards PVMs result in hierarchical DTs, while dependencies against feature models are just flat DTs by means of a list.

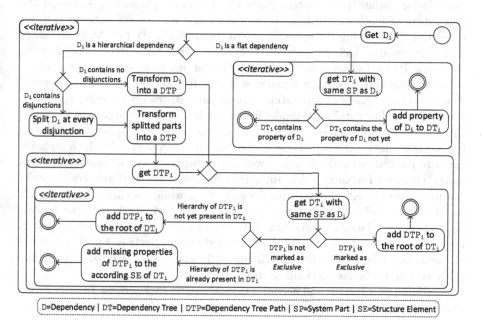

D=Dependency | DT=Dependency Tree | DTP=Dependency Tree Path | SP=System Part | SE=Structure Element

Fig. 3. Derivating DTs from a given set of dependencies

4.4 Detection of Mismatches

The resulting DTs will function as input to determine if the current PC is sufficient enough for the particular requirements of every system part. Therefore, an algorithm compares DTs and SPCs to detect any mismatches. Mismatches can occur in two ways: At first, properties within the SPC have to fulfill the boolean expressions defined in the DT. For instance, the selected platform *MPC5668G* has to provide a memory size of at least 512 as it is required by OSEK. Besides the validation of sufficient property values it is further necessary to check if a SPC covers the hierarchical structure of a *HierarchicalDependency*. This structural validation is especially important for hardware platforms as the hierarchy defines the context of a hardware element (e.g. *Microcontroller.Memory* vs *Microcontroller.Core.Memory*).

5 Discussion

The separation of a system into several system parts may increase the modeling effort as well as the complexity. However, we argue that this separation leads to several advantages. Firstly, according to the characteristics of a system part, a suitable type of variability model can be chosen. While feature models allow to model variant-rich system parts like software, PVMs have their focus on considering typed hierarchical structures together with properties and are therefore suitable for variant poor system parts like hardware platforms. Although the annotation of feature models with properties is a well known concept [14], we argue that introducing the specialized feature models, called PVM, is necessary as feature models lack support in describing hierarchical structures of typed elements. Using feature models to describe variant poor system parts, like a hardware platform, results in a model which is difficult to read and understand. The second advantage of separating system parts instead of covering the whole system variability within one model lies in the fact that this approach allows an easier exchange and reuse of system parts. Furthermore, it splits the complexity and information density of one model towards several models which makes it easier to understand and manage as well better supports a collaborative development. Thus, for instance, a domain expert for hardware platforms could model the hardware system part and its dependencies, while another domain expert could be responsible to define the operating system variants. Due to the generative dependency language and variability models, our approach is not limited to particular system parts. Beyond the described system parts in Fig. 1, which are common for embedded system development, it would also be possible to model other system parts like mechanical interfaces.

Configuring a system and according system parts by hand can be very error-prone and time-consuming. For this reason, our approach has an automatic compatibility check which evaluates a system configuration against the satisfaction of all relevant dependencies. This allows us to select those system part realizations (e.g. *MPC5668G*) from many other available (e.g. via a repository), which are sufficient for the specified requirements. We observed that our tool-based algorithm is sufficient enough for a compatibility check regarding suitable system part realizations, but lack support for additional analyses or automated product configuration. An example for an additional analysis could be the detection of an optimal configuration based on stakeholder preferences like low cost or high performance. For the future, a performance comparism between our implemented algorithm and a solver based solution has to be done. The use of solvers for product configuration has been often demonstrated [5,6,22,32]. However, whether a tool-based algorithm or solver is used for product configuration, the crucial point for a configuration support is the definition and maintenance of dependencies between system parts.

6   Related Work

The challenge to consider different domains in product lines has been described several times in the telecommunications and in the automotive domain [10,25].

AUTOSAR is a de-facto standard within the automotive industry to specify electrics/electronics architectures of an automotive by describing software, hardware and operating system parts in separate models. With the release of version 4.1 [2], AUTOSAR supports variants as well as their definition within feature models. However, it is not possible to define dependencies between variants of different parts.

Liebig et al. [24] dealt with the consideration of hardware aspects in the software product line development process. Therefore, they extended the process by another domain engineering phase for the hardware. This process contains the description of software and hardware variation points in different feature models, but they do not consider the replacement of hardware platforms or more than one nearly equivalent hardware platform. For this reason, they realize the dependencies between hardware and software as a direct dependency, which is not expedient if two hardware platforms or variation points have the same characteristics.

In order to add additional information like non-functional properties and attributes [4,29], for example costs, annotations are often used in feature models. Siegmund et al. [29] extended feature models by non-functional properties that are associated to code units, which allows a software product derivation.

Some approaches already dealt with the consideration of dependencies between different domains and product configuration support. Karatas et al. [22] proposed a mapping approach to use off-the-shelf constraint solver for an automated analysis of extended feature models over finite domains. Although their approach is able to cover different system aspects and allows an automatic check regarding valid product configurations, there are some differences compared to our approach. Firstly, their approach covers the whole system family in one model while our approach proposes one model for a system part, whereby different kind of variability models can be used to meet the characteristics of particular domains. Secondly, Karatas et al. describe cross-tree dependencies by mapping concrete attributes or features against each other which makes it difficult to reuse or exchange sub trees respectively validate against equivalent properties. Urli et al. proposed an approach to interrelate different feature model formalisms within one domain model to handle complex configurations [31]. Inter-model dependencies are defined through a kind of statements which restricts the selection of particular features. In contrast to our approach, inter-model dependencies in their approach are related to features. Although they separated the product line into several models, only one kind of variability model (feature models) is supported.

The process of configuring products in several stages where each stage resolves a set of configuration decisions refers to *staged configuration* [14]. White et al. mapped multi-step configurations to constraint satisfaction problems (CSP) to use CSP solver for an automated product configuration respectively optimization [32]. In [30], Tun et al. suggested to relate requirements with product configuration to generate an optimal configuration for given stakeholders requirements. Therefore, product lines are separated into three abstraction levels whereby each abstraction level is represented through a linked feature model. However, all of them neither distinguish between different system parts nor considering loosely dependencies.

Comprising several heterogeneous product lines in a multi product line (MPL) is often lead by the objective to configure large-scale systems in a distributed manner [17]. Holl et al. used multi-system requirements (MSR) within MPLs to describe dependencies between interrelated product lines [18]. To ensure valid system configurations, the definition and validation of constraints during distributed configuration is supported [16]. However, their approach focus on a distributed configuration where cross-dependencies are emerging through the configuration process, while our approach is centralized and based on the assumption that dependencies within system families are known in advance.

7   Conclusion and Future Work

In this paper, we analyzed dependency types between system parts of a system family by using an industrial use case. Furthermore, we proposed a concept to model different system parts by means of different variability models. As these models are not directly connected to each other, hierarchically structured property types specify requirements towards system parts. For system configuration, we proposed a tool-based algorithm that enables a common configuration of all system parts and checks the compliance with the specified requirements. Compared to other approaches, our concept avoids direct dependencies which makes an exchange of system parts such as hardware platforms easier and enables a further automatic verification of compliance with the requirements.

Due to the complexity of dependencies and requirements, we will continue to extend our concept by using solvers for the verification of requirements between system parts as well as for the verification of dependencies within a variability model. Our future work will further include the development of a change impact analysis method for system families. This will allow us to determine variants, which will not be supported by replaced system part realizations.

Acknowledgments. This research has been partly supported by the Federal Ministry of Education and Research (BMBF), project AMALTHEA4public (no. 01IS14029J).

References

1. Apel, S., Kästner, C.: An overview of feature-oriented software development. J. Object Technol. 8(5), 49–84 (2009)
2. AUTOSAR GbR.: AUTOSAR 4.1. Specification for the Feature Model Exchange Format (2013). http://www.autosar.org/fileadmin/files/releases/4-1/methodology-templates/templates/standard/AUTOSAR_TPS_FeatureModelExchangeFormat.pdf

3. Batory, D.: Feature Models, Grammars, and Propositional Formulas. In: Obbink, H., Pohl, K. (eds.) SPLC 2005. LNCS, vol. 3714, pp. 7–20. Springer, Heidelberg (2005)
4. Benavides, D.: On the Automated Analysis of Software Product Lines Using Feature Models. Ph. D. thesis, University of Sevilla (2007)
5. Benavides, D., Segura, S.: Automated analysis of feature models 20 years later: a literature review. Inf. Syst. **35**(6), 615–636 (2010)
6. Benavides, D., Trinidad, P., Ruiz-Cortés, A.: Automated Reasoning on Feature Models. In: Pastor, Ó., Falcão e Cunha, J. (eds.) CAiSE 2005. LNCS, vol. 3520, pp. 491–503. Springer, Heidelberg (2005)
7. Brink, C., Kamsties, E., Peters, M., Sachweh, S.: On hardware variability and the relation to software variability. In: 40th EUROMICRO Conference on Software Engineering and Advanced Applications (2014)
8. Brink, C., Peters, M., Sachweh, S.: Configuration of mechatronic multi product lines. In: Proceedings of the 3rd International Workshop on Variability and Composition. ACM (2012)
9. Brown, T.J., Gawley, R., Bashroush, R., Spence, I., Kilpatrick, P., Gillan, C.: Weaving behavior into feature models for embedded system families. In: Proceedings of the 10th International Software Product Line Conference SPLC 2006, pp. 52–64 (2006)
10. Broy, M.: Challenges in automotive software engineering. In: Proceedings of the 28th International Conference on Software Engineering, ICSE 2006, pp. 33–42. ACM, New York (2006). http://doi.acm.org/10.1145/1134285.1134292
11. Clements, P., Northrop, L.: Software Product Lines: Practices and Patterns. Addison-Wesley Professional, Reading (2001)
12. Czarnecki, K., Eisenecker, U.: Generative Programming Methods, Tools, and Applications. Addison-Wesley, Boston (2000)
13. Czarnecki, K., Kim, C.H.P.: Cardinality-based feature modeling and constraints: a progress report. In: International Workshop on Software Factories. ACM (2005)
14. Czarnecki, K., Helsen, S., Eisenecker, U.: Staged configuration through specialization and multi-level configuration of feature models. In: Proceedings of the 3rd International Software Product Line Conference (2005)
15. Ebrahimi, A.H., Johansson, P.E.C., Akesson, K.: Challenges in product family knowledge modeling and analysis: from product design to manufacturing. In: Proceedings of the 6th International Workshop on Feature-Oriented Software Development. ACM (2014)
16. Holl, G., Grunbacher, P., Elsner, C., Klambauer, T., Vierhauser, M.: Constraint checking in distributed product configuration of multi product lines. In: Proceedings of the 20th Asia-Pacific Software Engineering Conference (2013)
17. Holl, G., Grünbacher, P., Rabiser, R.: A systematic review and an expert survey on capabilities supporting multi product lines. Inf. Softw. Technol. **54**(8), 828–852 (2012)
18. Holl, G., Vierhauser, M., Heider, W., Grünbacher, P., Rabiser, R.: Product line bundles for tool support in multi product lines. In: 5th Workshop on Variability Modeling of Software-Intensive Systems (2011)
19. Jaring, M., Dannenberg, R.B.: Variability Dependencies in Product Family Engineering. In: van der Linden, F.J. (ed.) PFE 2003. LNCS, vol. 3014, pp. 81–97. Springer, Heidelberg (2004)
20. Kang, K.C., Cohen, S., Hess, J., Novak, W., Peterson, A.: Feature-Oriented Domain Analysis (FODA), Feasibility Study. Tech. Rep. CMU/SEI-90-TR-21, Software Engineering Institute (1990)

452   C. Brink et al.

21. Kang, K.C., Kim, S., Lee, J., Kim, K., Shin, E., Huh, M.: Form: a feature-oriented reuse method with domain-specific reference architectures. Ann. Softw. Eng. 5(1), 143–168 (1998)
22. Karataş, A.S., Oğuztüzün, H., Doğru, A.: Mapping Extended Feature Models to Constraint Logic Programming over Finite Domains. In: Bosch, J., Lee, J. (eds.) SPLC 2010. LNCS, vol. 6287, pp. 286–299. Springer, Heidelberg (2010)
23. Krueger, C.W.: Mechanical product lifecycle management meets product line engineering. In: Proceedings of the 19th International Conference on Software Product Line, SPLC 2015, pp. 316–320. ACM, New York (2015)
24. Liebig, J., Apel, S., Lengauer, C., Leich, T.: RobbyDBMS: a case study on hardware/software product line engineering. In: First Workshop on Feature-Oriented Software Development. ACM (2009)
25. Maccari, A., Heie, A.: Managing infinite variability. In: Workshop on Software Variability Management. The Netherlands (2003)
26. Pretschner, A., Broy, M., Kruger, I., Stauner, T.: Software engineering for automotive systems: a roadmap. In: Future of Software Engineering (2007)
27. Schäfer, W., Wehrheim, H.: The challenges of building advanced mechatronic systems. In: Future of Software Engineering (2007)
28. Shaw, M., Garlan, D.: Formulations and formalisms in software architecture. In: van Leeuwen, J. (ed.) Computer Science Today. LNCS, vol. 1000, pp. 307–323. Springer, Heidelberg (1995)
29. Siegmund, N., Kuhlemann, M., Rosenmüller, M., Kaestner, C., Saake, G.: Integrated product line model for semi-automated product derivation using non-functional properties. In: Workshop on Variability Modeling of Software-Intensive Systems (2008)
30. Tun, T.T., Boucher, Q., Classen, A., Hubaux, A., Heymans, P.: Relating requirements and feature configurations: a systematic approach. In: Proceedings of the 13th International Software Product Line Conference, SPLC 2009, pp. 201–210. Carnegie Mellon University, Pittsburgh (2009). http://dl.acm.org/citation.cfm?id=1753235.1753263
31. Urli, S., Blay-Fornarino, M., Collet, P.: Handling complex configurations in software product lines: a tooled approach. In: Proceedings of the 18th International Software Product Line Conference (2014)
32. White, J., Dougherty, B., Schmidt, D.C., Benavides, D.: Automated reasoning for multi-step feature model configuration problems. In: Proceedings of the 13th International Software Product Line Conference (2009)
33. Wozniak, L., Clements, P.: How automotive engineering is taking product line engineering to the extreme. In: Proceedings of the 19th International Conference on Software Product Line, SPLC 2015, pp. 327–336. ACM (2015)
34. Zeller, M., Prehofer, C.: Modeling and efficient solving of extra-functional properties for adaptation in networked embedded real-time systems. J. Syst. Archit. 59(10), 1067–1082 (2013)

Workshop on Human Factors in Software Development Processes

Toward a Meta-Ontology for Accurate Ontologies to Specify Domain Specific Experiments in Software Engineering

Waldemar Ferreira[1]([✉]), Maria Teresa Baldassarre[2], Sergio Soares[1], and Giuseppe Visaggio[2]

[1] Center of Informatics (Cin), Federal University of Pernambuco, Recife, Brazil
{wpfn,sbsc}@ufpe.cin.br
[2] Department of Informatics, University of Bari, Bari, Italy
{mariateresa.baldassarre,giuseppe.visaggio}@uniba.it

Abstract. Background: Experiments have been conducted in many domains of software engineering (SE). Objective: This paper presents a meta-ontology containing the common concepts present in any SE experiment. This meta-ontology aims at simplifying the proposition of accurate domain specific ontologies for the SE experiments. Method: The paper presents results of an exploratory study that proposes a general ontologyS and its specialization for the domain of coding experiments. Besides, we present how this domain specific ontology specifies a real experiment. Results: The ontology for coding experiments was modeled with few elements. Moreover, it focused only on elements specific to the coding activities. Conclusions: Our meta-ontology facilitates the development of a domain specific ontology in SE, however more research is necessary to evaluate our meta-ontology in other domains of SE.

Keywords: Meta-ontology · Experiment · Software engineering · Coding experiment

1 Introduction

In software engineering (SE) community, there is an increasing need for experiments to develop or improve the processes, methods, and tools [25]. For over a decade, the SE community has been discussing about how to provide a better support to experiments. With this goal, many researchers are proposing several approaches, such as guidelines [11,13,25] and tools [17,22,23].

Among those pertinent to support SE experiments, some propose a formalization of planning, execution, and data analysis [8,10,21]. In spite of all benefits provided by these approaches, they fall in the same limitation. Aiming in providing support for any SE experiment, they lack features to specify precisely the particularities of a specific domain. To illustrate these particularities we can take as example two experiments in SE, one on HCI (Human-computer Interface) domain [19] and other that evaluates two coding techniques [24]. While

© Springer International Publishing Switzerland 2015
P. Abrahamsson et al. (Eds.): PROFES 2015, LNCS 9459, pp. 455–470, 2015.
DOI: 10.1007/978-3-319-26844-6_33

the former focuses on the user interactions, then its relevant variables are mouse clicks and screen records. In the latter, the relevant variables are the lines of code changed by the user and the time spent to develop it.

With the current approaches, all the aforementioned variables are specified in the same way, leading to an inevitable loss of semantics. For instance, in the first experiment the researcher could be interested in only recording a small screen area (for privacy issues), and in the second experiment the researcher could be interested in which files the lines of code were changed. Such information cannot be specified in a general specification approach. However, it is fundamental for providing support to these experiments.

In this context, this paper proposes and details a meta-ontology to support accurate domain specific ontologies. Our meta-ontology describes only the concepts shared by any SE experiment. So that, a concrete ontology can reuse them, while it focuses only on the concepts that are relevant to its specific domain. Therefore, the concrete ontologies have enough expressiveness to specify all relevant characteristics of its domain. Moreover, it is easier to propose these concrete ontologies, because they can reuses the common characteristics of any experiment in SE from our meta-ontology. As example, we present a concrete ontology for the domain of coding experiments in SE. We define coding experiments as any SE experiment that evaluates coding activities (writing, testing, debugging, or maintaining code).

This article is organized as follows. Section 2 presents the related works. In Sect. 3, our meta-ontology is presented. Section 4 demonstrates the realization of our ontology to coding experiments domain. Finally, Sect. 5 presents some final remarks and directions for future work.

2   Related Work

As said in the previous section, the goal of this work is to provide a meta-ontology able to specify all characteristics share among any experiment in SE. Therefor, we have to identify all the mechanisms available to specify an experiment in SE. Besides we have to evaluate how these mechanisms specify the experiments and how they can be extended in order to specify the specificities of a specific domain. The mechanisms presented in the following were identified from two studies Borges et al. [3] and Freire et al. [9]. In the former the authors performed an extensive systematic mapping to identify the support mechanisms used by the empirical studies published in three important venues. In the latter, the authors performed a systematic mapping to identify the automated support mechanisms for SE experiments.

Some authors have proposed models to specify general empirical studies. Cartaxo et al. proposed a visual domain specific language (DSL) called ESEML, for modeling experiments in SE [6]. Based on this DSL, the authors proposed a tool to generate the experimental plan document. Garcia et al. proposed a ontology, called ExperOntology, that focuses on the documentation of SE experiments [10]. Based on this ontology, Neto et al. [17] proposed a tool to support conduction and data packaging of SE experiments. In similar work, Siy, H and Wu, Yan proposed an ontology that focus on experiment process [21]. A remarkable feature of this ontology is the fact that the researcher can apply restrictions regarding the threats to validity.

Other tools have been proposed to support SE experiments. The eSEE tool for example allows researchers to specify and to manage various types of empirical studies in SE [23]. SESE is a web-based environment that supports the management of the participants, it captures the time spent during each task, enables the collection of produced artifacts, and monitors the activities of each participant in a SE experiment [22].

Finally, we highlight a work that proposes both a tool and a DSL to support experimentation in SE [8]. Firstly, the authors propose ExpDSL, a language able to specify some elemental concepts of a SE experiment. Moreover, the authors outline a model-driven approach to manage activities execution and data collection in SE experiments.

Table 1. Related work comparison.

Works	Basic elements	Documentation	Process	Extensible
ESEML	X	X		
Garcia and Neto	X	X	X	
Siy's ontology	X	X		
SESE	X		X	
eSEE	X		X	
ExpDSL	X	X	X	

The goal of this work is to provide a meta-ontology for accurate ontologies in specific domain of SE. Therefor, this meta-ontology has to fulfill at least the following criteria: (i) Basic Element, it has to be able to specify all common characteristics of a SE experiment (variables, factors, parameters, etc.); (ii) Experiment Process, it has to be able to specify activities that the participants have to perform, as well as their execution order; (iii) Extensible, it has to allow extensions to a specific the characteristics of a domain in particular in SE. We believe that without fulfilling these criteria an approach cannot provide an accurate specification of a domain specific experiment. Table 1 presents the evaluation these criteria to the aforementioned works. As we can notice none of them can fulfill all the criteria. In the next section, we propose a meta-ontology that fulfills these criteria.

3   Meta-Ontology for Experiments in SE

One of the goals of this paper is to provide a system of meta-concepts with respect to SE experiment characteristics and how they can be reused to specify

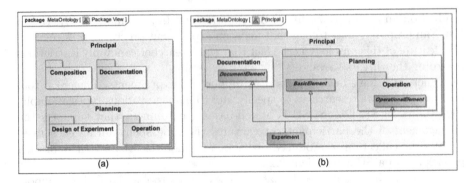

Fig. 1. (a) Meta-ontology package overview and (b) Principal package overview.

domain specific experiments. This meta-concept system is composed in packages. Figure 1a presents the nested hierarchy of our ontology's packages.

Each package in Fig. 1a is designed to stress the general concepts of each perspective in an experiment:

- **Composition** defines the constructs needed to specify experiments that are composed of other experiments (Sect. 3.1).
- **Documentation** defines the concepts to report and to document a SE experiment (Sect. 3.3).
- **Planning** defines the concepts to describe the plan or protocol that is used to perform and to analyze the experiment' results (Sect. 3.2). This package has two sub-packages: (i) *DesignOfExperiment*, describes the chosen design and therefore the statistical analysis; (ii) *Operation* describes procedures to apply treatments to subjects.

The Principal package has only one element (*Experiment*) that defines an experiment in SE (Fig. 1b). This element is a composition of three abstract classes (*BasicElement, DocumentationElement,* and *OperationElement*) that define each facet of an experiment. In the following sections, we present each one of these classes in details. Instead of a hierarchy of packages, we could organize our meta-ontology as a unique package with multiple views, as ExpDSL [8]. we believe that in a hierarchy of packages it is better to organize its content and extend it by adding new packages.

3.1   Composition

Some experiments in SE are a composition of other experiments. The Composition package defines the elements to specify such kind of experiments (Fig. 2a).

Basically, the package comprises two elements:

- **Replication:** Replications play a key role in Empirical SE by allowing the community to build knowledge about which results or observations hold under

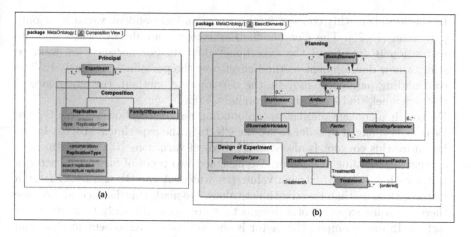

Fig. 2. (a) Composition package and (b) Planning package overview.

certain conditions. Therefore, we modeled a replication as an ordinary experiment with a relationship with other experiment; the one used a baseline for replication. Shull et al. [7] identified two types of replications in SE: exact replications, in which the procedures of an experiment are followed as closely as possible; and conceptual replications, in which the same research question is evaluated using a different experimental procedure. We modeled this characteristic as the *ReplicationType* enumeration.

- **Family of Experiment:** A family of experiments contains multiple similar empirical studies pursuing the same goal [2]. A family of experiment is defined as an ordinary experiment adding a composition of two or more experiments.

3.2 Planning

This section presents the *Planning* package. The experiment planning is sometimes refereed to as experimental design or protocol, it describes the plan or protocol that is used to perform and analyze the experiment results.

Figure 2b presents the main elements of the *Planning* package. According to several guidelines [11,13,14,25], experiment planning describe features such as: goal, participants, experimental material, tasks, hypothesis, parameters, variables, experiment design, procedure for conduction the study, as well as the analysis procedure. Elements that are not present in Fig. 2b will be described in the next sections.

The package components are:

- **Basic Element:** This component represents the most basic facet of an experiment. It is a composition of 4 fundamental components: *ObservedVariable*, *Factor*, *ConfoundingParameter*, and *DesingType* (Sect. 3.4).
- **Confounding Parameter:** This component models any characteristic (qualitative or quantitative) in the experiment that is to be invariable [25].

In the literature this concept is also know as independent variable or only parameter [13,25]. The *ConfoundingParameter* is an abstract class since its realization is specific of the experiment domain. For instance, we want to study a new development method effect over the personnel productivity. The confounding parameter may be the development method, the experience of the personnel, tool support, environment, etc.

- **Factor:** it a concept similar to confounding parameter, however this type of variable is changed in order to see the effects in the experiment [13,25]. In the literature this concept is also called Provoked variations [13]. A treatment is one particular value of a factor. We designed two types of factors: 2 Factor, a factor with only two treatment values (treatment A and B); and *MultFactor*, a factor with more than two treatment values. We made this distinction, because there are some experimental designs that are applicable only to 2 treatment factors. In our example, the factor is the software development method and it may have two treatments agile and traditional method.
- **ObservedVariable:** this component models the outcome of an experiment [25]. In literature, this concept is also known as dependent variable or response variable [13,25]. Therefore, those variables are observed to see the effect of the treatments. Considering our example, the outcomes are time and lines of code.
- **RelatedVariable:** This entity is an abstraction to allow other entities to make unified relationship with *ConfoundingParameter*, *Factor*, or *ObservedVariable*.

Many experiment guidelines suggest that the subjects have to be specified [13,25]. However, we did not specify any component to do so, since our meta-ontology aims at specifying the experiment before execution. Only after or during the execution we can know the relevant information about the subjects. However, the different skills and abilities have to be specified as a confounding parameter. Any other sorts of influence and threat that can impact on the subjects have to be considered in the confounding parameter specification.

3.3   Documentation

In an experiment, not only the operational information is important. Our meta-ontology is able to model all meta-elements of an experiment in order to provide information to enable any researcher to judge the reliability of the experiment and to replicate it. Therefore, we modeled the Documentation package to provide a description of the most common elements in a SE experiment (Fig. 3). Our package is based on various guidelines [11,13,25] and models [8,17].

Our ontology comprises the following elements:

- **Author:** This element defines the information about the experiment authorship. All individuals that made a significant contribution to the experiment should be modeled by this element. For the sake of simplicity, we did not presented all details about the definition of an author; this information includes e-mail, position, institution, etc.

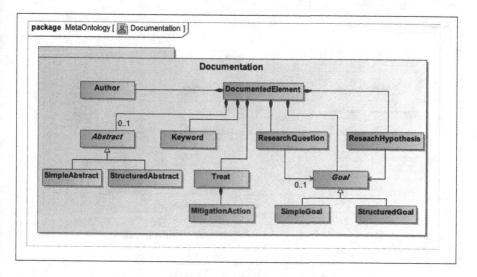

Fig. 3. Documentation package overview.

- **Abstract:** This element defines an experiment abstract. The abstract is an important source of information for any reader as it briefly summarizes the major points of the study. The exact format of the abstract is an open issue [5]. Therefore, we modeled two types of abstracts: (i) *CommonAbstract* represents the most common abstract with only the general text content; *StructuredAbstract*, such type of abstract is a composition of a brief description of the following classes: Background, Objective, Method, Results, Limitation, and Conclusion. This element was based on Jedlitschka et al. [11];
- **Keywords:** This element describes the keywords of the work. The keywords can describe areas of research, treatments, dependent variables, and study type. Besides, this element is not mandatory in an experiment, and therefore, we modeled the multiplicity {0..*} (zero or many).
- **Goal:** This element defines the research objectives, describing in more concrete terms the main manipulations of the experiment. Similar to Abstract, this element models two types of Goals: *SimpleGoal*, with only a description of the goal, and *StructuredGoal*, a goal based on the ExpDSL goal description [8];
- **ResearchHypothesis:** This element describes the experiment hypotheses. For each goal specified in the model, a null hypothesis and corresponding alternatives hypothesis need to be modeled. The description of both null and alternative hypotheses should be as formal as possible. Besides, it is also necessary to state treatments and control conditions (Sect. 3.2);
- **ResearchQuestion:** This element describes each research question of the experiment. The research question identifies the problems that the authors wish to work on. In each case, they could focus on a number of different research questions, each of which lead to a different direction in developing

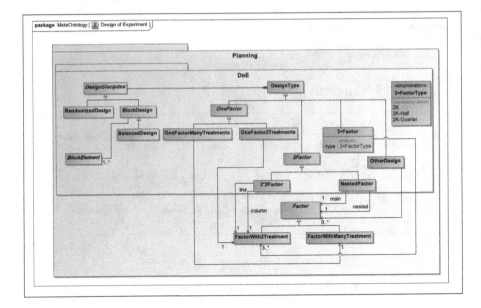

Fig. 4. Package design of experiment overview.

research strategies. The classification of research questions we use in ontology is adapted from Meltzof [16];

- **ThreatToValidity:** this element is used to specify the threats to validity of an experiment. Each threat is defined by an identifier, description, type of threat (Conclusion, Internal, Construct, External) [25], and, optionally, a mitigation action. A *MitigationActor* is used to specify any action taken by the researcher to reduce a threat that may compromise the experimental results validity.

We modeled the package into the Planning package, because many authors argue that goals, hypothesis, and research question are part of the experiment planning [11,25]. Besides, this ontology is complaint with the ExpDSL [8].

3.4   Experiment Design

To draw meaningful conclusions from an experiment, we apply statistical analysis methods on the collected data to interpret the results. To get the most of the experiment, it must be carefully planed and designed. Figure 4 presents our ontology's package designed to represent the experiment design.

This package is composed of the following entities:

- **Design Type:** this entity represents a generalization of the most common designs of experiments in the literature [13,25].
- **Design Principle:** this entity represents the manner of how the subjects have to be distributed among the groups. There are three options: *Randomization,*

with this principle the subjects, objects, and execution order are assigned randomly; *Blocking* is used to systematically eliminate the undesired effect in the comparison among the treatments; *Balanced*, this entity represents the scenarios where the treatments are assigned to equal number of subjects. A Blocking design (and Balanced) is associated with a *BlockElement* that represent what has been blocked by this design. For instance, in many experiments a blocking design is used to block the undesirable effect of subjects' experience. This element is Abstract since it is specific of the experiment domain.

- **OneFactor:** this entity represents the simplest design of Experiment, which compares a set of treatments of one factor against each other. There are two concrete classes that extend this class: the *OneFactor2Treatments*, this can be Complete Randomized design or a Paired Comparison; and the *OneFactorManyTreatments*, this can be Complete Randomized design or a Randomized Complete Block design.
- **2Factor:** this entity models the designs of experiments with two factors. Similar to *OneFactor*, there are two concrete classes for this entity: *2*2Factor*, that models the 2*2 factorial design when there are 2 factors and 2 treatment by factor; and the *NestedFactor*, that models the two-stage nested design when there are also 2 factors but it can support more the 2 treatments by factor.
- **3+Factor:** this factor models those experiments with more then two factors. Different from the previous entities, this class is directly concrete. Besides, it has an attribute to type that indicates which kind of the design: 2k Factorial complete, 2k Factorial half, and 2k Factorial quarters.
- **OtherDesign:** this entity represents other designs of experiments that are not being adopted in SE, such as, the Taguchi methods [18].

We modeled this package to stress the current literature about design of experiments [1,13,25]. Once a new design of experiment (such as the cited Taguchi methods) is implemented in SE, this design can be incorporate to our ontology by extending the class *DesingType* as all other designs.

3.5   Package Procedure

This package describes the procedure of the experiment in terms of activities that participants are subject to. Figure 5 presents the main elements of the package responsible for modeling the experiment procedure.

The package Procedure comprises the following elements:

- **Operational Element:** This component represents the operational facet of an experiment. It is a composition of two components: *Training* and *Process*.
- **Training:** this element represents the training that should be provided to the subjects before the execution of the tasks. This element is abstract, since the kind of training is strongly related to the domain of the experiment.
- **Process:** this element comprises all the activities that the subjects have to perform. There are three types of processes: sequential, random, and conditional. In the conditional process, the class *TaskCondition* represents the

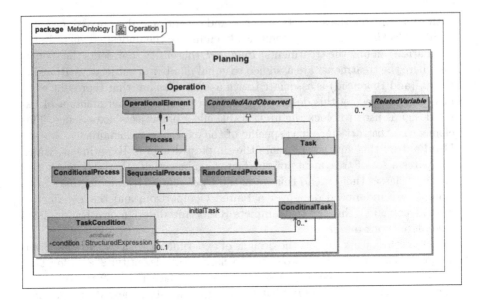

Fig. 5. Package procedure overview.

transition between the tasks. A condition can be specified by conditional logic or any other behavioral description (such as, petri net, graphs, etc.).

– **Task:** this element represents an atomic task that a subject has to perform.
– **ControlledOrObservedElement:** a Task or the whole process can be associated with a *RelatedVariable* (Reminding that a *RelatedVariable* can be a *ObservedVariable, Factor*, or *ConfoundingParameter*, Sect. 3.2). It means that a variable can be observed only on one task or during the whole process. The same applies to *ConfoundingParameter*.

Many authors argue that the experiment procedure should not only describe the training, the description of the tasks, and the schedule of the experiment, but also the details of the data collection method, including when the data should be collected, by whom, and what kind of support (e.g. tool). However, we did not model such information because it is specific of the experiment domain.

4   Ontology for Coding Experiments

Two packages in our ontology have incomplete elements that should be enhanced in a specific domain, the Planning and Procedure packages. This section describes an extension of our ontology to the coding experiments domain.

Coding experiments are SE experiments where the main activity of the subjects is coding. According to SWEBOK [4], coding or programming activities involves designing, writing, testing, debugging, and maintaining. Design is the conception or invention of a scheme for turning a customer requirement for computer software into operational software. It is the activity that links application requirements to coding and debugging. Writing is the actual coding of the design in an appropriate programming language. Testing is the activity to verify if the written code actually does what it was designed to do. Debugging is the activity to find and fix bugs (faults) in the source code (or design). Maintenance is the activity to update, correct, or enhance existing programs.

Usually, experiments that involve design activities do not produce source code, but only mechanisms to bridge the link between customer requirements and source code. Due to the nature of experiments that involve design activities, they are not considered as coding experiments. In the following section, we present the main packages of our coding experiment ontology.

4.1   Coding Experiment Planning Package

The first package is the Coding Experiment Planning Package. This package realizes the abstract classes in the Planning package of our ontology (Fig. 6).

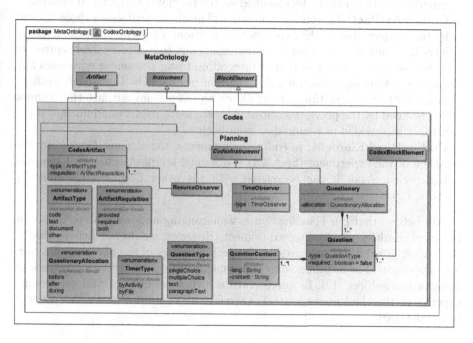

Fig. 6. Coding experiment planning package overview.

The main entities in the Coding Experiment Planning Package are:

- **CodingInstrument:** This entity represents the instruments used to measure the metrics of the experiment. According to our research the instruments in a coding experiment are classified as: *TimeObserver, ResourceObserver, Questionnaire,* or *OtherInstrument*. The *TimeObserver* is responsible to measure the time spent in an activity or in changing a file. An activity can be a task or the whole experiment process (a *Process* or a *Task*, Sect. 3.5). The *ResourceObserver* is responsible of tracking changes in an artifact, usually in coding experiments artifacts are source code, but it can also be a test or a user story. The *Questionnaire* represents all the instruments the subject is responsible for providing the data. In spite of the name adopted, this entity can represent instruments such as forms, sheets, text fields, etc. Moreover, it can be used to collect both quantitative and qualitative data. The attribute allocation presents the circumstance where the questionnaire should be applied, before, after, or during the activity (as *TimeObserver*, the activity depends on the owner of this entity). A *Questionnaire* is composed of many *Questions*. A *Question* can be mandatory and it must have a type. The enumeration *Question* type is based on the *Questionnaire* View of ExpDSL [8]. We decided to specify a *Question* with many *QuestionContent*, in order to allow our ontology to represent the same questionnaire in multiple languages. The *OtherInstruments* represent any other instrument used to measure metrics in coding experiments that cannot be classified as the previously mentioned entities.

- **CodingArtifact:** This entity represents all available artifacts or those created by the subject, during the experiment execution. The type of the artifacts in a coding experiment can be: *Code* represents any source code; *Test* represents since unit tests until validation or integration tests; *Document* represents any document that supports the task execution from a PDF Document, until an image with design of the system; *Other* represents any artifact that cannot be classified by the previous entities. The attribute requisition indicates if the artifact is provided or required or even both.
- **CodingBlockElement:** in coding experiments, the element blocked by the design of the experiment (Sect. 3.4) is obtained by questionnaires. Usually it is experience, but it can be related with any other *ConfoundingParameter* (Sect. 3.2).

We believe that our classification is wide-ranging and accurate to represent the particularities of a coding experiment. However, we do not believe that it stresses all possibilities to represent the particularities of the planning of a coding experiment. For instance, some experiments with usability uses eye-track to monitor the subject [12]. In our literature review we did not find any coding experiment that had used eye-track, therefore we could not model this concept in our ontology.

4.2   Coding Experiment Variables Package

This section describes the package Coding Experiment Procedure Package. This package describes the specification of the variables (dependent and independent) in a coding experiment. Figure 7 presents an overview of this package.

The Coding Experiment Variable Package comprises of:

- **ConfoundingParameter:** this abstract entity represents most common confounding parameters in a coding experiment. We propose 7 concrete classes

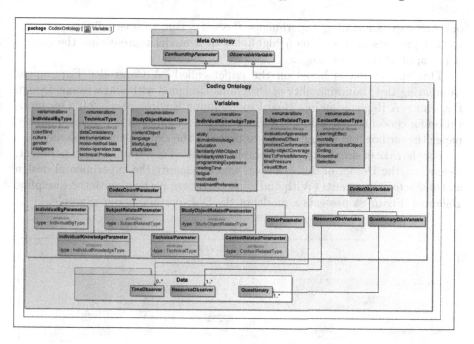

Fig. 7. Coding experiment variables package overview.

corresponding to each confounding parameter category proposed by Sigmund and Schumann [20]. Besides, we proposed the entity *OtherParameter* to represent any other parameter that was not identified by the literature yet.

– **SimpleVariable:** this entity represents the simplest variables in an experiment. The concrete entity *TimeObservableVariable* represents the variables those variable that the time have to be measured. Therefore, these variables have to be associated to an instrument *TimeObserver*. A common example of this variable is the amount of time to finish a task. This entity has two subtypes *ResourceObsVariable* and *QuestionaryObsVariable*. The former represents those variables measured based on the resource provided by the subject (for instance, number of LoC added). The latter those variables that are collect by asking the subject through a questionnaire (for instance, satisfaction).

We modeled the *ResourceObsVariable* and *QuestionaryObsVariable* as a subtype of *TimeObservableVariable*, because many variables in coding experiments make a correlation between the resource production and time to produce them, or the questionnaires and time to answer them.

4.3 Application

This section presents a demonstration of how our ontology has been used in a coding experiment. In particular, we selected a coding experiment from the literature, and demonstrate how this experiment could have been specified in

468   W. Ferreira et al.

our ontology for coding experiments (Sect. 4). Due to space limitation, this
section presents only the main highlights of a model representing the chosen
paper applied to the ontology.

This application is based on the paper called "A Controlled Experiment
Comparing the Maintainability of Programs Designed with and without Design
Patterns – A Replication in a Real Programming Environment" [24]. Our motivation for choosing this coding experiment is the assumption that being a journal
paper the author had enough space to describe the experiment completely.

For the sake of simplicity, our example is modeled as a traditional experiment.
Regarding the Design of our example, we can classify the experimental design
as *OneFactor2Treaments* (With and without Design pattern) with the discipline
Balanced. Figure 8a presents a model of the DoE pertaining our example.

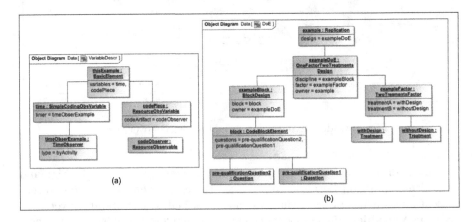

Fig. 8. Vokavc et al. [24]'s (a) experimental design and (b) observed variables.

All examples presented until here used only the concepts of our meta-
ontology. Now we present the specification of the observed variables that are
part of the specific ontology for coding experiments. In the paper, the authors
report that they observed two variables: time and correctness. Time is "The
time taken to complete each task, in minutes". Correctness is "Each solution
was evaluated on a five-point scale to assess to what degree it was functionally correct, regardless of whether it used the 'proper' design...". Based on this,
Fig. 8b presents a specification of the observed variables of our example.

While an ontology has to specify all relevant concept of the ontology's
domain, its application only specifies the concrete information of those concepts.
So that some concepts in the ontology are not relevant for some applications. For
instance, our example did not specify any *QuestionaryBasedVariable*. However,
such type of variables is common in coding experiments.

5   Final Remarks

This paper presents a meta-ontology containing a set of concepts common to any SE experiment. This meta-ontology aims at supporting the construction of domain specific ontologies for SE experiments. We believe that by reusing the concepts of our meta-ontology, the domain specific ontologies can focus on their domain particularities. So that, based on these domain specific ontologies the researchers can develop domain specific approaches that provide a precise support for the particularities of the experiment domain. Finally, we presented a domain specific ontology related to the domain of coding experiments.

As part of the future work of this research, we are developing a tool able to facilitate the specification of domain specific ontologies. Furthermore other SE domains must be covered by our ontology, such as HCI experiments. We are currently modeling our ontology using ontologies-specific languages, such as OWL [15].

References

1. Antony, J.: Design of Experiments for Engineers and Scientists. Elsevier, Oxford (2014)
2. Basili, V.R., Shull, F., Lanubile, F.: Building knowledge through families of experiments. IEEE Trans. Softw. Eng. **25**(4), 456–473 (1999)
3. Borges, A., Ferreira, W., et al.: Support mechanisms to conduct empirical studies in software engineering: a systematic mapping study. In: Proceedings of the 19th International Conference on Evaluation and Assessment in Software Engineering, p. 22. ACM (2015)
4. Bourque, P., Fairley, R.E., et al.: Guide to the Software Engineering Body of Knowledge (SWEBOK (R)): Version 3.0. IEEE Computer Society Press, Los Alamitos (2014)
5. Budgen, D., Kitchenham, B.A., Charters, S.M., Turner, M., Brereton, P., Linkman, S.G.: Presenting software engineering results using structured abstracts: a randomised experiment. Empir. Softw. Eng. **13**(4), 435–468 (2008)
6. Cartaxo, B., Costa, I., Abrantes, D., Santos, A., Soares, S., Garcia, V.: Eseml: empirical software engineering modeling language. In: Proceedings of the 2012 Workshop on Domain-Specific Modeling, pp. 55–60. ACM (2012)
7. Carver, J.C., Juristo, N., Baldassarre, M.T., Vegas, S.: Replications of software engineering experiments. Empir. Softw. Eng. **19**(2), 267–276 (2014)
8. Freire, M., Accioly, P., Sizílio, G., Campos Neto, E., Kulesza, U., Aranha, E., Borba, P.: A model-driven approach to specifying and monitoring controlled experiments in software engineering. In: Heidrich, J., Oivo, M., Jedlitschka, A., Baldassarre, M.T. (eds.) PROFES 2013. LNCS, vol. 7983, pp. 65–79. Springer, Heidelberg (2013)
9. Freire, M., Alencar, D., Campos, E., Medeiros, T., Kulesza, U., Aranha, E., Soares, S.: Automated support for controlled experiments in software engineering: a systematic review. In: SEKE, Boston/USA (2013)
10. Garcia, R., Hhn, E., Barbosa, E., Maldonado, J.: An ontology for controlled experiments on software engineering. In: SEKE, Boston/USA (2013)

11. Jedlitschka, A., Ciolkowski, M., Pfahl, D.: Reporting experiments in software engineering. In: Shull, F., Singer, J., Sjøoberg, D.I.K. (eds.) Guide to Advanced Empirical Software Engineering. Springer, London (2008)

12. Johansen, S.A., San Agustin, J., Skovsgaard, H., Hansen, J.P., Tall, M.: Low cost vs. high-end eye tracking for usability testing. In: CHI 2011 Extended Abstracts on Human Factors in Computing Systems, pp. 1177–1182. ACM (2011)

13. Juristo, N., Moreno, A.M.: Basics of Software Engineering Experimentation. Springer, Heidelberg (2013)

14. Kitchenham, B., Pfleeger, S.L., et al.: Preliminary guidelines for empirical research in software engineering. IEEE Trans. Softw. Eng. **28**(8), 721–734 (2002)

15. McGuinness, D.L., Van Harmelen, F., et al.: Owl web ontology language overview. W3C Recommendation 10(10), 2004 (2004)

16. Meltzoff, J.: Critical thinking about research: Psychology and related fields. American psychological association (1998)

17. Neto, J.P., Scatalon, L.P.: Exptool: a tool to conduct, package and replicate controlled experiments in software engineering. In: Proceedings of the International Conference on Software Engineering Research and Practice (SERP), p. 1 (2014)

18. Peace, G.S.: Taguchi Methods: A Hands-on Approach. Addison Wesley Publishing Company, Reading (1993)

19. Eustáquio Rangel de Queiroz, J., de Sousa Ferreira, D.: A multidimensional approach for the evaluation of mobile application user interfaces. In: Jacko, J.A. (ed.) HCI International 2009, Part I. LNCS, vol. 5610, pp. 242–251. Springer, Heidelberg (2009)

20. Siegmund, J., Schumann, J.: Confounding parameters on program comprehension: a literature survey. Empirical Software Engineering pp. 1–34 (2014)

21. Siy, H., Wu, Y.: An ontology to support empirical studies in software engineering. In: International Conference on Computing, Engineering and Information, ICC 2009, pp. 12–15 (2009)

22. Sjøberg, D.I., Anda, B., Arisholm, E., Others: conducting realistic experiments in software engineering. In: 2002 International Symposium on Empirical Software Engineering, 2002, Proceedings, pp. 17–26. IEEE (2002)

23. Travassos, G.H., dos Santos, P.S.M., Neto, P., Biolchini, J.: An environment to support large scale experimentation in software engineering. In: 13th IEEE International Conference on Engineering of Complex Computer Systems, ICECCS 2008, pp. 193–202. IEEE (2008)

24. Vokáč, M., Tichy, W., Sjøberg, D.I., Arisholm, E., Aldrin, M.: A controlled experiment comparing the maintainability of programs designed with and without design patternsa replication in a real programming environment. Empir. Softw. Eng. **9**(3), 149–195 (2004)

25. Wohlin, C., Runeson, P., Höst, M., Ohlsson, M.C., Regnell, B., Wesslén, A.: Experimentation in Software Engineering. Springer, Heidelberg (2012)

A Qualitative Empirical Study in the Development of Multi-platform Mobile Applications

Rita Francese[1], Michele Risi[1]([✉]), Giuseppe Scanniello[2], and Genoveffa Tortora[1]

[1] Dipartimento di Informatica, Universitá di Salerno, Fisciano, Italy
{francese,mrisi,tortora}@unisa.it
[2] Dipartimento di Matematica, Informatica Ed Economia,
Universitá della Basilicata, Potenza, Italy
giuseppe.scanniello@unibas.it

Abstract. We propose a qualitative study to assess an approach devised for model-driven development of portable applications that use native device features. A model is based on a finite-state machine which specifies a GUI and transitions and data-flow among application screens. We developed our approach in an integrated development environment. Both the approach and the environment have been empirically assessed through a qualitative study with low experienced developers. Participants in this study appreciated solutions we developed.

Keywords: Qualitative study · Multi-platform development · Mobile devices · Model-driven development

1 Introduction

We have previously proposed a model-driven based development (MDD) approach and a supporting environment for the development of multi-platform mobile apps based on finite-state machine [1]. This environment provides a finite-state machine editor and a generator, which produces source code starting from a model. The editor has been developed as an Eclipse plug-in. The editor also exploits PhoneGap[1] functionalities to access device native features and to manage app activities and transitions between app screens. Data-flow, control-flow, and user's interaction are automatically handled, while the application logic is written in Javascript. To assess the validity of our proposal, we have performed a preliminary empirical evaluation conducted with students. The obtained results are presented in this paper for the first time.

This paper is organized as follows. In Sect. 2, we discuss related work. Our solutions are highlighted in Sect. 3. Our empirical study is presented in Sect. 4. Remarks and future work conclude the paper.

---

[1] http://phonegap.com.

© Springer International Publishing Switzerland 2015
P. Abrahamsson et al. (Eds.): PROFES 2015, LNCS 9459, pp. 471–478, 2015.
DOI: 10.1007/978-3-319-26844-6_34

2 Related Work

In the recent years a number of research work has addressed the problem of the multi-platform development for mobile devices (e.g., [2–4]). The use of MDD to generate multi-platform mobile application is relatively new. Only a few approaches are based on MDD. For example, the modeling tool Mobile Applications (MobiA) is proposed by Balagtas-Fernandez and Hussmann [5]. The main idea is to adopt three different models: *(i)* for the GUI, *(ii)* for the navigation, whose model represents how navigating from one screen to another, and *(iii)* for the information, whose model indicates how the information is passed from a component to another. Limited access to native device functionalities is provided.

Choi *et al.* [2] present an application framework based on the Model-View-Control (MVC) architectural pattern. Each component in the framework has transformation rules corresponding to each mobile platform. A component has also an EXtensible Stylesheet Language (XSLT) code template for code generation. The differences are that our approach visually supports the GUI generation and the data flow among the screens of an app.

Cimitile *et al.* [3] propose an approach for the creation of multi-platform mobile applications based on the MVC architectural pattern and a framework for the generation of source code starting from a textual formal algebraic specification. The methodology is completely manual and requires the knowledge of formal languages, such as Linear Temporal Logic. Our solution is simpler since there is no need of to be skilled in formal languages, but only in Javascript development and offers graphical design support.

AXIOM [6] generates apps from a Domain Specific Language. This tool is based on the programming language Groovy and resembles features of the Unified Modeling Language (UML). Features are derived in a bottom-up manner from the functions provided by mobile devices, rather than from business requirements. However, transformations have several intermediary steps requiring additional decisions and are hence not fully automated. This represents the most remarkable difference with respect to our proposal.

The MicroApp Generator [7] is a graphical environment for generating mobile applications starting from their models. A model is directly composed on the smartphone by connecting services representing native functionalities of the device or web services. Colors are used to provide intuitive cues to correctly connect the inputs and the outputs of two or more services. Different types of data are supported. The model is translated in XML and is executed by the MicroApp engine on Android devices. The model is platform independent and can be executed on different platforms once the engine has been migrated. The difference here is that the mobile app is modeled in terms of service composition and is addressed to end-users, whilst the service logic cannot be defined.

Vaupel *et al.* [8] present an MDD approach based on the following different abstraction levels: compact modeling of standard app elements, detailed modeling of individual elements, and separate provider models for specific customers' needs. In particular, a data model, similar to a class diagram, an Interface model and the process model, describing the application behavior (in a BPEL-like way) have to be designed.

Abadi *et al.* [9] represent the application screens as states of a finite state machine, while events such as user's actions and communication-related triggers cause transitions between the states.

Several are the differences with the approaches introduced before. One of these differences is that empirical studies with human beings have not been conducted to assess the validity of proposed solutions. This lack might strongly affects their diffusion. In fact, the spread of a new technology/method is made easier when empirical evaluations are performed [10]. In this paper, we present an empirical study conducted with low-experienced developers to assess the validity of our solution. The used methodological approach is qualitative.

3   The Environment

Our graphical development environment supports a Javascript developer in the generation of a mobile application by designing a State Transition Diagram (STD) implementing a Finite State Machine [11]. The states of the STD represent screens of the app, while the transitions between the states represent events (i.e., user interaction with screen GUI elements) causing the navigation between screens. The environment graphically supports the developer in the generation of the GUI and in the parameter passage between screens. The developer has in charge to specify the logic of a screen.

The environment includes an STD editor. It has been implemented as an Eclipse plug-in by using features offered by the Graphical Editing Framework[2] (GEF). This editor allows developers to graphically specify finite-state machines. These machines manipulate one type of object at time, namely the state. It is possible to connect two states with one or more transitions.

The STD in Fig. 1 shows a finite-state machine associated to the *PictureEffect* app. This app accesses to the device camera, lets the user take a picture, and makes the picture preview by applying a graphical effect. PictureEffect is composed of four states. On the top left hand side of Fig. 1, it is shown the development process menu. It is composed of four buttons:

- *Info.* It allows specifying general information on the app, such as name, author, and release data;
- *Generate.* It is responsible for the source code generation, of its syntactic and semantic checks;
- *Edit.* It allows modifying source code. In this case, HTML, Javascript, CSS (Cascading Style Sheets), and jQueryMobile knowledge is needed.
- *Build.* It produces a project executable in the operating system of the app.

The editor allows the developer to specify additional properties of states and transitions, (i.e., GUI elements and variables), by adopting a form-based

---

[2] https://eclipse.org/gef/.

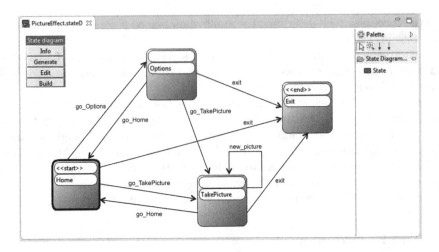

Fig. 1. An example of STD drawn with the generation environment.

GUI. Native functionalities can be also exploited. To this end, it is possible to access a menu listing available functionalities, including camera, accelerometer, geolocation, network, and sensors.

4   Empirical Study

We conducted a preliminary empirical study to assess the satisfaction in developing multi-platform apps by means of our solutions. Our study is questionnaire-based and its context is constituted of Bachelor students in Computer Science at the University of Salerno. Ten students were involved on voluntary basis. All the involved participants had Web programming skills. They also had software engineering skills and knew UML.

The study has been divided in three steps and performed in one-to-one session (i.e., a supervisor for each participant) using the think aloud technique [12] (i.e., participants thought aloud as they were performing a set of specified tasks). In the first step, a lesson of 30 min introduced to each participant the needed information for conducting the empirical study. Also an example of app generation was presented. This was different from that the participants had to use in the second step of our study. In this step, we asked to the participants to perform a task without time limit. The task concerned the creation of the *PictureEffect* app. The task involved the basic functions of the editor. During this step the supervisor did not provided any support. He only took note of comments and problems from participants, when they spoke aloud while performing the tasks. In the third step, the participants had to fill in a post-experiment questionnaire (Perception Questionnaire - PQ) to collect information on their satisfaction. This questionnaire is shown in Table 1. Questions from P1 to P3 were chosen to assess the clarity of the task, while questions from P4 to P11 to assess the

Table 1. The Perception Questionnaire

ID	Statements
P1	The objectives of the tasks were clear to me
P2	The material I received was clear to me
P3	The tasks to be performed were easy
P4	I am satisfied about the use of the development environment (satisfaction)
P5	It was simple to use the development environment (simplicity)
P6	I can effectively complete the tasks using the development environment (effectiveness)
P7	I am able to complete my work quickly using the development environment (efficiency)
P8	It was easy to learn to use the development environment (learnability)
P9	Whenever I make a mistake using the environment, I recover easily and quickly (recoverability)
P10	The organization of the information on the GUI of the development environment is clear (clarity)
P11	The interface of the development environment is pleasant (pleasantness)
P12	The finite-state machine definition rules are easy
P13	The number of steps to develop an app is appropriate
P14	The state attributes and its properties have a clear meaning
P15	Adding Javascript to model the application logic is easy
P16	The app matched your expectations
P17	In the future, I would like to exploit the environment to develop multi-platform apps (intention to use)

participants' satisfaction level. Questions from P12 to P16 aimed at obtaining feedback on the features of our development environment and the quality of the generated app. To understand whether participants had some interest in using our development environment in the future, we asked P17. All the questions in PQ admitted answers according to a 5-point Likert scale: from 1 (*Strongly Disagree*) to 5 (*Strongly Agree*).

The participants were provided with laptops having the same hardware configuration (i.e., a 2.93 GHz i3-560 Processor with 4 GB of RAM and Windows 7), while the generated app was deployed on an Android based Samsung Galaxy S4 device, SDK version 4.4.2.

All the participants completed the task. The histograms in Fig. 2 summarizes the responses to PQ. In particular, the clarity of the objective of the study (P1) and the provided material (P2) were positively judged. The task was considered easy for 60 % of the participants (P3). The results regarding the editor were positive in terms of effectiveness (P6), efficiency (P7), and clarity (P10); generally positive for simplicity (P5), recoverability (P9) and pleasantness (P11); less positive for learnability (P8). In any case, the greater part of the participants were satisfied of the development environment (P4). Concerning the specific editor features, the finite-state machine definition rules were clear for 90 % of participants (P12), also the effort needed to develop a mobile app is considered appropriate for 60 % of participants, while the remaining are neutral (P13). Further analysis on a more prolonged use of our development environment has to be conducted to verify whether the observed results change when developers have a better knowledge of our solutions. Two participants had some problems concerning the meaning of the state attributes, 4 where neutral and the remaining 4 positive (P14). Thus, improvements on the widgets describing state interface, variables and transitions have to be considered. The development of the specific app features in Javascript was considered easy for 40 % of the participants, while 40 % of the participants was neutral (P15). 9 participants were satisfied of the generated app (P16) and 80 % intended to use our development environment in the future (P17). This result is particularly relevant because it suggests that participants found our environment a viable tool for multi-platform mobile app development.

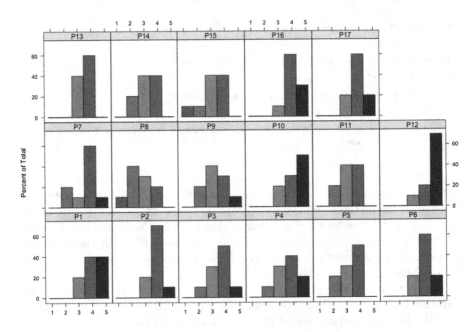

Fig. 2. The Perception Questionnaire results.

Results from the observation of the students, while performing experimental tasks, suggested that there were some problems in the design of multiple transition between two states, namely the lines overlapped and the text was too small and difficult to read. Also the menu buttons were all active and should be activated in a successive way, to properly follow the generation process (*Info*, *Generate*, *Edit*, and *Build*). Moreover, a participant forgot to assign a widget for the picture. This had the effect that the picture was not visualized in the app this participant generated.

5   Conclusion

In this paper, we recalled an MDD approach based on the design of a finite-state machine for supporting the generation of portable mobile apps. The definition of the data-flow and control-flow is managed by an environment intended as an Eclipse plug-in. A preliminary evaluation provided encouraging results, which revealed the adequacy of our development environment. Possible threats to the validity of our study are related to the kind and the number of participants involved. The use of students as participants may affect external validity. This threat has been mitigated because, we postulated that novice developers can master our solutions. To increase our awareness on the achieved results further investigations are needed with different kinds of developers (e.g., senior professional developers). We also plan to replicate our study with a larger number of novice developers. A possible threat to construct validity is concerned to the defined and used survey questionnaire. To deal with this kind of threat, we designed this questionnaire using standard methods and scales [13].

Future work will be also devoted to deeply assess the advantage offered by our approach by testing the generated apps on different devices. Also other types of widgets should be supported. To better support app development, also syntactic and semantic checks on the variable definitions and on their use will be took into considerations in the future versions of our environment.

References

1. Francese, R., Risi, M., Tortora, G., Scanniello, G.: Supporting the development of multi platform mobile application. In: 15th IEEE International Symposium on Web Systems Evolution (WSE), pp. 87–90 (2013)
2. Choi, Y., Yang, J.S., Jeong, J.: Application framework for multi platform mobileapplication software development. In: 11th International Conference on Advanced Communication Technology (ICACT), vol. 1, pp. 208–213 (2009)
3. Cimitile, M., Risi, M., Tortora, G.: Automatic generation of multi platform web map mobile applications. In: International Conference on Distributed Multimedia Systems (DMS), pp. 84–89 (2011)
4. Viana, W., Andrade, R.M.C.: XMobile: a MB-UID environment for semi-automatic generation of adaptive applications for mobile devices. J. Syst. Softw. **81**, 382–394 (2008)
5. Balagtas-Fernandez, F.T., Hussmann, H.: Model-driven development of mobile applications. In: 23rd IEEE/ACM International Conference on Automated Software Engineering (ASE), pp. 509–512. IEEE Computer Society (2008)
6. Jia, X., Jones, C.: AXIOM: a model-driven approach to cross-platform application development. In: 7th International Conference on Software Paradigm Trends (ICSOFT), pp. 24–33 (2012)
7. Cuccurullo, S., Francese, R., Risi, M., Tortora, G.: MicroApps development on mobile phones. In: International Symposium on End-User Development (IS-EUD), pp. 289–294 (2011)

8. Vaupel, S., Taentzer, G., Harries, J.P., Stroh, R., Gerlach, R., Guckert, M.: Model-Driven Development of Mobile Applications Allowing Role-Driven Variants. In: Dingel, J., Schulte, W., Ramos, I., Abrahão, S., Insfran, E. (eds.) MODELS 2014. LNCS, vol. 8767, pp. 1–17. Springer, Heidelberg (2014)
9. Abadi, A., Feldman, Y.A., Shagin, K.: A Screen-oriented representation for mobile applications. In: Companion Publication for Conference on Systems, Programming, & Applications: Software for Humanity (SPLASH), pp. 79–80 (2013)
10. Baldassarre, M.T., Carver, J., Dieste, O., Juristo, N.: Replication types: towards a shared taxonomy. In: International Conference on Evaluation and Assessment in Software Engineering, pp. 18:1–18:4 (2014)
11. Lee, D., Yannakakis, M.: Principles and methods of testing finite state machines-a survey. Proc. IEEE **84**, 1090–1123 (1996)
12. Nielsen, J., Clemmensen, T., Yssing, C.: Getting access to what goes on in people's heads? Reflections on the think-aloud technique. In: 2nd Nordic Conference on Human-Computer Interaction, pp. 101–110 (2002)
13. Oppenheim, A.N.: Questionnaire Design, Interviewing and Attitude Measurement. Pinter Publishers, London (1992)

If Usability Evaluation and Software Performance Evaluation Shook Their Hands: A Perspective

Tania Di Mascio$^{(\boxtimes)}$, Laura Tarantino, and Giovanni De Gasperis

Università degli Studi dell'Aquila, Via Vetoio, 1, Coppito, 67100 L'Aquila, Italy
{tania.dimascio,laura.tarantino,
giovanni.degasperis}@univaq.it

Abstract. The success of interactive systems depends on a variety of factors, including usability and system performances. The balance of these factors is more ideal than a practice, since traditionally these issues have been addressed by two distinct communities – Human-Computer Interaction and Software Engineering – using different processes, methods and tools. Consequently, the traditional approach is to separately address human performances and system performances. We argue that results from early-cycle system performance evaluation should be exploited by interaction designers to produce "performance-informed" design iteration, then leading to a performance-aware self-adaptive interaction environment, according to a vision bridging the two communities.

Keywords: Usability evaluation · System performance · Self-adaptive systems

1 Introduction

In the Human-Computer Interaction (HCI) research field, iterative design is nowadays indicated as the approach that most likely produces a successful interactive system (see, e.g., [1]). The design is in general conducted as a "test and make change" process, according to formative evaluation, which is "user testing with the goal of learning about the design to improve its next iteration" [2]. Notwithstanding some recognized criticality [2], the application of usability evaluation methods is identified as one of the primary key that allows designers to reveal and fix problems early or, to better say, at the right moment during the design of the system [3]. It has to be noted that does not exist such thing as "the method for all seasons" and the designer should accommodate his/her way of working to the nature and the features of the system under development. It is then useful to briefly overview the major intellectual waves that have formed the HCI field.

1.1 The Three Paradigms of HCI

Following Kuhn's view of scientific revolutions as a succession of overlapping waves in which ideas are re-framed [4] and with the aim of bringing clarity in the broad research in HCI and its evolution, Harrison et al. order the field into three "paradigms"

© Springer International Publishing Switzerland 2015
P. Abrahamsson et al. (Eds.): PROFES 2015, LNCS 9459, pp. 479–489, 2015.
DOI: 10.1007/978-3-319-26844-6_35

[5]. The paradigm shift from a wave to another is traced by tracing shifts in the underlying metaphors of interaction, according to Agre's theory of generative metaphors in technical work [6] developed for analyzing the typical questions of interest for a research stream and the corresponding methods and criteria for knowledge creation: each metaphor of interaction bring certain phenomena into the center of investigation, while marginalizing others. Phenomena of interest, questions, methods and validation procedures are the main constructs used by Harrison et al. to single out and characterize three paradigms in HCI literature (see Table 1).

Table 1. Synopsis of the three paradigms of the HCI according to [5]

	Paradigm 1	Paradigm 2	Paradigm 3
Metaphor of interaction	Interaction as man-machine coupling	Interaction as information communication	Interaction as phenomenologically situated
Main goals	Optimizing fit between man and machine	Optimizing accuracy and efficiency of information transfer	Support for situated action in the world
Appropriated disciplines	Engineering, programming, ergonomica	Laboratory and theoretically behavioral sciences	Ethnography, action research, practice-based research, interaction analysis
Methods	Cool hacks	Verified design and evaluation methods appliable regardless of context	Palette of situated design and evaluation strategies
Main values	Reduce errors	Optimization Generalizibily	What goes around the system is more interesting than what's happening in the interface

The 1st paradigm is based on the metaphor of *"interaction as man-machine coupling"*: the central goal of the design is to optimize the fit between man and machine and a typical question of interest would be *"how can we fix specific problems that arise in interaction?"*. This human factors perspective is an a-theoretic and pragmatic approach to which engineering, programming and ergonomics disciplines provide the grounding for empirically validated objective hypotheses.

The 2nd paradigm, which dominated the HCI discourse for a couple of decades, is based on the metaphor of *"interaction as information communication"*: the primary goal is optimizing the accuracy and the efficiency of information transfer among computers and their users, and typical questions of interest are *"how can we accurately model what people do?"* or *"how can we improve the efficiency of computer use?"*. This objective is achieved through the definition of abstract models of interactions that enable to systematically compare alternative design solutions.

The more recent 3rd paradigm, rooted in the concept of embodied interaction as introduced by Dourish [7], is based on the metaphor of *"interaction as phenomeno-logically situated"*: its main focus is on the construction of meaning and on the complexity around the system and typical questions of interest are *"what existing situated activities in the world should we support?"* or *"how do users appropriate technology, and how can we support these appropriations?"*. The paradigm refocuses attention from single user/single computer paradigm that dominated the 1st and 2nd paradigms towards collaboration and communication through physically shared objects. A specific characteristic of the 3rd paradigm is a preference for multiple interpretations and, for this reason, rather than adopting a single, correct set of methods and actions, it relies on a variety of approach that Harrison et al. denote *phenomeno-logical matrix.*

The three paradigms highlight different questions and methods for answering them, and may clash. While laboratory and theoretical behavioral science can be an appropriate discipline for the 2nd paradigm, the 3rd paradigm would rather rely on ethnography, action research, and practice-based research. It is emphasized in [5] that to allow the 3rd paradigm to bear full fruit, it is necessary to recognize and accommodate its notion of validity, and that it is desirable that research works in the 3rd paradigm explain their phenomenological matrix and their measures of success.

1.2 Assessment of Evaluation Methods Against the HCI Paradigms

One may observe that most used evaluation methods and practices originated within the 2nd paradigm of the HCI: human performances in performing tasks are the focus. With the advent of the 3rd paradigm, on the other hand, the nature of IT products changed: the adoption of novel architectural solutions for the new application domains, e.g., cloud computing, clusters, service oriented architectures (SOA), should put the system and its performances back in focus not only for Software Engineering (SE) issues but also for HCI issues. Traditional design approaches, however, separately address system performances, faced by Software Performance Engineering (SPE), and human performances, faced by Usability Engineering (UE). This is still one of the gaps between SE and HCI communities that hamper common efforts towards a unitary vision. The discussion in [8] singles out, among the causes of the gaps, the mismatches between the development processes and life-cycles they adopt, and advocates the idea of "boundary object", i.e., a flexible and adaptable enough representation to sit in between the two communities and retaining enough integrity to serve as a bridge. In our opinion the lack of an adequate bridge may bring, among others, to what we call "performance uninformed" design iterations and, consequently, to usability problems descending from performance failures.

As to *system performance evaluation*, two general approaches are followed: the most commonly used is a late-cycle measurement-based approach, applied when the system under development can be run but when changes in the design are too costly [9]. Conversely, the model-based approach uses predictive performance models early in the development cycle; unfortunately, in practice, according to [10], just a few model-based methods have explicitly addressed the issue of providing some sort of feedback from performance analysis to designers (e.g., information on software components or interactions responsible for some bad throughput figure).

As to *usability evaluation,* it has to be observed that, in general, guidelines discourage the involvement of large-numbers of users. For example, guideline n:18:6 of [11] goes: "Select the right number of participants when using different usability techniques. Using too few may reduce the usability of a Web site; using too many wastes valuable resources." Actually the issues related to 'how many users you need' keep being debated [12]: the early model from Virzi, suggesting that 80 % of usability problems can be detected with 4 or 5 participants [13], was followed by Nielsen's position [14] on usability testers needing to test with only five users to discover 85 % of the usability problems; Nielsen recently reaffirmed his tenet [15], opening to few exceptions (e.g., 39 users for eye-tracking studies or 20 users when the aim is statistics and not insights), while [16] calculated that to be 90 % confident of finding usability problems that will affect 99 % of users requires more like 112 representative test participants. In any case, considering also that usability tests are often conducted on an individual (or small users' group) basis, traditional usability evaluation cannot stress the system up to the point in which performance flaws emerge, with most interaction design choices ignoring altogether system performance issues: as a consequence, usability problems related to performance issues are seldom, if never, revealed and, then, taken into consideration by interaction designers.

Based on our experience about issues of this kind within a real project [17], we propose an enlarged concept of usability evaluation, including both human performance and system performance analysis, which can (1) serve as boundary object between the SE and HCI communities, and (2) lead to performance-aware self-adaptive interaction environments in which the interaction experience is dynamically configured according to, among others, system performances.

1.3 Structure of the Paper

The remainder of this paper is organized as follows: Sect. 2 reports on our experience within the TERENCE project and brings into focus the objective vision we pursue. Section 3 is focused on issues that mainly contribute to the attainment of our vision. Section 4 presentes and example scenario and, finally, in Sect. 5, conclusions are drawn.

2   The TERENCE Experience

TERENCE (www.terenceproject.eu) was a European FP7-ICT project placed in the area of Technology Enhanced Learning (TEL) aimed at developing an Adaptive Learning System for supporting 7–11 years old poor text comprehenders and their educators through a playful and enjoyable interaction experience including reading stories and playing with smart and relaxing games [17], conceived to be part of school activities. To evaluate usability, we used both expert-based and user-based usability evaluation methods [11, 18] to carry out formative small-scale and summative large-scale evaluations with end-users in schools in Italy and UK [17]. To evaluate system performances, according to the commonest approach [9], we conducted a stress test when the final system was realized and a measurement-based system performance analysis, with actual workload, in parallel to the large-scale usability evaluation.

As to **usability evaluation**, ethical issues prevented us from including TERENCE in regular school activities before it was finished (we note that it frequently happens that problems of different nature (e.g., ethical or security/privacy issues) prevent from introducing early prototypes in real settings and/or in the real information workload). The differences between the settings used for the small-scale and the large-scale usability evaluations, and between frequency and regularity in the use of the system in the two cases, allowed us to compare the two experiences and their results. While the small-scale evaluation was conducted in summer schools, with about 170 users, the large-scale evaluation was carried on in regular classes, with about 900 users during regular school activities. From the beginning of the large-scale evaluation it was immediately clear the different attitude of children towards the system, with kids developing affection towards avatars and books, engaging competition with each other and showing eagerness to play with the system; this finding complies with the results of a study [19] focused on Management Information System design, underlining that "earlier is not necessarily better", because users tend to become fully and truly engaged – and hence to provide feedback really useful for the design – only when the system "goes live" and impacts on their actual lives. Our experience with learners allows us to conjecture that results of [19] are generalizable to other application domains.

As to **system performance evaluation**, when moving from the small-scale set-up to the large-scale set-up, two important aspects emerged: (1) unexpected performance problems were observed (e.g., concurrent accesses to interactive books, which had passed the stress test, turned out to be a bottleneck of system responsiveness); and (2) system performances impacted on system usability. More specifically, evaluators observed children loosing concentration when system response time increased beyond some task-specific threshold, with a damage to both pedagogical stimulation and user satisfaction. The system, with this reduction of efficacy and effectiveness, might hence struggles in achieving its main goal. In other words, *HCI fails if performances fail*. A prediction of these conditions might have suggested us to design differently not only the system architecture, now implemented following the SOA approach, but also the stimulation plan and the interaction environment. For example, one may imagine, on the one hand, a different solution for the architecture, providing a combination of local and Internet-based services, and, on the other hand, the adoption of monitors that automatically launch relaxing games or other entertainment activities, based on local services, whenever detect failures in Internet-based service responsiveness.

All this given, we argue that since early stages of the design one should be able to predict which variables may, and to which extent, affect performances and usability and to use this information to guide an overall interaction design possibly based on an innovative *performance-aware self-adaptive interaction environment*.

3   Towards Performance Awareness

Since we wish to shape the interaction so to cope with performances, we need to assume a novel vision relying on (1) early-cycle methods/protocols that allow the design team to identify aspects (variables) that will affect system performances during the interaction sessions, and (2) architectural/interaction guidelines using such information to enable performance-informed design and system behavior.

When speaking about early-cycle methods and their feedback one naturally refers to the pioneer work on the model-based approach by [20]. According to this view, if the model indicates that there are performance problems two possibilities occur: (1) modifying the product concept if feasible cost-effective alternatives do exist, or (2) revising performance objectives, and then modifying performance goals, otherwise. We observe that while this approach is reasonable for 2nd paradigm IT products characterized by predictability of interaction sessions, typical of non-discretionary job use, it sounds unreasonably rigid for 3rd paradigm IT products allowing flexible, often non predictable, interaction sessions, typical of discretionary personal use of new application domains. More importantly, a view in which the system behavior constraints the design would contrast with one of the fundamental question to which 3rd paradigm researchers have to answer: *"how can we support interaction without constraining it too strongly by what a computer do or understand"?* [5]. We also observe that when aiming at defining performance-informed architectural/interaction guidelines, literature propose solutions still mostly 2nd paradigm-oriented, like in [21], thus offering just marginal contributions to our goal. A novel vision has to deal with uncertainty and dynamic changes because, at design time, the information about future interaction sessions is incomplete: it is not possible to precisely state when and to which extent system performance downgrades. This is the very nature of self-adaptive system.

Self-adaptation is defined, in general, as the ability of a system to adjust its behavior in response to its perception of *actors*, *environment* and the *system itself* (see, e.g., [22, 23]), which is appropriate for us to examine under an interaction environment perspective, to single out what has already been done and what it is instead an open research challenge.

As to *actors* – entities that interact with the system – in our vision we have to focus on users. This issue have been commonly addressed by adaptive user interfaces, which change their appearance according to users' profiles (see e.g., [24, 25]). This view is clearly positioned within the 1st and 2nd paradigms of the HCI, and related to their typical questions, like *"how can we optimize the fit between humans ad machines?"*, and *"how can we accurately model what people do?"*, respectively, without touching 3rd paradigm related issues.

As to *environment*, this aspect is somehow inherently addressed by 3rd paradigm IT products, which support situated action in the world and therefore environmental changes (think, e.g., of ubiquitous computing or ambient systems). An interesting example is provided by the MUSIC project [26], which faces the issue of selecting alternative application configurations in response to context changes. Indeed, under the 3rd paradigm we ask *"how does our design accommodate the context?"* [5]. Anyhow, it is worth notice that adaptation in MUSIC, at middleware framework level, is more on the functionality realization than on interaction design.

As to adaptation to the *system itself*, system performances are indeed recognized as a possible non functional cause of adaptation, computationally accessible and upon which behavioral variation may depend [22, 23]. Nevertheless, when focusing on this issue from an interaction environment perspective, to the best of our knowledge no proposal exists targeted at dynamically configuring the "interaction experience" according to system performances, which is the gap our vision aims to fill.

We envision an interaction designer who, benefitting from results in diverse fields (e.g., self-adaptive systems, software performance engineering, ontology, and goal-oriented requirement engineering [27]) (1) reasons in terms of specification of goals, properties, and constraints (to be considered as "adaptation targets") within a mission that the system has to pursue, and (2) conceives a system with choice of behavior, capable of preserving both its mission and the capacity of user involvement also in cases of dynamic changes (in our case, system performance downgrading risks), possibly degrading gracefully to meet end users requirements in a manner which is as good as possible under the circumstances (which also imply that is produced by the system in due time – according to the application domain). We underline the fact that the process is usually transparent to the final user.

Notice that with graceful degradation we do not mean a system performance degradation but rather a possible end-user goal relaxation. For example, in a children-oriented TEL system, like TERENCE, in which the main goal is "learning" and the stimulation plan sub-goals are "reading", "playing", and "enjoying", the system might dynamically select the sub-goal that better fits the system performance; in the case of TERENCE, the system may decide to propose relaxing games locally accessed (sub-goal "enjoying") in place of stories accessed via Web (sub-goal "reading"), when it detects network connection downgrades.

To make a different example, imagine an online store based on a cluster architecture and the specific end-user goal "find a black skinny pair of Gucci pants"; in case of excessive response time from the cluster node capable to satisfy this request, the system may decide to rearrange the steps of the sale process funnel by anticipating some possible user actions (e.g., filling a size form) so to maintain the user engaged in the interaction with the store while the system tries to satisfy the request.

Broadly speaking, from a conceptual point of view, we envision a *component-based dialog* generated by a *self-adaptive interaction environment*. This environment should dynamically configure the interaction experience that best fits for end-users goals, according to *plans* based on, among others, adaptation targets (which account for usability goals), utility functions, and "quality of service", using a repertoire of adaptation mechanisms from more traditional device and parametric adaptations to more innovative compositional adaptations, in which dialogue components may be added, removed, replaced, or re-arranged. Notice that this approach to interaction design fits the 3rd HCI paradigm providing answers to another question raised in [5]: *"what are the politics and values at the site of interaction, and how can we support those in design?"*.

As a final remark, we observe that one should not be worried by loss of consistency or predictability in such *"hic et nunc"* interaction experience, not only because a good adaptation should anyhow enforce appropriate consistency, but also because of the characteristics of 3rd HCI paradigm IT products we are dealing with. Consider, for example, the many one-visit mobile and web applications characterized by a high rate of "interaction with strangers", i.e., users who exploit a web site or an app just once as a "disposable object" (e.g., within the context of online searches targeted at finding a product) and cannot then perceive any change of behavior.

4   An Application Scenario in the Domain of Cultural Heritage Fruition

An ideal application domain for the concept so far discussed is that of the fruition of cultural heritage, like in a museum exhibition, through some kind of Virtual Assistant (VA). VAs, software systems that assist a user during tasks of knowledge browsing/information retrieval, appears in the literature under different forms and name, also depending on the application domain. Generalizing, we can describe the virtual assistant as *an interaction sub-system between a human user and a generic system, within a given context of use*. In more abstract terms, according to a recent definition [28], a VA is "*a person (or an agent) who is able to provide distinct help at a given time in a given activity context*".

In the identified application domain, the VA may be the interaction subsystem running on a mobile handheld device, between a (geolocalized) visitor and a content provider (see Fig. 1), with the mission of guiding the visitor throughout the museum by providing multimedia information (e.g., text, images and videos) about the museum exhibition, possibly at different levels of details, aggregated at different levels and channeled in different ways [29]. In this case, adaptation is related to the content (e.g., structural complexity of the presented information, level of detail of the presented information, media channel) and may be foreseen according to different perspectives, among which, visitor behavior (e.g., the VA may infer whether s/he is carrying on a quick shallow visit or a relaxed deep one), device characteristics (e.g., screen size/resolution), network connection performance (depending, e.g., on the number of visitors and bandwidth). Benefitting, e.g., from design space models proposed for large

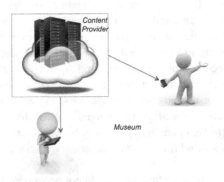

Fig. 1. Visitors at the museum

hypermedia information spaces (like the one in [29], a VA can be based on the architecture in Fig. 2 including two main components: the managed module is responsible for offering the interaction experience, while the adaptation module is responsible for dynamically configuring such experience while guaranteeing, *whatever the condition*, a guidance into the exhibition. Depending, e.g., upon the network connection quality, it may decide to rely on light weighted vs high weighted channels (text vs video), updated vs cached data, high density vs low density information presentation.

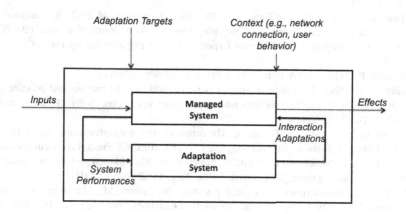

Fig. 2. The gross architecture of the adaptive VA

5   Conclusion

This paper builds on the necessity of re-balancing the focus on humans and systems as to usability issues. Besides agreeing with [19] on the necessity of legitimizing a design stage devoted to post-implementation activities, we go one step further in the reconsideration of UCD stages by proposing a vision in which human performances and system performances are not regarded as independent variables in the success of the system. With this vision in mind, it is mandatory to have HCI experts and SE experts working together to harmonize analysis and design choices. Our vision, requiring an *enlarged concept of usability evaluation* including human performance analysis and system performance analysis at every design and development iteration, positions experts coming from the two communities at the same level, shaking hands and exploiting each other know-how and results, thus lessening possible defensive attitudes. Predictive model-driven and measurement-based approaches for system performance evaluation offer consolidated complementary tools for both early and late life-cycles, to be used both for usability evaluation and dialog design, to produce "performance informed" design iterations with the final aim of a *component-based dialog* generated by a *self-adaptive interaction environment*.

References

1. Preece, J., Sharp, H., Rogers, Y.: Interaction Design: Beyond Human-Computer Interaction. Wiley, Hoboken (2015)
2. Redish, J., Bias, R., Bailei, R., Molich, R., Dumas, R., Spool, J.: Usability in practice: formative usability evaluations, evolution and revolution. In: International Conference on Human Factors in Computing Systems, pp. 885–890. ACM Press, New York (2002)
3. Holzinger, A.: Usability Engineering Methods for Software Developers. Commun. ACM **48** (1), 71–74 (2005)
4. Kuhn, T.S.: The Structure of Scientific Revolution, 2nd edn. University of Chicago Press, Chicago (1970)
5. Harrison, S., Sengers, P., Tatar, D.: The three paradigms of HCI. In: International Conference on Human Factors in Computing Systems. ACM Press, New York (2007)
6. Agre, P.E.: Computation and Human Experience. Cambridge University Press, Cambridge (1997)
7. Dourish, P.: Where the Action Is. MIT Press, Cambridge (2001)
8. Kazman, R., Bass, L.: Editorial: special issue on bridging the process and practice gaps between software engineering and human-computer interaction. Softw. Process Improv. Pract. **8**(2), 63–65 (2003)
9. Woodside, M., Franks, G., Petriu, D.: The future of software performance engineering. In: IEEE Future of Software Engineering, pp. 171–187. IEEE-CS Press, Los Alamitos (2007)
10. Balsamo, S., Di Marco, A., Inverardi, P., Simeoni, M.: Model-based performance prediction in software development. IEEE Trans. Softw. Eng. **30**, 295–310 (2004)
11. Leavitt, M., Shneiderman, B.: Usability testing. In: Leavitt, M., Shneiderman, B. (eds.) Research-Based Web Design and Usability Guidelines, vol. 18, pp. 187–198. U.S. Government Printing Office, Washington (2006)
12. Francik, E.: Five, ten, or twenty-five – how many test participants? Human Factors International Newsletter. http://www.humanfactors.com/newsletters/how_many_test_participants.asp
13. Virzi, R.A.: Refining the test phase of usability evaluation: how many subjects is enough? J. Hum. Factors and Ergon. Soc. **34**, 457–468 (1992)
14. Nielsen, J.: Why you only need to test with five users. http://www.useit.com/alertbox/20000319.html
15. Nielsen, J.: How many test users in a usability study? http://www.nngroup.com/articles/how-many-test-users/
16. Bailey, R.: The growing popularity of usability. Human Factors International Newsletter (2001). http://www.humanfactors.com/newsletters/the_growing_popularity_of_usability.asp
17. Di Mascio, T., Tarantino, L., Vittorini, P., Caputo, M.: Design choices: affected by user feedback? Affected by system performances? Lessons learned from the TERENCE project. In: 10th Biannual Conference of the Italian SIGCHI Chapter (2013)
18. Nielsen, J.: Usability Engineering. Academic Press, San Diego (1993)
19. Wagner, E., Piccoli, G.: Moving beyond user participation to achieve successful design. Commun. ACM **50**(12), 51–55 (2007)
20. Williams, L.G., Smith, C.U.: PASA: a method for the performance assessment of software architectures. In: 3rd International Workshop on Software and Performance, pp. 179–189. ACM Press, New York (2002)
21. Yang, Y., Cheng, J.X.: Applying software performance engineering methods to development of interactive software. J. Softw. **13**(10), 1921–1932 (2002)

22. Cheng, B.H.C., de Lemos, R., Giese, H., Inverardi, P., Magee, J. (eds.): Software Engineering for Self-Adaptive System. Springer, Berlin (2009)
23. de Lemos, R., Giese, H., Müller, H., Shaw, M. (eds.): Software Engineering for Self-Adaptive System II. Springer, Berlin (2011)
24. Greenberg, S., Witten, I.H.: Adaptive personalized interfaces: a question of viability. Behav. Inf. Technol. 4(1), 31–45 (1985)
25. Krzysztof, Z.G., Czerwinski, M., Desney, S., Daniel, S.W.: Exploring the design space for adaptive graphical user interfaces. In: International Conference of Advanced Visual Interfaces, pp. 201–208. ACM Press, New York (2006)
26. Rouvoy, R., Barone, P., Ding, Y., Eliassen, F., Hallsteinsen, S., Lorenzo, J., Mamelli, A., Scholz, U.: MUSIC: middleware support for self-adaptation in ubiquitous and service-oriented environments. In: Cheng, B.H.C., de Lemos, R., Giese, H., Inverardi, P., Magee, J. (eds.) Software Engineering for Self-Adaptive System, pp. 164–182. Springer, Heidelberg (2009)
27. van Lamsweerde, A.: Goal-oriented requirements engineering: a guided tour. In: 5th IEEE International Symposium on Requirements Engineering, pp. 249–262. IEEE Press (2001)
28. Milhorat, P., Schlogl, S., Chollet, G., Boudy, J., Esposito, A., Pelosi, G.: Building the next generation of personal digital assistants. In: 1st International Conference on Advanced Technologies for Signal and Image Processing, pp. 458–463. IEEE Press (2014)
29. Celentano, A., Dubois, E.: A design space for exploring rich and complex information environments. In: 11th Biannual Conference of the Italian SIGCHI Chapter (2015)

Quantitative Metrics for User Experience: A Case Study

Roberta Capellini[1,2](✉), Francesca Tassistro[2], and Rossana Actis-Grosso[1]

[1] Department of Psychology, University of Milano-Bicocca, Milan, Italy
r.capellini@campus.unimib.it
[2] Avanade Italy, Milan, Italy

Abstract. Improving the human aspects of the software product development requires to take into account the users. This can be done in several ways; here we investigate ways to involve them directly during the first phases of prototypical development. To this aim, rigorously constructed and validated questionnaires can help researchers, designers and developers in collecting opinions and feedback of users to inform design choices and implementation plans. We present a revised Italian version of a standard questionnaire that allows to measure with little effort both the overall User Experience of a product and the Workforce Experience. The idea is that both components are tightly intertwined and can affect each other. The questionnaire was adopted and tested to verify the quality of the redesign interventions on a working tool of an Italian Tour Operator. Results encourage the team to increasingly apply the questionnaire in other projects to collect feedback about users impressions.

Keywords: User experience · Workforce experience · Quantitative methods

1 Introduction

The Software Development process needs to consider and integrate lessons learnt from both the Software Engineering (SE) field and the Human-Computer Interaction (HCI) research area. To take into account human factors means to involve users throughout the entire development process in order to understand in depth their needs and requirements and to provide them with a good user experience (UX). This, in turn, is a consequence of (i) user's internal state, (ii) the main features of the designed system and (iii) the context within which the interaction occurs [5,6]. How is this possible and feasible? User-Centered Design (UCD) is an approach devoted to increase user experience through user participation in the design process. The UCD process can help software designers to develop a product fitting the needs of its users and tailored to satisfy their requirements [1].

One of the greatest challenges in UCD is how to measure the UX of a product. UX metrics show how users perceive an interface, reveal something about the

© Springer International Publishing Switzerland 2015
P. Abrahamsson et al. (Eds.): PROFES 2015, LNCS 9459, pp. 490–496, 2015.
DOI: 10.1007/978-3-319-26844-6_36

interaction between the user and the product, help researchers and designers to understand whether the design strategy is effective and give objective data on which to base the design recommendations [2,11]. Furthermore, the quality of UX has a direct impact on users' satisfaction and a good UX increases sales and improves brand perception.

However, while a number of standardized tests and rigorous methods are available for usability measuring, the measurement of UX is often achieved with ad hoc tools specifically designed for different products and scenarios, without any test regarding their reliability or effectiveness.

Here we present a case study where the UX has been evaluated for the two versions (i.e. before and after the re-design) of a working tool used by the travel agents of an Italian Tour Operator. Customer satisfaction, as perceived by the travel agents, together with the perceived quality of the working experience supported by the new version of the tool, have been evaluated as well.

To compare the UX for the two versions of the tool we selected 18 (out of the original 26) items from the UEQ questionnaire [8], and developed 10 new items to cover other complementary dimensions. The validation of the UEQ items has been verified for the Italian version by calculating the Cronbach's Alpha (which describes the consistency of the items of the scales) for each dimension. Cronbach's Alpha has been calculated also for the 10 new items. Values assigned to each dimensions have been compared for the old and new version of the tool, showing a good consistency and an improvement of the overall UX for both the end users and the travel agents. However, as it is better detailed below, the re-design of the tool did not improve travel agents UX along all the measured dimensions. This helped our team in better focusing future work to shape the product according to the customer UX, showing the importance of having quantitative metrics to measure UX.

2 Method

2.1 A Case Study

In the last months of 2014 our team (i.e. the Experience Design Team of Avanade Italy) was involved in a design project concerning the redesign of a working tool used by the travel agents of an Italian Tour Operator. The project aimed to create a new way of working for the operators, in order to support collaboration with end users and to help travel agents to be more productive and efficient, allowing a dynamic management of work. The design process was based on the User-Centered Design methodology and involved user research activities as stakeholders workshops, requirements analysis, observations of customers and travel agents and design activities as informational architecture, wireframes and visual design. Then, the interface was implemented by a developers' team.

In the early stage of the project, before starting the design process, we involved the travel agents in a general survey in order to understand their evaluation of the current version of the tool interface, which they used in their daily work, and to define users requirements.

After the redesign our point was that a quantitative measure of the possible improvement in both usability and UX for travel agents could have a twofold importance. On the one hand, it could help our team in focusing future work on the weaknesses that are not necessarily clear to end-user but that could emerge in a quantitative study; on the other hand it could add a "special value" to the product we give to our client, who could have a clear feedback regarding the quality of the work we did. To this aim we decided to use a questionnaire designed to measure the main dimensions involved in usability and UX for the tool we were working on, and to statistically compare the values obtained for the old and the new version of the tool interface.

For the construction of the questionnaire we reviewed and studied the relevant literature, relying on the standard usability questionnaires available. We then decided to extend the previous work in this field by adding a new set of items meant to measure four dimensions [7,12] mainly related to the quality of the workforce experience and the end-user satisfaction.

2.2   The Construction of the UX Questionnaire

Surveys and questionnaires are easy ways to collect data from users. They provide direct information about what users feel during the interaction with an interface or about the overall impression of a product and allow researchers to gather helpful feedback and insights by asking directly the users.

A questionnaire to measure UX for interactive products has been recently developed by Laugwitz et al. (2008). The User Experience Questionnaire [8] encompasses 26 pairs of opposite adjectives that cover both usability and UX aspects. Thus, UEQ is a semantic differential [9] (i.e. a type of a rating scale designed to measure opinions, attitudes and values on a psychometrically controlled scale). In particular, UEQ contains 6 semantic differential scales [3] designed to measure 6 different dimensions. An Italian version of the questionnaire is also available. The UEQ, which was originally developed in German, is freely available on-line in several languages [10]. We then decided to use this scale for our study, but we needed to shorten it, in order to add some new items meant to investigate other aspects specifically related to our client request.

We thus selected a subset of 18 pairs of constraint adjectives concerning the 6 dimensions measured by the UEQ: Attractiveness, (that concerns the general impression towards the product), Efficiency (whether a product or a service allows to work quickly and efficiently), Perspicuity (whether a product or a service is clear and intuitive), Dependability (whether a product or a service is reliable and safe), Stimulation (whether the use is interesting and exciting) and Novelty (whether the design of the product is innovative and creative). Our questionnaire included three items for each of Novelty, Efficiency, Attractiveness and Dependability scales, two items for Stimulation and four items for Perspicuity.

To check for possible improvement in cooperative work experience and in the end-user satisfaction (as perceived by travel agents), we created 10 items in order to measure 4 dimensions: Engagement (which includes one item), Productivity (which includes five items), Empathy with brand (which includes two items) and Perceived Customer Experience (which includes two items). Travel agents (n=84) have been asked to fulfill the questionnaire for both the old and the new version of the tool interface. The total number of items was thus 46.

3   Results

3.1   Confirming the Validation of UEQ Items

Below we present the main results of the analyses. First, we reverse scored the negatively worded questions. Then, we conducted reliability analysis on the responses to the 18 pairs of adjectives related to the assessment of the two interfaces, paired t-tests to compare the overall user experience and a Binomial Test on the responses to the 10 items related with the Workforce Experience.

After the transformation in standardized z-points, 8 participants were excluded from the analyses because they resulted outliers on the values of one or more dimensions ($|2.5|$ SD). Analyses were thus conducted on a sample of 76 participants. In order to calculate an index for each of the 6 dimensions for the assessment of the overall User Experience, we averaged the two Stimulation items because they were highly consistent both in the older interface dataset (Cronbach's $\alpha = .68$) and the newer one (Cronbach's $\alpha = .84$). For the same reason, due to the overall satisfactory reliabilities, we combined the three Attractiveness items (old interface Cronbach's $\alpha = .85$, new interface Cronbach's $\alpha = .86$), the three Efficiency items (old interface Cronbach's $\alpha = .72$, new interface Cronbach's $\alpha = .81$), the three Dependability items (old interface Cronbach's $\alpha = .75$, new interface Cronbach's $\alpha = .78$), the three Novelty items (old interface Cronbach's $\alpha = .78$, new interface Cronbach's $\alpha = .75$) and the Perspicuity four items (old interface Cronbach's $\alpha = .84$, new interface Cronbach's $\alpha = .89$).

3.2   Comparison Between the UX of the Old and the New Interface

We compared both the 6 indices related to the evaluation of the old interface and the 6 indices related to the evaluation of the new re-design by means of paired t-tests. The analysis revealed that the assessment of the redesign interface along the Novelty dimension ($M = 5.50$, $SD = 1.09$) was more positive than the assessment of the older interface along the same scale ($M = 4.72$, $SD = 1.45$), $t(75) = -4.81$, $p < .001$. The same pattern was revealed for the other dimensions; the new interface was perceived significantly more challenging ($M = 5.65$, $SD = 1.16$) than the older one ($M = 5.17$, $SD = 1.27$), $t(75) = -3,11$, $p = .003$, more trustworthy ($M = 5.43$, $SD = 1.17$) than the older one ($M = 5.09$, $SD = 1.22$), $t(75) = -2,66$, $p = .01$, more efficient ($M = 5.46$, $SD = 1.17$) than the previous interface ($M = 5.16$, $SD = 1.18$), $t(75) = -2,38$, $p = .02$ and more attractive ($M = 5.59$, $SD = 1.23$) than the previous one ($M = 5.08$, $SD = 1.35$), $t(75) = -3,53$, $p< .001$, (Fig. 1).

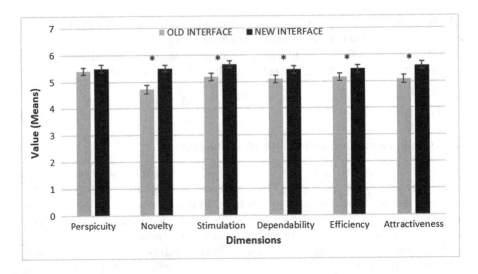

Fig. 1. Comparison between the old and the new interface

As shown in Fig. 1, participants assessed more positively the overall user experience of the new working tool. The design process allows the team to improve the interface, to achieve a better evaluation and to better answer the users needs.

The results shown in Fig. 1 did not show a significant difference between the evaluation of the new and the old interface along the Perspicuity dimension, $t(75) = -.85$, $p = .39$. This latter result can be interpreted due to the following reason: when participants answered the survey, the new interface was newly deployed and they did not receive any training about how to use it yet. This might have influenced their impression about the clearness and perspicuity of the interface and justify this finding. Further steps in the design have to consider this aspect and try to improve it.

3.3 Workforce Experience

Following the same procedure presented above, we collapsed over the evaluation that participants provided for each of the 10 items related to the Workforce Experience. Cronbach's alphas for the Productivity, .71, for Empathy with brand, .81, and for Perceived Customer Experience, .77, were sufficiently high to allow us to combine the traits of each dimension.

Following a technique introduced in [4], we then computed a Binomial Test on the proportion of responses on the Engagement, Productivity, Empathy for brand and Perceived Customer Experience. Clear responses polarizations have been detected for the following dimensions: Engagement (.07 vs. .93, $p < .001$), Productivity (.09 vs. .91, $p < .001$) and Perceived Customer Experience (.13 vs. .87, $p < .001$).

As shown, the new version of the tool supported travel agents in their daily work. After the re-design, participants felt to be more productive, to work in a more efficient way and to be able to provide a better service to their customers. Moreover, they felt more engaged and emphatic with their company brand. In line with the literature [7, 12], these aspects influence the overall quality of the workforce experience in a positive way.

4 Discussion

We presented a tool that allows researchers and designers to evaluate the user experience of a product. It measures both usability aspects like perspicuity, efficiency and dependability and user experience aspects like stimulation or originality. It allows also to measure the quality of the workforce experience perceived by the employees who use the interface under investigation in their daily work.

The case study we presented was our first application of the UX questionnaire in a design project; our aim was to measure the quality of our work. Results showed that the team was able to design an interface that helps travel agents to build a travel tour together with their customers, giving them the possibility to choose and customize itineraries, according to their wishes. The overall user experience of the working tool was improved, in terms of an enhanced attractiveness, higher levels of perspicuity, dependability, stimulation and novelty. The innovative interface enabled travel agents to work in a cooperative way with their clients and to experience a new way of working.

These challenging results encourage us to use always more frequently this UX questionnaire in our project. It should become usual the usage of surveys and validated questionnaire to gather objective data about the user experience of a product. Further, this should happen throughout a project; before starting the design phase, in order to obtain insights to guide the subsequent steps and at the end of a design project, in order to measure in a quantitative way the quality of your work.

Moreover, to gather users' requirements, to bring quantitative data and to base the design and implementation of a product "from the users' point of view" might create a bridge between designers and developers. It could be the ideal way to integrate Software Engineering and Human-Computer Interaction in the Software Development process.

Acknowledgments. We'd like to thank Avanade Experience Design Team, based in Milan (Italy) that actively participated to the project *(in alphabetical order)*: Arianna Angaroni, Marco Buonvino, Roberto Chinelli, Celeste Cirasole, Alice Deias, Giulia Delmedico, Luca Erbifori, Alessandro Fusco, Jessica Guizzardi, Lais Kantor Caserta, Angelo Oldani, Matteo Puggioni and Silvia Soccol. We thank also Federico Cabitza of the University of Milano-Bicocca for his help in regard to the non-parametric inference analysis and suggestions for the scale definition.

References

1. Abras, C., Maloney-Krichmar, D., Preece, J.: User-centered design. In: Bainbridge, W. Encyclopedia of Human-Computer Interaction, vol. 37(4), pp. 445–456. Sage Publications, Thousand Oaks (2004)
2. Albert, W., Tullis, T.: Measuring the user experience: collecting, analyzing, and presenting usability metrics. Newnes (2013)
3. Brooks, P., Hestnes, B.: User measures of quality of experience: why being objective and quantitative is important. IEEE Netw. **24**(2), 8–13 (2010)
4. Cabitza, F., Simone, C., De Michelis, G.: User-driven prioritization of features for a prospective InterPersonal Health Record: Perceptions from the Italian context. Comput. Biol. Med. **59**, 202–210 (2015)
5. Hassenzahl, M.: User experience (UX): towards an experiential perspective on product quality. In: Proceedings of the 20th International Conference of the Association Francophone d'Interaction Homme-Machine, pp. 11–15. ACM, September 2008
6. Hassenzahl, M., Tractinsky, N.: User experience-a research agenda. Behav. Inf. Technol. **25**(2), 91–97 (2006)
7. Keitt, T.J., Smith, A.: Measuring Your Workforce Experience: Use Customer Experience Insight As Your Guide. Forrester Research (2013)
8. Laugwitz, B., Held, T., Schrepp, M.: Construction and evaluation of a user experience questionnaire. In: Holzinger, A. (ed.) USAB 2008. LNCS, vol. 5298, pp. 63–76. Springer, Heidelberg (2008)
9. Osgood, C.E.: A Monograph on the Semantic Differential. University of Illinois Press, Urbana (1957)
10. Rauschenberger, M., Olschner, S., Cota, M.P., Schrepp, M., Thomaschewski, J.: Measurement of user experience: a Spanish language version of the user experience questionnaire (UEQ). In: 2012 7th Iberian Conference on Information Systems and Technologies (CISTI), pp. 1–6. IEEE, June 2012
11. Sauro, J., Lewis, J.R.: Quantifying the User Experience: Practical Statistics for User Research. Elsevier (2012)
12. Yates, S., Keitt, T.J.: Measure Workforce Experience Through Engagement. Productivity and Customer Impact, Forrester Research (2013)

Evaluating Mobile Malware by Extracting User Experience-Based Features

Francesco Mercaldo[✉] and Corrado Aaron Visaggio

Department of Engineering, University of Sannio, Benevento, Italy
{fmercaldo,visaggio}@unisannio.it

Abstract. The perception the user has about the performances of an application could determine the success of the application in the marketplace. The research community has made many efforts to understand out how to measure the user experience of mobile applications. In this paper we apply a set of features, typically used to evaluate mobile user experience (UX), with the aim at understanding whether there are differences in terms of usability between trusted and malware mobile samples. As a side effect we evaluate whether the feature set is useful to discriminate mobile malware. The experiment suggests that malware samples exhibit a better UX than legitimate ones. Furthermore we obtain, training several classifiers from UX-based features, a precision of 0.97 in malware identification.

1 Introduction

Smartphones have enriched the capabilities of mobile devices with advanced computing abilities and Internet connectivity: basically, they combine the functions of a personal computer with those of a mobile phone.

Current smartphones offer a number of native features, including high-resolution touchscreen, GPS navigation, Wi-Fi and mobile broadband access.

ISO 9241-210[1] defines the user experience (UX) as "a person's perceptions and responses that result from the use or anticipated use of a product, system or service".

Several works in literature evaluate user experience through resource-based features, i.e. monitoring memory [1], power consumption [2–5], CPU and network [6] but their experimental dataset is usually limited to a small set of applications ad-hoc developed by authors.

From another side, there is another problem plaguing the ecosystem of mobile applications: the increasing production of malware targeting the Android platform.

The most common mechanism employed by attackers to diffuse malware is represented by downloading popular apps, disassembling them, enclosing malicious payloads, re-assembling and then submitting the new apps to marketplaces. Usually, the best candidate applications to embed malicious payload are the top

---

[1] http://www.iso.org/iso/catalogue_detail.htm?csnumber=52075.

© Springer International Publishing Switzerland 2015
P. Abrahamsson et al. (Eds.): PROFES 2015, LNCS 9459, pp. 497–512, 2015.
DOI: 10.1007/978-3-319-26844-6_37

downloaded applications with a trivial business logic, such as applications to change ringtones or to change wallpapers. This happens because the attacker easily integrates the malicious payload into these basic applications.

In addiction to this trusted applications tend to exhibit an intrinsic complexity, because they are designed to satisfy the ever increasing needs of users. The distribution of the op-codes, as demonstrated in Canfora et al. [7], is revealing of legitimate samples complexity respect to malware ones. Conversely, as the malicious payload has not an articulated business logic except for the malicious payload [8], this difference tends to be less evident than in trusted applications.

Starting from these considerations, in this paper we investigate whether the user experience of malicious Android applications is different from that of trusted ones. Thus, we first observe the differences of user experience between trusted and malicious applications, evaluated by extracting a set of resources usage metrics. Then we build a classifier with these metrics for understanding whether such features are able to discriminate a malicious application from a trusted one.

The paper poses two research questions:

- RQ1: is there a difference in user experience between mobile malware and trusted applications?
- RQ2: are the features extracted able to distinguish a malware from a trusted application for Android platform?

The paper is organized as follows: the next section provides an overview of related work; the following section illustrates the proposed features set; the fourth section describes the experiment, the fifth section discusses the results and, finally, conclusion and future works are given in the last section.

2 Related Work

Different authors propose metrics for evaluating the user experience on mobile devices.

Authors in [1] developed a platform named ATE for supporting design of UX tests. ATE is able to test scenario in a script file, the test is performed without the human interaction, as the test execution is the launch and running of the script corresponding to the test scenario. User perception is obtained by measuring the smartphone's resources (i.e. time, memory occupation).

Wei et al. [5] propose an energy-based fair queuing as a pivotal instrument to increase the smartphone UX. Their approach represents a novel class of energy-aware scheduling algorithms that support proportional energy use, effective time constraint compliance and a flexible trade-off between them.

Wineguide [6] application assesses network resources as signal strength, monitored during usage of the applications. Higher signal strengths correspond with a better experience (e.g. speed). The aim of the method is to correlate UX to quality of service by taking into account both social and technical aspects.

Resources usage has been studied in literature for discriminating mobile malware from trusted applications.

Andromaly [9] considers several features, like CPU usage, number of sent packets through network, number of running processes and battery level. The authors obtained a detection rate of 94 %, but the apps used in the experimentation were ad-hoc developed by the authors.

Blasing and colleagues [10] use a combination of static and dynamic techniques. They first scan the code, then run the suspicious app in a totally monitored environment, catching all the events occurring in the sandbox such as files open operations and connections to remote server. The technique is evaluated using ad-hoc developed malware.

Shabtai et al. [11] use the knowledge-based temporal abstraction methodology. They detect suspicious temporal patterns to decide whether an intrusion is found, using memory, CPU and power related features, obtaining a detection rate above 94 %.

Researchers in [12] propose an Android malware detector evaluating permissions and system calls related to process management and to I/O operations. They obtain a precision equal to 0.74 using a dataset of 200 malicious applications.

TaintDroid [13] uses dynamic information flow tracking to detect sensitive data leakage. The dataset used included 30 popular third-party Android applications, and the method was able to recognize 20 apps with potential misuse of private information.

Reference in [2–4] consider the power consumption as the distinguishable feature between benign and malicious applications. The method of [3] produced 99 % true positive rate but using a sample of 3 malicious apps for validation; the experimentation of [2,4], did not evaluate the method performances.

3   The Features Set

We defined a set of features for evaluating UX on mobile devices that monitor resource consumption.

Features are retrieved using a tool chain while the application under analysis (AUA in the remaining of the paper) is running.

We extract features related to consumption of following resources handled by Android operating system:

– CPU load;
– memory usage;
– I/O storage;
– network, in terms of sent and received bytes.

The resources consumption is measured both at *AUA-grain* (i.e., only for the running application) and at *global-grain* (i.e., considering all the processes running). For instance, regarding the CPU load, we are interested in both the consumption of the resource by the application process when is running (at AUA-grain), but also in the total consumption of the monitored resource in the operating system while the AUA is running (at global-grain).

We consider the following features:

1. *TotalUserCPU* ($f1_{CPU}$): the percentage of CPU used by the AUA;
2. *TotalSystemCPU* ($f2_{CPU}$): the percentage of CPU used by all processes during the execution of the AUA;
3. *KBWRITTEN_IO* ($f1_{IO}$): the amount of information (expressed in Kilobyte) written on storage by all processes during the execution of AUA;
4. *KBREAD_IO* ($f2_{IO}$): the amount of information (expressed in Kilobyte) read from storage by all processes during the execution of AUA;
5. *RCHAR_PROC_IO* ($f3_{IO}$): the number of bytes which are read from storage from AUA: the value is represented by the sum of bytes which the AUA process passed to read()[2] and pread()[3] system calls;
6. *WCHAR_PROC_IO* ($f4_{IO}$): the number of bytes which are written into the storage from AUA: the value is represented by the sum of bytes which the AUA process passed to write()[4] and pwrite()[5] system calls;
7. *SYSCR_PROC_IO* ($f5_{IO}$): the value represents the number of read I/O operations, i.e. the occurrences of read() and pread() syscalls performed by AUA;
8. *SYSCW_PROC_IO* ($f6_{IO}$): the value represent the number of write I/O operations, i.e. syscalls like write() and pwrite() performed by AUA;
9. *GLOBAL_FREE_MEM* ($f1_{MEM}$): the global amount of idle memory;
10. *GLOBAL_MAPPED_MEM* ($f2_{MEM}$): the global amount of used memory;
11. *GLOBAL_ANOM_MEM* ($f3_{MEM}$): the global amount of anonymous mapping maps, i.e. an area of the process's virtual memory not backed by any file;
12. *VSS* ($f4_{MEM}$): the Virtual Set Size represents the total virtual memory size of the AUA process (i.e., the total amount of memory in swap and RAM);
13. *PSS* ($f5_{MEM}$): the Proportional Set Size is the amount of AUA memory shared with other processes, accounted in a way that the amount is divided evenly between the processes that share it;
14. *RSS* ($f6_{MEM}$): the Resident Set Size is the portion of memory occupied by AUA process that is held in main memory (RAM). The rest of the occupied memory exists in the swap space or file system, either because some parts of the occupied memory were paged out, or because some parts of the executable were never loaded;
15. *USS* ($f7_{MEM}$): the Unique Set Size is the set of pages that are unique for AUA process. This is the amount of memory that would be freed if the application is immediately terminated;
16. *GLOBAL_RX_BYTES* ($f1_{NET}$): the number (expressed in bytes) of the packets received from all the processes while the AUA is running;
17. *GLOBAL_TX_BYTES* ($f2_{NET}$): the number (expressed in bytes) of the packets transmitted from all processes while the AUA is running;

---

[2] http://linux.die.net/man/2/read.
[3] http://linux.die.net/man/2/pread.
[4] http://linux.die.net/man/2/write.
[5] http://linux.die.net/man/2/pwrite.

Table 1. Overview of the features involved in the study, each feature is associated to a monitored resource (CPU, I/O, memory and network); in addiction each feature is associated to the "grain" level of monitored resource (AUA-grain or global-grain) and to tool used to compute it.

Resource	Feature	Global	AUA	Tool
CPU	TotalUserCPU ($f1_{CPU}$)	X		top
	TotalSystemCPU ($f2_{CPU}$)		X	top
MEM	GLOBAL_FREE_MEM ($f1_{MEM}$)	X		vmstat
	GLOBAL_MAPPED_MEM ($f2_{MEM}$)	X		vmstat
	GLOBAL_ANOM_MEM ($f3_{MEM}$)	X		vmstat
	VSS ($f4_{MEM}$)		X	vmstat
	PSS ($f5_{MEM}$)		X	vmstat
	RSS ($f6_{MEM}$)		X	vmstat
	USS ($f7_{MEM}$)		X	vmstat
I/O	KBWRITTEN_IO ($f1_{IO}$)	X		iostat
	KBREAD_IO ($f2_{IO}$)	X		iostat
	RCHAR_PROC_IO ($f3_{IO}$)		X	*proc/[PID]/io* folder
	WCHAR_PROC_IO ($f4_{IO}$)		X	*proc/[PID]/io* folder
	SYSCR_PROC_IO ($f5_{IO}$)		X	*proc/[PID]/io* folder
	SYSCW_PROC_IO ($f6_{IO}$)		X	*proc/[PID]/io* folder
NET	GLOBAL_RX_BYTES ($f1_{NET}$)	X		DDMLIB libraries
	GLOBAL_TX_BYTES ($f2_{NET}$)	X		DDMLIB libraries
	RX_BYTES ($f3_{NET}$)		X	DDMLIB libraries
	TX_BYTES ($f4_{NET}$)		X	DDMLIB libraries

18. *RX_BYTES* ($f3_{NET}$): the number (expressed in bytes) of the packets received from AUA;
19. *TX_BYTES* ($f4_{NET}$): the number (expressed in bytes) of the packets transmitted from AUA.

Table 1 shows an overview of the features involved in the study, grouping them by the type of monitored resource and by the grain type (i.e., AUA-grain or global-grain).

We use different tools in order to monitor the resource consumption, each tool is related to the single monitored resource.

To retrieve information about the CPU consumption we use the top tool[6]. The top tool is able to provide an ongoing overview of the CPU activity in real time, i.e. while the applications are running. It displays a list of the most CPU-intensive tasks on the system, and it sorts the tasks by the CPU usage. with the top tool we extract the $f1_{CPU}$ and the $f2_{CPU}$ features.

---

[6] http://linux.die.net/man/1/top.

To extract the features regarding the global memory usage, we use the virtual memory statistics (vmstat) tool[7]. Vmstat is a system monitoring tool that collects and displays information on operating system memory, processes, interrupts and paging. Using vmstat we are able to extract the following global-grain features: GLOBAL_FREE_MEM ($f1_{MEM}$), GLOBAL_MAPPED_MEM ($f2_{MEM}$) and GLOBAL_ANOM_MEM ($f3_{MEM}$).

Using procrank[8] tool we retrieve a quick summary of the process memory utilization. Procrank is usually used to check if a process has memory leakage. The binary is located in /system/xbin folder on Android devices. With procrank we extract following AUA-grain features: VSS ($f4_{MEM}$), PSS ($f5_{MEM}$), RSS ($f6_{MEM}$) and USS ($f7_{MEM}$).

With iostat[9] we extract the following global-grain I/O features: GLOBAL_FREE_MEM ($f1_{MEM}$), GLOBAL_MAPPED_MEM ($f2_{MEM}$) and GLOBAL_ANOM_MEM ($f3_{MEM}$).

To retrieve information about the I/O usage related to the AUA we parse the proc/[PID]/io file, useful to extract the following AUA-grain features: KBWRITTEN_IO ($f1_{IO}$), KBREAD_IO ($f2_{IO}$), RCHAR_PROC_IO ($f3_{IO}$), WCHAR_PROC_IO ($f4_{IO}$), SYSCR_PROC_IO ($f5_{IO}$) and SYSCW_PROC_IO ($f6_{IO}$).

To extract the features related to the use of the network, we developed a tool that extends the Device Monitor[10] tool which can be found in the Android SDK. Using the DDMLIB libraries provided by Device Monitor we retrieve the AUA and the global-grain features network-related: GLOBAL_RX_BYTES ($f1_{NET}$), GLOBAL_TX_BYTES ($f2_{NET}$), RX_BYTES ($f3_{NET}$) and TX_BYTES ($f4_{NET}$).

We developed a script able to invoke the different tools while the application is running, in order to automatize the features extraction process.

The script developed is able to record the feature set 10 times while the AUA is running. Each application is run for 60 s, the script retrieves the features every 6 s, i.e. for each AUA we store 10 different measures for the full features set.

The final value of each feature is the arithmetic mean of the ten different values retrieved for each features while AUA is running.

Concerning the UI interactions and system events, we used the monkey tool of the Android Debug Brigde (ADB[11]) version 1.0.32. Monkey generates pseudo-random streams of user events such as clicks, touches, or gestures; moreover, it can simulate a number of system-level events.

Specifically, we configured Monkey to send 2000 random UI events in 60 s.

In order to collect the features for an AUA, we built a script which interacts with the emulator and performs the following procedure:

1. copies the AUA into the storage of emulated device;
2. installs the AUA (using the install command of ADB);

---

[7] https://www.freebsd.org/cgi/man.cgi?query=vmstat.

[8] http://elinux.org/Android_Memory_Usage#procrank.

[9] http://linuxcommand.org/man_pages/iostat1.html.

[10] http://developer.android.com/tools/help/monitor.html.

[11] http://developer.android.com/tools/help/adb.html.

3. gets the package name and the class (activity/service) of the AUA with the launcher intent (i.e., get the AUA entry point, needed for step 4);
4. starts the AUA (using the `am start` command of ADB);
5. gets the AUA process id (PID);
6. starts Monkey (using the `monkey` command of ADB), instructed to send UI and system events;
7. waits 60 s;
8. collects the features;
9. waits 6 s;
10. repeats ten times from step 8;
11. kills the AUA (using the PID collected before);
12. uninstalls the AUA (using the `uninstall` command of ADB);
13. saves the features extracted into the database;
14. deletes the AUA from the device.

4 Evaluation: Study Design

We designed an experiment in order to evaluate the effectiveness of the proposed feature set, expressed through the research questions RQ1 and RQ2, stated in the introduction.

More specifically, the experiment is aimed at verifying whether the nineteen features are able to highlight differences in UX between malicious and trusted mobile applications. Furthermore the classification step is carried out by using classifiers built with four groups of features (each group consists of features related to the same resource) and with the full features set.

The evaluation includes three stages: (i) a comparison of descriptive statistics of the populations of programs; (ii) hypothesis testing, to verify if the nineteen features have different distributions for the populations of malware and trusted applications; and (iii) a classification analysis aimed at assessing whether the features are able to correctly classify malware and trusted applications. The classification analysis was accomplished with Weka[12], a suite of machine learning software very popular and largely employed in data mining research and applications.

The dataset was made of 1,000 Android trusted applications and 1,000 Android malware applications: The trusted applications were downloaded from Google Play[13] between January 2015 and April 2015 and they were later analysed with the VirusTotal service[14], a service able to scan an application using simultaneously more than 50 antimalware, to confirm that the applications did not contain malicious payload. The malware applications belong to the Drebin project [14,15], a dataset that gathers the majority of existing Android malware families.

---

[12] http://www.cs.waikato.ac.nz/ml/weka/.
[13] https://play.google.com/.
[14] https://www.virustotal.com/.

With regards to the hypothesis testing, the null hypothesis to be tested is:

H_0: 'malware and trusted applications have similar values of the features'.

The null hypothesis was tested with Mann-Whitney (with the p-level fixed to 0.05) and with Kolmogorov-Smirnov Test (with the p-level fixed to 0.05). We chose to run two different tests in order to enforce the conclusion validity.

The classification analysis was aimed at assessing whether the features where able to correctly classify malware and trusted applications.

Six algorithms of classification were used: J48, LadTree, NBTree, Random-Forest, RandomTree and RepTree. These algorithms were applied separately to the full feature set and to four groups of features.

5   Evaluation: Analysis of Data

The results of our evaluation will be discussed reflecting the data analysis' division in three phases: descriptive statistics, hypotheses testing and classification.

5.1   Descriptive Statistics

In Fig. 1 the box plots related to the $f1_{CPU}$ and $f2_{CPU}$ features. The box plots related to the $f1_{CPU}$ feature shows a significant difference between malware and trusted samples, while the second one (related to $f2_{CPU}$ feature) do not produce a significant differences between the two distributions.

This means that the total CPU time ($f2_{CPU}$) used by all processes does not change between trusted and malware applications. The difference occurs in the CPU time used by the AUA ($f1_{CPU}$): trusted applications seem to be more CPU expensive than malware ones. This happen because trusted applications usually present a business logic more complex than malware ones, in fact the purpose of malware is usually information gathering that does not require CPU time.

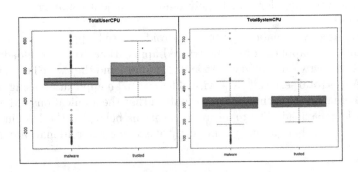

Fig. 1. Box plots for the features TotalUserCPU ($f1_{CPU}$) and TotalSystemCPU ($f2_{CPU}$).

Figure 2 shows the box plots related to global memory features. The box plots show that the execution of malware applications is much more expensive in terms of memory usage by all running processes compared to trusted applications.

The most discriminating feature is the $f3_{MEM}$: the use of pages saved to disk is higher in malware than trusted, this is symptom that most of malware applications do not save data to disk, but use more RAM memory to store the information to send to attacker.

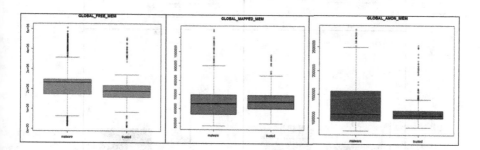

Fig. 2. Box plots for the features GLOBAL_FREE_MEM ($f1_{MEM}$), GLOBAL_MAPPED_MEM ($f2_{MEM}$) and GLOBAL_ANON_MEM ($f3_{MEM}$).

Figure 3 shows the box plots related to memory AUA-grain features.

The set of memory AUA-grain features show that the trusted applications are more memory-intensive at AUA-grain than malware ones. We note that the global-grain memory features instead show the opposite result. Probably malware applications are turning to intermediaries processes to load into memory the information retrieved to avoid detection by antimalware software.

Figure 4 shows the box plots related to I/O global-grain features.

Regarding the $f1_{IO}$ feature, the trusted applications perform many write operations with respect to the malware ones. This is because most of trusted applications are web-services based: they need to store the required information on storage, and then have a caching mechanism in order to optimize the user experience. The malware applications do not require these mechanisms, since they typically expose a trivial business logic. From the point of view of the attacker the information storing is a bad practice: it would leave imprints of malicious behavior.

The feature $f2_{IO}$ shows that read operations are very similar between the two distributions: this represents an interesting result, considering that the only information retrieved by malware applications are usually those related to smartphone owner.

The consideration for the $f2_{IO}$ feature, is confirmed from the analysis of box plots for AUA-grain I/O features ($f3_{IO}$, $f4_{IO}$, $f5_{IO}$ and $f6_{IO}$) in Fig. 5. The malware applications, that perform read and write operations just to send sensitive information to the attacker, call the I/O functions similarly to the

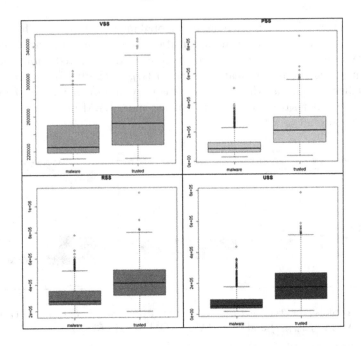

Fig. 3. Box plots for the features VSS ($f4_{MEM}$), PSS ($f5_{MEM}$), RSS ($f6_{MEM}$) and USS ($f7_{MEM}$)

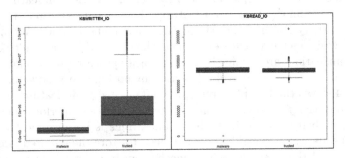

Fig. 4. Box plots for the features KBWRITTEN_IO ($f1_{IO}$) and KBREAD_IO ($f2_{IO}$)

trusted applications (which depending on the purpose of the application they use the I/O functions).

The box plots in Fig. 6 shows the malware and trusted distributions for global-grain ($f1_{NET}$ and $f2_{NET}$) and AUA-grain ($f3_{NET}$ and $f4_{NET}$) network features.

The distributions for $f1_{NET}$, $f2_{NET}$ and $f3_{NET}$ features appear to be similar, while for $f4_{NET}$ is different. We recall that trusted applications use intensively network resources, indeed mobile applications are usually web-service oriented. As for the AUA-grain I/O features, the distributions are similar

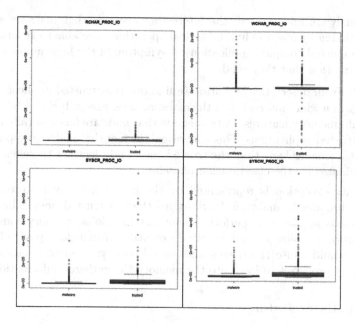

Fig. 5. Box plots for the features RCHAR_PROC_IO ($f3_{IO}$), WCHAR_PROC_IO ($f4_{IO}$), SYSCR_PROC_IO ($f5_{IO}$) and SYSCW_PROC_IO ($f6_{IO}$).

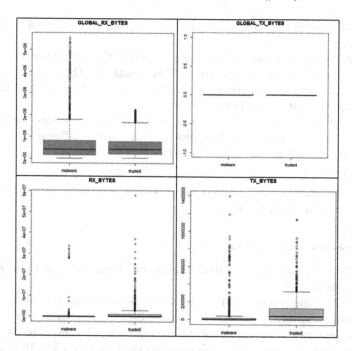

Fig. 6. Box plots for features GLOBAL_RX_BYTES ($f1_{NET}$), GLOBAL_TX_BYTES ($f2_{NET}$), RX_BYTES ($f3_{NET}$) and TX_BYTES ($f4_{NET}$)

between malware and trusted: the interesting result is that malware applications, consisting by few and limited logical operations, are able to generate data traffic like trusted complex applications, a symptom of the huge amount of sensitive information that they send.

Remark 1: From descriptive statistics we find out that trusted applications box plots range in a wider interval than the malware ones, except box plot inherent to global-grain memory features. Data suggests that malware has generally a better UX than trusted applications. This may reveal the fact that malware applications implement a smaller logic than the trusted ones, and identifies these features as good candidates for the classification phase.

The only exception is represented by the global memory features, whose values are broader in malware distributions than in trusted ones. This means that malicious applications performs many actions global memory consuming, a symptom of a prolonged and repeated execution of malicious payload, which over time would cause slowdowns and an UX decay: probably malware uses intermediary processes to load into the memory the gathered information.

5.2 Hypothesis Testing

The hypothesis testing aims at evaluating if the features present different distributions for the populations of malware and trusted applications with statistical evidence.

We assume valid the results when the null hypothesis is rejected by both the tests performed.

Table 2 shows the results of hypothesis testing: the null hypothesis H_0 can be rejected for all the nineteen features. This means that there is statistical evidence that the vector of features is a potential candidate for correctly classifying malware and trusted applications.

This result will provide an evaluation of the risk to generalize the fact that the selected features produce values which belong to two different distributions (i.e. the one of malware and the trusted one): those features can distinguish those observations.

Remark 2: the malware and trusted samples show a statistically significant difference by running both the tests.

5.3 Classification Analysis

The classification analysis consisted of building classifiers in order to evaluate features accuracy.

For the learning phase, we use a k-fold cross-validation: the dataset is randomly partitioned into k subsets. A single subset is retained as the validation dataset for testing the model, while the remaining k − 1 subsets of the original dataset are used as training data. We repeated the process for k = 10 times; each one of the k subsets has been used once as the validation dataset. To obtain a single estimate, we computed the average of the k results from the folds.

Table 2. Results of the test of the null hypothesis H_0

Variable	Mann-Whitney	Kolmogorov-Smirnov
$f1_{CPU}$	0,000000	p < .001
$f2_{CPU}$	0,000000	p < .001
$f1_{MEM}$	0,000240	p < .001
$f2_{MEM}$	0,000000	p < .001
$f3_{MEM}$	0,000000	p < .001
$f4_{MEM}$	0,000000	p < .001
$f5_{MEM}$	0,000000	p < .001
$f6_{MEM}$	0,000000	p < .001
$f7_{MEM}$	0,000000	p < .001
$f1_{IO}$	0,000000	p < .001
$f2_{IO}$	0,000240	p < .001
$f3_{IO}$	0,000000	p < .001
$f4_{IO}$	0,000000	p < .001
$f5_{IO}$	0,000000	p < .001
$f6_{IO}$	0,000000	p < .001
$f1_{NET}$	0,000000	p < .001
$f2_{NET}$	0,000000	p < .001
$f3_{NET}$	0,000000	p < .001
$f4_{NET}$	0,000000	p < .001

The results that we obtained with this procedure are shown in Table 3. Six metrics were used to evaluate the classification results: TP rate, FP rate, recall, precision, f-measure and roc area.

The true positive rate measures the proportion of positives that are correctly identified as such (i.e., the percentage of malware applications who are correctly identified as having the condition).

The true negative rate measures the proportion of negatives that are correctly identified as such (i.e., the percentage of malware applications who are correctly identified as not having the condition).

The precision has been computed as the proportion of samples that truly belong to class X among all those which were assigned to the class. It is the ratio of the number of relevant records retrieved to the total number of irrelevant and relevant records retrieved:

$$Precision = \frac{tp}{tp + fp}$$

where tp indicates the number of true positives and fp indicates the number of false positives.

Table 3. TP Rate, FP Rate, Precision, Recall, F-Measure and RocArea obtained by classifying malicious and trusted dataset, using features grouped by resource monitored (f_mem, f_net, f_cpu and f_IO) and using the full features set (f_tot).

Features	Algorithm	TP Rate		FP Rate		Precision		Recall		F-Measure		RocArea	
		M	T	M	T	M	T	M	T	M	T	M	T
f_mem	J48	0.907	0.884	0.116	0.093	0.888	0.903	0.907	0.884	0.897	0.893	0.919	0.919
	LADTree	0.886	0.883	0.117	0.114	0.885	0.884	0.886	0.883	0.885	0.883	0.938	0.938
	NBTree	0.888	0.887	0.113	0.112	0.889	0.886	0.888	0.887	0.888	0.887	0.927	0.927
	RandomForest	0.926	0.903	0.097	0.074	0.906	0.923	0.926	0.903	0.916	0.912	0.961	0.961
	RandomTree	0.875	0.867	0.133	0.125	0.87	0.872	0.875	0.867	0.873	0.869	0.871	0.871
	RepTree	0.89	0.868	0.132	0.11	0.872	0.886	0.89	0.868	0.881	0.877	0.924	0.924
f_net	J48	0.873	0.702	0.298	0.127	0.749	0.844	0.873	0.702	0.806	0.767	0.813	0.813
	LADTree	0.901	0.684	0.316	0.099	0.744	0.872	0.901	0.684	0.815	0.767	0.832	0.832
	NBTree	0.875	0.712	0.288	0.125	0.756	0.848	0.875	0.712	0.811	0.774	0.836	0.836
	RandomForest	0.749	0.735	0.265	0.251	0.742	0.742	0.749	0.735	0.746	0.739	0.793	0.793
	RandomTree	0.727	0.724	0.276	0.273	0.728	0.722	0.727	0.724	0.727	0.723	0.725	0.725
	RepTree	0.89	0.685	0.315	0.11	0.742	0.86	0.89	0.685	0.809	0.763	0.825	0.825
f_cpu	J48	0.848	0.54	0.46	0.152	0.652	0.777	0.848	0.54	0.737	0.637	0.733	0.733
	LADTree	0.809	0.565	0.435	0.191	0.654	0.743	0.809	0.565	0.723	0.642	0.751	0.751
	NBTree	0.893	0.452	0.548	0.107	0.624	0.806	0.893	0.452	0.735	0.579	0.705	0.705
	RandomForest	0.693	0.601	0.399	0.307	0.639	0.658	0.693	0.601	0.665	0.628	0.708	0.708
	RandomTree	0.643	0.613	0.387	0.357	0.629	0.628	0.643	0.613	0.636	0.62	0.629	0.629
	RepTree	0.823	0.577	0.423	0.177	0.665	0.763	0.823	0.577	0.736	0.657	0.745	0.745
f_IO	J48	0.938	0.887	0.113	0.062	0.895	0.933	0.938	0.887	0.916	0.91	0.923	0.923
	LADTree	0.922	0.869	0.131	0.078	0.878	0.916	0.922	0.869	0.899	0.892	0.952	0.952
	NBTree	0.925	0.884	0.116	0.075	0.89	0.92	0.925	0.884	0.907	0.902	0.944	0.944
	RandomForest	0.961	0.905	0.095	0.039	0.912	0.958	0.961	0.905	0.936	0.931	0.976	0.976
	RandomTree	0.911	0.895	0.105	0.089	0.898	0.908	0.911	0.895	0.904	0.901	0.903	0.903
	RepTree	0.923	0.886	0.114	0.077	0.892	0.919	0.923	0.886	0.907	0.902	0.944	0.944
f_tot	J48	0.974	0.969	0.031	0.026	0.969	0.973	0.974	0.969	0.972	0.971	0.974	0.974
	LADTree	0.971	0.959	0.041	0.029	0.96	0.97	0.971	0.959	0.966	0.965	0.989	0.989
	NBTree	0.96	0.965	0.035	0.04	0.965	0.96	0.96	0.965	0.963	0.962	0.986	0.986
	RandomForest	0.989	0.95	0.05	0.011	0.953	0.988	0.989	0.95	0.97	0.969	0.995	0.995
	RandomTree	0.931	0.923	0.077	0.069	0.925	0.93	0.931	0.923	0.928	0.926	0.927	0.927
	RepTree	0.958	0.962	0.038	0.042	0.963	0.958	0.958	0.962	0.96	0.96	0.984	0.984

The recall has been computed as the proportion of samples that were assigned to class X, among all the samples that truly belong to the class, i.e. how much part of the class was captured. It is the ratio of the number of relevant records retrieved to the total number of relevant records:

$$Recall = \frac{tp}{tp + fn}$$

where fn is the number of false negatives. Precision and recall are inversely related.

The f-measure considers both the precision and the recall of the test to compute the score. The score can be interpreted as a weighted average of the precision and recall:

$$F\text{-}Measure = 2 * \frac{Precision * Recall}{Precision + Recall}$$

The Roc Area is defined as the probability that a positive instance randomly chosen is classified above a negative randomly chosen.

The classification analysis suggests several considerations:

- when considering the classifier with all the features, the detection is highly effective;
- by using the memory-related features we obtain the best precision value (0.906) with the RandomForest algorithm:
- by using the network-related features we obtain the best precision value (0.756) with the NBTree algorithm;
- by using the CPU-related features we obtain the best precision value (0.665) with the RepTree algorithm:
- by using the I/O-related features we obtain the best precision value (0.912) with the RandomForest algorithm:
- we obtain the best precision value (0.969) with the J48 algorithm using all the features extracted in the study.

Remark 3: The full set features classification improves the detection capability, with a very high level of precision. If we consider the feature groups, the best in class are the memory related and the I/O related features.

6 Conclusions and Future Works

In this paper we evaluate how the user experience varies between the malware and trusted applications for the Android platform.

The results obtained show that malware applications tend to exhibit a better user experience than trusted ones, except for the use of the global memory. This usually happens because the malware applications are obtained by adding the malicious payload to legitimate applications with trivial business logic: the complexity of malicious apps resides more in the malicious payload added by the attacker. Usually the malicious payload is designed to leave no trace of its action, for instance it does not write on storage but considering the simplicity of its business logic, we notice that malware makes use of the network in the same way of trusted applications, moreover we highlight also that malware increases the global memory usage in the system during its execution.

The features extracted were used also to build a classifier for detecting malware applications: the results show a precision equal to 0.969 and a recall equal 0.989 in the best case. This result highlights the diversity in the usage of resources between trusted and malware applications.

Future works concern the adoption of clone detection techniques in order to isolate the malicious payload to evaluate the UX with regards to the implemented malicious actions. Furthermore we plan to extend the dataset of malicious applications in order to characterize the malware families.

References

1. Canfora, G., Mercaldo, F., Visaggio, C.A., D'Angelo, M., Furno, A., Manganelli, C.: A case study of automating user experience-oriented performance testing on smartphones. In: Proceedings of IEEE Sixth International Conference on Software Testing, Verification and Validation (ICST) (2013)
2. Dixon, B., Jiang, Y., Jaiantilal, A., Mishra, S.: Location based power analysis to detect malicious code in smartphones. In: Proceedings of the 1st ACM workshop on Security and privacy in smartphones and mobile devices (2011)
3. Kim, H., Smith, J., Shin, K.G.: Detecting energy-greedy anomalies and mobile malware variants. In: Proceedings of the 6th International Conference on Mobile Systems, Applications, and Services (2008)
4. Liu, L., Yan, G., Zhang, X., Chen, S.: VirusMeter: Preventing Your Cellphone from Spies. In: Kirda, E., Jha, S., Balzarotti, D. (eds.) RAID 2009. LNCS, vol. 5758, pp. 244–264. Springer, Heidelberg (2009)
5. Wei, J., Juarez, E., Garrido, M., Pescador, F.: Maximizing the user experience with energy-based fair sharing in battery limited mobile systems. IEEE Trans. Consum. Electron. **59**(3), 690–698 (2013)
6. Deryckere, T., Martens, L., De Marez, L., De Moor, K., Berte, K.: A software tool to relate technical performance to user experience in a mobile context. In: Proceedings of IEEE Sixth International Symposium on a World of Wireless, Mobile and Multimedia Networks) (2008)
7. Canfora, G., Mercaldo, F., Visaggio, C.A.: Mobile malware detection using op-code frequency histograms. In: Proceedings of International Conference on Security and Cryptography (SECRYPT) (2015)
8. Canfora, G., Mercaldo, F., Moriano, G., Visaggio, C.A.: Composition-malware: building android malware at run time. In: Proceedings of International Workshop on Security of Mobile Applications (ARES) (2015)
9. Shabtai, A., Kanonov, U., Elovici, Y., Glezer, C., Weiss, Y.: Andromaly: a behavioral malware detection framework for android devices. J. Intell. Inf. Syst. **38**, 161–190 (2012)
10. Blasing, T., Schmidt, A.D., Batyuk, L., Camtepe, S.A., Albayrak, S.: An android application sandbox system for suspicious software detection. In: Proceedings of 5th International Conference on Malicious and Unwanted Software (2010)
11. Shabtai, A., Kanonov, U., Elovici, Y.: Intrusion detection for mobile devices using the knowledge-based, temporal abstraction method. J. Syst. Softw. **83**(8), 1524–1537 (2010)
12. Canfora, G., Mercaldo, F., Visaggio, C.A.: A classifier of malicious android applications. In: Proceedings of the 2nd International Workshop on Security of Mobile Applications (ARES) (2013)
13. Enck, W., Gilbert, P., Chun, B.G., Cox, L.P., Jung, J., McDaniel, P., Sheth, A.: Taintdroid: An information-flow tracking system for realtime privacy monitoring on smartphones. OSDI **10**, 255–270 (2010)
14. Arp, D., Spreitzenbarth, M., Hubner, M., Gascon, H., Rieck, K.: Drebin: effective and explainable detection of android malware in your pocket. In: Proceedings of NDSS 2014, Network and Distributed System Security Symposium (2014)
15. Spreitzenbarth, M., Ectler, F., Schreck, T., Freling, F., Hoffmann, J.: Mobilesandbox: looking deeper into android applications. In: Proceedings of SAC 2013, 28th International ACM Symposium on Applied Computing (2013)

Information System Software Development with Support for Application Traceability

Vojislav Đukić[1], Ivan Luković[1], Matej Črepinšek[2],
Tomaž Kosar[2]([✉]), and Marjan Mernik[2]

[1] Faculty of Technical Sciences,University of Novi Sad,
Trg Dositeja Obradovića 6, 21000 Novi Sad, Serbia
{vdjukic,ivan}@uns.ac.rs
[2] University of Maribor, Slomškov trg 15, 2000 Maribor, Slovenia
{matej.crepinsek,tomaz.kosar,marjan.mernik}@um.si

Abstract. Information systems are rapidly changing since new requirements are emerging frequently in business processes. When incorporating changes in the system you should not underestimate the usability and personal satisfaction of the user. There are many variables that influence the success of evolving an information system from the user's viewpoint. In this paper we outline the problem of information system traceability, the ability of users to verify the history of information system and with that a possibility to check the differences between information system's versions. Unfortunately, most of the systems support traceability only at the level of the document. The novel approach presented in this paper is integrated within WISL, using our information system generator, and supports versioning control inside information systems. WISL introduces application traceability at the level of information systems' domain concepts which deliver versioning information to the users in a seamless manner.

Keywords: Program versioning · Information systems · Dynamic graphical user interfaces · Human-computer interaction · Domain-specific modeling · Domain-specific languages

1 Introduction

Software engineers are constantly dealing with new requirements and extending Information Systems (ISs). Usually, the success of an extension is recognized by the proper functioning and efficiency of the IS. Rarely is the success factor related to usability and the personal satisfaction of the users. The latter are often forced to unconditionally adopt the changes introduced in the ISs. Activities that would ease the transition between two versions of the same software are often not supported. The above-mentioned problems are topics of research within field of human-computer interaction (HCI) more specifically as an interaction design discipline, which focuses on how to design computer software so that it is as simple, intuitive, and comfortable to use as possible [1]. In this paper we suggest

© Springer International Publishing Switzerland 2015
P. Abrahamsson et al. (Eds.): PROFES 2015, LNCS 9459, pp. 513–527, 2015.
DOI: 10.1007/978-3-319-26844-6_38

improving the user's usability with a software development approach often used in model-driven architecture [2], a domain-specific language (DSL) [3].

In rapidly changing systems there are many variables that influence the success of IS development from the viewpoint of user's efficiency. We will outline traceability. An example of a successful implementation at the level of source code traceability is the Git versioning system [4]. Unfortunately, it only enables traceability at the level of the text, rather than on the level of IS domain concepts.

The idea of traceability in ISs is not new [5] but is rarely being implemented since it takes precious resources. We can find examples of such functionality within some development frameworks but it is usually limited to changes inside the log file, the source code with its comments, and the updated documentation that is not linked to the context of history. Such documentation is often a good support for a software developer but unfortunately not available to the user to understand the evolution of IS, evaluating/determining the price of changes for a customer, finding potential security holes for the security engineer, etc.

In order to overcome some of these problems, we have designed a tool WISL (Web Information System Language)[1] that is based on the centralized integration of changes at the level of domain concepts. In view of that, the feature of traceability is available throughout the whole process that includes documentation, metamodel, source code, user interface, and history-enriched user documentation.

In order to support users with the capabilities of tracing the IS versions and their functionality changes, we use DSL [6]. DSLs have become an important Software Engineering (SE) field and one of the vital elements of several software development methodologies, like Model-Driven Engineering (MDE) [7], Software Factories [8], etc. In this paper we first used the power of DSLs to generate an arbitrary IS. In this manner the software engineer can describe any IS with writing specification in WISL. The novel approach that we present in this paper, is the extension of this DSL to support version control inside IS similar to the Git versioning system. We believe that such interaction design of IS improves the user's perception on changes introduced in evolved IS.

The organization of the paper is as follows. Motivation is discussed in Sect. 2. The general overview of the WISL framework is given in Sect. 3. The language behind the WISL framework is presented in Sect. 4. An extension of the language from Sect. 4 that enables the construction of system traceability is given in Sect. 5. Finally, concluding remarks with future work are summarized in Sect. 6.

2   Motivation

Each approach to software development has its advantages and disadvantages. The design of our approach is based on the actual needs of the industry on the one hand and our expert knowledge on the other. The environment where we

---

[1] The project source is available at: https://bitbucket.org/work91/wis.

operate an economy is changing rapidly. Economy is changing enterprises from large to small and micro. Budgets for information technology are getting smaller, although there is a growing demand for ISs. Economy also changes the dynamics of the IS life-cycle. The frequencies of IS changes are increasing constantly. In practice, we meet the requirements, which are expected to change the IS not in a few days or weeks but within a few hours. The expectations of customer are often unrealistic and do not foresee the consequences they bring.

IS software development is becoming similar to the software prototyping in many aspect. In order to support our needs, the IS development framework needs to meet the following requirements:

- A high level of interactive integration of the customer, the developer, and the user.
- Support of traceability not only for the developer but also for the customer and the user.
- Support for the incremental development of domain specific concepts.
- Support for rapid implementation.

Customer and user are often the same person (Fig. 1) but this is not essential. In a simplified scenario, the customer is the one who is ultimately responsible for paying for the IS changes. Supporting aspects of billing system is very important, because requirements can grow out of proportion very quickly. The user is one who usually interacts with the IS user interface. However, the developer is usually the software engineer who adopts and implements a customer's requirements.

The described procedure is similar to the well-known issue-tracking systems [9], where the subscriber or user opens a new ticket to which developer responds

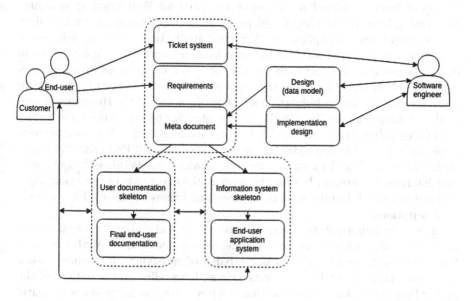

Fig. 1. Outline of WISL with traceability support

with a change in the IS or just a simple reply. Support of traceability is taking care of by including the ticket identifier in all documents of IS. The identifier of changes can be found in the description of the changes, over the source code to the user interface forms, or even reports.

In regard to the efficiency and transparency of incremental developing it is necessary to support the history of changes at the level of the domain concepts of IS not just at the level of text. Using such support IS can be returned to the previous version, review changes over time and link requirements not only on the level of specification but also at the level of graphical interface, database and associated documentation. These requirements of rapid development we have achieved with WISL by using a code generation, and concepts of DSL.

3   System Architecture

WISL is designed to be a comprehensive way of describing an IS in general (see Fig. 2). It combines the basic concepts from the entity-relationship model (ER model) but also includes some technical details about the end-system implementation. Comparing abstraction levels, WISL stays between ER and the relational data model. After creating the system description ("WISL Model" from Fig. 2), we have provided a process (see "IS Generation") for automatically generating a functional prototype ("IS Prototype" in Fig. 2). First of all, we used XText to implement WISL language and an editor as a plug-in for Eclipse IDE. Using the same tool we have defined a model to model transformation from WISL description to the WISL object model. The object model has been built within the Eclipse Modeling Framework (EMF) [10]. We used XTend to write code templates from the object model. Since we opted for Web-based applications, we have implemented two highly independent generator categories for the client and server sides of the application. WISL end application is built-up using some of the more widely used software frameworks mixed with our own extensions in order to support system extensibility. On the server side we used Spring Framework and Hibernate [11,12] together with a WISL data framework, in order to overcome problems with bidirectional relationships within the Hibernate framework. We have generated a JPA [12] data model, Spring repositories and Spring REST Controllers [11] from the WISL object model. On the client side we have implemented a highly decoupled Single Page Application (SPA) using the AngularJS framework [13]. In addition, we have provided the WISL with a dynamic user interface framework. In order to support the client side of the application, we have generated Angular routers, services, and menus but also WISL dynamic UI descriptions.

It is very important to mention some of the techniques for integrating a generated code with a hand written code. We are aware that WISL can build functional applications but it is not capable of satisfying all customer needs in commercial projects. On the server side we have relied on the options of the Spring Framework. Using configuration files it was possible to exclude some parts of the generated code or to include custom written code and combine it with

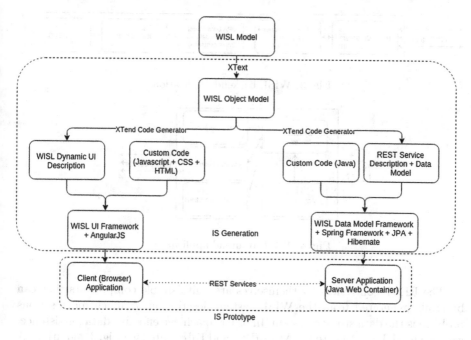

Fig. 2. WISL system architecture

the generated one. On the other hand, the WISL UI framework enables simple extensions of a client side application just by following the project structure.

3.1 WISL Backend Application

The WISL system follows the SPA architecture. It means that a server side does not generate HTML code, as in traditional web applications. The main idea is to write HTML templates that are going to be delivered to the client side as a bundle together with Javascript code. By using the Javascript code, it is possible to fill the templates with data retrieved by the server REST controllers. A big advantage of this approach is that it allows browsers to cache a client-side application. It leads to much more effective bandwidth usage and simpler server side code.

In order to support SPA architecture, the WISL backend is a REST application based on the Spring Framework (see Fig. 3). This framework has a well-defined code structure that allows developers to modify or to easily add custom code. What is more important, it separates the generated and custom code. Newly generated code will not overwrite the hand-written parts and violate a previous structure. On the other hand it is possible to use generated code within other custom parts using the Spring framework features. By changing the configuration files, a developer can substitute or exclude some parts of the generated code.

Fig. 3. WISL backend application

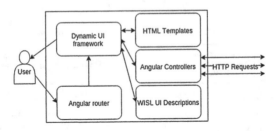

Fig. 4. WISL frontend application

The REST controllers by themselves are quite simple components that can be easily generated from the WISL system description. A much more serious problem is the data storage system. In order to achieve effective data persistence, we have used Java Persistence API (JPA) and Hibernate (see Fig. 3, again). JPA relies upon Java Database Connectivity (JDBC) drivers that allow usages of many different Relational Database Management Systems (RDBMS).

3.2   WISL Frontend Application - WISL Dynamic UI Framework

The WISL Dynamic UI framework is the most important part of the WISL client application (see Fig. 4). It is capable of generating the complete functional web user interface just by using the WISL UI description model. The framework is implemented as a group of AngularJS directives. They are independent components that contain HTML templates as static view descriptions and Javascript controllers that define the behavior of a component. We have implemented directives for the global entity view, detail entity view, entity create, entity update, show entity relationship, and edit entity relationship. There is also a general directive that encapsulate the previous ones. If a developer is satisfied with the default functionalities it is enough to call a general directive for each entity. Otherwise, it is possible to use only some of the directives or to write the entire user interface from scratch. For example, write a completely new global entity interface but after that just include buttons for entity editing.

Each of the UI directives is based on the WISL UI description model. It is a description of the user interface on an abstract level. The description is in the JSON format (see Fig. 5). The directives parse the description and use it to generate different user interface components dynamically. It is also possible to change this description during the run-time. The framework will recognize the changes and will reorganize the user interface.

```
1.  angular.module('WIS.projectManagement')  36.      relationships:[
2.  .controller('ctrlProject',['$scope',       37.      {
3.    function($scope){                         38.        entity: {
4.      $scope.model={                          39.          label:'Employee',
5.        label:'Project',                      40.          serviceName:'ServiceEmployee',
6.        serviceName:'ServiceProject',         41.          fields:[
7.        fields:[                              42.          {
8.        {                                      43.            label:'First name',
9.          label:'Name',                       44.            name:'firstName',
10.         name:'name',                         45.            type:'text',
11.         type:'text',                         46.            important: true
12.         important: true,                     47...          },...
13.         validation:{                         80.          ]
14.           required: false,                   81.        },
15.           vType: 'stringsingleline',        82.        label: 'Project manager',
16.           customValidation:[                 83.        name: 'projectManager',
17.           ]                                   84.        editable: true,
18.         }                                     85.        type: 'one'
19...       },...                                86...      },...
35.       ],                                     137.     ]
                                                 138.   };
                                                 139.}]);
```

Fig. 5. WISL UI description

The UI description provides technical details about UI components (e.g. type of component - see that the component "name" is presented as a "text" type in Fig. 5) and interfaces of Spring REST services on the server side of an application. The description could be custom-written or generated from a WISL model. The description in Fig. 5 corresponds to the WISL model described in the following Sect. 4.

4 WISL IS Definition

As was mentioned previously, WISL is a solution for a comprehensive description of IS. The WISL abstract syntax (metamodel [14]) has been created using ECore and EMF (see Fig. 6). The concrete syntax is textual and is implemented in XText. The WISL metamodel shares some of the basic concepts with the ER data model. As in ER, WISL contains entities (WEntity in Fig. 6) and relationships (WConnection in Fig. 6) with slightly different properties. Each entity, except its own name, contains zero or more attributes similar to ER. However, the attributes (WAttributs in Fig. 6) are much different. They play an important role for the most part in end-system generation. Hence, at the attribute level it is possible to configure name, type, label, validation rules, and much more properties which can affect the user interface and user experience. WISL also provides the possibility for defining a new enumeration type together with suitable UI component and validation rules and then assign it as a type to some attribute. The other very important concept is the link. The link can be defined between two and only two entities. Each side of the link has minimal (zero or one) and maximal cardinality (one or many). Unlike in the ER, n-ary relationships and categorization are not supported. Also, it is not possible to bind attributes to a relationship. If the concept of a gerund is not directly supported then it should

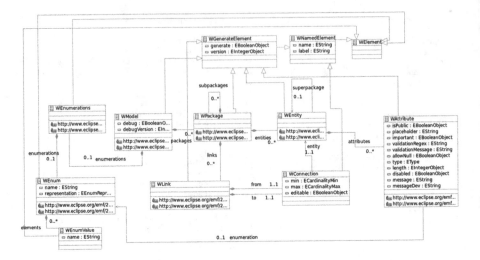

Fig. 6. WISL metamodel

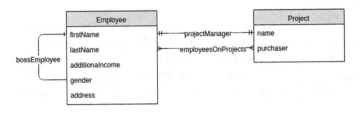

Fig. 7. Employee salary ER diagram

be implemented as a new entity. Also, the solution is the same for relationships with attributes. The inheritance is supported in the WISL metamodel but it is not implemented in the end system due to technical reasons. In addition to the mentioned concepts, WISL extends the existing ER data model with a concept of package (WPackage in Fig. 6). By using packages, the user is able to build a system as a hierarchical structure.

4.1 WISL Use-Case Scenario

As an example of WISL application we can consider a very basic use case - manager attaching employees to different projects. Each employee is described by the following attributes: first name, last name, wage, additional income, date of birth and gender. A project is defined with the name, and purchaser. A corresponding ER schema to this scenario is the one shown in Fig. 7.

The same semantic as described in WISL language is in Fig. 8. Note that entities and links are defined separately within individual blocks of code. Each link has a name (e.g. projectManager) and two related entities - the first entity (construct "from") and second entity (construct "to"). It is necessary to assign

```
 1. entities{                          25. links{
 2.     employee{                       26.     projectManager{
 3.         attributes{                  27.         from employee as projectManager {
 4.             firstName,                28.             min one
 5.             lastName,                 29.             max one
 6.             additionalIncome{         30.         }
 7.                 type Double           31.         to project as managedProjects
 8.             },                        32.     },
 9.             gender{                   33.     employeesOnProjects{
10.                 type Enumeration      34.         from employee as employees
11.                 enumeration EGender   35.         to project as projects
12.             },                        36.     },
13.             address                   37.     bossEmployee{
14.         }                             38.         from employee as boss{
15.     },                                39.             max one
16.     project{                          40.         }
17.         attributes{                   41.         to employee as subworker
18.             name,                     42.     }
19.             purchaser{                43. }
20.                 type StringMultiline
21.             }
22.         }
23.     }
24. }
```

Fig. 8. Employee salary system in WISL

a role name for each entity (e.g. from employee as projectManager). This is particularly important in case of a recursive relationship.

Entities in the WISL can have type, length, placeholder and many other properties. Each of these properties has a default value. Note the difference between attributes "firstName" and "additionalIncome" (see Fig. 8). Using the default values wherever possible, we have tried to decrease learning time for the system developer.

4.2 IS Generation

The WISL is capable of generating fully functional prototypes. The generated system supports basic CRUD operations (create, read, update and delete) [11] for each defined entity and relationship. An entity has two views - a global and a detailed view (see Fig. 9). The global view shows only the important attributes - attributes that are marked as important in a model. This concept of a way to narrowing entities with a very extensive number of attributes. It makes user interface much clearer. Search queries are only possible regarding important attributes (by default).

In order to make the user more comfortable, the WISL provides a global search, entity pagination and sorting. These operations are usually very time-consuming for implementation, but they are an infallible part of every modern IS.

Each time a developer changes a WISL model, it is necessary to generate a system again. If a custom code is written properly, the process of generation will not violate a project's structure and functionalities. In regard to the simple example from Sect. 4 (employee <-> project), the generation process lasts only a few seconds and creates 17 files with 973 lines of code.

Fig. 9. Generated system - global view (upper part) and detail view (lower part)

5 IS History Support

In the previous Sects. 3 and 4 we introduced the WISL system, which is able to generate arbitrary IS. However, the original architecture does not have any kind of support for traceability. The implementations of these WISL functionalities are presented in the following section where advice is given on how we extended the metamodel behind WISL. The outcome of this extension is IS with integrated versioning support on the levels of domain concepts.

An IS model can be viewed as a state of a metamodel. Making changes to the model has similar properties as modifying the state (data) within database. Any change must be atomic, consistent, isolated and durable. In order to change the model we used the operations of deletion and insertion. While the concept of update is interpreted as a combination of deletion and insertion.

Each operation has parameters that describe the domain concept. So you could say that the version of the model changes after each operation but such an interpretation could lead to inconsistencies of the model. Therefore a set of operations is carried out during a transaction. All changes within a transaction are identified with the same id version. Update of the concept in a model is always performed as a transaction.

In order to support the suggested approach, we needed a relatively small change of the metamodel (see Fig. 10). All we had to do was to expand the

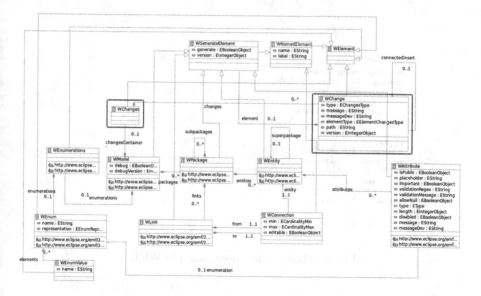

Fig. 10. WISL metamodel with history support included

metamodel with WChange and WChanges classes, where WChange includes the concept updates and WChanges is just a container for changes (Fig. 10). In order to achieve transparency of the changes arguments are introduced for the user (message), developer (messageDev), identifier changes, and the like.

Changing the metamodel has two aspect. The first aspect is changing the user interface and second is changing tts IS data. In order to achieve full history backtracking, data transformation needed to be provided (for example transforming integer to real data type). Modifications that need complex transformations will be the subject of future work.

5.1 Example

Imagine a real case-scenario which extends the IS defined with specifications from Fig. 8. In this scenario we would like to insert new attributes (e.g. "wage", "date of birth") and delete some attributes (e.g. "address") inside entity "employee". Note, that we would like that WISL automatically inserts/deletes concepts in the user interface, insert new entities in the database, etc.

Normally, one would insert just the attribute inside the specifications in Fig. 8. In this way the system would be fully functional but the history of the changes would be absent. Using the extension that corresponds to the new metamodel (see the concept WChange in Fig. 10, again) we are able for instance, to insert attribute "wage" in a way that will support traceability for the developed IS.

The concept "history" in Fig. 11 contains several block sections that correspond to individual change in the IS. Each block contains the same attributes.

```
{
    ticketId 2
    message 'Wage added'
    messageDev 'Wage added development'
    path 'package.projectManagement.entity.employee.attribute.wage'
    type Insert
    elementType Attribute
},
{
    ticketId 5
    message 'Address delted'
    messageDev 'Address delted'
    path 'package.projectManagement.entity.employee.attribute.address'
    type Delete
    elementType Attribute
    element attribute {
        address
    }
}
```

Fig. 11. Traceability specification in WISL

```
entities{                                links{
    employee{                                projectManager{
        attributes{                              from employee as projectManager {
            firstName,                               min one
            lastName,                                max one
            wage{                                }
                ticketId 2                       to project as managedProjects
                type Double                  },
            },                               employeesOnProjects{
            additionalIncome{                    from employee as employees
                type Double                      to project as projects
            },                               },
            dateOfBirth{                     bossEmployee{
                ticketId 3                       from employee as boss{
                type Date                            max one
            },                                   }
            gender{                              to employee as subworker
                type Enumeration             }
                enumeration EGender    }  }
            }
        }
    },
    project{
        attributes{
            name,
            purchaser{
                type StringMultiline
            }
        }
    }
}
```

Fig. 12. History aware specifications

In our case-scenario attribute "ticketID" is set to value "3", which means that this change has been done for user request id "3". Attribute "message" contains the message that will be presented in user interface beside the concept that is going to change. Our system also supports messages that can be seen only by a software developer (attribute "messageDev"). The next attribute that needs to be set in history is the name of the concept that is going to change (attribute "path"). Here, the full path is expected - package name, entity name and finally, the name of the attribute. Next attribute is "type", the value of which represents the operation of the change in IS. The last attribute is "elementType" which contains the information about the changing concept. Note, that deleting the concept is very similar to inserting a new concept, the only difference is in the value of the attribute "type" (see the second block inside the history in Fig. 12).

After generating a new version of IS, the user interface has been changed (see Fig. 13). The deleted fields are marked with red rectangles and new ones with green. For every changed field you can get additional information in the form of the hint (black bar with text).

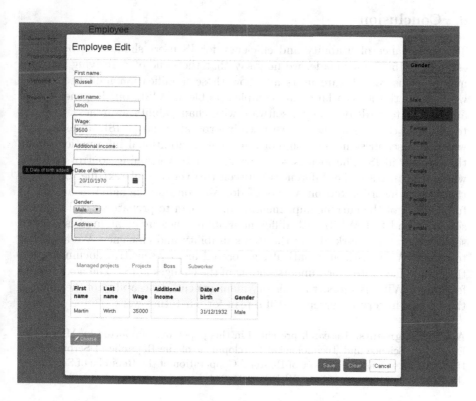

Fig. 13. Interface and help changes in IS (Color figure online)

5.2   Discussion

IS history support in WISL has been shown on a very simple use-case scenario where text fields have been added/deleted from our IS in previous subsection (see Fig. 13, again). The difference of the last two instances of IS is shown in this figure. But the essence and the real power is hidden behind this figure and WISL implementation. The user can always select two arbitrary versions of IS and check the differences between them. Imagine a real-case scenario where user might miss several versions of the IS. IS developed with WISL has a support for such user which can check the differences between the current and a specific version of the IS. Note that this is supported with keeping information of IS instances in our modified WISL metamodel (see Fig. 10, again).

Of course, the history-aware view in the IS is optional. User that understands the newly introduced changes in IS can easily turn off support for traceability. An interesting research question would be how long to show new changes visible to the user and when to automatically hide traceability support.

6   Conclusion

The importance of usability and efficiency for IS users should not be under-estimated [15]. To conclude, we may say that the issue of perceiving software modifications by software users and how those modification influence human work and activities is a large and complex problem. WISL, our IS generator, is an attempt towards developing software with changeability awareness. In order to visualize changes in the IS, we have incorporated into WISL an extension, which in a seamless manner supports users with additional information about the changes in IS. The idea is somehow similar to versioning control systems, where we can trace the differences between two versions of text file. In WISL, this idea is incorporated on a level of domain concepts included in an IS. As future work of the current implementation, we plan to prepare several use-case scenarios and test WISL with different usability measurement models [16], to see how our framework affects the user's usability and efficiency. We also plan to extend WISL with automatically generated history-sensitive documentation that would facilitate users' understanding of the changes in ISs. The next desired feature for WISL is support for history management - traceability of the changes throughout history is currently still a plan for our future work.

Acknowledgments. Research presented in this paper was supported by Ministry of Education, Science and Technological Development of the Republic of Serbia, Grant III-44010, as well as the Project of Bilateral Cooperation of the Republic of Serbia and the Republic of Slovenia, Grant BI-RS/14-15-034.

References

1. Preece, J., Sharp, H., Rogers, Y.: Interaction Design-Beyond Human-Computer Interaction. Wiley, New York (2015)

2. Abrahão, S., Iborra, E., Vanderdonckt, J.: Usability evaluation of user interfaces generated with a model-driven architecture tool. Maturing Usability: uality in Software, Interaction and Value. Human-Computer Interaction Series, pp. 3–32. Springer, London (2008)

3. Mernik, M., Heering, J., Sloane, A.: When and how to develop domain-specific languages. ACM Comput. Surv. **37**(4), 316–344 (2005)

4. Lawrance, J., Jung, S.: Git on the cloud. J. Comput. Sci. Coll. **28**(6), 14–15 (2013)

5. Tang, A., Jin, Y., Han, J.: A rationale-based architecture model for design traceability and reasoning. J. Syst. Softw. **80**(6), 918–934 (2007)

6. Kosar, T.: Martínez López, P.E., Barrientos, P.A., Mernik, M.: A preliminary study on various implementation approaches of domain-specific language. Inf. Softw. Technol. **50**(5), 390–405 (2008)

7. Stahl, T., Völter, M.: Model-Driven Software Development. Wiley, New York (2006)

8. Greenfield, J., Short, K.: Software Factories: Assembling Applications with Patterns, Models, Frameworks, and Tools. Wiley, New York (2004)

9. Aggarwal, A., Waghmare, G., Sureka, A.: Mining issue tracking systems using topic models for trend analysis, corpus exploration, and understanding evolution. In: Proceedings of the 3rd International Workshop on Realizing Artificial Intelligence Synergies in Software Engineering, RAISE 2014, pp. 52–58, New York, NY, USA. ACM (2014)

10. Steinberg, D., Budinsky, F., Paternostro, M., Merks, E.: EMF: Eclipse Modeling Framework, 2nd edn. Addison-Wesley, Boston (2008)

11. De, A.: Spring, Hibernate, Data Modeling, REST and TDD: Agile Java Design andDevelopment. CreateSpace Independent Publishing Platform (2014)

12. Bauer, C., King, G.: Java Persistence with Hibernate. Dreamtech Press, New Delhi (2006)

13. Freeman, A.: Putting AngularJS in Context. Apress, Berkeley (2014)

14. Atkinson, C., Kuhne, T.: Model-driven development: a metamodeling foundation. IEEE Softw. **20**(5), 36–41 (2003)

15. Hering, D., Schwartz, T., Boden, A., Wulf, V.: Integrating usability-engineering into the software developing processes of sme: a case study of software developing sme in Germany. In: Proceedings of the Eighth International Workshop on Cooperative and Human Aspects of Software Engineering, CHASE 2015, pp. 121–122. IEEE Press (2015)

16. Shawgi, E., Noureldien, A.: Usability measurement model (umm): a new model for measuring websites usability. Int. J. Inf. Sci. **5**(1), 5–13 (2015)

Characterising Users Through an Analysis of On-line Technical Support Forums

Solomon Gizaw, Jim Buckley, and Sarah Beecham[✉]

Lero - The Irish Software Research Centre,
Department of Computer Science and Information Systems (CSIS),
University of Limerick, Limerick, Ireland
{solomon.gizaw,jim.buckley}@ul.ie,
sarah.beecham@lero.ie

Abstract. Users of software systems need support. When users choose to go directly to online forums rather than report issues to the source of the problem, the development organization loses out in terms of gathering information on where their systems could be improved, and can lose customer loyalty and goodwill. This in turn will have a negative effect on future sales and system enhancements.

The objective of this study is to examine online forums in order to characterize technical support (TS) users, and create a framework that allows commercial organizations (and other interested parties) to identify types of users and how best to address their needs.

One hundred and sixteen threads (3,064 messages) from eight online open source forums were analysed using a grounded theory approach. Also the literature on human factors, and personalisation was examined to elicit information on how people can be categorized.We found that users of TS systems can be grouped according to their level of expertise and what they value. Additionally we identified characteristics of the communication handling process that influence desirable and undesirable outcomes.

The contribution of this research is an empirically derived framework that identifies TS users according to groups of characteristics. We hypothesise that a user will be more satisfied when the TS service provider recognises concepts such as what they personally value, their level of expertise and how best to manage emotions.

Keywords: Information technology · Technical support · User characteristics · Online technical support forums · Individualisation · Human factors · Grounded theory

1 Introduction

1.1 Context

Technical Support (TS) is a post sales service provided to users of Information Technology (IT) products where, ideally, TS advisors respond to users' needs in a timely and effective way when they have problems using a product [1]. One of the goals of TS is to maintain a high level of customer satisfaction by providing quality answers to technical questions.

© Springer International Publishing Switzerland 2015
P. Abrahamsson et al. (Eds.): PROFES 2015, LNCS 9459, pp. 528–545, 2015.
DOI: 10.1007/978-3-319-26844-6_39

According to Posselt and Gerstner [2] post-sale factors are considerably more influential than pre-sale factors with respect to retaining customers, and TS is an important component of post-sale service for IT technologies. A quick and accurate response to the users' problems ensures user satisfaction and a good reputation for the company [3]. Negash and his colleagues concluded in their service quality measurement study that the good reputation gained through TS is also used to build a long-term relationship with the users [4].

Additionally, in the software and hardware industries efficient TS can be considered a major revenue stream in itself, where payments can entitle users to TS, patches, and minor upgrades [5, 6]. As a result software product firms are taking advantage of TS services as a necessary cost centre [6, 7]. It follows that a TS system provider must ensure that it doesn't bury key information; that it has an appropriate response time; that it can be trusted with a good level of privacy and security; that it has a well-designed interface and that it provides individualized service [8, 9].

The literature suggests that users are not fully satisfied with company-based TS services; partially due to the lack of guidance and support on how they should use information to learn about their software systems and how to assist them when problems arise [10, 11]. According to Len-Rios [12] who conducted a study on consumer expectations from corporate websites that include TS, users isolate themselves because of a series of unsatisfactory interactions, which do not fulfill their expectations [12]. Indeed, there is some evidence to suggest that companies are failing in their efforts to provide effective TS, as users are ignoring company-based communication channels such as documentation, FAQ, chat, call centres, email and websites. They seek out alternatives in the form of community forums where they appear to be better supported [8, 13, 14].

1.2   Problem

The dismissal of company-based TS, in favour of open-source, non-proprietary alternatives is not an optimal solution for the IT company, since users who remain loyal to the company build and maintain long-term relationships, continue to purchase their products and services and spread good-will to enhance the company's reputation [8, 13–15]. Additionally, companies may lose control over user experience information and information on the source of problems, and thus where their systems could be improved [16].

A review of the literature suggests that a core problem is the neglect of user characterisation in TS, where, at best, a user's characteristics are captured in an ad hoc fashion [17–19]. This is somewhat surprising given that the user experience can be enhanced by channeling support to meet the user's individual needs [13, 14, 17]: Providing an individualised response to each user is an effective user-satisfaction strategy [20]. The literature shows that individualised value-added services can meet users' requests at a deeper level than that of traditional TS services by providing accurate information and processing the information to satisfy user requirements [19]. Other CRM research [21], suggests that individualising TS can improve customer acquisition, customer retention, customer loyalty and customer profitability through individual information to be administered in the right context and at the right time [22]. Users expect individualised services and two-way communication [12]. Wang et al. [23] suggests that successful communication with users can even reduce software failure rates and produce better versions of the application [23].

1.3 Objective

The literature indicates that, to achieve a much better user experience, TS should consider the individual characteristics of the user [4, 11, 19, 22, 24]. Research that does address this issue in this field does so in an ad hoc fashion and is not based on *in vivo* empirical evidence. Defining user characterisation in an ad hoc fashion is unreliable, and not repeatable, resulting in inconsistencies, and a weak understanding of user characteristics.

Empirically derived and evaluated characteristics of users may determine prevalent user attributes, which enhance the process of implementing personalised TS. Empirically derived personalised attributes could reinforce our current understanding of how to characterise users and, by taking a more inductive approach, may possibly provide novel perspectives and new attributes that may in turn improve TS. Furthermore, these individual characteristics should be empirically derived based on *in vivo* practice to truly reflect the user needs. Without such empirically grounded characterization efforts to individualise TS may be misguided. The fundamental question that the research tries to answer is:

- How can we improve TS systems to satisfy user requirements in a more targeted and personalised manner?

    In order to address this research question, we consider the following:

- What are the individual characteristics found in TS?
- How are the observed individual characteristics handled during the TS process?
- What are the success scenarios in TS that satisfy user satisfaction?
- What can we learn from the unsuccessful scenarios in TS?
- How can the observed scenarios be used to more effectively construct TS systems for improving individualised services in TS?

    This study is organised as follows: Sect. 2 describes the grounded theory method that underpins this study. Section 3 presents the results where the user characteristics are categorized, and combined to define a *Personalisation in Practice* framework. In Sect. 4 the limitations of the study are stated, and finally Sect. 5 concludes and summarizes this study.

2   Method

The purpose of this study is to inductively generate theory to gain a deeper understanding of the interaction of individuals in the context of TS forums. We generate theory so as to inform a framework for how the user characteristics identified and the

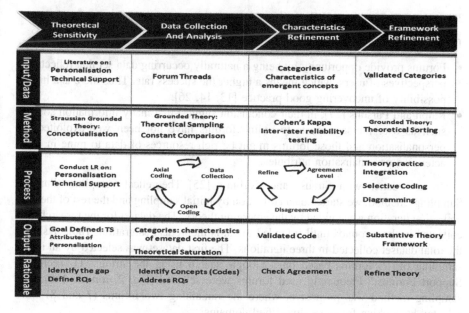

Fig. 1. The research method

communication handling process affect future communication. Threads from TS forums are analyzed to understand what is happening in the forums, and what people understand about a given issue through text-based communication. In this way we elicit information on how people can be grouped together in a more comprehensible and manageable way.

The research method is shown in Fig. 1. The methodology process is iterative whereby we continue to investigate the phenomena until tending to saturation (i.e. where after several analyses of the data no new theme emerged). Theoretical sensitivity was gained during the initial literature review, which provided conceptual clarity of concepts that might be relevant to guide the research. Theoretical sensitivity is the ability to see relevant data and to reflect upon empirical data material with the help of theoretical terms [25]. To keep an open mind in the field of interest, the study uses existing related literature on human factors and personalisation to elicit information on how users can be modeled and grouped together [13, 14, 26].

2.1 Grounded Theory Method

A qualitative grounded theory approach is adopted according to Strauss and Corbin [25] to developing a theory (or framework) that specifically informs company-based TS systems and actors. The main distinguishing features of the Grounded Theory Method (GTM) include the continuous undertaking of theoretical sensitivity, data collection, coding and analysis, memo-ing, sorting and constant comparison, theoretical sampling, and theoretical saturation [25] as discussed in the introduction to the method Sect. 2.

2.2 Data Collection and Sampling

TS forums are selected as a data source mainly due to:

- Forums provide opportunity by being a naturally occurring data set that reflects the perspectives of users, which means a higher the success rate. Thus there is a higher possibility of uncovering good practice [13, 14, 26].
- Ralph and Parsons [27], in their conclusion suggest that many information sources such as user message posts to online forums have not been well-exploited for personalisation and those forums might be rich resources of data to mine in characterising personalisation attributes.

In accordance with Strauss and Corbin's [25] Theoretical Sampling (Purpose Sampling) method, we started data collection by initial sampling and the rest of the data collection iteration was guided by the emerging theory. The dataset for the research was collected in three rounds until it tended towards theoretical saturation. Table 1 shows the total dataset collected in three iterations. The first dataset was selected by an initial sampling of TS forums based on a Google search using the string: "IT Technical Support Forums." Frequently used forums were selected (Fig. 2, forums 1–6). The sampling method was purposive, where the remaining two forums (7 and 8) were selected by looking for more diversified domains.

Table 1. Dataset sampling

Dataset	Description	# Forums	# Threads	# Messages	# Messages per Thread
1	Exploratory sample	6/8	40	747	1-54 (range)
2	Focussed set	8/8	61	1217	1-87 (range)
3	Long interactive threads	8/8	15	1100	51-127 (range)
Total		**8**	**116**	**3064**	**1-127 (range)**

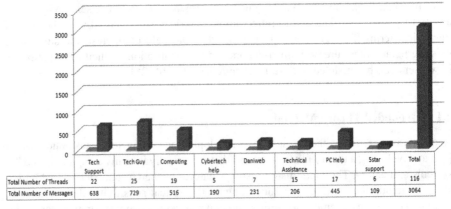

Fig. 2. The eight TS forums used in the study

The eight technical support forums as shown in Fig. 2 are selected due to their support for many diversified IT domains, bearing in mind more interaction patterns can be found and different user characteristics can be identified. In total 116 threads were collected within the three iterations; 3064 messages were found within these 116 threads.

2.3 Data Analysis

According to the GTM of Strauss and Corbin [25] data interpretation involves three stages of coding: *open coding* to discover categories, *axial coding* to further develop and relate the categories and finally *selective coding* to integrate and refine the theory. The three coding techniques are not necessarily sequential analytic steps. For example, open and axial coding overlapped in this study and were iterative, as categories were developed and refined. In addition, axial and selective coding overlapped as categories were related and integrated into an explanatory theory.

In this research *open coding* began with the first thread and a message-by-message analysis. The purpose of open coding was to identify codes in the data and to begin to discover categories and their properties and dimensions [25]. Table 2 presents an example of open coding that began with a simple interpretation of each message that summarises the underlying concept (shown by the square bracketed text). For instance line 072 is coded as "**Problem of user not stating the question properly**". Consequently a memo about the concept is created as shown in line 073. We use Atlas.ti V 6.2 (http://atlasti.com) to manage and analyse the textual data. The tool also helped to connect and visualize files as well as index the data.

After identifying categories through the open coding process, the next step is an intermediary coding process known as *axial coding* [25]. In axial coding, concepts are sorted, synthesised and reassembled. Each property of a given concept is grouped into a new set of categories that represent the ideas. Strauss and Corbin [25] define a *property* as a general or specific characteristic of a category and a *dimension* as a location of a property along a continuum or range. For example, 'credibility', is one of the categories identified as something that is important to a user in this study. It has a dimension ranging from trust to mistrust. A property of 'credibility' is the differentiator *cause*, where

Table 2. Open coding examples

Line	Text and [open code]
072	"Had you explained what your reason was we could have advised you sooner". **[Problem of user not stating the question properly]**
073	**Memo:** *The respondent reminded the questioner it would have been better to state the question and reason in the first place*
078	"I think this poster is not reading the answers" **[Novice]** **Memo:** *Prior discussion shows the questioner has low level experience*
080	"It's hard to soar like an Eagle when you are flying with Turkeys" **[Insulting]**

credibility can be 'caused' by the product, the vendor, the respondent, the instruction, the consequences of executing the instruction, or the software that diagnoses the problem.

Selective coding is the final coding process in GTM, and involves the selection of core categories of the data. *Selective coding* systematically relates the categories identified in axial coding, and integrates and refines them to derive theoretical concepts. This is achieved according to a coding framework that captures the phenomenon in terms of context, causal conditions, intervening conditions, action/interaction and consequences. The *context* captures the environment within which decisions and actions take place; the *causal and intervening conditions* reflect the why, when, how come, and where the phenomenon occurs; these culminate in a portrayal of *actions/interactions* of the people in response to what is happening in the situations (answers the questions 'by whom' and 'how'); and finally we consider the *consequences* of the action taken or inaction (answers what happen as a result of the actions/interactions).

Our method also included an inter-rater reliability test to validate the first author's interpretation and findings. Such tests also help to define refinement of the findings. After theoretical saturation, we conducted an inter-rater reliability test evaluation using Cohen's *kappa* [28]. Even though GTM itself does not call for the calculation of inter-rater reliability specifically verifying coder interpretation can validate the grounded categories for further analytic steps. Cohen's *kappa* inter-rater reliability test was performed using IMB SPSS version 20.0. Initial results produced an inter-rater agreement of $0.673k$ value, where disagreements and assumptions were exposed. Subsequent discussions between the 'raters' led to refinement of some category definitions. A further independent inter-rater test was performed which achieved an agreement score of $0.797k$ which according to Landis and Koch [29] is a "substantial agreement".

3   Results

3.1   Categories

Emergent concepts are categorised according to their properties and dimensions. These concepts are grouped into three main categories according to similar characteristics as outlined below:

- A user characteristics category which has two subcategories: level of expertise sub category that contains attributes that define the users' level of knowledge and/or experience in the specific field and user-values sub category, which contains attributes that determine users' judgment on information provided.
- A Communication process category which has four subcategories: an *activity* sub category that contains attributes which define actions performed by the users during communication; a communication issues sub category that contains attributes which define problems that occurred during the communication process; a technical issues sub category that contains an attribute which defines the technical problems which

affect communication and an emotions sub category that contains attributes which defines the emotional conditions of the users during the communication process.

- An Outcomes category which has two subcategories that we analyse: *successful* sub category which contains the positive consequences or outcomes of the communication handling process and *unsuccessful* sub category which contains the negative consequences of the communication handling process.
  - A successful scenario is one where the user's question is answered to their satisfaction e.g. *"yep, seem to have fixed it. And a fine job, he did at that. Thanks"* (p11: f19: s231) or where a good communication handling process occurred e.g. *"ok. thank you for your help anyways, much appreciated"* (p15: f23:s432).
  - An unsuccessful scenario is one where the user's question is not answered to their satisfaction e.g. *"its starting to get on my nerves"* (p19:f27:s048), *"I think I need to take it to a tech bc this is way over my head.."* (p22: f3: s064) or where the user showed a negative emotional response: *"Please tone down your language"* (p45: f100: s50), *"A pre-formed opinion is harder to crack than an atom (paraphrase of a statement by Albert Einstein)"* (p93: f148: s82)
- There is a third category, *unknown outcomes* that we do not include in our analysis since it does not help develop the theory, where we are interested in the effects of personalising the TS service on the user.

The prevalence of the categories suggests that the user characteristics are applicable at persona level, where a persona (in the context of this work) is defined as a way of creating a category to define attributes of personalisation, where groups of people are aggregated into clusters based on their essential commonalities and differences. A persona is a precise description of whom the user is and what the user wants to accomplish [30]. The term persona is a way of creating user profiles [31]. For example, prevalent characteristics are novice, intermediate and experienced. These characteristics suggest three grouping of individuals that occur frequently and this can be taken as the basis of content that is generically appropriate to each group. The communication and outcomes characteristics can be viewed as indicators/guidelines towards effective communication and the interplay between the user characteristics and communication process.

Table 3 shows the occurrence of each concept, labelled as an attribute in each sub category. Definitions of each attribute and categories are presented in Appendix A: Glossary of Terms. Table 3 also shows the frequency counts of each attribute that occurred during the process of coding. Typically GTM does not use quantifying data to obtain meaning, and this study applies counting the frequency with which categories occur in the dataset only as it was found to be useful to highlight patterns in the data, where frequency is used as a proxy for prevalence; not to give meaning by statistically analyzing it.

There were different outcomes of the TS forum threads, with some ending up as '*successful*', others as '*unsuccessful*' and the remaining were those that were labeled as 'unknown' (as shown in Fig. 3 in terms of percentages). However, from the interaction

Table 3. Nominal list of categories

Category	Sub Category	Attributes	Number of Occurrence
			User
User Characteristics	Level of expertise	Novice	47
		Intermediate	11
		Experienced	16
		Total	74
	User Values	Loyalty	24
		Value for Money	27
		Credibility	26
		Security	10
		Total	87
Observations made during the Communication Process	Activity	Emphasis	50
		Procedure	18
		Total	68
	Communication Issues	Misinformation	9
		Misunderstanding	22
		Confusion	12
		Total	43
	Technical issues	Multi-Component	22
		Total	22
	Emotions	Frustration	18
		Anger	12
		Total	30
Outcome (at end of Communication process)	Successful	Satisfaction	141
		Total	141
	Unsuccessful	Insult	5
		Frustration	10
		Anger	9
		Total	24

data it was observed that most of the threads that ended up with a status of "unknown" finished after the right information had been posted. So indirectly, it could be assumed that participants just did not acknowledge it, or had maybe left the forum before the

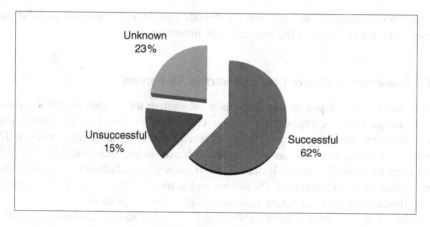

Fig. 3. The outcomes of the threads

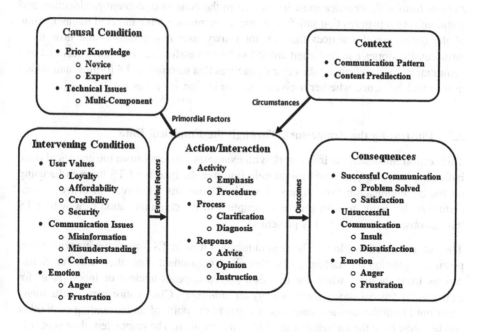

Fig. 4. *Personalisation In Practice* framework

response was posted. Questioners usually will not come back to the thread after they have solved their problem to inform the respondents. Hence we can assume that most of the threads of status "unknown" can be considered as successfully ending threads.

Despite this assumption, we only use the threads with known outcomes to build our theory since the outcome of the interaction is important.

3.2 Framework – of User Characteristics in TS Forums

The framework developed in this study is a substantive theory that provides a theoretical interpretation or explanation of user characteristics found in TS forums and communication handling process. Figure 4 presents the substantive framework in TS forums, and the relationships among categories based on the Strauss and Corbin [25] predefined framework schema. It depicts the framework of attributes of persona and their characteristics involved in TS forums and a model representing the communication themes that resonate across personas involved in the process.

Considering the research question, *Personalisation In Practice* was identified as the central phenomenon because it links the categories derived from the coding process. The term *Personalisation in Practice* emerged from the data analysis to describe the many successful practices of the personalised communication handling process. This *Personalisation In Practice* must be viewed in the context of content predilection and communication patterns that satisfy user requirements in a more targeted manner, some of the unsuccessful practices that do not satisfy user requirements, and how these unsuccessful stories can be turned around to be successful. Individualised services and communication handling are the central practices that resonate in TS forums, and which in turn will influence whether a given communication is successful.

3.3 Illustrating the Framework Through the Empirical Data

This section illustrates the framework with examples extracted from the empirical data, indicating how the framework might help improve the quality of TS through focusing on the communication flow observed within TS forums. However, in order to contextualize this work, a short generic description of the communication flow within TS threads observed in this data is presented.

The communication Flow: The communication flow in TS forums begins with a user posting a question by starting a new thread. A respondent then often asks for clarifications from the user when the question posted appears unclear or incomplete: for example, "*A few questions, just to clarify the situation*". Clarification may iterate many times until both the user and respondent come to the point of understanding each other and feel they have the knowledge to address the problem. The respondent then proceeds to diagnosis and instruction. However, clarification iterations are not always present in the threads. The respondent may bypass this step if the question is clear enough to him/her and may proceed directly to the diagnosis steps of the communication.

Empirical Illustration: Initially the data suggests that by-passing clarification doesn't prove very successful, the subsequent responses being premature and leading to misinformation. This is well illustrated by the frustrated comments of users as the threads proceed: "*Just trying different fixes willy-nilly in hopes of resolving the problem is a waste of time and energy and more likely to make things worse than better*", and, "*My father had a piece of advice you need to hear and it is*, and, "*Better to keep quiet and be thought a fool, than it is to open your mouth and remove all doubt*".

However, of all the successful threads, only 23 % had clarification iterations, indicating that mis-information may be a frequent component of (ultimately) successful communication. When communication was unsuccessful, the point at which it became unsuccessful was during initial clarification (29.4 % of the threads), during diagnosis (23.5 % of the threads) and during instruction (47.1 % of the threads). These figures include instances when threads may have just been abandoned, and so should be considered approximate, since abandoned instructions may still have been read and used, but not responded to.

The data suggests that being able to gauge the level of the user's expertise greatly influences the personalised communication handling process and the success of the outcome. For example, of the 47 threads where the user declared themselves as novices, the respondent tended to provide procedural instructions (74.5 % of the time - 35 threads). Of these 35 threads that were answered procedurally, 31 had successful outcomes with, on average, 5 messages per thread. This is a high success rate, over a short message span, suggesting that procedural instructions suit novice users. In contrast, the 12 novice queries that were not answered procedurally had a success rate of 33.3 % and took, on average, 10 messages to reach a conclusion. This, allied with the comments of some of the novice users when not provided with procedural instruction, re-enforces the impression that procedural instruction suits novice users: "*WHAT THE HELL IS GOING ON?[1]*", "*You seem to think that everyone thinks as you, well, <NAME> we don't GO AND PLAY WITH YOUR TOY!!!!!*"

On the other hand, when it becomes clear that the user has a high level of expertise (we categorise as *experienced*), different patterns are observed. The respondents enquire as to the diagnostics performed by the user and provide a greater proportion of declarative answers, only providing procedural answers 50 % of the time (in contrast to the 74.5 % associated with novice users). Also when users declare themselves as experienced (16 threads) the problem is solved quickly and the number of messages in the thread is typically low: Of the 16 threads where the user declared themselves as experienced, 12 had successful outcomes, and only 31 % of the threads were above 10 messages long.

These patterns, while providing only a small set of examples support the assertion that the framework and dataset can provide important insights into how user profiling and communication handling in TS forums can impact on success.

---

[1] The use of capitalisation is taken directly from the forums, in this context suggests anger, as a textural form of shouting.

3.4   Implication of the Framework to TS Practitioners

The results of this study have implications for personalisation practice in TS. Specifically the results of the grounded analysis suggest the following guidelines:

Prompt User to Provide Individual Context: While this guideline is generic across all users it does address the individuality of their context and the importance of respondents understanding that individual context. TS advisors should prompt the user to provide information regarding the steps they have tried and action taken to try to solve their problem; the tools used to diagnose the problem, and detailed information regarding what happened at each stage of the problem. In this study, a detailed clarification process preceded a successful outcome the majority of times. Unsuccessful outcomes were more frequently associated with queries where clarification was not sought. Out of all 116 threads, 53 had clarifications and 46 of these were successful. 63 threads did not have clarifications and only 26 threads were successful.

Avoid Premature Response with Respect to the Problem Context: On a related point, TS advisors might think they understand the context of a question, but not. This assumption frequently led to anger and misunderstanding. Again, this suggests that the advisor should be aware of trying to obtain full context before committing to a diagnosis or solution. In fact, in situations where a premature response was given by the respondent, there was a successful outcome in only 2 out of 12 episodes.

Managing the User's Level of Experience: An important aspect is considering the level of experience of the user. For example, out of the 26 clarification processes observed in threads, 13 of them involved the responder checking the users' levels of experience. In those 13 instances the ultimate success rate was 77 % whereas in the other 13 instances the success rate was 61 %. Likewise, as mentioned in Sect. 3.3 responders are more likely to issue step-by-step instructions to novice users and this has a high success rate. In episodes where TS advisors did not capture the user's level of experience it frequently led to confusion, misinformation and misunderstanding. For example, of those threads where the users experience was captured 8 threads went through periods of confusion, misinformation or misunderstanding. In contrast where the user's experience wasn't captured 20 threads went through periods of confusion, misinformation or misunderstanding, showing that it is better to obtain the users' levels of experience.

Several other more provisional guidelines can be determined from the analysis of the data to date:

- **Managing Emotions:** TS advisors should be trained in the ability to understand the emotional situation of the user from the written submissions provided by the user. For example questioners often showed their anger by capitalising words. The data suggests that it is better for a responder to address the emotions (by for example calming the user down) before providing further instructions to solve the problem, as this course of action was associated with a higher success rate.

- **Building Trust:** The findings indicate that trust should be built by empathizing with preferences of the users, such as the affordability of the product, the credibility of the respondent to the user and the perceived quality of the brand. In doing so, there seems to be a smoother communication, in terms of lack of anger, and implicit increased mutual respect.

- **Augment Step-by-step procedural instruction:** When providing instructions for the question asked, the respondent might, for example, explain or illustrate the GUI changes for each step. The empirical study shows that TS advisors often include a screenshot of the GUI for each step of the instructions, pointing out where the users should take the next action. In these cases there was a 72.2 % success rate in the threads. Likewise respondents used emphasis techniques to augment procedural instructions. Instructions that the user should follow were emphasized by stating them in capital letters or changing the color of that part of the message. The evidence suggests that emphasizing important parts of the instructions helps the questioner to follow the instruction accordingly.

4 Limitations

This research is limited by the choice of forum datasets, which in turn were in some ways limited by our access to them. The characteristics of online users may differ from the user that will interact directly with a development organization. While, data collected from our 8 selected forums (comprising 116 conversation threads from 116 different users) allowed us to identify characteristics across a range of different user types, and may share the characteristics of the wider population of TS users; we do not suggest that these findings can be generalized outside of the context of 8 Open Source forums. Future work could include a triangulation of data sources to include interviews with the TS experts giving advice, as well as the users asking for advice to gain further confidence in our interpretations.

Some the practices identified as leading to success in an Open Source forum (such as multiple responders engaging with the user at run time) may not be feasible in a company based TS scenario. Future work could include a validation of our findings through a comparison of company-based datasets to produce more externally valid results.

Data derived from the TS forums contained different types of expression such as texts, symbols, and gestures and abbreviated words. This research only concentrated on analysing text since the core purpose of this research is text-based communication in TS. The other expressions (such as emails, telephone calls, gestures and symbols in the text) have not been collected or analysed in this empirical study. These complementary expressions could be included in the future studies to find more concrete and rich set of individualised characteristics.

Since the success of a given interaction is determined by a clear sign-off from the user, there were many threads that were indeterminate (we class as outcome 'unknown').

While we were careful not to use these data in our analysis, it may contain patterns of communication that run counter to our findings.

5 Conclusion

In conclusion, based on the empirical study of 8 open source forums we addressed our research question, which was to investigate how we can improve technical support systems to satisfy user requirements in a more targeted and personalized manner.

We first focussed on identifying individual characteristics that emerged in TS forums. Our empirical study indicates that user's can be characterized not only according to a level of expertise, but also according to how they value system security, credibility of the service, and whether the system represents value for money to them personally. These emerging user characteristics can be considered during company-based TS system development to enhance the service in a more targeted, personalised manner.

We observed successful scenarios of the TS forum communication process. Successful scenarios are those where a conclusion is reached that satisfies the user. For example, the data analysis indicates that, respondents may respond in a procedural way, offering step-by-step instructions suited to the novice user characteristic. Observing how questioners (or users) are handled in scenarios provide good guidelines to better understand the user-respondent communication process.

We traced all the successful scenarios to identify whether there was any clear patterns between how the respondent offered solutions (e.g. in procedural or declarative manner) and the user's characteristics. The study also observed reasons why unsuccessful communication occurs and what can be learnt from these scenarios in future TS advisor/user interactions in a company-based context.

This resulting empirically derived framework highlights that users of TS systems can be identified according to groups of characteristics. The framework also supports the idea that a successful communication handling process, based on these emerging user characteristics, provides a degree of manageable individuality with economies of scale. Groups of people can be aggregated into persona clusters to customise systems or content for their intended users. That is, content can be made accessible to all groups of users based on assumptions about common characteristics, irrespective of their locale, where the focus of these groupings are now based on shared individual characteristics (personas).

Acknowledgments. This work was supported, in part, by Science Foundation Ireland grant 10/CE/I1855 to Lero - the Irish Software Engineering Research Centre (www.lero.ie). This research is also supported by the Science Foundation Ireland (Grant 07/CE/I1142) as part of the Centre for Next Generation Localisation (CNGL) at the University of Limerick.

APPENDIX A: Glossary of Terms

Term	Definition
Anger	An interpretation or perception of emotion, which is a strong feeling of displeasure and unhappiness as the result of communication issues.
Confusion	A lack of clarity or distinctness of the information provided.
Credibility	User's perception of the source of information that ranges from trust as a reliable, competent source based on some kind of relationship, and mistrust as untrustworthy or a source that prefers to exploit the other's user's trust.
Emphasis	Intensity or force of expression, or an action to highlight a point of discussion as a note, reminder or warning or to indicate their emotional situations.
Experienced	A user who is skillful or knowledgeable as shown through extensive contact or participation or observation.
Frustration	Users' negative emotion following from unfulfilled expectations or dissatisfaction in which the expected goal or reward is not reached.
Insult	Deliberately treating with gross insensitivity, insolence, or contemptuous rudeness, behaving arrogantly and causes an offensive action or remark as the outcome of the communication process.
Intermediate	A user who is not familiar with a given domain but have skills in using different software applications.
Loyalty	A user perception of the quality of service/product or specific brands.
Misinformation	A communication process issue where an action of after incorrect or misleading information which may cause uncertainty about the information provided; create communication difficulties and loss of confidence and delays in finding a solution.
Misunderstanding	The wrong perception of someone's intention or communication, which creates a condition or fact that often, determines an inappropriate course of action.
Multi-component	A technical issue where the solution for the problem includes the combination of two or more domains.
Novice	A user who is new or inexperienced in a certain task or situation.
Online community forums	A place where users are able to share their bad or good experiences on various products or services with a large number of unknown people
Procedure	A sequence of action or a set of instructions to be followed in solving a problem
Satisfaction	Users' level of approval when comparing perceived performance with his/her expectations results in successful completion of the solution and/or good communication process.
Security	Users' concern to protect from harm, risk or danger caused by the actions of attackers that ranges from worry to warning.
TS Staff	When a problem is reported by the user, TS staff will provide a series of suggestions to the users to implement or check as a means of rectifying the reported problem. TS staff are labeled differently: analysts , operators, and staff , computer support specialist and service engineer
TS system	TS systems are a software system that encompasses communication, providing a platform for receiving queries from the user and manage the resources, response and delivering information.
User values	The preferences of the user in the product or services provided
Users	As one of the stakeholders in TS systems, users report technology problems, issues or faults. Users are given different labels such as 'client', 'customer', 'end-user'; in this paper the term *user* is applied.
Value for money	The inclination of the user to pay for the service/product that ranges from free, cheap and costly, that might influence the decisions to get the service.

References

1. Das, A.: Knowledge and productivity in technical support work. Manage. Sci. **49**(4), 416–431 (2003)
2. Posselt, T., Gerstner, E.: Pre-sale vs. post-sale e-satisfaction: impact on repurchase intention and overall satisfaction. J. Interact. Mark. **19**(4), 35–47 (2005)
3. Heras, S., et al.: Multi-domain case-based module for customer support. Expert Syst. Appl. **36**(3), 6866–6873 (2009)
4. Negash, S., Ryan, T., Igbaria, M.: Quality and effectiveness in web-based customer support systems. Inf. Manage. **40**(8), 757–768 (2003)
5. Durcikova, A., Fadel, K.J.: Knowledge sourcing from repositories: the role of system characteristics and autonomy. In: 2010 43rd Hawaii International Conference on System Sciences (HICSS). IEEE (2010)
6. Cusumano, M.: The changing software business: moving from products to services. Computer **41**(1), 20–27 (2008)
7. Raninen, A., Merikoski, H., Ahonen, J.J., Beecham, S.: Applying software process modeling to improve customer support processes. J. Softw. Evol. Process **27**(4), 274–293 (2015)
8. Stefani, A., Xenos, M.: E-commerce system quality assessment using a model based on ISO 9126 and belief networks. Softw. Qual. J. **16**(1), 107–129 (2008)
9. Bivall, A.-C., Mäkitalo, Å.: Re-visiting the past: how documentary practices serve as means to shape team performance at an IT help desk. Learn. Cult. Soc. Interact. **2**(3), 184–194 (2013)
10. Smart, K.L., Whiting, M.E.: Designing systems that support learning and use: a customer-centered approach. Inf. Manage. **39**(3), 177–190 (2001)
11. Lee, Z., Kim, Y., Lee, S.-G.: The influences of media choice on help desk performance perception. In: Proceedings of the 34th Annual Hawaii International Conference on System Sciences. IEEE (2001)
12. Len-Ríos, M.E.: Consumer rules and orientations toward corporate websites: a pilot study. J. Promot. Manage. **9**(1–2), 125–143 (2002)
13. Oxton, G.: The Power and value of on-line communities. In: 2010: Consortium for Service Innovation, Keynote address in Centre for Next Generation Localisation Public Showcase, Localisation Research Centre CSIS Department, University of Limerick, 27 April 2010
14. Steichen, B., Wade, V.: Adaptive retrieval and composition of socio-semantic content for personalised customer care. In: International Workshop on Adaptation in Social and Semantic Web (2010)
15. Massey, A.P., Montoya-Weiss, M.M., Holcom, K.: Re-engineering the customer relationship: leveraging knowledge assets at IBM. Decis. Support Syst. **32**(2), 155–170 (2001)
16. Gorla, N., Somers, T.M.: The impact of IT outsourcing on information systems success. Inf. Manage. **51**(3), 320–335 (2014)
17. Wu, D., Im, I., Tremaine, M., Instone, K., Turoff, M.: A framework for classifying personalization scheme used on e-commerce websites. In: Proceedings of the 36th Annual Hawaii International Conference on System Sciences. IEEE (2003)
18. Viviani, M., Bennani, N., Egyed-Zsigmond, E.: A survey on user modeling in multi-application environments. In: Proceedings of the 2010 Third International Conference on Advances in Human-Oriented and Personalized Mechanisms, Technologies and Services, pp. 111–116. IEEE Computer Society (2010)
19. Na, C., Yalin, L., Haizhong, A., Yue, W.: A value-added service model of mining right information. In: 2010 International Conference on E-Business and E-Government (ICEE). IEEE (2010)

20. Kim, W., Song, Y.U., Hong, J.S.: Web enabled expert systems using hyperlink-based inference. Expert Syst. Appl. **28**(1), 79–91 (2005)
21. Fan, W., et al.: Customer relationship management for a small professional technical services corporation. In: Systems and Information Engineering Design Symposium, 2004. Proceedings of the 2004 IEEE. IEEE (2004)
22. Tam, K.Y., Ho, S.Y.: Web personalization: is it effective? IT Prof. **5**(5), 53–57 (2003)
23. Wang, G.A., Jiao, J., Abrahams, A.S., Fan, W., Zhang, Z.: ExpertRank: a topic-aware expert finding algorithm for online knowledge communities. Decis. Support Syst. **54**(3), 1442–1451 (2013)
24. Gao, N., Zhao, S., Jiang, W.: Researched customer requirements representation and mapping on ontology. In: 2011 International Conference on Management and Service Science (2011)
25. Strauss, A., Corbin, J.M.: Basics of Qualitative Research Techniques and Procedures for Developing Grounded Theory, 2nd edn. Sage Publications, London (1998)
26. Vesanen, J.: What is personalisation? A conceptual framework. Eur. J. Mark. **41**(5–6), 409–418 (2007)
27. Ralph, P., Parsons, J.: A framework for automatic online personalization. In: Proceedings of the 39th Annual Hawaii International Conference on System Sciences (HICSS 2006). IEEE (2006)
28. Cohen, J.: Weighted kappa: nominal scale agreement provision for scaled disagreement or partial credit. Psychol. Bull. **70**(4), 213 (1968)
29. Landis, J., Koch, G.: Measurement of observer agreement for categorical data. Biometrics **33**, 159–174 (1977)
30. Blomquist, Å., Arvola, M.: Personas in action: ethnography in an interaction design team. In: Proceedings of the second Nordic conference on Human-computer interaction. ACM (2002)
31. Cooper, A.: The Inmates are Running the Asylum. Sams, Indianapolis (1999)

Software Developers as Users: Developer Experience of a Cross-Platform Integrated Development Environment

Kati Kuusinen[✉]

Tampere University of Technology, Korkeakoulunkatu 1, Tampere, Finland
kati.kuusinen@tut.fi

Abstract. Software development is professional activity that demands a plethora of skills and qualities from the developer. For instance, developers need technical skills to create the code that implements the running software and social skills to be able to collaborate with peer developers and with various stakeholders. Development is an endeavor towards building complex systems that realize user and business requirements in technologically sophisticated manner. Considering the challenges of software development, developer experience is a highly unstudied topic. Developers are users of multifaceted development tools such as integrated development environments. Yet, little is known of how to support developers in their demanding tasks. This paper presents early results towards increasing the understanding of developer experience in order to enable improvement of development tools to better support software developers in their activities. We present qualitative results of a survey study with 45 developers from 21 countries considering developers' perception of a particular integrated development environment.

Keywords: Software development · Human factors · Human-Computer interaction (HCI) · Developer experience · User experience (UX) · Development tools · Integrated development environment (IDE)

1 Introduction

An integrated development environment (IDE) is a collection of development tools such as code editor, compiler, debugger, and graphical user interface builder in a software application [16, 17]. IDEs automate common development tasks such as refactoring and correction of compilation errors [17]. Productivity goals of using an IDE include decreasing the error proneness of the developer and increasing development speed [17]. Developers perform a plethora of tasks with the IDE. For instance, they create new code to add features to the software under development, and fix defects in the existing code [11]. Developers typically work on several tasks during a day and thus the support of task switching and recall are important [11]. The core of software development work is writing the program code that constitutes the running software, which demands the ability to concentrate and work alone for several hours at a time [2]. Moreover, programming work necessitates having a logical mind and the ability to pay

© Springer International Publishing Switzerland 2015
P. Abrahamsson et al. (Eds.): PROFES 2015, LNCS 9459, pp. 546–552, 2015.
DOI: 10.1007/978-3-319-26844-6_40

attention to details [2]. Developers need to be analytical, capable of making decisions, independent, creative, tenacious, and be able to tolerate stress [1].

Although qualities of both developers and development work have been studied, developers are rarely seen as users of development tools. Thus, what is true to any user according to UX definitions, should apply also to software developer. However, the dualistic role of developer as both a user and a designer makes the developer special: Developers should be also able to understand the human user to be able to fulfill their needs with the software under development. In this paper, we discuss developer experience in terms of user experience (UX) and as a distinct concept and developers' needs as IDE users. We present preliminary results of our survey study considering developers perception of a particular cross-platform IDE, its best qualities and subjects for improvement. Altogether, we got 45 responses from 21 countries.

2 Background

Commonly, UX is understood as *subjective, context dependent, and dynamic* [14]. It is affected by users' expectations, needs and motivation, system's characteristics such as its purpose and functionality, and the context of use including physical, organizational and psychological aspects [8]. It has temporal dimensions: it can happen before usage (*anticipated* UX), during usage (*momentary* UX), after usage (*episodic* UX), or over time (*cumulative* UX) [12]. Moreover, being dynamic, UX changes constantly while interacting with a product [14]. The standard definition of user experience (UX) is as follows: "*person's perceptions and responses resulting from the use and/or anticipated use of a product, system or service*" [9]. The definition is ambiguous and numerous others exist [12, 14].

Despite the context dependence, researchers have aimed at a general conception of UX. According to a recent study by Law et al. [13], in academic research the most commonly utilized frameworks for UX are the *hedonic-pragmatic model* [6] and *sense-making experience* [15]. The hedonic-pragmatic model divides user experience into *hedonic* or non-utilitarian dimension and *pragmatic* or instrumental dimension [6]. Hassenzahl [6] further divides the hedonic into two sub-dimensions of identification and stimulation while the instrumental contains mostly items related to usability and usefulness. McCarthy et al. [15] describe that UX construes of compositional, emotional, sensual, and spatio-temporal threads of experience.

Although early HCI studies concentrated almost exclusively on task- and work-related usability issues and achievement of behavioral goals [8], UX research has mainly concentrated on consumers and leisure systems [3]. Especially, studies in the software development context are lacking. Thus, it is unclear how these models and measurement scales serve the research of developer experience.

Fagerholm and Münch [4] understand developer experience as a construction of developer's perception of the development infrastructure, feeling of their own work, and conception of the value of their contribution. Thus they state it has cognitive, affective, and conative factors [4]. Conative factors in their model seem to relate to motivational and goal-oriented aspects while affect is related to feeling of the social context and relation to others. Finally, cognitive factors are related to the execution of the development work itself. Gass et al. [5] discuss characteristics of platform as a service (PaaS) in terms of development productivity. They divide those characteristics into shared components, extensibility, development tools, and learnability. Finally, Palviainen et al. [18] construe the concept of developer experience via activity theory and thus divide it into categories related to tool, object, actor, rules, community, and division of labor. Moreover, they [18] discuss the support of development environment to developer experience with regard to operation, action and activity-level support.

3   Method and Participants

We surveyed software developers of a particular cross-platform integrated development environment utilizing a web survey with the following two open-ended **questions**:

1. *"In your opinion, what are the best qualities of* [the IDE]*?"*
2. *"How could* [the IDE] *better support your development work?"*

The concept of "[the IDE]" was replaced with the name of the IDE in the survey. We accompanied the survey with a front page presenting informed consent statements adopted from World Health Organization's Informed consent form template for qualitative studies [21]. We approached the developers via a global online developer community targeted to users of the IDE of our interest and via Twitter. In total, we received responses from 57 developers. Of those, 40 responded to the first question and 45 to the second. The survey contained also three validated structured scales to measure the experience of flow state [10], intrinsic motivation [19], and user experience [7] which we will exclude from this paper.

Respondent population was as follows: We got responses to questions 1 and 2 from 21 different countries. Of the respondents, 13.3 % were from France, 13.3 % from Germany, 11.1 % from Italy, 8.9 % from Norway, 6.7 % from each of the following: Finland, Switzerland, and United States, 4.4 % from Australia, and 2.2 % from each of the following: Algeria, Andorra, Austria, Bulgaria, Brazil, Belarus, Denmark, Indonesia, Iran, Poland, Russia, Sweden, and United Kingdom. Respondents had on average 12.6 years of working experience in software development, standard deviation was 6.5 years. Of the respondents, 82.2 % had been using the particular IDE for over a year and 15.6 % had been using it for over a month but less than a year. Thus the respondents can be considered expert users. 37.8 % of the respondents considered themselves as front-end developers, 22.2 % as back-end developers, 22.2 % as architects, and 17.8 % considered themselves as other types including either a combination of the aforementioned roles, or hobbyist, or teacher.

We utilized an approach similar to emergent coding as **analysis method**. However, we interpreted the data in terms of adjectives that describe the qualities of the IDE as the respondent had experienced it. We utilized a list of UX adjectives from [20] to support interpreting the responses according to adjectives that are commonly used in UX research when feasible. Thus, we first read through the data and formed an overall understanding of it. Then we transformed each item into an adjective. For instance, when a respondent had written: *"Speed, scale on big projects"*, we coded it as follows: *"fast"*, *"scalable"*. Moreover, we left all the objects and descriptions out, thus, for instance we coded *"scale on big projects"* to *"scalable"*. We coded such items as *"code highlight"* to *"informative"* and *"I wish I could better integrate it with my favorite text editor"* to *"extensible"*. Adjectives, for instance, *"good"*, *"nice"*, and *"easy"* were usually coded as such.

For the second question *"How could* [the IDE] *better support your development work?"* we coded adjectives in their positive basic form. Thus, for instance, for item *"the debugger could be nicer"* we coded *"nice"* and for "[the IDE] *is not stable"* we coded *"stable"*. For bug complaints we coded *"faultless"*.

For both the questions, we categorized the formed codes based on their semantic similarity using the categorization utilized in the analysis of [20]. 15 categories were formed. After that, we went through the data again and categorized each response individually under the formed categories, this time taking the objects and descriptions of the responses into account. Finally, we counted the number of items in each category and included those with more than one item into our result set. One researcher planned, conducted, analyzed and reported the study alone, which is to decrease the confirmability of the results. However, the analysis was conducted carefully and results were double-checked.

4 Results

Developers regarded *efficiency, flexibility, informativeness* and *intuitiveness* as the best qualities of the IDE whereas it was mentioned the most often that the IDE should be more *flexible, informative,* and *reliable* (Fig. 1). Thus, although the IDE was considered both flexible and informative, those were also the areas requiring improvement the most. The result might indicate that these concepts are central for an IDE. On the other hand, developers considered efficiency as one of the best qualities most often (37.9 % of respondents mentioned it), and it rarely was considered as subject for improvement. In contrast, reliability was rarely mentioned as a good quality whereas 35.9 % of the respondents thought that the IDE should be more reliable, mostly in terms of stability and faultlessness.

For the first question: *"In your opinion, what are the best qualities of* [the IDE]*?"* the developers considered the IDE fast and easy to use. Fastness was mentioned often with no description but it also referred to launching the IDE and to search features. Easy to use was also mentioned as such but also in relation to making configurations, using editing tools, and to novice users. Respondents also saw the IDE simple, good, and unbloated. Thus, they thought it does not contain unnecessary features and that it is well-designed. They also saw the ide as flexible and supporting their work. Other mentioned qualities included that the IDE is customable, flexible, powerful, compatible, and efficient.

For the second question: *"How could* [the IDE] *better support your development work?"* the developers wished that the IDE was more flexible, i.e. it would offer more extensive or easier integration with other tools and better plugin support. Respondents wanted the IDE to be more stable, especially the debugger stability was complained. Both poor flexibility and instability was reported to break the workflow as the developer needs to switch between tools either because it needs to be done manually or

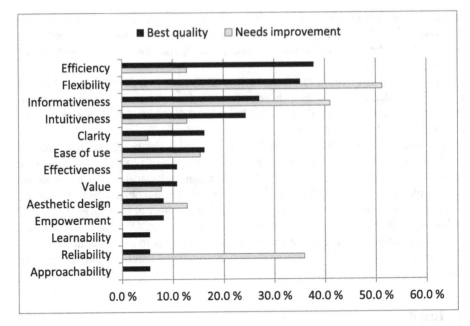

Fig. 1. Qualities of the IDE respondents considered the best and those qualities that need improvement categorized in terms of UX adjectives. N = 45.

because the developer needs to wait or use another debugger, respectively. Moreover, respondents desired better visibility on their work in terms of presentation of information. For instance, they asked for more code formatting options, better code highlighting, improvements in the code coloring theme, and intelligent code completion. Considering feature support, developers desired for easier to include plugins, better support for desktop development, and better support for large projects. Regarding the debugger, they wished that it was more informative, integrated better to the IDE, and was more powerful and stable.

5 Discussion

For a developer, a good IDE should be efficient and flexible, informative and intuitive to use. Moreover, it should also support the development workflow, let the developer be in control and offer clear visibility to the code and the situation. An IDE should also be reliable in use. We believe that studying both best qualities of the IDE and those that need improvement offered us a rather rich peek to developers' needs considering IDEs. Developers used rather rich vocabulary in describing the best qualities of the software. The presence of UX scales might have had an impact on their thinking. However, they utilized their own words and did not repeat those on the presented scales. In addition, responses concentrated mostly on pragmatic qualities of the IDE instead of the hedonic. However, some developers also described the IDE with affection: they expressed that the IDE made them to feel at home and created a friendly atmosphere.

Our presumption is that the resulted qualities support developers' ability to concentrate on the task at hand and thus they might also support the likelihood of developers to experience being in the flow state during development. Flow state is characterized by deep concentration, involvement and enjoyment of the task [19]. Its components are related to perceived challenge-skill balance, person's ability to act spontaneously and automatically, getting unambiguous feedback, sense of being in control, transformation of time, and feeling that the experience is highly rewarding [19]. Thus, we relate easiness to use and simplicity with perceived challenge-skill balance and to person's ability to act spontaneously. Developers' appreciation of the feeling of being in control is one of the core components of flow. Being informative and offering visibility is related to unambiguous feedback, and finally, supporting the task flow is related to acting spontaneously and most probably to rewarding experience. We got some evidence of the connection of task flow distraction and feeling frustration in regard to debugger instability and poor extensibility in our data. However, it should be noted that at this point our reflections are highly speculative.

6 Future Work

We continue the study with analyses of the quantitative data on flow state, intrinsic motivation, and UX. Our goal is to understand factors of developer experience and enablers of flow state and intrinsic motivation in software development work and in IDEs. In addition, we will survey also users of other IDEs to improve the generalizability of our results. Later, we will deepen our understanding of the phenomena by interviewing developers about their work. Our aim is at enabling the creation of better development tools in that they would help the developer to focus on the current task, and on the other hand to help to collaborate with other developers. Moreover, the interplay of these two is on our focus: how to support developer collaboration without disturbing the developer flow.

7 Conclusions

We conducted a survey study of developers' experiences considering a particular cross-platform integrated development environment. We asked the developers to describe in open-ended questions the best qualities of the IDE and on the other hand, how the IDE could better support their work. 45 developers from 21 countries responded to those open-ended questions. We analyzed the responses and found that developers appreciate an IDE that is efficient to use, flexible, informative, intuitive, and reliable.

References

1. Acuna, S.T., Juristo, N., Moreno, A.M.: Emphasizing human capabilities in software development. Softw. IEEE **23**(2), 94–101 (2006)

2. Capretz, L.F., Ahmed, F.: Making sense of software development and personality types. IT Prof. **12**(1), 6–13 (2010)
3. Diefenbach, S., Kolb, N., Hassenzahl, M.: The 'hedonic' in human-computer interaction. In: Proceedings of Designing interactive systems (DIS), pp. 305–314. ACM (2014)
4. Fagerholm, F., Münch, J.: Developer experience: concept and definition. In: Proceedings of the International Conference on Software and System Process, pp. 73–77. IEEE Press (2012)
5. Gass, O., Meth, H., Maedche, A.: PaaS characteristics for productive software development: an evaluation framework. Internet Comput. IEEE **18**(1), 56–64 (2014)
6. Hassenzahl, M.: The interplay of beauty, goodness and usability in interactive products. Proc. HCI. **19**(4), 319–349 (2004). (Lawrence Erlbaum Associates)
7. Hassenzahl, M., Monk, A.: The inference of perceived usability from beauty. Hum. Comput. Interact. **25**(3), 235–260 (2010)
8. Hassenzahl, M., Tractinsky, N.: User experience - a research agenda. Behav. Inf. Technol. **25**(2), 91–97 (2006)
9. ISO 9241: Ergonomic Requirements for Office Work with Visual Display Terminals (VDTs) – Part 11: Guidance on Usability. International Organization for Standardisation, Genève (1998)
10. Jackson, S.A., Martin, A.J., Eklund, R.C.: Long and short measures of flow: the construct validity of the FSS-2, DFS-2, and new brief counterparts. J. Sport Exerc. Psychol. **30**(5), 561 (2008)
11. Kersten, M., Murphy, G.C.: Using task context to improve programmer productivity. In: Proceedings of the 14th ACM SIGSOFT International Symposium on Foundations of Software Engineering (SIGSOFT 2006/FSE-14), pp. 1–11. ACM, New York, NY, USA (2006)
12. Lallemand, C., Gronier, G., Koenig, V.: User experience: a concept without consensus? Exploring practitioners' perspectives through an international survey. Comput. Hum. Behav. **43**, 35–48 (2015)
13. Law, E.L.C., Hassenzahl, M., Karapanos, E., Obrist, M., Roto, V.: Tracing links between UX frameworks and design practices: dual carriageway. In: Proceedings of HCI, Korea, pp. 188–195. Hanbit Media, Inc (2015)
14. Law, E., Roto, V., Hassenzahl, M., Vermeeren, A., Kort, J.: Understanding, scoping and defining user experience: a survey approach. In: Proceedings of CHI 2009, pp. 719–728. ACM (2009)
15. McCarthy, J., Wright, P.: Technology as experience. interactions **11**(5), 42–43 (2004)
16. Murphy, G.C., Kersten, M., Findlater, L.: How are Java software developers using the Elipse IDE? Softw. IEEE **23**(4), 76–83 (2006)
17. Muşlu, K., Brun, Y., Holmes, R., Ernst, M.D., Notkin, D.: Speculative analysis of integrated development environment recommendations. ACM SIGPLAN Not. **47**(10), 669–682 (2012)
18. Palviainen, J., Kilamo, T., Koskinen, J., Lautamäki, J., Mikkonen, T., Nieminen, A.: Design framework enhancing developer experience in collaborative coding environment. In: Proceedings of the Annual ACM Symposium on Applied Computing, pp. 149–156. ACM (2015)
19. Ryan, R.M., Mims, V., Koestner, R.: Relation of reward contingency and interpersonal context to intrinsic motivation: a review and test using cognitive evaluation theory. J. Pers. Soc. Psychol. **45**, 736–750 (1983)
20. Sundberg, H.-R.: The importance of user experience related factors in new product development – comparing the views of designers and users of industrial products. In: 23rd Nordic Academy of Management Conference, Copenhagen, Denmark, 12–14 August 2015
21. World Health Organization: Informed consent form template for qualitative studies. http://www.who.int/rpc/research_ethics/informed_consent/en

Workshop on Software Startups: State of the Art and State of the Practice

Ways to Cross the Rubicon: Pivoting in Software Startups

Henri Terho[✉], Sampo Suonsyrjä, Aleksi Karisalo, and Tommi Mikkonen

Tampere University of Technology, Korkeakoulunkatu 1, 33720 Tampere, Finland
{henri.terho,sampo.suonsyrja,aleksi.karisalo,tommi.mikkonen}@tut.fi

Abstract. Startup, or a potential company looking for form and repeatable, scalable business model, has become an advocated mechanism for embracing high ambition, innovativeness, and growth. The success of a startup is often related to the time it takes the startup to develop their business model. When the entire business is based on extreme uncertainty the main business hypothesis of the business model must be continuously tested and improved. This main business hypothesis can be split into smaller business hypotheses and when one of these business hypotheses proves to be false, a change in the direction of the company – so-called pivot – must be considered. Readily made approaches exist to accomplish this, including in particular the Lean Startup framework, that aims at iteratively developing, experimenting, and validating business hypotheses. In this paper study how pivots can change business hypotheses shown as a segments in Lean Model Canvas, a strategic management tool for developing nbusiness models. As an empirical contribution, we describe this definition of pivots with three case companies – all small software startups from Tampere region, Finland – and map the pivot effects on the business hypotheses. We found out that the pivots can be identified by changes in the Lean Model Canvas, that pivots typically take place in groups, and that comprehensive pivots happen early in the startup's life, whereas once the business model is clarified, fine-tuning is more likely to take place.

Keywords: Lean Startup · Pivots · Startups · Business model hypothesis · Lean Model Canvas · Case study

1 Introduction

Startup, or a potential company looking for form and repeatable and scalable business model, has become an advocated mechanism for embracing high ambition, innovativeness, and growth [2,5,14]. The success of a startup is often related to the time it takes the startup to develop their business model. Consequently, the value of fast iteration cycles is intensified, as the entire business model can be unclear or at least remain under constant development. To find a fast-track to profitability, a startup needs to streamline and speed up two vital processes –

© Springer International Publishing Switzerland 2015
P. Abrahamsson et al. (Eds.): PROFES 2015, LNCS 9459, pp. 555–568, 2015.
DOI: 10.1007/978-3-319-26844-6_41

developing novel products and finding new markets for their products. Mastering these requires optimized techniques and methods for product and customer management [3]. An emerging choice for such a management method is the Lean Startup framework [5,14], which aims at iteratively developing, experimenting, and validating business hypotheses. Moreover, when a product is deemed failed, a pivot – or, in other words, a change designed to test business hypotheses – is encouraged. That is a structured course correction designed to test a new fundamental hypothesis about the product, strategy, and engine of growth [14].

In general, Lean Startup is a relatively novel framework for business development. As such, there are few validation studies regarding the approach, and to the best of our knowledge, in particular pivoting and the pivots that Ries establishes in [14] have never received focused research attention. Given this gap in research, while Lean Startup has received a lot of attention from the industry [4], there is a need to define the concept of pivoting in a more rigorous fashion. Moreover, we aim at connecting pivots to Lean Model Canvas created by Ash Maurya [11], a technique for elaborating startups' business plans.

In this paper we validate the definition of pivoting and show how we can identify different pivots through three case study companies. The three companies are all startups created in Tampere region, Finland, and all three companies share some similar characteristics – established recently, aim at following Lean Startup ideals, and personnel that is highly motivated in their participation in startup activities. Similarly, all the studied companies have had a short runway that enables rapid evolution in both architecture of the business system and time-to-market product cycle [6].

The rest of this paper is structured as follows. In Sect. 2 we go through startups and the Lean Startup framework. In Sect. 3, we introduce Ries's definition of pivoting. In Sect. 4 we have the descriptions of our three case study companies and of their business decisions. In Sect. 5 we go show the identified pivots from the business decisions. In Sect. 6 we analyze the case companies through our pivot definition and show what kind of pivots the case companies have made. In Sect. 7, we introduce some directions for future work aiming at establishing pivoting as a recognized, well-understood practice. Finally, in Sect. 8 we summarize the identified pivots from cases, and draw some final conclusions.

2   Lean Startup Framework

The core idea of the Lean Startup framework is to define a process for validation through an iterative build-measure-learn cycle, which transforms new ideas into products [5,14]. The main phases of the cycle are learn, build, and measure (Fig. 1), and they are executed in the following fashion [11,14]. The first state one enters the loop is in the ideas state. This means that one has an assumption, a hypothesis of a business plan that is being refined into the first product. This idea is then turned into a product by the startup. When customers interact with the product, they generate feedback. Then based on this feedback, the startup learns more about their business space and the performance of their products. If

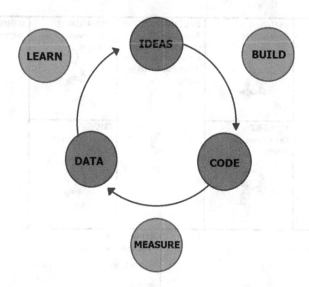

Fig. 1. Build-measure-learn loop

the hypothesis is supported by the gained data, the company should persevere. However, if the hypothesis is not supported, a pivot should be considered on its business plan.

A business plan consists of the key hypotheses of the startup. The business plan of a startup can be described with tools such as the Lean Model Canvas. The Lean Model Canvas collects all the hypotheses and allows easy communication of the whole business plan. In relation to other approaches, the goal of the Lean Model Canvas is to make tools such as the Business Model Canvas by Alexander Osterwalder and the Lean Startup toolkit by Rob Fitzpatrick fit to the startup's business plan [9,13].

The Lean Model Canvas can also help the startup to shape the necessary aspects of its business plan [1]. These aspects of the business plan, presented in Fig. 2 [11], form a hypothesis for each sector. Together, these hypotheses define the general hypothesis for the startup's repeatable business model.

For some of the fields the explanations in the Fig. 2 are sufficient, but others require more explanation. One of them is key metrics, which should be given at a level of detail and precision, that by observing them it is obvious if the startup is making progress. These metrics should present actionable knowledge, that helps in deciding to whether to pivot or not, and therefore the key metrics field is tightly coupled with the measure phase of the build-measure-learn cycle.

Key metrics also affect how easily a startup can execute more comprehensive pivots, where several changes are made at the same time. When key metrics are unrefined and informal the pivots are also wide and have a tendency to contain several other pivots. When key metrics have evolved it needs a validating system to collect the validated data. When this data shows that a pivot is needed, that pivot often focuses to change only a certain section of the business. In this case

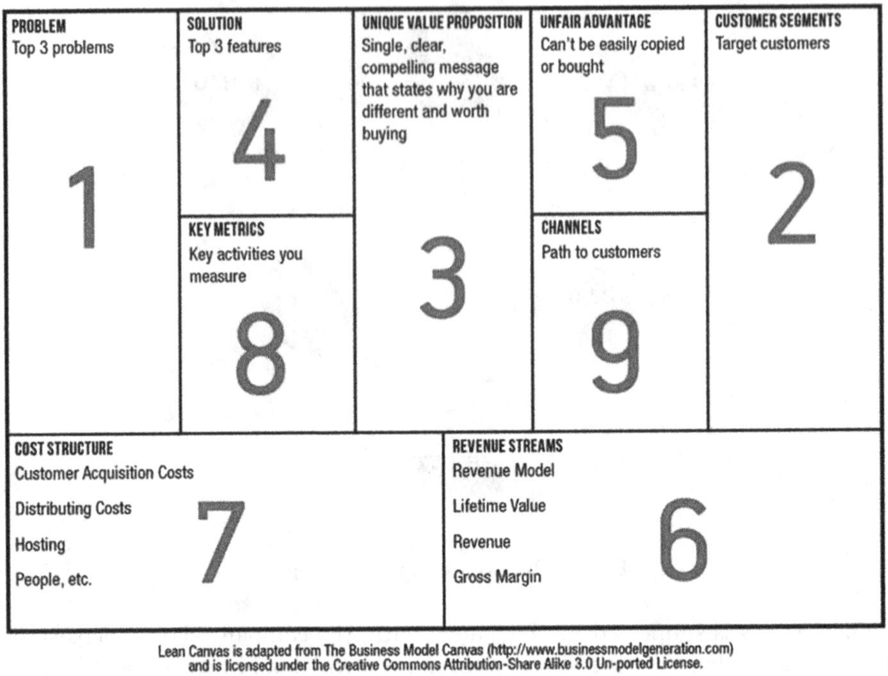

PROBLEM	SOLUTION	UNIQUE VALUE PROPOSITION	UNFAIR ADVANTAGE	CUSTOMER SEGMENTS
Top 3 problems	Top 3 features	Single, clear, compelling message that states why you are different and worth buying	Can't be easily copied or bought	Target customers
1	4		5	2
	KEY METRICS	3	CHANNELS	
	Key activities you measure		Path to customers	
	8		9	

COST STRUCTURE	REVENUE STREAMS
Customer Acquisition Costs	Revenue Model
Distributing Costs	Lifetime Value
Hosting	Revenue
People, etc.	Gross Margin
7	6

Lean Canvas is adapted from The Business Model Canvas (http://www.businessmodelgeneration.com) and is licensed under the Creative Commons Attribution-Share Alike 3.0 Un-ported License.

Fig. 2. Lean model canvas (http://findingferdinand.com/blog)

the validating system is hard to abandon and leaving all existing behind is much harder decision. In the following research cases we will show how key metrics effected the startup pivots.

3   Pivots and Pivoting

At first, a pivot sounds a lot similar to a plain change in the company setup. However, when considered more thoroughly, there is a major difference: a pivot is a change that is specially designed to test a new fundamental hypothesis about the company direction [14]. With this definition, a pivot can be defined as an action to change the current direction of something in the company to a new course in [12].

A pivot is a way to manage the change and it is closely related to Lean Startup working and most important decisions making. It can happen, for example, when a product is rejected in market testing [7]. Different pivots presented in [14] are listed below. These different types of pivots are linked to the different sections of the Lean Business Canvas and correspondingly to the different hypotheses.

- **Zoom-in Pivot** raises one feature on top of others and the feature becomes the actual product.
- **Zoom-out Pivot** is the reverse. The product needs more functions to successfully fill the desired customer need.

- **Customer Segment Pivot** is done when a company has proven that a customer need is filled, but on a different customer segment. Therefore such a pivot is needed to change the customer segment.
- **Customer Need Pivot** is sometimes needed when a startup works with the customers and it becomes clear that the problem being solved with the product is actually a minor facet of the problem. A pivot is made to solve this actual problem.
- **Platform Pivot** refers to the change from one application platform to another.
- **Business Architecture Pivot** is done when a company changes their targets from the masses to a niche or when old business model is changed from business to business model to business to consumer model or vice versa.
- **Value Capture Pivot** refers to the monetization methods of the company. This is the case when the way the company collects funding or revenue is changed.
- **Engine of Growth Pivot** refers to the three primary engines of growth that power startups: viral, sticky and paid growth models. In this pivot a company changes its growth strategy.
- **Channel Pivot** is done when a company abandons a previous sales process, for example to sell directly to users or if a delivery channel is changed.
- **Technology Pivot** is done when a company discovers that the same solution can be achieved much easier with another technology. This new technology is providing superior price or performance or both when comparing to existing technology.

The boundaries between the different types of pivots can be blurry, and sometimes it may even be difficult to determine into which category a pivot belongs to. Moreover, pivots need not be independent of each other; rather one pivot can imply several other pivots, following each other in domino effect – in essence a chain reaction triggered by one pivot that sets off a chain of further pivots. In this paper, we call such phenomena a domino-pivots.

4 Research Approach and Case Company Overviews

The objective of this paper is to find out how software startups are developing their business and do they actually perform pivots. A case study was done to find out new insights into pivoting and generating new ideas for research into the subject.

4.1 Research Approach

For this study we studied three software startups from Tampere region, Finland. We interviewed the personnel involved in the startups. Then, based on these interviews, we attempt to understand the theory of pivoting in their context. [15]

The three companies that were chosen were startups where at least one author was personally involved in. This makes the study unique and gave the researchers easier access and deeper views on the phenomena. The validity of this research is thus partly compromised, but on the other hand the participants understand the study way better than in a more typical study situation, and they can be more open on some subjects.

The study was executed by performing unstructured interviews based on the Lean model canvas as a discussion point. In general, a case study approach is particularly useful in situations where the phenomenon and context are difficult to separate [16]. These unstructured interviews also allowed for more in-depth discussions, which in turn made it possible to gather more information from the processes of the companies than pre-selected questions would have enabled.

Interviews were carried out during Spring and Summer 2015. All the interviewed persons held a high position in the interviewed companies. These startups were small, as only one person from them was interviewed. Interviews were recorded with detailed notes and at least two of the authors that were not involved with the interviewed company conducted the specific interview.

The selected company for the interview was interviewed once and the interview concerned both the initial business situation of the startup and the current business situation of the company. All of the companies were founded after 2013 and their business had gone through changes. Based on the interviews detailed case descriptions were written. In the cases the initial pivot identification was also done by authors not involved with the specific case. Afterwards the findings were validated with all authors and all the analyses were combined together.

These concrete cases – companies Illegal Alien Studios (IAS), Taplia, and Movendos – are introduced in the following subsections. As already mentioned, all these startups have been recently established in Tampere region, Finland, and follow Lean Startup ideals. However, all the companies have also had enough time to gather experience regarding pivots.

4.2 Illegal Alien Studios

Founded 2013, Illegal Alien Studios specialized in mobile software programming. Founders of the company were all 5th year students in Tampere University of Technology, Tampere, Finland. The main motivation for founding the company was to boost owners' experience in the field of ICT.

IAS has successfully launched one mobile game on the windows phone platform[1]. The original business model was to take the advantage of new and fresh marketplace and also to test and develop skills of the team. Business model contained iteration cycles that resemble those used in agile software development [10]. The goal of these iteration cycles was to be able to test the product with customers and continue developing the application based on the feedback collected. This kind of development helped to validate the interest of the customers. In this business model monetization was based on the freemium model. After releasing the first product IAS had successfully tested their team.

---

[1] https://dev.windows.com/en-us/.

After the development of the first product the market situation was changed. Moreover, other issues also emerged, as the customer segment was not clear for the company. Before starting the next game project, IAS got an offer for the development of a mobile user interface for consumer automation system. Based on the experience that IAS had gathered they decided that it was time to change their solvable problem and monetization model. They had proven their team and the core development model with mobile software. That model was preserved but the platform and the nature of the applications was changed completely.

IAS decided to start the customer project to create a user interface application for the automation system that contained some low level interfacing code. IAS also decided to keep a close relationship with the customer. The initial unique value proposition of IAS high usability was maintained also for this project. Feedback from the product was collected during the development process as before.

Such project required different network code for the program, and consequently IAS had to learn programming approaches related to several new technologies, such as Bluetooth. At the start of this project IAS had already made several big decisions to change their business model and the area of expertise. The first and maybe biggest of them being business model change that changed doing for masses to creating new for a niche. Changing from windows phone platform to Android[2] and including networking code was also a big change for the company. Later on the development has continued to use the old Lean strategy where development is done in a customer-centric way.

This customer project was supposed to be ending at the beginning of 2015 but a second agreement was found and development is still continuing. In the second stage of this project customer decided to change the hardware platform of the project. The new technology was Raspberry Pi[3]. This opened an opportunity for IAS to increase their role in the project. Now the development has continued in close co-development for both platforms Raspberry Pi and Android. This was a smaller technological change that helped IAS to continue and grow their part in the project.

4.3 Taplia

Taplia is a software services startup founded 2013 by three Tampere University of Technology, Tampere, Finland students (two full time, one part time). The company was based on the perceived need of one of the founders in his previous job. An electrical company had a problem that their hour logging was tedious and expensive. Based on this Taplia started to create a solution for the problem.

The first product of Taplia was an hour logging software done with mobile web technologies. The first version was a quickly done version made with ready made UI libraries and web technologies that allow fast prototyping. This version was ready in under a month. These prototypes were shown to the customer

---

[2] http://developer.android.com/index.html.
[3] https://www.raspberrypi.org/.

and this included the customer in the development right from the start. The monetization model was based on a customization fee and subscription based fee. When the first version of the product was done, the electrical company decided not to buy the product.

At this point Taplia made a business decision to abandon the original customer segment of construction companies and look for some other field where the same ideas could be applied. Similar problems were found from the gym industry. A potential customer was looking for a hour logging service, but using physical access cards. The old system was branched and a version supporting these cards was made.

However, an another construction company expressed their interest at this point in the original hour logging software aimed at the construction industry. An extra feature that they needed was text message confirmations. A decision was made to develop both these branches at the same time to sell the software to the third company and to develop the gym branch at the same time. The first decision to not to develop the construction version was overruled by this decision.

At this point both companies bought the solutions from Taplia based on these initial versions. This caused problems for Taplia which only had 2 persons working full time and the workload of creating two different products overwhelmed them. After the construction version of the software was ready and given to the customer and in use for a couple of months, the personnel involved in the construction company changed. This led to a situation where nobody was using the solution in the construction company. A business decision was made by Taplia not to try to improve the situation and let the product fizzle out because of the workload involved and focus on the gym product.

Also at this point the personnel in Taplia changed so that only one person was doing the development full time. This employee quickly realized that his effort was not enough to run the company, so a decision was made to get more part time employees to the company. After new persons were hired, a focus shift was made to try to sell the gym software to other clients as well, which changed the style of Taplia from a software house type to a product based business.

4.4   Movendos

Founded 2013, Movendos is a software startup focusing on creating tools for health and wellness coaching. They started their business by first analyzing potential business cases with the Lean Model Canvas. After initial review of the ideas, the ones that seemed the most potential were chosen and screened for potential customers. Customer validation was included in the process from the start. The wellness sector was chosen because of the potential customers seen in that market.

The original business model for Movendos was to develop a mobile application for a single company to track patient exercise outside their private rehabilitation facilities. The software was developed as an Android application with a web server backend. The monetization model for Movendos was a subscription based model. Many features of this initial product were spoofed and many features were left as just concepts. This version only enabled the clients to track their training, no coach views were yet done.

After the initial proofing of the business model with one company, Movendos made a business decision to start the development of an enlarged version of the mobile tracking application, this time featuring an actual web portal for coaches to track the customer training data. This was designed to be a hybrid Android application, using web technologies inside an Android program to enable portability to other platforms in the future. Some technology choices were made that were known to be unscalable, but this was overlooked for the time being, in exchange for faster time to market. The new version had an extended set of features, and it was tested with multiple clients. The actual usage for coaches was also enabled in this version.

Again when the version of the software proved to be actually useful, a business decision was made to enlarge the scope of the product to target more wellness and occupational health providers. This meant that the original Android technology was not scalable enough and was redone as a web based portal. At this point the monetization model of the application was finalized to be a subscription based model, based on the number or clients the coaches had in the system.

5   Identified Pivots

Based on the above, case companies have executed several types of pivots, some in domino effect and some in isolation. Moreover, the different types of pivots based on different rationale, requiring different types of actions. In the following, we go through each pivot that has been addressed above one company at a time, and map the pivots to the Lean Model canvas described above. An overview of the pivots in these cases are outlined in Table 1. The numbers in the table represent the different pivot groups, which consist of the pivots following the domino effect as made by the different case companies. In this paper we call these larger group of pivots domino-pivots, where the first pivot in the group causes the others. Based on the table, we can see that in case of IAS first larger pivot and in case of Taplia the first two pivots consisted of several other pivots. In IAS case we identified that the first group of pivots contained four different pivots. The decision to pivot the business architecture can be seen as a starting point which required other pivots to support. Also in case of Taplia the business architecture pivot led to other pivots. This pivot was smaller than in case of IAS. We identified that these domino-pivots are also changing multiple sections in Lean canvas model.

These identified pivots reflects business decisions that has some actual impact in the company. The impact can be seen in working routine or in our case when looking through their Lean canvas model. We are sure that in the companies decisions have been made that have not introduced changes – or, within the scope of this paper, pivots. The pivots highlight the important business decisions found in the interviews.

Table 1. Pivots in case companies

Pivots	IAS	Taplia	Movendos
Zoom-in		T3	M1
Zoom-out	I3	I1, I2	M2
Customer segment	I1	T1	
Customer need			
Technology			M3
Platform	I2		
Business architecture	I1	T3	
Value capture	I1		
Engine of growth			
Channel	I1		

5.1 Illegal Alien Studios

When considering IAS, we can identify three different pivot groups. These are addressed in the following.

IAS Pivot 1(I1): From Appstore to B2B. The first pivot group happened when the customer project offer was accepted, a business decision was made to change from application store to niche. This caused a business architecture pivot, customer segment pivot and a channel pivot. These pivots affected the problem, solution, channels and customer segments parts of the canvas. This pivot is largest that IAS has done in their startup runway. It is also largest pivot in this scope of startups and describes the way how radically a startup can change what they are doing.

IAS Pivot 2(I2): Windows to Android. The second pivot group consisted of a platform pivot. It was made when the company decided to change their supported mobile platform from Windows phone to Android. This affected the problem part. This pilot also challenged the employee knowledge and skills. Android platform uses totally different developing channels and languages.

IAS Pivot 3(I3): Additional Platforms. The third pivot group consisted of a zoom out pivot and was done when the application was extended to include Raspberry Pi. Adding another technology expand the core knowledge even further and helped IAS to attain even bigger role in the project.

5.2 Taplia

Taplia Pivot 1(T1): Construction Sites to Gyms. The first pivot group can be identified as a customer segment pivot, where business decision was made to leave the construction sites out and focus on gyms. This also caused a zoom out pivot because of the need for the access cards at the gym.

Taplia Pivot 2(T2): Expand to Two Segments. As the business decision to include the construction sites back was made, a second pivot group, consisting of a business architecture pivot, was made when it was decided that there would be 2 products. Consequently this caused a zoom out pivot to include new features for the construction site segment.

Taplia pivot 3(T3): Fallback. When the construction branch withered out a third pivot group, a zoom in pivot, was made to focus back on the gym sector. This affected the customer segment section and cost structure parts of the canvas. The latest decision to seek new customers for the gym product is such a new one that its actual consequences remain to be seen and is not included in the analysis.

5.3   Movendos

Movendos Pivot 1(M1): Finding the First Product. The first pivot group was a zoom-in pivot as many product features were tested, but never finished. For example a UI prototype of a food diary was done, but no actual functionality was implemented beyond the UI. Through these concepts, key features were chosen for zoom-in. This affected the problem of the Lean canvas.

Movendos Pivot 2(M2): From Freelancers to Companies. The next pivot group can be seen as a zoom-out pivot when based on the initial product they decided to enlarge it to encompass a larger customer segment. The change in customer segments was to scale up the companies that were targeted, originally just freelance personal coaches were targeted, then the focus was changed to include larger companies providing occupational health services.

Movendos Pivot 3(M3): Prototype to Maintainable Development. The third pivot group to be identified from the Movendos case is the technology pivot when it was seen that the original Android solution was not scalable. The database solution which mirrored the database to all the devices in use was changed a more conventional SQL database. At the same time the whole back-end architecture was refactored and made into an actual maintainable product, most of the MVP shortcuts taken were fixed.

6   Discussion

When considering the changes that the different domino-pivots caused to the Lean model canvas hypotheses, it can be seen that IAS and Taplia made much more radical pivots than Movendos. These pivots led to multiple changes in the Lean Canvas hypotheses. In total, the first IAS pivot changed four different fields of the canvas, the second Taplia pivot changed three different fields, and in Movendos, only at most two fields changed. These changes to the canvas values by pivot group are listed in Table 2.

Based on our research customer segment pivots are linked to the change of solution in Lean Canvas Model. This kind of change took place in both IAS

Table 2. Lean Model Canvas changes in case companies

Lean model canvas	IAS	Taplia	Movendos
Problem	I2		M1
Customer segments	I1	I2, T3	M2
Unique value proposition			
Solution	I1	T1, I2	M2, M3
Unfair advantage			
Revenue streams	I1		
Cost structure	I3	T1, I2, T3	M3
Key metrics			
Channels	I1		

and Taplia. In IAS and Taplia a zoom-out pivot, and in Movendos a technology pivot affected the cost structure. In Taplia and Movendos a zoom-out pivot also changed both the customer segment and solution in the Lean Canvas Model.

Based on case studies, zoom-out pivots seem to cause cost structure pivots, because of the larger scope of the new product requiring more investments. The same can be said of technology pivots, where the foundations of the product are changed and these affect the cost structure typically in some way, be it a earlier investment going to waste, or the change from cloud servers to a local application.

When looking at the domino-pivots done by IAS and Taplia, the larger pivots radically changed the direction of the companies. The reasoning for these larger pivots was mostly based on the gut feeling of the founders and were done, when the company needed a new source of revenue. This need for instant revenue was driven by the fact that IAS and Taplia had no external sources of funding for their startups. Thus the main key metric that these companies were measuring at that time was the revenue of the company so that the startup could continue living. In fact, Taplia and IAS did not have the resources to actually establish any measuring frameworks for their key metrics, so they relied on the easily measured revenue as a metric. This caused the key metrics of IAS and Taplia to be quite informal and unrefined.

In Movendos, the company had established external sources of funding and their pivots were more focused on product iteration. All the pivots Movendos made were tied to product improvements, whereas IAS and Taplia pivots were more focused on revenue generation.

More detailed key metrics often require a system to collect validated data about the product or service. This validated data helps to identify problematic sectors and areas that still need improvement. Data collection also enables more focused pivoting and the effect of pivots can be validated through key metric data collection systems. When it comes to pivots these systems also make it harder to pivot and abandon all existing to start something again from the scratch.

This focusing effect can also be seen in the case studies. When IAS and Taplia made their first domino-pivot it changed multiple sectors in their business model. In both cases the existing key metric was unrefined and data collection was quite informal. After doing the domino-pivot their key metrics evolved and data collection improved. Based on this more validated data focusing pivots could be done. As identified above these follow-up pivots were more detailed and changed less their Lean Model Canvas.

7 Future Work

In the future we plan to analyze more deeply how different pivots affect startup business hypotheses, in particular from the viewpoints of iteration and validated learning. Moreover, we also want to study how these pivots are linked together in order to investigate correlation and potential causalities between linked pivots.

On a more methodological side, we wish to test the hypothesis that pivots cause changes to specific Lean Model Canvas segments. Moreover, it would also be interesting to investigate if the amount of changes caused to the Lean Model Canvas can be used as a metric for the severity of the pivot, thus helping startups to understand how big a leap they are taking. In general, a step to this direction has been taken by accepting that pivots can act in accordance to the domino effect, with one pivot spurring more pivots within the company. Our hypothesis is that the more established the company gets, the less pivot groups will emerge. Rather, it is possible to focus on validated learning, where, in order to iterate, at least some of the underpinnings of the startup must go unchanged.

Finally, defining a research agenda for going beyond the present in general in the startup genre is a part of future research. While we do not believe there is a ready-made recipe for creating successful startups out of scratch, there already is data regarding patterns on how startups operate [8].

8 Conclusion

In this paper we defined pivots to be changes in the business hypotheses of the startup. The Lean Canvas Model was used to describe the different business hypotheses that form the overall business hypothesis of the startup. With this definition, we evaluated three case companies, and found several pivots that are linked to business decisions the startups made. We also identified the changes to the Lean Model Canvas segments these pivots caused.

Research done in this paper showed researchers that existing startups share similar properties when considering pivots and changes in their business plan. These pivots reflects the natural need of change to sustain the business. Researchers are convinced that these are not the only startups that has done pivots and similar business decisions that lead to pivots and has effect in Business Model Canvas.

References

1. Barquet, A.P.B., Cunha, V.P., Oliveira, M.G., Rozenfeld, H.: Business model elements for product-service system. In: Hesselbach, J., Herrmann, C. (eds.) Functional Thinking for Value Creation, pp. 332–337. Springer, Heidelberg (2011)
2. Blank, S.: Search versus execute (2012). http://steveblank.com/2012/03/05/search-versus-execute/
3. Blank, S.: The Four Steps to the Epiphany. K&S Ranch, Pescadero (2013)
4. Blank, S.: Why the lean start-up changes everything. Harvard Bus. Rev. **91**(5), 63–72 (2013)
5. Blank, S., Dorf, B.: The Startup Owner's Manual. K&S Ranch, Pescadero (2012)
6. Bosch, J., van der Veen, J.S.: Pivots and architectural decisions: two sides of the same medal? In: Eighth International Conference on Software Engineering Advances, ICSEA 2013, October 27-October 31 2013, Venice, Italy (2013)
7. Callele, D., Boyer, A., Brown, K., Wnuk, K., Penzenstadler, B.: Requirements engineering as a surrogate for business case analysis in a mobile applications startup context. In: IW-LCSP@ ICSOB, pp. 33–46. Citeseer (2013)
8. Dande, A., Eloranta, V.P., Kovalainen, A.J., Lehtonen, T., Leppänen, M., Salmimaa, T., Sayeed, M., Vuori, M., Rubattel, C., Weck, W., et al.: Software startup patterns-an empirical study. Tampereen teknillinen yliopisto. Tietotekniikan laitos. Raportti-Tampere University of Technology. Department of Pervasive Computing. Report; 4 (2014)
9. Fitzpatrick, R.: The startup toolkit: a canvas for you to sketch your business framework (2010). http://readwrite.com/2010/06/15/the-startup-toolkit-a-canvas-f
10. Martin, R.C.: Agile Software Development: Principles, Patterns, and Practices. Prentice Hall PTR, Upper Saddle River (2003)
11. Maurya, A.: Running Lean: Iterate from Plan A to a Plan that Works. O'Reilly Media Inc., Sebastopol (2012)
12. Münch, J.: Evolving process simulators by using validated learning. In: Proceedings of the International Conference on Software and System Process, pp. 226–227. IEEE Press (2012)
13. Osterwalder, A., Pigneur, Y.: Business Model Generation: A Handbook for Visionaries, Game Changers, and Challengers. Wiley, New York (2010)
14. Ries, E.: The Lean Startup. Penguin, New York (2011)
15. Runeson, P., Höst, M.: Guidelines for conducting and reporting case study research in software engineering. Empirical Softw. Eng. **14**(2), 131–164 (2009)
16. Yin, R.K.: Case Study Research: Design and Methods. Sage Publications, Thousand Oaks (1994)

On the Feasibility of Startup Models as a Framework for Research on Competence Needs in Software Startups

Pertti Seppänen[✉], Kari Liukkunen, and Markku Oivo

Department of Information Processing Sciences,
University of Oulu, FI 90015 Oulu, Finland
pertti.seppanen@oulu.fi

Abstract. *Background*—Until recently, mainstream research on software engineering targeted software development in established companies. However, startup companies have become more important in developing new software-intensive products and services. Consequently, research focusing on software startups has emerged. Understanding competence needs during the evolution of a software startup company is crucial to its success. Competence needs are, however, a difficult topic to study because software startups are rapidly and constantly changing. *Aim*—This paper presents the preliminary results of our on-going research on competence needs in software startups, compares them to the startup models identified in the recent literature, and figures out the feasibility of the models as a research framework. *Method*—We interview key persons from nine software startup companies in three European countries. From the interview material, we identify characteristics of competence needs. We investigate the recent literature models created for software startups. We then compare our empirical findings to the models identified in the literature and conclude with the feasibility of the models as a framework for the future research. *Result*—The results of our preliminary study indicate a need for a new startup model that combines aspects of the existing models in order to get a comprehensive framework for the research of competence needs in software startups.

Keywords: Startup company · Software engineering · Software startup · Startup model · Competences · Competence needs · Research on competences

1 Introduction

A startup is a company founded to create new business and rapid growth. It is typically small, has short operational history [4], and develops a new product marketed and sold to customers. Until recently, mainstream research on software engineering targeted software development in established companies. However, because software startups have become more important in developing new software-intensive products and services, research on them has increased. Research to gain understanding of characteristics specific to software startups and their operational environments has been conducted to identify success factors [2] and challenges [3–5, 13]. Furthermore, several models have been created to describe software startups [9, 11, 12].

© Springer International Publishing Switzerland 2015
P. Abrahamsson et al. (Eds.): PROFES 2015, LNCS 9459, pp. 569–576, 2015.
DOI: 10.1007/978-3-319-26844-6_42

Understanding competence needs is a crucial factor in the success of a startup company. In a startup, not only the products but also the processes and practices need to be developed. Establishing such processes and developing the first product require substantial knowledge, skill, and effort from the startup's core team. Distinct competence areas, such as software engineering, have been studied [7, 10], but comprehensive competence research covering the evolution of startups is still scarce.

We define the term competence needs as a complete set of skills and knowledge required for successful progress of a startup along its evolutionary path.

In this paper, we present preliminary results of our on-going research on the competence needs in software startups. We analyze the interview data from nine different software-intensive startup companies in three European countries. We identify characteristics of the competence needs that the interviewed companies have in common. We conduct a preliminary literature study to find publications on the models and characteristics of software startups. We compare the findings from the interviews to the models identified in the literature in order to figure out the feasibility of the models as a framework for research on competence needs in software startups.

The study seeks to answer the following research questions:

RQ1:   What are the key characteristics of the competence needs identified from the interview data?

RQ2:   Are the models defined for software startups from the literature able to describe the competence needs identified from the interview data?

The results indicate that the key characteristics of the competence needs in software startups reflect the volatile and immature nature of the evolutionary path of a software startup. They also indicate that no single startup model analyzed in this study addresses all the key characteristics of competence needs, especially the interdependencies between different competence areas. Thus, a new comprehensive startup model is needed as a framework for future research.

The rest of the paper has the following structure: Sect. 2 defines the problem area, Sect. 3 introduces the research approach, Sect. 4 summarizes the findings from the industry interviews, Sect. 5 presents the findings of the literature study on software startup models, Sect. 6 summarizes the comparison of the interview findings to the literature, and Sect. 7 concludes the study and provides suggestions for future research.

2   Problem Definition

A software startup company faces many challenges [3–5, 7]. The team is small and possibly inexperienced, the company is developing its first product, and software development practices and processes are not yet established. Besides software development, many other tasks must be conducted successfully, including gaining application area understanding, building the company, hiring the core team, creating the customer base, and finding the needed funding Research on software startups must thus address a multitude of research topics and viewpoints. Addressing the multitude of potential research topics and viewpoints can be done at each stage of the startups' evolutionary path [3] according to discipline, such as software engineering [7], according to success factors and challenges, [2–5], or according to the modeling of the evaluation path of the startup [9, 11, 12].

In spring 2015, as members of an international research community focused on software startups, we started research on the competence needs of software startups. The long-term aim of our research is to gather new knowledge on the competence needs of software startups that can be utilized by both academics and practitioners to improve the success of new startups. The key research approach is empirical—we gather the raw data via industry interviews and analyze it in accordance with the research literature.

Our research on competence needs is also facing challenges caused by the multitude of research topics and viewpoints: how to structure and address the different areas and viewpoints and how to conduct future research.

One approach to managing different research topics and viewpoints is to create models describing the problem area and utilize the models as a framework for identifying the potential areas of interest and their interconnections. To gain an understanding of the model-based approach, we conducted a preliminary study on the feasibility of existing startup models identified in the literature. For the study, we analyzed the characteristics of the competence needs of the nine companies that we interviewed during summer 2015. We made a preliminary literature study to find publications on the models and characteristics of software startups. By comparing the findings from our interview data with the models and characteristics identified in the literature, we gathered preliminary understanding of the feasibility of the model-based approach as a framework for our future research.

3 Research Approach

We started conducting interviews with software-intensive startup companies in spring 2015. The interviews were semi-structured, and the competences and competence needs were addressed in the interviews at a high level without an in-depth focus on any specific competence area.

For this study, we included the first nine companies of our on-going interviews. The geographical distribution of the cases is two interviews in Trondheim, Norway; one interview in Bolzano, Italy; four interviews in Oulu, Finland; and two interviews in Helsinki, Finland. The applied areas of the companies interviewed are different. Five develop pure software products, while four develop embedded products with mechanics, electronics, and software. The maturity and complexity of the deployed technologies also varies, from straightforward service implementation to the utilization of technology that was virtually nonexistent at the beginning of the startup's development.

In order to get an overall picture of the companies, persons having CEO or CTO roles were interviewed. They were all the founders or co-founders of the companies in question. The interviews were conducted face-to-face in 1–2 h on the company's premises. The focus of the interviews was on the evolutionary paths of the companies until the first product was produced. The interviews were recorded and annotated with written comments.

Identifying competence-related topics from the interview data was conducted in the following steps: (1) identifying the type of the first product, (2) identifying the overall evolution path towards the first product, (3) identifying discontinuation points along to the evolution path if any, (4) identifying the role of competence issues to the progress of the evolution path, and (5) concluding a set of preliminary findings that the interviewed companies have in common.

We gathered a preliminary set of literature on the models and characteristics of software startups by applying the snowballing technique to recent literature [6, 14]. We conducted backward and forward snowballing, starting with four recent papers written by recognized software startup experts [4, 5, 7, 10]. In backward snowballing, we went through 320 publications; in forward snowballing, we went through 37 publications. The small amount of papers in forward snowballing was due to the recent publication date of the original four papers. The main criterion for selecting the papers for this study was the relevance for modeling software startup companies. Papers identifying and modeling (1) success factors, (2) problems and challenges, (3) the evolution paths and processes, and (4) software engineering in software startups were included in the analysis. Additional criteria for the selection focused on the big picture of software startups instead of a specific area or a recent publication date.

4   Characteristics of Competence Needs Identified in Industry Interviews

4.1   Interview Results

Companies 1 and 2 developed systems that provided mass-market customers with Internet services. Company 1 developed the system smoothly but faced difficulties in creating the customer base, which lead to discontinuation of development. In company 2, both the original customer discovery and the first software development work failed. The difficulties with the customer base were overcome by succeeding in searching for new customers. The difficulties with the software development were due to gaps in programming skills in the original team. The founder stated, "They were Google programmers looking for sample code pieces on the Internet." Company 2 had to lay off the first team and hire a new team with a carefully selected software head. The new team re-started software development from the beginning.

Company 3 developed a pure software system, providing a combined service to both mass-market customers and institutional customers. The idea refinement and customer discovery went without problems. But even in company 3, the first software development team did not succeed in developing quality software. The reason was the same as that for company 2: gaps in programming skills. The solution was the same: a new experienced software head, a new team, and a re-start of development. In both cases with incompetent original teams, the company founders had engineering degrees in other disciplines but not computer science or software engineering.

Company 4 developed a software system for a single big customer with highly customer-specific and application-specific functionality. The founder had earlier work experience in a customer-centric company, knew the application area well, and had established contacts with both the users of the system and the decision-making managers. He was an experienced software developer and hired a successful development team. The system definition, software development, piloting, and system launch progressed smoothly. The founder stated, "I looked for people [that were] not only skilled programmers but interested in the application area, too."

Company 5 developed an operating system component for smart devices. The software was highly adaptable, and it was offered to smart device vendors on an OEM basis. Before founding the company and hiring developers, the founder ran an unsuccessful trial with open source software. The quality of the available open source solutions turned out to be too low. After that, the founder, having over 20 years' experience in software development, conducted the basic development by himself and made smooth progress in the work. He emphasized the importance of the programming skills by explaining: "Missing programming skills—that is why three MBAs fail in founding a software startup."

Companies 6, 7, 8, and 9 developed embedded devices for different application areas. In all companies, the application area, the device architecture, and the solutions in other technology areas affected the software development. In company 6, the team was highly experienced, worked as a spin-off of a bigger company, and deployed known technologies. In that company, software development ran smoothly. In companies 7, 8, and 9, difficulties in other technology areas caused changes and a rework of the software development. In the extreme case of company 7, the whole development was discontinued due to a sensor solution that did not reach the required quality level. In company 9, difficulties in other technology areas increased the software development time by 1–2 years due to a series of reworks on the software side.

4.2   Preliminary Findings from the Interviews

The key findings we derive from the above interview results are that (1) competence needs are volatile and change as a company evolves; (2) evolution is not linear, meaning neither are competence needs; (3) software engineering competences are essential, but competences in many other disciplines are also needed; and (4) competences and competence needs are strongly interdependent. We can also conclude that missing competences are one reason for nonlinear progress and discontinuation points of the evolutionary path. The smoothest progress were encountered in companies 4 and 6 where the personnel's software development experience, application area knowledge, awareness of the used technologies, and customer needs were well balanced.

In the interview data, software development competences are dominant. In companies developing embedded products, competences in other relevant disciplines are also highlighted. Competences in pure programming are strongly highlighted in the interviews. Several other software engineering disciplines, such as requirements management or project planning, do not arise in the interview data.

5   Software Startup Characteristics and Models in Literature

Giardino et al. [4, 5] studied the characteristics of software development in startups, identifying 15 typical attributes of software startups. Most of them are challenges, such as lack of resources, uncertainty in business and technology, time pressure, dependency on external parties, small size, having only one product, lack of experience, and high risk. Sutton [13] also defines four characteristic challenges: little or no operation history, limited resources, multiple influences, and dynamic technologies and markets.

Crowne [3] defines a three-plus-one stage model for a startup that includes the startup phase, the stabilization phase, the growth phase, and maturity. The model defines specific challenges, called symptoms, for each phase. He identifies five symptoms of the startup phase, six symptoms of the stabilization phase, and four symptoms of the growth phase.

Klotins et al. [7] and Paternoster et al. [10] studied the knowledge and skills required for software engineering. They note that mainstream software engineering research doesn't focus on startups. For instance, the mapping study [7] indicates that only 28 of 62 knowledge areas of IEEE Computer Society's Guide to the Software Engineering Body of Knowledge (SWEBOK) [1] were covered in startup-specific research in 2015.

Chorev and Anderson [2] propose a static model for startup success containing 16 critical factors. Two factors are related to the idea, three to the external environment, and the rest to the company itself, such as core team expertise, customer relations, and product development.

Giardino et al. [5] studied why software startups fail and propose a behavioral framework defining two evolution stages: the exploration stage and the validation stage. Each stage is further divided into the four dimensions, which were originally proposed by [8]: market, product, team, and business.

The early phases of a startup are dominated by continuous change, which is described by dynamic process models, such as [3, 9, 11, 12].

Crowne [3] proposes a four phase model for a startup that includes the startup phase, the stabilization phase, the growth phase, and maturity.

In *The Lean Startup*, Ries [11] proposes a looped evolution path for software startups, one that includes the steps of idea, build, product, measure, data, and learn. This model covers the actions in the evolution steps and addresses the non-linear progress typical of software startups by, for instance, defining a restart, pivoting, and the loop from learning to a refined idea.

Steinert and Leifer [12] define two different action modes: (1) innovative and seeking hunting and (2) analytic and systematic gathering. Hunting refers to the innovation needed to identify the technologies, products, and business ideas, while gathering refers to traditional engineering work.

Nguyen-Duc et al. [9] expand on the idea of hunting and gathering from the innovation process to include the whole evolution of a startup. The authors identify a set of actions conducted in the early phases of a startup and propose a division into hunting- and gathering-type actions.

6   Comparison of the Interview Results and the Literature

The key findings from the interview data are that (1) competence needs in a software startup are changing along an evolutionary path, (2) software development skills are essential, and (3) there are strong interdependencies between the competence areas.

The static models [2, 4, 13] are not able to describe the dynamic nature of the competence needs, but they address many key characteristics of software startups, such as personnel experience, limited resources, and dependency on external parties. With the dynamic process-like startup models [9, 11, 12], the situation is the opposite. They address the evolutionary path, even taking nonlinear progress into account. However, they fail to describe many characteristics addressed by the static models.

Our findings highlight the importance of software development skills, which is also addressed in the literature [7, 10].

The interdependencies between the competence areas identified from the interview data are not addressed by any model we identified from the literature study.

7   Conclusions and Future Research

Our study indicates that using startup models as a framework is a feasible approach to identifying areas and viewpoints for the research on competence needs in software startups. All the models included in our study give valuable viewpoints, although no individual model addresses the whole spectrum of the competence needs. The results also reveal that models included in our study do not address the interdependencies between different competence needs.

Thus, the results indicate that there is a need for a comprehensive model that combines the viewpoints of the models analyzed in this study. Defining such a model and validating it with broader empirical data will be a key area of our future research. Furthermore, deploying this new model as a research framework will likely support a multitude of other interesting research topics in the future.

Limitations on the validity of this study are due to the limited number of company cases and a possible lack of coverage in the literature included in the study. However, the aim of this paper is to present the preliminary results of our on-going research and figure out future research directions. From that point of view, the included sample size seems to be enough to identify some new, interesting research topics, such as a comprehensive model for competence needs and interdependencies between competence areas. In the same way, the selected literature seems to support use of a model-based approach for creating a framework for our future research on competence needs in software startups.

Acknowledgements. Software Startup Research Network supported this study and made it possible for us to conduct it. We thank all the members of the network, especially Anh Nguyen-Duc and Pekka Abrahamsson for their support in gathering the empirical data. Research was partly funded by TEKES as part of the HILLA Program.

References

1. Bourque, P., Fairley, R.E.: Guide to the Software Engineering Body of Knowledge (SWEBOK (R)): version 3.0. IEEE Computer Society Press, Washington (2014)
2. Chorev, S., Anderson, A.R.: Success in Israeli high-tech start-ups; critical factors and process. Technovation **26**, 162–174 (2006)
3. Crowne, M.: Why Software Product Startups Fail and what to do about it. Evolution of software product development in startup companies, 1 (2002)
4. Giardino, C., Unterkalmsteiner, M., Paternoster, N., et al.: What do we know about software development in startups? IEEE Softw. **31**, 28–32 (2014)
5. Giardino, C., Wang, X., Abrahamsson, P.: Why early-stage software startups fail: a behavioral framework. In: Lassenius, C., Smolander, K. (eds.) ICSOB 2014. LNBIP, vol. 182, pp. 27–41. Springer, Heidelberg (2014)
6. Jalali, S., Wohlin, C.: Systematic literature studies: database searches vs. backward snowballing. In: Proceedings of the ACM-IEEE international symposium on Empirical software engineering and measurement, pp. 29–38. ACM (2012)
7. Klotins, E., Unterkalmsteiner, M., Gorschek, T.: Software engineering knowledge areas in startup companies: a mapping study. In: Fernandes, J.M., Machado, R.J., Wnuk, K. (eds.) ICSOB 2014. LNBIP, vol. 210, pp. 245–257. Springer, Heidelberg (2014)
8. MacMillan, I.C., Zemann, L., Subbanarasimha, P.: Criteria distinguishing successful from unsuccessful ventures in the venture screening process. J. Bus. Ventur. **2**, 123–137 (1987)
9. Nguyen-Duc, A., Seppänen, P., Abrahamsson, P.: Hunter-gatherer cycle: a conceptual model of the evolution of software startups. In: ICSSP 2015 (2015)
10. Paternoster, N., Giardino, C., Unterkalmsteiner, M., et al.: Software development in startup companies: a systematic mapping study. Inform. Softw. Technol. **56**, 1200–1218 (2014)
11. Ries, E.: The Lean Startup: How Today's Entrepreneurs Use Continuous Innovation to Create Radically Successful Businesses. Random House LLC, New York (2011)
12. Steinert, M., Leifer, L.J.: 'Finding one's way': re-discovering a hunter-gatherer model based on wayfaring. Int. J. Eng. Educ. **28**, 251 (2012)
13. Sutton, S.M.: The role of process in a software start-up. IEEE Softw. **17**, 33–39 (2000)
14. Wohlin, C.: Guidelines for snowballing in systematic literature studies and a replication in software engineering. In: Evaluation and Assessment in Software Engineering (2014)

Towards a Software Tool Portal to Support Startup Process

Henry Edison[✉], Dron Khanna, Sohaib Shahid Bajwa, Valery Brancaleoni,
and Luca Bellettati

Free University of Bozen-Bolzano, Piazza Domenicani 3, 39100 Bolzano, Italy
{henry.edison,bajwa}@inf.unibz.it, dron.khanna@unibz.it,
{valery.brancaleoni,lucabelles}@gmail.com

Abstract. Despite their popularity and growth, startups still face many
challenges to keep survived in highly dynamic and turbulent environments. With limited time and resources, they must develop products
or services that solve real problems. Today, various software tools have
been provided to help entrepreneurs to tackle these challenges and speed
up their processes. However, how to effectively find and use these tools
are not clearly understood either by entrepreneurs or in literature. The
purpose of this research-in-progress paper is to apply design science principles to develop a software tool portal to support the startup processes.
The initial results reveal the need of tool recommendation as part of
software the portal for entrepreneurs to find the right tools effectively in
order to meet their specific needs.

Keywords: Startups · Software tool portal · Entrepreneur

1 Introduction

Startup is not only about developing innovative product or service, but also
about business development [1]. To enter into an existing market or a new market, a startup often develops technologically innovative product which requires
disruptive technologies. The entrepreneurs should ensure that the product they
build targets at solving a real problem. It means that there is somebody out there
who will pay for and use it to solve their problems. To do this, entrepreneurs
should go out of the building to involve the customers since day one [2].

Most of startup founders are young and inexperienced. Moreover, they have
limited resources. To overcome these challenges, finding and using the right tools
have become critical for entrepreneurs to build and grow their startups. Entrepreneurs need tools to assist them in managing the team, finance, product or
service development and marketing. Choosing the right tools will not only allow
them to speed up their product or service development but also to commer-
cialise it. In this study, we focus on software tool which defined as a software
application (including mobile, desktop and web application) that supports a
well-defined startup activity [3].

© Springer International Publishing Switzerland 2015
P. Abrahamsson et al. (Eds.): PROFES 2015, LNCS 9459, pp. 577–583, 2015.
DOI: 10.1007/978-3-319-26844-6_43

Today, the growth of web technology has made available a plethora of software tools that can be useful for entrepreneurs. Knowledge of what others may be doing helps them to make startup process less painful, more productive and effective. Various web portals have been also developed to serve as the gatekeepers to the existing software tools for startups. Entrepreneurs may begin their searching for tools by visiting a portal and obtain information about the tools and the links to get the tools.

Most of the existing portal provides a collection of a huge number of tools and organised them into a certain category. Moreover, each portal offers different features for entrepreneurs to find a tool for them e.g. tool search, forum, etc. However, it is still unresolved how these portals can suggest right tools for the entrepreneurs to support their activities. Hence, the research question in our study is *how do we implement a portal that satisfy the entrepreneurs' needs of finding the right tools?*

The solution we propose is based on the following argument. Different tools have been developed and published over the world wide web. New entrepreneurs might not have sufficient knowledge what tools they need in their circumstances as compared to experienced entrepreneurs. In this case, we advocate a new categorisation of existing tools. In addition, not all of tools are good enough to help entrepreneurs in certain tasks or situations. The entrepreneurs' experience of using the tools will serve as the basis to evaluate and recommend certain tools.

The remainder of this paper is structured as follows. Section 2 discusses the related work of this study. Section 3 presents the research approach proposed. The preliminary results of this study are explained in Sect. 4. Section 5 describes the immediate next steps.

2   Literature Review

2.1   Startup Process

Startups are newly created companies tend to grow fast in extreme uncertainty. According to Sutton [4], startups have the following characteristics: (1) young and immature (2) limited resources (3) multiple influences from stakeholders and (4) dynamic technologies and market.

In order to grow and attain a sustainable business model, startups go through different phases. Crowne [5] defines the startup life cycle into four stages: The first stage is startup stage starting from idea conceptualisation to the first sale. The stage starting from the first sale until the product is stable enough to present to new customers without effecting development process is second (or stabilisation) stage. The growth phase beings with growth, getting share in the market. The final stage is when a startup becomes a mature company and follows proven process to develop an innovative product.

During the life cycle, startups perform different activities. These activities are related to product development, business and customer development etc. Software tools can be helpful for entrepreneurs to effectively perform and thus accelerate these activities. However, little is known about what are the software tools that startups are using to accelerate performance during their daily activities.

Tools are used to facilitate people to perform, manage and control different tasks and activities. For example, project management tools can help entrepreneurial team to effectively manage and utilise their resources. Another example is development tools that can be helpful to support different software development activities. Keeping in mind the dynamics and fast nature of startups, it is important to identify the tools that entrepreneurs can use to accelerate their startup processes.

2.2 Portal

Over the past decade, the popularity of web portal has increased considerably. Organisations use web portals to compliment, substitute and extend existing services [6]. The idea of a web portal is to provide an access to different data providers via online [7] and an environment which allows users to find the data and information needed to support their operational or strategic decisions [8]. Therefore, web portals serve as a gateway to explore and access information on the Internet.

Collins [8] defines a set of basic functions that are provided by web portals, as follows:

- Data points and integration. Web portal provides information from a wide range of sources, which should be correct, up-to-date and complete.
- Taxonomy. The information published in the portal should be arranged and ordered so that users can easily use the portal.
- Search capabilities. Users can search the information throughout the portal.
- Help features. Users should be able to ask and get answers when using the portal.
- Content management. This function allows users to create/modify content.
- Process and action. Users can be involved in the portal business process.
- Collaboration and communication. This function facilitates sharing of innovative ideas, information or resource.
- Personalisation. Web portal allows each user to organise and configure a specific working environment.
- Presentation. The information provided should be presented in flexible format and intuitive so that it is easy to navigate.
- Administration. This function refers to the deployment and maintenance of the portal.
- Security. This function defines the level of access and portal features that each user has.

3   Research Methodology

To answer our research question, we employed design science approach [9] (see Fig. 1). Design science approach is a problem-solving paradigm which creates

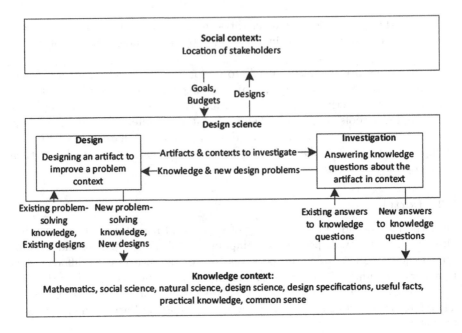

Fig. 1. Design science framework [9]

artefacts to solve a problem in a certain context [10]. The artefacts can be represented in various structured forms, e.g. software, formal logic, method, technique or conceptual structure [9]. Each problem has a root in a certain context so that the artefacts are designed to understand that context. Design science involves two main activities: designing and investigating (see Fig. 1).

In this study, the stakeholders in the social context are startuppers or entrepreneurs. The goal of this design science study is to understand and meet the needs of entrepreneurs regarding software tools to support their activities and access to them. Hence, we analysed the existing software tool portal available online. To be qualified as a software tools portal, a web page should meet the following criteria [6,11,12]: (1) collection of links to multiple sources in the world wide web, (2) the links are organised based on a certain structure for navigation. We used Google search engine to perform the selection. The generic search string with combination of keywords we used to find the software tools portal is *("startup" OR "startups" OR "start-up" OR "start-ups") AND ("Tools" OR "Tool")*.

Our selection with Google search engine discovered 15 tool portals, which offer thousands of tools available online that one can use for different purposes (see the complete list of the portal in the following link: http://figshare.com/ articles/List_of_software_tool_portals/1540679. For startuppers, it becomes very crucial to find a suitable tool quickly because of fast and dynamic nature of startups. Currently, we do not see any solution that is primarily developed by

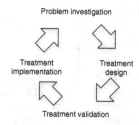

Fig. 2. Design cycle [9]

keeping in mind startups nature and involving several startuppers to overcome this problem.

To fill this gap, we started designing a new software tool portal. We follow the four steps proposed by Wieringa [9] iteratively (see Fig. 2): (1) problem investigation, (2) treatment design, (3) treatment validation and (4) treatment implementation. To better understand the problem, we performed interviews with five different startups. Semi-structured face-to-face interview with a mix of open-ended and specific question is employed to elicit information. Based on the interview, we found out that the entrepreneurs are not aware of these portals and the list of tools available. They tend to use only the tools they are familiar with.

Based on tool portal analysis, we designed a new web portal, called MineToolz and asked the experts to foresee how the portal can satisfy their need. Three criteria were posed: (1) the positive aspect, (2) the negative aspect, (3) additional feedback for the design. The first validation with the experts signalled a positive impression about our design. The three level designed are insightful for new entrepreneurs who are looking for tools systematically. Only one expert thought that we were showing our own tools. All the experts agreed that our design was simple and enabled the users to go through the categories and list of tools.

One of the experts suggested to implement a questionnaire to know a user's need and based on that, suggest the right tools for him (can be a recommender system). Besides, this feature also allows the users to directly find the desired tools rather than browsing all the pages. The experts also suggest to have two types of rating: the user rating and the admin rating. User rating is given by users based on their experience using certain tools. For admin rating, the experts suggest to have a certain mechanism to evaluate the tools which is supposed to be more objective than user rating.

4   MineToolz

MineToolz (www.minetoolz.com) is designed by following the three-tiered architecture design: presentation layer, business logic layer and data layer (see Fig. 3). The presentation layer is the first layer where users can see the list of the tools. Users can also read the description about each tools. The presentation layer is further divided into three levels. The first level consists of the landing page and

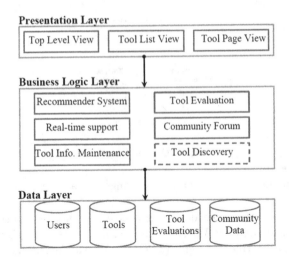

Fig. 3. MineToolz architecture

the four categories (product, market, team, finance) in which the list of tools are categorised. Also, the landing page consists of several features e.g. suggesting a tool, contact form, connecting with social media etc.

The business logic layer is responsible for two important features: recommender system and automated tool evaluation. Recommender system is designed to generate a list of recommended tools for entrepreneurs. Automated tool evaluation is handling all the process of evaluating newly added tools into the portal. Another component of business logic layer is an independent tool discovery component that helps to discover the new tools that are available on the Internet with the passage of time. The data link layer is used to manage the information about different tools with their evaluations, users of the portals etc.

The curated list of tools are shown in the second level. This level serves as the hub of all the software tools. When a user enters a category, the corresponding tools are displayed. Each tool displayed at this level consists of the tags, tool description, rating etc.

The third level gives the detailed view of a specific software tool. After logging in, a user can give comments and rate a specific tool. Tools are also recommended to users at this level by implementing a tool recommender system.

We classified the users into newbie, intermediate and advanced users. For newbies, a minimum set of tools are offered to build the business idea into startup. For intermediate users, an additional list of tools are provided that assist the startup to follow their flow after business idea validation. The advanced user tool section is: when the startup is in the scalable phase.

5   Next Step

In this paper, we have described an outline of the design of a new software tool portal, called MineToolz. The following premises stipulate the need of such systems. First, a huge number of software tools have been published online the world wide web. A software tool portal plays an important role as the gateway to the huge collection of tools. Second, every entrepreneur has different needs. A tool recommender system will be beneficial for entrepreneurs to find the right tools effectively.

Further research will entail several new studies. First, we are still working on the implementation of the system. The implementation will also include the tool recommendation system. Second, we will collect empirical evidence of validity and reliability of our solution.

References

1. Ries, E.: The Lean Startup: How Today's Entrepreneurs Use Continuous Innovation to Create Radically Successful Business. Crown Business, USA (2011)
2. Blank, S.: Why the lean start-up changes everything. Harvard Bus. Rev. **91**(5), 63–72 (2013)
3. Kitchenham, B.A.: Evaluating software engineering methods and tool part 1: the evaluation context and evaluation methods. SIGSOFT Softw. Eng. Notes **21**(1), 11–14 (1996)
4. Sutton, J.S.M.: The role of process in a software start-up. IEEE Softw. **17**(4), 33–39 (2000)
5. Crowne, M.: Why software product startups fail and what to do about it. evolution of software product development in startup companies. In: IEEE International Engineering Management Conference, vol. 1, pp. 338–343 (2002). doi:10.1109/IEMC.2002.1038454
6. Caro, A., Calero, C., Mendes, E., Piattini, M.: A probabilistic approach to web portal's data quality evaluation. In: 6th International Conference on the Quality of Information and Communications Technology, QUATIC 2007, pp. 143–153, September 2007
7. Yang, Z., Cai, S., Zhou, Z., Zhou, N.: Development and validation of an instrument to measure user perceived service quality of information presenting web portals. Inf. Manage. **42**, 575–589 (2004)
8. Collins, H.: Corporate portal definition and features. AMACOM (2011)
9. Wieringa, R.J.: Design Science Methodology for Information Systems and Software Engineering. Springer, Heidelberg (2014)
10. Hevner, A.R., March, S.T., Park, J., Ram, S.: Design science in information systems research. MIS Q. **28**(1), 75–105 (2004)
11. Xiao, L., Subhasish, D.: User satisfaction with web portals: an empirical study. In: Gao, Y. (ed.) Web Systems Design and Online Consumer Behavior, pp. 192–204. Igi Global, Hershey (2005)
12. Udgata, S., Vanam, S., Madhav, M.: Regression based automated test tool for web portals. In: TENCON 2008–2008 IEEE Region 10 Conference, pp. 1–6, November 2008

What Can Software Startuppers Learn from the Artistic Design Flow? Experiences, Reflections and Future Avenues

Juhani Risku[✉] and Pekka Abrahamsson

Department of Computer and Information Science,
Norwegian University of Science and Technology, Trondheim, Norway
juhani.risku@idi.ntnu.no, pekkaa@ntnu.no

Abstract. **[Context and motivation]** Startups are one of the most important economic drivers in today's economy. The high failure rates have not discouraged communities, cities or universities from investing in startup ecosystems. We know that the great majority of startups today are software based. **[Problem]** It is equally well acknowledged that the early stage concept design and validation plays a key role in getting the first customers and ultimately attracting funding for the survival and possible success of a startup. Very little research, however, exists to support starttuppers in developing their early-stage ideas into concepts efficiently. **[Results and contribution]** This paper aims contributing to this gap by studying the artistic design flow and the tools utilized by architects, industrial designers and artists, and as a result proposes concrete ways to improve the current state-of-practice. However, it is argued that borrowing techniques, approaches and ideas will not be sufficient, and a change in software education culture is required.

Keywords: Artistic design flow · Lean startup · Software startup · Systemic design

1 Introduction

Software startup is all about design: you need an idea to start with, you have to refine the idea into a crystallized concept which is then developed into a prototype. The prototype, whether it is on a paper, a simulation or a partly functioning application, is later realised and published as a software solution in the form of an application, a service or a large systemic solution. Design, as a historical entity and industry from early pyramids through Leonardo da Vinci's art and machines, has their design origins in arts, architecture and craftsmanship.

During Nokia Corporation's golden age 2004–2009, the money-maker was the so called Symbian based mobile phones. Phones became all-the-time software intensive

---

J. Risku spent 9 years in Nokia Corporation in various design related roles where he also served as an innovation director. P. Abrahamsson has researched and taught software startups since 2011.

© Springer International Publishing Switzerland 2015
P. Abrahamsson et al. (Eds.): PROFES 2015, LNCS 9459, pp. 584–599, 2015.
DOI: 10.1007/978-3-319-26844-6_44

products, in which usability and visualisation grew in importance. In Symbian core teams, the designers (artists, industrial designers and visual designers) had a twofold role: design individually holistic user interfaces so that several proposals were evaluated during one session. Then the proposals were merged into one version, which was developed both into a simulated version on a laptop and a functional version in an existing phone.

We observed then that a single designer can, at its best, design nearly everything from abstract to detail-level solution for a mobile application by herself. This means that a typical designer team of 5–7 designers can together cover up to 85–90 % of the application, in some days, to be put forward for coding. What is even more worth-noticing is that, designers are able to start any work initiatively alone as well as in a team. This may be because of their educational background in design and forward-looking attitude. If there were engineers or psychologists in the team they could participate right after the designers had produced the design. Engineers or psychologists seldom had a plan or design even in a raw format to be discussed. Now it seems that the idea of initiators and followers also scale to a single team level [1]. The initiators start and lead the creation and development process, and the followers participate mostly on technical implementation details. This detailed level is often divided according to educational and professional background to roles like user-interface designer, tester, coder, etc. The ideas of *first movers* and *second movers* emerge.

The notion of a first-mover can be found in Aristotle's idea of the prime mover. Aristotle's Metaphysics ("after the Physics"), develops his theology of the prime mover, as πρῶτον κινοῦν ἀκίνητον: an independent divine eternal unchanging immaterial substance [2]. Aristotle's Prime Mover causes the movement of other things. The Prime Mover is the purpose and the teleology of the movement when creating it. The Second Mover observes, waits and stays on the background. The Second Mover never starts the process and gives a meaning to it. But, as we know that both fast followers and late movers can profit from the first-movers' mistakes.

A person, who takes the initiative in a product creation process, needs a wide skillset of the product related factors from idea conception, crafting, building and finishing the product. He (she) needs not only a deep understanding of the user needs and market demand, but also an ability to lead the creation and development process. In startup context, one person may have such responsibilities but may fall short in actual skills. Current research on software startupper competencies emphasizes software engineering skills but acknowledges a need for a broader skillset [3]. Seppänen et al. do not however indicate what these broader skills may be [3]. We hypothesize that first-movers are more likely to possess horizontal artistic and design skills, which means in practice having a deep knowledge in ideation, sketching, concepting, planning, design workflow, leadership, crafting and human understanding.

Universities play a major role in educating startuppers. Today's software startuppers often have a computer science education. When observing computer science master students of their fourth academic year at NTNU we noticed an interesting issue. Very few students if any take regularly notes during the lectures although it is well grounded that note-taking is essential in a learning process [4]. Based on our initial observation only one or two from 50 students are making notes, writing or drawing structures during the lectures. One worth-mentioned observation is that only small

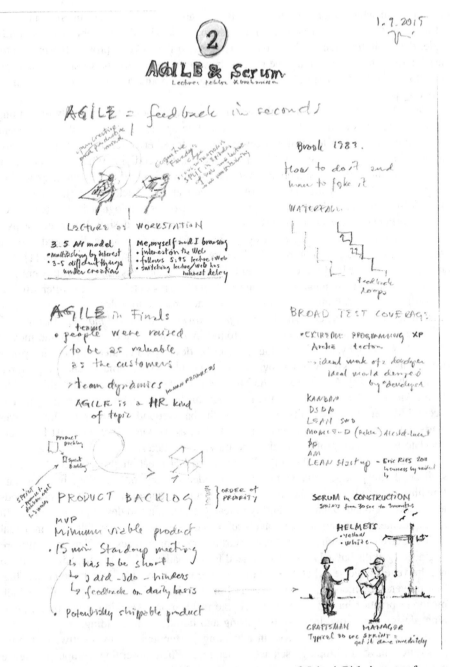

Fig. 1. Designer's main tool is his notebook. An excerpt of Juhani Risku's notes from a computer science lecture.

portion of students follow the lecture and something visible from it. In one lecture at NTNU, we have seen c.a. two thirds of the students appear to be sitting two hours listening or just eyeballing the wall behind the lecturer. When asked, other lecturers confirmed our observations. As a contrasting example, Fig. 1 shows a picture of a designer's notebook when following a computer science lecture.

When pulling together the Nokia and university experiences we formulated a hypothesis: It appears that designers have a proper skill-set to start to work with even the blue-sky ideas and that this skill-set is different from those of computer science students. Computer science students may be active, but they don't take the initiative to start designing early on, which in this context means envisioning, planning or sketching as it is not part of their educational background.

We propose that the present day startup ideas and software solutions in general are based on ideas and solutions which have similar ideation and development processes like the arts or any design. Whereas smartphones as an example are certainly designed by industrial designers having artistic education, do the core elements like mobile applications, services and systems have an origin in the arts and artistic creation methods in their early phase of the development process? Are the art-based design methods applicable to software design? If we can find a working, perhaps a separate and independent design methodology in software development, does it scale to the arts?

The remainder of this paper is organized as below: Sect. 2 presents the background for artistic design, Sect. 3 reflects the current design process in modern software development considering from the startup viewpoint and finally Sect. 4 proposes alternative avenues to improve the current state of practice.

2 Considering an Artistic Design Flow

In this section an artistic design flow, including the art creation principles and artistic creation processes are depicted. A comparative reflection on design thinking and designer thinking is also presented.

2.1 Art Creation Principles as Basis for Architecture and Design

The artist, when starting to paint or to sculpt, has either an ideation session or just starts to craft. Crafting rarely starts from a scratch, however. The years of artist's experience have prepared the artist to the task at hand. The ideation session may consist of sketching and composing by drawing or with materials or items. Ideation and sketching before the practical crafting is a separate planning and design phase to structure the later work. Typically complex projects like house and car construction need to carefully plan and design in advance.

When giving a form to a car, a house, or a sculpture, artist needs several form-giving operations like moving, rotating, mirroring, breaking, cutting, drilling, joining, stretching, bending and resizing, as shown in Fig. 2. These are operations to mold the structural form of the object, and the operations have their origin in sculpture. When the outward appearance, the surface, walls, priming coats and flat details on a

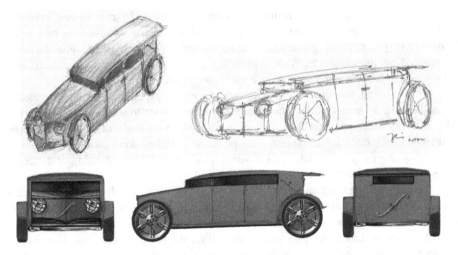

Fig. 2. Form-giving with artistic methods: Juhani Risku, RodMobile 2015

car, house or a sculpture need color, coating or graphic figures—the work follows classical painting methods like sketching the structure of the figure, drawing details, mixing colors and coloring separate pictorial items. The outer form coating and decoration happens with 2D artistic methods of drawing, painting, graphic design and typography.

The creation process of the most noticeable buildings, cars and sculptures of the 20th and 21st century have been following the form-giving methods from classical arts and crafts, as described in Fig. 2. When crafting, the artist may take drawing pauses to create or check details of the artefact. Iterative pauses and checking draft forms are similar to testing in software development. In both processes corrective actions and decisions for continuing the work are made by evaluating errors, need for changes and fine-tuning.

Direct crafting is "sketching and freezing form" simultaneously. Direct crafting differs from art category and material to another e.g. giving form in clay allows additions, cut offs and reforming until the clay is dry or fired. Stonecutting and sculpting is all about cut off and giving form by diminishing the megalith.

Form-giving operations like moving, rotating, mirroring, breaking, cutting, drilling, joining, stretching, bending and resizing have been used by engineers and designers working with CAD (Computer Aided Design).

CAD allows, as direct crafting in sculpting, try-outs and experimental form-giving using solid object modification without preceding plans or sketches. When giving form to everyday items and complex systems, such a teapot or a car, drawing and sketching by hand ensures that the 3D modelling with CAD software is easier and more efficient.

When considering the automotive industry, the general appearance of the car is studied and developed and details created (Fig. 2). The car gets its forms during a process where the primary idea is in the form of a written synopsis. The birth of the car is given sketching by hand and crafting by clay, 3D models and prototypes. The car reaches the level of an entity when the industrial production line produces the first

Fig. 3. Form-giving from sketch to a stained glass: Juhani Risku 1995 Stone Chapel, Vivamo, Finland

street legal versions. When the designers end the creation process of a car model they lose their grip on the car and it becomes an autonomous entity. The car manufacturer together with the design team create a brand philosophy, and the successful car becomes a part of the design history with a specific essence. This applies to other artistic domains as well. Figure 3 shows a result of a time consuming sketching period. During drawing a sketch turns to a stained glass window.

Industrial design applies artistic form-giving principles and practices from the classic handicraft and its modern formats of digitalized 3D design methods. Industrial designers often have a thorough education in art, crafts and design with traditional Bauhaus methods [5]. Bauhaus's main objectives were to unify art, craft, and technology. This is still seen as an ideal for architecture and industrial design education.

2.2 Artistic Creation Process

Artistic creation process can be seen as an evolutionary pattern from an idea into a real world artefact. After initiating, the idea evolves either in a waterfall process or iteratively through several increments. When the artist is working alone (which is close to a standard), all feedback, iteration loops and test sessions are made in seconds inside the designer's brain. Similarly to writers, artists are sometimes faced with a "writer's block" in which they experience a creative slowdown. These are typically caused by external events and for example in Nokia some persons had encountered 12 lay-off warnings and being under subsequent co-operation negotiation processes diminishing their creative capacity to very low.

Figure 4 depicts a typical iterative creation process from an idea to an independent product takes a full iteration round. The round is simultaneously a knowledge gathering

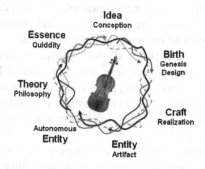

Fig. 4. Artistic design circle: The creation process in art and architecture [6].

session as well as a waterfall-like development process. The second round iterates the first round, the third the second and so on. This way we got e.g. the best violins by Antonio Stradivari. The violins differ from each other only one to two mm variation and the evolution in quality from the first Stradivarius to the 960th version of it.

Artistic design process is also closely connected to the concept of first-mover and second mover introduced in the introduction section. As proposed, the first-mover has the ability of pioneering firms to earn positive economic profits. The pioneering happens through advantages arisen from technological leadership, pre-emption of assets and buyer switching costs. Also advantages derived from a "learning" or "experience" curve, the success in patent or R&D races ensures first-mover advantages.

The second mover doesn't act in this way. The second mover rather observes, waits and stays on the background. A second mover never starts the process or gives meaning to it. But, as we know that fast followers and late movers can profit from the first-movers' mistakes. Facebook overtook Myspace and Skype overtook the VoIP service providers. In both cases the second mover had time to conceptualize a more competitive solution, Facebook was a better fit for big audiences and Skype was free and it worked.

Artists, architects and designers act like first-movers when they are ideating and envisioning new things and objects. The artist's mind-set is based on originality, creation or even abiogenesis in the first place. Copying is not an option for a real artist. A second-movers role for an artist is a loser's role, despite you make money with the copies. Here, copies are usually edited and transformed to look different than the original ones, because the shame may be mortal.

An ideal software startup as a first-mover would be presenting an epoch-making application of an everyday action, which is overpriced and arrogant, and all this in a disruptive way. Do we have any examples of epoch-making startup incidents? Yes, Apple's iPhone was made when the company still was in startup mode, Uber reorganizes the transportation business starting from the most conservative one, the cabs.

When the artistic creation process normally happens in silence and solitude (solitary artistic workflow) all decisions are being made without interaction with the outer world or interfering people. Quick and straight-forward decision-making is an important part of artistic quality and productivity. Quick decisions mean early "right or wrong" solutions. As a possible outcome can be an early sketch, illustration or a draft similar to the one presented in Fig. 5, which is the result of a few minutes of ideation regarding lecture recording. This means either a fluent progress or early corrections to get back on track. This serves as a concrete example of how a design-driven startupper moves rapidly, facilitates communication, creates a solid plan from sketches and ideas thus enabling fast validation of the idea with real customers.

The artist has always been the leader of her own creation, design, execution, implementation and manufacturing process, alone. In case of Leonardo, Picasso and Dali, it is a question of detail and lifelong production, which scales into software design in the form of systemic solutions. Design output for Leonardo were ideas and drawn lines and systemic solutions in the form of helicopters, bridges and artwork to the creation of fundamentals of art by surgery.

Regarding the development and skill in artistic processes, seniority and mastery ensure quality. A senior, when being creative, active and diligent after getting the best

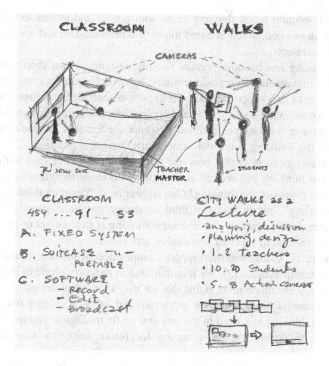

Fig. 5. Early sketch of lecture recording scenarios

education and criticism by peers and masters, is free from practical obstacles to produce individualistic art. Creativity is often connected to young artists but more equitable would be to see creativity as a function of novel ideas, full professional skill set, courage and diligence to work. If so, the youngster has years ahead to work hard.

As a summary, designers mainly think and act according to design culture's centuries-old ways of working and education. Design is based on artistic creation and craftsmanship. The young person studied as an apprentice under a master's supervision learning all skills needed for the profession. When the apprentice was better than her master, she could continue her independent career. His target is to develop his design thinking capacity, which will be addressed in the following section.

2.3 Design Thinking and Designer Thinking

Design thinking is a description of how designers think when creating. Design thinking refers to design-specific cognitive activities that designers apply during the process of designing [7].

Present design thinking has its origin in the psychology of science [8] and design engineering [9]. Rowe, in his book about Design Thinking [10], described methods and approaches used by architects and urban planners. Design thinking has two different goals: to help solving problems and to help creating solutions. In the problem-solving process, seven stages can be used: define, research, ideate, prototype, choose, implement, and learn. Creative solution-based thinking starts with a goal and strives to get alternative solutions to be developed. Solution-based thinking is problem-free and is commonly used by artists and architects.

Design thinking has become popular outside designers' own discipline. We may see it also as a movement (with positive goals, however) to smuggle design principles and habits in weeks as a superficial skill-set to persons outside the design culture. More importantly, we maintain that there is a danger when importing design thinking in a lightweight manner without professional designer's education or traditional apprenticeship work, the thinking is not the same as the designers practise.

An important question is that how far does design thinking lead without design skills? Does the thinking just remain as thoughts without further development? If not, who realises the results of the thinking? One answer is: A "designer thinking" is always a "designer crafting", but an "outsider thinking design thoughts" usually doesn't craft the ideas further. In the outsider's case design thinking is in a danger of remaining as a superficial and inefficient layer of knowledge and skills.

Seppänen et al. claim that startuppers competence needs are volatile and may change as the startup evolves [3]. We maintain that in the early phase of the startup, the competence needs are much more stable that we may think. The design skillset broadly considered represents those expertise areas required when acquiring funding for the startup. Design thinking is rooted in the arts and crafts traditions, and as such, offers a fruitful avenue to consider when planning for future computer science education curriculums.

The value of design thinking is at its best when proper professional design work is executed by the new-born thinkers. This is possible for the young startuppers because they haven't forgotten art classes at the elementary school and senior high school. If the startuppers have a continuum in art and design education at university level they become more than design thinkers, they will become thinking designers.

3   Design in Software Development and Startups Today: Communicability Should Be the Key

Modern software development has adopted several design principles from the traditional arts and design field. Usability, User Experience and User Centric Design have been in the core of industrial product and services design for decades. Graphic design of Web pages, icons and visuals is a centric component in creating attractive Web presence. These design dimensions are also crucial for startuppers when considering the quality of achieved applications, services and software.

Flow charts, paper prototypes, simulations and scale models are commonly used. Paper prototyping can be seen as a modern and simplistic way of developing even complex systems. This practice should not however be confused with ideation sessions with sticky notes or using them to monitor the progress of the project on a team room's wall for example. Paper prototyping (or prototyping on paper) should primarily be seen as a designer's planning tool for the product or service, not the project itself.

In paper prototyping non-artist people practice with artistic methods without necessarily knowing it. Generally there is no training to use these methods and developers learn from the experience. The underlying question here is naturally to what extent their capacity would improve if they would have better artistic and design skills.

The artists and designers, when creating their solitary artefacts, can use more profound tools for organising complexity than those with paper prototypes. The "paper prototyping alike" methods of artists are structural sketching, visual versions of a product in drawings and scale models, storyboards, collages and iterative improvisation. Sketching allows the fail quickly method for the artists and designers to imagine the prototype, test immediately its structural entities and fine-tune, correct or restructure it in seconds.

Artistic methods are quicker, more informative and already close to 80 % of a functioning prototype, not just stickers on the wall. Those methods are also easier to communicate so that all parties can understand the goal better. Paper prototype needs always several design iteration rounds, several professionals and time to be taken seriously and being useful for the development process.

Figure 6 presents planning and design tools employed by software developers including the Gantt-chart, flow-chart, paper prototyping, storyboard, mind-map and sticky note ideation. All tools can be useful for a specific purpose but they should employed with care. For example, sticky notes with relations, text and hierarchy form a complex system, which may be difficult to communicate. A drawing with real world look and feel is a prototype on a higher design abstraction and easier to communicate. We maintain that design skills are needed to ensure the efficient use of the selected tools.

When a startup team presents their proposal for a solution to the prospective funders, they face a test of efficiency in communication: Is a well-engineered structure good enough to get a positive funding decision or would a visible and touchable mock-up be better? We believe that the latter is more viable, tolerates more error, is producible faster and finally is more open for continuing the product development.

Major differences between the engineering thinking and the design thinking are: the engineering design is more difficult to communicate in two minutes, but for example a real world clay model of a smartphone engages the executives for several hours. The charts, diagrams and graphs of the same smartphone are too generic and dull. The model

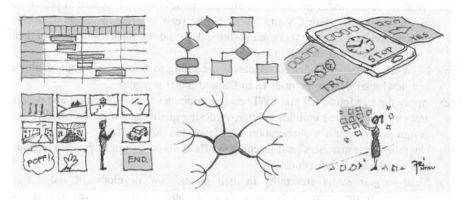

Fig. 6. Planning and design tools employed by software developers.

is touchable and highly crafted like a jewel. This is the difference between software and design thinking, design is sensual and charts are engineered. We believe that design thinking is actually closer to the startuppers' workflow than engineering thinking. Design thinking is, however, currently only superficially included in universities' curricula beyond designers' education.

4   Four Alternative Avenues for Design and Software

We propose that software development and startups have four different directions to go when dealing with the design opportunity:

1. (Radical) Embed designers' ideal as an integral part of software creation and development
2. (Conventional) Keep design as a separate area of the development process and use it when needed
3. (Arrogant) See design as an entity which already has an application in software development and merely needs improvement
4. (Ignorance) Ignore design as a systematic power player in software development.

The four future scenarios of software with or without design culture in depth are outlined below.

4.1   Embed Designers' Ideal as an Integral Part of Software Creation and Development

Embedding designer's ideal as an integral part of the process means that computer science (CS) and software development (SWD) take part in the creation and evolution of design and apply all design principles that have their origins in design, as shown in Fig. 7. However, it is proposed that software development would rather approach design discipline rather than vice-versa. This approach causes several needs and actions:

(a) Need for fundamental program of research and development of design principles in CS and SWD. Here CS and SWD can be seen as prior inventors of design principles which can't be found on traditional art and design areas because of their "non-software thinking" abilities.
(b) Need for fundamental design education according to traditional design methods and newfound design methods from CS and SWD research
(c) Apply the newfound CS and SWD design principles to traditional art and design areas to support their abilities to improve design quality and to ease CS/SWD and design professionals' collaboration with lever and pulley effects.
(d) Upgrade the researchers' and teaching staff's skills in design to provide relevant and newfound design education
(e) Need to gain street credibility in their overall SW development and design approach by delivering software applications and solutions related to research findings. CS and SW professors may have ideas, skills and brainpower to

Fig. 7. Lever and pulley analogues showing CS and SWD possible newfound design principles improving SW design and traditional design as interactional systems.

outperform and beat present operating systems and platforms like iOS and Android, and games like Angry Birds.

The first two points can be realised in weeks or for next season's curriculum, especially at universities with design education programs (e.g. NTNU, Aalto, and Stanford). Point c is a game changer and future success story of CS's and SWD's impact in general design principle evolution. It is also a probable area of competition between universities and criteria for ranking their quality. The newfound CS and SWD design principles as an area of research and development is totally new and its value for diverse businesses is of millions and billions of euros. No university has leadership in this design approach or strategies to tackle the approach.

Point d is a simultaneous program to Point a and Point b. Point e is the hard one and gets possibly the most resistance. Practical output of research results in the form of applications and solutions can be seen as irrelevant effort of a free researcher's role in science. Practical solutions may also be too demanding horizontal strives for highly vertical scientific targets. Or maybe the scientists merely get measured by "wrong" outputs. Alternatively, maybe the comfort zone reached is a direct hindrance for CS and SWD progress in general and an indirect barrier against advancement in university rankings.

4.2   Keep Design as a Separate Area of Development Process

We can remain conventional and continue treating design as a tool, and use it when needed. Indeed, this is the present day mind-set and practice at universities, software intensive companies and startuppers alike. Design in the form of graphics, visuals, usability, User Experience, and hardware like devices, accessories and mechanics is ordered separately from small-scale design consultant companies. Design is usually outsourced into part time and split sessions. Design services are also under high cost-reduction pressure. Those make design as a buyable entity for the host company and design becomes a subjugated and uncertain party. We however argue that this is in conflict with the idea that design could be a key competitive factor and a change maker for the host company. In other words, as subcontractors, design companies can't give their best to their paying customer.

Continuing with design as a separate and subcontracted area for CS and SWD causes:

(f) Inefficiency in getting best design solutions and details to CS and SWD.
(g) Larger gap between CS/SWD and design collaborative interaction in agile and lean approaches, in human efforts and commitment, and holistic development and progress in quality.

Threats (or opportunities), if design would be embedded into CS and SWD:

(h) CS and SWD as an area of discipline would grow stronger. One will not take over the other one but in either case, people would lose their *"governance by subjugation"* mentality, which is not necessarily a bad thing.
(i) Trained designers could replace several "non-designers performing design duties" who have gained their positions as granted in a CS/SWD society or company. The latter type designers would be exposed but they would also learn novel ways of working.
(j) On the background (when continuing to see design as an outsource opportunity) the designers' justified and positive impact would grow outside the CS/SWD community.
(k) Design would be a success factor for CS/SWD research and development and every CS/SWD student would get professional skills of a newfound CS/SWD designer.

4.3 Considering Design as an Entity, Which Already has an Application in Software Development

A basic set of design and design principles already are in CS and SWD. Design in its classical principles is adopted to Usability, User Experience Design (UXD) and User Centric Design[1] (UCD, HCI, cognition psychology). HCI and cognition psychology have separate CS/SWD formulations and conventions like Man-Machine-language MML, use cases and task flows as design. Certainly, these software related design areas are researched and developed in scientific circumstances, and taught for students. But the question is that are they researched and developed in a closed and hermetic vertical environment without influence from outside? Examples of outer influence are: reading

---

[1] User Centric Design (UCD), Human Computer Interaction (HCI or CHI), and cognition psychology have a scientific approach to understand the human being and her needs, expectations and actions in contexts of systems, machines and daily Use Cases and task flows. UCD and HCI are typically developed by designers at e.g. mobile device and solution companies (Apple, Google, ex-Nokia).

design literature, practicing design form-giving techniques, taking design classes and having design people working, teaching and researching at CS/SWD institutions.

4.4 Ignoring Design as a Systematic Power Player

Ignoring design as a systematic power player in software development means that present day CS/SWD methods would be seen as self-sufficient and a hermetic attitude without external input. Interaction would be seen unnecessary or even hostile. This would cause degeneration and a slow withering would take over the CS/SWD community. Points presented in Sects. 4.3 and 4.4 are relatives with only a slight difference: In Sect. 4.3 the CS/SWD community is self-contained and self-contained with their superiority. Both in Sects. 4.3 and 4.4 it is a question of gained comfort zone and arrogance to not to renew and have constant progress.

5 Conclusions and Concrete Steps to Take

When considering the possible futures and trends when combining software development and design principles we observe that there is an immense opportunity to improve the current-state of praxis and the existing design habits in software development.

Embedding design principles into software development is a future strength especially for the first-movers. A fundamental new strategy, however, is needed here. The strategy describes goals and provides a roadmap, organising patterns, participating organisations and people.

We propose that software development, startuppers and design can join their forces in combining design thinking and practices to software thinking and practices. To be successful this research and development approach requires the following:

(a) Start: Get an overview of present day students' awareness and skills to plan and design necessary entities in software development; envision the possible futures of new design skill-set need and form, set short and long term targets for the envisioned outcome, create a strategy to realise the development project. Find an owner for the project.
(b) Research: Recruit eligible faculties, departments and people from the university to participate in structuring the project. Ownership at computer science departments sounds natural.
(c) Development: Beside the research project establish a development project to pilot, experiment and test the research results and give further input for the researchers.
(d) Piloting: Deliver the research and development results to participating faculties, departments and people to support their own education and training sessions.
(e) Education: Start simultaneous classroom training for acquisition of information from all participating faculties and departments.
(f) Joint projects: Find appropriate peer and partner courses to be in collaboration during the research, development and education phases.

We could call this novel type of software education by the Design Software Thinking and Praxis Program (DSTPP).

From the four alternative avenues for design and software the ideal choice would be the first, radical, way. When embedding designers' ideal as an integral part of software creation and development software startuppers would act as more independent creators and leaders during their products' lifecycle. For a startupper a designer's skill-set would give advantage in speed in product development, launch and go to market. The designer's skill-set helps communication to the investor and customer, because the product is well structured and clearly organized with accurate design principles. And the most important outcome for a design-skilled startupper is that she gets a whole portfolio of sketches, organised ideas in structured format, interconnected product concepts to be scaled and further developed. As a by-product of design-thinking with design skills the startupper, very early, gets a holistic and forward-looking mindset, which helps her to succeed in the business.

The designer-developer-startupper, as the mindset and skill-set shows, is a systemic combination of wide and highly professional capabilities. Design, like planning, refers to broader contexts, more flexible and creative attitude [11, 12].

The nature of systemic design process to be an integrated, holistic, multidirectional approach to the design (of instruction). In a systemic approach the designer is frequently conscious of the correlation of the total (instructional) system, and all its details [13]. Therefore design should be applied in its systemic form to startuppers' skill-sets. This systemic and multidirectional design approach influences software development research and education in a very positive way.

Acknowledgements. We want to thank the Software Startup Research Network and especially Dr. Anh Nguyen-Duc for his inspirational ideas on this work.

References

1. Leonard, L.: FLOSS strategic thinking: a proposed framework to support strategic decision for commercial open source companies. In: 4th FLOSS International Workshop on Free/Libre Open Source Software, Jena, Germany (2010)
2. Ross, S.D., Ross, S.D.: Aristotle, 6th edn, pp. 188–190. Psychology Press, Hove (2004)
3. Seppänen, P., Liukkunen, K., Oivo, M.: On the feasibility of startup models as a framework for research on competence needs in software startups. In: The 1st Workshop on Software Startups: State of the Art and State of the Practice, Bolzano, Italy (2015)
4. Richards, J.P., Friedman, F.: The encoding versus the external storage hypothesis in note taking. J. Contemp. Educ. Psychol. 3(1), 136–143 (1978)
5. Bergdoll, B., Dickerman, L., Buchloh, B., Doherty, B.: Bauhaus 1919–1933: Workshops for Modernity. The Museum of Modern Art, New York (2009)
6. Risku, J.: The critique of architecture. Keynote held at the Critique on Finnish Modern Architecture Seminar (in Finnish), Joensuu, Finland (25–26 April 2003). Digitally available at http://tinyurl.com/o4khz9l
7. Visser, W.: The Cognitive Artifacts of Designing. Lawrence Erlbaum Associates, Mahwah (2006)

8. Simon, H.: The Sciences of the Artificial. MIT Press, Cambridge (1968)
9. Faisandier, A.: Systems Architecture and Design. Sinergy'Com, Dehradun (2012)
10. Rowe, G.P.: Design Thinking. The MIT Press, Cambridge (1987)
11. Romiszowski, A.J.: Designing Instructional Systems. Kogan Page, London (1981)
12. Thomas, M., Mitchell, M., Joseph, R.: The third dimension of ADDIE: a cultural embrace. TechTrends **46**(2), 40–45 (2002)
13. Molenda, M., Pershing, J.A., Reigeluth, C.M.: Designing instructional systems. In: Craig, R. L. (ed.) The ASTD Training and Development Handbook, 4th edn, pp. 266–293. McGraw-Hill, New York (1996)

Designing a Maturity Model
for Software Startup Ecosystems

Daniel Cukier[1]([✉]), Fabio Kon[1], and Norris Krueger[2]

[1] Department of Computer Science, University of São Paulo, São Paulo, SP, Brazil
danicuki@ime.usp.br
[2] Entrepreneurship Northwest, Boise, ID, USA

Abstract. Resulting from the technological revolution from the last decades, we observed many software startup ecosystems emerging around the globe. Having tech entrepreneurs as their main agents, some ecosystems exist for more than 50 years, while others are newly born. This difference in terms of evolution and maturity makes the task of comparing different tech hubs a challenge. Moreover, nascent ecosystems need a clear vision of how to develop their community to evolve towards a fruitful and sustainable ecosystem. This paper proposes a maturity model for software startup ecosystems based on a multiple case study of two existing ecosystems. By determining the maturity level for each ecosystem, it is possible not only to compare different realities, but mainly to identify gaps and propose customized practical actions that can lead to real improvements in the existing ecosystems, taking it to the next level of development, promoting innovation.

Keywords: Startup ecosystems · Maturity model · Entrepreneurship

1 Introduction

In the last two decades, we observed the rising and maturation of many software startup ecosystems around the world. The Global Entrepreneurship Monitor shows that human capital and social capital co-evolve [21,23]. Given the existence of hundreds of technological clusters in different countries, it is difficult to identify what is the level of development of each ecosystem. This paper proposes a methodology to measure each Ecosystem's level of maturity with respect to multiple factors. By determining the maturity level for each ecosystem, it is possible not only to compare different realities, but mainly propose practical actions that can lead to real improvements in the existing ecosystems.

As our previous research has identified [16,17], software startup ecosystems are a complex social structure where entrepreneurs and their tech ventures are the main actors. Some of these high tech ventures will evolve to high-growth firms, which make a disproportionate impact to economic growth [19]. By identifying opportunities in the market, an entrepreneur creates a startup. Startups face multiple challenges to discover its market fit [13] and be successful. For

© Springer International Publishing Switzerland 2015
P. Abrahamsson et al. (Eds.): PROFES 2015, LNCS 9459, pp. 600–606, 2015.
DOI: 10.1007/978-3-319-26844-6_45

that, the entrepreneur gets support from family, friends, and other personal connections, who are part of a society and culture that influence the entrepreneur's behavior. Demographics characteristics such as language, race, religion, and gender influence the culture and creates opportunities and barriers to the entrepreneur. The geopolitical status also influences the culture and creates opportunities and barriers for the startup. Universities and research centers provide knowledge in technologies that enable the startup, by preparing the entrepreneur and providing networking possibilities. Universities and research centers also guide entrepreneurs on the technology transfer process [3]. Successful, experienced entrepreneurs serve as mentors to novices. Universities and established companies run incubators and accelerators that train and instrument the startup with methodologies such as agile methods [1], lean startup [22], customer development [5], and disciplined entrepreneurship [2]. Eventually, established companies buy, compete, or collaborate with the startup. Private funding bodies like angels and venture capitalists mentor and invest on startups, which can also get financial resources from governmental programs through R&D funding agencies or tax incentives. The existing legal frame (labor laws, tax laws, IP, patents, and its associated bureaucracy) influences costs and frames the startup business model.

2 Related Work

Startup ecosystems cannot be analyzed as static entities. Similar to biological ecosystems, they behave like living organisms, changing over time. Some changes are planned or somehow controlled, while others are results of unexpected forces acting within and outside the ecosystem. Although startup ecosystems are a novel object of study, we already have enough examples to state that these ecosystems pass through the following phases: **Nascent**, **Evolving**, **Mature**, and **Self-sustainable**. There are also examples of ecosystem **degradation** or **illness**, like what has been reported in Atlanta [7].

Frenkel and Maital propose a methodology for mapping national innovation ecosystems [12]. The methodology is based on a workshop with experts on the ecosystem. They identify anchors and processes that characterize that particular ecosystem, leading to a visual innovation ecosystem map. Their methodology was applied to several countries and it resembles, in some aspects, the methods we use in this research. The major difference is that our work extends their approach by also including meetings and interviews with ecosystem players, while Frenkel and Maital's methodology is based on a single workshop with experts. Another difference is that our study focus only on software startups.

The World Economic Forum mapped eight pillars of entrepreneurial ecosystems [11], namely (1) accessible markets, (2) human capital workforce, (3) funding and finance, (4) mentors and advisors support system, (5) regulatory framework and infrastructure, (6) education and training, (7) major universities as catalysts, and (8) cultural support. All these eight elements are present in our proposed maturity model and conceptual framework.

Lemos mapped entrepreneurship ecosystems based on the perspective of a research university [18]. In another approach trying to understand ecosystems,

Brad Feld presents the "Boulder Hypothesis" [10] with four essential characteristics in a successful startup community: (1) it must be led by entrepreneurs and not by other important players such as government, universities, service providers, big companies, etc., which Feld call feeders; (2) the leaders (entrepreneurs) must have a long term commitment with the community (at least 20 years); (3) it has to be inclusive, which means that everybody who wants to participate must be welcome; and (4) it must have high quality events to engage people, specially acceleration programs and mentoring sessions. Less fragmented ecosystems would score higher on all 4 elements. Feld's model challenges the triple helix model (governments, universities, and industries) [6]. Recent studies show that policies with focus on bottom-up approaches are more efficient when developing startup ecosystems [24], putting the entrepreneur as the main change agent, while the traditional triple helix model tends to discard the entrepreneurs focusing only on government, university, and industry.

Changes in ecosystems are observed over time, and some differences can take years or sometimes decades to be observed. Ecosystems have a dynamic and evolutionary nature rather than a static phenomenon that can be captured by a snapshot at a given point in time [19]. The startup ecosystem report 2012 [15] proposes a ranking of the top 20 ecosystems in the technologic economy. It puts Silicon Valley as a benchmark and compare other ecosystems to it. Three years later, another report, The global startup ecosystem ranking 2015 [14], revises the 2012 version, presenting a new landscape of ecosystems, showing new technological hubs entering the ranking as well as old startup agglomerations that did not evolved enough to enter in the new top 20. The questions that arise are: what happened to those ecosystems that felt out of the ranking? What did the ecosystems that entered in the ranking performed to scale up? Being higher in the ranking means to get better? Being lower means to get worse? Could the evolution across maturity levels stages be an evidence of a virtuous cycle [4]?

3   Methodology

The maturity model proposed in this paper is based on a conceptual framework for startup ecosystems that we developed after an extensive literature review about existing ecosystems and a detailed qualitative research we performed in two existing ecosystems: Tel Aviv [16] and São Paulo [9]. Our qualitative methodology was based on two different techniques: (1) a multiple case study [25] based on more than 80 semi-structured interviews with key players (entrepreneurs, investors, educators, executives, etc.) in both ecosystems; (2) a systematic workshop / focus group that we executed in São Paulo [9].

The conceptual framework contains core elements that relate to each other. We can analyze the level of development of each core element, as well as the quality of the relationship between them to measure some degree of maturity in each aspect. For example, there is the funding bodies core element. The development level of the funding structure inside the ecosystem is a measurement of maturity. The presence of technical talent, provided by high quality educational

Table 1. Ecosystem maturity factor classification

Factor	L1	L2	L3
* Exit strategies	0	1	>= 2
* Global market	<10%	10–50%	>50%
Entrepreneurship in universities	<2%	2–10%	>10%
* Number of startups	<500k	500–3k	>3k
* Access to funding in USD/year	200M	200M-1B	>1B
Access to funding in # of deals/year	200	200–1000	1000
Mentoring quality	<10%	10–%50%	>50%
Bureaucracy	>40%	10–40%	<10%
Tax burden	>50%	30–50%	<30%
Incubators / tech parks	2	2–10	>10
Accelerators quality	<10%	10–50% success	>50% success
* High-tech companies presence	<10	10–50	>50
Established companies influence	<20	20–80	>80
* Human capital quality	>20th	15–20th	<15th
* Culture values for entrepreneurship	<0.5	0.5–0.75	>0.75
Technology transfer processes	<4.0	4.0–5.0>5.0?	
Methodologies knowledge	<20%	20–60%	>60%
Specialized media players	< 3	3–5	>5
* Ecosystem data and research	not available	partially available	fully available
* Ecosystem generations	0	1	2

institutions, or access to educational resources are other examples of factors to measure the ecosystem maturity. Thus, we propose, for each core element, a scale to evaluate its state. The scale contains three levels of development: **L1**, **L2**, and **L3**. We then propose a metric to classify ecosystems for each core element maturity, described in Table 1. This table was generated after a series of iterations with specialists and confirmation of what they considered the right measurement of **L1**, **L2** and **L3** in each aspect. The full explanation of each factor scale and measuarements can be found in the Startup Ecosystem Maturity Model Technical Report [8].

4 Results

Some factors in the ecosystem comparison table are crucial to be considered when an ecosystem has reached a certain level of maturity. Not achieving a specific grade in any of these factors keeps the ecosystem on a lower level of maturity. Thus, we divided the factors in two categories: **essential** and **summing**. The summing factors are important to "upgrade" the ecosystem to the next level.

Our proposal of maturity model is divided into four levels as described below:

- **Nascent (M1):** usually when the ecosystem is already recognized as a startup hub, with some already existing startups, a few investment deals and maybe government initiatives to stimulate or accelerate the ecosystem development, but no great output in terms of jobs generation or worldwide penetration.

- **Evolving (M2):** ecosystems with a few successful companies, some regional impact, job generation and small local economic impact. To be in this level, the ecosystem must have all essential factors classified at least at L2, and 30 % of summing factors also on L2.

- **Mature (M3):** ecosystems with hundreds of startups, where there is a considerable amount of investing deals, existing successful startups with worldwide impact, a first generation of successful entrepreneurs who started to help the ecosystem to grow and be self-sustainable. To be in this level, the ecosystem must have all essential factors classified at least at L2, 50 % of summing factors also on L2, and at least 30 % of all factors on L3.

- **Self-sustainable (M4):** ecosystems with thousand of startups and financing deals, at least a 2nd generation of entrepreneur mentors, specially angel investors, a strong network of successful entrepreneurs compromised with the long term maintenance of the ecosystem, an inclusive environment with many startups events and presence of high quality technical talent (as proposed in the Boulder Thesis by Brad Feld [10]). To be in this level, the ecosystem must have all essential factors classified as L3, and 80 % of summing factors also on L3.

After generating the classification table for each factor, we filled the table with data about the ecosystems we analyzed, also using the help of two specialists in each ecosystem. The resulting Table 2 shows data collected from both the Tel Aviv and São Paulo Ecosystems.

Table 2. Startup ecosystem comparison table

	Tel Aviv	São Paulo
* Essential factors	L3 (9)	L2 (9)
Summing factors	L2 (5), L3 (6)	L1 (8), L2 (3)
Maturity level	Mature (M3)	Evolving (M2)

As a secondary metric, we can use the ecosystem progress within a certain level to understand how far it is from being upgraded to the next level. For example, Tel Aviv has all essential factors in L3 and 54 % of the summing factors in L3, which suggests the ecosystem is almost reaching the M4 maturity level. On the other hand, São Paulo has no essential or summing factor on L3, suggesting that the ecosystem just entered the M2 level and needs more effort to reach the next level.

5   Conclusions and Future Work

This paper proposes a novel maturity model for software startup ecosystems based on an extensive literature study as well as a multiple case study of two existing ecosystems. A conceptual framework of software startup ecosystems was created from these studies and the maturity model was validated with specialists from these ecosystems. The findings show that Tel Aviv is considered a **Mature (M3)** ecosystem, while São Paulo is **Evolving (M2)**.

The maturity model can be used to identify gaps in each ecosystem, showing a direction on which the local community should concentrate, promoting initiatives to take the ecosystem to the next level.

A missing element in the current version of the maturity model is the measurement of interconnectivity between agents within the ecosystem. Literature shows that this is a very important aspect [20] to analyze the ecosystem maturity and, thus, should be included in the evaluation criteria. Future work should investigate how to measure the quality of the entrepreneurship network and how to fit it into the whole maturity model.

As a next step in this research, we will carry out a new round of interviews in the New York ecosystem, classifying it according to the maturity model. These new findings will then be used to further adapt the model towards a refined version. We will then invite specialists from different ecosystems around the world to perform the exercise of classifying their ecosystem using this model, criticizing the criterion we proposed and helping to improve it collaboratively.

References

1. Abrahamsson, P.: Agile Software Development Methods: Review and Analysis. VTT Publications, Espoo (2002)
2. Aulet, B.: Disciplined Entrepreneurship: 24 Steps to a Successful Startup. Wiley, New York (2013)
3. Berbegal-Mirabent, J., Sabaté, F., Cañabate, A.: Brokering knowledge from universities to the marketplace: the role of knowledge transfer offices. Manage. Decis. **50**(7), 1285–1307 (2012)
4. Björklund, T., Krueger, N.: Generating resources through co-evolution of entrepreneurs and ecosystems. J. Enterprising Communities 9 (2015)
5. Blank, S.: The Four Steps to the Epiphany. K&S Ranch, Pescadero (2013)
6. Brannback, M., Carsrud, A., Krueger, N., Elfving, J.: Challenging the triple helix model of regional innovation systems: a venture-centric model. Int. J. Technoentrepreneurship **1**(3), 257–277 (2008)
7. Breznitz, D., Taylor, M.: The communal roots of entrepreneurial-technological growth - social fragmentation and stagnation: reflection on Atlanta's technology cluster. Entrepreneurship Reg. Dev. **26**(3–4), 375–396 (2014)
8. Cukier, D., Kon, F., Krueger, N.: Software Startup Ecosystems Maturity Model Technical Report. Technical report, June, University of São Paulo, São Paulo (2015). http://ccsl.ime.usp.br/startups/files/MaturityModelTechReport.pdf
9. Cukier, D., Kon, F., Maital, S., Fenkel, M.: Innovation and Entrepreneurship in the São Paulo Metropolis - The role of its major university. Submitted to the Int. J, Entrepreneurship Small Bus (2015)
10. Feld, B.: Startup Communities: Building an Entrepreneurial Ecosystem in Your City. Wiley, New York (2012)

606   D. Cukier et al.

11. Foster, G., Shimizu, C., Ciesinski, S., Davila, A., Hassan, S., Jia, N., Morris, R.: Entrepreneurial ecosystems around the globe and company growth dynamics. In: World Economic Forum, vol. 11 (2013)
12. Frenkel, A., Maital, S.: Mapping National Innovation Ecosystems: Foundations for Policy Consensus. Edward Elgar Publishing, London (2014)
13. Giardino, Carmine, Bajwa, Sohaib Shahid, Wang, Xiaofeng, Abrahamsson, Pekka: Key Challenges in Early-Stage Software Startups. In: Lassenius, Casper, Dingsøyr, Torgeir, Paasivaara, Maria (eds.) XP 2015. LNBIP, vol. 212, pp. 52–63. Springer, Heidelberg (2015)
14. Herrmann, B.L., Gauthier, J.F., Holtschke, D., Berman, R., Marmer, M.: The Global Startup Ecosystem Ranking 2015. Technical report, Compass (2015)
15. Herrmann, B.L., Marmer, M., Dogrultan, E., Holtschke, D.: Startup Ecosystem Report 2012. Technical report, Telefónica Digital (2012). http://bit.ly/teleco2014
16. Kon, F., Cukier, D., Melo, C., Hazzan, O., Yuklea, H.: A panorama of the israeli software startup ecosystem. Technical report, University of São Paulo (2014). http://bit.ly/israeli-startup-ecosystem
17. Kon, F., Cukier, D., Melo, C., Hazzan, O., Yuklea, H.: A Conceptual Framework for Software Startup Ecosystems: the case of Israel. Technical report. June, University of São Paulo, São Paulo (2015). http://bit.ly/iframework
18. Lemos, P.: Universidades e Ecossistemas de Empreendedorismo. Unicamp (2012)
19. Mason, C., Brown, R.: Entrepreneurial ecosystems and growth oriented entrepreneurship. Final Report to OECD, Paris (2014)
20. Motoyama, Y., Watkins, K.K.: Examining the connections within the startup ecosystem: A case study of st. louis. Louis (September 1, 2014). Kauffman Foundation Research Series on City, Metro, and Regional Entrepreneurship (2014)
21. Reynolds, P., Hay, M., Bygrave, W.D., Camp, S.M., Autio, E.: Global entrepreneurship monitor. Executive Report (2000)
22. Ries, E.: The lean startup: How today's entrepreneurs use continuous innovation to create radically successful businesses. Random House LLC (2011)
23. Singer, S., Amoros, E., Moska, D.: Global entrepreneurship monitor 2014 global report (2015)
24. Stam, E.: Entrepreneurial ecosystems and regional policy: a sympathetic critique. Eur. Plann. Stud. **23**(9), 1759–1769 (2015)
25. Yin, R.K.: Case Study Research: Design and Methods. SAGE, Thousand Oaks (2013)

A Conceptual Framework of Lean Startup Enabled Internal Corporate Venture

Henry Edison[✉]

Free University of Bozen-Bolzano, Piazza Domenicani 3,39100 Bolzano, Italy
henry.edison@inf.unibz.it

Abstract. It has been perceived that innovation has been dominated by startups and new small companies whereas large companies struggle with balancing the challenges of operational excellence and product innovativeness. Internal corporate venturing has been promoted as one way to foster radical innovation in corporation. Lean startup suggests that internal corporate venturing can be managed through engineering science, which can be taught. However, the importance of the learning gained by small innovative and entrepreneurial teams has yet to be fully conveyed to the whole organisations. To investigate this complex phenomenon, a conceptual framework combining internal corporate venture and Lean startup has been developed based on the literature review. The framework will serve as a theoretical lens to collect and analyse empirical evidence through a multiple case study approach. It enables a better understanding of the potential benefits and challenges of practising Lean startup in large companies.

Keywords: Software product innovation · Internal corporate venturing · Lean startup

1 Introduction

Product innovativeness is a vital tool to seek growth and survival, which is suggested in literature (e.g. [1,2]), together with operational excellence and customer intimacy [3]. In reality, many companies are too risk-averse to engage in any innovation initiatives [4]. It has been perceived that innovation is dominated by startups and new small companies whereas large companies struggle with balancing the challenges of operational excellence and product innovativeness [5]. Moreover, in large companies with well-aligned processes and strategies, any endeavour to change the status-quo will emerge resistance. Even when the environment and the infrastructure are already in place, the implementation of an innovative idea must compete with other product development activities [6]. This is also the case in software industry. Little attention is given to product innovativeness. For example, the well-known Capability Maturity Model (CMM - which is later replaced by CMMI) is mostly concerned with operational excellence [7].

© Springer International Publishing Switzerland 2015
P. Abrahamsson et al. (Eds.): PROFES 2015, LNCS 9459, pp. 607–613, 2015.
DOI: 10.1007/978-3-319-26844-6_46

To address these issues, internal corporate venturing (ICV) has been promoted as one way to foster radical innovation in corporation [8–11]. Although the new venture is still operating within the corporation, the way of working is different with respect to the traditional research and development (R&D) system. ICV is responsible from end to end, from developing new products to finding business ideas and introducing them to the markets [9]. Therefore, ICV is seen as a learning process to create new competence different from the main business [12]. Competence makes difference among companies in yielding the outputs.

Eric Ries introduced Lean startup as a new way of innovation [13]. He contends that startups and corporate ventures can be managed through engineering science, which can be taught. However, the important learning gained by small innovative and entrepreneurial teams has yet to be fully conveyed to large organisations. The objective of this study is to unveil the potential benefits and challenges of practising Lean startup inside large companies. Therefore, this study aims at investigating the following research question: *"How to develop innovative software products through internal corporate venture in large companies?"*

As the initial contribution, a conceptual framework combining internal corporate venture and Lean startup has been developed to guide the study process. Therefore, the framework needs to be evaluated empirically. The remainder of this paper is structured as follows. Section 2 discusses the related work of this study and Sect. 3 proposes the conceptual framework. Section 4 presents the approach to apply the framework. The summary of this study is covered in Sect. 5.

2 Related Work

2.1 Internal Corporate Venturing

ICV involves an entrepreneurial effort which attempts to integrate small initiatives into established companies to generate innovation through a separate and dedicated internal entity [14,15]. The characteristics of ICV are semi-autonomous groups within the corporate entity, aimed at exploring new or exploiting existing competence, led by venture manager and using resources that are solely under the control of the companies [16].

Different models have been developed to explain the actual process of ICV in corporation. The study by Burgelman [12] examines the ICV processes in a large diversified company. He finds that there are two processes of ICV: core process (definition and impetus) and overlaying process (strategic context and structural context). He argues that the idea for new business comes by combining the available technology and the market needs. The idea should not be inline with the current corporate strategy. To turn the idea into real project, a product champion is required. If management approves the idea, the new venture concentrates on strategic forcing where the focus is on commercialising the new product or process. Once the strategic forcing is successful, the venture looks for a strategy building. In this stage, the venture needs more support from the corporation to grow. To establish its sustainability, the new venture must be integrated into the corporate strategy. Organisational champion plays an important role to convince top management that the venture opens new field of business and then request to extend the strategy to protect the initiative. Since any ICV efforts may emerge from the bottom, only the ones that show the potential for fast growth have more opportunities to survive. This is how selecting mechanism is applied to control the ICV.

The study by Garud and Van de Ven [17] develops a model based on trial-and-error learning to overcome the uncertainty and ambiguity of the ICV process. In this model, before embarking on next activities, an entrepreneur evaluates the outcomes of prior activities. When the outcome is positive, the entrepreneur proceeds to the next activities, otherwise a change to plan is needed. A champion from corporation is needed when a series of negative outcomes occur or major environmental changes happen. In this period, the plan is reviewed to seek for alternative activities. In addition, the champion serves as a mentor to guide the changes in the plan.

A recent corporate venturing model was introduced by Breuer [5]. She argues that there are five activities in specifying business model for a new venture: exploration, elaboration, evaluation, experimentation and evolution. However, the framework assumes that the entrepreneurs have identified the values that will be delivered to the customers.

In summary, the current ICV process models focus more on the resource-based view of the firm. Burgelman's model [12] acknowledges that the idea of new business is the combination of technology and market needs. However, the model does not give any clue how this can achieve the product/market fit. Both models from Garud and Van de Ven [17] and Breuer [5] are taking into account the learning process to create knowledge. They are able to describe the dynamics of creating new business but fail to explain the interaction between the new venture and the parent company.

2.2 Lean Startup

Inspired by lean manufacturing principles from Toyota, Eric Ries introduced a new way of innovation [13]. Lean startup focuses on the efforts that create value to customers and eliminate waste during the development phase. However, since the customers are often unknown, what customers could perceive as value are also unknown. Therefore, entrepreneurs should "get out of the building" to involve the customers since day one [18]. Instead of emphasising on business plan, Lean startup advocates to build the product iteratively and deliver to the market for earlier feedback. Gilb et al. [19] refer Lean startup as a more "extreme" agile approach than XP or Scrum to manage system building processes.

Lean startup is based on a hypothesis-driven approach [20] which aims at achieving product/market fit (see Fig. 1). To perceive customer value, an entrepreneur should start a feedback loop that turns an idea into a product then learn whether to pivot or persevere. This can be done by developing a minimum viable product (MVP) using an agile method as a tool to collect customer feedback on

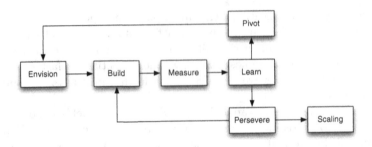

Fig. 1. Lean startup process model [20]

the product. The feedback becomes the input to improve the product and validate the hypotheses. As the result, the startup might pursue a new direction of the business or continue and scale it. Pivot is common to any startup, since it will help the startup from bankruptcy if time between pivots is minimised.

3   The Conceptual Framework

Originally, Lean startup approach is designed to manage startups to speed up the product/market fit [13]. The approach helps entrepreneurs to find out whether a product should be built. Eric Ries argued that large companies can also benefit from practising Lean startup [13]. However, startup is not the small version of corporation and corporation is not the large version of startup. Since large companies rely on management structure, they tend to be bureaucratic. Any attempt to change the stability will be considered as a violation to certain territorial rights [21]. Therefore, ICV is seemed as the ideal environment to nurture the innovation and entrepreneurship in large companies. Even though entrepreneurs also can be found in large companies, they do not have the same degree of freedom as in startups. Lean startup approach does not consider the interaction between the startup process and the current process in the companies. Therefore, we argue that Lean startup approach needs to be adjusted to the corporate culture.

Inspired by Burgelman's ICV process model [12] and the Lean startup approach [20], a new model of innovation in large companies is proposed in this paper, called Lean-ICV (see Fig. 2). The new model acknowledges the dynamics of both the process in the innovation team level to achieve the product/market fit and in the corporation level to keep the innovation initiative still within the corporation strategy. In this model, there are three main processes: definition, impetus, portfolio. Adopting the Lean startup model, the innovation initiative starts with envision, where the entrepreneur sets the vision and translates the vision into hypotheses. To do this, the team needs two important things: the authorisation from corporate management and coaches from new venture division (NVD) management on how to turn the vision into successful business.

The initiative needs a product champion to get further resources. Once it gets approval from top management, the build-measure-learn loop takes place to validate the hypotheses. When all the hypotheses are valid, then it is the time to integrate the new business into the company portfolio. In this process, the entrepreneurial team must convince corporate management to change the strategy to accommodate the new business. On the other hand, the NVD management plays an important role to map the new business in the current strategy. Therefore, organisational championship is needed to continuously communicate with corporate management about the development of the new business area. To control the innovation initiative in the company, top management use selecting mechanism. Only the initiatives that have greater potential impact are getting continuous support.

4   Applying Lean-ICV

Lean-ICV (as shown in Fig. 2) serves as the theoretical lens for the investigation of the research question through a multiple case study. It is a sensitising and sense-making device that guides the data collection and analysis processes. As a result, the framework will be instantiated, modified or extended to better explain the empirical observations.

A multiple case study is undertaken by following the guidelines in [22]. Three selection criteria are employed to select case companies: (1) companies develop software in-house, (2) companies have at least one dedicated team who is responsible from ideation to commercialisation of a new software; and (3) the area of the new software product falls beyond the current main product line. The unit of analysis in this study is a team of software product development.

The primary data for this study is collected through semi-structured interviews, where a mix of open-ended and specific question is employed to elicit information. Each interview lasts between 45–60 min and is recorded for further analyses. Interviewees are selected only if they have involved in any software

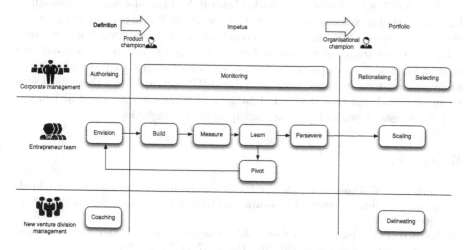

Fig. 2. The Lean-ICV process model

product innovation project, ideally in the development roles e.g. developers, product owners, etc. To complement our primary data, any related documents to the project are collected.

To manage the in-depth data analysis, NVivo is used since it allows a better manipulation of codes and identification of common patterns. All interviews are transcribed verbatim and coded using Corbin and Strauss [23] technique. The main ideas and concepts are identified using open and axial coding. The conceptual framework is used as the seed for categorisation to further data analysis.

The first case study had been done in one of the large software companies in Europe. In 2012, the top management decided to create an internal startup team to develop a new product for end users. It was an experiment to generate radical innovation since it was a new product line and was targeted at new market segment. It took three months to turn the idea into the app and release it to the internal market. Eight employees with different roles in the company were interviewed. The questions were focused on discovering the presence of the key activities as shown in Fig. 2 in the real process and to identify the emerging ones. As the preliminary results, two key findings were identified. First is the absence of coaching and delineating activities from NVD management. The second is the absence of organisational champion. A year after its introduction, the startup project was terminated and the product was released as an open source software.

The next step of this study is to extend and refine the conceptual framework and to conduct the in-depth data analysis. The protocol for case study will be improved for the next case study. A cross-case comparison will be performed to see the commonalities and differences among the cases.

5   Summary

The contribution of this research-in-progress paper is a conceptual framework combining ICV and Lean startup, called Lean-ICV. The following premises stipulate the need of such framework. First, the existing ICV process does not give any clue to achieve product/market fit. Second, Lean startup approach has received a lot attention from entrepreneurs but mainly as the approach to build and grow independent startups. This study tries to fill the gaps by investigating the same phenomenon in large companies. Lean-ICV serves as the theoretical lens to guide a multiple case study that targets at revealing the potential benefits and challenges of practicing Lean startup in large companies.

References

1. Muller, A., Välikangan, L., Merlyn, P.: Metrics for innovation: guidelines for developing a customized suite of innovation metrics. Strategy Leadersh. **33**(1), 37–45 (2005)
2. Kuratko, D.F., Hornsby, J.S., Covin, J.G.: Diagnosing a firm's internal environment for corporate entrepreneurship. Bus. Horiz. **57**(1), 37–47 (2014)

3. Treacy, M., Wiersema, F.: The Discipline of Market Leaders: Choose Your Customer, Narrow Your Focus, Dominate Your Market. Addison-Wesley, Reading (1995)
4. Ahmed, P.K.: Culture and climate for innovation. Eur. J. Innov. Manag. **1**(1), 30–43 (1998)
5. Breuer, H., Mahdjour, S.: Lean venturing: entrepeneurial learning to model and grow new business. In: Proceedings of ISPIM Conference, vol. 24 (2012)
6. de Ven, A.H.V.: Central problems in the management of innovation. Manag. Sci. **32**(5), 590–607 (1986)
7. Rifkin, S.: What makes measuring software so hard? IEEE Softw. **18**(3), 41–45 (2001)
8. McGrath, R.G.: Advantage from adversity: learning from disappointment in internal corporate ventures. Bus. Ventur. **12**(5), 121–142 (1995)
9. Bart, C.K.: New venture units: use them wisely to manage innovation. Sloan Manag. Rev. **29**(4), 35–43 (1988)
10. Kuratko, D.F., Covin, J.G., Garret, R.P.: Coporate venturing: insights from actual performance. Bus. Horiz. **52**(5), 459–467 (2009)
11. Morse, C.W.: The delusion of intrapreneurship. Long Range Plan. **19**(6), 92–95 (1986)
12. Burgelman, R.A.: A process model of internal corporate venturing in the diversified major firm. Adm. Sci. Q. **28**(2), 223–244 (1983)
13. Ries, E.: The Lean Startup: How Today's Entrepreneurs Use Continuous Innovation to Create Radically Successful Business. Crown Business, USA (2011)
14. Narayanan, V.K., Yang, Y., Zahra, S.A.: Corporate venturing and value creation: a review and proposed framework. Res. Policy **38**, 58–75 (2009)
15. Roberts, E.B., Berry, C.A.: Entering new business: selecting strategies for success. Sloan Manag. Rev. **26**(3), 3–17 (1985)
16. David, B.L.: How internal venture groups innovate. Res. Technol. Manag. **37**(2), 38–43 (1994)
17. Garud, R., de Ven, A.H.V.: An empirical evaluation of the internal corporate venturing process. Strateg. Manag. J. **13**, 93–109 (1992)
18. Blank, S.: Why the lean start-up changes everything. Harvard Bus. Rev. **91**(5), 63–72 (2013)
19. Gilb, T., Gilb, K.: Lean Startup - The most extreme agile method by far. Agile Record (9), 53–54 (2012)
20. Eisenmann, T., Ries, E., Dillard, S.: Hypothesis-driven entrepreneurship: the lean startup. Harvard Business School Entrepreneurial Management Case No. 812–095 (2012)
21. Shepard, H.A.: Innovation-resisting and innovation-producing organizations. J. Bus. **40**(4), 470–477 (1967)
22. Yin, R.K.: Case Study Research: Design and Methods, 3rd edn. Sage Publications, Thousand Oaks (2003)
23. Strauss, A., Corbin, J.: Basic of Qualitative Research. Sage Publications, London (1998)

Author Index

Printed in the United States
By Bookmasters